# RECONFIGURATIONS

# RECONFIGURATIONS:

## Canadian Citizenship
## and Constitutional Change

Selected Essays by

### ALAN C. CAIRNS

Edited by Douglas E. Williams

Canadian Cataloguing in Publication Data
Cairns, Alan C.
Reconfigurations: Canadian citizenship and constitutional change

Includes bibliographical references.
ISBN 0-7710-1879-7

1. Citizenship – Canada. 2. Canada – Constitutional history. 3. Canada – Constitutional law. 4. Minorities – Government policy – Canada. 5. Multiculturalism – Canada.– I. Williams, Douglas E., 1949–   . II. Title.

JL.187.C35 1995    323'.0971    C94-932314-4

McClelland & Stewart Inc.
*The Canadian Publishers*
481 University Avenue
Toronto, Ontario
M5G 2E9

1 2 3 4 5   99 98 97 96 95

# Contents

*Editor's Preface*

# In Praise of Hedgefoxes: Alan Cairns's Contribution to Canadian Constitutionalism

*He viewed Canada as an inherited public good, of which he was one of the custodians – patching, mending, prescribing, and trying to get the patient to give up those bad habits that reduced life expectancy.*

– Alan Cairns, Tribute to Donald V. Smiley [1]

*The science of politics is the one science that is deposited by the stream of history, like the grains of gold in the sand of a river; and the knowledge of the past, the record of truths revealed by experience, is eminently practical, as an instrument of action and a power that goes to the making of the future.*

– Lord Acton, Inaugural Lecture on the Study of History (delivered at Cambridge, June, 1895) [2]

This is the third volume of essays by Professor Alan Cairns of the University of British Columbia to be published in less than a decade, all three of which I have had the honour of editing and introducing to a wider readership than might otherwise have been their fate. [3] For as his friend of some thirty years and former colleague, the late Don Smiley, observed in concluding the third edition of his highly regarded text on Canadian federalism, Cairns's contributions to our understanding of the political system "are not as available as easily as they might be because they are published in various journals and collections of papers." [4] Little has changed during the fifteen years since Smiley pointed this out, except for the deeper diversity and complexity of the issues and audiences, and the often dizzying pace of the occasions for which the essays collected here originally were prepared.

Readers familiar with the study of intellectual history will recognize immediately the intention of this brief introduction from its title. It attempts to situate Alan Cairns's work – its style and underlying structure – in the context of the well-known distinction between "hedgehogs" and "foxes." For those unacquainted with the previous work of Alan Cairns, or with the distinction between intellectual hedgehogs and foxes drawn by Sir Isaiah Berlin, a few additional words of background may be helpful. Cairns's own introduction, written especially for this collection, makes it superfluous for the editor of such a book to address the specific themes and concerns that unite and animate individual chapters gathered here. This brief discussion will be devoted instead to the matter of Alan Cairns's overall contribution and approach to Canadian constitutionalism.

In his now-classic study of Tolstoy's view of history, Berlin begins with a line from the fragments of the Greek poet Archilochus, which reads: "The fox knows many things, but the hedgehog knows one big thing."[5] To some commentators, these words may mean no more than that the fox, for all his cunning, is defeated by the hedgehog's one defence. Berlin, however, goes on to suggest that, taken figuratively, the words of Archilochus "can be made to yield sense in which they mark one of the deepest differences which divide writers and thinkers, and, it may be, human beings in general." On this account, there exists a

> great chasm between those, on one side, who relate everything to a central vision, one system less or more coherent or articulate, in terms of which they understand, think and feel – a single, universal, organizing principle in terms of which alone all that they are and say has significance – and, on the other side, those who pursue many ends, often unrelated and even contradictory, connected, if at all, only in some *de facto* way.

The latter, Berlin continues,

> lead lives, perform acts, and entertain ideas that are centrifugal rather than centripetal, their thought is scattered or diffused, moving on many levels, seizing upon the variety of experiences and objects for what they are in themselves, without, consciously or unconsciously, seeking to fit them into, or exclude them from, any one unchanging, all-embracing, sometimes self-contradictory and incomplete, at times fanatical, unitary vision.[6]

Without much fear of contradiction, Berlin concludes, Dante embodies the intellectual and artistic personality of a hedgehog, while Shakespeare embodies that of the fox. Similarly, in varying degrees, Plato, Lucretius, Pascal, Hegel, Dostoevsky, Nietzsche, Ibsen, and Proust are best thought of as hedgehogs, while Herodotus, Aristotle, Montaigne, Erasmus, Molière, Goethe, Pushkin, Balzac, and Joyce are foxes.

In the Canadian case, one might say that the late C.B. Macpherson was a hedgehog, a thinker who knew "one big thing" – forever warning us of the structural incompatibility between capitalist market relations and our ability to achieve a truly egalitarian, participatory democracy. Conversely, the McGill University political philosopher, Charles Taylor (himself a student of Isaiah Berlin's at Oxford and his successor there as Chichele Professor of Social and Political

Theory from 1976-79), can be said to reflect the dominant intellectual personality and style of a fox – underscoring the pluralistic "diversity of goods," the multiple sources of the malaise we call modernity, as well as the alternative visions and "deep diversities" that currently inform constitutional discussions and debate in Canada.[7]

In his graduate seminar in Canadian politics at the University of British Columbia, Alan Cairns has been fond of bringing Isaiah Berlin's distinction to the attention of those struggling to find their own scholarly identities.[8] Such counsel, and an abiding concern for the scholarly enterprise, is typical of Cairns's deeper interest in discouraging intellectual conformism and what Thorstein Veblen – whom Cairns cites approvingly on a number of occasions – called the "trained incapacity" to see things clearly and creatively that academic disciplines often engender. As Cairns has observed:

> one of the most difficult challenges for an academic is to bring an authentic, personal voice to the collective task of research and writing. Finding and keeping alive the always precarious balance between personal expression and disciplinary constraints is a subtle matter both of judgement and of having something worthwhile to say. Since clones are useless colleagues, the most serious mistake is to sacrifice individuality for disciplinary conformity.[9]

A sympathetic review of the recently published book version of his 1987 Kenneth R. MacGregor Lectures delivered at Queen's University, *Charter versus Federalism: The Dilemmas of Constitutional Reform*,[10] contends that in this collection, "as he has for much of his academic career, Cairns brings the perspective of the fox to his subject."[11] While what another reviewer of the same volume refers to as the "rather uncompromising tone of the book's title"[12] may account for some of this tendency to read Cairns's work through a single lens of Berlin's dichotomous distinction, such a view finds little support from a systematic appreciation of the dialectical nature of his thought.[13]

What Cairns characterizes as his "historical perspective on the dialectic between states and peoples" was the product of the broadly historical, institutional, and philosophical training he received as an undergraduate and Master's student at the University of Toronto in the early 1950s. This broadly based, humanistic orientation, in turn, was reinforced by the unstructured nature of his Oxford D.Phil. with its lack of compulsory course work and flexible attitude toward disciplinary boundaries.[14] Clear indications of this fundamentally interdisciplinary, dialectical approach to states and peoples, governments and citizens, can be found in virtually all of Cairns's major writings.

For example, in a section unfortunately cut from the published version of his 1983 Killam Lecture delivered at Dalhousie University, Cairns notes that he simultaneously sees "the interaction of powerful forces, coexisting with the chaos and confusion of weaker, marginal actors pursuing smaller purposes. It is this dialectic which I wish to explore."[15] Having devoted the first several pages of his lecture to a critique of the hedgehogs and foxes of the day, he characteristically observed, "the most accurate perception of my own position may be that I am a fox trying to be a hedgehog, or only a half-believing hedgehog with an atypical sympathy for foxes." Perhaps, he goes on to remark, "in a world of bioengineering I am a new species waiting to be born, a hedgefox if you like."[16] The scholarly tendencies of a hedgefox are notable in Cairns's well-known elaboration of the dialectic between "citizens (outsiders) and governments (insiders)" in the constitutional misadventures of the past decade and in his conception of the autonomy of political institutions and their ongoing interaction with various social movements and actors, among many other areas of his diverse body of work.[17]

While hedgehogs run the risk of subordinating the particularities of events to some overriding formula or universal theory, and foxes are often unable to discern much pattern at all amidst the "blooming, buzzing confusion" of disjointed events and the Babel of alternative discourses we call reality, hedgefoxes, like Cairns, thrive on the creative tension between the universal and the particular, ultimately producing a powerful variety of what Robert Merton aptly has characterized as middle-range theorizing.[18] For example, in a recent study of competing nationalisms in Canada, characteristically leavened with a strong dose of comparative experience, Cairns observes, "the seeker of comprehensive contemporary generalizations of state-society interactions is easily defeated by the plethora of particulars." He nonetheless goes on to underscore the fact that "several common themes, tendencies and developments can be found."[19]

Typical in this context of Cairns's frequent emphasis on what might be called political dynamics, he writes that nationalism "should always be thought of as expanding or contracting." Accordingly, when a "nationalism of the centre is contracting, this can mean either that its hold over the citizenry is weakening, or that it is retreating to a more compact population base, following the actual or anticipated defection of one of its components."[20] Another generalization of broad significance he expounds upon is that "when long established patterns of governance are broken, previously suppressed or concealed ethnic/national cleavages emerge." This is evident, he notes, "in Canada, in the demise of the USSR, in former Czechoslovakia, and in the bitter conflicts in what used to be Yugoslavia. In each of the preceding cases, a former constricting order is either gone or seriously challenged."[21]

Hedgefoxes like Cairns often find themselves straddling several academic disciplines as they try to grasp and give expression to the dialectical interplay between institutional structures and civic identities. Virtually all of his major writings reflect a deep historical, sociological, and comparative understanding of the problems they address. This was equally as true of one of his earliest emblematic essays, "The Living Canadian Constitution" – where the wisdom of the great American jurist, Oliver Wendell Holmes, and the evolutionary approach to the law of Karl Llewellyn, one of the pioneers of anthropology, figure prominently – as it is today of more recent reflections on the ambiguities of citizenship in Canada.[22] As he observed in a comparison of leading textbooks in Canadian politics, "an escape from linguistic and cultural ethnocentrism to an examination of the non-English-speaking world, and the scholarship of that world, would improve our capacity to understand Canada."[23]

Like his long-time friend, the late Don Smiley, Cairns, too, has had "a remarkable capacity to coin new terms, highlighting emerging tendencies in Canadian public life, and addressing the big issues troubling Canadians."[24] Our intellectual landscape and self-understanding would be greatly diminished without such notions as "province-building" (jointly minted with another former colleague and friend, Edwin Black), the "embedded state," "Charter Canadians," "constitutional minoritarianism," "Charter-federalism," "citizens' constitution," and "citizens plus" (a term introduced by Cairns in 1966 to describe the appropriate civic recognition of Indian peoples), to name the more prominent contributions.[25] Each – in its own distinctive hedgefox manner – captures a deep structural, dialectically open-ended transformation occurring between different orders of government, the ongoing dynamic of domestic and international influences on the structure of Canadian politics, and the state's interdependence with an increasingly diverse and complex citizenry.

In philosophical circles, it is commonplace to note that one may philosophize *for* or *against* Kant, the towering figure of the late German enlightenment, but that one may not philosophize *without* him.[26] There are continuing signs that much the same can and will continue to be said of the work of Alan Cairns in the study of Canadian politics. Both his early work on the electoral system, Canadian federalism, the Judicial Committee of the Privy Council, the study of politics and more recent writings on the impact of the Charter of Rights and Freedoms and the rapidly changing nature of Canadian citizenship have all been at the centre of constructive though spirited scholarly debate.[27] This catalytic influence of Cairns's work in part reflects the effect that hedgefoxes can have on disciplines more accustomed to the alternative callings and rewards of "grand theorizing" and "crawling-the-earth empiricism."[28] It serves also as testimony to Cairns's courage and persistence in reminding his colleagues of "debates that have yet to occur" and of the costs that scholarly rituals and taboos can exact on their imaginations and interpretations of events.[29]

As he poignantly observed in an issues paper prepared for the Royal Commission on Electoral Reform and Party Financing, "the issue of aboriginal self-government [is] a policy area hedged in with taboos that undermine honest analysis."[30] Elaborating on this point below (Chapter Ten) with respect to the remarkable recent evolution of the constitutional status of Aboriginal peoples, Cairns writes, "the quality and openness of the debate are both damaged by taboos that inhibit serious public examination of questions in ways that might challenge the feasibility or desirability of Aboriginal goals." The source of these constraints, he continues, "lies in some combination of liberal guilt and the inchoate acceptance of the voice appropriation thesis that disadvantaged 'others' should be allowed to speak for themselves." Cairns goes on to note that past failures, of the intellect and public policy alike,

> leave non-Aboriginal Canadians impotent before the challenge "What is to be done." Guilt weakens their ability to resist Aboriginal claims, and taboos inhibit their willingness to ask questions that might appear to be negative. At the same time, the relative absence of a shared sense of community and citizenship facilitates acceptance of constitutional provisions that will constitutionalize and reinforce difference.

These are the reflections of a challenging, constructively critical mind at work.

The work of Alan Cairns is perhaps best read in the company of a long line of Canadian liberalism, the most notable example of which was the late J.A. Corry of Queen's University, in whose honour Cairns delivered one of his most important public lectures, "Constitutional Minoritarianism in Canada," reprinted below as Chapter Four. Throughout his own illustrious career of scholarship and public service, Corry never tired of reminding us of the need to foster an ethos of "constitutional morality" with which to restrain the excesses of intergovernmental competition in the interest of promoting the long-term well-being and civility of the constitutional order as a whole.[31] For example, in his Massey Lecture of some twenty-five years ago, presented against the backdrop of an upsurge in strained relations between Quebec and the rest of Canada, Corry observed, "it would be easy to show with many examples that English-speaking Canadians have been thoughtless (people who are out of sight are likely to be out of mind) and naturally insensitive to the natural sensitivities of French-speaking Canadians in Quebec." He went on to remind us, however, that "this cannot be cured by constitutional edict but only by an enlargement of sympathies and fellow-feeling."[32] For all their power, the law and the constitutional order from which it derives its overall sense of purpose and proportion have their limits, limits easily lost sight of in the day-to-day competition of political elites and an increasingly politicized, fragmented society.

The essays gathered here, as well as a great deal of Cairns's earlier work, share many of the same concerns. In the context of underscoring the need for a constitutional rapprochement – a "creative constitutional symbiosis" – between federalism's emphasis on community and alternative spatially diffuse civic identities, partly stimulated by the Charter of Rights and Freedoms, he observes, "constitution-makers seeking agreement at one minute to midnight may privilege the momentary and the trivial and undervalue more enduring forces." Or, as he wrote in his introduction to *Constitution, Government, and Society in Canada*, for the past twenty-five years "numerous domestic equivalents of border incidents threatened to get out of control." In the spirit of Corry, he continues, "in the same way as the study of war helps us to understand the conditions of peace, a more elaborate study of . . . constitutional breakdown . . . would illuminate the contrasting conditions that sustain constitutional civility." [33] While many of the essays in this volume were occasioned by particular events and recent constitutional skirmishes, they continue to reflect Cairns's oft-stated concern for the long run, a concern especially attuned to the well-being and health of the pan-Canadian political community as a whole.

Consider the example of Aboriginal peoples once again. Cairns recently noted that one of the reasons our political elites were prepared to go such a distance in recognizing "an extraordinary degree of differential treatment for aboriginal peoples in the Constitution that would have flowed from [the] Charlottetown [Accord]" derived from the fact that "we did not consider aboriginal peoples really to be a part of our community." Revealingly, he continues, "I fear that we were possibly creating a future situation in which the capacity of aboriginal peoples to make claims on the rest of us would be gravely attenuated and the feeling of obligation on the part of non-aboriginal Canadians towards aboriginal Canadians would be profoundly weakened." The former, he fears, would simply say, "You are not part of our community. The Charter has a very limited application to you. You have a differential relation to the House of Commons, a differential relation to the Senate, a differential relation to the amending formula, and so on." Cairns concludes, "you can go through the whole constitutional package of the Charlottetown Accord and read it as a way of, in a sense, taking aboriginal peoples out of the pan-Canadian community." [34]

One of the great political philosophers of the century, Michael Oakeshott, once observed that "the arrangements which constitute a society capable of political activity, whether they are customs or institutions or laws or diplomatic decisions, are at once coherent and incoherent." He went on to note that "they compose a pattern and at the same time they intimate a sympathy for what does not fully appear." [35] Throughout his now long and extraordinarily productive career, Cairns also has underscored the "at once coherent and incoherent" or dialectical tensions of the evolving Canadian drama we call constitutional change. More than many of his peers, he has given sympathetic voice to various social forces and trends struggling to find their place on the scholarly and political agenda of our time. As he has never tired of reminding us, and notwithstanding the well-known perils of such an enterprise, "a case can be made that the times and our situation defy comprehension if we rely on yesterday's intellectual frameworks."[36] Regardless of where Canadians ultimately find themselves in the decades ahead, few will know, let alone be able to assess candidly and wisely, how they've gotten there without the aid of that hedgefox I've briefly tried to describe. Having taken the time to chart his temperament and the terrain he explores, it is now high time to let him lead the way.

# Author's Introduction

## Whose Side Is the Past On?

*Appeals to the past are among the commonest of strategies in the interpretations of the present. What animates such appeals is not only disagreement about what happened in the past and what the past was, but uncertainty about whether the past really is past, over and concluded, or whether it continues, albeit in different forms, perhaps. This problem animates all sorts of discussions – about influence, about blame and judgement, about present actualities and future priorities. [1]*

– Edward Said

At first glance what appears to hold these essays together is their largely contemporary focus. They were written in response to the ongoing crisis of Canadian statehood, most crucially indicated by the unending and largely unsuccessful attempts to amend the constitution. While our constitutional *angst* was detrimental to the peace of mind of most Canadians, it was indirectly a full employment policy for academics specializing in the understanding of constitutional complexities. That understanding, however, mirroring constitutional realities, lacks coherence. Canadians are in the midst of a potential constitutional paradigm shift, a vantage point that obscures our future. These essays attempt to clear away some of the obscurity.

Although the obvious purpose of constitutional debate is to influence the future, much of its content is historical. On rereading these essays, and faced with the task of writing an introduction, I was struck by the pervasive presence of the past. In nearly every essay, the past is a brooding visitor, shaping the issues we confront, influencing the criteria and processes by which we respond, defining the communities that struggle for constitutional living space, or surviving as memories in the minds of the constitutional participants. In fact, much of our agonized constitutional introspection could be mistaken for an excessively partisan seminar in Canadian history. History is one of the many battlegrounds on which the struggle to control the future takes place. Hence, many of the following essays focus on the competitive efforts of rival groups to get history on their side in the service of various desired constitutional futures. Others describe the institutional, policy, and constitutional inheritance that constrains us as we try to change constitutional direction.

"The Embedded State" is described in the opening chapter as a sprawling giant, deeply entangled in society as a result of past policies, and with little room for manoeuvre. The next chapter amplifies this message by underlining "the pastness" of the Canadian state, the reality that, as one author puts it, "We have become more and more governed by old decisions."[2] The title and theme of the following chapter, "The Constitutional World We Have Lost," draw attention to the way in which the continuities and discontinuities between where we constitutionally were and where we constitutionally now are contribute to our constitutional confusion.

While Part III, "The New Constitutional Culture," as the heading suggests, is less historically oriented, the past remains a central player in one essay. "Barriers to Constitutional Renewal" attributes much of our difficulty in achieving formal constitutional change to a pervasive, historically derived distrust and suspicion of each other that the major players, non-governmental included, bring to the politics of constitutional reform. Although a later essay on "Aboriginal Canadians" argues that the constitutional policy goal is to repudiate a colonial and stigmatizing past, there is no clean slate to write on, for the very identities of the Aboriginal peoples have been shaped by the past, especially the past policies, including denial of the franchise until 1960, that turned status Indians into a legally differentiated category of Canadians with inferior civic rights.

While the presence of the past is perhaps less pervasive in the remaining essays, they constantly return to the tension between new and older definitions of Canada that are now at the centre of our constitutional discourse. Indeed, the resolution of that tension is perhaps the major constitutional task confronting Canadians. Hence the following essays, from one perspective, are ruminations on our constitutional past, how we use the past, how we are conditioned by it, how we argue over its meanings, how we struggle to relax its grip on us, and how, in trying to shape our own constitutional future, we are creating new pasts to guide, constrain, and perhaps liberate our grandchildren.

The formal constitution is the primary focus of our attempted transformation because it is the repository of official past definitions of who we are as a people. Indeed, a written constitution is always an attempt of yesterday to control tomorrow. Its definitions, because of their official nature and their historical embeddedness in institutions and practices, have a potency denied to the more informal constitutional understandings that flourish in any open society. Further, when they are incorporated in the written constitution, their status protects them against easy change by requiring the use of complex, inherited formal amendment procedures for their displacement, a barrier that is reinforced by the support offered the official status quo by its contemporary beneficiaries.

Resistance is likely to be especially strong when proposed constitutional change deals with how a society sees, understands, and interprets its own essence, for such proposals are freighted with weighty symbolism. The combination of symbolism and the complexities of the amending process explains the frequent description of written constitutions as higher law, explicitly and appropriately shielded from the erratic enthusiasms of ephemeral majorities. This biases the formal constitutional order in favour of its own continuity, and thus in favour of the past.

The grip of the constitutional past on the present illustrates the inescapable fact that confronts state policy-makers in all fields – they never have clean slates; they always inherit going concerns. In more conventional, extra-constitutional policy areas, society and state have become so intertwined as a result of past state action that when the state approaches society with reforms in mind, it confronts the inherited web of state-society interdependence produced by its predecessors. One aspect of that interdependence is the extent to which collusive special interest organizations have managed to bend state policy to their benefit to the detriment of economic growth. As Mancur Olson notes, the extent tends to be correlated with how long a society has enjoyed stability and continuity. Hence, an unanticipated by-product of defeat in war or revolution may be rapid economic growth, as attested by post-war Germany and Japan, precisely because, as in these two cases, growth-suppressing linkages between the state and special economic interests had been cleared away by the fresh start following defeat.[3]

An adaptation of Olson's theory may have some applicability to our constitutional difficulties. Not only is Canada an ancient polity, in comparative terms, but our three-decades-long binge of constitutional introspection has multiplied the number of interests seeking to employ the constitution for their own purposes. The result is a blockage and rigidity in the state-constitution-society linkage similar to what Olson found in the state-economy nexus. Thus far, in constitutional politics we have felt the shaking of the earth but our constitutional buildings have only tottered, not fallen. Our crises have been insufficient to liberate us from ancestral constraints. Consequently, inertia and momentum, conservative defenders of the past, have successfully resisted major formal constitutional change, 1982 excepted. Indeed, it is now almost conventional wisdom that we are imprisoned in the constitutional status quo, incapable of responding to Quebec's demands by major changes within the system. One might say that Québécois nationalists, having concluded that a convulsive exit is the only way to clear the air, are Olsonites.

The constitutional past is not a straightforward, uncontested inheritance of institutions and rules, but rather the subject matter of often heated controversy. In our first century, our rampant constitutional debates focused on the question of how we had originally agreed to live together as a federal people. What had

Macdonald and his colleagues really meant or intended in establishing a parliamentary federalism? Constitutional history in this period dealt with the genesis and evolution of the institutions of the constitutional order. It focused on the relations between official state actors – Canada and the mother country, federal and provincial governments, Senate and House of Commons, courts and legislatures, monarchical representatives and their elected advisers. It was, of course, recognized that the central institutions – the "natural habitat" of the politician in Mallory's apt phrase [4] – were instruments for the governance of a people. It was clearly understood that controversies between federal and provincial governments over the division of powers were simultaneously about the shifting salience of Canadian and provincial senses of community and identity in the people governed through federalism.

With the possible exception of the imperial relationship in our first half-century, the dominant and most strident constitutional debate until very recent decades focused on federalism. This focus defined Canadians in terms that were deferential to governing elites, for it took for granted that our main cleavages were federal – the interaction between a federal society and a federal framework, the latter, of course, including a strong central government. The resulting debates were, in a sense, official, for the logical and leading participants were those who wielded state power on behalf of the provincial and Canadian communities. These meta-debates were containers for competing narratives, macro-portraits of our past and future existence, in which lesser identities were subsumed or dwarfed by such encompassing rubrics as province, nation-building, founding peoples, and divisions of power.

These debates linked us to the two large civic communities, Canadian and provincial, established by the constitution, and to the two basic linguistic-national communities derived from the earlier competition of two European empires. Simultaneously, they had a teleological dimension for their concerns were the creation of a great new country, or the protection and strengthening of an historic minority language community on an English-speaking continent. These debates, therefore, associated us with epic processes of growth and survival. They floated above the many smaller specific identities that constituted our individuality, and they entirely ignored the Aboriginal dimension of Canada. The cues coming from the political environment encouraged citizens to define themselves in terms of the complex dual identities of a functioning federalism.

The key participants in the unending controversies were the successive federal and provincial leaders from 1867 to the present. Every generation of leaders ransacked the words and actions of all its predecessors for rhetoric and examples in the service of its own constitutional objectives. Constitutional and historical scholarship played a supportive role, adding academic credibility to the aspirations of governments. In the 1880s, Judge T.J.J. Loranger published a vigorous defence of provincial autonomy and the priority of the provinces in the constitutional order.[5] Donald Creighton provided another classic illustration of scholarship in the service of constitutional purpose by contributing to a strengthened central government with his massive two-volume biography of John A. Macdonald in the 1950s.[6]

The great state papers of the mid-twentieth century, the Rowell-Sirois Report[7] and the Tremblay Report,[8] were steeped in history, about which they disagreed, basing their analyses on the premise that an historical rationale going back to Confederation was a prerequisite for effective constitutional advocacy. "Every generation," asserted the economic historian John Dales, "*should* write its own history," as the authors of the Rowell-Sirois Report had done. Their achievement "was ... intellectual ... [they] succeeded in writing a history for their own times ... in giving their contemporaries a coherent picture of themselves – of where they had been and how they got where they were ... and of where they seemed to be going."[9]

The long-running debate over the validity of the compact theory as an interpretation of Confederation was simultaneously a debate about our past, about what constitutional futures were legitimate, and how we should seek them.[10] Was the federal government the child of the provinces, as Quebec Premier Maurice Duplessis commonly argued? Was Confederation a solemn pact that could only be altered with the explicit assent of the original signatories? What about the provinces that joined later, or were created by the federal government? Was it legitimate for the federal government to employ cultural policy to foster a pan-Canadian identity, as the Massey-Lévesque Commission asserted in 1951[11] and as the Tremblay Report vigorously denied?[12] Related controversy over the role of the Judicial Committee of the Privy Council (JCPC) was frequently conducted as an historical debate over what the founders had intended and had achieved. If the JCPC's interpretation of the division of power was erroneous, was it simply because they were bad historians?[13] Given this focus on the founders and their handiwork, it is unsurprising that four or five years in the mid-1860s have generated incomparably more attention and controversy from later students of federalism and of judicial review than any fifteen-twenty subsequent years. What kind of country did the founders have in mind? How faithful should judges be to their prescriptions, if these could be discerned, when the founders, like the rest of us, had only limited foresight? Did they provide us with a fundamentalist creed to which we should religiously adhere, or only a sense of direction that we should feel free to modify in the light of our later knowledge and experience?

Canada is a classic illustration of the thesis that federal polities with written

constitutions are almost compelled by the ongoing significance of their founding origins to revisit the past when a change of constitutional direction is being
debated.

The traditional constitutional past embracing federalism, the compact theory, French-English relations, and judicial review can reasonably be described as
"official (governments') constitutional history." It is now supplemented by new
subject matter for historical constitutional introspection, focusing on gender,
ethnicity, and Aboriginal peoples, among other things. To oversimplify somewhat, while both contemporary and previous historical controversies focus on
our peoplehood, they approach it from different perspectives. The perennial,
historically informed federalism controversy, for which Confederation was the
seminal event, was over how we should handle coexisting Canadian and provincial definitions of identity and community. It is now joined by historical debates
about male patriarchy and the subordination of women, for example, for which
Confederation is almost an irrelevance, except for the reminder that women
were absent from that formative event.

The redefinition of what is in our constitutional past responds to the concerns
of women, Aboriginal peoples, ethnic communities outside the mainstream,
and other minorities whose status or interests were previously not thought of as
overtly constitutional. This emerging perspective can usefully be called "citizens'
constitutional history," thus differentiating it from the "official constitutional
history" that dominated what we defined as our constitutional past until recent
decades. The appropriateness of the new label may be questioned on the ground
that the link to the constitution of women's history or of bias against Asians in
immigration policy appears problematical. In fact, however, the central question
addressed by the newer explorations of our past is the old question – who are we
as a people? Thus, how do we combine our particularities and our differences
with a common citizenship? And pointedly, how can we explain and how should
we judge past constitutional understandings and practices that excluded
women, status Indians, and non-European minorities from the franchise? Once
it is recognized that the formal text of written constitutional documents is filtered through an informal constitutional culture of meanings and assumptions,
then attempts to transform the latter through reinterpretations of the past
should be understood as constitutional history.

The emergence of an enlarged and transformed constitutional past is an indirect consequence of the democratization of the constitutional order or, less
grandiosely, of the changed relation of the post-1982 constitution to the Canadian people. Formerly, the written constitution spoke to governments in
general, and to those who played leading roles in the constitutional system in
particular. In Canadian constitutional matters, Theda Skocpol's admonition to
scholars to bring "the state back in"[14] was irrelevant for most of our history,

for it was widely understood that the state already occupied most of the available space. Accordingly, constitutional history and controversy were largely restricted to the distribution of power within governments, the relations among governments, and, in general, to the concerns of governments. From this elitist constitutional perspective, society was primarily background, and the citizenry rarely left the audience when the constitutional past was examined for answers to questions of governance.

The changed relation of the constitution to Canadian society signalled by the 1982 Constitution Act – and earlier anticipated by the 1960 Bill of Rights, by the role of referenda in Newfoundland in 1948 and in Quebec in 1980, and by the effective mobilization of status Indians against the federal government's 1969 termination proposals – necessarily redefined the scope and content of history that were seen as constitutionally relevant. According to V. Seymour Wilson, the interaction of their "long memories" with "Charter recognition" propelled ethnocultural minorities from the audience into new roles as "serious players in the constitutional stakes." In his presidential address to the Canadian Political Science Association, of which a central theme was "history denied or ignored can easily lead to history relived," Wilson documented a "tradition of racism and ethnocentrism amongst Canada's founding groups."[15] Since the Charter and Aboriginal clauses now spoke directly to Canadians, often addressing their particularities, and did so in the language of rights, it encouraged the new constitutional actors to think of themselves historically in several ways.

The 1982 Constitution Act played the same role for some of the new constitutional actors that 1867 did for later federal and provincial politicians. They produced narratives of how they had gained constitutional recognition, status, and rights. Feminists could now see the past in terms of a steady but halting progression from the gaining of the franchise to *The Taking of [Section] Twenty-Eight* of the Charter.[16] They and others worked to establish the most favourable interpretations of "their clauses," given the hopes that had brought them into overt constitutional politics. Further, if only indirectly, the simple fact of their new constitutional prominence gave a new importance to their past history. To become more important in the present sustains the satisfying belief, by a kind of reflex action, that one's past significance must have been under-appreciated and therefore should be illuminated. Aboriginal peoples, given the section 35(1) Constitution Act statement that "The existing aboriginal and treaty rights of the aboriginal peoples of Canada are hereby recognized and affirmed," received an explicit invitation to document those rights to their fullest by historical research. This invitation has been accepted with alacrity. A recent discussion paper of the Royal Commission on Aboriginal Peoples, directed to fleshing out the content of s. 35(1), asserted that "Aboriginal peoples are the bearers of ancient and enduring powers of government that they carried with them into Confederation and retain today. . . . Aboriginal governments provide the Constitution with its deepest and most resilient roots in the Canadian soil." [17]

Alternatively, past inequities and injustices, previously overlooked or downplayed, were researched and publicized to become the basis for redress claims. The Charter, designed as an integrating mechanism to transcend our cleavages in the future, elevated the status of equality as a constitutional principle and, paradoxically, contributed to a transformed historical self-consciousness that underlined how badly we had treated each other in the past. By a seemingly odd but understandable psychology, constitutional affirmation of our present and future equality was transformed into a searchlight to expose past inequalities. For example, the Charter's equality clauses provided the women's movements with explicit criteria by which the past as well as the present could be judged and found wanting. Such findings could then be employed as rationales under s. 15(2) of the Charter for compensatory treatment or affirmative action in the present.

The constitutionally significant past now encompasses episodes formerly thought of as conventional political history, such as the cultural assault on the Indian people via the residential school system and the racial and cultural preferences embedded in immigration policy, including the head tax imposed on Chinese immigrants. It also includes past social practices, such as discrimination against gays and lesbians, and the distribution of power and authority between husband and wife in the family, previously relegated to the social history of the private realm. Many formerly settled practices and standards dealing with how we treated and evaluated each other – men and women, the able and the disabled, conventional heterosexuals and the sexually different, indigenous peoples and newcomers, early newcomers and later arrivals – are now either explicitly or implicitly constitutional. They are explicit when they are elevated to the constitutional level by the Charter and by Aboriginal constitutional clauses, or by the efforts of gays and lesbians to gain inclusion in the s. 15 equality rights clause. The re-evaluation of the past is implicitly constitutional when it focuses on redress issues recently and still on our agenda, issues raised by groups who see particular episodes of their past treatment by the majority society as demeaning and wounding reminders of their former inferior civic status.

Claims for symbolic apologies from the federal government, with or without financial compensation, are surprisingly frequent. The high-profile and successful Japanese-Canadian claim for compensation and apology for their World War Two displacement and relocation in camps is not unique. [18] A non-exhaustive listing of issues supporting analogous ongoing claims for redress would include the imposition of the head tax on Chinese immigrants (rising from $50 in 1886 to $500 in 1903, paid by over 81,000 Chinese between 1885 and 1923) and the virtual exclusion of Chinese immigration from 1923 to 1946, [19] the detention of about

5,000 Ukrainian Canadians in work camps during World War One,[20] similar treatment of smaller numbers of Italian and German Canadians in World War Two,[21] and the relocation of Inuit to the High Arctic in the early 1950s.[22] The successful campaign of the Métis to rehabilitate Louis Riel as a founder of Manitoba is perhaps the most striking example of triumphant historical revisionism – the transformation of yesterday's "traitor" into today's "founding father."[23]

These redress claims are typically couched in powerful emotional language that underlines the humiliation, shame, and stigma experienced by the original victims, subsequently diffused throughout the ethnic community and inherited by later generations. Japanese Canadians were left with "an unjustly shattered community. . . . [They] suffered immeasurable shame and grief at having their families torn apart, their citizenship denied, and their dignity undermined."[24] "Lasting scars [were left] on the Ukrainian-Canadian community,"[25] who suffered "traumatic . . . long-term consequences."[26] The Second World War was a "dark age" for the Montreal Italian community.[27] The Chinese Canadian National Council refers to "the continuous impact" of the head tax and punitive immigration restrictions on the self-esteem of Chinese Canadians,[28] a legacy of the "social stigma" attached to "early immigrants . . . labelled . . . inferior and undesirable."[29] The official apologies employ similarly dramatic language. Mulroney's apology to Japanese Canadians was intended to remove "a stain on [Canada's] reputation,"[30] while his apology to Italian Canadians referred to the "unspeakable act" of their war-time treatment.[31]

In the absence of an elaborate comparative study of these Canadian redress claims, only a few tentative interpretations of their meaning and significance can be offered. (1) War, which imposes the highest demands on citizenship, is often the catalyst that fractures community cohesion along ethnic lines. It invites majoritarian abuses under the banner of patriotism that generate long-standing senses of grievance and resentment among unjustly treated ethnic minorities. John Herd Thompson's summary, dealing with World War One, is apt: "the treatment afforded enemy-alien minority groups had little or no relationship to their supposed threat to Canada or to their behaviour during the war, but was instead the product of prewar nativism legitimized by an atmosphere charged with patriotism."[32] (2) Collective memories are long lasting. The events in question may be more than a century old, as in the execution of Riel. (3) Issues generating redress claims appear to involve a tension between ethnic membership and full citizenship recognition. The deprivation of the latter, therefore, is experienced by the community as if their "ethnicity itself . . . was *put on trial*."[33] Symbolically, the assault on minority citizenship is often accompanied by physical removal from the community (Japanese, Ukrainian, Italian, and German Canadians). Tension that follows ethnic lines translates social distance into geographic distance when passions are inflamed. Alternatively, access to the community is impeded, as in the case of the Chinese. (4) The publicizing of past injustice is experienced as a catharsis – an act of courage, integrity, and honesty, often following decades of a political forgetfulness motivated by insecurity. "The most important thing," according to a Ukrainian-Canadian spokesperson, "is [to] ... bring the historical facts in from the cold," and thus throw light on a "hidden period of Canadian history." [34] Going public may be preceded by a period of ambivalence about one's ethnic identity and silence about past injustices, [35] which makes going public something akin to coming out of the closet, even if the shame formerly felt was considered unmerited. Conversely, the positive recognition of a once maligned figure such as Riel, according to Joe Clark, at the time Minister Responsible for Constitutional Affairs, would help the Métis to "generate pride in their history, in their heroes, and in their country." [36] Redress was received by Japanese Canadians as a restoration of their honour. [37]

The re-examination of the past from the vantage point of the formerly silenced, the dispossessed, and the politically marginal is not driven by idle curiosity. Such historical research, including much academic scholarship, is purposively driven in at least three ways. (1) It is central to the efforts of the still disadvantaged to find the historical explanation of their present situation, on the premise that greater understanding will contribute to healing and to a more dignified future. (2) In some cases, especially when there are explicit, discrete instances of maltreatment – as is true with redress claims – the goal is to obtain public, official apologies from government and sometimes financial compensation. This is adversarial, accusatory history. [38] It challenges the majority society through its government to reprove what are now viewed as nefarious acts committed by its ancestors. The admission of intergenerational guilt, or vicarious responsibility, followed by absolution, will wipe a moral stain from the past, to the end of a more harmonious existence in the future as the justification for divisive memories is removed. (3) More broadly, it is understood that constitutional orders rest on historical underpinnings and that major changes in the former require revisions of the latter. For example, the contemporary label First Nations is given additional substance if it can be shown that Aboriginal peoples had flourishing societies before the arrival of Europeans, or that the model of the Iroquois Confederacy was influential in positively shaping the American constitutional order. [39] Such positive histories add a reassuring dignity to minorities seeking to enhance their contemporary status. They are domestic versions of what Edward Said observed throughout the post-colonial world – "tremendously energetic efforts to engage with the metropolitan world in equal debate so as to testify to the diversity and differences of the non-European world and to its own agendas, priorities and history." [40] This was phrased even more succinctly in the title of another book, *The Empire Writes Back*. [41]

The distinctiveness of this expanded constitutional history needs stressing. It neither addresses the past from the perspectives of governments and their concerns, nor is it much concerned with the particulars of what was achieved in 1867, for the new constitutional players underline their absence from the bargaining that produced the British North America Act. The contemporary presence of the past, therefore, is much more than the inherited institutional arrangements of federalism and Parliament and, since 1982, the Charter, that define us and shape us.

The past also exists as memory, as a key source of our identity, and as a contributor to whether we feel valued or unrecognized. The past is the raw material from which senses of pride or alienation derive or are fabricated. Definitions of who are "we" and who are "other" evolve from an infinity of past encounters in our own lives and in the lives of those with whom we are linked by such ties as kinship, gender, linguistic community, and ethnicity. Such encounters are not accompanied by their own ready-made interpretations and evaluations. The latter are created and contested by the generations that follow. The past is an inexhaustible resource in the struggle for self-esteem, or to have the leading role of one's party, class, ethnic group, or sex accepted as right and proper, or, conversely, to make compelling claims for compensatory treatment in the present for past injustice whose lingering effects are still visited on survivors.

"If we can get the past with us, who can prevail against us?" is a commonplace assumption in constitutional politics. A supportive past can wear many masks and lead in many directions. At one time, when the British Empire was still substance, it supported Anglo-Saxon hegemony. More recently, a different past, seen as confirming the impossibility of a harmonious coexistence of Québécois and other Canadians within federalism, has been mustered as a rationale for an independence-seeking Quebec nationalism. In an even more recent incarnation, which might appropriately be labelled the anti-Christopher-Columbus-past, it is a key component in the rebirth of once ignored Aboriginal peoples as First Nations. We do not, therefore, face the future as if we are coming together for the first time, devoid of historical connections with each other. We are not a randomly selected aggregation of individuals sharing no more than proximity, who face the task of constructing from scratch a new political people. Rather, we confront our fragile togetherness trailing contested historical memories. How we interpret yesterday, therefore, is integrally linked to our search for a better constitutional tomorrow.

An American writer recently revised the aphorism of the American historian Carl Becker, "Everyman His Own Historian," to "Every Group its Own Historian," which he thought more accurately described the contemporary condition of American historical writing.[42] The Canadian situation is no different.

A cogent illustration is provided by four of the chapters in a recent volume on Canadian citizenship. In each case, the reader is taken on an historical pilgrimage documenting the maltreatment, persecution, and indifference visited on marginalized groups prior to their more recent progress. The flavour of these accounts provides deep insights about the divisions in contemporary Canadian constitutional culture.

The chapter on New Brunswick Acadians, commencing with Acadian settlers in 1604, reports a history of endurance through centuries of injustice or official indifference (up to the reforms instituted by the first Acadian premier, Louis-J. Robichaud in the 1960s), including deportation to the American colonies in the mid-eighteenth century.[43] The chapter on Franco-Ontarian history, going back to before the Plains of Abraham, describes a prolonged, grim existence as an oppressed minority until recent decades. The remembered Franco-Ontarian past includes the "deliberate attempt of ['Le Reglement 17' of 1912] to destroy our language and our culture," which up to the 1950s "made us hate the English majority in the province . . . 'les maudits Anglais' – our enemy."[44] The racism chapter traces restrictive immigration laws back to the 1840s, cites subsequent restrictions in detail, and chronicles the discrimination against black Canadians.[45] The chapter on First Nations stresses their long pre-Columbian history, the equality of status in the early alliance of the Haudenosaunee with the British, and later, when the balance of power had shifted, the cultural assault on the Indian people embodied in the Indian Act. "The prevailing Canadian mythology," Darlene Johnston argues, "portrays a transition from ally to subject to ward to citizen. In First Nations circles, this is often referred to as 'the Big Lie.'" The history of deprivation of the rights of indigenous people explains "the ambivalence and resistance that First Nations display toward Canadian citizenship."[46]

This fragmentation of history reflects and contributes to the fragmentation evident in contemporary constitutional politics. It provides the intellectual infrastructure for the constitutional objectives of the new constitutional players. The Canadian state plays a supportive role in this endeavour with its funding contribution to ethnic chairs (now twenty-six) in universities across the country. Further, the federal Multiculturalism program funds short histories of ethnic groups, more than twenty thus far, published by the Canadian Historical Association. Aboriginal history flourishes, stimulated by Native Studies departments, by journals devoted to indigenous issues, and by the necessary resort to history in the documentation of claims and in litigation. Compared to a quarter of a century ago, when the *Report of the Royal Commission on the Status of Women*[47] appeared, women's history, feminist journals, and women's studies programs challenge the exclusion of women from who we were, and thus from who we now are.

The simple fact of having one's history recognized in a university system is, by itself, reassuring. It also reinforces the distinctive identities of the groups that are studied, although probably not to the extent formerly true of the teaching of

Canadian history in elementary and secondary schools to "French Canadians and English Canadians." The latter, according to a 1970 study, "tended to set one group against the other" with its dramatically divergent portrayals of the Canadian past.[48]

The search for a new past, driven by the socio-intellectual movements of those who were formerly relegated to the sidelines, is functionally analogous to the post-colonial literature of previously colonized peoples. This literature seeks to underline and then undermine the imperialist bias in the literature emanating from the imperial centres that once justified their peripheralization and subjugation. The counterattack they launch against the link Edward Said detected between culture and imperialism[49] indicates that the formerly colonized – the wretched of the earth, in Fanon's phrase[50] – seek not only an end to imperial rule by national independence. They also wish to replace imperialist narratives such as "Christianity, Civilization and Commerce," the interventionist justification by the missionary explorer of Africa, David Livingstone, which treat them as objects in someone else's grand design, with more pluralistic multi-hued portraits of the post-imperialist diversity of peoples. They insist on having voice, the recognition and the respect that imperial rule denied. The colonized know that the challenge to imperial rule requires "extending decolonization . . . into the past." National liberation movements see "history as contested terrain, they recognize the writing of history and the constitution of memory as means to political power."[51]

The domestic analogy is precise and highly appropriate. In the case of status Indians, historically an administered people, it is almost a perfect fit, with the exception that sovereign independence is not an available option. They shared the fate of other colonized peoples. The assault on their cultures, identities, and dignity turned them into "temporal refugees . . . exiled from the past of their ancestors and the posterity they once looked toward."[52] Not surprisingly, status Indian political advocacy responds to the obliteration of their past with a denigration of Euro-Canadian culture, which is compared unfavourably with positive portrayals of the pre-European Indian past.[53]

Adjectives such as forgotten, overlooked, invisible, silenced, and isolated recur as the contemporary descendants of the formerly excluded look back on the history of their peripheralization. Their working premise is that the conventional past descriptions of who Canadians were, and of who counted, filtered out or devalued women, Aboriginal peoples, non-European minorities, and others in ways that directly paralleled their long exclusion from the franchise and from the category of desirable immigrants.

The new constitutional voices, accordingly, seek to end not only past practices but also the cultural assumptions that formerly restricted their social roles and then minimized the visibility of what they were allowed to do. Their immediate goal is to break the cultural mould that historically denied them equal participation in the shaping of society. This inexorably leads to a reinterpretation of the past in which they can find either more positive reflections of who they were or irrefutable evidence of their maltreatment as measured by contemporary standards, or both. Their more fundamental goal is to fashion a more equitable *modus vivendi* between disparate groups who have little alternative but to continue to live together in the same society. Formal constitutional reform is one of the means to achieve their objectives. In a larger sense, however, regardless of the means employed in its achievement, their goal of refashioning society or of remaking a people is the ultimate constitutional pursuit.

To understand where we are and where we have come from requires a complex appreciation of a remarkable conjuncture in our constitutional life. From the official perspective natural to governments – the Trudeau government's attachment to an entrenched Charter being an important exception – the central concern has been to accommodate Quebec and, more generally, to modernize the federal system. While much of the response has been to "work" the federal system, there has been a thirty-year preoccupation with formal constitutional change.

In addition, however, to this historical agenda, a different constitutional reform agenda, not always immediately seen as constitutional, has been under way. Its main objective is a new inclusive definition of contemporary Canadians that is sensitive to their diversities. Its achievement requires a revisiting of the past. This activity may be variously described as cultural-constitutional, or societal-constitutional. It involves the efforts of yesterday's outsiders to be fully and positively included in society's view of its past and present. Its field of action is almost as broad as society itself, including more egalitarian marriages, the tolerance of differences once castigated, and the demise of beliefs supporting racial hierarchies. In general, the goal of the new agenda, if only a single phrase is allowed, is a more egalitarian society in which authentic expressions of diversity are more highly valued than deference to majoritarian conformity.[54]

Much of this agenda is pursued in normal politics, leading to changes in divorce legislation, to a proliferation of rights commissions, to affirmative action, to the symbolic presence of the formerly excluded on the Supreme Court, in cabinets, and in official roles as Lieutenant-Governors and as Governors General – the list is very long. Doubtless even more important are the cumulative consequences of the judgements implicit in how we interact with each other in our daily life. Here, often unconsciously, we contribute to the evolution of society. Gramsci said it best:

> Since all men are 'political beings', all are also 'legislators'. . . . Every man, in as much as he is active, i.e. living, contributes to modifying the social

environment in which he develops (to modifying certain of its characteristics or preserving others); in other words, he tends to establish 'norms', rules of living and of behaviour.[55]

These mundane activities are constitutional in the sense that they contribute to the shaping of what Shils called "the constitution of society through the formation of an image of the society in the minds of its members; [and] . . . the consequences of that formation for the effectiveness of authority and the maintenance of order in society."[56] These images in turn may influence the interpretation of the written constitution by judges and politicians, and thus acquire, over time, a semi-official status.

This agenda, the requirement for a people constantly to revise its self-conceptions, may also be pursued in formal constitutional politics by the citizenry, although the wisdom of that route is challenged by believers in the virtues of ordinary, participatory majoritarian politics. The obvious recent examples are the interest group pressures that helped to shape the 1982 Charter and the pressures for public involvement in the amending process to reflect the enhanced status of the citizenry. Further, the rambling, chaotic, and yet incomplete inclusiveness of the Canada clause in the Charlottetown Accord was a response to pressures from a battery of constitutional lobby groups, with differential access to the process, for favourable inclusion of their clientele in the listed categories.[57]

The constitutional agendas of governments focusing on their own governmental concerns and on historic definitions of community, and the citizens' constitutional agenda focused more on readjusting the image of society and how we value and treat each other, have surprising similarities when closely examined. Both can be pursued either by formal constitutional means or by practical arrangements or developing understandings – ranging from intergovernmental agreements to changes in rhetoric, "Indians" to "First Nations," for example – that come to be widely accepted. When the constitution is formally opened up, the concerns of both citizens and governments appear on the constitutional agenda. Indeed, our difficulty in achieving large-scale formal constitutional change is a by-product of our inability to find a synthesis of the not always complementary objectives of their separate but overlapping constitutional agendas.

Any claim to provide a definitive explanation of how history enters into our constitutional consciousness, and of how the constitutional order is challenged as historical understandings evolve, might seem to require the kind of meta-narrative against which the flourishing particularistic histories of the present are reacting. The traditional big-picture narratives – nation-building, the expansion of Europe, the discovery of America, and capitalism's mastery of nature – are now seen as rhetorical devices to deflect our attention from the marginalization of Aboriginal people, the subordination of women, the assessment of non-European peoples as inferior, and the treatment of gays and lesbians who dared leave the closet as pariahs. Such meta-narratives are now on the defensive, viewed as the ideology of the beneficiaries of historical (and still continuing) injustice and inequity. The particularistic counter-reaction is clear – women's studies, Native studies, a flourishing ethnic studies, gay and lesbian readers. We are in the midst of a great unsettling – hence the excitement, but also the ambiguities and insecurities of the present era.

Any attempt to put all of the above into a single framework, one final meta-narrative to explain the displacement of all other meta-narratives by the triumph of particularity, is probably doomed to fail. It may even be politically challenged if it appears to threaten the integrity of the social-intellectual movements now seeking to establish themselves. Encompassing explanations are sometimes wrongly interpreted as "explaining away," especially if they pay little attention to particulars that dominate the attention of activists. Or, as I heard at a conference, explanation can be construed as appropriation of someone else's hard-earned existential pain and suffering. Probing for data and for subtle indicators of meaning may even appear distasteful, out of tune with the situation – analogous to the stereotypical sociologist asking enraged rioters against some profound injustice to stop for a moment and fill out her questionnaire. Nevertheless, while our attempts to understand should not ignore certain proprieties, we should not slacken in our efforts to see ourselves in the large. A country and a people are more than a smorgasbord of particular items.

In concluding this introduction, I find it necessary for a limited retreat from the concentration on the past that I have tried to highlight as an integrating theme for the essays that follow. This is not a retreat from the assertion that understanding the influence and uses and abuses of the past is essential for students of our constitutional malaise. It is only a distancing from the impression that may falsely have crept into the preceding pages, that the past provides sufficient lens for constitutional self-understanding. It does not. We need to employ many lenses, of which history is only one.

The essays that follow do not pretend to provide an entirely consistent or comprehensive analysis of how we got to "here." They are essays, not treatises. They are suggestive, not definitive. They were written at different times for different occasions, and they reflect that fact. Even the casual reader will probably detect contradictions in essays that were often written on the run. In many cases, they are more intuitive and speculative than empirically based. They do, however, have a unity of purpose – reducing the Canadian constitutional equivalent of the blooming, buzzing confusion that William James saw as the infant's view of the world.

PART I

THE PAST, PRESENT, AND FUTURE OF
THE CANADIAN CONSTITUTIONAL STATE

Chapter One

# The Embedded State:
# State-Society Relations in Canada

## Introduction

Modern social science lacks the capacity to see society as a whole. The academic division of intellectual labour multiplies the lenses through which we view society, contributes to specialization, and discourages speculation that does not fit neatly within disciplinary boundaries. This bureaucratization of thought contributes to microprecision at the expense of macroclarification. The cost of trying to overcome this preference for the manageable is an unavoidable intrusion of a personal, somewhat intuitive approach, wide open to the arrows of critics because it is so little subject to the possibility of systematic empirical verification. While this might seem reason enough to shy away from big pictures, the fact remains that we *do* live in the large world, as well as in specific sectors of it; where we are, who we are, and where we are going *do* concern us. Indeed, the larger perspective through which we try to answer such questions invades the particulars of our existence, informs our propensity to optimism or pessimism, and contributes to feelings of anomie or empathy with and connection to the larger social order.

This is a corner of the social science enterprise where it is appropriate to stray beyond the hard data and the clear correlations, and to move in realms where the ratio of evidence to statement is precarious. Such approaches were, of course, common among the nineteenth-century founders of social science; they have always been prominent in Marxist analysis; sociology has not been immune

31

from the lure of trying to see society in the round; while historians have often been comfortable with encompassing centuries and whole societies within the covers of a single book. Yet in mainstream contemporary social science there remains a hint of illegitimacy about such enterprises, a suspicion that they are a front for smuggling in ideologies, and that they cross the dividing line between "science" and politics. These concerns are justified.

As the great burst of sociological theorizing in the nineteenth century suggests, such macro approaches have flourished at transitional times in the evolution of societies, when conventional wisdom seems irrelevant and the sense of the world is hard to find. Although it may seem like exaggeration – or a self-serving justification for this essay – to suggest that this is one of those periods in Canada, a case can be made that the times and our situation defy comprehension if we rely on yesterday's intellectual frameworks.

Consider only the most obvious points: the development of a rights-seeking entitlement society; the feminist challenge to the gender division of labour; the transformation of Quebec and the development of a state-centred nationalism that, until recently, pursued independence; the ethnicity explosion, manifested in multiculturalism and in Aboriginal demands for self-government and self-determination; the looming appearance of race relations as "visible minorities" emerge on the public agenda; the startling discrepancy between the size and the weakness of the modern state; a growing deficit, the politics of which hamper its reduction; the more general difficulty that the state experiences in changing policy directions; and, in the public sector of the federal system, a congestion of programs that defy rationalization. This list, which could be extended over pages, suggests that it would be reasonable to step back and try to find some common threads in the interdependencies, contradictions, and emergent phenomena of late twentieth-century Canada.

The primary tasks of the state are the creation and maintenance of internal order and the protection of its own territorial integrity in the international system. A related task is the integration of the regions, classes, ethnicities, lifestyles, generations, and gender and other cleavages that always threaten to pull society apart, erode the sense of community, and weaken the capacity for effective collective action. A history of Canada could easily be written around previous state efforts directed to this integrative purpose: the national policy, the post-war welfare state and the Keynesian role of government, cultural policies to generate national distinctiveness, and most recently, language policy and the Charter. An overarching state task is the provision of policy leadership for society in those areas where private actors are incapable of responding successfully.

In a comparative sense, the Canadian record of achievement on these dimensions is not to be belittled. When measured not against standards of utopia but against real-world comparisons, we have been a civil non-violent society; we are wealthy, and through the welfare state we make collective provision for one another. In our second century of existence, we are one of the oldest continuing political systems in the world.

Yet it is the theme of this essay that the tighter fusion of state and society engendered in recent decades by activist national and provincial governments simultaneously fragments the state and contributes to the multiplication and increased political salience of socio-economic cleavages. The overall Canadian federal state has become a sprawling diffuse assemblage of unco-ordinated power and policies, while the society with which it interacts is increasingly plural, fragmented, and multiple in its allegiances and identities. The more we relate to one another through the state, the more divided we seem to become. Somewhat paradoxically, however, the web of state-society interdependencies is in one way stabilizing, for it locks state and society in countless discrete overlapping linkages; this makes it necessary for us to rethink the meaning of societal integration and of community.

We must learn to think in terms of politicized societies caught in webs of interdependence with the state, and we must think of the latter as an embedded state tied down by its multiple linkages with society, which restrain its manoeuvrability. In the midst of this fusion of state and society it is increasingly appropriate to think of ourselves in terms of a growing characteristic of our lives, as political man and political woman. If other eras have been summed up by other attributes – feudal, renaissance, capitalist – our era merits the label "political" to identify its defining characteristic.

The overall task of this essay, therefore, is to undertake a preliminary exploration of the embedded state and the politicized society, of the fragmentation of both state and society that they have brought in their wake, and to reflect briefly on the impact of the preceding developments on the state's capacity for policy leadership.

## The Politicized Society and the Embedded State

The traditional state-society dichotomy invites us to view these two spheres as separate, overlapping of course, and somewhat interdependent, but still capable of being viewed essentially as distinguishable systems with distinctive principles of organization, and as transmitting their own appropriate incentives to the key actors whose activities they encompass and regulate. In the earlier history of liberal democratic states, this view had considerable plausibility. In the contemporary world, however, such a perspective subtly but seriously misleads, for it implicitly postulates a separateness that no longer exists and thus gives inadequate recognition to the new state-society fusion of the last half-century. B. Guy Peters and Marten O. Heisler correctly observe:

There is a commonplace assumption that what is public can be differentiated from what is private. In fact, that distinction is generally very elusive;
and in some circumstances it cannot be made meaningfully at all. Perhaps
the most outstanding feature of the mixed economy welfare state is the
blending and confounding of public and private. [1]

The state, of course, is not a single monolithic actor, and society is not a homogeneous mass of undifferentiated interests and values. The Canadian state is
multiple, scattered, and diffuse. Its post-war growth has produced an immense
complication of the public sector and of the machinery and institutions through
which the state seeks to manage itself and society. The combined Canadian state
at both levels is characterized by a centrifugal scattering of public authority. This
fragmentation manifests itself in federalism, in the more than 260 cabinet ministers and their departments of its eleven senior governments, and in a proliferation of government agencies and corporations only loosely connected to the
traditional responsible government focus of executive authority. Countless programs, mostly old, occasionally new, and frequently contradictory, are applied
by the thousands of separate bureaucratic units of the eleven governments. The
result is a fragmented state with a fragmenting impact on society. Social actors
are pulled in multiple directions by the scattering of state structures and policies.
The cues that the state transmits are hostile to the idea of the citizenry conducting themselves with a sense of obligation to the larger community and instead
encourage a fragmented self-interest of particular concerns.

Of course, societal fragmentation does not derive entirely from the state.
Society has its own divisive tendencies, and they contribute to the centrifugal-
ism within the structure of the state. Contemporary Canadian society is plural,
heterogeneous, and characterized by multiple cleavages. The territorial communities that required the adoption of a federal system in 1867 – and the others that
were added as Canada expanded from four to ten provinces – still exist, although
in changed form; so, too, do the cleavages associated with an economic system
that distributes income and power unequally. It is no longer possible, however,
to capture Canada's main cleavage structures by concentrating on the interaction between the continuing vertical territorial cleavages of federalism and the
cross-cutting horizontal class cleavages of capitalism. While these remain, they
have been joined in the political arena by cleavages associated with gender, age,
lifestyle, and ethnicity – including Québécois nationalism, multicultural
groups, visible minorities, and Aboriginals. This diversity has penetrated the
state structure in terms of agencies, personnel, and policy, and contributes to the
state's lack of cohesion. Neither state nor society is immune from fragmenting
tendencies in the other.

The multiple politicized cleavages of modernity intertwine with the state's internal divisions, which they both reflect and foster. The state is no longer meaningfully visualized as an aloof, distant, unitary actor presiding over a relatively autonomous society and economy for which it provides a limited bundle of public services and enforces a few durable rules of the game. Even to speak of its positive, *dirigiste*, interventionist role is to fail to grasp the new reality, for this seeming updating of the descriptive language of modern state purposes continues to suggest a no longer valid distinction between the state as actor and society as the subject of its actions. When the state is viewed as the sum total of the programs it administers, most of them the contemporary expression of yesterday's policy decisions, it is clearly seen as embedded in, or tied down to, the society it serves and has a responsibility to lead. In the crisp language of a Swedish scholar and politician, "We have become more and more governed by old decisions." [2]

New governments inherit massive program commitments put in place by their predecessors. These programs are enmeshed in bureaucracies; they are supported by clientele expectations; they are protected by the incremental processes of policy-making and budget decisions; their sanctity is preserved by their number and the crowded agenda of cabinets and legislatures that can only focus their attention on a minuscule proportion of ongoing state activity; except in revolutionary times, their existence is usually equivalent to their survival. To turn around a huge loaded oil tanker steaming full speed ahead is child's play when contrasted with the difficulty of engineering a significant change of direction for the great ship of state. The latter task is beyond the capacity of particular governments between elections. It is a task for decades of clear-sighted leadership possessed of a vision of an alternative relationship between state and society. Competitive democratic politics, the short-run perspective of most politicians concerned with the next election, and the sheer difficulty of visualizing such an alternative in the face of the intimidating complexity and interdependence of what exists all foster a pragmatic conservatism over major innovations. [3]

The conceptual necessity is to generate a style of thinking that focuses simultaneously on the politicized society and its counterpart, the embedded state. The contemporary state manoeuvres in an ever more extensive policy thicket of its own creation, interacting with a society that is tied to the state by a complex network of benefits, dependent relationships, and coercions. From this perspective the state, in confronting society, confronts its own past, and the society that seeks to influence the state directs its efforts to transforming the multiple linkages that interpenetrate and affect almost every facet of its functioning.

Public and private decision-makers collude and collide. Socio-economic actors increasingly pursue their objectives by political means. They devote ever more resources to manipulating the state or escaping from its intended reach. State actors pursue their objectives in that overlapping state-society territory created by past state efforts to lead society in preferred directions. State and societal actors, drawn into each other's orbit, jostle and intermingle in that extensive, expanding middle ground that binds and fuses them together in multiple bonds of inescapable interdependence. In the language of Claus Offe:

> In an era of comprehensive state intervention, one can no longer reasonably speak of "spheres free of state interference" that constitute the material base of the "political superstructure"; an all pervasive state regulation of social and economic processes is certainly a better description of today's order.[4]

The relationship between state and society is not one in which an active vanguard state moulds the responsive clay of an inert society willing to be fashioned according to state dictates. Neither is the state a neutral executor mechanically implementing societal choices and choosing among competing demands by some agreed calculus. It has some autonomy, and its leaders have goals for their people, but goals and autonomy operate primarily at the margin, skirmishing around the edges of the existing network of established policies linking state and society.

The interaction between the multiple power structures of the modern Canadian state and the heterogeneous interests of an open society is a complicated multi-partnered dance in which the roles of leaders and followers shuffle back and forth over time and across issues. It is simplistic to inquire who leads and who follows in the never-ending *pas de deux* of state and society. Actors in both are involved in an endless game of mutual influence. At any given time the capacity of each actor is a product of all the past games they have played together, games whose results are embedded in past policies that define the situation for each actor, games that were played out in institutional arenas derived from history and that had and have their own rules and conventions. The latter structure the game, facilitating some outcomes and inhibiting others. Yet in another sense, the game is always changing, for the actors in state and society are driven by multiple purposes, which evolve in response to restless striving and human ingenuity. The actors differ in the intelligence and skill with which they play the evolving game. As in other activities, they can improve their performance by practice and by deploying more resources.

Because both state and society are multiple, it is common for one state actor to involve segments of society in competition primarily directed against another state actor. It is equally common for private socio-economic actors to involve the state to their own advantage relative to other private actors. Crosscutting alliances, accordingly, are standard. There are winners and losers. There are negative sum, zero sum, and positive sum games. There are biases in the rules of the game and attempts to modify the rules to influence future outcomes are never-ending. The centrifugal state and the fragmented society, locked in multiple embraces and exchanging reciprocal influences, meet in many arenas. One of these is an evolving federalism.

## Contemporary Federalism and Community in Canada

To make sense of our contemporary Canadian condition it is essential to be clear on the nature of the processes at work in the interaction between the Canadian federal state and Canadian society. An historical perspective is helpful, for the relations between state and society in the federalism of 1867 are not those of the federalism of the mid-1980s. Unfortunately, too much of our thinking about federalism is still appropriate to 1867.

The federalism of 1867 was a response to regional diversities that, over and above the recognition they received at the provincial level, were also to be incorporated for national purposes into a new national political community. In 1867, the sociological bases for provincialism did not confront the reality of a coexisting national community but rather the aspiration to create such a community. Provincialism rested on historically generated territorial diversities. The Canadian community was a project for the future. Although the provincialism of 1867 was clearly political, in that it represented the continuation of the former British colonies (with the Province of Canada redivided into Ontario and Quebec, the successors of Upper and Lower Canada), it was political in a restricted sense. Provincial societies had a high degree of independence from provincial governments, which performed only limited functions. Even the central government, in spite of its nation-building responsibilities, impinged on society and economy in early post-Confederation decades with, from our contemporary perspective, a light hand. For the Laurier administration, from 1896 to 1911, "the distribution of patronage was the most important single function of the government." [5] The taxing system was primitive: income tax was not introduced at the federal level until 1917. Welfare was primarily a private matter. Regulatory activity was scant by modern standards. The modern state churning out legislation was still far in the future. Political careers were part-time, and professional bureaucratic influence on state activity was not pronounced.

For the great bulk of social and economic activity, therefore, federalism mattered little. However, as the tempo of state activity accelerated, especially after World War Two, the socio-economic impact of federalism dramatically increased. As the policy output of the state grew – with the central government in the vanguard in the 1940s and early 1950s, and with the provincial governments reasserting themselves in the 1950s and 1960s – a federalism of big governments emerged, big relative to their own past and big relative to society. Political activity and political calculation by both government and non-government actors grew as a proportion of total goal-directed activity. The two orders of government pulled society and economy into the framework of Canada-wide concerns emanating from Ottawa and provincial concerns emanating from ten provincial political executives.

The shifting balance between public and private can be seen in the ratio of total government expenditure to gross national product (GNP), which increased from 5.6 per cent in 1867, to 22.1 per cent in 1950, to 47.4 per cent in 1982. In a federal system the division between levels of government is also critical. In recent decades expenditure growth has been most pronounced at provincial and local levels. The share of the latter increased from 48.1 per cent of total government expenditure in 1950 to 56.3 per cent in 1982, after intergovernmental transfers, while the federal share declined from 51.9 per cent to 43.7 per cent over the same period.[6] The shifting shares of federal and provincial/local governments reveal the changing policy significance of membership in national and provincial communities for the citizenry. As a necessary by-product of shifts in the exercise of power by each order of government, citizens experience transformations in the relative importance of their coexisting membership in provincial and national communities.

Coexisting interventionist governments in these circumstances do not so much reflect underlying national and provincial communities, but continuously recreate them and enhance their practical significance for the citizenry. This does not necessarily mean that the process is purely state-led, but that it is institutionally structured by the forms of federalism. Citizens and groups who seek to advance state activity into new policy areas contribute as a side effect to provincializing or Canadianizing a sphere of activity formerly private and apolitical. As a consequence, the national and provincial communities are increasingly the product of the policy output of the two orders of government. Individual citizens and interest groups are induced to define themselves in provincial terms for one purpose, in national terms for another. An ever-diminishing proportion of socio-economic activity lies outside the federal system, the governments of which have been drawn ever more deeply into societies and economies subject to growing state authority.

In a unitary state, the subjection of society and the market to political authority is relatively straightforward. In a federal state where both levels of government are activist, the decline of the market and of traditional private resolution of social problems increases the significance of the federal-provincial fragmentation of public authority. Self-regulation in market and society is replaced not by a single government with at least a theoretical capacity for policy co-ordination, but by a pluralism of government power centres, which then act on society and economy to produce politicized and overlapping national and provincial societies and economies. Thus the move from private to public not only politicizes society, but at the same time divides it into national and provincial components for policy purposes.

Federalism inherently divides legislative authority and makes citizens and groups members of different communities for different purposes, and this is the reason for its choice as a system of government. The ultimate consequences for society of federal forms, however, are profound or trivial depending on the extent of state involvement in society. The ratio of nationalizing to provincializing consequences for society reflects federal/provincial differences in the exercise of authority. As more and more of society and the economy are brought within the scope of government activities, the underlying societies and economies of Canada are incorporated into national and provincial frameworks at differential rates.

The existence of strong provincial governments, and provincialized societies and economies in the sense just described, is not incompatible with the fact that in many ways interprovincial differences of values and policy choices are of diminishing significance. Unquestionably, homogenizing tendencies have been at work over the post-war years. Up until the late 1950s a conventional wisdom identified such tendencies at the level of society and centralizing tendencies at the level of elites. This was held to undermine the historic regional diversities on which federalism was assumed to be based. Subsequently, the Quiet Revolution in Quebec in the 1960s clearly reflected and contributed to a decline in the cultural distinctiveness of Quebec on which the Tremblay Report had lavished attention in its multi-volume analysis of Quebec specificity.[7] Recent scholarship portrays an increasing similarity of preferences in major policy areas.[8]

That increasing similarities may induce convergence in the policy outputs of governments does not mean that the federal system is rootless. The eleven governments are rooted in power, jurisdiction, capacity to extract resources, and in the elemental fact that they have integrated their peoples by multiple policies into national and provincial frameworks. In this policy sense, the federal state continues simultaneously to provincialize and Canadianize the citizenry, as a by-product of its routine interventionist activity, thus dividing and combining us at the same time as the more traditional bases of community are attenuated by modern conditions.

Governments also occasionally seek to modify the relative importance of national and provincial communities directly and deliberately. The national government has repeatedly attempted to limit the provincializing of the Canadian community that develops from the provincial governments' exercise of their constitutional authority. In the last half-century the federal government has fought against the balkanization of the tax system; struggled to create a welfare state in which social rights will not differ from province to province; worked obsessively under Mr. Trudeau to gain acceptance of a Charter of Rights and Freedoms to prevent the provincialization of rights, differing from province to province, that would otherwise ensue; and pushed vigorously and successfully to entrench minority language rights in the Charter. The list could be extended. In general, many of the conditional grant programs in the post-World War Two period were the result of a national government frustration with the fact that as the role of the state increased, many policy areas relevant to its conception of a national community were under provincial jurisdiction, as a result of a constitution drawn up in earlier times when different conceptions of government responsibility prevailed.

Basic to the consistent federal purpose behind these efforts has been the concept of a national community whose integrity – from the federal government perspective – is threatened by the growing role of provincial governments. The enhanced capacity of provincial governments to penetrate and mould their societies generates a counter tendency for the federal government to attempt to preserve and foster a Canada-wide community. This necessarily involves constraints on the capacity of provincial governments to employ their jurisdictional authority according to their preferences. The national government's purpose is to inject the concerns of the national community, as it views it, into provincial political arenas and to modify the policy output of provincial governments accordingly. The federal government concern over the balkanization of the economic union in the years leading up to the Constitution Act, 1982, derived part of its urgency from these political considerations. From the federal government's pan-Canadian political perspective, its opposition to the balkanization of the economic union by various provincial economic development strategies was based not only on considerations of market efficiency, but also on its opposition to the negative effects on a common Canadian citizenship implicit in provincial borders becoming barriers to the pan-Canadian mobility of labour, services, capital, and goods. Its own contribution to balkanization was of lesser concern, since it was not accompanied by rival conceptions of political community sustained by provincial governments.

The most dramatic recent example of government efforts to shape conceptions of community is found in the constitutional struggles of the past two decades. The conduct of governments in this period reveals their clear understanding that varying definitions of community have differential consequences for their own effective authority as governments, particularly in situations of intergovernmental competition. The competition between the Quebec and federal governments for citizen allegiance is especially instructive, for it reveals the penetrative efforts of the modern state to modify our self-conceptions as citizens and the nature and significance of the national and provincial communities to which we relate. That competition graphically underlined the politicization of community and identity. It revealed competitive struggles of state authorities to transform the symbolic order of the provincial state in Quebec, of the national state, and indirectly of the overall federal system. The struggles did not leave Canadians unchanged; they left us a different people in our varying collective identifications with national and provincial communities.

The country-wide image of Canada as a British country was rendered obsolete by the growth of a state-centred Quebec nationalism, which drew Francophones in that province into tighter links to and identification with the Quebec state, a term that acquired increasing currency in the 1960s. This development attenuated their country-wide linkage with a French Canada that transcended provincial boundaries, reduced the role of the Catholic Church in education and welfare, and, most importantly, led to the use of the provincial state to modify the socio-economic order in Quebec in the interests of the French-speaking majority. Among its other consequences, this entailed a political, economic, and status reduction for the English-speaking minority in Quebec and the use of provincial language policy to reduce the propensity for non-British immigrants to enter the minority English-language community rather than the majority French-speaking community. As a by-product of the tighter bonds between the Quebec government and the province's Francophone majority, Francophones elsewhere in Canada were required to redefine themselves. No longer could they view themselves as belonging to a country-wide French Canada from which four-fifths of their linguistic brethren had psychologically seceded. They, too, came to define themselves in provincial terms as Franco-Manitobans, for example, and most evocatively of all as Francophones outside of Quebec.

The emergent linkages of the French-speaking Quebec majority with the provincial state revealed that the existing federal system and the national government's weak incorporation of the Francophone side of Canadian dualism were no longer adequate. Token symbolic recognition, limited bureaucratic participation, and negligible opportunities to use French in the national capital and in the institutions of the central government were not major concerns as long as the Quebec government was weak and the French-speaking majority relatively apolitical. However, the historic poverty of the central government's recognition of the French fact and the unacceptability of the assimilation of French-Canadian minorities in the provinces of English Canada were emphasized by nationalist developments in Quebec.

Reduced to its essentials, the political agenda became starkly simple: refashioning the central government and Canadian federalism, or accepting the possible fragmentation of Canada into two or more successor states. The primary struggle was over the boundaries of community, and over the relationships – hostile or complementary – between Canadian and provincial identities and loyalties. From the federal government's perspective, the task was to refashion the symbolism and practice of the central government and the overall federal system, which could no longer be based on British imagery of who Canadians were as a people. The Bilingualism and Biculturalism Commission, the new flag, the official languages policy, the prominent roles of Quebec cabinet ministers (notably, of course, Prime Minister Trudeau), the unremitting federal government support for a Charter of Rights and Freedoms with special stress on its language provisions, and other less prominent policy thrusts were all driven by a need to construct new symbols and new practices within governments and between governments and linguistic communities, which would restore the faltering allegiance of Québécois to the central government and federal Canada.

Symbolic resources, like other resources, are scarce; consequently, the reconstruction of a symbolic order involves winners and losers. The transformation of the overall symbolic order from a British to a dualist cast clearly resulted in a status decline for British Canadians, although they remained one of the two founding peoples, or charter groups. However, the growing multicultural components of Canada – Ukrainians, Germans, Italians, East Europeans, and many others – seemed to be relegated to the status of second-class citizens outside the charmed circle of the two founding peoples.

In western Canada, status resentment was aggravated by the fact that the non-British, non-French members of the population, who were numerous, had in recent decades improved their status as they advanced economically and politically in the Prairie provinces.[9] Concurrently, they had benefited at the national level under the Diefenbaker regime, the cabinet of which was unusually ethnically heterogeneous by Canadian standards and was led by a Prime Minister inspired by an ideology of pan-Canadianism that was reflected in the 1960 Bill of Rights. The status order within which they had been making headway was abruptly deflected in another less appealing direction by the federal government response to Quebec. Their sense of displacement and exclusion was exacerbated by the fact that the Francophones in their midst, whose status was to be relatively enhanced, were a small minority in western Canada. The concern of the national government for their linguistic future was a by-product of its efforts to shore up the faltering allegiance of Quebec Francophones to Canada. Their numerical and political weakness in the provinces of western Canada was countered by their possible contribution to the resolution of political problems whose source was elsewhere – problems that were not accorded high salience by the provincial governments of the communities in which they lived.

Multiculturalism emerged as a policy requirement to alleviate the unanticipated negative consequences of singling out for privileged treatment the two official-language communities and the British and French charter groups from which they sprang. Once the federal government had begun to travel the route of recognizing ethno-national linguistic duality, it responded, through the policy of multiculturalism, to the political necessity that it encompass the ethnic heterogeneity of the country within the evolving definition of Canada it was attempting to fashion.

This complicated dance between state, language, and ethnicity was joined by another stream of development. To the Bilingualism and Biculturalism Commission the threat to Canadian unity lay in Quebec nationalism. Ten years later the Pepin-Robarts Task Force on Canadian Unity saw the threat in terms of regionalism, as well as dualism; by "regionalism" they meant centrifugal provincializing tendencies sustained and driven by activist provincial governments. Rhetorically, this was manifested in conceptions of Canada as a community of communities, which in some versions accorded primacy to provincial communities and the provincial governments based on them. Politically, it was evident in the efforts of some provincial governments to mobilize their populations in contests with the federal government. In terms of the constitutional reform agenda, this thrust was revealed in various proposals to restructure the institutions of the central government to make them more sensitive to regional needs (as defined by provincial governments) – the various Bundesrat proposals – or, as in Alberta, to erect protective barriers against federal intrusions by means of such instruments as the spending power and the declaratory power.

These manifestations of provincialism challenged the legitimacy of the federal government and the ideology of pan-Canadianism, which, in admittedly differing versions, was held by Diefenbaker, Pearson, and Trudeau from the late 1950s to the mid-1980s. The logic of intergovernmental competition when the stakes were so high induced the federal government under Prime Minister Trudeau to elaborate a counter-definition of Canada: a comprehensive conception of a national community based on individual citizen allegiance, a constitutional order in which the country was more than the sum of its provincial parts, and a society in which the rights of official-language minorities (including rights to minority-language education) were to be given constitutional recognition by both orders of government.

The constitutional compromise that emerged after protracted controversies and passionate intergovernmental exchanges included an amending formula, a resources clause, and the Canadian Charter of Rights and Freedoms. It has been discussed in numerous publications[10] and will not be explored in detail here. However, the Charter itself is unusually revealing of the relationship between socio-economic cleavages and state policies. In intent the Charter was a nation-building, and nation-preserving, as well as a rights-protecting instrument. However, the complex political process out of which it emerged produced a Charter in which many interval divisions and cleavages were accorded recognition and sometimes stimulation.

As a concession to some of the provinces, the Charter contains a *non-obstante* override clause, which allows governments that meet certain procedural requirements to enact legislation notwithstanding the provisions of section 2, dealing with fundamental freedoms, sections 7 to 14 (legal rights), and section 15 (equality rights). To the extent that the notwithstanding provision is used – and so far it has been used to exempt all legislation in Quebec from these sections, but not elsewhere – it undermines the Charter's efficacy as a nation-building instrument based on a uniform possession by Canadian citizens of rights guaranteed against both orders of government. A high incidence of use of the override by the Quebec government and its negligible utilization by other governments will reinforce dualist elements and underline the singularity of Quebec.

The inclusion of a "notwithstanding" clause was, in retrospect, not surprising, given the unquestioned nation-building purposes of the Charter to limit provincial diversity and the prominent role of provincial governments in the final constitutional settlement. Somewhat more surprising, and revealing of the politicization of an ever-increasing range of cleavages and identities, is the extent to which the Charter supplemented its basic recognition of individual rights with a singling out for special constitutional recognition of a number of particular groups. That the linguistic dualism of Canada would receive special attention and protection (sections 16 to 23) was to be expected, as it related directly to the overriding federal government purpose of giving Francophones in Quebec a stake in the whole country and of shoring up the English-speaking minority in Quebec. But the Charter also instructs the courts to interpret the Charter "in a manner consistent with the preservation and enhancement of the multicultural heritage of Canadians" (s. 27). It also protects "aboriginal, treaty or other rights or freedoms that pertain to the aboriginal peoples of Canada" (s. 25), a section supplemented in the Constitution Act (s. 35), which defines the Aboriginal peoples to include "the Indian, Inuit and Métis peoples of Canada," thus giving the Métis a constitutional recognition they previously lacked.

Perhaps most significant as an indication of the tendency of the Charter to provide constitutional support to particular groups is the affirmative action clause (s. 15(2)), which allows, as an exception to the equality clause (s. 15(1)), programs or activities that are directed to "the amelioration of conditions of disadvantaged individuals or groups including those that are disadvantaged because of race, national or ethnic origin, colour, religion, sex, age or mental or physical disability." This clause is an invitation to both orders of government to engage in micro social engineering to readjust the status order produced by history. Whatever the ultimate utility of affirmative action in overcoming unjustified inequalities, it clearly has the potential to involve the state in never-ending interventions in the public sector, in education, and possibly, by contract compliance, in the private sector on behalf of particular groups. The task is never-ending because the state, no matter how fine-tuned and successful its interventions, can never catch up with the capacity of society and the economy to generate new inequalities the justice of which can be challenged. Moreover, the pursuit of equality by affirmative action will produce

> new winners and new losers; in short, new inequalities will result from the state's interventions, and the problem of "equality versus equality" will remain a permanent one. The state will always be vulnerable to criticism in the name of equality; however, it can also always justify itself in the same name. The debate that has been opened in the name of equality is a debate *sine die*.[11]

The constitutional recognition afforded particular categories of Canadians illustrates a recurring tendency of the Canadian state. By singling out particular groups or categories for individualized treatment, it simultaneously attracts those particular groups or categories to it as patron to client, accords political salience to some and not to others, and fractures the possibility of a common citizenship focusing on more abstract and more general concerns. Moreover, it encourages the emergence of additional divisions in society to which it is pressured to provide another round of particular responses. Thomas Flanagan has recently analysed the manufacture of minorities by Canada's eleven human rights commissions, which have displayed "an extraordinary tendency to enlarge their mandate." The first comprehensive human rights legislation in Canada, the 1947 Saskatchewan Bill of Rights, prohibited discrimination on grounds of race, colour, ethnic and national origin, creed, and religion. Prohibited grounds in the eleven jurisdictions now number thirty, and have progressively moved from stigmatic criteria such as race, through life-cycle criteria such as age, to lifestyle criteria such as sexual orientation and alcohol and drug dependence.[12] Many of the nineteenth-century social theorists feared the levelling effect of the democratic state whose emergence they observed. The modern democratic state seems equally capable of multiplying differences and hiving off groups from the general community.

Taken as a whole, the exercise in constitutional renovation revealed with disturbing clarity the driving force of self-interest when the basic rules of the game are in question. In such circumstances, governmental and private interests recognize the possibility of tilting the fundamental arrangements of the state to their long-run advantage. The basic goal of governments was to enhance their control over their own societies and economies and their own constitutional position relative to that of other governments. Constitutional arrangements were viewed as tools to restructure relationships between governments and peoples and to transform citizen identities and conceptions of community. As a quick constitutional solution proved unattainable, more and more actors appeared on the scene. What began primarily as a contest between governments in Quebec City and Ottawa steadily expanded to encompass all eleven governments along with women, Aboriginals, numerous ethnic groups, the handicapped, and others. A struggle that began over the status of Quebec and French Canada ultimately produced, among other consequences, the first constitutional recognition of Métis and a generally heightened political salience for Aboriginals, women, other probable beneficiaries of affirmative action and, to a lesser extent, for non-charter ethnic groups. None of them were significant participants when the process began in the late 1960s, and their concerns were absent from the goals of the earlier players of the constitution-making game. A process intended to unite us produced a Charter of individual rights and an amending formula, but it also constitutionalized many of our differences. It did so, partly, in recognition of the increasing ethnic heterogeneity of the Canadian mosaic and, especially with the equality clause (15(1)) and the affirmative action clause (15(2)), in recognition of the claims of equality and the argument that preferential treatment by the state in the service of the disadvantaged was the vehicle for its achievement.

Whatever its long-run contribution to our evolving conceptions of equity,[13] the increasing resort to affirmative action that the constitution now invites will engender political conflict along whatever cleavage lines it singles out for attention. It will involve the state more deeply in societal conflicts, add to the politicization of society, and thus encourage the belief that society is a political artifact to be engineered by governments responding to political pressures. In conjunction with the general thesis of our discussion of federalism and community, it confirms how far removed we are from the 1867 world of state-society relations when our journey as Canadians began. In the words of Léon Dion: "Whoever we may be, whatever our profession, whatever the area of the country we inhabit, politics has invaded our lives and it is virtually impossible to escape its hold. This political invasion of our daily lives is a new phenomenon in history."[14] In this new world, our conceptions of community and identity are increasingly the result of state policy, consequences sometimes deliberately sought, but more often inadvertent by-products of the massive role of the state in our day-to-day existence.

## Intragovernmental Divisions, Incrementalism, and the Fragmentation of Community

The constitutional system is more than federalism; it is also parliamentary responsible government. To both of these institutional arrangements the Canadian Charter of Rights and Freedoms has recently been added as a third pillar. The theory of responsible government suggests the existence of an energizing central political executive based on the relatively predictable support of a parliamentary majority and thus able to translate its policy initiatives into legislation. By so doing, a cabinet is supposed to bring unity and coherence to its overall conduct of the business of government. The performance belies the theory.

As a federal public servant, H.L. Laframboise, observed recently, the federal bureaucracy is becoming analogous to a mini-international system where a corps of interdepartmental diplomats engages in negotiation with other departments in the same jurisdiction.

> This activity is becoming increasingly formalized through written contracts between parties such as memoranda of understanding between ministers, and letters of agreement between deputy heads. The form and content of these various pacts and treaties have reached a level of fastidious refinement that would do credit to Talleyrand . . . this unfortunate trend toward formality . . . reflects a prevailing, and often warranted, distrust of one another's motives within the same jurisdiction. [15]

The cabinet is thus more like a holding company of competing departments than like a football team directed by a quarterback who calls the plays and expects clockwork precision of performance from his teammates. One reason for this difference is that for a real quarterback every play is a new beginning. For cabinet, it is otherwise. All the past plays, except those few that have been repudiated, are still being played again and again by units of government who still, in 1985, respond to the legislative quarterbacking of prime ministers long departed. Any prime minister in an established political system, therefore, sits atop a pyramid of the policies of many yesterdays, the administration of which is relatively impervious to his or her role as chief executive officer of the modern state. There is neither time nor knowledge available to overhaul more than a minuscule fraction of the policies bequeathed by those who went before. Further, yesterday's policies are embedded in bureaucracies composed of career officials who view their specialized knowledge as a guarantee of tenure and promotion. They are linked in symbiotic relationships with clientele groups who have become habituated to the program in question and have probably managed to shape it increasingly to their advantage as it has undergone incremental change since its inception.

Change, therefore, operates at the margin. There is no divorce from the past. Government is a continuing organization, deeply embedded as a result of ongoing past policies in the society and economy of the country. There is a further complication: many of the government players are not on the team. They are playing different games in hundreds of Crown corporations and regulatory agencies that have been given varying mixes of actual and/or legal independence from the direct political supervision of prime ministers and cabinets.

Thus quarterbacks and prime ministers should have different skills and different ambitions. If they do not, one of them is playing in the wrong game. The quarterback has the advantage of a clean slate with each new play, but his touchdown pass is history once it is completed. Clean slates that are followed by other clean slates facilitate only ephemeral triumphs for those who write on them. Prime ministers and cabinets do not have clean slates, but their two-yard gains will influence posterity, for they will be as relatively impervious to modifications by their successors as the handiwork of their predecessors is to them.

The consequences for relations between state and society are many. First, since the major part of the state's activity at any given time is the result of continuity rather than innovation by those now in charge, most of the citizens' linkages with the state are habitual. Second, and as a consequence, the links are with the bureaucracy rather than with parties in legislatures and cabinets. The thrust and focus of the latter, which is future directed, is in normal times not of direct concern to most of the citizens and interests who are the recipients of ongoing policies and programs. Third, unlike potential new policies that retain an element of playfulness and unpredictability in their formative process, existing policies are defended by administrators and recipients, who are amenable to what they regard as improvements but quick to resist change that they define as unwelcome. Fourth, the program links between citizens and the state are highly specific. The citizens and socio-economic interests interacting with the state are not only fashioned into eleven territorial and jurisdictional communities by federalism, but they are also further subdivided into multiple categories by the departmental system of cabinet government, the sub-bureaucratic units within each department, and the host of specific policies that the latter administer. They are linked as well, in areas large and trivial, to the amoeba-like proliferation of hundreds of regulatory agencies and Crown corporations (of both orders of government), which have been deliberately distanced from cabinets and legislatures. To the academic social scientist, the fate of the Social Sciences and Humanities Research Council of Canada (sshrcc) is of vital concern, the fate of egg-marketing boards of little interest. To egg producers, the reverse is true, and the very existence of the sshrcc is probably unknown.

In terms of ongoing programs, therefore, the citizens and socio-economic interests of the country are first grouped into overall national and provincial communities by the federal division of powers, and then further subdivided in terms of innumerable specialized administrative units and the particular programs that the latter administer.

Through the lenses of federalism, the citizen can be viewed as simultaneously belonging to a national and a provincial community, both of which are increasingly politicized, and both of which fluctuate in relative importance as federalism evolves. These communities, however, are internally fragmented by their interaction with the centrifugal structure of each government and the multiple programs it administers. The citizens, in their normal interaction with the state, receive negligible incentives to view themselves as other than the aggregate of their individual linkages with governments of either order. A calculating spirit of political self-interest, the components of which differ from individual to individual and from group to group, pushes the public arena toward being another marketplace in which exchanges are mediated by power and votes rather than by dollars.

## Politicized Fragmentation

As the societies and economies of the country become inextricably entangled in the policy output of the state, political calculation occupies an ever-increasing significance in the pursuit of individual goals. Powerful incentives increase the deployment of political skills in society. Self-regarding behaviour becomes politicized. The affirmative action provisions of the Charter open up new opportunities for disadvantaged groups to bring the resources of the state to their assistance in labour markets and, possibly, in systems of higher education. Political preference becomes an alternative to market performance in the pursuit of economic survival and profitability. Firms devote considerable time to responding to government bureaucracies. Intermediaries emerge to enhance the benefits of individual and group interactions with the state. Some 480 "nationally relevant" business-interest associations have emerged in order, among other purposes, to manage relations with the state. The majority have been founded since the beginning of World War Two, with the highest rate of growth between 1961 and 1975.[16] They are particularly effective at the level of subsectoral issues, but are less so at the macro level, where they are plagued by internal divisions and contradictory interests.

Political calculation is diffused to realms of society and the economy for which it was historically irrelevant. It is manifest not only in attempts to extract benefits from the state, but also to avoid state obligations. The accounting profession, dispensing helpful advice to minimize financial obligations to the state, rides the crest of a wave. For accountants, April is the month of shortened nights and profitable days as the deadline for filing income tax approaches. Political advisers become executive assistants to corporation presidents. Faculties of Commerce and Business Administration increasingly employ political scientists and devote major attention to business interactions with the state. A late December flurry of marriages to take advantage of the tax system reveals the interaction of private planning and state planning in the most intimate areas of our existence. The sale of registered retirement savings plans (RRSPs) greatly increases in January and February in response to tax considerations. We now operate in terms of many state calendars indifferent to the movements of the solar system.

The state is not only obeyed and co-opted, it is also evaded. The most striking evidence of the latter is the underground economy, which represents an attempt to escape state regulation and state taxation. The underground economy is a response to unwanted state intrusions that cannot be successfully manipulated. It becomes a subterranean area of freedom operating beneath the surface of officially recognized and sanctioned activities. It is a phenomenon most widespread in the Communist world, but it also has a significant existence in democratic societies where state burdens of a regulatory or fiscal nature are considered oppressive. Its extent is also positively related to the laxity of each state's administrative system and the amount of corruption characteristic of each.

By its very nature, an underground economy that seeks to escape official definition and detection is not easily measured. In the Canadian case, estimates of its size are varied, but it almost certainly constitutes a significant portion of total economic activity. Economic activity that exists outside the effective purview of the state, and that in the nineteenth century was natural and legal, has now gravitated to a realm of covert exchanges, the extent of which is debatable but which is clearly massive. A recent study by Rolf Mirus put the "true size of the invisible money-based sector of the economy" in the range of 10 to 15 per cent of GNP, and growing. [17]

Further, evasive behaviour is learned. As it diffuses through those segments of the economy where its detection is most difficult, it is increasingly accepted as normal behaviour. Differences in the possibilities of participating in the underground economy foster envy and resentment in those least capable of benefiting from it. Speculatively, it may also be suggested that the underground economy is state-threatening, since its participants clearly view the state, in selective areas, as a burden to be evaded. In a profound sense it reveals the limits of successful state action. One consequence of the underground economy is that official data describe only a diminishing portion of economic activity. The extension of the state produces, in selected spheres, a dangerous unreliability in the data base for state operations. The state becomes, in part, a negative pied piper to the extent that its tunes fall on unreceptive ears. Its attempts to control and extract resources are met by selective counterattempts to escape and hide in the nooks and crannies that the arm of the state cannot reach. The underground economy merits extensive examination as a key indicator of a significant tendency in the political sociology of the contemporary Canadian state.

The state has become a ubiquitous factor in our calculations. Power, influence, income, and status are no longer seen as the product of anonymous impersonal forces of the market or of tradition. S.M. Lipset, after approvingly citing Max Weber's thesis that class action requires that "the fact of being conditioned must be distinctly recognizable,"[18] explained agrarian protest by the visibility of the market and price system by which farmers felt themselves oppressed. The Winnipeg grain exchange, the CPR, the elevator companies, and the tariff all seemed to exemplify the manipulation of the price system by powerful interests who controlled the state. The visibility of the enemy facilitated agrarian mobilization by generating the assumption that a change in political power relationships was the route to enhancement of economic status and security.

The visibility of the state's role in distributing advantages and disadvantages has grown enormously since the agrarian protest movements of the decades up to World War Two. The state has become the arbiter of competing conceptions of social justice incapable of permanent resolution. The result is a process of competing claims powered by the recognition that the state can be an ally in the search for equality and privilege. The state, from this perspective, becomes a series of hurdles or opportunities, or barriers and loopholes, with respect to which we pursue our purposes. The opening up of the constitutional issue, and the self-interested bargaining it unleashed and revealed, were especially pointed lessons of what citizens and groups had been learning since the Great Depression: that the state is more than an umpire, and that it is not exclusively an instrument that involves our better selves playing civic roles and making disinterested contributions to the public weal. Rather, it is intimately involved in what William Goode reminds us is the ubiquitous societal process of constant renegotiation of the status of the members of society.[19]

The politicization of ethnicity noted above made it clear that the overall symbolic order of the state was a politically created artifact and that the ethnic distribution of power, income, status, and language use was subject to political modification. Simultaneously, an awakened Aboriginal self-consciousness led to demands for major strides in self-government, up to and including self-determination.[20] Aboriginals, of course, were subject to deep internal fissures derived from history, geography, and differences of legal status. In the last fifteen years the political activity of Aboriginals has greatly increased, partly as a result of state financial support, partly because of the opening up of the constitutional issue, which provided them with a forum they were quick to exploit. As the definition of Aboriginals expanded to include Métis, given constitutional recognition for the first time by the Constitution Act, 1982, the stimulation of their self-consciousness was accompanied by an increase in their political demands.

Concurrently, the gender division of power in society – including politics, the work force, the economy, and the family – was challenged by the women's movement. Lifestyle groups challenged the normative dominance of heterosexuality and asserted a right to free choice of sexual partners and sexual practices. The handicapped have emerged to challenge the stigmata and socio-economic penalties attached to their physical or mental disabilities.

It is tempting, but misleading, to focus solely on the domestic sources of our internal diversities. The federal state, with its two orders of government, and the Canadian society with which it interacts are caught up in international forces that play on governments and peoples. While our economy has been internationalized by the post-war, liberal international economic order, our society has also been caught up in international forces. The women's movement, for all its national variations, challenges the gender division of labour and of society itself throughout the democratic capitalist world. The politics of Canadian Aboriginals cannot be understood without reference to the organizational links and psychological affinities with Aboriginals in other countries who are undergoing a similar ethnic revival. More generally, Aboriginal demands for self-government derive sustenance from the ending of European empires in Africa and Asia and the overthrow of the racial hierarchies on which they were based. Gays, who challenge both the traditional definition of the family and the dominance of the norm of heterosexuality, are linked with similar movements outside Canada from which they derive ideas, strategies, and moral support. The United Nations Universal Declaration of Human Rights and numerous special international covenants are quickly transformed into domestic political demands by citizens in Canada and elsewhere. In sum, political aspirations, alternative identities, competing values, and new definitions of the appropriate relations between men and women, young and old, workers and employers, parents and children, the able and the handicapped, and citizens and states sweep across national borders. The contemporary internationalization of social movements and political life, stimulated by the penetrative power of contemporary media of communication, is integrally linked to centrifugal tendencies in contemporary democratic politics that complicate the role of governments.

These centrifugal tendencies derive from a pluralistic explosion of self-consciousness organized around cleavages and differences that do not emerge directly from class or from the economy. This self-consciousness refers initially to a particular group or social category – women, Aboriginals, Francophones outside Quebec, the disabled, and many others – and secondly, to the now commonplace understanding that the state is the relevant agent for remedial actions. The particular form of contemporary political self-consciousness in Canada is partially shaped by the diffusion of a rights mentality in the last quarter-century.

Many of the rights are positive rights in that they require action by the state if they are to be honoured. Recognition of a right and its honouring by the state are complex phenomena. From a narrow utilitarian perspective, rights can be reduced to a transaction between the state and a citizen, in which money in the form of Old Age Security is transferred from the former to the latter, or the occupational position and income of a member of a disadvantaged group is improved by affirmative action. Equally important, however, is the state role in conferring status, recognizing identities, and providing meaning for the citizenry. As the state role increases, the symbolic order in which it is situated becomes much more consequential. The symbolic order is now a prominent arena within which there is competition for the scarce goods of recognition and status.[21] At the time of writing (May, 1985), the issue of compensation and public apology to Japanese Canadians for their wartime treatment by the Canadian government nearly half a century ago is on the public agenda. The role of Riel as martyr, scapegoat, or recipient of a fair trial in the 1880s is hotly debated. Leaders of women's groups and Aboriginal movements seek to change our understanding of the past. Ethnic studies flourish, and the state funds ethnic histories. The competitors for social recognition realize that history is not dead, but is a resource that can be put to use for contemporary purposes. Since the state is the major actor in education and is centrally involved in research funding, its policies are subject to political challenge by numerous groups who see justice and advantage in particular changes involving curricula and subjects for research.

Our multiple interactions with the state do not leave us unchanged. Our very identities are transformed. Our political, social, and economic selves are brought together in the state arena where they are shuffled, combined, and divided by the multiplicity of state linkages with our no-longer-private selves. The public and the private are intertwined. In recent years we have seen the politicization of language, the politicization of ethnicity and civic identities, the politicization of sex and gender through the feminist movement and the abortion issue, the politicization of rights, the politicization of ownership and control of the economy, the politicization of research through the strategic grants programs of the SSHRCC, and the politicization of medicine and hospital care. As we move from cradle to grave, we move through successive stages of age-related state-welfare schemes. The point at which life begins in the transition from conception to birth is now a political decision. The point at which life ends is indirectly a state decision, mediated through funding decisions and state criteria, direct or indirect, which ultimately dictate when life-support systems should be shut down.

The preceding and other indications of politicization are not all completely new, but most of them are new in terms of extent and visibility. Most important, the cumulative effect is profoundly new. We have experienced, to borrow a phrase, a Quiet Revolution.

Centrifugal tendencies in the state and the multiplication of cleavages in society reinforce one another. Part of the centrifugal tendencies within governments represents state efforts to establish linkages with the evolving cleavages within society. Thus the older client departments of Veterans Affairs and Indian Affairs have been supplemented by new state agencies that single out women, youth, consumers, regional development, small business, and multiculturalism. In addition, the commissioners of official languages, human rights, and privacy play watchdog roles on behalf of the clientele or values they are mandated to preserve and foster.

Most of these new advocacy departments and commissions have limited line responsibilities. They scrutinize and monitor policy development from the vantage point of multiple special interests. From one perspective, this represents the invasion of the state by society; from another, it represents the politicization of society. From both perspectives, it represents the linking of political/bureaucratic struggles with underlying societal conflicts over the distribution of status, power, and privilege within society. The result is a species of bureaucratized pluralism that reinforces and reflects the societal fragmentation it singles out for special attention. The regulatory arm of the state attracts another cluster of specialized interests to agencies such as the CRTC and the CTC. In these discrete regulatory arenas highly focused conflicts are played out with their own rules for participation, representation, and policy formation.

We approach the state through a multiplicity of classificatory systems (derived from state policies, state agencies, and the discretion of administrators) that define us by gender, age, ethnicity, region, and producer or consumer status and whether we are French-speaking or English-speaking. We are politicized and fragmented simultaneously. Some of our traits are privileged; others are ignored. We approach the state as fragmented selves, calculating the advantages of stressing our ethnicity, our age, our gender, our region, our language, our sexual preferences, our doctorates, or our disabilities.[22] Shifting self-definition in response to state cues increases the size of any non-ascriptive group to which the state hands out privileges and reduces membership in non-ascriptive categories subject to penalties and disadvantages.

The multiple classificatory paradigms of the modern state are subject to constant evolution. The significance of those that exist is subject to modification by organizational change. Cabinet and administrative changes are closely watched by relevant clientele to see if their power and status are rising or falling. Appointments of ministers to particular portfolios, or of the heads of agencies visibly identified with a particular interest, are observed with pleasure or chagrin, depending on the higher meaning that can be read into them. Now that the Charter is in effect, appointments to the Supreme Court will be closely monitored by groups with a stake in Charter interpretation. A socio-psychological history could be written of the mix of rumours and proposed policies attending the future of the federal role in Indian affairs. Its projected or rumoured demise or cutback results in angry mobilization by Indians in its defence, followed by reassurance that the rumours are unfounded, that the policy has only been proposed, not accepted, and that nothing will be done without consultation. The only certainty is that the cycle will be repeated.

Each bureaucratic rearrangement or policy change by the state has an unequal incidence on diverse social actors. When, in 1966, the federal government changed its policy of direct subsidization of universities to channelling financial support through provincial governments, the Canadian Union of Students, which had located itself in Ottawa in response to the previous policy, was left stranded. It collapsed three years later, as it no longer had a *raison d'être*.[23] New state categorizations change our behaviour and our self-definition. They modify the relationship among the varied multiple identities that we carry through life. At the same time, society and economy, driven by their own imperatives, unceasingly churn out new distinctions and new patterns of inequality, which interact unpredictably with existing state categories and generate pressures for their redefinition or supplementation.

In political terms, we come to exist as a multiplicity of those discrete selves that the state has singled out for attention. We act as managers of our shifting selves in the same way that business adjusts to changes in tax laws and regulations. We are like Kremlinologists constantly looking for clues. The flexible multiple identities fostered by our interactions with the state work against our civic sense of wholeness.

It is not irrelevant to inquire in particular cases whether state cleavages generate social cleavages or the reverse. That question, however, is a subject for case studies. To step back and attempt to see the process whole is to conclude that what exists is a complex system of exchanges in which the state is likely to recognize and sustain cleavages that are to its advantage, and that private interests, defined in innumerable ways, seek recognition and support. They will redefine themselves if a redefinition is plausible and increases the chances of state support. The competition is unequal. Producers carry more weight than consumers, although both are recognized. The disabled are defined as candidates for affirmative action by section 15(2) of the Charter. Gays are not. The overall tendency is for the state to pick up and recognize more and more identities and cleavages that are reinforced by their association with the state.

## Where Are We Now?

The nature of the state-society symbiosis that this essay has explored is a fascinating subject in its own right, justifying its examination for all the reasons that lead us to try to satisfy our curiosity about the way we live. Beyond that, however, an understanding of its nature, more profound than this speculative essay can provide, is essential to our understanding of contemporary citizenship and community, and of the capacity of the federal state to provide the policy leadership that future domestic and international concerns will unquestionably require.

It may be useful to put the changes in state-society relationships in broad historical perspective. The thrust of the transition period as Western society moved from feudalism to a system of competitive capitalism under the aegis of the nation-state was to free the competition for social status, income, and economic power from the hampering entanglements of feudal social arrangements and ascriptive criteria. The freeing of the economy and the ideology of markets and competition produced, from the vantage point of a broad historical sweep, a remarkable separation and distinctiveness of the spheres of the state on the one hand, and society and economy on the other. That period proved unstable.

The disintegrating consequences of the market for society threatened to generate a pervasive anomie destructive of community, or to set class against class as market-generated inequalities proved unacceptable to the working class. The last half of the nineteenth century in the United Kingdom, as Dicey noted, was characterized by a growth of collectivist sentiment and legislation. In Germany, Bismarck introduced social legislation in the 1880s to pacify and integrate the working class into the German nation. The world wars of the twentieth century and the Great Depression of the 1930s further exalted the state's role, reduced market autonomy, and brought state, economy, and society into a closer nexus. In Canada, J.A. Corry wrote perceptively in 1936 of the independent public corporation under the apt heading of "The Fusion of Government and Business."[24] Polanyi's *Great Transformation* was being reversed in Canada as elsewhere.[25] The progressive expansion of the welfare state and the increasing social role of the state in response to new cleavages not directly derivative of the economy or the class system pushed state and society to a higher level of mutual interaction and penetration.

The focus on Canada in the preceding pages too easily leads to an insularity of perspective that should be resisted. As John Boli-Bennett concludes, after a comprehensive examination of national constitutions from 1870 to 1970, a "progressive" global ideology has developed that "calls for continual expansion or growth of state authority . . . for an augmentation of state jurisdiction over society and citizens that, like economic growth, population, and pollution, appears to follow an upwardly accelerating curve." That world ideology is a product of a global process that is "largely independent of, and strongly shapes, particular national processes." Individual states and peoples respond to evolving international definitions of what it means to be a state.[26] For any particular state, these definitions are largely given, and they limit the extent of national variations in state-society relations. The Canadian example, accordingly, is a case study of the impact on one country of global forces to which we have added idiosyncratic variations derived from the particulars of our situation.

To capture the contemporary interpenetration of state and society in descriptive language is not easy, for our language, including the language of the social sciences, posits a separateness of state from society and the economy that no longer exists. The recent literature positing the autonomy of the state[27] is a welcome advance from assumptions that the state is no more than a reflecting mirror, or a neutral arena where contending social interests struggle ceaselessly for advantage. The state is unquestionably actor as well as umpire. Political and bureaucratic elites have their own goals for society, as well as their own interests to protect. And, given the massive resources at their disposal, they frequently get their way. However, the stress on autonomy can lead to an uncritical view of the state as aloof and distant. Realistically, autonomy exists only at the margin where the state can play a catalytic role with new ventures. The overriding reality, therefore, is not state autonomy, but interdependence. The state, as a result of past performance, is embedded in society, linked in thousands of ways to interests in society that no longer can meaningfully be described as private.

The state-society symbiosis derives from the elementary consideration that, especially in an era of big government, changes in state structure and policies always produce changes in the behaviour of social actors. Equivalently, changes in society and the economy, whatever their source, have repercussions on the state and on existing policies when society and the state are deeply intertwined. The declining isolation of state and society from each other means that each is now caught in a network of subtle moves and countermoves in a never-ending game of shifting competition and collaboration. When both society and state are broken down into their numerous respective interests, ambitions, and identities, the game is more correctly seen as a gigantic chessboard in which no player can clearly grasp the future moves of the other players and hence can make only a tentative assessment of the probabilities of winning and losing.[28]

From one perspective, the multiple fragmentation of society to which the state-society symbiosis has led is not without its advantages for integration. The non-territorial distribution of the emergent structure of multiple cleavages, with the partial exception of Aboriginal communities, inhibits secessionist tendencies and forces the interests concerned to struggle with one another within the framework of given national and provincial communities. In addition, multiple cleavages contribute to cross-pressures, thus reducing the intensity of demands. The nationalist pressures of the Parti Québécois government were ultimately constrained by the Canadianism of a majority of the referendum electorate. By the same token, defeat in one arena can be compensated for by victory in another. Finally, multiple cleavage structures provide state elites with manoeuvrability and discretion in their response to specific demands.

The relationship of the cleavage structure of society to national unity and integration has been a recurring concern to students of Canadian politics. Horowitz, Porter, and others have argued the desirability of strengthening the class cleavage that would integrate Canadians across provincial boundaries by stressing the class differences of income and power generated by a capitalist economy. The democratic class struggle, John Porter's creative politics, would shift debate to the national level and thus have centralizing consequences for the federal system. Moreover, classes, lacking a territorial base, cannot threaten secession and thus pose a lesser challenge to the integrity of the Canadian state than do cleavages coinciding with provincial boundaries.

The class cleavage, however, was viewed as a single cleavage. The cleavages fostered by the social role of the modern state, interacting with a society for which gender, ethnicity, language, competing lifestyles, and other cleavages and divisions have supplemented class, are multiple. The emergent nationalist community, therefore, promises to be more internally fragmented and plural than was assumed by those who asserted the integrative capacities of the democratic class struggle. This also holds true for provincial communities, which are subject to similar multiple cleavages, although on a smaller scale.

The consequences for the state of its own fragmentation, whether they are deliberately sought or inadvertently produced, are ambiguous. As Peter Hall argues with respect to France, there are political advantages accruing to a state that does not overcome its internal divisions:

> A state faced with multiple tasks and well-defined conflicts of interest among the social classes it governs, or the groups within these, may find it necessary to maintain a degree of deliberate malintegration among its various policy-making arms so that each can mobilize consent among its particular constituencies by pursuing policies which, even if never fully implemented, appear to address the needs of these groups. In many cases the pursuit of incompatible policies renders all of them ineffective, but this strategy prevents any one group from claiming that the state has come down on the side of its opponents. [29]

This, however, is a type of integration or social pacification by deception. It keeps us together by separating us from one another. It fragments our civic wholeness by parcelling out our various discrete concerns to multiple separate agencies, which neither we nor the state can bring together again. As we shall note below, this form of integration by fragmentation comes at a price, for it is more likely to preserve policy rigidities derived from the past than to support policy initiatives that require changes of direction or policy reversals. The mobilization of diffuse support for major policy change is frustrated by the typically greater countermobilization of the beneficiaries of specific existing programs, in government and society, who resist change considered detrimental to their particular concerns.

The contemporary Canadian state manoeuvres gingerly through the minefield of its own past decisions. As it scans the socio-economic environment, it encounters its former self, and it approaches society through structures beset by contradictions that are themselves resistant to change. In the words of a political scientist who was involved in the 1973 Working Paper on Social Security, "to characterize Canada's tangle of federal-provincial and interdepartmental jurisdictions as a fragmented decision system is to understate the case."[30] In a period of economic recession and in an international setting that imposes severe adjustment demands on society, economy, and polity, the costs to the contemporary Canadian state of rigidities and internal contradiction threaten to become inordinately high. The virtues attributed to a system of parliamentary government resistant to tying down the future become almost irrelevant in the face of the multitudinous entrenchments of past policies, the beneficiaries of which resist adjustment. Society and polity experience a diminished manoeuvrability, the unanticipated consequence of past decisions undertaken in a more optimistic climate in which the future was to generate a sufficient surplus to allow a necessary flexibility at the margin.

We have long known that institutions represent a mobilization of bias, that states are historical products whose evolution is subtly channelled by the incentives and disincentives of their institutional arrangements, arrangements that are usually peculiarly resistant to change. Institutional congealment and the mobilization of bias to which it contributes are supplemented by the congealment of past policies, which, deeply entangled with society, require Herculean efforts for their modification. In the real world, the analytical distinctions among the institutions of the state, the past policies it has pursued, and the society/economy of the country cannot be located. What now exists is a series of overlapping governmentalized societies in which the limits to the effective exercise of political authority are set not by society or economy conceived as autonomous entities, but by the embedded enduring interactions between government and society/economy. The growth of government, as Peters and Heisler observe, produces a

> certain paradox of power. At the same time that government has been growing in terms of the number, range, and extent of its regulations of society, it appears to have lost effective power and authority over the society and indeed its broader environment. It is perhaps the very extent of its activities, their frequently unintended consequences, the presence of contradictory goals of agencies, and the extension of activities to include policy areas not obviously amendable [sic] to collective control or the quick technological fix that have led to this unhappy situation.[31]

When the requirement is for policy manoeuvrability in a period of straitened circumstances, the contemporary state finds retreat much less manageable than were the previous advances whose contemporary consequences now strain its resources. The difficulties of retreat or major change have been vividly manifested in the failure of tax reform after the Carter Commission, the difficulty of bringing the deficit under control, and the resistance to attempted changes in family allowances in the early 1970s and more recently. The repetition of yesterday's policies continues, despite their often partial obsolescence and their often negative consequences.

In these circumstances of built-in rigidities and vetos, it is scarcely surprising that federal and provincial political elites increasingly resort to a unilateralism of "act first and pick up the pieces afterwards."[32] The *fait accompli* takes its place in the arsenal of democratic statecraft – hence the manner of Ottawa's introduction of wage and price controls, the Trudeau announcement of massive federal budgetary cutbacks, in 1978, against self-protective instincts of government departments, the unilateral change in fiscal arrangements in 1977, the federal unilateralism threatened throughout the recent constitutional exercise, and the leadership style of the British Columbia government in a period of cutbacks. A Gaullism of action, supplemented by demagoguery, is no longer an isolated tendency in contemporary statecraft. This type of response to a Byzantine blockage that threatens paralysis may, in particular circumstances, be necessary and efficacious. It has little to offer as a long-run recipe, for it destroys civility, undermines the spirit of constitutionalism, and encourages a reciprocity of competing unilateralisms that no interdependent political economy can digest.

The thesis of the women's movement – "the personal is political" – is of general application. The magnification of political calculations as we go about our daily rounds does not leave us untouched. Political man and political woman have distinctive characteristics. They constitute a new species qualitatively different from their predecessors, who could be defined by the adjective "economic" or "religious." Whether they are more or less lovely or unlovely than the predecessors they have displaced can be left to the moral philosophers. That they are a new creation whose emergence is a happening rather than a deliberate product of conscious choice is clear. That we shall have to come to grips with this new phenomenon is also clear. Its emergence changes the nature of the state, of politics, and of society, and thus changes the subject matter of the social sciences. From the perspective of democracy, the problem is that the politicization of multiple cleavages, in conjunction with the extensive social differentiation characteristic of modern society, erodes our identity as citizens concerned with the whole. "Typical for subsystems in differentiated societies is that they combine high sensibility for specific problems with indifference toward all other problems."[33] The fragmentation of society simultaneously generates an urgent need for political leadership and social cohesion, and works against their appearance. Our political selves get in the way of our civic selves.

It remains true that in most ways contemporary Canada is more humane, more democratic, and, it has been debatably suggested, Canadians are "certainly ... [a] happier" people than they were in the world in which our parents were young.[34] These achievements are neither to be lightly dismissed nor casually overturned. Nevertheless, it is also true that the road we have travelled has led us to a new agenda of problems with which Canadians must now grapple.

In responding to this new agenda it is necessary not to shelter every activity of modern government in Canada under the rubric of the welfare state, and thus impervious to criticism. It is far from evident that the major beneficiaries of modern state activity are the poor, the downtrodden, the disadvantaged, and the helpless. The complexity of the modern state puts a premium on the possession of political skills, organizational power, financial resources, and insider knowledge. J.S. Woodsworth had other recipients in mind.

It is also necessary not to caricature the state-society fusion under conditions of political democracy, and thus unwittingly equate it with the attempted annihilation of civil society by the state, as in the Soviet Union.[35] State power in Canada is so widely dispersed and its application so fragmented that the state is incapable of achieving anything approximating total control of the citizenry. It can scarcely keep its own house in order. Its inefficiency, combined with the culture and practices of democracy, makes its relationship with society loose and relatively benign rather than malign.[36]

Beyond the question of the domestic distribution of the advantages and disadvantages of modern state activity and the comparative mildness or rigour of the state's grip on society there is another issue. In some sense the world of nations, states, economies, and societies is Darwinian. The world will not leave us alone. The domestic political economy of a successful response to the openness and interdependence of the modern world requires a discriminating reappraisal of the institutional and policy legacy of yesterday. This is a task not for the bulldozer, but for rational analysis that must include the particulars of the state-society symbiosis we have inherited in the light of the challenges we have to meet. The intellectual task, by itself, is overwhelming. Unfortunately, it is relatively easy compared to the daunting political task of doing whatever it is decided should be done.

The world of politics is not an academic seminar but a political world of interests whose advocates focus on the short run. To them analysis is good or bad, depending on its utility for their goals. Nevertheless, disciplined inquiry remains our most significant tool in that difficult search for a society that is simultaneously humane and adaptive to the world of the future that is now, as always, knocking at our door.

Chapter Two

# The Past and Future of
# the Canadian Administrative State

A few years ago Albert O. Hirschman published a collection of his essays under the title *Essays in Trespassing: Economics to Politics and Beyond.* He described "their unifying characteristic [as] the propensity to trespass from one social science domain to another and beyond."[1] Such intellectual trespassing is sometimes functional, always difficult, and frequently disastrous for those who lack Hirschman's intellectual dexterity and imaginative flair. Nevertheless, we are compelled to trespass because the shifting reality outside our windows is disrespectful of the disciplinary categories and boundaries we employ. This is especially so for students of the state, which has re-emerged as a major focus of interdisciplinary attention. Hence the dramatic growth in Canada of an interdisciplinary political economy orientation focusing on the state, and the emergence of the law and economics movement. Further, the Canadian Charter of Rights and Freedoms has reinvigorated the constitution's role in Canadian life and has stimulated intellectual links between law and political science. More generally, the recently formed Canadian Law and Society Association is remarkably eclectic in disciplinary terms. Thus, the interdisciplinary nature of this conference is to be applauded.

The central focus of the conference is the administrative state, its likely evolution, alternatives to its commanding presence, and its compatibility with the theory and practice of constitutional government in Canada. My approach to these concerns reflects the revival of political scientists' interest in the state. A flourishing literature has developed around the theme of the autonomy of the democratic state, a literature that takes for granted that democratic office-holders are more than puppets of the influences that flow through the system of elections and party competition, and more than some version of an executive committee of the bourgeoisie.[2] My task is to portray selectively the past, present, and future administrative state in Canada, underlining aspects that might otherwise escape attention. Since any state is constantly redefining its purposes, and indeed its nature, in the light of shifting cues from the domestic and international environments, including the intellectual environment of competing efforts to understand its development, I do not consider the observations that follow as tedious preliminaries to examination of the "real" thing – the state existing in splendid isolation from the buffeting world and from its own history.

Unfortunately, several approaches that in an ideal world might commend themselves would exceed my space limitations and my command of the relevant literatures. Thus, I cannot provide in a few pages a detailed interpretive survey of the burgeoning literature on the state, much of it Marxist, or even a less ambitious dispassionate appraisal of the ideological controversies that seem inseparable from the study of the state. Nevertheless, the intrusions of ideology appropriately remind us that the understandings we seek emerge from our citizenship and involvement as well as from the more purist concerns of the academic cloister. Indeed, we are so shaped by the state that we are unavoidably engaged in self-discovery as we explore the Leviathan that pervades our existence.

The kind of large macroperspective appropriate to a focus on the state is a particular genre of social science in which intuition and world views have a more pervasive influence than they do in more focused, empirical microstudies. This reflects both the shapelessness and the many-sided nature of the modern state. The developed Western state is a sprawling, labyrinthine giant, with numerous dispersed power centres, a limited capacity for co-ordinated action, and a ubiquitous presence in the societies for which it plays a fragmented leadership role. It is a complex mix of historic institutional arrangements and evolving normative concerns. It is the source of one of our most significant identities, citizenship. It outlasts the transient generations successively subject to its sway. Canada, we too infrequently remember, has one of the oldest uninterrupted constitutional systems in the contemporary world. In constitutional terms, Canadians are an historic people.

The Canadian state is not a distant Olympian presence but an omnipresent factor shaping the way we pursue every one of our objectives.[3] In Canada almost a quarter of the labour force is employed in the public sector, defined broadly to include public enterprise, health, and education,[4] and workers in this sector thus have a dual relation to the state, as employees and as citizens.

An excessive concentration on the boundaries between state and society or state and economy, or on the division of labour between them, distracts attention from the fact that the society and economy of contemporary Canadians have been profoundly shaped by past state actions.[5] We are born into a going concern – a state-society symbiosis – that is the product of all the past encounters of our predecessors with the predecessor to the Canadian state of the 1990s.

That symbiosis is not the result of a plan or design of a founder, or the conscious pursuit by several single-minded generations of a dominating, guiding vision. The policies we encounter in the welfare state, in transportation, in the Criminal Code, and elsewhere are classic examples of an incrementalism whose overall ragged pattern is a happening, not an intended outcome. The aggregate product of the endeavours of our ancestors, the contemporary administrative state in Canada, is the cumulative consequence of thousands of past decisions and actions, scattered over more than a century, by political and bureaucratic elites who necessarily had little appreciation of the state-citizen relationship to which they were contributing.

Writings on the administrative state, particularly if they take the individual as the unit of analysis, are prone to analyse the state as a structure of incentives and disincentives within which individuals manoeuvre if their life chances are likely to be significantly affected. From this perspective, state structure and state policies are simply changing contexts within which unchanging individuals pursue their goals. This approach implicitly sees behaviour variations as purely instrumental, as irrelevant to the inner person. This, however, is falsely to assume that feudal man, capitalist man, and Soviet man differ only with respect to the externals of their behaviour rather than, as is surely the case, that they are anthropologically differing versions of our common humanity. Accordingly, it behooves us to ask what the administrative state does to the character, identity, and values of the citizenry. To ask these questions is only to suggest that we become anthropologists of our changing selves. Not to ask them may be to miss the essence of the change we are experiencing.

## Preliminary Reflections on the
## Administrative State in Canada

In the nineteenth century, all governments were small. Now all governments are big. We cannot return to simpler times. The size of contemporary government in Canada, as elsewhere, is not the result of intellectual error, of idiosyncratic factors, or of the personal goals of particular politicians. The basic similarity of trends in democratic capitalist nations clearly indicates that in general, Canadians are dealing with broad systemic factors within which limited national variations are played out.[6]

The modern administrative state defies simple description. V. Seymour Wilson and O.P. Dwivedi provide a helpful definition: "[T]he administrative state denotes the phenomenon by which state institutions influence many aspects of the lives of citizens, especially those aspects which relate to the economic and social dimensions. It describes a system of governance through which public policies and programs, affecting almost all aspects of public life, are influenced by the decisions of public officials."[7]

The attempt to pin down the contemporary administrative state is doomed to failure. Its very boundaries become unclear as the state increasingly involves numerous private actors in its pursuit of goals by joint ventures, contract compliance in the service of disadvantaged minorities, and extensive and discretionary funding of many of the pressure groups that then appear before parliamentary committees seeking policy changes advantageous to themselves. An emerging category of instrument choice that further blurs the public-private dividing line is that of "chosen instruments," defined by John L. Howard and W.T. Stanbury as "privately owned corporations which are systematically favored by government in order to achieve public policy objectives."[8] Finally, by the socialization processes directly under its control in education, supplemented by its extensive powers of suasion, exhortation, and manipulation of symbols, the state seeks to mould the citizen's perceptions of self, community, and rights and duties in line with the requirements of the constitutional order.

From the vantage point of the state almost no realm of individual behaviour is entirely outside its orbit of control. From the perspective of the individual no major purposes can be pursued without encountering the state as an enemy or an ally, existing or potential. As Claus Offe observes, "In an era of comprehensive state intervention, one can no longer reasonably speak of 'spheres free of state interference' that constitute the material base of the 'political superstructure'; an all-pervasive state regulation of social and economic processes is certainly a better description of today's order."[9]

The instruments employed by the modern state are so various and incommensurable, its programs are so frequently unco-ordinated and often contradictory, so much of its behaviour now lies outside the system of accountability supposedly sustained by the practice of responsible government, and so intimately and reciprocally is it intertwined with society that it is better to multiply vantage points for its examination than to seek the spurious simplicity of a single defining characteristic.

The contemporary Canadian administrative state is made up of not one but many actors, not only because of the obvious presence of federalism and the inescapable relative autonomy of departments headed by ministers, but also because of the vast system of "structural heretics" (regulatory agencies and Crown corporations) whose autonomy is no less real for being deliberately granted. This organizational pluralism of the contemporary state is supplemented by a pluralism of policies, both of which have historical roots. The passing parade of office-holders operates only at the margin. They preside over a pragmatic smorgasbord that includes legacies from every year of our existence as a people. The contemporary manifestations of the administrative state can no more be understood by analysing those who now wield bureaucratic, political, and judicial power than the essence of the Vatican can be extracted by concentrating on the contemporary pope and his advisers. "Tradition," as Chesterton put it, "refuses to submit to the small and arrogant oligarchy of those who merely happen to be walking around."[10]

I will employ a handful of organizing rubrics to underline key aspects of the reciprocities of influence between the contemporary administrative state and the society and economy of the country. This focus reflects my belief that we require bridging perspectives focusing on the meeting ground of state and society. Those perspectives must go beyond the mediating role of parties and intermittent elections so beloved by political scientists, and the court decisions minutely examined by lawyers, to encompass the day-to-day totality of the ubiquitous embrace of these Siamese twins destined never to be separated. Further, the approach should partake of the *Annales* historical school and search for the profound historical patterning that states and societies have imprinted on each other, leaving ephemera to the journalists.

I cannot, of course, live up to my own injunction, but it may be possible to be suggestive and even provocative. Initially, however, it is necessary for me to present some elementary data to indicate the scope and diversity of the contemporary Canadian administrative state.

Students of the administrative state need to heed the wise admonition of Richard Bird that significant aspects of contemporary state activity "do *not* lend themselves to systematic quantitative treatment," although they may be no less important than those that do.[11] An assessment, let alone a measurement, of the activities of the state is further complicated by the tendency of governments to employ indirect means and oblique instruments to attain their goals.[12] However, the admitted inadequacy of statistics in portraying the reality of the Canadian administrative state is surpassed by the even greater inadequacy of approaches that eschew completely such aids to understanding. While the "indicators" noted in the following paragraphs "cannot be 'added up' as they are incommensurable,"[13] their presentation helps to underline both the magnitude and the diversity of the contemporary administrative state in Canada.[14]

Although firm estimates are lacking for the earlier period, one leading scholar states that "we can confidently assert that the *ratio* of [government expenditures] to GNP in Canada has increased at least seven times over a period of 116 years, that is, from 4 to 7 per cent of GNP in 1867 to 45 per cent of GNP in 1983,"[15] with the relative share of provincial and local levels of government having increased in recent decades. Crown corporations have grown rapidly in number in the last quarter of a century and pursue more diversified purposes than they formerly did, including entrepreneurial roles in resource sectors. As of May, 1980, 454 federal public corporations were identified by two authors who noted that the federal government had listed a slightly larger number; they added that "there are still a large number of corporations unidentified."[16] Provincial Crown corporations numbered 233 in 1980; nearly half of these were created in the previous decade, and three-quarters in the previous two decades. About 10 per cent of GNP *may* be produced by federal and provincial Crown corporations together.[17] More Canadians are now employed by federal Crown corporations than by federal departments.[18]

The explicit regulatory arm of the state has experienced marked growth in recent decades, and the purposes of these "governments in miniature" have evolved from policing to promoting and planning in sensitive socio-economic and cultural areas.[19] Between 1970 and 1978 more new federal regulatory statutes were enacted than in the previous three decades, and nearly a third of 1978 provincial regulatory statutes had been enacted since 1960.[20] Figures collected by Stanbury indicate that the average number of federal and provincial regulatory statutes enacted per decade was less than 100 before 1900, 137 per decade from 1900 to 1949, more than 200 per decade in the 1950s and 1960s, and 324 in the period from 1970 to 1978.[21] According to Richard Schultz, regulation "has come to rival, and in some respects eclipse" spending and taxing as instruments to modify social and economic behaviour.[22] Its scope is so extensive "that it is difficult to think of an activity, good, or service that is *not* subject to government regulation, directly or indirectly."[23] As the regulatory agency performs the indisputably political task of choosing between rival claimants, its quasi-independence inevitably comes under greater scrutiny.

An additional interventionist strategy of growing significance is the acquisition of equity interests in the private sector by federal and provincial agencies. A recent estimate suggests that as of 1983 this had led to more than 300 mixed enterprises. Equity in 183 companies was held by the Caisse de Dépôt et placement du Québec in 1982, which had over $3 billion in its equity portfolio the following year.[24] "Tax expenditures" is a further category of state intervention to influence individuals and firms that grew dramatically in the 1970s and 1980s. These taxes forgone, the practice of including in the tax system various exemptions, deferrals, and tax credits, amounted to $13.8 billion in personal tax expenditures in 1979, an amount equal to 81 per cent of the federal personal income tax collected. Corporate tax expenditures also grew dramatically in the 1970s.[25] Stanbury attributes the "enormous erosion" of corporate income tax by tax expenditures directly to business lobbying.[26]

One final set of indicators of the pervasive influence of the contemporary state is in the income security field. The number of recipients of major income security payments is striking: 2.4 million received old age pensions in 1981 and 1.2 million received guaranteed income supplements; 1.7 million received payments from the Canada or Quebec pensions plans; 2.4 million received unemployment insurance; and (in 1980) 1.3 million received social assistance.[27]

While the figures above are illustrative of state growth and the contemporary state presence and may appear dramatic from a purely Canadian perspective, their impact is muted when they are viewed comparatively. There are significant variations in public spending as a proportion of gross domestic product among OECD nations, from a high of 63.7 per cent in Sweden to a low of 33 per cent in Spain. In this league, Canada is a modest spender.[28]

Such variations in spending patterns are not idiosyncratic, although the correlations that sustain variations remain matters of debate. One highly influential study by David Cameron identifies high spending with small nations with relatively open economies, a highly unionized and well-organized labour force, leftist governing parties, and unitary rather than federal systems of government.[29] These conditions, with the exception of an open economy, do not apply to Canada.

Significantly, there is no trend toward spending pattern convergence. As Manfred Schmidt has observed, "the combination of a capitalist economic structure and democratic political arrangements seems compatible with widely divergent policy stances."[30] From a slightly different perspective, Alex Inkeles repudiates the thesis that global interdependence homogenizes humankind and erodes national identities. Resistance to these tendencies comes from "the distinctive cultural traditions which different national populations bring to the contemporary situation, and in the array of historically determined institutional arrangements with which they enter the contemporary era. These traditions and forms seem remarkably adaptable, and a high degree of variability in economic and political arrangements seems compatible with the management of a modern industrial society."[31]

## Readjustment of Government-Market and Government-Society Relations

Faith that an activist state could resolve the pressing problems of modern society ... has receded in the last decade ... the optimism of the early postwar years has given way to lowered expectations, renewed emphasis on the limits of public policy and greater stress on the negative consequences of an enlarged public sector.[32]

In a recent volume assessing the attitudes of English-Canadian intellectuals to the role of the Canadian state from 1900 to 1945, Doug Owram captured the orientation of his subjects under the label *The Government Generation*.[33] On the whole, the intellectual community he examined had a beneficent view of the state (especially if its policies could be informed by intelligences such as theirs) and a somewhat technocratic, managerial view of government. Their views triumphed in the middle decades of the century, initially in the federal government where the successes of wartime administration during the Second World War were followed by post-war reconstruction, and subsequently at the provincial level.

In the immediate post-war years, as the fears of depression did not materialize, business and government worked out a *rapprochement* on the terms of the mixed economy and the incremental development of the welfare state. The federal government was seen positively as a humane and competent manager of the affairs of Canadians. The dialectic of intergovernmental competition and the continuing significance of their jurisdictional powers induced provincial governments to build up their own bureaucratic capacity. The process of transforming provincial societies and economies under the aegis of provincial government leadership came to be labelled province-building in academic accounts and occasionally in public discourse. The process was developed most vigorously and aggressively in post-Duplessis Quebec as another "government generation" took power. Under the rubric of the newly labelled *état* of Quebec, operating on behalf of a new political people whose territorial civic identity was simultaneously being redefined as "Québécois," various well-known *dirigiste* state policies accelerated the process of secularization and modernization.

Given the pervasive state-market, public-private dualism of the political thought of the contemporary Western capitalist democracies, it was probably inevitable that a counter-reaction would develop. The Great Depression, the memory of which informed the initial post-war generation of state-builders, receded into history. At the same time the experience of living in the era of the "big government" welfare state was almost bound to draw attention to state failures, especially in view of the continued vitality of the market as a functioning and hence an alternative institution for tasks that could be undertaken by either state or market. Reversion to the market was facilitated by the fact, noted by Ramesh Mishra, that the welfare state in Canada and elsewhere lacked a theoretical basis.[34] Further, a general phenomenon, brilliantly described by Hirschman, no doubt played its part – an oscillation in the relative attractiveness of the public or private realms triggered by the inevitable disappointments that follow a one-sided concentration on one or the other.[35]

That binge of post-Second World War state worship, in Donald Smiley's phrase,[36] has ended, and a reassessment of state-market and state-society relations is under way. In Canada some of the widespread support for the Charter draws on these sentiments. The advance of the state has halted, at least temporarily, especially in the realm of economic policy and the fine-tuning of the economy. The phenomenon is pervasive. It is on the ascendancy in the Soviet Union, the People's Republic of China, several of the East European countries, and considerable parts of the Third World, often under the prodding of the International Monetary Fund, as well as in the capitalist democracies of Europe, North America, Australia, and New Zealand. Even in Quebec, where a particular history and an ethnic division of labour combined to give the provincial state an exalted status in the 1960s and 1970s that had no parallel in earlier Canadian history, the intellectual and political climate had clearly changed by the 1980s and a cautious, selective cutback of the state role was pursued by the Bourassa government. Another Quebec politician, Jacques Parizeau, described "proposition 13, adopted in California in June 1978 [as] the single most significant event of our time as far as the relationship of the citizen and the state is concerned. For the first time in thirty years, the citizens showed unambiguously that they were ready to jeopardize what politicians and public administrators had assumed they wanted . . . it had the impact of an earthquake." [37]

The domestic role of the state is also informed by the lessons derived from examples of state-society relations elsewhere. The Soviet experiment of domination of society by the party-state, whether feared or admired, appeared for half a century as a plausible alternative to the Western wedding of liberal democracy and capitalism. Now with "'existing socialism' increasingly moribund, both materially and spiritually . . . the military question apart, the challenge of socialism has for the moment dwindled to nothingness. This is an important – indeed the essential – context against which the resurgence of neo-conservatism generally and the appeal of a return to market approach has to be understood." [38]

This external validation of the corrupting effects of total state power was supplemented by the much milder but still pregnant lesson that individuals and corporations quickly learn to "work" government programs to their advantage and thus generate outcomes not intended by policy-makers. According to Douglas Hartle, the regulatory process has spawned fortunes by making it "possible for the well-to-do, the well-connected and the well-informed to glide quickly and silently through seemingly impenetrable barriers, like pike through a weedbed, with their eyes fastened on their prey. The unnumbered minnows have disappeared without a ripple on the surface." [39] A classic confirmation of Hartle's thesis is what Stanbury has called "the most extreme case of a tax expenditure run amok . . . the Scientific Research Tax Credit (SRTC), which has been described as 'almost an invitation to fraud.'" This program was intended to stimulate research; it was initially estimated to cost $100 million, but escalated to $2.6

billion. Fifty-seven per cent of SRTC transactions (nearly 1,800) were "quick flips," and had little visible effect on research.[40] The cost approximated the annual expenditures of the government of Newfoundland and five times the annual expenditures of the government of Prince Edward Island.

The SRTC case, like the example of unemployment insurance noted below, underlines the extent to which there is a never-ending dialectic in state-society interactions. State actions generate counter-actions by goal-seeking private actors. The response of the state to the latter is followed by another round of responses by the interests its policies affect. In this dialectic the state is at a disadvantage, for, except in emergencies, it is incapable of a rapid response. For business, in particular, interactions with government are now managed by a veritable army of lobbyists, public consultants, and trade associations. In extreme cases the attempts of the state to control are countered by systematic evasion. The underground economy that seeks to escape the regulatory and taxing power of the state is steadily growing, and in Canada already is equal to 10 to 15 per cent of GNP.[41]

More generally, it is unsurprisingly the case that the multitude of government programs emanating from eleven major jurisdictions often work at cross-purposes. Economists argue that structural rigidities in labour markets that are sustained and fostered by government policies keep the rate of unemployment higher, given the complementary goal of a non-accelerating rate of inflation, than would be the case if such policy contradictions were eased or eliminated.

The state's difficulty in developing and applying finely honed instruments directed successfully at specific targets has contributed to a reassessment of state-market relations among both elites and citizens. The recent advocacy of an enhanced role for the market by the Macdonald Commission, in language that occasionally verged on the evangelical, not only was a reflection of the influence of classical economists who dominated the economics research stream, but also drew from an intellectual climate less willing than it had been several decades earlier to give governments the benefit of the doubt. Neither politically nor intellectually does the "government generation" portrayed by Douglas Owram dominate the scene.

A final point is relevant here. However much the line between state and market shifts to the advantage of the latter, the market will not have the sanctity or sense of natural "givenness" that it possessed for a brief period in Western history. This is so for three reasons: (1) it is evident that the freeing of the market is a political act that requires an ongoing state-supported infrastructure and managerial role for its effective functioning; (2) whatever the retreat of the state, its former roles survive as a memory against which market performance will be assessed; (3) the extensive continuing state role in other arenas means that the market's relative autonomy will always appear somewhat exceptional and conditional, as a matter of choice. In that sense, the freeing of the market is correctly seen as a state-allowed experiment.

The Canadian state will not lack tasks to occupy itself. Retreat, withdrawal, and privatization will operate at the margin. The welfare state role, that bundle of social programs made available on the basis of citizenship that serves the end of social integration, may be modified in its particulars but not in its essentials. The environmental role of the state is likely to increase rather than diminish. The state's traditional role in the international system in the "high politics" of peace and war is now supplemented by the "low politics" of managing international economic transactions in the service of domestic economic goals. More generally, the international role of the state now encompasses halting attempts to manage the global economy and emerging roles in the management of the global environment. What may be called the social role of the state – the management of a rights-conscious society of increasing diversity and particularistic self-consciousness based on ethnicity, race, language, sex, and age – is not going to abate. Indeed, as I will argue later, the developing role of the state will be much influenced by the transformations in Canadian political and constitutional culture deriving from the Charter, race, and ethnicity.

## Rights, Race, Ethnicity, and the Administrative State

### THE ADMINISTRATIVE STATE, THE CHARTER, AND RIGHTS

The *Canadian Charter of Rights and Freedoms* has changed the political and legal landscape of this nation. [42]

The 1982 Charter, with its enumeration of fundamental freedoms, democratic rights, mobility rights, legal rights, and equality rights and its references to race, sex, ethnicity, official-language minority populations, and disabilities, makes the written portion of the Canadian constitution a much more comprehensive document than the uninspiring and spare British North America Act, which did constitutional service for more than a century. In its new guise the constitution undoubtedly will come to play a role in Canadian constitutional culture similar in magnitude, if different in particulars, to the role of the U.S. constitution in symbolizing and defining the nature of the American political community and the experiment it is engaged in. Our understanding of the nature of that major change in Canada's constitutional evolution is hindered by intellectual conservatism and by the prior habituation of most adult Canadians, some immigrants excepted, to the theory and practice of parliamentary supremacy. The tendency of early academic and journalistic reactions to the 1982 Constitution Act to stress the limited nature of the change achieved, contrasted with the various ambitious agendas out of which it emerged, further contributed to a playing down of the Charter's significance. Behind this difficulty of appreciation, of course, was the exclusion of the Quebec government from the ranks of Charter signatories, which made it appear that the *raison d'être* of two decades of agonizing constitutional introspection had been ignored.

A further factor that discouraged comprehension of the Charter's likely impact was the prominence of lawyers in its discussion. As R.A. Macdonald has said, lawyers played "the predominant role . . . in selling the country on the idea of a Charter."[43] Prominent exceptions to the contrary, most legal analysis almost totally ignored the fundamental political purposes of the Charter as an instrument of nation-building, as a device to reshape the very identity of Canadians. The linking of the Charter to the "general theme of rights of individuals in opposition to the State,"[44] or, in the language of the Chief Justice, the viewing of it in terms of its purpose as "intended to constrain governmental action,"[45] clearly captured one dimension of the Charter. It is this aspect of the Charter that lies behind the apprehensions of legal scholars such as R.A. Macdonald and Andrew Petter and the more gently expressed preliminary concerns of the Law Reform Commission of Canada that the Charter might become a vehicle for the return of the limited state.[46]

This, however, was and is an unhelpful vantage point from which to appreciate the Charter's political purposes: to tie Canadians more tightly to the state – and especially to the federal government and the national community – by explicitly linking rights to the constitutional order. As Peter Russell has noted, the strong support of the federal government under Pierre Trudeau for a Charter derived from its "national unity function" rather than from its capacity to protect rights and freedoms.[47]

Viewed as an instrument to counter the centrifugal pressures of provincialism, the Charter was intended to link individuals and groups more tightly to the state and to embed them in a strengthened pan-Canadian community. In part this would occur from the Charter's stimulation to pose issues in terms of citizen-state relations rather than in the language of federalism. The overall purpose was to strengthen the civic, or citizenship, component of the identity of Canadians, and thus to integrate them more closely into the constitutional order. No one who has sampled the proceedings of the various legislative committees that have examined the Meech Lake Accord can doubt the success of that effort, at least as far as the elite of the women's movement, "third-force" Canadians, visible minorities, official-language minorities, the disabled, and numerous others are concerned. In all but the most superficial senses, therefore, the Charter illustrates the growth of the state, not its retreat. It enhances the civic component of our lives at the expense of the private and the personal.[48]

Although political scientists were more likely than lawyers to stress the Charter's political purposes, their powerful traditional commitment to federalism and parliamentary government, both of which were weakened by the Charter, has delayed their recognition of the Charter's fundamental importance.[49] To put it differently, both disciplinary insularity among lawyers and the socialization of political scientists in the values of the constitutional world we have lost have been impediments to a comprehensive appreciation of the Charter.

Both federalism and parliamentary government, the leading organizing principles of the Canadian constitution since 1867, lost constitutional status to the Charter. The Charter's confrontation with parliamentary supremacy, somewhat modified by section 33 and its "notwithstanding" clause, is self-evident. It is also worth noting, however, that the enhancement of the judicial role at the expense of Parliament is accompanied by the stimulation of interest group activity focused on the courts, thus weakening the role of parties whose concentration is fixed on Parliament. Feminist groups have devoted considerable resources to the legal arena as a means of advancing their interests.[50]

In retrospect, it is striking how limited the support for parliamentary supremacy, the symbol of our former Britishness, turned out to be in the final debates leading up to the Charter. The political defenders of parliamentary supremacy, such as Sterling Lyon and Allan Blakeney, were clearly on the defensive. The mother country and the Westminster model with which it was linked had already receded in psychological and intellectual prominence in Canadians' self-consciousness. Without always knowing it, Canadians have experienced a progressive decomposition of their constitutional Britishness. With hindsight, as the support for the Charter suggests, it now appears that the backing for parliamentary supremacy derived from the imperial connection and lacked indigenous roots.

The relation of the Charter to federalism is straightforward. In general, it was a device to limit the creation of provincial diversities by the exercise of provincial jurisdictional power – a consequence that has already appeared in several areas, such as Sunday closing and provincial film censorship, where Canada-wide standards are emerging from court decisions in areas where provincial variety formerly flourished.[51] The Charter was to induce citizens to evaluate the conduct of provincial governments through the lens of a rights-oriented Canadianism. In the future, provincial policies were to apply not to distinctive provincial communities but to the provincially resident members of a national community of rights-bearers. Thus it was entirely predictable, in terms of the structure of federalism, that the consistent push for an entrenched Charter or Bill of Rights binding on both orders of government came from the central government, and that opposition was concentrated in governing provincial elites. Although the latter employed the language of parliamentary supremacy in their defence, that language "was a rhetorical device to protect province-building against the nationalizing philosophy of the Charter."[52] The national purposes of the Charter were further underlined by the minority-language educational rights (section 23). The section's straightforward objective was to require provincial governments to do what Canadian history and the bias of provincial politics suggested was unlikely to be a result of provincial voluntarism, especially in English Canada – to provide primary and secondary school instruction to English and French minority populations in their own language. The purpose was to keep alive a conception of French Canada that transcended Quebec and a conception of Quebec that was hostile to the systematic attrition of the minority Anglophone population. These political purposes behind the Charter overwhelmed the consideration, noted by Macdonald, that the Canadian civil libertarian record would stand up well against any country with a Bill of Rights, and that there was no reason to believe that an entrenched Charter would improve the quality of Canada's fundamental freedoms.[53]

While the final drive for the Charter was the product of political imperatives of the Trudeau government, which saw it as an instrument to weaken centrifugal forces in English Canada and nationalism within Quebec, the momentum behind it was sustained by various domestic and international forces.[54] The establishment of the United Nations in 1945 and the 1948 Universal Declaration of Human Rights, against the backdrop of the state-engineered atrocities and inhumanities of the previous quarter of a century, gave the Charter idea an enhanced legitimacy and weakened the legitimacy of parliamentary supremacy regimes, whatever their actual record of rights observance.

Domestically, the Charter was part of a broader intellectual and political movement that had various manifestations. One stream was a steady progression of human rights commissions that over time incrementally developed their mandates to encompass more and more minorities. This process, labelled "the manufacture of minorities" by Thomas Flanagan,[55] is fed by the expansionist desires of human rights commissions with permanent staff, the existence of more "advanced" commissions in other jurisdictions of federalism that inspire emulation, the availability of commissions as lobbying targets for groups who seek inclusion in a commission's categories of coverage, and the occasional emergence of human rights issues in election campaigns. Flanagan's expansionist thesis is amply confirmed by the example of the Ontario Human Rights Commission, which began in 1962 with one staff member and a part-time secretary, and which two decades later had a staff of 101 and an expanded jurisdiction in terms of "both the prohibited grounds and the social areas in which discrimination was forbidden."[56]

Another rights stream was "concentrated in the administrative field" in many Western nations and contained, according to a recent Law Reform Commission

working paper, "an ombudsman; freedom of information and access to administrative documents; reasons for administrative action; non-curial administrative
procedures; consultation and participation; a right to privacy and confidential-
ity; creating rights for users; maintaining 'essential' services; simplifying formal-
ities; administrative decentralization; and additional safeguards in judicial
proceedings (such as class actions)."[57]

In spite of the Charter's affinities with earlier or concurrent developments,
including provincial Bills of Rights, the Charter is not just a marginal modification of the constitution. As it progressively works its way into our understanding,
transforms the language of political discourse, and shapes our conceptions of
who we are as a people, the magnitude of the change it has brought about will
become increasingly evident. On the one hand, Peter Russell is correct in his frequently cited observation that the major impact of the Charter does not lie in the
creation of new rights, but in giving judges an enhanced role in their application
and evolution.[58] On the other hand, as F.L. Morton and Leslie A. Pal point out,
when the Charter pits rights against administrative logic the processes of reasoning are very different between judges and administrators, with the former typically ignoring many concerns that are central to the logic of administrators who
work within the confines of legislation and are concerned with values such as
costs and efficiency.[59]

The Charter legitimizes and strengthens a rights-oriented discourse in Canadian political culture. As early as 1968 Maxwell Cohen observed how human
rights in the previous two decades had become "an important piece of 'debating'
language," which Canadians had turned into a "large 'catchall' for social
claims."[60] Since Cohen wrote, the 1982 Charter, binding on both levels of government, introduced as the centrepiece of the federal government's constitutional strategy, and sensitive to the wishes of a growing civil rights constituency,
has turned Canadians, especially "the intellectual classes," into a "constitutional
people" who think of themselves as part of the constitutional order and deny that
the constitution is only an affair of governments.[61]

This constitutionalizing of a people is most evident in the way the Charter
links numerous non-governmental groups to its specific clauses – Aboriginals,
official-language minorities, women, visible minorities, the disabled, third-
force Canadians, and others – and by so doing changes over time their innermost
self-conceptions. By acquiring niches in the constitution these groups have been
given constitutional identities. For women's groups, the inclusion of section 28
(the sexual equality clause) in the Charter and its exemption from the section 33
override play a role "in the mythology of the women's movement similar to that
of victorious past battles for the inheritors of a military tradition. . . . Feminist
activists view s. 28 not as something granted to women, or as the automatic and
logical application of a principle to women, but rather as something seized, in a

way akin to a trophy. Thus the language of the women's movement tends to describe s. 28 as being possessed by women, or as a beachhead occupied by women in a not altogether friendly land." [62]

At the operational level, the Charter will have major consequences for the administrative state. For the president of the Law Reform Commission, the Charter poses an "unprecedented challenge for law reform" in coming decades with its requirement that laws be re-examined for their compatibility with the Charter. [63] The Charter, according to a Law Reform Commission report, "dramatizes the importance of procedure in any governmental decision-making process and invites the expression of its values in the procedures that apply whenever private rights are affected by statutory decision makers." [64]

One plausible impact of the Charter on administrative law will be the "constitutional entrenchment of a number of restraints upon administrative action that had previously been only a matter of common law and, therefore, capable of statutory exclusion." [65] J.M. Evans suggests that section 2(b) (freedom of expression), section 7 (the right to life, liberty, and security of the person), and section 15 (equality rights) will probably be the provisions most frequently used against administrative bodies. [66] The Charter has already had an impact on parole practices. "It has accelerated the acceptance and propagation of the previously recognized duty to act fairly and elevated it from a common law concept, subject to the will of Parliament, to an enshrined right, inviolable by legislation or executive action." [67] The right to be secure against unreasonable search or seizure (section 8) has been changed "dramatically" by the Charter's introduction of a "constitutional threshold of *reasonableness*." [68] Two researchers who studied the first four years of the Charter discovered that 90 per cent of the Charter arguments were based on the legal rights sections (sections 7-14). [69] Nearly three-quarters of Charter litigation in the early years involved criminal law enforcement, and two-thirds of Charter cases challenged the behaviour of public officials, primarily policemen. F.L. Morton has noted that courts are not normally defying legislative policy when they check police or bureaucratic excesses. [70]

These specific illustrations of the Charter's practical impact should not deflect attention from its less tangible and larger consequences. As precedents accumulate and constitutional commentary flourishes, the rights and obligations of citizenship and the way in which our Aboriginal, multicultural, bilingual, provincial, sexual, and other constitutional categories relate to each other and to the Canadian community will become more explicit, philosophical, and theoretical. The leadership role of courts will follow from the pressure of growing constitutional litigation, which "is bound to require them to think harder, and to write more overtly, about some important issues of law and government, including, of course, their own rule." [71]

In the long run the actual protection of rights may not be advanced by the

Charter, but citizens will "possess" such rights differently from the way they possessed them under the former regime of parliamentary supremacy. "For a parliamentary people, tradition and practice are the basis of rights; it is not easy to catalogue these rights, and citizens may not be particularly aware of them. For such a people, the protection of rights occurs in the interstices of judicial and political processes."[72] Although many of the Charter's rights are the historic rights of Englishmen, the Charter gives them an explicit constitutional and institutional support and a degree of specificity they previously lacked. The Charter is a deliberate departure from the unwritten constitution of Canada's British heritage.

For a Charter people, rights are explicit.[73] This explicitness will increase the propensity to litigate when they are challenged. Rights are identified as belonging to "everyone," "every citizen," "any person," "every individual," "any member of the public," and "citizens of Canada." Over time these rights will flesh out "citizenship" as a constitutional category, not just in the legal sense but in the political sense of one's having a role in the constitutional order. The Meech Lake proceedings make it clear that this has already begun to happen, that what may be called a citizens' constitution has emerged that denies the legitimacy of government domination of amendment processes.[74] The Charter lessens deference to elites and governments, stimulates pressures for citizens' participation in the public realm, and suggests that working the constitution and governing should be more of a partnership between office-holders and citizens than formerly.

THE EMERGING SALIENCE OF RACE AND ETHNICITY

In the past three-quarters of a century, three great events – depression, war, and the survival of the Canadian state – have given pride of place in our perceptions of the primary roles of the state to (1) economic management and the welfare state (Keynes plus Beveridge), (2) defence, participation in international conflicts, and peacekeeping, and (3) nation-saving and constitutional change to accommodate dualism and regionalism. The high profile of these areas derives not only from their substantive importance but from their possession of convenient rubrics – economic management, welfare state, defence, constitutional crisis – that help us to see various separate policies as directed to a common goal. The integrating capacity of a convenient label for our perceptions is strengthened if particular academic disciplines focus on the policy questions the label encompasses; this is true for the economic role of the state by its association with the prestige of economics as the most technically advanced of the social sciences, for the constitutional crisis by law and political science, for war and defence by international relations and strategic studies, and, less prominently, for the welfare state by social work. Other policy areas that may possess a potential underlying unity may have a lesser visibility, and the state's response may remain as an aggregation of separate policies if they lack a compelling label and the focused attention of a prestigious academic discipline. This is the case with the state's handling of our ethnic and racial diversity outside of French-English dualism, a task that will almost certainly grow in scope and difficulty in the future.

A diffuse policy area relating to our ethnic diversity, to cultural pluralism, to the potential divisiveness of race, and to the terms of coexistence between Aboriginal Canadians and later arrivals – in short, to our identity as a people – has commanded extensive if piecemeal attention since the Second World War. Even a limited list of policies addressing ethnic diversity is impressive: the postwar extension of the franchise to formerly excluded groups; the pan-Canadianism that lay behind the Diefenbaker Bill of Rights; the failed assimilationist thrust of the 1969 policy paper on Indians; the changed immigration requirements of the 1960s; the 1971 policy of multiculturalism; Quebec language policies aimed at channelling immigrants into the French-speaking community; the development of human rights commissions and codes at the federal and provincial levels and the steady expansion of their jurisdiction; patriation and the ending of the British role in Canadian constitutional evolution, which complemented the declining Britishness in the population; the 1982 Constitution Act and the Charter of Rights with its clauses pertaining to Aboriginals, multiculturalism, and, in section 15, to "race, national or ethnic origins, [and] colour"; parliamentary committees on visible minorities and Indian self-government; a succession of constitutional conferences devoted to Aboriginal self-government; and the appointment of Canadians of Aboriginal, black, and Chinese background to the office of lieutenant-governor.

The Canadian state has been busily engaged in refashioning the collective identity of Canadians to make it more congruent with the changed ethnic composition of Canadian society. This is in addition to federal policies directed to the accommodation of Quebec and French Canada. The 1982 Constitution Act, modified by the Meech Lake Accord if it passes, gives constitutional status to a discourse focusing on ethnicity, race, culture, and communal identity – subjects that, apart from the historic French-English dualism and a minimal focus on status Indians, have had only a weak presence in our constitutional discussions.

Policy in these areas has both practical and symbolic aspects; the latter is typically under-appreciated. An *economisme* that stresses the "material basis of social life" tends to crowd out what Raymond Breton calls the "symbolic dimension of social organization."[75]

The formation of societies consists, at one level, in the construction of a symbolic order. This construction entails, first, the definition of a collective identity which, with time, becomes articulated in a system of ideas as to who we are as a people. This identity is represented in the multiplicity of symbols surrounding the rituals of public life, the functioning of institutions, and the public celebration of events, groups and individuals... individuals expect to recognize themselves in public institutions. They expect some consistency between their private identities and the symbolic contents upheld by public authorities, embedded in the societal institutions, and celebrated in public events. Otherwise, individuals feel like social strangers; they feel that the society is not *their* society.[76]

The recent volatility of the symbolic order, in contrast to its relative stability in earlier periods, reflects the heightened self-consciousness of various social groupings defined by language, ethnicity, and race. The self-confidence and political aggressiveness of third-force Canadians, visible minorities, and the Aboriginal peoples draw their inspiration from the shifting ethnic and racial demography of the Canadian population, which in turn derives from more liberal immigration laws, including refugee policy. Ethnic political demands are stimulated by the progressive shrinking of the proportion of the population of British and French background. One-third of Canadians now fall outside of the charmed circle of the two European founding peoples, a ratio that will reach 40 per cent early in the twenty-first century, by which time more than 10 per cent of Canadians, excluding Aboriginals, will be visible minorities.[77]

The politicization of ethnicity was stimulated by the declining significance of Britishness for Canadian constitutional identity as Great Britain receded in psychological and practical importance for Canadians, and even more so by the redefinition of the Quebec French-speaking majority as a political people seeking a nationalist state of their own. The latter, along with the various responses of the federal government to these challenges to the country's integrity, triggered the counter-mobilization of traditional third-force Canadians and subsequently of racial minorities.

In the background is the sustenance given ethnic and racial minorities, especially those from the Third World, by the demise of the great European empires and the defeat of the implicit and explicit racial hierarchies on which they were based. There is a clear link between the numerical dominance of Third World countries in the global international order, whose international rhetoric is informed by the psychological legacy of imperialism, and the contemporary tensions in domestic policy areas pertaining to visible minorities and Aboriginal peoples.

The results of these developments for Canada parallel the impact on Western Europe of what has been described as

one of the most important social changes that has occurred ... since the war; every reasonably populous state now has ethnic minorities of considerable size within its borders. The permanent settlement, not merely migration, of workers – and their families – from Third World and poorer European countries, and the resurgence of long-quiescent or defeated indigenous groups, has combined to bring this about. In my view this change is irreversible. [It contributes to] what has become the dominant characteristic of twentieth-century states: ethnic pluralism within the framework of a united polity.... Political theory and jurisprudence are.... largely unprepared to answer what has become one of the most pressing issues of liberty in these times: how, within the over-arching political unity, are conflicts engendered by the co-existence of diverse and at times opposed, cultural values and ways of life to be resolved?[78]

For most of humankind these developments put the Wilsonian ideal of the ethnically homogeneous national state on the shelf as an anachronistic vision. In Canada, the ethnic and racial diversification already achieved, and the recognition that we are still in the early stages of its growth, weakens the viability of dualism, whether linguistic, cultural, or historical, as a defining characteristic of Canada. It also requires the Quebec component of the French-language side of dualism to come to grips with the multicultural and multiracial composition of the Quebec Francophone community, toward which its own policies, especially in education, lead.

For the Canadian administrative state the proliferation and assertiveness of ethnic and racial minorities generate numerous challenges, which in general will require the state's future ethnic sensitivities to extend beyond dualism to include those Canadians who do not identify with the contestants on the Plains of Abraham more than two centuries ago.

(1) The issue of "appropriate" ethnic and racial representation in all branches of government, including the judiciary, cannot be avoided in staffing the administrative state.

(2) The constitution is and will continue to be deeply embroiled in the tensions of an ethnically and racially plural society. It is already a battleground for struggles between competing ethnic, racial, and Aboriginal communities for relative status vis-à-vis each other and with the two founding peoples, who are privileged both by past history and by the contemporary constitution. The Charter and the 1982 Constitution Act draw explicit attention to ethnic, racial, and Aboriginal components of the Canadian community. Demographic projections guarantee that the impact of ethnicity and race on the theory and practice of the Canadian constitution can only increase.

(3) Ethnic diversity not only leads to a relative downgrading of dualism as a constitutional organizing principle, but weakens the relative weight of the constitutional characteristics that are intimately linked to the French-English

dominance of the original Confederation settlement. The declining support for
parliamentary supremacy and the growth of support for the Charter reflect the
ethnic diversification of Canada and the relative decline in the numerical presence and political power of Canadians of British background. The 1960 Bill of
Rights, introduced by the first Canadian Prime Minister whose ancestry was not
entirely British or French, was explicitly intended to be a political instrument for
a pan-Canadianism that would enhance the status and recognition of those with
other than French or British heritage. Further, the ethnic and racial diversity that
leads to strong support for the Charter contributes to a weakening of the status of
federalism as an organizing principle in the constitution.

(4) Depending on the pattern of future immigration and the extent to which
cultural assimilation does or does not occur, Canadians will have to face the tensions between the individualism of the liberal tradition, "which exalts conscience and intellect and deprecates collective identity and loyalty unless centred
upon the state," and the loyalties, identities, and group-based behaviour of ethnic communities.[79] A related concern, attributable to the pressures of other
minorities as well, is what Ian Hunter has discerned in the development of
human rights legislation in Ontario – the encroachment of equality on liberty.[80]
The constitutional sanction of affirmative action held out by the Charter in section 15(2) leads in the same direction.

(5) The coexistence of the shaping penetrative powers of the contemporary
positive state with an increasingly plural society weakens the status of majoritarianism as an acceptable governing formula. Already evident in the desire of Quebec *indépendantistes* for a country of their own, and in one of the Trudeauite
responses – the use of the Charter to require provincial governments to provide
official-language minorities with educational facilities that could not be left to
the sensitivities of provincial majorities – a hostility to majoritarianism is also
behind Aboriginal demands for self-government and the steady development of
support for the theory and reality of bills of rights and charters to protect minorities against the abuse of state power.

The coincidence of the ethnic transformation of Canadian society with the
opening up of the constitution to respond to centrifugal pressures in the federal
system pushed the constitutional package of 1982 toward a fuller recognition of
ethnic diversity than had been originally intended. Section 27, dealing with the
multicultural heritage of Canadians, and the various clauses pertaining to
Aboriginals, as well as the listed categories in section 15 of the Charter, have
accorded a degree of constitutional recognition to ethnicity and race that was
formerly absent. These clauses have given niches in the constitution to Aboriginal Canadians, traditional third-force Canadians of European background, and
visible minorities. They have acquired, along with women by section 28 and official-language minorities by section 23, constitutional identities. They view these

clauses as theirs. Their presence in the constitution is the state's response to one of its central tasks, the symbolic representation of the "unity of the political community."[81] The Meech Lake discussions show that Canadians are deeply divided over the way in which they should think of themselves as one political people. The relationship between older French-English cleavage lines, the Aboriginal components of Canadian existence, the third-force European minorities, and the older and newer visible minorities is far from settled.

## State-Society Relations in the Era of the Administrative State

### THE "PASTNESS" OF THE CANADIAN STATE: ITS STRUCTURES, POLICIES, AND RELATIONS WITH SOCIETY

In strictly constitutional terms, and compared with most of mankind, Canadians are an historic people whose uninterrupted constitutional existence since 1867 is a rare achievement. Federalism, parliamentary government, the constitutional monarchy, an independent judiciary, and competitive elections in a pluralistic society, all of which characterize our contemporary constitutional system, are in a direct line of descent from their origins at Confederation and earlier.

Many of the policies administered by the state are equally venerable. In the Criminal Code "archaic sections dealing with witchcraft, duelling, cockpits, three-card monte and other similar hoary relics of the past remain in force." In the words of Vincent Del Buono, "To wander through the present Code is to stare into the face of the ghosts of all the social evils thought, at one time, to threaten the very fabric of Canadian society."[82] The general "pastness" of policy is also evident in the age of regulatory statutes. Of the provincial regulatory statutes in existence in 1978, one-quarter could trace their statutory origins (or that of a predecessor) to a time before 1910, 50 per cent to a time before 1930, and 70 per cent to a time before 1960. Nearly 40 per cent of the federal statutes in existence in 1978 appeared "in some form" before 1910, 50 per cent before 1920, and 77 percent before 1960.[83]

This pastness of institutional arrangements and of the policies applied through them does not always reflect a positive appreciation of their virtues by those who inhabit the former, apply the latter, or are subject to the shaping effects of both. At the highest level, the durability of the constitutional order, its resistance to change when besieged on all sides in the 1960s and 1970s, and the "constitutional conservatism" it displayed[84] were based less on its intrinsic virtues than on the procedural hurdles to its formal modification, the competing and thus mutually exclusive objectives of those who sought change, and the massive supports of inertia that cluster around any ongoing system that performs tolerably. As Roger Gibbins has said, "Federal constitutions have a life of their own ... a resilience that makes them very resistant to social change." Federalism in Canada survives not because of its functional congruence with an underlying deeply federal society, "but because the governments of the Canadian federal state are able to defend their constitutional position."[85]

This survival capacity of inherited institutions, given the changing environment they encounter over long periods, means that we should expect a certain degree of disharmony between governing institutions and their environment. "The state as administrative apparatus and legal order will *not* smoothly adjust to changes in its domestic environment. Once institutions are in place they will perpetuate themselves. ... The natural path for institutions is to act in the future as they have acted in the past."[86] The potential disharmony this threatens is modified by the practices of a "living" constitution that often introduce behaviour modifications at the margin, and by the tendency of master institutions to shape society in a manner consonant with their own requirements. Nevertheless, it is a reasonable working assumption that any long-established political order will display a certain internal incoherence and some abrasiveness in the interactions of its major governing institutions with the underlying society.

Perhaps the most striking example of such incoherence is what J.E. Hodgetts called "structural heretics," the sprawling mass of regulatory agencies and Crown corporations that lie outside the conventional channels of control by responsible ministers and Parliament. The reports and working papers of the Law Reform Commission on the administrative law project constitute a litany of laments over these constitutional anomalies and proposals to address them. The basic issue was identified by Claus Offe:

> It is my thesis that both the location of major political conflicts and struggles and the institutional location at which state policies are formed shift away from those institutions which democratic theory assigns to these functions. As a consequence, the mediation that democratic theory postulates between the state and the individual breaks down as an operative mechanism, without, however, being formally abolished. At the same time, *alternative political forms* of both the articulation of conflict and the resolution of policy issues appear for which at the present there exists no normative political theory. Behind the façade of parliamentary democracy, both political conflict and the resolution of policy issues increasingly take place within organizational settings which are unknown to democratic theory.[87]

At a less exalted level, as incisively noted by Stephen D. Krasner, elected and appointed state officials are hemmed in by the administrative, legal, and constitutional arrangements they have inherited and the political culture in which they are set. Political resources and the way in which they can be combined are constrained by institutional arrangements. In sum, "the ability of a political leader to carry out a policy is critically determined by the authoritative institutional resources and arrangements existing within a given political system,"[88] and these are largely historical givens.

A similar conservatism of policy exists when ancient programs persist less because of their utility than because of bureaucratic rivalries, congested political and parliamentary timetables, the relative invisibility of the policy area in question to all but the immediately affected, who may have developed coping mechanisms, and the momentum that comes from being in place with bureaucratic units, personnel, and rules to apply. According to Douglas Johnston, writing in 1985, much marine legislation, including the federal Fisheries Act and the Canada Shipping Act, is simultaneously ancient and hopelessly inadequate.[89]

This policy durability, more a product of inertia than of conviction, limits the manoeuvrability of contemporary government. In the succinct summary of a Swedish academic and politician, "We have become more and more governed by old decisions."[90] The pastness of the state and its policies tends to escape our attention because its existence is relatively independent of the more visible features of our political life – the world of parties, elections, and legislatures, and in general the world of talk, of adversary politics, of the crisis of the day, and of the never-ending competition for the favour of the voter. It is too easy to forget that the contemporary administrative state is an inheritance that owes much to Macdonald, Laurier, and Borden as well as to their most recent successors. We focus too much on change at the margins and thus under-study and under-value the sheer "ongoingness" of established policy regimes.

Accordingly, when the contemporary Canadian state opts for policy change, the society it confronts has no pristine status but has adapted to, and perhaps been shaped by, the policies now to be modified. To put it differently, the state manoeuvres in a minefield of its own creation. In confronting society it confronts its former self. There is no clean slate. We cannot begin anew in response to the unceasing changes in our desires, our needs, and our capacities. We are custodians of a heritage, not scribblers on an erasable blackboard. Past choices inhibit subsequent flexibility, or exact penalties on those who wish to repudiate them.[91]

Elsewhere I have described this version of state-society relations as the "embedded state," tied down by, if not mired in, the entanglements of its established program links with society.[92] Would-be radical reformers of unemployment insurance, according to Leslie A. Pal, are likely to be defeated by "tremendous counter-pressures from affected provinces, regions, unions, employers, and social advocacy groups." Serious change is virtually ruled out for a scheme "so deeply and widely embedded in the Canadian political economy."[93]

As the Macdonald Commission summarized the situation, innovation:

> operates at the margin. It is countered by the massive inertia of big govern-
> ment. Yesterday's ideas and values are already bureaucratized and embed-
> ded in programs that are resistant to change. Most of what governments do
> represents the continuation of earlier programs. New programs always
> form only a small proportion of total government activity. Established
> governments are thus unavoidably instruments of conservatism, more
> responsive to habit than to innovation. Further, given the extensive exist-
> ing program links between government and society, nearly all new pro-
> grams affect activities that are already subject to various policies.[94]

For the citizen this means that most of his or her interactions with the state and
the bureaucracy are habitual. For the reformer, keen to improve the quality of
citizen-state interactions, it logically follows that the civility and fairness of
encounters with the administration will be crucial in informing the citizen's conceptions of the state. Such a focus, therefore, at least as much as the more exciting
frontiers of new legislation, deserves our attention.

## FRAGMENTATION OF STATE AND SOCIETY

The contemporary Canadian state is not a unitary actor, but rather a fragmented,
sprawling colossus. It manifests itself through the central government and the
governments of ten provinces and two territories. Since this fragmentation of
jurisdictional authority is frequently dysfunctional for the prosecution of particular goals, it has to be worked or managed or bypassed in the interest of programs
that cannot easily be implemented by a single government. The fleshing out of
the intergovernmental arena by federal-provincial agreements, often sustained
by the federal government's use of the spending power and by elaborate intergovernmental committee networks, was one of the great achievements of politicians and mandarins after the Second World War. By these means the constitutional impasse of the 1930s was broken, an impasse that was based on the too narrow premise that constitutional amendment and a judicial review that fostered
flexibility should be the major vehicles of constitutional change. The shattering
of those restrictive assumptions and their replacement by a view of federalism as
a system to be worked were essential mind-clearing exercises for the expansion of
the administrative state that spilled across the boundaries of federalism. A learning process changed the lens through which federalism was viewed, led to the
development of new instruments for its management, and facilitated its adaptation to the enlarged goals of the post-Second World War Canadian state.

Success is only relative, however. A recent summary of the literature on federalism describes it as indecisive, paralysed in controversial areas, and only "moderately successful" in managing conflict, and describes federal-provincial negotiations as normally closed to and thus often insensitive to non-governmental interests.[95]

Each government is internally fragmented. At the elementary level of the number of cabinet ministers with separate portfolios, the combined cabinets of the nine provinces and the national government contained only 118 ministers in 1945; four decades later, with Newfoundland now a province, the combined figure was 269. The internal division of labour triggered by the enhanced role of the state goes well beyond the multiplication of cabinet portfolios. State policies are applied, enforced, and adapted by hundreds of thousands of functionaries scattered in a bewildering variety of units, agencies, departments, Crown corporations, and commissions. Many of these bodies are deliberately removed from the possibility of ongoing ministerial supervision on the ground that the values or purposes they serve – efficiency, equity, and impartiality, or entrepreneurial risk-taking activities – are incompatible with the kinds of electoral and partisan concerns that are natural to politicians or with the constraints that inhere in conventional departmental structures.

These various fragmentations generate counter-trends to overcome or alleviate their worst efforts – in the federal system by the methods described above, in cabinets by a succession of experiments with central agencies and cabinet committees in pursuit of the elusive holy grail of an effective cabinet political control that is not undermined by the centrifugal pressures of departmentalism,[96] and in Crown corporations and regulatory agencies by a variety of specific practices that nevertheless operate on the fringes of the relative autonomy these bodies have been granted. Unfortunately, as J. Stefan Dupré has pointed out, the attempt to check fragmentation within governments by subjecting operating departments to certain kinds of central agency control can constrain the cross-jurisdictional departmentally based networks that transcend the division of powers in functional areas.[97] Correspondingly, as Donald Smiley noted long ago, conditional grant federalism based on the spending power weakens the collective control of cabinets over departments with policy and financial links with the other jurisdiction.[98]

Some of the proliferation of autonomous actors, such as Crown corporations and regulatory agencies, reflects conscious political choice; some, such as the system of courts staffed by an independent judiciary, reflects historic principle; in other cases, the *de facto* limited autonomy of operating departments of government is based on specialized knowledge and the partial world views to which it leads. The departmental basis of public authority attracts relevant clientele interests that interact with its specialized bureaucratic expertise to produce what

Dupré calls a "portfolio loyalty" in ministers, who depend on their clientele for public support and their bureaucrats for the expertise they do not personally possess.[99]

In the bureaucratic politics to which this leads, the "maximum and minimum objectives . . . [of the contending organizations] . . . will be at least partly shaped by institutional self-preservation and institutional self-aggrandizement."[100] Conflicts between departments such as Agriculture and Consumer and Corporate Affairs, however, are also conflicts between the different social blocs (e.g., farmers versus consumers) that they represent.

The sprawling administrative state scatters the capacities for autonomous action, exercise of leadership, and use of discretion across hundreds of offices and agencies. The focused executive leadership that parliamentary government, which links the governing cabinet with the elected Commons, is to bring to the conduct of public affairs is belied by many of the realities of the contemporary administrative state. Those realities militate against leadership with a synoptic vision of the role of government that encompasses more than a limited spectrum of what government does. A further consequence is that very frequently state policies, even within the same government, work at cross-purposes.

The fragmentation of public authority does not leave the underlying society unaffected. State fragmentation selectively reinforces societal fragmentation. It is self-evident that federalism sustains territorially based provincial communities by its continuing reinforcement of the significance of provincial boundaries and also separates provincial membership from citizenship in the larger Canadian community. The policy and bureau pluralism of the state also selectively links Canadians defined by economic interests, by ethnicity, by Indian status, by sex, by language concerns, by age, and by one's status as, for example, a welfare recipient or a veteran to particular branches of government. These classification schemes, at least instrumentally, structure the identities of those they cover or exclude. The new label of "allophones" in Quebec is a residual category of those who fall outside the historically based and rights-possessing Francophone and Anglophone communities and who must, by state compulsion, be deprived of choice in the language of their children's education in order to swell the population of French-speakers. The socio-linguistic category of "Francophones outside Quebec" is an explicit by-product of intergovernmental competition between Quebec and Ottawa, of the Quebec government's efforts to fashion Québécois – at the expense of French Canada – out of its provincial Francophone population, and of the language policies and political goals of recent federal governments directed to the linguistic survival of Francophone communities in English Canada. Canadians other than those ascended from the founding peoples have been relabelled under the rubric "multicultural," a word unknown thirty years ago, coined in the 1960s, and now accorded constitutional recognition in section 27 of the Charter. Human rights commissions, the first of which was created in Ontario in 1962, have steadily expanded their coverage of minorities to be protected. Prohibited grounds for discrimination covered by one or more jurisdictions have grown from six in the original Ontario Act to thirty in total. The average in the thirteen human rights acts is 12.3.[101]

The status Indian category and the division it creates within the Aboriginal population are products of the constitutional division of jurisdiction and the federal Indian policy that flows from it. Although we are too close to the 1982 Constitution Act and the Meech Lake Accord to speak conclusively of their effects, it is at least plausible to assert that the constitution has now been enlisted in the service of fragmentation and divisiveness. Constitutional clauses pertaining to women, Aboriginals, "multicultural Canadians," official-language minorities, and the disabled single out the social categories they cover from the general status of citizenship. The constitutional inclusion of Métis in the category "aboriginal peoples" in section 35 has enhanced Métis self-consciousness and apparently driven a wedge between Métis and non-status Indians.

These multiple discrete links with the policies and organs of the state condition the underlying society to define or redefine itself in ways that facilitate optimum interactions with the state. Corporate actors in particular will rearrange their affairs to benefit from tax expenditure policies. Simultaneously, private actors, especially the well-organized, apply constant pressure to modify the content and coverage of the existing rules, seeking inclusion or exclusion as self-interest dictates. In sum:

> We approach the state through a multiplicity of classificatory systems (derived from state policies, state agencies, and the discretion of administrators) which define us by gender, age, ethnicity, region, producer or consumer status, and whether we are French-speaking or English-speaking. We are politicized and fragmented simultaneously. Some of our traits are privileged; others are ignored. We approach the state as fragmented selves, calculating the advantages of stressing our ethnicity, our age, our gender, our region, our language, our sexual preferences, our doctorates or our disabilities. Shifting self-definition in response to state cues increases the size of any non-ascriptive group to which the state hands out privileges, and reduces membership in non-ascriptive categories subject to penalties and disadvantages. . . . In political terms, we come to exist as a multiplicity of those discrete selves that the state has singled out for attention. We act as managers of our shifting selves in the same way that business adjusts to changes in tax laws and regulations. We are like Kremlinologists constantly looking for clues. The flexible multiple identities fostered by our interactions with the state work against our civic sense of wholeness.[102]

Although fragmentation within government is typically deplored, normally because of an implicit premise that coherent integrated purposes could be effectively pursued by the state in its absence, it is not without its benefits. Peter Hall has suggested that malintegration contributes to the appearance of responding to the needs of competing groups with conflicting interests. While the result may be ineffective policies, neither of the competing groups will have experienced a defeat. [103] A more significant benefit emerges if, instead of dwelling on the way in which fragmentation frustrates the state from acting as an efficient agent of our interests, we remember that its internal confusions and inefficiencies save us from the threats to liberty that its tremendous power would otherwise bring.

## POLITICIZATION

In 1865 farmers in the Maritimes were described as "the great body of settlers in the country whose backs are covered with woollens of their own production, whose feet are shod with the hides of their own cattle, who sleep between blankets of their own wool and their own weaving – on feathers from their own farmyards." [104] A century later Léon Dion described our condition: "Whoever we may be, whatever our profession, whatever the area of the country we inhabit, politics has invaded our lives and it is virtually impossible to escape its hold. This political invasion of our daily lives is a new phenomenon in history." [105]

As the state extends its tentacles of coercion, inducement, incentives, and obligations to more and more areas of socio-economic functioning, private actors in the society and economy are not simply passive recipients of the state's imperatives. On the contrary, they engage in adaptive behaviour designed to turn the existing array of state programs to their advantage, and to influence emerging policy before it crystallizes. Kenneth Bryden's description of pensioners – "it took the shared experience of being pension recipients to create a perception of common interest sufficient to provide a basis for organized action" [106] – is of more general application. The increased scope of the interventionist state and its highly visible role in distributing advantages and disadvantages transmit the message that status, power, influence, income, and recognition are not to be viewed as the products of tradition or of anonymous market forces, but rather and increasingly as political creations to be won by manipulating the state.

The consequences of the pervasive interaction between the citizens and the governments of the federal system for the underlying experiences of living in national and provincial communities are not always appreciated. In practical terms, the exercise of state power by either the federal or provincial government has the necessary consequence of enhancing the significance of membership in the national or provincial community to which it is directed.

When governments rested much more lightly on society, federal-provincial differences affected a relatively limited sphere of the citizen's daily round. However, the accelerated politicization of society extends the consequences of federal and provincial jurisdictional differences to ever deeper and more profound levels of our existence, as it creates a national or provincial dimension to the activity that is regulated, the income that is taxed, or the behaviour that is subsidized. The sphere of society, or activity, outside the political, and therefore outside the federal system, undergoes constant shrinkage.

Sometimes political and bureaucratic elites at both levels are acting out the Canadian version of the Italian aphorism: "We have made Italy, now we must make Italians." At other times the impact of their actions in shaping our community memberships is only an accidental by-product. In either case, in the second century of Canadian federalism it is appropriate to think of the provincial and national communities served by the two orders of governments not as pre-existing communities to which federalism is a response, but as communities shaped and given political meaning by the penetrative powers of the governments created by the Constitution Act.

The circumstances in which the pursuit of private goals increasingly involves political calculation and interaction with the state may be called politicization. The state comes to be viewed as a potential ally to be influenced, as a source of opportunity to be exploited, or as a threatening force to be thwarted or evaded, legally by the employment of lawyers and tax accountants or illegally by participation in the burgeoning underground economy. Exit is a blunt response widely employed by both capital and citizens, as the dramatic decline of the Anglophone population of Quebec suggests.

For both individuals and corporate actors the state's programs and the discretion wielded by its officials become alternatives or supplements to market profitability and employment as sources of income. The inducements to influence the state are greatly enhanced by the ubiquity of state discretionary powers involving an element of judgement or choice. A catalogue compiled on the basis of the 1970 Revised Statutes of Canada indicated nearly 15,000 discretionary powers explicitly conferred by federal legislation on public authorities. [107]

Individuals troubled by the complexity of the state and its bureaucratic processes inundate their members of Parliament with a "staggering" volume of constituency work – some 5,500 cases a year, for example, for Mark MacGuigan, a former MP. Constituents pressure their MPs to intercede on their behalf when problems or conflicts arise with the bureaucracy. [108]

One measure of the state's significance to individuals is its contribution to personal income. Government transfer payments as a percentage of total income grew from 6.6 per cent in 1971 to 10.9 per cent in 1982. [109] For the lowest quintile

of the population, the payments grew from 53.3 per cent in 1971 to 61.4 per cent in
1982. Equally striking is the marked difference in income security payments as a
proportion of total personal income by province – from 29.4 per cent in Newfoundland to 10.7 per cent in Alberta in 1978.[110] In numerous communities in
Atlantic Canada, unemployment insurance is the most significant source of
income. Its major contribution to personal income helps to explain the intervention of provincial governments from eastern Canada when the program is
threatened with rationalization.[111]

Where it is feasible, collective strategies are devised to maximize community
income. Newfoundlanders, according to the Newfoundland Royal Commission
on Employment and Unemployment, have developed two strategies "to maximize the number of people that qualify for UI benefits." Given the scarcity of
jobs, employers in small communities experience community pressure "to qualify as many people as possible for UI" by laying off individuals as soon as they
qualify and replacing them with a new crop of potential eligibles. The other strategy, employed by both federal and provincial governments, is make-work
job-creation programs lasting just long enough to build up entitlements to
unemployment insurance.[112]

The state and its programs are also a ubiquitous presence for business. For
many firms, the treatment they receive from government determines their
profitability and survival. Books are written on ways to turn the system, including regulatory agencies, to their advantage.[113] On the one hand, business sees
itself as pressured by the "demands of consumers, environmentalists, various
types of 'rights' organizations, and other interest groups [that] have been
translated into an unprecedented amount of government intervention."[114] On
the other hand, given the prevailing system, "why not try to get government to
provide one with cash subsidies, institute protective regulation, grant a tax
incentive, or provide capital at less than market rates?. . . It is irrational . . . to
forgo an opportunity to exploit political markets. . . . Those who play the game
with relatively greater effectiveness will be able to increase their incomes by
means of government bounties."[115]

Elections are not won by prayers; neither are contests with government.
When the anticipated return is positive, the expenditure of time and money to
influence government decisions by a corporate executive is "just part of the job."
For regulated industries interaction with government is a first-order priority.
"Entrepreneurship capacity is primarily directed toward devising the most effec-
tive strategies for dealing with government."[116]

Success in the "government game" requires the establishment of government
relations units within business, frequent use of the private consulting firms that
offer access and insider information, resort to advocacy advertising, and a proliferation of trade associations or business-interest associations.[117] One of the

most insightful students of the welfare state asserted that the "vast growth in organized interest groups" has greatly reduced the manoeuvrability of governments. [118] Another author estimated that in 1981 there were approximately 300 "professional and trade associations in Ottawa employing 2,000 people and spending $100 million-plus a year getting their message across to ministers, MPS and bureaucrats." [119] Other studies have suggested that the numbers of these intermediaries and lobbyists have significantly increased since the 1950s. [120] It is logical to assume that the proliferation of specialized intermediaries to facilitate advantageous business interactions with governments is directly related to the much greater government discretionary potential to harm or benefit business. In some cases silence is the requisite business strategy. The Macdonald Commission noted that on occasion major private economic actors whose profitability was linked to discretionary government decisions "were afraid to voice in public their opinions of government policies for fear of the consequences," [121] a situation in which silence is almost literally golden.

Individuals and businesses operate in political as well as economic markets. The range of concerns we address through the state goes well beyond our economic interests to include a battery of high-profile social concerns relating to language, ethnicity, sex, age, disabilities, race, and sexual preference. We live not only in a political economy but in a political society. The attempt to get the state on side now includes the constitution as the supreme instrument of political leverage. As the constitutional agenda lengthened from the mid-1960s to Meech Lake, more and more groups sought and often attained the enhanced status and rights the constitution could offer. By the time of Meech Lake, groups that before 1982 had no explicit constitutional recognition – such as women, third-force Canadians, and visible minorities – and Aboriginals, whose constitutional recognition was enhanced by the 1982 Constitution Act, were enraged and despondent at the weakening of their constitutional recognition that they saw in the Meech Lake Accord.

For most of the purposes for which individuals and groups interact with the state, infrequent elections characterized by vague party platforms are inadequate vehicles to seek the highly specific results that are typically sought. Accordingly, a vast system of continuing reciprocal exchanges between groups (especially business) and the state, often facilitated by intermediaries, has grown up. In general, these transactions occur outside the party system and thus contribute to its diminished status.

The innumerable transactions of the administrative state with the economy and society work on the behaviour and beliefs of the participants. For example, from the perspective of individuals, the existing income security programs clearly weaken the achievement ideology that relates income to effort in the market. As John Keane, summarizing the work of Claus Offe, observed, "State policies considerably decommodify the daily lives of the population by replacing 'contract' with political status and 'property rights' with 'citizen rights.'" Thus, "'work' and 'pay'" are partly severed from each other for the temporarily or permanently unemployed. [122] In like manner, market profit and firm income also become disconnected.

The inducements held out by the administrative state lead to an increased role for political calculations in our daily lives and therefore in our perceptions of ourselves and our environment. As our life becomes "life by political design," [123] fewer and fewer practices can be unthinkingly left to the authority of tradition and custom. On the one hand, the fact that those practices evolved and were not produced by state action makes them appear to be without justification; on the other hand, the knowledge that the state has intervened so extensively elsewhere makes them potentially subject to state intervention in the future. Politicization reduces the incidence and acceptance of the simply "given." As Anthony King graphically put it in 1975, "Once upon a time man looked to God to order the world. Then he looked to the market. Now he looks to government." The redress of problems, accordingly, is the responsibility of the last. [124]

The change of focus from God to market to government brings with it a change of human type. Political man and political woman differ from economic and religious man and economic and religious woman, whom they have displaced. The relation between the administrative state and the character, values, and identities of Canadians is not an easy subject to research. Nonetheless, the version of Canadianness we bequeath to our children is our most important legacy and should not be left unexamined.

## Conclusion

While the attempt to characterize the administrative state and its relation to the society and economy of Canada in a few paragraphs can only lead to over-simplifications, the latter may nevertheless help to focus on the recurrent themes, implicit and explicit, of this paper.

(1) The state has some autonomy and plays a leadership role, or what Deutsch called a "steering" role for society. [125] The state also operates by means of historic constitutional arrangements and institutional structures not amenable to easy modification; these facilitate some kinds of responses and inhibit others. Also, in almost any seemingly new area of endeavour the state does not encounter an untouched segment of society or behaviour, but rather one that its existing policies already affect. In most cases of policy development the state is rearranging its relations with society, not establishing them for the first time. The state constantly encounters its own pastness in both its structures and its policies.

(2) Given the coexistence of institutional conservatism and changes in the environment of politics, there is an inevitable discordance between the pattern of governing institutions, including the constitution, and pressures deriving from new intellectual, technological, and economic tendencies thrown up by socio-economic change. The massive presence of "structural heretics," state responses to new pressures that have bypassed our textbook constitutional theory, is one measure of the extent of the problem in the Canadian case.

(3) The state's involvement in society and the economy is so extensive, and thus beyond the effective monitoring reach of cabinets and legislatures, that the bulk of state activity is traditional and habitual. For established states the inheritance of old programs is always infinitely larger than the annual incremental additions. This pastness of programs is the essence of the administrative state, for it is the source of the bureaucracy's prominence in modern government.

(4) The realities of the administrative state belie the focused executive leadership that parliamentary cabinet government is supposed to provide. Even within single jurisdictions the state is not a unitary but a multiple actor. This fragmentation of the state fragments the political activity directed to influencing it. Given the extent of discretionary activity in the outreaches of the modern state in regulatory agencies and Crown corporations, the capacities of elections, political parties, legislatures, and cabinets to symbolize the unity of the state and to provide coherence to its programs are seriously attenuated.

(5) The administrative state modifies the theory and practice of federalism in two ways: first, the intergovernmental arena becomes a significant forum for policy co-ordination between federal and provincial governments, thus changing the practical meaning of the division of powers and weakening parliamentary controls over political executives; second, for an old federal system characterized by interventionist governments, both the contemporary provincial and national communities are very much the products of past state activity. They are shaped and given political meaning by the penetrative powers of the governments created by the Constitution Act.

(6) In the administrative state the governing elites work the constitution, frequently shuffle their internal administrative arrangements, especially in cabinets, and devise new policy instruments to enhance their governing capacities. Analogous efforts, with varying degrees of sophistication, are undertaken by private actors who develop increasingly complex coping mechanisms to handle and manipulate the state as the pursuit of self-interest increasingly acquires a political dimension. Individuals redefine themselves and rearrange their affairs to generate optimum interactions with the state. For businesses, especially those involved in regulated industries or heavily dependent on government contracts, a sophisticated capacity to deal with government is essential. These responses to

the interventionist state have produced a proliferation of intermediaries between private actors and the state – professional and trade associations and consulting firms for business and the well-endowed, occasional contacts with lawyers and accountants for the middle classes, social workers and community lawyers for the disadvantaged, and MPs and MLAs for a broad range of constituents. These phenomena are all examples of politicization, indicators of the increased role of political calculation as we pursue our goals.

(7) The fragmentation of the modern state and the varieties of its programs reduce private actors to the aggregation of those distinct facets of their existence to which the state has responded. Individuals therefore approach the state in a spirit of calculation, as managers of their fragmented selves, deciding which traits should be stressed and which concealed. These system-induced tendencies frustrate a civic sense of wholeness in the citizenry.

(8) Two recent phenomena will significantly influence the future evolution of the Canadian administrative state. First, the Charter has made Canadians a constitutional people; it has distributed constitutional identities to women, Aboriginals, and others. Its political purpose as an instrument of national unity, always more important to its creators than its role as protector of rights, was and is to create a floor of Canadianism below which neither order of government could go. [126] In particular, the objective was to penetrate the psyches of the citizens so that they would view and judge provincial policies through the lens of a rights-bearing pan-Canadianism. Over time, the Charter will tend to make Canadians, in constitutional terms, a more philosophical, theoretical people. The Charter stimulates citizens' allegiance to the constitution but weakens deference to political authority. Its tendency is to suggest that governing and working the constitution should be more of a joint affair between authorities and the citizenry than it has been. Second, the society of the future that interacts with the administrative state will be multicultural and multiracial and characterized by a more politicized ethnic and racial self-consciousness than has been true in Canadian history. This ethnic and racial pluralism is hostile to majoritarianism and unsympathetic to constitutional and political practices that accord superior status to French-English dualism.

(9) One of the most demanding tasks confronting the state in coming decades will be the management of an ethnically and racially plural society in the context of a numerical decline in the population of British and French descent, and of a citizenry digesting its new Charter-derived status as possessors of enforceable rights. The 1982 Constitution Act, supplemented or not by the Meech Lake Accord, is both a major beginning and an incomplete answer to the question raised by the changing social composition of Canada: how are we to think of ourselves as a people now that our British past has been cast aside and dualism is self-evidently too restrictive?

# PART II

## WHERE WE HAVE COME FROM

Chapter Three

# The Constitutional World We Have Lost

*At Charlottetown, 128 years ago, the Fathers of Confederation had names like Brown and Macdonald and Cartier and McGee – French names, English names, Irish or Scots. All men.*

*In August, this year, in Charlottetown, were Canadians with names like Rosemarie Kuptana and Ovide Mercredi, and Roy Romanow and Joe Ghiz. They came from a very different country, a modern Canada. The Charlottetown Accord lets the Constitution catch up to the country we have become.*[1]

– Right Honourable Joe Clark

*One hundred years ago, the role for women was almost exclusively domestic; 50 years ago, some visible minorities were disenfranchised; 25 years ago, native peoples lacked a policy voice; and 10 years ago, disabled persons were routinely kept dependent. Today, none of these exclusionary assumptions is acceptable.*[2]

– Judge Rosalie Silberman Abella

# Introduction

"The Constitutional World We Have Lost" may suggest a Creightonian lament for the Macdonaldian constitution displaced by appeasers, the historically illiterate, and Privy Council incompetents. In fact, this paper is in no sense an attempt to turn back the clock to a constitutional garden of Eden that we have regrettably let slip from our fingers by sins such as eating the forbidden fruit of the Charter, thus elevating the status of the citizenry in the constitutional order. At the level of the individual, such nostalgia may be an effective coping mechanism, a kind of opting out from whatever aspects of constitutional modernity, or post-modernity, threaten one's sense of personal continuity with a comfortable past. For society as a whole, however, a pervasive nostalgia is dysfunctional if it inhibits sensitive adaptation of a constitutional inheritance to new social forces. At our present juncture, constitutional imagination is a greater need than the historian's expertise in our traditions. While ours is not the naive or utopian task of wiping the slate clean, we do need to prevent the inertia of our traditions from impeding necessary adjustments.

An analysis of, not nostalgia for, our constitutional past can be instructive, however, if (1) its marked contrast with the contemporary constitutional world illuminates where we are and underlines how far we have travelled in a relatively short time; it can be doubly instructive if the contrast informs us of the dramatically changed relationship of the constitution to Canadian society, and thus of the new functions the contemporary constitution performs; or (2) it helps to explain some of our difficulties in working the new constitutional arrangements because of the still powerful, if diminishing, impact of the past on our assumptions, identities, and behaviour; or (3) if it cautions us that our constitutional future may differ from the constitutional present just as much as the latter contrasts with yesterday's constitutional world. A reminder of the world we have lost may tame the natural arrogance of the living that they can bend the future to their dictates, constructing regimes that will last a thousand years. To look back is to be reminded that even as enduring a constitutional regime as Canada's surely has been, rests partly on granite and partly on quicksand, the underground constitutional location of which eludes our unavoidably imperfect understanding.

## Yesterday's Constitutional World

Whether yesterday's constitutional world was better or worse than the one we now inhabit is not germane to my purposes. It was, however, very different. Its guiding constitutional principles responded to different criteria and social forces. Its central written component, the BNA Act, was a much more spartan instrument than its contemporary successor. Further, the constitution's role was much less comprehensive and its symbolism much more muted than our post-1982 constitutional instruments. Nevertheless, most of our past constitutional practice survives, since the 1982 additions were a rearrangement or supplementation of an historic constitutional system, not a revolutionary repudiation.

If we ascend to a mountaintop to survey our constitutional past, the Olympian vantage point Tocqueville recommended to the student of American life, the loss in detail is amply compensated by the stark outlines that monopolize our vision. The resultant landscape may be viewed from a distant perspective unimpeded by distracting particulars. Inevitably, the resulting picture risks our seeing the past through the eyes of the present, rather than as it was viewed by those who lived it. The description that follows also doubtless stresses difference rather than similarity, and thus minimizes the continuities that have survived. That bias, however, is positively helpful, given our objective of underlining the extent of Canada's recent constitutional transformations, by contrasting where we were with where we are. The constitutional world we have lost was simplicity itself compared to the constitutional world we have gained.

## THE SENSE OF HISTORY

The constitutional scholars and activists of our first constitutional paradigm, which I date from Confederation to roughly 1960, were profoundly historical, rooted in a legacy they updated with contributions consonant with its spirit. They viewed existing institutional arrangements as contemporary expressions of an inheritance. For the Quebec constitutional class, that meant adherence to the original understanding of Confederation and its practical updating to respond to new pressures while remaining faithful to its spirit.

There was much looking to the past for understanding and for guidance. For Dawson's *Government of Canada*, first published in 1947, heredity or parentage was one of the two powerful forces shaping the character of a government, along with the environment, although only limited attention was paid to the latter.[3] Constitutional prescriptions displayed a fascination with origins. The Rowell-Sirois Report, after a long introductory chapter on the background to Confederation and the contested meanings attributed to it, settled down to a decade-by-decade political economy analysis of the development of Canadian federalism into the 1930s. Its recommendations were guided by its historical interpretations.[4] The Quebec government's Royal Commission rival to Rowell-Sirois, the 1956 Tremblay Report, was equally immersed in history, looked back to Confederation for the true meaning of the French-English *entente*, went on to construct its own rival analysis of Canada's post-Confederation evolution, and based its recommendations on an understanding of Confederation that it chastised English Canadians for ignoring.[5] The 1939 O'Connor Report to the Senate on judicial interpretation of the BNA Act simplistically recommended that the judicial task required little more than a return to the clear and correct interpretation of the obvious, explicit, original centralist understanding of Confederation. To O'Connor, if the courts could only get their history right, their damaging misinterpretations would surely end.[6] In a similar fashion, English-Canadian critics of the compact theory appeared to believe that Duplessis would give up his espousal of the theory if he would simply read their works that gave him a failing grade in Canadian history. Compact theorists and Macdonald centralists, such as Donald Creighton, agreed that the past was the essential validation for their constitutional preferences, although they diametrically disagreed on its interpretation.

The one area where change was most visible, and explicitly sought, the ascent from colony to nation, was viewed as a journey or pilgrimage, whose direction was still conditioned by origins. The colony-to-nation theme inevitably provided a pervasive historical dimension to constitutional theorizing. This profoundly historical orientation also gave strong emotional sustenance to a British definition of a Canada fashioned by or after the model of the Imperial Mother. "Britishness" in personnel, in academic training, and in the orientation of the infant social science disciplines in English Canada made an independent contribution to bolstering a British definition of the constitution. The Department of Political Economy at the University of Toronto, the most prestigious Canadian department in that field, was headed by British academics from its 1888 founding to the 1937 appointment of Harold Innis as the first Canadian head. In Anglo-Canadian scholarship, an historical orientation typically elicited laudatory appreciation of the monarchical tradition, generally of "a constitution similar in principle to that of the United Kingdom," and specifically of parliamentary government, seen as the core of that similar constitution. After all, institutionally, "colony to nation" meant the progressive filling out of responsible parliamentary government, satisfying its insatiable urge to encompass more constitutional territory.[7]

Colony to nation applied no similar principle of growth or progressive change to federalism. Further, for several reasons the Canadian experience of federalism did not link its constitutional assumptions to the American practice of federalism in the way that parliamentary government established links with the United Kingdom. Not only had the Canadian founders explicitly and deliberately rejected crucial doctrines of American federalism, but unlike responsible government, the nature of Canadian federalism was explicitly laid out in the BNA Act, and thus did not require resort to a foreign model for its understanding. Therefore, American federalism was not the mother of Canadian federalism in the way that Westminster was the mother of Canadian parliamentary practice. In

spite of the twin British and American roots of the two main pillars of Confederation, parliamentary government and federalism, resort to constitutional history stressed the British, not the American, contribution to our constitutional
package. By the same token, as we evolved and history's grip relaxed, the British
component of our constitutional self-image receded.

### THE INSTITUTIONAL HERITAGE AND ITS EVOLUTION

The institutions that collectively comprised the constitutional framework were
in place from the beginning – federalism, parliamentary government, the constitutional monarchy, and the judiciary. And, although it was often argued that federalism and parliamentary government were an ill-matched pair,[8] their long
coexistence suggested that the tension between them was manageable.

Federalism was the main component of the written constitution. Hence,
survey texts in constitutional law were essentially commentaries on judicial
interpretation of the division of powers,[9] sometimes interspersed with a nation-
alist/imperialist debate about the JCPC role in strengthening provincial jurisdiction. The constitutional role of the Supreme Court, established in 1875 and the
apex of judicial power in Canada, was accordingly seen as the umpire of federalism. When and whether it should replace the Judicial Committee as the final
appellate court was debated in terms of the prospective consequences for the
federal-provincial division of powers and for Quebec's cherished provincial
autonomy, as well as the nationalist/imperialist dimension.

Federalism, which had been viewed as transitional by some of the more
centralist inclined English-Canadian politicians at Confederation, rooted itself
deeply in Canadian society. Its natural and strong Quebec base of support was
supplemented by the institutional self-interest of the political and administrative class that operated the provincial order of governments. Further, as the
country expanded from four to ten provinces, the increasingly complex tasks of
managing space and accommodating territorial diversity enhanced the utility of
federalism.

By the mid-twentieth century, a particular reflection of French-English differences was implanted in the constitutional structure. The federal government
had become an instrument for English-Canadian purposes to a degree that far
exceeded the English-Canadian proportion of the population. The introduction
of the merit principle decades earlier dramatically reduced French-Canadian
representation in the federal bureaucracy, especially at the senior levels. Quebec's real influence in the federal government, in spite of its important numerical
contribution to a succession of Liberal governments, was severely limited.
Although Trudeau's characterization of backbench Liberal MPs as "trained

donkeys" may have been exaggerated, the marginalizing of Quebec cabinet ministers into the minor patronage portfolios was undeniable. In sum, "English-speaking Canadians," as Trudeau phrased it, "have long behaved in national politics as though they believed that democracy was not for French Canadians."[10] Relatedly, as the Royal Commission on Bilingualism and Biculturalism reported, to "very many [English-speaking Canadians] Canada appears as essentially an English-speaking country with a French-speaking minority, to which certain limited rights have been given."[11]

The unsympathetic face offered to Quebec by the federal government and to French-speaking by English-speaking Canadians inevitably strengthened the allegiance of Francophone Quebecers to the one province where they were in a majority. The B&B Commission was struck by "the extreme suspicion with which a large part of Quebec looks on anything that is initiated by Ottawa, and [by] its considerable scepticism as to English Canada's ability and desire to understand French Canada."[12] The resultant siege mentality made provincial autonomy the primary constitutional principle of Quebec political leaders and deflected attention, until the Quiet Revolution of the sixties, from the democratic shortcomings of Quebec provincial politics.

These components of this lost constitutional world, so congenial to English-Canadian centralists and nationalists, rested, as noted below, on an acquiescent, non-assertive Quebec, which was on the verge of disappearance by the time of the Diefenbaker governments of the late fifties. By the sixties, the ethnic assumptions underpinning the previous federal-provincial division of labour turned out to be based on sand. This, in turn, undermined the constitutional assumptions based on a superior (English)-inferior (French) or dominant-passive ethnic constitutional equilibrium.

The English-Canadian counterpart to Quebec's principled adherence to federalism for Canada's first century was a racial pride in the positive heritage of parliamentary government.[13] However, as parliamentary government was battered by crude democratic assumptions over time, it was translated into legislative majoritarianism that, given party discipline, meant executive (or Prime Minister or Premier) dominance. Thus a consistent trend over the first century was the systematic erosion of checks on legislative majoritarianism.[14] This required unleashing federal and provincial legislatures from the restraints of supervision by the Crown in Canada and the United Kingdom.[15] The empowering of provincial legislatures required the relaxation or elimination of federal government supervision by means of disallowance and reservation and, to a lesser extent, the declaratory power.[16]

In sum, up to the 1950s constitutional change was seen as an evolutionary unfolding, as responses to the system's inner logic. Hence, the relaxation both of imperial controls and of constraints on legislatures was seen as an indicator of a natural maturing process. The progressive moves to a universal federal and provincial franchise were also, in a broad sense, in the nature of things – elaborations of what had already been achieved. The fluctuating fates of federal and provincial governments, their alternating cyclical rise and fall in response to domestic and international pressures, were not constitutionally threatening. Rather, excepting the depression of the thirties, they were evidence of the system's adaptive flexibility. By and large, therefore, yesterday's constitution was a living constitution that responded successfully to within-system challenges that presupposed constitutional continuity.

## CONSTITUTIONAL SHORTCOMINGS

The constitutional order bluntly and briefly described above lasted for more than a century. It had many virtues, not least its durability. Under that constitutional order Canada grew in population, in territorial expanse, in wealth, and in international recognition. However, the longevity of the old constitutional order rested on practices and arrangements we can no longer employ – the avoidance of fundamental issues, such as the location of sovereignty and how, constitutionally, we see ourselves as a people; the luxury of a custodial mother to look after some of our constitutional requirements, constitutional interpretation, and formal constitutional amendment, for example, while we slowly got our act together; the restriction of the social base of the political order and hence the constitution to the politically acceptable by exclusionary practices; and the employment of an elitist style of ordinary and constitutional politics that restricted constitutional issues to those that concerned elites and were politically manageable.

## THE AVOIDANCE STRATEGY

From one perspective, the practice of incremental constitutional change driven by no teleological sense of destiny can be a cause for self-congratulation, an appropriate philosophy for a "living" constitution that responds to the requirements of the moment, but no more. From a negative perspective, however, to look back on our constitutional history up to the post-1960 modern period (defined below) is to be struck by the conscious and habitual practice of avoidance by which many of the big questions were put aside or the response interminably delayed until some acceptable state of ripeness had developed. Although all constitutions are living, and hence always in transition, the Canadian constitution, and therefore the Canadian people, was in transition in a more fundamental sense. Basic constitutional issues were repeatedly shelved.

The colony-to-nation route, a consequence of the deliberate incompleteness of Confederation, meant that for most of our history, and for a dwindling minority still, the boundaries, and hence the very nature, of the Canadian community were ambiguous. The unending debate over the appropriateness of any particular boundary between imperial and domestic always had one set of protagonists arguing, in effect, for a transnational definition of community that encompassed United Kingdom kin. Whether this should simply be labelled the colonial mentality, or the natural community conceptions of a diaspora, it rendered impossible even the simple acceptance that Canada's boundaries were also those of the Canadian community.

Psychologically, the absence of an amending formula in the original BNA Act that could be operated entirely in Canada, and the subsequent inability to agree on such a formula after the 1931 Statute of Westminster, meant that the elementary question of the appropriate location of sovereign power was left in abeyance until 1982. As recently as 1980-81, various provincial governments and some Aboriginal organizations opposed a threatened Trudeau unilateralism by arguing that the British government had a discretionary trustee role that might require the refusal of a federal government request for particular amendments.

The inability to agree on an amending formula, and thus on where sovereignty resided, was from a different perspective an inability to agree on what kind of political people Canadians were. This inability rested on four unresolved tensions: (1) the conflict already noted between those who for long saw themselves as British Canadians, still linked emotionally to the United Kingdom and Empire as well as to Canada, and those, including virtually all French Canadians, for whom Canada was their undisputed homeland – while ultimately time was on the side of the Canadian identifiers, the bitterness of the flag debate as recently as 1964, and the British imperialist sentiments it aroused, underlined the deep attachment of many Canadians to the British connection; (2) the conflict between federal and provincial governments for influence, control, or protection in the amending formula, and the Canadian versus provincial conceptions of community for which the contesting federal and provincial governments were proxies; (3) the conflict between Quebec and the rest of Canada over the amending formula and over a definition of Canada acceptable to both linguistic communities; (4) a tension to which almost no attention was paid in the pre-Diefenbaker constitutional era, whether Canada was to be thought of constitutionally as a system of governments or as a political nation of citizens, the response to which would inform the relative roles of citizens and governments in constitutional change. The almost obsessive concentration on process in the criticisms of the Meech Lake misadventure and the post-Meech difficulty in finding an acceptable division of labour between governments and citizens in formal constitutional change give this final concern a prominence equal to the federalism conflict among governments and the Quebec-driven two nations conflict.

The formal sovereignty answer provided by the 1982 Constitution Act is clearly incomplete, given its rejection by Quebec and its inadequacy from the perspective of a participant citizenry stimulated by the Charter. The shortcomings in the 1982 amending formula response to the sovereignty question have left its resolution to our generation in a context in which the number of claimants to a share of sovereignty threatens to become unmanageable.

While a constitutional strategy of avoidance clearly had its short-run attractions for the politicians who practised it, its long-run viability as a constitutional strategy depended on the capacity of succeeding generations of politicians also to avoid the same or other big constitutional issues. It therefore rested on the faith that the future would be equally user-friendly, a phrase that does not come easily to the lips of the students or practitioners of post-Meech constitutional politics, who confront a daunting agenda of problems, much of which is the legacy of the avoidance strategy of our predecessors.

### THE EXCLUSION STRATEGY [17]

The second basic constitutional strategy was the practice of an extensive exclusion, varying from relative to absolute, of significant segments of Canadian society from full active political membership in the community. For most of our first century, the living constitution rested on a restricted social base. Presumably, this eased the task of working and periodically updating the constitution by reducing the number of interests that had to be accommodated. This, too, however, was a strategy that visited major problems on future generations – the task of incorporating the formerly excluded once the diffusion of the democratic ideal and egalitarian values rendered continuing exclusion illegitimate.

*Aboriginal peoples.* Aboriginal peoples, a rubric not then employed, existed in the shadows, devoid of public voice. With the exception of three Aboriginal MPs from Manitoba in the 1870s, when the Métis were a provincial majority, there were no self-identified Aboriginal persons elected to the House of Commons until 1968. [18]

Eskimos, now Inuit, were constitutionally and territorially peripheral, although a 1939 Supreme Court decision subsumed them in the category "Indian" of s. 91(24) of the BNA Act. Until the 1950s, Inuit contact was restricted to missionaries, the RCMP, the Hudson's Bay Company, and a few government officials. To the extent that any government policy existed, it was to "keep . . . the native native." Prime Minister St. Laurent stated in 1953 that government administration of the North until then had occurred "in an almost continuing state of absence of mind," a policy dereliction whose overcoming formally commenced with the establishment in that year of the new Department of Northern Affairs and National Resources.[19] There was, however, no Eskimo Act to parallel the Indian Act, and Inuit were considered full citizens. Whatever special services they received were not seen as indicating any special status, but as transitional arrangements until they became self-sufficient.

Status Indians were subjects, deprived of the federal and provincial vote with a few exceptions. Denial of the franchise was a symbolic statement that status Indians were not considered full members of the political community of citizens, a perception shared by Indians. They showed little concern over their subordinate civic status. In fact, for many the "combination of political exclusion and a special system of administration came to be psychologically coupled with a lack of identification with the political system of the larger society, and with a tenacious emphasis on their own unique status. The extent of this was dramatically revealed when the extension of the federal and provincial franchise to Indians was met with little popular acclaim, much suspicion, and occasional hostility."[20] Their demise – the "passing of the Indian race" – or their assimilation was variously anticipated or hoped for. "I want to get rid of the Indian problem," Duncan Campbell Scott, Superintendent-General of Indian Affairs, stated in 1920. "Our objective is to continue until there is not a single Indian in Canada that has not been absorbed."[21]

Indians were conventionally described as wards or children. Their culture was stigmatized, and several of their customs with high symbolic value were banned. Their administration was custodial, and their administrators were very often authoritarian, a posture protected from attack by the marginal status of their subject clientele. Overall, Indians were subjected to a system of "coercive tutelage,"[22] "involuntary ... [and] imposed upon an entire people virtually in perpetuity. ... From birth to death most Indians ... [have been assaulted by] ... one unvarying and unceasing message – that they are unacceptable as they are and that to become worthwhile as individuals they must change in the particular manner advocated by their current tutelage agents."[23] Memories of their past humiliation explain the passionate resistance of contemporary Indian political leaders to policy proposals that appear to be instruments of assimilation.

Up until World War Two there was a negligible parliamentary interest in Indian issues.[24] At least up until then, "Indian administration was a version of colonialism. The [Indian Affairs] Branch was a quasi-colonial government dealing with almost the entire life of a culturally different people who were systematically deprived of opportunities to influence government, a people who were isolated on special pockets of land and who were subject to separate laws. Throughout this period a dominating Branch concern was simply to keep the peace and to prevent unruly clientele reactions to Branch policy."[25]

The Métis had no explicit constitutional recognition. Officially, they were treated as and considered to be ordinary Canadians, albeit with a unique background. Unofficially and socially a Métis identity was perceived negatively in the surrounding white society. This provided a practical encouragement to "pass for white" and to merge into the larger society. The Métis National Council recently referred scathingly to the historical federal policy of non-recognition, which meant "that no official statistics were kept for the Metis people, so that Canada did not know who, how many and where the Metis were. Metis culture was ignored by the country's museums and galleries. Metis historical contributions were ignored by the country's educators. As far as Canada was concerned, the Metis, like the buffalo, had disappeared."[26]

In general, Aboriginal political organizations were weak. Status Indians, lacking the vote, were more likely to turn to the courts for redress than to the more overt political process. The limited political pressure applied by status Indians showed little of the aggressive self-confidence of the Aboriginal political elite of the last two decades. For example, Indian presentations to a 1946-48 Joint Parliamentary Committee on Indian Affairs were noticeably "deferential, humble and shy. In many cases [Indians] prefaced their remarks by reminding parliamentarians that they were uneducated, that they spoke and read English poorly, and that in general they lacked the experience to assume a confident demeanour when appearing before M.P.'s and Senators."[27] Finally, of course, there was no constitutional category of "Aboriginal peoples," as in s. 35 of the 1982 Constitution Act, which brings Indian, Inuit, and Métis together, thus facilitating the use of intra-Aboriginal comparisons as levers to advance the less favourably treated, a strategy now vigorously employed by contemporary Métis leaders.

The background, off-stage existence of Canada's indigenous peoples reflected global trends in the distribution of power and status among what were thought of as the races of humankind. The domestic treatment of indigenous peoples paralleled the socio-political hierarchies of imperialism through which a handful of European powers held sway over what was to become the Third World. The powerlessness and subject status of the colonized peoples of Africa and Asia reinforced, by their prestigious example and global extent, a similar position for indigenous Aboriginal Canadians.

*Women.* The face of yesterday's politics was male. Although the franchise was progressively extended to women, with Quebec responding last in 1940, public life was monopolized by men. While there were individual victories and firsts – the election of the first woman, Agnes Macphail, to the House of Commons in 1921, the Privy Council decision in the *Persons* case in 1929 (leading to the subsequent appointment of Cairine Wilson to the Senate in 1930), and the appointment in 1957 of the first federal woman cabinet minister, Ellen Fairclough – these were lonely triumphs.

For those women who pinned their hopes on the franchise or on the influence of initial examples, the subsequent statistical record was singularly depressing.

From 1917 to June, 1970, 6,845 individuals were elected in 134 federal and provincial elections, of whom sixty-seven were women, less than 1 per cent. Women constituted 2.4 per cent of candidates in federal elections from 1921 to 1968, and 0.8 per cent of the elected members. In the forty-year period from 1930, when the first woman senator was appointed, 227 men and only eight women were appointed. In 1969 only fourteen of the 889 judges and magistrates in Canada were women, only one of whom was on a superior court.[28]

The 1970 *Report of the Royal Commission on the Status of Women in Canada* succinctly summarized half a century of very limited progress:

> The last 50 years, since woman suffrage was introduced, have seen no appreciable change in the political activities of women beyond the exercise of the right to vote. In the decision-making positions, and most conspicuously in the government and Parliament of Canada, the presence of a mere handful of women is no more than a token acknowledgement of their right to be there. The voice of government is still a man's voice. The formulation of policies affecting the lives of all Canadians is still the prerogative of men. The absurdity of this situation was illustrated when debate in the House of Commons on a change in abortion law was conducted by 263 men and one woman.
>
> Nowhere else in Canadian life is the persistent distinction between male and female roles of more consequence. No country can make a claim to having equal status for its women so long as government lies entirely in the hands of men.[29]

*Ethnic and racial minorities.* Up to the 1950s, *The Race Question in Canada*[30] remained what it had been in Siegfried's day, the relationship between the French and the English peoples. The major texts of the forties by Brady, Clokie, Corry, and Dawson saw Canada in essentially dualist terms, with the French Canada/Quebec component downplayed, supplemented by sporadic references to Indians and to the ethnic composition of immigrants.[31] The long history of anti-Orientalism in British Columbia, the war-time internment of Japanese Canadians, widespread anti-Semitism, and restrictive immigration policies up to the 1960s all reflected the dominance of the British and to a lesser extent the French founding peoples in the Canadian pantheon. Immigrants who came in large numbers from Southern, Eastern, and Central Europe prior to World War One were treated as inferiors who, according to English-speaking Canadians, should be raised to the values and behaviour of Anglo-conformity. In each of World Wars One and Two, ethnic minorities that could be linked by ancestral origin to wartime enemies – those of German, Ukrainian, Italian, or Japanese background – experienced discrimination, were put in camps in considerable numbers, and lost both property and legal rights.[32] This was the precursor of the world that John Porter brilliantly dissected in *The Vertical Mosaic* of the sixties. [33] Until Diefenbaker took office, public life was still dominated by the two founding peoples. Of the thousands of elected MPs from 1867 to 1964 less than 100 had ethnic origins outside the founding French, British, and Aboriginal peoples. [34]

Thus, three of the more influential and highly visible constitutional participants of the past decade and a half – indigenous peoples, Canadians who lacked founding people status, especially Asians and Africans, and women – were marginalized in public life prior to the 1960s. In different terminology, representation in public life was biased by various filtering systems that accorded disproportionate weight to some and minimized, sometimes to the point of virtually silencing, the voice and presence of others. For example, according to the *Royal Commission on Electoral Reform*, Canada's "past is replete with symbols of . . . [Aboriginal people's] . . . exclusion from the Canadian polity." [35] Unless they had served in the Armed Forces, Canadians of East Indian, Chinese, and Japanese ancestry could not vote until after World War Two.

The relative stability of yesterday's constitutional world was sustained by exclusionary practices that masked much of the underlying heterogeneity of Canadian society. The famous brokerage politics partly succeeded by artificially reducing the number and diversity of the interests that had to be brokered.

Additional aspects of the constitution we have left behind distance our situation from that of our predecessors, reduce the availability of lessons in constitutional management from the past, and suggest that forgetting may be more important than remembering as we confront the constitutional agenda of the nineties.

### CONSTITUTIONAL ELITISM

In the first ninety years of Canada's existence there were no counterparts to the large package of constitutional change in the 1982 Constitution Act, to the proposed Meech Lake Accord, or to the post-Meech Lake package enshrined in the Charlottetown Accord. Equally, with the exception of the World War Two conscription referendum, there was no equivalent in explicitly constitutional matters to the widespread public participation from the Quebec referendum of 1980 to the 1992 demise of the Charlottetown Accord. [36]

Formal constitutional change was an affair for elites, who squabbled among themselves as to how much intergovernmental agreement was needed before a formal request for an amendment could appropriately be transmitted to Westminster for British parliamentary passage. Whether the United Kingdom Parliament had any discretion, any obligation to ensure that the procedural proprieties had been observed in Canada before the federal government formally requested a British response, was a contested issue, but not one that extended the circle of concerned interests to include citizens. The search for an amending formula acceptable to Canadians, one that would relieve the United Kingdom of its thankless role, overwhelmingly defined the problem as determining the extent of the necessary intergovernmental agreement before an amendment would pass. Even the Fulton-Favreau amending formula of the mid-1960s rose and fell without any formal opportunity for public input.[37] Indeed, the Gang of Eight's amending formula, devised as recently as 1980-81, was fashioned in private interprovincial meetings of governments, who never questioned the premise of governments' virtually total domination of the process of formal amendments, a premise that became anachronistic almost as soon as it received constitutional sanction in 1982.

Formal constitutional change was not seen as a matter for citizens. The constitution addressed them through the lens of federalism, and hence in terms of those territorial conceptions of community for which the governments of Canadian federalism assumed a natural leadership role. As is noted immediately below, the absence of an entrenched Charter was probably the major reason for the constitution's inability to engage the citizenry directly in terms of nonfederal criteria, and thus to bypass governments.

## A CONSTITUTION WITHOUT CHARISMA

Unlike the post-1982 constitution with its Charter, the founders' constitution, especially the BNA Act, its key written component, had a very low profile. Its nonrevolutionary origins as an elite creation, its non-inspirational workmanlike language, and the absence of a Bill of Rights conspired to minimize the constitution's impact on public consciousness. The fact that so much of the effective constitution, especially parliamentary government, was found in custom and convention made an independent contribution to the constitution's relative invisibility. Citizen rights and parliamentary practice were sustained by understandings that influenced behaviour, rather than being responses to a binding, written text. More generally, as the phrase went, "the rights of Englishmen" travelled with them. The diffuse nature of constitutional norms may or may not have affected adherence to them; unquestionably, however, it lowered their profile.

The constitution's derivative status contributed to its low profile. It linked Canadians not to an autonomous past, or to a time when freedom's bells signalled the creation of a new people, but to a mother country. Parliamentary government was a British cultural transplant. The specifics of Canadian federalism were laid out in a British statute. The monarchical role again was explicitly derivative. Thus, although the form of the constitution was chosen by Canadians and adapted to Canadian conditions, the overall heritage was British and imperial, with a sensitivity to the distinctive requirements of Quebec.

## A DIVIDED BRITISH-CANADIAN IDENTITY

At least until World War Two, many British Canadians had a composite civic identity. Their Canadianness shaded comfortably into a Britishness that had imperial connotations. A 1910 defence of the Judicial Committee of the Privy Council by Justice W.R. Riddell referred to the British court in glowing terms, "sitting to decide cases from every quarter of the globe, administering justice to all under the red-cross flag and symbolizing the mighty unity of an Imperial people. . . . One name we bear, one flag covers us, to one throne we are loyal; and that Court is a token of our unity." [38]

British Canadians were linked by a common allegiance to the centre with the other white Dominions of the Empire. Democracy in the four Dominions of Canada, Australia, New Zealand, and South Africa was the product of "transplanted Britons," and reflected the "ascendancy of British liberal ideas" in sympathetic settings, according to Brady. [39]

The existence of this divided or fused allegiance, a complex, composite national-imperial identity that could not be shared by French Canadians, meant that psychologically the two European founding peoples lived in different constitutional worlds and had different constitutional identities. French-Canadian leaders frequently pointed out that British Canadians did not completely identify with and devote themselves entirely to Canada. [40] Finally, this constitutional division between French and English Canadians, which threatened Canada's stability in both world wars, along with the ambiguity at the heart of the British-Canadian identity, contributed to the failure of Canadians to constitute themselves a sovereign people.

Yesterday's constitutional world did not disappear overnight. The constitution and Canadian society had adapted to each other, albeit selectively, as already noted. The constitution had deep roots in many segments of society. Canada was a success story. In the decade and a half after World War Two, with Europe still recovering from the ravages of war, Canada had a significant international presence. Canada was a leading player, only marginally behind the United Kingdom, in the emerging multiracial Commonwealth. The addition of Newfoundland in 1949 rounded out Canada's territorial domain. The abolition of appeals to the Privy Council in the same year and the 1952 appointment of Vincent Massey as the first Canadian Governor General were comfortably fitted into the colony-to-nation evolutionary development that gratifyingly differentiated Canada from its republican neighbour.

## The Diefenbaker Transition to the New Constitutional World

The portents of a new era, however, were not long in appearing. The six years of Diefenbaker's prime ministership, 1957-63, were transition years from a constitutional order that had lasted nearly a century to a chaotically emerging new order whose shaping still continues three decades later. At its onset, and still today, the new order incorporated most of Canada's constitutional inheritance. Nevertheless, the cumulative impact of a battery of changes justifies labelling Diefenbaker's government as a vanguard government presiding over a transition in which the significantly different constitutional world of the present began to surface in hydra-headed fashion.

The Diefenbaker portrait that follows is, no doubt, one-sided. His One Canada concept had anti-French overtones, and a balanced judgement of his career, especially his prime ministership, would conclude that his theatrical skills far exceeded his government management skills. It remains true, however, that in various fields the elaboration of his policies by following generations led directly to our present constitutional world.

(1) The 1960 Diefenbaker Bill of Rights, weak instrument that it may have been, signalled the weakening hold of parliamentary supremacy on the Canadian constitutional imagination.[41] It contributed to the rights consciousness that, further catalyzed by the 1982 Charter, subsequently transformed Canadian constitutional culture.

(2) The franchise extension to status Indians in 1960 repudiated previous policy defining Indians as wards who could only attain the franchise by graduating from their backward condition and giving up Indian legal status. The ending of that requirement gave a major boost to the explicit Indian involvement in conventional politics that served as a bridge to subsequent involvement in the politics of constitutional reform. Two years earlier, Diefenbaker had appointed James Gladstone as the first Indian senator. Both initiatives were clearly responses to the post-imperial international climate, particularly the moral influence of the United Nations on behalf of domestic as well as colonial Third World peoples. The demise of a world in which white skin colour and the unquestioned possession of political power and superior status were clearly correlated had domestic consequences.

(3) Diefenbaker appointed the first woman cabinet minister, Ellen Fairclough, in 1957. While it would be far-fetched to describe this as the direct precursor of the later feminist movement, it was at least an early, if mild, response to the challenges to male political hegemony that were to become stronger in later decades.

(4) Diefenbaker had little sympathy for or understanding of French Canada or Quebec nationalism. However, partly due to his own ethnic background and

his experience of Saskatchewan's richly varied immigrant population, he was acutely sensitive to the failure to recognize Canadians who lacked founding people status. Given his One Canada concept, he was "inordinately proud . . . of [the] eighteen different racial origins" in the Conservative caucus in the 24th Parliament.[42] His appointment of the first Ukrainian Canadian, Mike Starr, to the cabinet, was well received by "New Canadians," especially of Ukrainian background. In one sense, his ethnic views and the constituencies he spoke for were early warning signals of the "third-force" ethnic challenge of the sixties to the dualist, two nations/founding peoples definition of Canada that informed the terms of reference of the Royal Commission on Bilingualism and Biculturalism. Here, too, Diefenbaker was readjusting a long-established status hierarchy on behalf of relative outsiders whose political strength, public profile, and pressures for recognition and inclusion have dramatically grown in subsequent decades, partly as a response to the change in the source of immigrants.

Diefenbaker's early contribution to the emergence of the modified constitutional world we now inhabit was impressive. He changed the cast of players to the benefit of the formerly excluded or marginalized. His obsessive devotion to the strengthening of rights, which, language rights excepted, was the equal of Trudeau's, gave official sanction to the rights revolution that is the greatest break in Canada's constitutional continuity since Confederation. More generally, he clearly recognized the symbolic role of the written constitution for the citizenry and thus contributed to the greatly enhanced status of contemporary citizenship that, flowing from the Charter and Aboriginal constitutional clauses, now successfully challenges government domination of the constitutional reform process.

Diefenbaker was also acutely conscious of the impact of international developments on citizen-state relations in Western countries – the end of empire and of racial hierarchy, the relatively diminished status of the former white Dominions in the increasingly multiracial Commonwealth, and the moral leadership and symbolic influence of the United Nations and its missionary proselytization on behalf of rights. Here, too, he was a modernizer in his recognition that the conditions of successful statehood are, in the last analysis, set by the international community of states, and the norms it establishes are not static.

Two other developments during the Diefenbaker years, attributable neither to his prescience nor to concordance with his policies, help to underline the magnitude of the socio-political forces that were challenging the old constitutional order.

Most crucially, the 1960 victory of the Lesage Liberals in Quebec is conventionally dated as the beginning of the modern, secular Quebec nationalism, whose subsequent development remains the most serious challenge to Canada's survival. The almost unremitting constitutional preoccupation with Quebec over the past three decades, which derives directly from Quebec's nationalist challenge to the constitutional status quo, too easily blinds us to the very different pre-Quiet Revolution reality. According to Mallory, "even the most liberal" English-speaking Canadians for most of Canada's first century "regarded French Canada as little more than a transitory source of trouble and discomfort which, in the long run, would somehow be solved by the ultimate penetration of the forces of 'progress' into Quebec. Meanwhile it was best to let sleeping dogs lie."[43] Consequently, the accommodation of Quebec in the old constitutional order was much easier than the as yet unrealized accommodation of its contemporary successor.

A closely related phenomenon, the attenuation of federal dominance, in Smiley's terms,[44] resulted from a centrifugal, challenging provincialism that acquired visibility during Diefenbaker's terms of office, supplementing the Quebec nationalism just mentioned. Jointly, these led directly to the Pepin-Robarts analysis of the late seventies that the twin forces of duality and regionalism (meaning provincialism) were the major challenges to the constitutional order.[45]

The Diefenbaker government, therefore, was a watershed not only in ending the long Liberal hegemony in office, but also in presiding over or stimulating, across multiple fronts, the transition to a decisively transformed constitutional order. Diefenbaker's constitutional world, therefore, is ours in a way that King's and St. Laurent's are not.

## Then and Now

The contrast between our constitutional world and that of our predecessors is so striking that their sequential existence in the same country, separated by only three to four decades, appears scarcely plausible. The contrast graphically underlines how far we have travelled in a few decades, and thus indicates the uniqueness of our situation in the light of our history. The contrast also logically cautions us that our own future is inherently unpredictable – that the forces that buffet constitutions have a cunning that will outwit the shrewdest constitution-maker seeking to master the future.

The extent of the difference between the constitutional past and the constitutional present is dramatically underlined by the dual facts that we now confront the issues our predecessors avoided for the sake of constitutional peace, and those who were formerly excluded or marginalized are now key constitutional players – Aboriginal peoples, women, and multicultural Canadians of neither British nor French background. They compensate for their past exclusion with a tenacious constitutional participation driven by the mistrust of official elites that our predecessors bequeathed to them. Our constitutional world is more

pluralistic, more participatory, and in general more democratic. Formerly muffled voices now utter strident claims for recognition. Status Indians have moved
from an imposed wardship status to self-chosen nationhood in one generation.
They are supported in the latter national identity by similar claims of the Inuit
and the Métis. However, our democratic pleasure at how far we have come is
accompanied by at least mild apprehension that the longevity of our original
constitutional arrangements was perhaps sustained by exclusions and avoid-
ances that we can no longer practice. [46]

The main constitutional paradigm from the 1860s to the 1950s successfully
kept many of the big issues at bay, an unwelcome gift for future generations; our
avoidance capacity is much more limited. Our predecessors' constitution not
only was elitist and kept the people out of formal constitutional politics – a practice tried in Meech Lake but repudiated by public opinion as no longer legitimate
– but also rested on a limited social base that excluded many Canadians; by contrast, we have no alternative but to be democratically pluralist, open to all the
interests of a heterogeneous society possessed of a universal franchise, and in
many cases psychologically empowered by the Charter and the rhetoric of rights.

The relatively integrated historical package of constitutional management
strategies employed by our predecessors in the first nine or so post-Confederation decades presupposed a domestic and international environment that has
vanished. As a result, we are on our own in more than the platitudinous sense
that since 1982 all amending power is domiciled in Canada. Equally important,
the guidance we can get from history is reduced by the extent of our divorce from
our constitutional past. In fact, for our generation the fundamentals of our predecessors' paradigm are the source of some of our most difficult problems.

The previous constitution could be thought of as the governments' constitution because its main concerns of parliamentary government and federalism
were especially salient for governing elites. The contemporary constitution,
however, has a citizen base derived from the Charter and Aboriginal constitutional clauses, reinforced by the history of citizens' constitutional participation
over the last decade and a half. Whereas the evolution of our original constitution after 1867 was toward the weakening of the controls and external checks on
legislatures in the service of majoritarianism, we now seek to check majority
power by Charters and courts, by a revived Senate with real blocking power, by
denying governing elites the power to control unilaterally the process of formal
constitutional change, and by sophisticated litigation and lobbying practices
that bypass legislatures.

The modified constitution of the nineties has the function of providing a
democratic legitimation for the entire constitutional order that was not required
of the top-down constitution of most of our first century. The resultant constitutionalization of society or socialization of the constitution makes it potentially

misleading to discuss the original and contemporary constitutions as if both were similar entities performing similar functions, for clearly they are not.

The past constitutional world was crucially different from ours, especially up to World War Two, in one additional way. It was relatively sheltered from international opinion. Or, more accurately, the international opinion of consequence was generated within Western civilization and thus reflected values that were natural for Canadian elites. In a world of essentially European states, there was no significant external source of standards available to judge their domestic treatment of their own people. Countries with a European heritage judged countries and peoples that lacked it, by and large pronounced them inferior, and proceeded to dominate or ignore them. The judgement of the dominated others, prior to the end of empire, was muffled, a concern of anthropologists and missionaries, and had negligible impact in shaping world opinion on the domestic politics of the European powers.

Our predecessors did not have to justify themselves, as we now do, to a world of nation-states in which white governments are a minority. Ours is a world in which memories of racism, of European imperialism and its accompanying humiliation, generate critical international scrutiny of the manner in which all of the European countries treat their domestic, especially non-white minorities. Political executives now operate in the glare of an international public opinion sensitive to rights, to racial inequalities, to women, and to indigenous minorities. Particularistic concerns are mobilized behind United Nations covenants, behind International Women's Year (1975) and the Decade of Disabled Persons (1983-92). Cumulatively, the preceding give the constitution a much higher profile for the citizenry than was ever enjoyed by the BNA Act, its spare, prosaic predecessor.

Our predecessors' constitutional self-image was profoundly historical, and they worked a living constitution that they thought would continue to serve them indefinitely; they had not yet felt the domestic shaking of the earth in constitutional matters; the French-English tensions of both world wars and the apparent message of the depression of the thirties that the constitution was out of date, in spite of their seriousness, did not generate the degree of doubt about the constitutional future that we have recently come to regard as normal; we no longer have a living constitution, one that presupposes continuity can be maintained by incremental adjustment and piecemeal accommodation at the margins; we now assume the possibility of serious rupture or discontinuity simply by clinically observing the objectives of some of our fellow citizens; we no longer debate our future by appealing to the other party to accept our interpretation of a common past event, such as the Compact Theory debate about the intent of the Fathers of Confederation; we now have separate constitutional pasts for the multitude of new non-governmental actors with constitutional concerns – women,

Aboriginal peoples, the disabled, and others. Their particularistic constitutional histories are tales of rebuffs, exclusions, and the occasional heady triumphs. They look back not to Confederation but to the 1763 Royal Proclamation for Indians, to the 1929 *Persons* case for feminist groups, to the winning of the multicultural heritage clause (s. 27 of the Charter) for ethnocultural communities, and to their inclusion in s. 15 of the Charter for the disabled. These histories do not unite. Status Indians have turned their history of separate treatment on segregated reserves as a stigmatized people into contemporary claims for positive constitutional and institutional recognition of their status as internal "nations" apart from the general mass of the Canadian citizenry. Not surprisingly, the "relentless assault on their autonomy, communities, and culture"[47] has generated a nationalism that prides itself on difference and contrasts Euro-Canadian values unfavourably with Indian values.

These histories are weapons, and they occupy a different discursive terrain than the self-interested histories of governments. These histories, the passionate attachment to specific constitutional clauses by particular groups, and the evocative constitutionally sanctioned rhetoric of rights give the constitution a symbolic potency its predecessor lacked. Thus one strand of constitutional rhetoric is now replete with an emotional language of shame, honour, and dignity. Since this language taps and expresses powerful sentiments of identity, it facilitates popular constitutional mobilization around symbolic concerns. The distrust of governing political elites is led by the formerly excluded, who tend to adhere to a mirror theory of representation and who challenge the legitimacy of executive federalism as the central deliberating arena for fashioning constitutional change. The lengthy socialization that drove home both the difference and the inferiority of the formerly excluded poisons the atmosphere of contemporary constitutional politics.

The profound differences between where we were constitutionally, and where we now are, are key factors in explaining our difficulties in working the constitution, especially when symbolically salient issues of constitutional reform have to be addressed. Governments, the traditional constitutional actors, have been slow to recognize the new constitutional interests. Spokespersons for the latter often display little empathy for (especially provincial) governments and the territorial cleavages they stress. In many cases, governments and the new constitutional actors confront each other as rivals. This is strikingly true for Aboriginal peoples and provincial governments. The different worlds of the old and the new constitutional actors are especially evident when constitutional discussion moves from the governments' executive federalism arena to the multitudinous discordant voices of the new constitutional players making claims before legislative constitutional committees.

The legacy of the composite strategy of avoidance and exclusion haunts the contemporary search for a revised, enduring constitutional arrangement. The formerly excluded, who have not shed the suspicion and mistrust derived from their past treatment, now join the traditional constitutional players to grapple with the issues we formerly avoided, particularly who we are as a people and the location of sovereignty.

# PART III

## THE NEW CONSTITUTIONAL CULTURE

Chapter Four

# Constitutional Minoritarianism in Canada

*Ultimately, that which either holds society together or takes it apart is senti-
ment, and the chief instrument with which such sentiment may be aroused,
manipulated, and rendered dormant is discourse.* [1]

– Bruce Lincoln

*When someone with the authority of a teacher, say, describes the world and
you are not in it, there is a moment of psychic disequilibrium, as if you looked
into a mirror and saw nothing.* [2]

– Adrienne Rich

## Introduction

I thank Queen's University for the opportunity to deliver the annual Corry lecture. Professor James Alexander Corry bridged law and political science in a long
and productive scholarly career. He was an adviser to governments. Indeed, he
was one of the key academics who, in the 1930s, left their intellectual imprint on
one of the great state documents in Canadian history, the Rowell-Sirois Report.
In a broader and more diffuse sense, he was ever conscious of the public obligation of the scholar to educate the citizenry whose taxes supported the privileged
life of thought and research from which he benefited. J.A. Corry was also a

devoted citizen of the academic community and in particular of this university, which he served as Principal for many years.

From a political science perspective, he was one of the "founders," a member of that small group – it numbered only about thirty after World War Two – who extricated political science from its colonial beginnings as an offshoot of British academic life, and who simultaneously worked to establish its autonomy and separate identity from Economics, with which it was often linked in universities. In his roles as scholar, administrator, and citizen he was, as he reminds us in his autobiography,[3] a happy warrior, one whose life and work were harmoniously blended.

For all of these reasons, I am honoured to give this lecture. Such named lectures are the vehicles by which we pay tribute to our illustrious predecessors. We employ ceremony and occasion in the service of the scholarly vocation that always needs bolstering against the market's narrow conceptions of utility.

## The Fragmentation of Constitutional Discourse

The subject of my lecture is constitutional minoritarianism, the basic constitutional world view held by the various groups that were explicitly brought into the constitution in 1982. Although my list could be extended, I will confine myself primarily to women, the disabled, Aboriginals, official-language minorities, and "third-force" ethnic Canadians and visible minorities who lack founding people status.

These are the new actors on the constitutional stage who received some kind of recognition in 1982. They do not exhaust the category "minority," which also includes political scientists, left-handers, trade unionists, gays or lesbians, and many others. Although these latter groups may have views on and talk about the constitution, they lack the compelling focus of attention that explicit inclusion in the constitution provides, for example, to women and Aboriginals. The minorities on which I am focusing, especially their elites, now see themselves as part of the constitution. They see their fate as affected by the evolving meaning attached to particular constitutional clauses. They monitor the developing judicial interpretation of their clauses. They fear that constitutional reform processes that exclude them will rearrange the constitutional order in a manner detrimental to their interests. In sum, their particular constitutional concerns generate a higher profile for the constitution in their lives than is the case for the general citizen body.

Explicit constitutional status elicits constitutional introspection and an elaboration of the group's constitutional interests. The inclusion of section 27 in the Charter, with its reference to the multicultural heritage of Canadians, inevitably generates a specific debate on the relevance of ethnicity for how we treat each other in the public domain and how we view ourselves as a people. Section 28, which guarantees the Charter's rights and freedoms "equally to male and female persons," in conjunction with the section 15 inclusion of "sex" as one of the categories not to be used to discriminate against individuals, gives to the male-female cleavage a constitutional dimension that it formerly lacked. Consequently, there is now a constitutional discourse organized around gender, along with an ethnic constitutional discourse stimulated by section 27, both of which join the well-developed historic constitutional languages of federalism and parliamentary government.

It now makes sense, accordingly, in a way that it formerly did not, to think of the constitution as the home of a variety of constitutional discourses, many of which were triggered into existence by the constitutional changes of 1982. There is also an Aboriginal discourse, internally differentiated into sub-discourses separately responding to the distinct concerns of the Inuit, Métis, status, and non-status Indians. This shades into the more encompassing ethnic constitutional discourse that debates the proper relationship and status differentiation among third-force Canadians, visible minorities, and the French-English and Aboriginal founding peoples. [4] Another discourse deals with the language rights of the two official linguistic communities, further broken down by the crucial distinction between minority and majority situations for each language group. Yet another constitutional discourse addresses the significance to be attached to the presence or absence of mental or physical disabilities – although this constitutional orientation is not yet strongly developed.

This multiplication of constitutional vantage points underlines the new role of the constitution in Canadian society. It now plays a symbolic role in discriminatingly fine-tuning the relative status to be derived from such basic personal attributes as race, ethnicity, gender, and language in contemporary Canada. Their salience is heightened by their incorporation into a rights-awarding Charter. The citizenry's possession of rights transforms the relation between the governors and the governed, most importantly by reducing the deference accorded the former by the latter. Relatedly, as Robert Vipond recently argued, and as the Meech Lake drama convincingly confirmed, the coexistence in the same constitution of a Charter that accords rights to citizens and an amending formula that presupposes the leading role of governments in formal constitutional change puts the issue of sovereignty directly on the Canadian constitutional agenda. [5]

Challenging and stimulating as it might be to grapple with all of these phenomena in one lecture, the risks of failure, superficiality, or both would be inordinately high. Instead, I will portray certain common characteristics of the constitutional orientations of these fledgling constitutional actors. Indeed, my ambition is anthropological – to enter sympathetically into the constitutional worlds of these new players on our constitutional stage. It is, of course, obvious that women, Aboriginals, ethnic groups, and official-language minorities are separately engaged in constructing constitutional arguments specific to themselves. Not only do their constitutional interests differ, but they are occasionally in competition. Nevertheless, there are common features in their thought and behaviour, the analysis of which, I hope, will add to our understanding of the emerging constitutional order that we are gropingly learning to work.

One of our difficulties in working the modified constitutional order we were bequeathed in 1982 is that the traditional languages of federalism and parliamentary government are deeply embedded in the inherited mindsets of politicians, bureaucrats, and scholars. Inertia and our investment in the historically developed intellectual capital appropriate to the constitution we have left behind get in the way of grasping the meaning of the new constitution we now possess. Further, there is an uneven distribution of rapport with the new and old elements of the constitutional order scattered throughout the structures of the contemporary state and among the citizen body. The assimilation of the Charter by the Quebec Francophone majority is clearly impeded by the consistent hostility of successive Quebec governments since 1982 to the Constitution Act of that year of which it is a part. Federal Liberal Party members are more favourably disposed to the Charter than are Conservatives, presumably reflecting the divergent roles the two parties played in its creation. Consciousness of the rights revolution has been more fully assimilated by the judiciary than by the intergovernmental affairs specialists that seek to manage federalism. Hence, those who plan constitutional change from the vantage point of the old norms, identities, and practices are prone to privilege federalism as the institutional arrangement on which attention should be lavished and to underestimate the extent to which the Charter has transformed the constitutional culture of Canadians, particularly in English Canada. That the managers of federalism, including first ministers, have been astonished and taken aback by the resistance to Meech Lake suggests a remarkable lack of sympathetic comprehension in the highest quarters of the Charter's psychological impact on the citizenry.

## Societal Pluralism and Constitutional Pluralism

In the 1960s, when we began the round of constitutional introspection that is now entering its fourth decade, we thought our task was to replace or update a no longer viable version of French-English and of Quebec-Ottawa relations that was challenged by a modernizing Quebec nationalism. As we entered the seventies, centrifugal provincial pressures in English Canada enlarged the constitutional agenda, but did not discourage most scholars and policy-makers from defining their primary task as the repair of a faltering federalism, for which the appropriate physicians were governments. By the late eighties, with the Charter firmly in place and the Meech Lake package apparently unravelling, it became evident that the cast of constitutional actors had expanded and, accordingly, that the constitutional agenda could no longer be controlled by governments. How did this happen?

Various social transformations in the sixties and seventies that initially had no obvious connection to our constitutional agonies were pulled into the constitutional arena, as is noted below, by the Charter project. The essence of the social change of that period is captured by the powerful phrase "coming out," initially employed by the gay community. The ambit of the phrase can appropriately be extended to include the coming out of women, of Aboriginal peoples, of third-force Canadians, of visible minorities, of linguistic minorities, and of the disabled. In each case, their coming out challenged the comfortable assurance by which yesterday's dominant elites and majorities had defined the boundaries of acceptable, normal behaviour and had transmitted their definitive cues of who was significant and who was not.

We turned out to have more closets in our background than we had been aware of, and they sheltered more of our fellow-citizens than we had appreciated. The opening of closet doors, and the coming out that followed, challenged the stigma that formerly attached to disapproved lifestyles and identities, and weakened the incentive to pass for something or someone else – as white, as heterosexual, as non-Aboriginal, or as fully able rather than disabled. The resultant increased availability of options stimulated changes in behaviour and identities, as the feminist movement graphically revealed. A related result was the proliferation of self-conscious demanding minorities.

These profound social transformations derive from domestic and international phenomena and the interaction between them. The ebbing of imperialism eats away at the status of those with ethnic or cultural affinities with what Victor Kiernan called *The Lords of Human Kind*.[6] Those of British background in Canada and elsewhere no longer gain an unearned boost to their self-esteem from the large swatches of reassuring imperial red on the world's map; the experience of our public and private selves throughout Western societies is no longer one of unquestioned male privilege – what may be called the gender aristocracy of males is under sustained attack; and cultural relativism has invaded the realms of sexual choice and behaviour so that heterosexuality is no longer a compulsion but only one option in a smorgasbord of choice.

Adjustment to these challenges is not easy, for they involve our deepest sense of self. They challenge our core identities, whether we are the challenged or the challenging. To those of us who are WASPS, or WASMAS, as is the author – white, Anglo-Saxon, male agnostics – the message is that the old order is gone and we must change, that we can no longer be the beneficiaries of an edifice of privilege

constructed over recent centuries, privilege that rests on the exploitation or
exclusion of those who are "other" – such as visible minorities, women, Aboriginals, and the disabled. To feminists, the society they challenge is not neutral or
impartial, but rather is "a finely tuned affirmative action program" for men.[7] To
another feminist scholar, the "'main enemy' of women's equality [is easily iden-
tified]: men, and the State which has upheld the continued exercise of male
authority over women, creating women as a subordinate and certainly a disadvantaged class."[8] Aboriginal peoples nod their agreement that this society is
biased, which in their case means the inequitable distribution of its advantages
and disadvantages between those who are really founding peoples, indeed are
"First Nations," and those who are later arrivals.

These identity transformations and value changes would unquestionably
have occurred even if the constitution had displayed a rock-like stability. Further,
by themselves they would have been insufficient to open up the constitution.
However, the coincidental opening up of the constitution, and the fact that the
federal government under Trudeau saw a Charter as a vehicle to weaken the
power of a rampant provincialism, produced a symbiotic reciprocity of interest
between a federal government looking for allies for its Charter project and the
emergent minorities avidly seeking the status and recognition that had been too
long denied. They were encouraged to cast their objectives in constitutional
terms. The affinity of these groups, excluding Aboriginals, for the Charter was
reinforced by the Charter's anti-majoritarian thrust that overlapped their own
similar attitudes. This mutuality of interest, modified by the trade-offs that
occurred with provincial governments in the politics that produced the Constitution Act, 1982, resulted in the enshrinement in the constitution of an orientation that can appropriately be called constitutional minoritarianism.

To put this point somewhat differently: the attempt to refashion the constitutional order to accommodate linguistic duality and to contain centrifugal pressures in federalism was partly derailed because dualism and federalism had no
answers for an explosive minority self-consciousness organized around gender,
ethnicity other than French and English, aboriginality, and the possession of
physical or mental disabilities. The bearers of these newly aggressive identities
jostled with dualism and federalism for space in the new constitutional order
that was emerging. These minorities are hostile to conceptions of community
that appear to marginalize them, that exclude them from the official portrait of
who we are as a people. Their utility as allies to the federal government helped
them to gain a foothold in the constitution, mainly via the Charter, from which
they could further pursue their objectives. In section 37 of the 1982 Constitution
Act, the Aboriginal peoples were guaranteed a constitutional conference – that
ultimately became four conferences – to identify and define their rights. The
constitutional arena thus became one of the ongoing sites at which adjustment,

responsiveness, and sensitivity to these new socio-intellectual forces would occur, or would be resisted. [9] With the minoritarian impulse deeply entrenched, that arena now became host to anger, resentment, bitterness, and frustration.

Intellectual currents in a complex modern society do not uniformly support or "help . . . [to] replicate the *established structures* of society," but on the contrary, as Bruce Lincoln reminds us, are a mix of "tensions, contradictions, superficial stability, and potential fluidity." [10] The striking feature of the present Canadian situation is that the "potential fluidity" and "contradictions" are within the constitution where they directly confront establishment thought, rather than being isolated in private realms or confined to an underground existence from which they rarely surface. Thus, the constitution has become one of the central arenas within which social conflicts are played out. Various counter-discourses critical of established hierarchies and hegemonies have been constitutionalized. Unlike past counter-discourses that derived from federalism, the new ones link up with basic societal cleavages. The route from closet to constitution has been short, rapidly traversed, and fraught with unsettling consequences we are still digesting.

The controversies precipitated by these developments straddle the political and academic arenas. In a recent lecture I argued that the quality of public constitutional discussion in Canada was threatened by the near monopolistic possession of the right to speak on particular subjects by particular groups – section 28 and the sex equality provision of section 15, for example, by women. I suggested that men, or women who do not espouse feminist perspectives, are looked on coolly, somewhat as interlopers or intruders if they enter, uninvited, this discursive terrain. I went on to assert the need to keep alive a disinterested scholarly discourse with no connection to causes or movements, but rather an approach committed to understanding and that focused on the constitution as a whole. [11] I was informed at the time that I was simply using the standard technique by which dominant males protect their privileges by pretending to speak *ex cathedra* from some genderless Olympian mountaintop, one that existed only in my imagination. [12] I appreciate the criticism, which is not the same as accepting it, and I am still mulling it over.

Given the politicization that is thus clearly invited by my subject, what follows may not be received as dispassionate, unassailable truth convincing to all. I will be content if it is accepted as a helpful vantage point from which something useful can be said in the service of our constitutional self-education.

## Constitutional Identities

Aboriginals, women, official-language minorities, and others have constitutional identities. They have been named – singled out for recognition – in the written component of the constitution that emerged in 1982. The inference is that they are constitutional somebodies. Their constitutional connection can be variously described, and it is worthwhile to linger on a few of the terms that can be employed.

We might say that they have niches in the constitution, that a particular clause (or clauses) is occupied or possessed by them. Indeed, the language of occupation or possession is widespread. It derives from the perception of the groups involved that they had to fight their way into the constitution. For example, "mental or physical disability" is included in the section 15 equality rights because of the persistent and powerful lobbying of organizations speaking for persons with such disabilities. Section 28, in spite of its gender neutrality phrasing, is the women's clause. It is there because women's groups successfully fought for its inclusion and its wording, and not surprisingly they have a proprietary attitude to its interpretation and development.

These groups can be described as having constitutional identities. This may seem trivial until we remember the pride and status enhancement English Canadians long enjoyed from living under a constitution "similar in Principle to that of the United Kingdom." The "distinct society" label in the Meech Lake Accord is a contemporary example of a naming clause that was sought partly because of its status-giving properties. It is bitterly resented by many outside Quebec for the status deprivation they feel it visits on them. The Preamble of the Charter, stating that "Canada is founded upon principles that recognize the supremacy of God and the rule of law," was recently described as historically inaccurate from an Aboriginal perspective and "insensitive to cultural differences."[13] On the other hand, in the original BNA Act, "Indians, and Lands reserved for the Indians" (section 91(24)) was the constitutional basis for the construction of a people – "status Indians" – who do not relate as other Canadians do to the jurisdictional divisions of federalism. Status Indians have always viewed section 91(24) of the BNA Act as giving them a special constitutional identity and a resultant entitlement to distinctive treatment that they do not wish to relinquish, no matter how much they try to alter its specifics. The category, status Indians, which generates a political identity, is legal, not ethnic. Its members include many, especially women, who have no Indian ancestry; hundreds of thousands of others whose Indian ancestry, in whole or significant part, is impeccable, are excluded as falling outside the criteria that determine who does and who does not have legal status.

The significance of constitutional naming was driven home recently by the breakup of the Association of Métis and Non-Status Indians of Saskatchewan (AMNSIS). A bitter split was precipitated by the Métis leadership following the section 35 recognition of the Métis in the 1982 Constitution Act as part of the Aboriginal peoples of Canada – what a Métis leader described as constitutional recognition of the Métis "as a distinct people." [14] The Métis leaders concluded that this separate constitutional status and the goals it legitimated had to be served by a separate Métis organization.

Groups with constitutional identities occupying constitutional niches inevitably have stakes in the constitution. They have developed mini-histories of how their clause was won against strong odds. In official settings they tend to preface their remarks by reciting the landmarks in their evolution to constitutional recognition. They tend, in other words, to have their own Whiggish versions of colony-to-nation ascents appropriate to their achieved constitutional status as, for example, women (s. 28) or third-force Canadians (s. 27). The constitution that gives them status matters to them. They have made constitutional investments and they expect appropriate returns.

Consequently, they, and especially their official spokespersons, have powerful incentives to foster beneficial interpretations of "their" constitutional clause(s). Accordingly, they see themselves as legitimate participants in elaborating the various languages that envelop the constitution and thus influence its evolution. They think they have constitutional standing.

So, the groups concerned occupy niches in the constitution, possess constitutional clauses, carry constitutional identities, own stakes in their constitution, and in their own eyes have constitutional standing.

## New and Old Constitutional Discourse

The contemporary Canadian practice of federalism and parliamentary government rests on an extensive literature now in its second century. Thus Ed Black did not lack for material as he deciphered and analysed the principal criteria by which Canadian federalism has been evaluated. [15] The traditions of parliamentary government, likewise, have their expositors, from Alpheus Todd, [16] who tried to instruct the rude inhabitants of a frontier society in the practices of responsible government in the nineteenth century, to Ned Franks, who instructs the present generation in its practice in the closing decades of the twentieth century. [17]

Indeed, from one perspective, the living nature of the constitution formerly rested on little more than the evolved understanding of these arrangements. Further, federalism and parliamentary government are functioning systems that are daily worked by politicians and civil servants. They constitute, in Mallory's apt language, the habitat of the politician. [18] They have, accordingly, been lovingly explored by those who tend our constitutional arrangements.

This is not the case with the newer constitutional categories. While to think of the significance of gender for the constitution, or of the constitution for gender, or of how Aboriginal self-government might or might not fit into our constitutional system does not require us to start from scratch, such thought is inevitably less rooted, more experimental, and more open and indeterminate than is the case with such historic practices as federalism. Even the discourse of rights, although not without deep roots in our British and French constitutional traditions, is, in its Charter-derived present form, clearly a departure from the historic theory and practice of our constitution.

It is possible, of course, that an unbiased re-examination of the past may supplement the available stock of intellectual resources for these and other "newer" constitutional subjects. We may rediscover traditions we had lost. The major practitioners of these emerging constitutional conversations often engage in an historical revisionism as they seek to portray a past in which their kind of people or aspirations feature more prominently than in conventional accounts; they also search for and find predecessors who struggled for the same or similar goals as they do. Clearly, however, much of these pursuits can be brought under the copious umbrella of what Hobsbawm and Ranger have helpfully labelled *The Invention of Tradition*. [19]

Such attempts to create a usable past are the hallmarks of social movements. Even should they succeed, however, these new usable pasts will be thinner and shallower than the historic roots that sustain the more traditional themes of constitutional discussion. Antecedent discourses on federalism and parliamentary government do not have to be rescued or salvaged from an unfriendly past; they already dominate our constitutional past and our constitutional bookshelves.

In other ways, however, new and old constitutional discourses are not dissimilar. In both cases, discussion by self-interested participants rarely focuses on the constitution as an undifferentiated whole. Since the constitution is an aggregation of particulars, the organized interests that cluster around it always devote special attention to the clauses particularly germane to their goals. Thus in the early post-Confederation decades Premier Oliver Mowat of Ontario assiduously devoted himself to the protection and expansion of provincial jurisdictional rights under section 92 of the BNA Act. Prior to the return of their natural resources in 1930, the governments of the Prairie provinces vigorously fought for the equal treatment in the possession of natural resources under section 109 that had been denied to them by the original terms under which they entered Canada or were created. At various times, components of the business community have fought, as self-interest dictated, for generous or restrictive interpretations of clauses impinging directly on their pursuits.

The tendency for the organized interests of a free society, including governments, to line themselves up like iron filings responding to a powerfully discriminating constitutional magnet continues under the Charter and the 1982 Constitution Act of which it is a part. Not only do the existence and even wording of individual clauses reflect the lobbying activities of particular groups in the frantic environment out of which the Constitution Act emerged, but their victories are followed by organized efforts to gain the maximum subsequent advantage from the clauses most linked to their constitutional fate. Thus, Aboriginal organizations invested their aspirations, subsequently dashed, in the section 37 requirement of the Constitution Act that a constitutional conference, with Aboriginal participation, would be held to identify and define the rights of Aboriginal peoples; while Anglophones inside and Francophones outside Quebec view the section 23 clauses dealing with official minority-language education rights as constitutional entitlements and recognitions of which they are the guardians.

The Charter has called forth an interest group structure that parallels the cleavages and interests that it singles out for attention, especially in sections 16 to 28. Indeed, it is not unrealistic to speak of the competitive colonization of the constitution by organized interests, most notably governments of course, but since the 1982 Constitution Act, extensively supplemented by organized private interests.

## The Minoritarian Impulse

The style and emotional overtones of the discourse of these new constitutional participants display striking similarities, whether the speaker is making claims for the Aboriginal people, women, the disabled, or the others who fall into the categories I have been discussing. They are not confident elites accustomed to wielding power and taking for granted that their views will have an impact on the subject under discussion. On the contrary, theirs is the language of minorities, of outsiders self-consciously aware that their concerns may be knowingly or inadvertently overlooked. [20]

The self-descriptive labels they employ underline their exclusion or their less than full status. Thus feminists not only frequently refer to Simone de Beauvoir's *The Second Sex*, [21] but employ self-descriptions that invariably agree with its thesis of the discriminatory treatment of women. In the sixties, those who were neither British nor French, and thus excluded from the privileged circle of founding peoples, coined the phrase the "third force" to describe their status as late arrivals who feared exclusion when the descendants of those who did battle on the Plains of Abraham met to do constitutional business. A Canadian Aboriginal leader surveying the status of indigenous Native peoples around the globe described them as belonging to the Fourth World. [22] The Métis are often described as *The Forgotten People* [23] and even as *The Non-People.* [24] In the mid-seventies the president of the Inuit Tapirisat described the Inuit as living in "a forgotten colony . . . in the sense that when it's out of sight, it's out of mind." [25] Indian women who formerly lost their status when they married non-Indian men were labelled *Citizens Minus* [26] in an account of their condition. Immigrant women, often described as doubly oppressed as women and as immigrants, or as trebly oppressed if they are also visible minorities, were recently called "the 'muted shadows,' the silent partners of our society and the women's movement."[27]

These labels, of course, are more than simple descriptions, and less than identities proudly assumed. They are resentful accusations at the society that inflicts such injustice on the group concerned.

Particular groups are sometimes defined by what they are not – non-status Indians, and the (mentally or physically) (dis)abled; or by where they are not – Francophones outside Quebec; or by identities they cannot shed – visible minorities; or, as in the case of allophones, as a leftover category after the boundaries and rights of the more prestigious Anglophones and Francophones have been constitutionally determined.

These labels all suggest marginality and not getting full measure. The rhetoric of these constitutional minorities is a litany of such words as forgotten, ignored, subordinated, and exploited. They nurse memories of past maltreatment, of having been wronged for too long. This is cogently illustrated, for example, by a 1978 publication of the Federation of Francophones outside Quebec, with the haunting title *The Heirs of Lord Durham: Manifesto of a Vanishing People*.[28] Past injustice often generates demands for some tangible or symbolic compensatory response in the present. At this time, Chinese Canadians, Italian Canadians, and Ukrainian Canadians all have made public claims for the redress of particular instances of historical maltreatment, presumably encouraged by the success of Japanese Canadians in getting a settlement for their World War Two experience of relocation, internment, property seizure, and deportation. Aboriginal peoples, of course, have innumerable historical claims to be resolved by negotiation or in the judicial arena. Further, affirmative action is often justified as an appropriate rectification of the surviving effects of past discrimination. Thus, for many Canadians, historical memories provide a constant reminder that earlier versions of the society in which they now live dealt unkindly with their ancestors or their younger selves. In general, the elites of these groups have little sympathy for former Prime Minister Trudeau's assertion that "we must forget many things if we want to live together as Canadians," and that we can only be just in our time, based on the premise that the past is a minefield in which it is better not to tread.[29]

The sense of injustice and marginality, of being the new kids on the constitutional block, gives the constitutional contributions of these new constitutional actors a certain biting edge. Although they are in the constitution, they are cognizant of the relative weakness of the organizations that speak for them, compared to governments. Unlike governments, whose historic bureaucratic base provides resources for the long haul, the nascent bureaucracies of these new constitutional actors are fragile, and their practice amateurish and somewhat volatile.

They often have limited private resources and are thus subject to the vagaries of government funding. Their staff and clientele are prone to mood fluctuations ranging from the exultation of heady triumph to the gloom of bitter despair when they encounter rebuffs. Often their clientele is heterogeneous and divided over strategy and objectives, which makes leadership very difficult.

Cumulatively, the preceding considerations generate a rather shrill, aggressive discourse, a product of their sense that their presence in the constitution/Charter is precarious. Consequently, their attention is directed unremittingly to their own precise constitutional concerns, not to the larger claims of the community or to the overall health of the constitutional order. Such concerns are left to others.

## The Challenge To Majoritarianism and To Traditional Patterns of Representation

Precisely how these tendencies to constitutional minoritarianism will develop is unclear. However, the general direction of the pressure they will apply to our constitutional governing arrangements can be discerned.

Criticisms of majoritarianism are natural to peoples possessed of the federal condition. Quebec nationalist pressures for sovereignty or special status are attempts to eliminate or restrict the application of Canada-wide majorities to Quebec. Similarly, the pressures for a triple-E Senate are fed by the fears of the numerically weaker provinces of outer Canada that their interests are likely to be ignored in a population-based majoritarian system, especially one where executive power is sustained by party discipline. These are the classic apprehensions of territorially grouped peoples in a federal system that, although designed to remove such peoples from the application of country-wide majority rule in matters given to the states or provinces, nevertheless leaves a central government with powers whose exercise may appear regionally biased.

The minoritarianism that is of concern in this lecture, however, is not that of Nova Scotians, Albertans, or Québécois – provincial peoples with governments at their disposal – but of women, Aboriginals, ethnic Canadians, and others who exist as minorities within provincial, territorial, and national boundaries.[30] With rare exceptions, such as a possible Inuit-dominated province of Nunavut or possibly some of the larger First Nations governments, these minorities cannot hope to wield significant power as majorities in newly devised political arrangements. It is likely, given the constitutional identities these groups now possess and their historically rooted suspicion of the state as an instrument of others, that the legitimation of public policies whose justification resides in majority support will be increasingly challenged.

Self-perceived minority status and an ideology of being second class, victimized, or ignored slip easily into a distrust of representatives dissimilar from themselves. Such attitudes are sustained by their relative absence from governing elites. When they look at the state they do not see it as mirroring their proportion of the population. Historically, they were late arrivals in obtaining the franchise, Quebec women not receiving the provincial vote until 1940 and status Indians not receiving the federal vote until 1960. These historical reminders of the recency of their full political citizenship underline the negative evaluations placed on their civic capacities in, for many, their own lifetime. That they have doubts about the wisdom of leaving their fate in what they define as other hands is scarcely surprising.

They are suspicious of theories and practices of representation that imply or assert that representatives can be trusted to speak for citizens/constituents when they lack the defining characteristics of the latter. Their distrust is not confined to legislatures, but extends to all institutions that have a representative component, including courts and the elite-dominated practices of executive federalism, perhaps especially when constitutional amendments are on the agenda.

To Aboriginals and women's groups, the making of the 1982 Constitution Act provided wounding evidence that when their backs were turned recognitions and rights they thought they had won could be removed in a closed meeting of first ministers. Meech Lake has received a barrage of criticisms that eleven able-bodied white males cannot be trusted to represent and protect the constitutional concerns of women, Aboriginal peoples, visible minorities, and others who were not represented at the bargaining table by politicians who shared their defining characteristics. As Stefan Dupré gloomily observes, the sequel to the Meech Lake/Langevin meetings that produced the Meech Lake Accord is the reviling of executive federalism, viewed as "secretive and manipulative." He continues: "The eleven 'men' at the apex of our constitutional executives are not viewed as having either a duty or a capacity to discern the public interest." This is evidence, he concludes, of a serious "degree of alienation from the values that underpin the Canadian constitutional marriage of cabinet-parliamentary government and federalism."[31] In a nutshell, the dominance of governments in formal constitutional change is no longer sustained by an automatic deference of the citizenry. Thus an attempted *fait accompli* approach to constitutional amendment typified by the early stages of Meech Lake is incompatible with the kind of constitutional people Canadians have become.

Courts are subjected to the criticism that minorities are not proportionately represented in their ranks, resulting in a lack of empathy for the concerns of such underrepresented groups. Thus, the Canadian system of courts was recently criticized by an Aboriginal professor of law for its "elitist and culturally-specific (European) character ... a formalized adversarial and impersonal institution ... unknown amongst Aboriginal peoples," and one in which "the representatives of

the dominant (settler) communities write and 'interpret' the law for all Canadians. . . ."[32] Comments on judicial decisions not infrequently refer to the class,
ethnic, religious, or gender composition of the court. For example, when the
injunction prohibiting Chantal Daigle from having an abortion was upheld by
the Quebec Court of Appeal, her sister stated: "It's the decision of a group of
men. . . . If there were four women and one man on the panel, it would have been
different."[33] In more measured tones Madame Justice Bertha Wilson in a recent
address titled "Will Women Judges Really Make a Difference?" responded with
an emphatic if qualified "Yes!" Among other supporting evidence, she cited the
recent work of Carol Gilligan, whose "central thesis [is] that women see themselves as essentially connected to others and as members of a community while
men see themselves as essentially autonomous and independent of others."[34]
Madame Justice Wilson also drew extensively on the chapters of a recent volume
on *Equality and Judicial Neutrality*, which stated in its preface that "As the vast
majority of Canadian judges are appointed from the privileged elite class of
white, male, able-bodied persons, it is appropriate and inevitable that equality
seekers question the judiciary's ability to be neutral on legal issues which challenge the disproportionate distribution of power and wealth to their class."[35]

The minoritarian critique of majoritarianism and of the capacity of representatives to speak for minority perspectives that are absent from or only weakly
present on representative bodies will not quickly disappear. It is sustained by the
politicization of minorities, their constitutional recognition, and their (somewhat precarious) self-confidence that has already been discussed. It is also linked
to a pervasive characteristic of contemporary culture that questions the capacity
and right of one individual to speak for and represent someone else whose sex or
ethnic background, for example, is not the same.

The issue of who should have "voice" or who can speak for whom is a hotly
debated issue in scholarship,[36] literature, and the theatre.[37] In history, travel literature, and social commentary, "Westerners had for centuries studied and spo-
ken for the rest of the world. . . ." However, since mid-century, "Asians, Africans,
Arab orientals, Pacific Islanders, and Native Americans have in a variety of ways
asserted their independence from Western cultural and political hegemony and
established a new multivocal field of intercultural discourse."[38] The same
author, James Clifford, continues: "The time is past when privileged authorities
could routinely 'give voice' (or history) to others without fear of contradiction."[39] The change is neatly summed up in the aphorism that formerly anthropologists had their tribe; now tribes have their anthropologist. For the Western
anthropologist, according to Clifford Geertz, "the very right to write – to write
ethnography – seems at risk. The entrance of once colonialized or castaway
peoples (wearing their own masks, speaking their own lines) onto the stage of
global economy, international high politics, and world culture has made the

claim of the anthropologist to be a tribune for the unheard, a representer of the unseen, a kenner of the misconstrued, increasingly difficult to sustain."[40]

Placed in this larger global context of exploding change and politicized internal minorities and external majorities who formerly were mute but are no more, the issue of representation is no longer straightforward, particularly in heterogeneous societies characterized by multiple forms of self-consciousness. It would be naive to assume that these profound cultural changes will leave the world of politics, government, and the constitution untouched. Geertz recently stated that "The end of colonialism altered radically the nature of the social relationship between those who ask and look and those who are asked and looked at."[41] The functionally equivalent and equally true domestic statement would be that the emergence of voice for formerly quiescent domestic minorities in Canada alters radically the nature of the relationship between those who represent and those who are represented. In each case, the authority of a formerly dominant "other" is challenged.

## The Staying Power of the New Constitutional Actors

Given the marginality of the groups I have been discussing, it is nevertheless reasonable to inquire further if they might not fade away and be reduced to the status of a minor sideshow far removed from the settings where the big constitutional battalions do business. What, in other words, is their staying power? At the risk of adding to the graveyard already overflowing with wrong-headed social science predictions, my answer is that they will have considerable staying power – that they constitute permanent additions to our cast of constitutional actors. I have several reasons for my prediction.

(1) The simple fact that these groups have constitutional identities, status, rights, and claims provides a high probability that they will survive. Their placement in the constitutional firmament gives them a permanent rallying point around which they can reorganize following fallow periods. In addition, of course, the ongoing life of the constitution guarantees that constitutional issues directly affecting or indirectly impinging on their constitutional interests will recurrently emerge in the judicial arena, in discussions of constitutional amendments, and in public constitutional debate. Consequently, they will experience constant pressure and incentives, particularly their elites, to be constitutionally involved.

(2) The social movements and intellectual tendencies that lie behind the high profile of Aboriginal, gender, and the other concerns of this essay are not idiosyncratically Canadian and thus are not exclusively dependent on domestic factors for their ebb and flow. On the contrary, they are intimately connected to

transformations in the legal, socio-political, and normative components of the international environment that individual states cannot ignore.

A common approach of international lawyers to the significance of the international dimension is to argue that the evolution of international law, especially in those areas where Canada has ratified United Nations covenants, constitutes a source to which Canadian judges and legislators should look when interpreting Charter rights in the Canadian context. Essentially, this argument asserts that Canada and other states are part of a normative, legal network of evolving understandings of citizen-state relations, to some of which, especially those fashioned by the United Nations, Canada has officially subscribed and is therefore obligated to observe. [42]

An alternative approach, adopted here, is to stress the social, emotional, and psychological consequences for the citizenry of post-World War Two changes in the international environment. Here, the significance of the United Nations Charter, for example, or of the United Nations Convention on the Elimination of all Forms of Discrimination against Women (adopted by the General Assembly on December 18, 1979, and ratified by Canada on December 10, 1981) [43] is not how they should inform judges and legislators, but rather their availability as political resources and their role in contributing to the self-confidence and identities of the groups to whom they refer. They constitute reassuring reminders that one is not alone. More generally, women's groups and Aboriginal organizations are at least loosely integrated into international movements. It is not unreasonable to talk of a feminist international or of an international of indigenous peoples. The international literature, comparative examples, and role models to which women and Aboriginals look, provide positive comparisons that can be exploited, expand their horizons, and give them emotional support at the Canadian site where their particular struggles are engaged. In the most general sense, therefore, the international environment is broadly supportive of the domestic struggles and ambitions of women, indigenous peoples, the disabled, and ethnic minorities that challenge unsympathetic hegemonies.

(3) In several cases, especially with respect to women, third-force Canadians, visible minorities, Francophones outside Quebec, and Aboriginal peoples, a scholarly infrastructure has developed that on balance lends credibility to their grievances. This is partly because of the propensity for the relevant professoriate to be drawn from the group concerned. In recent decades there has been a proliferation of journals, scholarly chairs, academic programs, and institutes that accord a sympathetic and high profile to the minority groups they study. In a remarkably short period, impressive literatures have emerged. These scholarly developments undoubtedly add staying power, credibility, and legitimacy to the minorities concerned and their objectives.

(4) A relevant factor for those minority claims that are driven by the ethnic transformation of Canadian society is that immigration is clearly pushing Canada in a more multicultural, multiracial direction. The population of British and French background continues to shrink, as more generally does the European background population. Particularly in the great metropolitan centres of Montreal, Toronto, and Vancouver, the emerging populations are, in David Cameron's evocative phrase, "riotously multicultural."[44] These recent arrivals will almost certainly invigorate an ethnic debate that will challenge the constitutional hegemony of the French and English founding peoples. In a nutshell, the social forces behind multiculturalism/multiracialism will be strengthened and those behind a founding people dualism will be weakened.

Relatedly, the high birth rate of the indigenous peoples and the constitutional stimulation of the category Aboriginal by the inclusion of Métis as one of the Aboriginal peoples of Canada indicate that the varied demands of the Aboriginal people will be part of the Canadian constitutional condition for the foreseeable future.

(5) Finally, there is an imitative, contagion effect. Each group's activities and demands support an overall orientation to the constitution that is sympathetic to minorities.

The strong likelihood, suggested by the preceding, that these new, minority-syndrome constitutional actors are here to stay is also supported by a conjectural detour with which I will conclude this section.

The eagerness and stridency with which women, Aboriginals, ethnics, and others have come forth in response to the opportunities provided by the 1982 constitutional change suggest the prior existence of frustration and resentment that was waiting to be tapped. Was our previous constitutional order perhaps less healthy than we have been led to believe? Did we perhaps misconstrue as supportive if mute acquiescence what was in reality an indifference or alienation that lacked constitutional outlets? How else do we explain the proliferation of groups throwing themselves into the constitutional game, especially that of the Charter, with such zest?

One answer is provided by Mary Douglas, who notes that as government statistical data mushroomed in nineteenth-century Europe and as "new medical . . . criminal . . . sexual or moral categories [were invented] new kinds of people spontaneously came forward in hordes to accept the labels and to live accordingly." There was, she suggests, a dramatic "responsiveness to new labels [that] suggests extraordinary readiness to fall into new slots and to let selfhood be redefined."[45]

The Douglas thesis clearly has considerable cogency. Canadians have been remarkably fertile in developing new rubrics, either directly in the constitution or, even more impressively, in less formal constitutional discourse around which the citizenry has regrouped and acquired new identities. The labels First Nations, Inuit, Dene, Aboriginal, Québécois, Third Force, Visible Minority, Multicultural, Official Language Minorities, and Francophones outside Quebec illustrate the point. None of these labels would have found their way into a Canadian dictionary of political terminology as recently as thirty years ago. Those labels that get into the written constitution have perhaps a more persuasive shaping capacity than those that do not, but the latter often serve as the vehicles of constitutional ambitions not yet realized. Of course, not all the labels are new – race, colour, sex, mental or physical disability, male and female persons, Indian, and Métis are standard designations. Their placement in the constitution does not provide their bearers with new identities, but it does enhance the salience of identities they already had.

A second possible answer is provided by Timothy Garton Ash, a student of Central Europe who writes of "the split between the public and private self, official and unofficial language, outward conformity and inward dissent – in short, the double life . . . a phenomenon common to all Soviet-bloc countries."[46] In such repressed societies, there are covert, long submerged identities that will chaotically burst forth in propitious circumstances. This is graphically revealed in a description of what happened after the workers organized against the armed forces in the Spanish Civil War. "Virtually overnight the rules and habits of centuries dissolved, and a sweeping transformation in the conduct of human relations was accomplished. Suits and neckties disappeared, and overalls became the preferred dress. Women took to the streets and catcalls were forgotten. Waiters stared customers in the eye and spoke to them as equals. Bootblacks refused tips as signs of condescension and charity."[47]

To put it differently, outward conformity always exceeds private belief in any society; there is always much quiet desperation, repressed anger, and sense of injustice, even in open and democratic societies. Such sentiments may be relatively invisible for long periods, but they always constitute a latent source of disruptive potential when the structure of incentives changes. While the Canadian case is not properly to be compared to Central Europe or to the Spanish Civil War, a milder version of a similar process appears to have taken place – one in which the activity of "coming out" described earlier revealed tensions that had previously been hidden and which, because of the accident of timing, were given constitutional expression.

Yet a third vantage point, which in a sense combines the two preceding suggestive answers, and does so from a more overtly political perspective, is offered by Samuel LaSelva. Federalism, he observes, speaks only to the territorial dimensions of our existence – our membership in Canadian, provincial, and territorial communities – while the Charter addresses us as individuals and members of groups who are indifferent and sometimes hostile to federalism's categories.

Federalism, he asserts, "lacks the conceptual resources" to respond to the claims of individuals and groups for justice and freedom. "That is why a Bill of Rights is so important in a federal state. Through it, individuals and groups are given recognition in a federal system, and their interests are placed on the same footing as those of other constitutional actors."[48]

If LaSelva's answer is, as I believe, correct, then the support for the Charter in the kind of heterogeneous society with multiple non-territorial cleavages that Canada is becoming is not an occasion for surprise. Rather, the Charter, the possibility of a more precise and generous recognition of Aboriginal rights, and the general opening up of the constitution from which they both emerged were positively liberating. They were welcomed by those Canadians who did not find it easy to give voice in the constitutional order of parliamentary government and federalism. The chaos and babble of discordant voices to which this opening up seems to lead in the short run is in reality the early stage of a process of honest self-discovery on which we have embarked.

I conclude, therefore, that minoritarianism will be an enduring constitutional presence in our future, and that it is a profoundly important modification of our constitutional order. Whether we will successfully respond to its imperatives is a difficult and open question. As Meech Lake makes clear, the strident and multifaceted emergence of minoritarianism makes a negative contribution to our capacity to respond to the older, more traditional concerns of dualism and regionalism. Nevertheless, an ostrich approach that denies and ignores these changes is no recipe for success in managing our constitutional affairs. Finally, no matter how much our existence may be disturbed by what I have called an emergent minoritarianism, surely its appearance is to be welcomed. For women, Aboriginals, the disabled, minority ethnic Canadians, visible minorities, and others to have received constitutional sanction as they emerge from the background, drop their masks, and seek to be more authentically themselves is surely to be welcomed. As Jan Smuts once said, "the caravan of humanity has packed its tents and is on the move again."[49]

## Conclusion

In 1963, J.A. Corry delivered the Alan B. Plaunt Memorial Lectures under the title *The Changing Conditions of Politics.*[50] What I have tried to do in this lecture is a sub-category of Principal Corry's theme – The Changing Conditions of Constitutional Politics. Our lectures identify instabilities in our respective situations, and if not a nostalgia for an order that is disappearing, at least a recognition that past guidemarks will no longer fully serve.

The constitutional world we have lost was simplicity itself compared to the constitutional world we have gained. One of its organizing rubrics, federalism, was the vehicle through which we discussed the relation between our federal and provincial selves, both as governments and as peoples, as well as how the two historic founding French and English peoples should relate to each other. A second rubric, responsible government and parliamentary supremacy, provided us with a focus for organizing our thoughts on the appropriate relationship between executive leadership and representative democracy. A third organizing rubric, now departed but a significant if admittedly diminishing presence until only a few years ago, was how we were to manage or modify the coexistence of our Canadian selves and our inherited constitutional links to the mother country.

By and large, all three of these foci for constitutional introspection were elitist and governmental. Governments played the leading role in the great battles over federalism in our history. They fought each other in court, bargained with each other in executive federalism, and commissioned the great official inquiries, such as the Rowell-Sirois and Tremblay Reports, that sought to impart new senses of direction to our federalist future. Responsible parliamentary government raised crucial constitutional questions, but they all presupposed the centrality of relations among the institutions at the top of our political pyramid – cabinet, Commons, Senate, and representative of the Crown, or their provincial equivalents. The colony-to-nation focus, to simplify only slightly, addressed the pace at which imperial functions performed by British constitutional actors should be devolved to governments in Canada, or in the case of the Judicial Committee, to the Supreme Court.

What was strikingly absent from this constitutional world? Gender, the status of Aboriginal peoples as a constitutional concern, the relationship between the two founding peoples and the "others," and indeed virtually all the minoritarianisms that I have been discussing in this lecture. Finally, and directly related to the preceding of course, there was no Charter or Bill of Rights that explicitly incorporated the citizenry into the constitutional order. Thus, the constitutional law that preceded the Charter rarely addressed "relationships . . . between governments and citizens . . . because the Constitution Act, 1867 was virtually silent about those relationships."[51]

The constitutional world we have lost had many virtues, as our evolution from four small struggling colonies in 1867 to the prosperous, democratic Canada we have inherited testifies. On the other hand, it bequeathed us an impoverished constitutional theory. Our long quasi-colonial status deflected our attention from indigenous constitutional concerns, or transmuted them into issues in colonial-imperial relations. For example, the debate about the role of the Judicial Committee of the Privy Council in constitutional interpretation, and whether Canadians should assume the task of judicial interpretation for themselves, became an issue of nationalism versus imperialism that deflected attention from the fundamental jurisprudential questions of the appropriate role, composition, and constitutional status of an autonomous Canadian Supreme Court that could be overruled by no higher authority. The continuing British role in amending the Canadian constitution until 1982 prevented us from recognizing, and confronting, the even more fundamental question of where sovereignty should reside in Canada once the role of the Westminster Parliament had been finally eliminated. More generally, the very British absence of a Charter until 1982 not only deprived us of a rich constitutional language organized around "rights," but, in conjunction with the absence of a revolutionary tradition, left us with only a very thinly developed conception of citizenship. These characteristics of the constitutional world that we have lost ill-prepared us for the new constitutional world that we gained by the 1982 Constitution Act providing us with a Charter and a purely domestic amending formula.

Success in manoeuvring through the new constitutional world will not come easily. The cultural support base of the constitutional order has been irreversibly modified. The constitutional hegemony of the concept of founding peoples restricted to the British and French is in retreat, encroached on from one side by Aboriginal peoples who claim real founding status and from the other side by a rapidly growing multicultural, multiracial population that resists linking status to the length of one's Canadian ancestral line.

The elitisms of cabinet government and executive federalism – including the amending formula – presuppose a deferential citizenry that is not yet gone but that is in retreat. Representative practices based on women deferring to men, and on those who were neither British nor French deferring to those who were, can no longer be taken for granted. In our new constitutional world, majorities will be less easy to create and to maintain; elites will have to be more sensitive to the suspicious minorities that have come out of the recesses of our society; in brief, we will have to pay more attention to the citizen base of the constitutional order.

No better proof of that requirement could be provided than the difficulties encountered by the Meech Lake Accord. Fashioned in back rooms, unanimously agreed to by eleven first ministers, supported originally by all three parties in the House of Commons, engineered at the federal level by a party less committed to the Charter than were its Liberal sponsors, indulgently described in its early days as a constitutional miracle by its creators, with the process that led to it being singled out for special praise by its chief federal government architect, Lowell Murray,[52] Meech Lake now appears, as this lecture is being given in March, 1990, to have been based on a profound misreading of the constitutional culture that the Charter had influenced.

That the elitist practices of parliamentary government and executive federalism could not prevail against an unco-ordinated gaggle of minorities is a clear indication of the constitutional disarray in which Canadians find themselves. A healing response will require a scrupulous sensitivity to the varied minoritarian-isms that I have impressionistically described in this lecture.

The approach of this lecture has been sociological, or anthropological, a piece of reportage, as it were, of some of the fault lines in the Canadian constitutional order. A different and tougher task remains to be done: the elaboration of a polit-ical theory appropriate to the need for *rapprochement* between the majoritarian and minoritarian elements in contemporary Canada, and the devising of institu-tional arrangements for its expression.[53]

Chapter Five

# Barriers to Constitutional Renewal in Canada: The Role of Constitutional Culture

## Introduction

The plan of this lecture[1] is relatively straightforward. After some preliminary introductory comments I will assess the contribution of our constitutional culture, broadly conceived, as an underexamined source of our difficulty in achieving comprehensive constitutional change.

My purpose is to set the constitution in the context of the values, cultural assumptions, identities, and implicit meanings that lie behind its official, public face. As a result of the preceding, I hope to make clear that the constitution thus conceived is the source of fundamental cues and messages that inform the citizens of who counts and how much in the constitutional order. The constitution, to put it differently, should be thought of as an instrument of recognition or its denial. It has immense social and psychological impacts on the citizenry. How else do we explain the fact that our recent constitutional discussions have been replete with the language of shame, betrayal, dignity, identity, rejection, and honour? Thus Quebec and its people are said to have been betrayed in 1980-81, and then rejected by "English Canada" over their modest Meech Lake proposals. This is neither the technical language of constitutional lawyers nor the practical federal language of the division of powers. Rather, it is a melodramatic, theatrical, or operatic language of the emotions, of the feeling side of citizenship.

This paper, then, may be thought of as a few preliminary faltering steps to do for Canada what the American scholar Michael Kammen sought to do for the

United States, "to describe the place of the Constitution in the public consciousness and symbolic life of the American people."[2] My focus is, however, much narrower than Kammen's, as I am primarily concerned with the relationship between constitutional culture and constitutional change, and my focus is contemporary. Indeed, I will not be able to escape the hovering ghosts of the Meech Lake catastrophe, nor our pending constitutional agonies.

Explanations for the failure of Meech Lake flourish. Often, of course, they are the servants of unrealized constitutional ambitions as the actors in our constitutional drama position themselves for the next round. Those who play the constitutional game, whether governments or interest groups, know full well that if they can get their "explanation" accepted the likelihood of their future success is enhanced. Accordingly, the responsibilities of constitutional scholars and constitutional players differ. The former should be less partisan, less involved, more concerned with the whole, more attentive to deeper underlying social forces, and in general simply more academic. What is the point of having a division of labour between scholars in their study and the active players on the field if the former simply duplicate the often self-serving analyses of the latter, without the benefit of equivalent insider knowledge.

For the players, the search for a way out of our constitutional impasse naturally tends to focus on rules and procedures – Should the three-year ratification period be changed? Is unanimity a constitutional albatross? – for they are manipulable. Modified rules can change the structure of incentives and thus increase or decrease the chance of getting an agreement.

Such a focus is unquestionably important, but it needs to be supplemented by a searching consideration of the changing constitutional culture within which the rules operate. In fact, of course, as all good institutionalists know, there is an unending reciprocity of mutual influence among the applicable rules, the performing players, and the social forces that buffet both rules and players, such as broad cultural changes and the constrained creativity of such constitutional guardians as the judiciary. Concurrently, however, the rules shape the identities of the actors, distribute advantages and disadvantages unequally, determine who is in the game and who is not, and affirm some social forces and cultural tendencies and stigmatize others. Thus our constitutional culture is an ever-changing evolutionary creation, not a static historical given.

The focus of this paper on constitutional culture, therefore, is not intended to privilege attitudes, values, and identities over the institutions, constitutional arrangements, and official rules with which they are symbiotically linked. It is, instead, a simplifying stratagem and an attention-getting device designed to highlight one of the diffuse, background sources of our constitutional malaise. Accordingly, it pays less attention to governments and more to society than is customary in analyses of constitutional change.

## Change in the Implicit Constitution

The formal arrangements of a constitutional order are embedded in a larger context of implicit meanings that constitute, so to speak, certain guiding assumptions that are simply taken for granted. As long as their naturalness is unquestioned, such implicit meanings may not even rise to the level of consciousness. In the era of their hegemony, their status is more like the law of gravity than a contestable human artifact. If they are mentioned in constitutional documents they appear as a recitation of fact, as the universe making a statement rather than human actors making choices. Surrounding or pervading the sparse unemotional text of the BNA Act and the conventions of responsible government, therefore, there was an implicit constitution that can now, in retrospect, be read between the lines of the written rules and established constitutional practices. Many of the implicit understandings of yesterday's constitution are now explicit, and they are challenged by the new constitutional actors. Yesterday's taken-for-granteds are no longer part of the natural order. They are contested territory.

The constitution we are leaving behind was traditional, derivative, colonial, and British. Its roots, "a Constitution similar in Principle to that of the United Kingdom," were across the oceans in the mother country. Until 1949 final constitutional interpretation was entrusted to a British judicial body, the Judicial Committee of the Privy Council. Until 1982, formal constitutional amendments in key areas remained the responsibility of the British Parliament. The ethos of constitutional Britishness was viewed as a priceless heritage by Anglo-Canadian scholars up to the fifties.

Ordinary Canadians of British background received an unearned increment of status and prestige from living under a British constitution, and from surveying a global map so much of which was painted a reassuring red. Psychologically, the civic identity of many British Canadians linked them simultaneously and harmoniously to the "old country" and to its Canadian offshoot. Their attitudes might best be summed up as diaspora constitutionalism. Further, up to at least the middle of the twentieth century, before the upsurge of modernizing Quebec nationalism, British Canadians could think – automatically assume would be more accurate – that the federal government was essentially theirs, even although their hegemony was not total.

Although the constitution responded to two European founding peoples, French as well as English, the former were accommodated by rather than dominant in the overall constitutional order, a status reserved for the latter. Quebec might not be a province like the others, but until the last three decades it was constitutionally of greater importance that the British were not a founding people like the other. From the perspective of the two founding European peoples, the major challenge in recent decades has been to refashion the constitutional order in the interest of the historically weaker French partner. This was the driving theme of the two great state papers on the constitution of the fifties and sixties, the Quebec Tremblay Report[3] and the Report of the Royal Commission on Bilingualism and Biculturalism.[4] It was the guiding premise from which competing conclusions were drawn by the Trudeau federalists and the Québécois nationalists.

Until comparatively recently, another founding people existed on the constitutional sidelines. Status Indians had a form of constitutional recognition in the s. 91(24) allocation of "Indians, and Lands reserved for the Indians" as a federal jurisdiction. This, however, was not a badge of honour but a vehicle for wardship status and a separate system of administration that implicitly defined Indians as constitutional outsiders, as subjects rather than fully participant citizens. They did not receive the federal vote until 1960.

Canadians who were neither French or British nor indigenous were numerically insignificant at Confederation and existed in the constitutional shadow of the French and English founding peoples until the middle of the twentieth century. Particular ethnic groups, especially Asians, were subjected to various forms of discriminatory, stigmatizing treatment.

The working constitution was also, at its beginnings, a male constitution. Women received the vote belatedly and participated minimally in the representative structures of the Canadian state. The first woman was elected to the House of Commons in 1921, appointed to the Senate in 1930, became a federal cabinet minister in 1957, was made a Lieutenant-Governor in 1974, a Supreme Court judge in 1982, and Governor General in 1984.

Finally, the constitution we are leaving behind was a governments' constitution. Its two basic pillars – federalism and parliamentary government – divided the power to govern between two orders of government reflecting the Canadian and provincial dimensions of our existence and laid out the pattern of relationships between the executive and legislative branches of governments. That dominance or priority of governments in the constitutional order was strikingly revealed in the long search for a domestic amending formula, which until the late seventies automatically assumed that governments would decide how to distribute formal power in the amending process among themselves.

Yesterday's constitution, consequently, privileged the British-French dimension of Canada's existence, especially the former, over those of all other backgrounds, including indigenous peoples, implicitly defined the constitutional world as primarily a male prerogative, accorded extensive attention to the concerns of governments by means of federalism and responsible government, and paid minimum explicit attention to the citizen-state dimension.

For the last half-century, Canadians have attempted to redress these founding biases with varying degrees of success. The Parti Québécois pursuit of sovereignty-association, Meech Lake, the distinct society, and the Bélanger-Campeau Commission are the most recent attempts to deal with the eighteenth-century heritage of French-English duality in the interest of the no longer acquiescent junior founding partner. A third of a century ago, Duplessis and the Tremblay Report pleaded with the rest of Canada to adhere strictly to the Confederation agreement and to remain faithful to the principles of federalism. Now we are told that existing federalism is dead, and the most that can be hoped for is an asymmetrical federalism in which Quebec wields extensive jurisdictional powers unavailable to the other provinces. The allegiance of the majority of Québécois in the early days of the post-Meech Lake era to whatever can be salvaged from the existing system appears to be essentially conditional, contingent, and calculated.

Status Indians are no longer voteless and voiceless. They employ the rhetoric of First Nations in the service of a greater autonomy that, in words at least, often verges on sovereignty. They do not dispute, they simply deny the Mayflower claim of the British and French to be founding peoples, with the caustic reminder that they were waiting on the beach when these early European immigrants arrived. They have been joined in the constitution by the Métis and the Inuit under the new constitutional rubric of "aboriginal peoples." [5]

Non-founding peoples have gained their own constitutional recognition in the s. 27 multicultural clause of the Charter and in several of the categories of the s. 15 equality rights clause. Demographic projections, they incessantly remind their fellow citizens, support the claims of ethnocultural Canadians of European background other than French and British and of the rapidly growing metropolitan population of visible minorities that the constitution cannot restrict its sensitivities to the shrinking British and French proportion of the population. [6] Hence their recurrent and telling labelling of the Meech Lake Accord as backward-looking, as seeing Canada through a rearview mirror.

Women, too, have come of constitutional age. They have tasted constitutional recognition; they have their own constitutional interest groups and their own well-trained lawyers to defend their constitutional concerns. They lay claim to sections 15 and 28, in the making of which they played a key role. Feminist groups in particular view these clauses as weapons in their ongoing assault on a society that some of them view as a massive affirmative action program for men.

Finally, the Charter sends a powerful message to its many believers, especially in English-speaking Canada, that the constitution no longer belongs to governments, indeed that citizens are now part of the constitutional order, and thus that deference to the leadership role of governments in constitutional matters is not any more an unquestioned constitutional norm. The fact that Aboriginal, female, ethnocultural, visible minority, the disabled, and other Canadians successfully wielded the phrase "eleven able-bodied white males" to underline the illegitimacy of the Meech Lake process cogently confirms the decline of deference among the new constitutional players. A quarter of a century ago, such a phrase, deprived of its contemporary message of cultural arrogance, would have been virtually meaningless.

Now, at the beginning of the last decade of the twentieth century, Canadians can look back on a range of once-sacred constitutional hierarchies that have either crumbled or are under attack – an ethnic, racial hierarchy with the British at the top, and a sexual division of constitutional and political labour that privileged men over women. Finally, the hierarchy of authority and elitism sustained by deference, which assumed formal constitutional change was a matter for responsible governments to handle, has been badly shaken by the insouciant response of a society that would not accept a Meech Lake package that commenced its life with the support of eleven governments and all three major parties in the House of Commons.

This new constitutional culture, sustained by the Charter and Aboriginal constitutional clauses, greatly reduces the flexibility of the governments outside of Quebec in responding to Quebec claims for some form of distinctive treatment. In functional terms, the Charter, its allies, and its supporters restrain the federal government and the remaining provinces in the same way that Quebec nationalism keeps the Quebec government tightly leashed in the constitutional bargaining arena. Quebec nationalism led to the withdrawal of support for the Fulton-Favreau formula by Jean Lesage, to the later unwillingness of Premier Bourassa to proceed with the Victoria Charter, and to his posture of rigid inflexibility two decades later in the Meech Lake negotiations. It appears, then, that changes in the constitutional culture of English-speaking Canada, combined with the nationalist restraints on the government of Quebec, increase the likelihood that intergovernmental agreements will be repudiated if public opinion is given time to mobilize. Once that mobilization has occurred, the flexibility necessary for compromise is redefined by the purists as weakness.

## The International Dimension of Our Constitutional Difficulties

It is tempting, even natural, to locate the roots of our contemporary constitutional malaise in domestic factors, to assess our difficulties as the product of an inadequate response to the evolution of those domestic cleavages that have constitutional consequences. Such explanations, however, founder as we soon discover that many of the constitutional pressures playing on us have international roots. Francophone Quebec nationalism, the assertiveness of indigenous peoples, and the claims of multiracial and multicultural Canada for constitutional recognition all draw on global trends of ethnic revival, the post-World

War Two attack on imperialist racial hierarchies, and a growing international consciousness of indigenous peoples. Further, the emergence of numerous small states encourages concentrated minorities of national, ethnic, and indigenous peoples to view independence or self-government as much more feasible, as more in accord with the nature of things, than was true in the immediate aftermath of World War Two.

These global trends are supplemented and reinforced by an international explosion of rights consciousness stimulated in part by the United Nations. Its many consequences include a reduction in the deference accorded elites, pressures for Charters and Bills of Rights, and redefinition of the relative significance of governments and citizens in democratic constitutional orders to the benefit of the latter. Specifically, and as examples only, the women's movement and the activism of the disabled are inexplicable if external social forces, international intellectual climates, and a multitude of international organizations, both governmental and non-governmental, are not considered central links in any chain of causation.

Accordingly, the pressures playing on the Canadian constitution result from the interaction of domestic and international factors. State elites in the international system are recipients and senders of an unending series of cues from and to each other that provide evolving definitions of what statehood is. The citizenry, particularly of wealthy, open, and democratic societies, subliminally receives and purposefully selects messages and identities from the global environment that they then feed into the citizen-state axis of their domestic polity. Thus, the Canadian constitution, like all others, exists in and is responsive to an international environment of other states and of international organizations that transmits evolving definitions of citizenship and statehood.

In a country like Canada, democratic assumptions incline the student to see constitutional change as shaped by a domestic dialectic between citizens and their governments. This, however, is to forget that the state is in constant interaction with other states and that its citizens are bombarded by values, identities, and social forces that transcend frontiers. The international environment is a depository of resources that can be skilfully deployed at home. Aboriginal organizations bring the papacy and the United Nations to the support of their causes. The heroines of the feminist movement are international.

## Disarray about the Formal Rules and the Politics of the Amending Process

The 1982 achievement of an amending formula that can be operated entirely in Canada no longer appears as a triumph, but rather as an interim agreement. At a minimum, Meech Lake suggests that Canadians are still painfully learning how to work the new 1982 formula. More plausibly, I would argue that the formula's guiding philosophies verged on obsolescence before the constitutional ink was dry. The formula was devised as a response to the requirements of federalism, viewed as an affair of governments, albeit modified by the concession to responsible government involved in the new requirement of legislative ratification. Given the fashioning of the formula by the "Gang of Eight" provincial governments, who were adamantly opposed to Trudeau's competing formula with a referendum component, it was to be expected that the formula would be sensitive to governments, not to citizens. Further, the history of the search for a made-in-Canada amending formula had focused almost exclusively on the respective roles of the federal and provincial governments once the United Kingdom Parliament's role had been rendered obsolete by patriation. Indeed, the eventual sorting out of those roles among governments was viewed as *the* amending problem requiring solution. Consequently, the amending formula was not fashioned with a view to its congruence with the Charter or with a Charter-influenced constitutional culture.

However, no sooner had the new amending formula been installed than the constitutional culture in which it was to operate began to diverge from the formula's implicitly elitist assumptions. The basic premise that governments were the key, and virtually the exclusive players in generating and implementing formal constitutional change, was challenged by a new cadre of constitutional actors who denied legitimacy to a process that left them in the audience.

In that sense Meech Lake reiterated one of the recurrent lessons of our past efforts at constitutional reform. It is the most recent illustration of the inveterate Canadian tendency for the substantive issues of constitutional change to be embroiled in a debate about the legitimacy of the process of their attempted resolution. Indeed, fundamental disagreement about the rules that should govern the process of constitutional change has acquired the status of a Canadian tradition, dysfunctional though it may be.

Prior to Meech Lake, the proposed unilateralism route threatened by Prime Minister Trudeau in 1980-81 was fought before Canadian courts and before the British public and parliamentarians by provincial governments and Aboriginal peoples. After the passage of the 1982 Constitution Act, the government of Quebec unsuccessfully challenged the constitutionality of the process on the ground that it had not respected a constitutional veto claimed by the Quebec government. Just a few years earlier, the Senate proposals of the federal government's Bill C-60 reform package in 1978 were successfully challenged in court as exceeding the federal government's amending jurisdiction under a 1949 amendment to the British North America Act, which allocated specified powers of unilateral amendment to the federal government.

Any belief that the 1982 amending formula, especially if employed in the attempted fashion of Meech Lake, would provide the long-awaited answer to the need for a legitimate formula has been belied by the reaction to Meech Lake. Polls indicate that most Canadians, Québécois included, support the idea of referenda by large majorities.[7] After the week-long First Ministers' Conference in June, 1990, there was virtual unanimity among the exhausted political leaders that never again would they participate in such an isolated and secretive executive federalism bargaining session from which constitutional *faits accomplis* were supposed to emerge.[8]

The federal government discussion paper "Amending the Constitution of Canada" (1990) underlines the now recognized need for "public participation," "public involvement," and "public hearings." The key process criticism throughout the Meech Lake period, it concluded, was that the amending "procedures have not provided for public involvement in the examination and determination of constitutional amendment proposals prior to the formal amendment text being put forward for acceptance or rejection."[9]

The Citizens' Forum, whose hearings are now under way, is described and justified as a medium through which the people can speak and commissioners can listen.[10] A press release describes the Forum as providing a "framework for an unprecedented exercise in democracy" and as "reaching out for the insights and inherent wisdom of the citizens of Canada."[11] A more dramatic contrast with the philosophy of executive dominance that first ministers sought, ultimately without success, to apply to the Meech Lake process could scarcely be imagined. Prime Minister Mulroney's rhetoric suggests that he will consult and listen *ad nauseam* from now on, until the last voice has been heard.[12] The Charter constituencies and Aboriginal peoples presumably will resist any attempted repeat of the government monopolization of the process that characterized the early stages of Meech Lake.

Some of these reactions are, no doubt, the bitter or chastened responses of individuals, groups, and governments still reeling from the debacle so recently behind us. It would be wrong, however, to write them off as ephemeral, driven by momentary passions of despair or enthusiasm that will not survive the cold light of day. Meech Lake provides us with insights into our constitutional existence that could remain hidden through decades of constitutional placidity. The Meech Lake outcome can be explained in various ways: as a conflict between older and newer definitions of the constitution that I have elsewhere somewhat grandiosely described as the governments' constitution versus the citizens' constitution;[13] as executive federalism versus the Charter; as the old duality of founding peoples versus the new ethnic, racial, and indigenous complexity of contemporary Canada; or as the culture of deference and authority versus an emergent culture of constitutional participation.

These antitheses – and others could be constructed by those who are dichoto-
mously inclined – reveal how far we are from agreement on how we should proceed with the task of formal constitutional change, or who should participate
and how. Even if we were to try and exclude the citizenry again in Meech Lake II,
Premier Bourassa has made it clear that he rejects intergovernmental bargaining
on constitutional reform among eleven governments. From now on he will
negotiate only on a one-to-one basis with the federal government – nation to
prospective nation.[14] However, we have neither constitutional theory nor procedures to guide legitimate one-on-one Quebec-Ottawa bargaining directed to
fundamental constitutional change. To structure the bargaining in such a way
assumes the existence of an English-speaking Canada equated with the rest of
Canada and represented by the federal government, an assumption that could
not withstand the most cursory examination. In a corporate, institutional, or
governmental sense, English-speaking Canada does not exist. It is voiceless and
headless. If, therefore, we are playing the two-nations game rather than the federalism game, our disarray is little short of paralysing.

Our lack of consensus on the process of formal constitutional change is not
restricted to a few minor details to be tidied up by legal draftsmen; rather, it is one
of the paramount constitutional issues, for to agree on the participants and their
roles is to structure the outcome. If the game is to be a two-nations version of the
intergovernmental game restricted to two actors, Quebec City and Ottawa,
presiding over the demise of federal Canada, the federal government is not sym-
metrically related to the rest-of-Canada constituency for which it would, *de
facto*, be speaking. If the game is still a federalism game, the other nine provincial
governments will not be willing to delegate the refashioning of Canada to Quebec and a federal government facing the erosion of its own power in Quebec,
even if the formal rules sanctioned such a procedure, which they do not.[15]

In any event, Meech Lake makes clear that governments do not exhaust the
cast of constitutional actors. We need, accordingly, to find a process that is sensitive to the participant constitutional culture that the Charter and Aboriginal
aspirations have stimulated, and that has been legitimated, at least for its believers, by the role of Charter supporters and Aboriginal leaders in fashioning parts
of the 1982 Constitution Act and by their role in the defeat of Meech Lake. The
amending process, in other words, must be moved in the direction of reconciling
the traditional dominance of governments with the emerging challenge of a no
longer deferential citizen-body.

That the governments of Canadian federalism will continue to be central
players is obvious, for federalism and the Canadian and provincial communities
it reflects and nourishes remain crucial to our identities. That the government
and people of Quebec, if a revised constitution can contain their ambitions,

might require some unique status in the amending process is also evident. But the accommodation of Quebec, the federal government, and the other nine provinces is no longer enough.

The necessary rearranging of the respective roles of citizens and governments in the amending process would be difficult at the best of times. It is doubly so when the Quebec government is driven by a desire for national self-affirmation, following on the perceived humiliation of Meech Lake, that precludes a return to federalism's intergovernmental constitutional bargaining table. It is trebly difficult when put in the context of the widespread suspicion so many of the constitutional actors have for each other, to which I now turn.

## The Absence of Trust

The constitutional amendment process is profoundly hampered by the pervasive distrust of so many of the participants for each other. The evidence is lengthy and discouraging. The widespread resort to the courts to challenge the legality of particular constitutional reform packages, noted previously, is one telling illustration.

Distrust lies behind the progressive introduction of rigidities into the amending formula, from the relatively flexible Victoria Charter proposals of 1971 to the unanimity provisions in the 1982 Constitution Act and their further extension in the Meech Lake package. The assumption that a central criterion of a good amending formula is to alleviate insecurities, to reduce the possibility that a particular government might be a loser, was the implicit assumption behind Mulroney's reiterated defence of the Meech Lake unanimity requirement for Senate reform. Unanimity, he claimed, doubtless for the benefit of Premier Getty of Alberta, would guarantee Alberta against having the wrong kind of Senate reform imposed on it. This was a protection that Quebec had not had when the 1982 Constitution Act was fashioned and implemented.

Those who forged ahead with the Constitution Act in 1982 without Quebec's participation did so in the belief that the Parti Québécois could not be trusted to bargain honourably for renewed federalism. The Parti Québécois government and the nationalist elite responded by accusing the Trudeau Liberal government of betrayal, of a breach of trust, for failing to deliver the kind of renewed federalism they claimed that Quebecers justifiably assumed as inherent in Trudeau's referendum campaign commitments.[16]

The interpretations of our recent constitutional evolution by feminists, Aboriginal leaders, non-founding European ethnic groups, and visible minorities are a litany of bitterness, accusation, and distrust of governments. This bitterness, which has historic roots, burst forth in the Meech Lake episode in a battery of recriminations against an executive federalism first ministers' process dominated, as we were repeatedly reminded, by eleven able-bodied white males.

The absence of trust lies behind the widespread implicit acceptance of a mirror theory of representation that presupposes a decline of deference and suggests that only representatives cloned from the same stock as the groups that felt excluded could be trusted to speak for women and Aboriginals, for example. The implicit thesis that you have to be one to know one and to represent one draws powerful support from moral and intellectual trends in contemporary culture.[17] In the Meech Lake process it gained additional justification from the widespread view that the federal government failed in its duty to defend the Canadian community, Charter interests, and its own future status as a government.[18] In the absence of evidence that the federal government was a reliable proxy for their concerns, Meech Lake opponents simply denied the legitimacy of a process that tried to exclude their participation.

Mistrust leads to a constitutional paranoia ever on the lookout for slights and indignities, fearful that one's fate will be decided in a bargaining session to which one was not invited, when one was sleeping in Hull, for example, or apprehensive that the male bargainers will simply forget about women's constitutional concerns, as feminists assert, or convinced that the commitment to hold a constitutional conference on Aboriginal matters can only be relied on if it is written into the constitution itself.

This lack of trust, this ubiquitous paranoia, has major constitutional consequences, not only for the constitutional reform process itself but for the objectives of the participants. It easily gets translated into an unceasing search for the maximum constitutional protection. Hence, the successful efforts of women's groups to exempt s. 28[19] from the ambit of the s. 33 notwithstanding clause.[20] The women's s. 28 clause contained its own "notwithstanding anything in this Charter," partly to ensure that the s. 27 multicultural heritage clause[21] could not be used to justify sexual inequalities on the ground they were sanctioned by traditional cultural practices. The desire of Anglophone women's groups to protect s. 28 and s. 15[22] of the Charter from the distinct society clause was based on the same fear that cultural imperatives could be used on some future occasion to subject Canadian women living in Quebec to an inferior rights regime in the interest of cultural and linguistic survival.

In the constitutional politics between the Meech Lake and Langevin House meetings, ethnic and Aboriginal groups succeeded in exempting their constitutional clauses from the ambit of the distinct society clause.[23] Aboriginal groups had earlier sought and gained in s. 25[24] protection of their Aboriginal, treaty, or other rights or freedoms from abrogation or derogation by the Charter. The Assembly of First Nations tried without success in 1983 to gain a right of veto over constitutional amendments that might affect the rights of First Nations.[25]

The lack of trust is driven by disagreement over the formal rules and the accompanying political process for amending the constitution. The 1982 amending formula presupposes the dominance of governments, modified by the requirement of legislative ratification, in the amending process. The Charter, however, generates a new set of constitutional interests, as do Aboriginal constitutional clauses and the ambitions they sustain, that convinces their advocates that they should be more than onlookers when the constitution is being amended. The Quebec government, based on its Francophone majority, assumed that its turn had come, following its 1982 exclusion. In addition, the Charter had a weaker hold on Québécois, outside of Anglophones and allophones, than was true elsewhere in the country, and this hampered the Bourassa government's appreciation of Charterism in the rest of Canada. In any event, the fundamental social force that the Quebec government had to represent, or gingerly not offend, was nationalism, not the Charter and its pan-Canadian ideology. Meech Lake foundered on these competing understandings, with the Quebec government assuming it had a priority claim, all governments assuming the constitution was theirs to amend and resenting the interference of the new constitutional stakeholders, and the latter truculently non-deferential and insisting that their concerns also had to be met.

A constitutional amendment process built on mistrust is likely to display the following biases: (1) it multiplies the number of would-be constitutional players by undermining the belief that X can be trusted to represent the concerns of Y; (2) it generates a competitive search for ironclad constitutional protection in the form of vetoes, notwithstanding clauses, etc.; (3) on the flexibility/rigidity scale it will be heavily biased toward the latter; (4) it will encourage the search for loopholes and unilateralism options to break out of its confines; (5) it will lead to ingenious attempts to work the constitution, to achieve by political processes what cannot be achieved by formal amendments. However, for many of the constitutional objectives that Canadians now pursue, the less constraining political process cannot be substituted for change by formal amendment.

## Conclusion

The constitution we have left behind was sustained by an ethnic hierarchy in which the British assumed pride of place, the French a close second, and those communities that came to be labelled multicultural and multiracial in recent decades were clearly above the Aboriginal peoples, although not in the charmed circle of European founding peoples restricted to French and English. From a different perspective, a gender aristocracy of males monopolized the affairs of state at our beginnings and even now wields vastly disproportionate numerical power.

The constitutional culture that lay behind a constitution similar in principle to that of the United Kingdom has been convulsed by Québécois nationalism, by a changing ethnic demography and the politicization of ethnicity, by the awakening of the indigenous peoples, by the rights revolution and the Charter that is its most visible instrument, and by the attack on the constitutional and political role hitherto granted to men. Many of these trends derive support from an international environment that is broadly sympathetic to what I have elsewhere called "constitutional minoritarianism."[26] The Charter and Aboriginal constitutional clauses have been crucial catalysts in reducing deference and challenging the dominance of governments in the constitutional reform process.

We have more constitutional players than ever. Many of them speak the uncompromising language of rights, nationalism, and sovereignty. Governments and citizen groups disagree on what the constitution is about, and hence on how it should be changed. Even among governments, the criteria for formal amendment that were fashioned in 1980-81 are discredited. We look back on a succession of failed efforts interspersed with isolated successes before 1982. The 1982 achievement now seems to have been a Pyrrhic victory, as the exclusion of Quebec became a political resource to delegitimate the Constitution Act, 1982, and thus open the way for the mismanaged Meech Lake affair that has grievously damaged the constitutional order.

The somewhat antiseptic language of jurisdictional conflict has been overtaken by a passionate language of identity, honour, shame, betrayal, and status. This language of pride and affirmation gets in the way of compromise. Pervasive suspicion and distrust, which feed on historical grievances, compound the difficulties of constitutional reform.

We are caught in a vicious circle. While some of my observations can be characterized as disputes about rules and procedures, they are in fact reflections of a much deeper and more profound malaise. The crisis we face is one of community and identity. Our constitutional behaviour lacks fraternity, sorority, mutuality, and trust. Our multiple fragmentation corrodes the process we employ in the search for an accommodation that will overcome our divisions.

We would be better off if we had a clean slate on which to write our constitutional future, for then the compulsion of necessity would drive us toward agreement. Situated, however, as we are, in the midst of an incomplete constitutional experiment and surveying our condition as an unfinished people, we are hindered in our efforts to escape by the inertia of a decaying constitutional order.

PART IV

CITIZENSHIP AND THE CONSTITUTION

Chapter Six

# The Fragmentation of Canadian Citizenship

The theory and practice of Canadian citizenship, in the broadest political sense, have been not eternal, unchanging verities but rather materials for an unending debate. The pre-First World War debates between the imperialist British Canadians and the rival liberal nationalists were, although the word may not have been used, about citizenship, about whether the boundaries of political community and civic allegiance were restricted to Canada or also, through ties of kinship and political tradition, encompassed the mother country. The debates surrounding the conscription crises of both world wars were citizenship controversies about the extent and nature of civic obligation.

Citizenship has always been central to the debates about who Canadians were and what they should become. Nevertheless, in spite of its centrality, it has been an underexamined constitutional category. This essay provides an interpretive commentary on some of the tensions of contemporary Canadian citizenship, especially as reflected in constitutional politics. While this may seem a limited vantage point, constitutional politics is the supreme vehicle by which we define ourselves as a people, decide which of our present identities we should foster and which ignore, and rearrange the rights and duties of citizen membership. This essay considers citizenship from an historical, political, and sociological perspective rather than from a legal perspective.

The two major portions of this essay, following several brief introductory sections, discuss "A Three-Nations View of Canada" and "The New Diversity and Citizenship." A short conclusion brings the threads of the argument together. The pressures of time and the essay format, along with the fundamental indeterminacy of where Canadians are and where we might be heading, have engendered more speculation and conjectures in the following pages than is customary in academic analyses. Many of the unqualified statements that follow are "iffy," or are drawn from imagined futures that may never happen, or rest on implicit social theories that may well be wrong. I agree with Casey Stengel – or was it Yogi Berra? – that prediction is always difficult, especially when it deals with the future. Prediction, however, is not therefore to be avoided, but is to be taken with a grain of salt.

## Introduction

### THE NEW SALIENCE OF CITIZENSHIP

A few preliminary comments on the enhanced visibility and prominence of citizenship will set the stage.

(1) The gradual weaning of (especially British) Canadians from the British connection – the historic progression from colony to nation, culminating in the 1982 Constitution Act – confronts Canadians with basic questions of sovereignty, identity, and their place in the world, answers to which must address our citizenship.

(2) Globalization presents people with an unending stream of products, ideas, values, and new identities that threatens to destabilize links between citizen and state unless they are constrained by the positive identification with the polity that an enriched practice of citizenship can generate.

(3) The threatened breakup of Canada – a crisis of citizenship and community – raises the fundamental question: to what community or communities do Canadians wish to give their allegiance?

(4) Citizens are made as well as born. Immigration-induced change in our ethnic demography makes citizenship a crucial instrument for bridging cleavages between old and new Canadians who decreasingly come from the traditional "supply" sources of our country's first century.

(5) The behaviour that the modern state requires of its citizens cannot be achieved by coercion, an increasingly inefficient instrument for securing compliance in a complex contemporary democratic society. Meeting economic competition, responding to environmental threats, and sustaining the civic empathy that a multiracial society needs require autonomous civic behaviour that alienated subjects will only grudgingly provide.

(6) The constitutional recognition vigorously demanded by Aboriginal peoples will require unique citizenship status.

(7) The Charter of Rights and Freedoms of 1982 has profound effects on citizenship. Pierre Trudeau saw it as an instrument to transfer sovereignty to the people. Although the simultaneous introduction of an amending formula designed as an instrument of governments frustrated that goal, the Meech Lake fiasco suggests that governmental control of the amending process is illusory. That an amendment package with the noble intent of returning Quebec to the constitutional family with honour and enthusiasm foundered on widespread public opposition indicates that the ultimate authority over constitutional change is slipping away from the governing elites of executive federalism to the citizenry. Significantly, Charter supporters in the "rest of Canada" (roc) were key players in the defeat of Meech Lake, and the Charter's possible erosion by the "distinct society" clause was their leading concern.

(8) The constitutional crisis has undermined the authority of elites and of executive federalism. In a democratic era, citizens cannot be treated as chattels whose fate can be determined behind closed doors and announced as a *fait accompli* to a deferential and grateful public. A mandate obtained through a referendum was an essential requirement for legitimation of the extensive constitutional change of sovereignty-association that the Parti Québécois government sought in 1980. That same pressure to give citizens the last say lies behind the proposed Quebec referendum on sovereignty or renewed federalism in 1992. In general, the attention devoted to referenda and constituent assemblies in the past few years, more than in the entire previous century,[1] suggests a profound change in Canadian constitutional culture. The deference formerly accorded governing elites has been replaced by suspicion and distrust.[2] While agreement is lacking on the amending process appropriate to the new constitutional people that Canadians are becoming, the starting point is recognition that citizens are now constitutional actors to a degree that our predecessors in the first century after Confederation could not have predicted.

These challenges can be met only by changes in the very conception of citizenship – changes of citizens' behaviour, identity, and values that can be implemented not from above, but only by a co-operative enterprise of citizens and governments.

While comprehensive analysis of the above catalogue of pressures playing on citizenship would require a monograph, a more limited focus on the fragmentation of citizenship by multiple nationalisms and by the politicized diversity of modernity will capture much of the tension surrounding citizenship in Canada. It is our fate to have to think through the possibility and acceptability of a citizenship that is not the same for everybody at a time when the burdens of citizenship are increasing.

## THE FRAGMENTATION OF CITIZENSHIP

The tendency to think of citizenship as a single, uniform status is not surprising. Citizenship is the legally defined status of official membership in the political community, one that by its nature we would expect to be unvarying.

The angry use of such phrases as "second-class citizens" and "second-class provinces" as indicators of injustice reveals the powerful hold of equality, defined as sameness, on our constitutional imagination. Indeed, from one perspective, Canadian history is a record of positive responses to the tight linkage of the powerful norm of equality with that of universalism; hence the steady move to a universal franchise as former restrictions were dropped and the move toward a colour-blind immigration law, which suggests the triumph of the equal-treatment norm applied to the pool of potential citizens. More recently, the Charter, though not without special categories that speak to some but not all of us, clearly had levelling implications. In particular, it was explicitly hostile to diversities in the availability of rights based on province of residence.[3] Finally, the attempt of Trudeau's Liberal government to end special status for Indians, though unsuccessful, was based both on a principled aversion to categorizing people by race and on the belief that special status was a millstone that held those very people back.

These examples all suggest the historical potency of the egalitarian impulse in opposition to special status and differentiated treatment of the core components of citizenship. Inequalities were increasingly put on the defensive in areas where citizenship symbolism was involved. In each of the above cases, the challenged inequality was viewed as detrimental or demeaning to those subjected to it. Hence, its removal was considered as liberating, as rejection of inferior treatment – although status Indians obviously disagreed. While in the long sweep of history an egalitarianism tending to uniform treatment may be the dominant trend, a powerful counter-trend is now gathering momentum in Canadian and other Western societies.

This essay is directed to that counter-trend – to those who argue that uniformity of status is a hegemonic instrument of the numerically or politically strong; to those for whom the claim that Canadians are a single people obfuscates the deeper reality that Canada can survive only as a multinational state; to those for whom differentiated treatment, special status, and affirmative action are variously justified as compensation for past injustice, as necessary to overcome systemic barriers, or as required to produce greater equality of result or condition. To the purveyors of the counter-trend, perhaps the central characteristic of modern society is diversity, a gallery of discordant voices issuing from fundamentally divergent ways of seeing the world. Modernity, or post-modernity, from this perspective, is inescapably plural and should not be compressed into a single mode or manner of expression, thinking, being, and feeling. The Canadian citizenship of the future, accordingly, must seek accommodation with this diversity, both of internal nations and of the multiple identities and cleavages within them.

Historically, and even now in the 1990s, the major diversities whose successful accommodation was the supreme task of Canadian statecraft have been the territorial particularisms of federalism. Indeed, for our first century, students of the constitution strayed little beyond federalism. Canadian commentators eulogized or vilified the Judicial Committee of the Privy Council of Westminster in terms of its impact on federalism. The institutional management of the permanent French-English dualism of Canadian life was seen largely as a problem of federalism, with Quebec's provincial autonomy as the central response. Federalism was the key institutional variable facilitating expansion from four provinces to ten provinces and two territories. Would Newfoundland have joined Canada in 1949 had provincehood not existed to allow significant powers of self-rule to accompany extension of federal jurisdiction to these new Canadians?

Thus the claim that Canadians are a federal people is profoundly true. However, federal and provincial memberships do not exhaust Canadians' salient civic identities. In this essay I shall give the well-known features of federalism less than their proportionate due in order to focus on newer phenomena, where our understanding is limited and where conventional wisdom has not yet emerged from the competitive political-intellectual struggle to define who we are. Although Canadians are still deeply influenced by their federal and parliamentary past, viewed either as a heavy burden or as a rich heritage, their civic identities and patterns of community affiliation are changing rapidly. Even the basic challenge posed by Quebec to our constitutional continuity is much more than a standard provincial challenge to federalism. At a deeper level, it fits into a three-nations version of Canada (Quebec, Aboriginal, and rest-of-Canada) that now vies with the more conventional ten-provinces, two-territories federal version that we have inherited.

## A Three-Nations View of Canada

From a non-federal perspective, Canada is the home for three sociological nations – Quebec, the rest of Canada, and Aboriginal.[4] Their boundaries are unclear or contested; the extent and nature of their political organization vary; their members belong to and identify with the pan-Canadian community with differing degrees of enthusiasm. Their nationalisms are dissimilar and generate distinctive constitutional ambitions. That of Quebec is the contemporary expression of an historical community, the Francophone majority that has long nourished a national identity, though previously less attached to the state than now, when it has a powerful government at its disposal. That of the Aboriginal peoples is relatively new, although experiences of dispossession, subordinate status, and unjust treatment are of long standing.

The modern roots of Aboriginal nationalism lie in the status-Indian nationalism born of reaction to the assimilating proposals of the 1969 federal White Paper[5] and its subsequent, contagious diffusion to Inuit and Métis. It is powerfully expressed by Aboriginal political organizations. Both Aboriginal and Québécois nationalisms are ascending, nation-preserving, or nation-creating. Their adherents sense that history is on their side, and they are the vanguard of stronger, liberating nationalist governments of the future. Their political elites employ the language of nationalism both as an automatic ritual incantation and as an aggressive challenge to what they view as an assimilating pan-Canadian nationalism.

For the ROC, nationalist self-identification is more potential than actual, more reluctant than striving, for the majority's preference would be to leave things as they are. ROC nationalism is defensive and unorganized. Essentially, it is Canadian nationalism in retreat, besieged by rival Québécois and Aboriginal nationalisms. The acronyms that describe it – ROC (rest of Canada) and CWOQ (Canada without Quebec) – clearly indicate its residual, salvaging character and ambitions.

Ambiguities and imprecisions abound in a three-nations view of Canada, as the politics and sociology of community are at variance. The rough nationalist equation of Quebec with its Francophone majority is an injustice to Anglophone and allophone Quebecers and reduces one million Francophones outside Quebec, primarily in Ontario and New Brunswick, to an irrelevant diaspora; the casual identification of the ROC with Anglophone Canada or, worse, English Canada leaves Quebec's Anglophones outside the community with which they strongly identify, overlooks non-Quebec Francophones, and chills the Acadian heart by its non-recognition of New Brunswick's distinctive and proportionately large French-speaking community. It also suggests a homogeneity in Anglophone Canada that in reality is now multicultural and multiracial, albeit with English as the unifying language.

Federalism fits only crudely and imperfectly with the three-nations reality of Canada. It confines nearly two million Anglophone and Francophone Canadians to the provincial territories of the other majority. And, with the exception of the Northwest Territories, it is more an unsympathetic container for than sensitive expression of Aboriginal realities. "Unfortunately for cultural nationalists, and fortunately for supporters of cultural diversity and pluralism," states Peter G. White, "there is no part of Canadian territory, except for aboriginal reserves, that is the exclusive preserve of any one cultural group."[6] Further, the Aboriginal "nation," as noted below, is in fact a diversified array of communities and identities, not a cohesive or coherent, united single nation. While the lack of congruity between political and ethno-national boundaries poses major challenges to future constitution-makers, it inhibits expression of, rather than denies the reality of, the contemporary existence of the three national communities of identity and sentiment, coexisting with a challenged pan-Canadian political nationalism. To put it differently, the exceedingly difficult constitutional challenge is to adapt the constitutional structures of federalism, which are appropriately sensitive to provincial territorial pluralism, to the untidy three-nations reality briefly described above. That adaptation will almost certainly require an entrenched third order of Aboriginal government.

While non-Aboriginal Canada has long been seen through a dualist lens, as two founding peoples, as *The [French and English] Race Question in Canada*,[7] or as René Lévesque's two scorpions in a bottle,[8] the contemporary two-nations view has moved on. Its accommodation within a reconstituted Canada is problematic. A succession of commissions, task forces, attempted constitutional settlements, and inquiries – the Royal Commission on Bilingualism and Biculturalism, the Pepin-Robarts Task Force on Canadian Unity, the Meech Lake Accord, the Bélanger-Campeau Commission – has documented the escalating intensity of Quebec's demands. The no-longer junior Quebec partner, expressing a Francophone nationalist political consciousness that has retreated from French Canada to Quebec, appears ready to translate its nationhood into independent statehood if necessary. As Quebec's goals appear less and less capable of federal accommodation, a parallel, incipient political identity of the "other" slowly crystallizes, now conceived as the ROC, a revealing new designation, rather than English Canada. The citizenry of the ROC is induced, initially reluctantly, to see that the comfortable Canadianism natural to the majority, in which it had merged itself, indeed lost itself, is eroding under the impact of Quebec nationalism. Accordingly, the ROC begins to see itself as a potentially distinct political entity.

For Quebec's nationalists, a two-nations view is an aggressive posture, a vehicle for making claims for equality of national status within a reconstituted Canada or outside it. It suggests the terms on which Quebec will stay. For the ROC, however, Quebec's dualist demands suggest terms that may be impossible to meet within Canada. For Québécois, dualism is an attempt to make the country conform to their historical vision of a binational partnership, hitherto imperfectly realized. For the ROC, Quebec's challenge is a jolting reminder that its empathy for the French fact was always subordinated to its more passionate allegiance to Canada as a whole. Contemporary Quebec's attachment to Canada is clearly conditional. The ROC's allegiance to a Canada in which Quebec is a province rather than a nation now verges on the anachronistic. However, the ROC's potential support for a two-nations-inspired transformation of the Canadian constitutional order is problematical at a time when standard provincehood no longer appears acceptable to Québécois.

The search for a constitutional agreement between Quebec and the ROC is complicated immensely by the emergence of a set of Aboriginal national players to constitutional prominence. The Aboriginal First Nations "embraced the death of the [Meech Lake] Accord . . . wholeheartedly and joyously . . . [as] the rejection of a constitutional lie – the lie of only two founding nations in Canada."[9] As a result, the arrangement that Canadians seek has to encompass three, not two nations.

In fact, of course, it makes no sense to regard the Aboriginal peoples as a single nation. Not only are there the three basic categories of Aboriginal peoples identified in the Constitution Act of 1982 – Indian, Inuit, and Métis – but the word "Indian" itself is a legal fiction, behind which there are numerous distinct Aboriginal nations with their own histories and separate community identities.[10]

Aboriginal nationality is a label for an indeterminate number of nations divided by tribe, treaty status, location, presence or absence of a land base, and by a history of separate administration for status Indians that Inuit and Métis lacked. Given the absence of a land base for Métis and non-status Indians, except for a few isolated cases, their nationalist ambitions for self-government are more limited and difficult to achieve than are those of their more fortunate, landed indigenous kin.

Aboriginal nationalism, therefore, is the aggregate reaction of many indigenous peoples to their shared experience of historical subordination. That experience receives contemporary expression in the constitutional category "aboriginal" in the Constitution Act, 1982, which brings the national organizations of Indian, Inuit, and Métis peoples to the constitutional bargaining table under one constitutional rubric. This elite interaction, however, and overlapping Aboriginal objectives generate no vision of a single pan-Aboriginal political community with its own government. In that sense, Aboriginal peoples are unlike many Third World peoples who, faced with analogous divisions, had the prize of a single government left by the departing imperial power as an incentive to overcome historical tribal and other invitations to fission.

The high Aboriginal profile today is the legacy of the defeat of the assimilationist policy of the 1969 White Paper aimed at status Indians, the subsequent dawning recognition that some form of Indian special status is here to stay, the over-spill of that recognition to the Inuit and Métis, the deployment of the new constitutional label "aboriginal peoples" in the Constitution Act, the holding of four Aboriginal constitutional conferences (1983-87) to define Aboriginal rights, and the crystallization of Aboriginal demands around the concept of Aboriginal self-government. Given the momentum behind the last named, the Aboriginal drive for self-government is unlikely to be checked. The prospective third order of government to accommodate it will express Aboriginal values and will reinforce Aboriginal identities.

Contemporary pressure for Aboriginal special status is extensive. The Supreme Court's *Sparrow* decision of 1990 makes it clear that the federal government has a responsibility "to act in a fiduciary capacity" for Aboriginal peoples: "The relationship between the Government and aboriginals is trust-like, rather than adversarial, and contemporary recognition and affirmation of aboriginal rights must be defined in light of this historic relationship."[11]

Demands for self-government are accompanied by parallel support for an Aboriginal justice system.[12] The federal government has proposed separate Aboriginal representation in the Senate.[13] A prestigious Aboriginal task force reporting to the Royal Commission on Electoral Reform has advocated separate Aboriginal representation in the House of Commons.[14] A degree of Aboriginal exemption from the Charter is already provided for in section 25. Further exemptions will be sought as Aboriginal self-government develops, although federal support may not be forthcoming. A *de facto* if not *de jure* Inuit quasi-province is likely to appear reasonably soon in the eastern half of the NWT. A royal commission with a daunting mandate on Aboriginal affairs is now under way. The new president of the Native Council of Canada has bluntly asserted his desire to gain the same perquisites now enjoyed by on-reserve status Indians for non-status and off-reserve Indians, so as to end what he called the government-imposed apartheid system among Aboriginal people.[15]

Historical revisionism now reaches into the highest ranks of government, with the Minister Responsible for Constitutional Affairs, Joe Clark, reminding Canadians of the many Aboriginal contributions to Canadian history, including "the fact that Louis Riel is a Canadian hero."[16] The federal Minister of Justice has indicated that limited versions of self-government for Aboriginal "groups" without a land base are possible.[17] In sum, there is a massive, broadly based battery of developments taking place – all heading in the same direction, to different degrees of positive, permanent, unique constitutional treatment for about one million Aboriginal Canadians.[18]

The more overtly political and institutional proposals noted above are given momentum by a supportive intellectual and moral climate. Recent task forces and royal commissions have documented prejudice, discrimination, and a depressing litany of indicators of social disorganization and anomie in many Aboriginal communities that give legitimacy to extraordinary measures. Sympathetic scholarship on Aboriginal issues, Aboriginal political organizations, special university programs, reinterpretations of history, and the development of Aboriginal nationalist doctrine[19] all contribute to an encouraging climate for

Aboriginal nationalism. Additional sustenance comes from the vigorously exploited access to international forums and the skilful manipulation of international support, from the pope to the United Nations. [20]

The differences between Aboriginal and Francophone Québécois nationalism are profound – most crucially between a numerically decisive provincial majority, with a cohesive sense of historic collective identity, in control of a large and powerful province, and the differently constituted, heterogeneous assemblage of Indian, Inuit, and Métis, each capable of further subdivisions, and with a dispersed and scattered existence across a continent. They also, however, share many similarities. The assimilating objective of the White Paper of 1969 replicated Lord Durham's very similar attitudes to French Canadians more than a century earlier, and his similar recommendation. Both assimilationist policies were resisted by their intended beneficiaries and are retrospectively defined as misguided attempts to achieve unrealizable goals.

Under the label "founding people" or "First Nations," both link their right to distinctive survival to historical priority. Both groups have coined new labels – Québécois, First Nations, Inuit, Dene – that symbolize their nationhood. Both Aboriginal peoples and Francophone Québécois are national minorities worried about cultural and linguistic assimilation. Each resists submergence in an undifferentiated Canadianism. Each stands outside multiculturalism and denies its application to themselves. Both groups envisage a special status for themselves; both seek government power appropriate to their situation; they see government as a vehicle not only for self-expression but for ensuring an ongoing distinctive existence.

The three-nations view of Canada is implicit in the constitutional process now under way. The Quebec government's official posture is to bargain only one on one, nation to nation, with the federal government. The unique Aboriginal status in the constitutional process is evident in the four parallel Aboriginal constitutional task forces that are consulting their separate indigenous constituencies on their preferred constitutional futures. Aboriginal specificity is equally evident in the understanding that Aboriginal leaders will participate in a first ministers' conference on the constitution, a status accorded to no other non-governmental group.

The Aboriginal position, based on joint proposals in 1990 from the Assembly of First Nations, the Native Council of Canada, and the Inuit Tapirisat, demanded "a full, ongoing role in future constitutional discussions as of right and on the same footing as the provinces. This submission also made it clear that the national aboriginal organizations view all constitutional amendments as important to aboriginal people, not only amendments that mention aboriginal people." [21] Thus Ovide Mercredi informed Constitutional Affairs Minister Joe Clark "that natives are not just a special-interest group in this constitutional round; that they will be dealing government-to-government in these national-unity discussions."[22] Recognition that Aboriginal peoples are not simply another ethnic group in multicultural Canada or just another interest group – labels they resolutely resist – is also evident in the federal constitutional proposals, *Shaping Canada's Future Together: Proposals*, where the section "Shared Citizenship and Diversity" devotes more space to "Canada's First Peoples" than to "Recognizing Quebec's Distinctiveness."[23]

Significant, and revealing, in the present constitutional round is that both Quebec and Aboriginal peoples prepare separately and self-interestedly for their constitutional futures. In Quebec, the Allaire and Bélanger-Campeau inquiries saw constitutional change almost exclusively from the perspective of Quebec. In fact, the indifference toward Canada (or the ROC) in these reports was monumental. The Allaire Report, in particular, was a self-indulgent exercise in narcissism. While Bélanger-Campeau was a more serious enterprise, a reader would find in it little internal evidence that its writers were Canadians as well as Québécois, for the latter identity had vanquished the former. Aboriginal peoples were (as of January, 1992) conducting their own constitutional inquiries, separated from the main federal parliamentary committee on a renewed Canada. The latter committee, by default, duplicating the experience of the Spicer Commission, gravitated toward becoming an outlet for the voice of non-Aboriginal ROC.

The nation-to-nation bargaining strategies of Quebec and the Aboriginal peoples are acts of powerful symbolism. Their behaviour as nations in the bargaining process is an anticipatory assertion of the status they seek to have recognized in the outcome. In each case, the strategy is designed to weaken the legitimacy of or redefine the Canadian bargainer across the table. Quebec nationalist strategy in the post-Meech round is the contemporary version of the strategy that successfully trivialized the support of Trudeau and the federal Quebec Liberal caucus for the 1982 Constitution Act by contrasting it with the claimed true voice of Quebec in the National Assembly that decisively opposed the 1982 package.

Quebec's position, with conscious inaccuracy, treats the federal government as a surrogate for Anglophone Canada, or the ROC, implicitly discounting Quebec's numerically strong caucus representation in the governing Conservative Party. The clear purpose is to eliminate or weaken Ottawa's capacity to represent and speak for the federalist component of Québécois identity. That component has been provincialized, controlled by Quebec's provincial politicians who deploy their conditional, profitable federalism in battle with the *indépendantistes* at home, while proffering it to the ROC as an arrangement that can continue only if the latter's offers are sufficiently attractive. The federal government's role, from the Quebec nationalist perspective, is to act on behalf of the ROC and thus to deny its constitutional obligation to speak for all of Canada, acting on the advice of all MPs and cabinet ministers, including those from Quebec.

An analogous assumption is implicit in Aboriginal strategies that have their leaders attend first ministers' conferences in a nation-to-nation role. According to the Native Council of Canada, by 1980 Aboriginal leaders decided to get involved because "it was very clear that we could not trust others to protect Aboriginal interests," and it was "our right" to be at the table, because the future of "our people and land is at stake."[24]

Both Québécois and Aboriginal nationalists act as if their people did not have dual identities and loyalties, one of which is Canadian and is legitimately represented by the federal government. Instead, they implicitly deny, or at least downgrade, the "other" identity of Québécois and Aboriginal peoples as Canadians. They treat the Canadian identity as that of the other, of the external party that sits on the other side of the table and therefore speaks as an outsider, to the official Quebec and Aboriginal leaders, who fully and legitimately represent Québécois and Aboriginal peoples. In 1987 the Assembly of First Nations asserted that the "federal government's relationship is to First Nations as collectivities, not to our citizens as individuals." As Cassidy and Bish note, "from this perspective, Indian people are, first and foremost, citizens in their First Nations. Their primary relationship with the federal government, with Canada, is as part of these First Nations."[25] This approach by status Indians is clearly a legacy of the Department of Indian Affairs' historic policy of viewing citizenship, specifically the franchise, and retention of Indian status as incompatible. Until 1960, enfranchisement meant relinquishment of Indian status. Contemporary Indian attitudes to the franchise, and to the parliamentary representation to which it leads, are still shaped by the recollection of its former use as a coercive instrument of assimilation.

Since the federal government acts on behalf of an older order that still survives, and is based on the coast-to-coast representation of all Canadians as individuals in Parliament, the theory and practice of representation are in disarray. The question of who speaks for whom, and in what capacity, no longer has an accepted answer for Québécois and Aboriginal peoples. Their nationalism has eroded the capacity of the federal Parliament and cabinet to speak for and effectively represent them, and the Canadian component of their civic identity is accordingly diminished and on the defensive. Changes in the relative status of the Canadian and Québécois, or Aboriginal, components of individual civic identity mirror the larger struggle by competing elites to dominate the "voice" of their people.

These realities are sensed but seldom articulated in public. They belong to the category of tacit constitutional silences, the discreet acceptance of contradiction and ambiguity that surfaces in transitional eras. Formally, Parliament based on universal suffrage (for the Commons) and cabinet still occupy the stage, capable in theory of speaking for all Canadians. In reality, the federal Parliament and the community conceptions on which it is based are on trial. Quebec's nationalist elites no longer view theirs as an ordinary province, no longer fully accept Ottawa's role of speaking for all Canadians, including Québécois, and implicitly attribute to that government an identity and a capacity that it lacks – spokesperson for and government of the ROC.

Politically, of course, emasculation of the federal role in Quebec extends the political reach and bargaining power of the provincial government and places Quebec's federal MPs in limbo. Similarly, Aboriginal leaders act on the premise that their peoples are not conventional citizens. The leaders are the vanguard of a new order of government that will diminish the authority of the traditional federal and provincial governments over their peoples. The roles they now assume are anticipatory, not reflective of offices and statuses that now exist. Aboriginal leaders seek to monopolize the voice of their peoples and minimize the capacity of the elected elites of federalism to speak for them.

The cumulative and composite message of Québécois and Aboriginal weakening of Ottawa's capacity to speak authoritatively for either group is to underline a three-nations definition of Canada and to press for redefinition of the federal government as the government of the rest of Canada minus its Aboriginal population. Simultaneously, of course, Aboriginal nationalism denies the capacity of the government of Quebec to treat the Aboriginal nations in its midst as minorities that can be compelled to participate in a Quebec independence they categorically reject. Hence the conflict between Québécois and Aboriginal nationalism is unusually intense, for they may confront each other in a "when the chips are down" scenario.[26]

Implicit recognition of the three national communities emerged from the 1990-91 hearings of the Spicer Commission. The Spicer Report noted that the commissioners had made only limited and ineffectual contact with Francophones in Quebec and more generally with Aboriginal peoples across the country.[27] Consequently, the document became an ROC report, excluding Aboriginal peoples. The commissioners, reflecting their own hearings, noted a developing self-consciousness in the ROC, clearly a by-product of the disappearing evidence of Quebec's positive allegiance to Canada,[28] coupled with the recognition that some "special place"[29] for Aboriginal peoples lies ahead.

ROC nationalism has special characteristics. It has a clear territorial location – Canada outside Quebec. Psychologically, it is an imitative reaction to the Quebec government's attribution of nationhood to its people and, to a lesser extent, to Aboriginal nationalism. Prospectively, it is an anticipatory nationalism getting ready for a future it may reluctantly inherit. Retrospectively, it is a residual nationalism, a second choice that emerges because the Quebec partner no longer appears willing to adhere to the pan-Canadian nationalism that the ROC would prefer to retain. The ROC inchoate nationalism is thus based on a hesitant retreat from a faltering pan-Canadian vision, to whose survival a mix of serious effort, lingering hopes, and nostalgia is still directed. It is a nationalism by default, created on the rebound. However, whether or not Quebec departs, ROC nationalism is here to stay. If Quebec cannot be accommodated within a revised federalism, the rest of Canada will also emerge as one or more independent countries, at which time it will either sport the institutional and constitutional clothing it has inherited or devise arrangements appropriate to its new circumstances.

If Quebec remains, the ROC will still have a distinctive sense of itself, as a counterpart to whatever explicit status Quebec has achieved. The constitutional history of recent decades has driven home the fragility of the bonds between Quebec and the ROC. For the foreseeable future, their cohabitation within the same polity will be perceived as precarious. The presence of a Quebec that remains with unique status will be a daily message that the surviving, formal Canadian unity is calculated, conditional, and reasoned, rather than emotional. Such a Quebec will be a clear reminder that the ROC, too, is a nation in waiting.

The national status and identity of the rest of Canada, however, at least until it inherits a post-secession Canada without Quebec, are ambiguous and uncertain, for the ROC has no corporate existence. It is headless and officially voiceless. The federal government cannot and will not now speak for it, not because the leaders of the two major Canadian parties have leaders from Quebec[30] but because Ottawa's mandate is to govern for all of Canada and to transmit the peoples and territories that it has inherited intact to future generations. The provincial governments cannot speak for the ROC because their mandate is provincial, and each of them speaks only for a territorially delimited segment of the Canadian population. Even an aggregation of the nine provincialisms and two territories does not constitute the ROC.

One of the crucial, overlooked tensions in the present situation, therefore, is the inchoate nature of the ROC. As a future without Quebec is a distinct possibility, the ROC has the same need for self-expression, self-education, and socialization for independence as Quebec has for its possible future outside Canada. Quebec builds on a long history of introspection; the rest of Canada does not. The Francophone Québécois identity has been strengthened by the enduring and ever-renewed self-consciousness of a minority. The ROC identity is shapeless, ambiguous, and devoid of historical roots. Québécois now have a government that reminds them of who they are, and thus of what they might become. The ROC now has no government that addresses it as such. Quebec openly juggles two futures – renewed federalism and independence – through National Assembly committees examining their relative strengths and weaknesses. The ROC, as part of Canada, prepares seriously for only one of the two main futures

– renewed federalism – that await it. The ROC is gravely weakened by its majority control of all governments outside Quebec, the NWT excepted, and its majority share of federal government representation. Structurally, the ROC is weakened, not strengthened, by its control of so many governments.

If Quebec remains in Canada, the rest of Canada, made conscious of its existence by the constitutional perils through which it has lived, will experience a certain lack of identity, ambiguity in its self-perception, and frustration of its political selfhood, for it will have no single lever exclusively available to promote, shape, and then preserve an identity kept indistinct by the absence of supportive cues to give it definition. Unless the accommodation of Quebec is based on a decisive asymmetry, with Quebec wielding powers possessed by no other province, and in which the federal government in most policy areas becomes the instrument of the ROC, the latter people will be frustrated by its elemental inability to act collectively, by the absence of the routine daily reminders that it exists. This absence will be poignantly underlined for the ROC by the high profile of a Quebec government fashioning its people, of Aboriginal governments giving sustenance to aboriginality, and of the province-building activities of the provincial governments in the ROC's midst, and by the memory of a not-too-distant past when it was the governing majority in coast-to-coast Canada.

In the Canadian past, it was Quebec or French Canada that argued for enhanced recognition of dualism in order to strengthen its own status and power against a majoritarian pan-Canadianism at the service of English Canada. For English Canada, in the past, dualism was not a natural inclination born of a need for self-expression but was rather, when recognized, a concession by the numerically strong. At least until the 1960s, however, dualism did not detract from the reality that English Canada could view the central government as an instrument for its national purposes, which were thought of as Canadian purposes. If Quebec remains, at the cost of a gravely weakened centre, dualism in the form of ROC nationalism is likely to become the rhetoric of the numerically strong but institutionally incomplete. Dualism may well become the ideology of the ROC majority seeking equality. The rest of Canada, frustrated by the discrepancy between its numbers and its enfeebled capacity for collective self-expression through government, may not readily adapt to its condition in a constitutional order whose flexibility has been deployed in accommodating Québécois and Aboriginal nationalism.

If the Canada of the future is to be made up of three national communities, Canadians will have to learn to live with fundamentally divergent notions of citizenship. In Charles Taylor's terms, both Quebec's Francophone majority and the Aboriginal peoples are bearers of or possessors of "deep" diversity that goes beyond the shallow "first-level" diversities of multicultural/multiracial Canada.[31] Whether their deep diversity is in fact qualitatively more profound and more integral to their identity than Sikh identity is to Canadian Sikhs is both doubtful and irrelevant. They have more history on their side than later arrivals. They are not newcomers on whom the primary burden of adapting to the host society is placed. More important, their employment of the language of nationalism is considered legitimate, as is their search for enhanced governing powers for their advancement and protection as national minorities in an unsympathetic environment. They are not minorities like the others, which come to a country that is an ongoing concern and that sets the terms for those who are not "first" or "founding" peoples.

It is already evident that the uniform application of the Charter to Quebec and to Aboriginal peoples is challenged,[32] although there is some evidence of support for it among Aboriginal women,[33] and "Inuit are willing to consider the application of the Charter ... to self-government arrangements."[34] The Charter, which has become a symbolic signifier of citizenship for many ROC Canadians, may come to apply fully to only a limited, albeit the largest, component of a reconstituted Canada sensitive to the three national communities in its midst.

A positive response to a three-nation definition of Canada is also likely to challenge the norm of equality of the provinces, which has become practically an icon, especially in western Canada. Although *de jure* equality may be preserved in formal obeisance to the principle, *de facto* inequality is likely to emerge with Quebec assuming more responsibilities than other provincial governments. The dynamism of Quebec's differentiation will be driven by the continuing presence of a strongly nationalist or *indépendantiste* party in an adversarial political system, with parties alternating in office. No other provincial system will have these characteristics.

Although we are only in the early stages of our understanding, it is probable that the self-governing status of Aboriginal peoples will create a third order of government. Tony Hall correctly observes: "It is no longer sufficient to envisage federal-provincial relations as the sole axis of governmental authority in Canadian federalism. Aboriginal-federal relations constitute the hidden axis of our federal system."[35] According to the Penner Report, "Self-government would mean that virtually the entire range of law-making, policy, program delivery, law enforcement and adjudication powers would be available to an Indian First Nation government within its territory."[36] Aboriginal governing powers will almost certainly be constitutionally entrenched, unlike those of municipalities, which are delegated from the provincial governments. Following on the recommendations of the Penner Report directed to status Indians,[37] self-governing Aboriginal peoples will wield a unique mix of jurisdictions, employing some powers that are otherwise federal and others that are otherwise provincial. There will be marked diversity in the powers wielded by individual Aboriginal peoples, varying from near-provincehood in a Nunavut that will emerge when the NWT is geographically split up, to off-reserve Aboriginal agencies administering limited services to Aboriginal peoples scattered across a metropolitan region.

Thus the third order of Aboriginal governments will be unlike the second provincial order in two ways. The powers that such governments wield will transgress the federal-provincial division of powers, and unlike the rough equality of the provinces, various Aboriginal governments will display marked inequalities of jurisdiction. Integration of that third governing order into the constitutional framework will be a demanding process.

Aboriginal peoples will have a different relationship to the traditional federal and provincial orders of government than other Canadians – differences that range from the trivial to the substantial. Aboriginal peoples, therefore, like the Québécois of the future, will not be citizens like the others. The federal and provincial governments will not hold the same significance for them as for ROC Canadians. Their constitutionally entrenched Aboriginal governments, with their unique jurisdictional levers, will be focal points of identity and self-assertion. Such governments will be theirs in a way that can never be true of the federal and provincial governments. Their governments will be to them as Quebec's government already is and will increasingly be to the French-speaking majority of that province.

According to a recent study that pushed Aboriginal self-government to the limit: "Their [Aboriginals'] primary allegiance will be to native communities and governments. Since neither the federal nor provincial government reflects their communities, they will enjoy special, separate rights in all matters where cultural values count. . . . To the extent that they will look to their own governments to make decisions and provide services, aboriginal peoples will have no need to participate in other governments, either by way of voting or running for office."[38]

If the different relationship of Québécois and Aboriginal peoples to the governments of Canadian federalism is reinforced by differential application of the Charter, the norm of a uniform citizenship based on the equality of the provinces and of citizens' Charter rights will no longer hold. Further, at some future breaking point, Quebec's enhanced jurisdiction, in law or in fact, may lead to challenges to the role of MPs and cabinet members from Quebec. It is too easily forgotten that the equality of the provinces is not just a norm of federalism but is simultaneously the essential support for the norm of equal status for MPs. Rough equality of provincial powers is an indirect way of saying that federal jurisdiction applies equally across the country, which, in turn, is the prerequisite for undifferentiated roles for MPs, regardless of their province of origin. Jurisdictional equality of the provinces and the equal capacity of MPs to act in Parliament across the whole range of federal jurisdictions are two sides of the same coin.[39] To offer to all what only Quebec is expected to take may blur the constitutional issue for a transition period, but if the long-run trend is for Quebec to leap ahead of the other provinces in powers and responsibilities, the obfuscation will be seen through and resisted.

The issue of Aboriginal parliamentary representation is also likely to arise, given the premise that Aboriginal governments will handle functions that are dealt with for other Canadians by federal and provincial governments. Somewhat paradoxically, however, the drive to remove Aboriginal peoples, to a greater or lesser degree, from the jurisdiction of federal and provincial legislatures by self-government is accompanied by political pressures to strengthen Aboriginal representation in both the Senate and the House of Commons. If Aboriginal communities come to exercise special, extensive, entrenched powers, the constitutional appropriateness of Aboriginal peoples exercising the same voting rights as other members of the electorate will emerge as an issue. If there is special separate Aboriginal representation in Parliament, the participation of Aboriginal members in discussions and voting over laws that do not apply to their people will have to be reconsidered.

At some upper limit, the extent of the powers wielded by Aboriginal governments will erode the legitimacy of Aboriginal senators or MPs playing vigorous parliamentary roles concerning policies that do not apply to their voters. In response, it can be argued that an apparently privileged role for Aboriginal peoples and their representatives is simply a logical and just recognition of "their special constitutional position as peoples within the Canadian federation."[40] An apparent anomaly can thus be made legitimate by an encompassing historic exceptionalism. Alternatively, Aboriginal parliamentarians could be viewed as akin to ambassadors who participate and vote only on explicitly Aboriginal matters. Such a solution would stress their separate status in Canada at the expense of attributes shared with other Canadian citizens.[41]

Significant readjustments of the constitutional order to accommodate Aboriginal peoples and Quebec nationalism go beyond rearranging the powers of governments to the creation of differentiated categories of citizens, possibly to differential application of the Charter and, depending on the extent of special jurisdictional powers, the emergence of differential status for MPs.

The stability of such a constitutional order will be maintained only by unceasing statecraft and self-restraint; it will not be held together by rights and civic identities held in common; the social obligations of responsibility for the disadvantaged will presumably weaken toward those who are outside the nation of one's primary membership. Such wide divergences among the citizenry will displace the sense of sharing and caring for one's own that is generated by a relatively uniform citizenship and replace it with the much less compelling requirement, outside of one's own group, of caring for and sharing with an ambiguous category halfway between fellow-citizens and strangers.

The voyage on which we are embarked is designed to make the constitutional order more sensitive to our coexisting nationalisms. It will necessarily make us less sensitive to other values linked to sharing common citizenship. This may be most serious for Aboriginal peoples. Creation of a unique constitutional status that distances them unduly from majority conceptions of citizenship may conflict with their need for extensive financial resources from federal and provincial governments.[42]

Since the present disharmonious coexistence of an historic, now decentralized, federalism with the three nationalisms now struggling, if not warring, in its midst was not predicted by even the most learned of our predecessors, modesty cautions against the soothsayer role. The likelihood, however – assuming that a recognizable version of Canada survives – is that the future challenge to Canadianism will come not from centrifugal provincialism alone, but from its interaction with the powerful forces of internal nationalisms. Within that latter development, the least developed nationalism of all, that of the ROC, retreating from a no-longer viable version of pan-Canadian nationalism that was its first choice, will be pushed by nationalist contagion toward a more coherent sense of itself. Since, numerically, the ROC will possess the biggest battalions, the nature of its future transformation is one of the most crucial and unpredictable variables in Canada's constitutional evolution. Its present weakness reflects its residual status – an unsought condition thrust upon it by the more aggressive nationalism of Quebec and Aboriginal peoples. For reasons already noted, however, its incoherence will not be easily overcome. It may become a fragmented, lurching, unpredictable giant, the raw material for ROC nationalist leaders preaching, to borrow a phrase, "Equality or Independence."

## The New Diversity and Citizenship

The nationalisms of Quebec, Aboriginal peoples, and the ROC are not the only contemporary challenges to the idea of a single standard of citizenship.[43] Another comes from the political articulation of various social, ethnic, and gender diversities of modern society. While the latter do not threaten the survival of the constitutional order, they do challenge the norms of a universal, common citizenship. This is especially evident with respect to the theory and practice of representation and makes increasingly difficult the task of the state, via the politician, of representing, accommodating, and transcending the diversities of Canadian society.

This difficulty reflects the convergence of three phenomena. (1) The ethnic, social, and cultural diversity of Canadian society is increasing. (2) These diversities, based on gender, ethnicity, lifestyle, and so on are now politicized and indeed, in some cases, constitutionalized. (3) The politicized identities and group self-consciousness building on these diversities support the assertion that X cannot represent Y, if X does not share/possess the characteristics that Y considers essential to his/her identity and as necessary for the vigorous pursuit of Y's political goals.

The perceived inability of X may be attributed either to lack of empathy, derived from an absence of essential shared characteristics that limits understanding, or to a deficiency of trust that leads Y to believe that X, not being part of the Y group, will be ready to sacrifice the interests of Y more casually than Y would prefer.

The diversification of Canadian society is most dramatically evident in terms of race and ethnicity. Changes in the source countries of immigrants are pushing Canada in a multicultural and multiracial direction. The population of British and French background – the original European founding peoples – continues to decline in percentage terms, as does the population of European background in general. The British component, which was about 60 per cent at Confederation, fell below 50 per cent in 1940 and will soon be below 40 per cent. The segment of French origin fell below 30 per cent in the early 1960s and is now nearing 25 per cent. By 1981, the "other" had passed the French, and in the 1986 census it amounted to 38 per cent of the Canadian total. The "other" component is growing rapidly and by the turn of the century is projected to surpass 40 per cent. The great metropolitan centres of Vancouver, Toronto, and Montreal are already, in David Cameron's evocative phrase, "riotously multicultural." [44] Within the ethnocultural category, the multiracial component – the visible minorities – constitutes a growing percentage. Whereas formerly almost 80 per cent of immigrants came from countries with a European heritage, now almost three-quarters come from Asia, Africa, and the Caribbean. Almost half of Canadian immigrants now come from Asia. Visible minorities, exclusive of Aboriginal peoples, are expected to reach more than 10 per cent of the total by the end of the century, almost double their percentage in 1986. Nearly half of Vancouver school children have English as a second language, and they are predominantly of Asian background.

This ethnic transformation of Canada will almost certainly continue. Our immigration needs cannot be met from the traditional suppliers of our first century. Ethnic and racial minorities who are already here are advocates for those they left behind. Given the ethnic composition and distribution of the world's people and the exceptionally privileged position of the relatively small Canadian population, neither immigration nor border controls can prevent an influx, legal and illegal, of new arrivals that will add to Canada's ethnic heterogeneity.

The ethnic diversification has led to new labels – third force, visible minorities, allophones, multicultural peoples, and others – in the search for identities outside the French-English-Aboriginal circle of "founding" or "first peoples." Thus Canadians are grappling with what L.S. Lustgarten, referring to the changed ethnic demography of Western nations, described as "irreversible . . . [and] the dominant characteristic of twentieth century states: ethnic pluralism within the framework of a united polity."[45]

The articulation of diversity does not stop at the boundaries of race and ethnicity. It extends to women, the disabled, gays and lesbians, proponents of alternative lifestyles, and others. In each case, their articulation challenged historic assumptions of what was acceptable, normal behaviour, and of who counted and why. In some cases, their emergence is accompanied by a sense of uniqueness and difference and by challenges to previously dominant ways of viewing the world. Thus, according to Jill Vickers, feminist scholarship has recently demonstrated "that knowledge, which is apparently unisex, neutral and universal, is in fact biased by the point of view of the knowledge creator . . . few of us doubt that 'knowledge' about most human endeavours has been biased by the race, sex, and class of the dominant knowledge makers, not to mention their sexual orientation, their location in the northern hemisphere and other elements of their historical locatedness."[46]

In general, these groups have a sense of being marginal, of having been historically maltreated, or of having experienced wounding discrimination. They nurse a sense of grievance – their political language is replete with such phrases as "exploited," "overlooked," "left out," "dominated," "abused," "second class," and other negative rubrics used to describe their past experience. Thus Monture and Turpel note that it is impossible to threaten Aboriginal people who "do not have anything to lose anymore."[47] Ovide Mercredi, national chief of the Assembly of First Nations, recently attacked the distorted view of Canada "as only consisting of French and English peoples," and he asserted that Aboriginal languages, cultures, governments, and spirituality are "excluded by the Canadian constitution" and "continue to be despised and rejected," so that Aboriginal peoples are "viewed as strangers in our own land."[48] Aboriginal and other marginalized groups speak the language of minorities, of those whose sense of status and recognition is precarious, who have been taught by history to be watchful lest their concerns be sacrificed by indifferent majorities.

Their suspicions are grounded in contemporary realities and historic memories. When they look at the contemporary state they do not see themselves proportionately represented. When women, for example, look at the gender distribution of political power within political parties they see the confirmation of Putnam's "law of increasing disproportion" – that is, "the higher one goes in party elites, the fewer women are to be found."[49] In 1984, 9.6 per cent of MPs were women; in 1982 only 6.2 per cent of the members of provincial legislatures were women.[50] The number of women legislators increased to 13.2 per cent for the House of Commons in 1988 and to 13.9 per cent in provincial and territorial legislatures by 1989.[51] Women and others remember that they were not among the early recipients of the franchise – women in Quebec not receiving the provincial vote until 1940, and status Indians not receiving the federal vote until 1960. The recency of their acquisition of full citizenship status attests to the pejorative view of their civic capacities only a few decades ago. As Boyle notes, women's political history is different from that of men; they lack a long tradition of political activity: "In fact, their tradition is marked by the absence of political role models and by opposition to their efforts at emancipation."[52]

Thus the specific constitutional past of yesterday's constitutional outsiders is not of colony to nation but of historic events particular to themselves, a set of living memories that conditions their interactions with the state today. The 1929 *Persons* case occupies a prominent place in the feminist historical past and is the occasion for an annual commemorative breakfast organized by LEAF (Women's Legal Education and Action Fund). The exemption of section 28 of the Charter from the override is recalled with pride as a hard-won achievement by the women's movement.

Every ethnic association that appeared before the Joint Senate and House of Commons Committee on the Constitution of 1980-81 "began with a recitation of their members' arrival in Canada, their contribution to the development of the nation, and the trials and tribulations they endured along the way . . . . In every tale . . . there are epic heroes, early leaders of settler communities who saved their people from near catastrophe at the hands of ruthless villains – usually bigoted 'WASPs' who wanted to preserve the British character of Canada from the onslaught of foreign immigration."[53]

For Aboriginal peoples, the Royal Proclamation of 1763 far surpasses the Constitution Act of 1867 as a statement of their constitutional significance. In a recent dialogue, Turpel and Monture respectively described 1867 as "a date which I hate to use" and said that "Canada's birth is not something I celebrate."[54] For Métis, inclusion in the Constitution Act of 1982 is a signal achievement – a lever of immense potential that will be wielded to enhance access to entitlements now normally restricted to status Indians. Particular ethnic groups recall when they got the vote, how long they were deprived of it, and other indicators of citizenship deprivation. For decades, the Franco-Ontarian sense of minority status and unjust treatment was nourished by the memory of the attack on French-language schooling embodied in the infamous Regulation 17 of 1912.

The constitutional history of some groups, especially visible minorities, focuses on changes in immigration law – punctuated by moves from stigmatic exclusion to universalism. Particular communities, or at least custodians of official memories, keep alive past instances of maltreatment for which contemporary redress and apology are sought and, with partial success, gained – Japanese Canadians and relocation and internment, Chinese Canadians and the head tax, and the internment of Ukrainian and Italian Canadians in the First and Second

World Wars, respectively. These histories are stimulated by the overall salience of ethnicity, by a contagion effect, by their utility as tools of ethnic mobilization, and, of course, by the historical evidence.

The Canadian state of the 1990s governs a variegated assemblage of peoples who do not share a common past and whose historical memories are instruments of group affirmation and differentiation. *Je me souviens* is a motto for more than Francophone Québécois, and functional equivalents of the conquest are widespread.

Today's politicization of diversity is broadly based. It draws sustenance from basic changes in Western culture. The feminist movement, the aspirations of indigenous peoples, and the demands of gays and lesbians for acceptance of their preferred sexual practices and family patterns, for example, all have an international dimension. They are not ephemeral local phenomena, and they express themselves in many arenas. In universities, black studies, Native studies, women's studies, and ethnic studies, with professors normally if not exclusively drawn from the group concerned, struggle to give recognition and voice to identities and experiences that it is claimed were overlooked when their representation was in the hands of outsiders. The connection of these phenomena with citizenship in Canada may not be immediately apparent, but they are integrally linked to political assertions that query the legitimacy, capacity, or propriety of a "non-A" to speak for, give voice to, or represent an "A." As a consequence, the nature of citizenship and representation is no longer straightforward in heterogeneous societies where personal civic identity is informed by patterned differences in assumptions, memories, and goals.

A recent paper by Iris Young severely and lucidly criticizes the ideal of a universal citizenship on the ground that different social groups with different life experiences necessarily bring different needs and perceptions to the analysis and advocacy of public policy.[55] Young's paper helps us to appreciate the profound diversity of modern society, with the concomitant variety of world views in the electorate, and she concludes that citizenship is or should be a many-splendoured thing – a status that does not hold everyone to precisely the same civic rights and duties.

Pressure for recognition of diversity contributes to the enhanced symbolic role of the constitution. It has become the vehicle that confirms (or not) one's acceptance by society and the relative status enjoyed by particular groups vis-à-vis others. The written constitution is no longer only or primarily a functional instrument for the management of federalism but also a powerful symbolic statement of inclusion or exclusion. Hence constitutional battles are now fought over status, and the language of constitutional politics is replete with emotionally powerful words – shame, dignity, honour, and so on. Historic offices of high symbolic value – most prominently governors general and lieutenant-governors – are now employed to remind Canadians of, and accord public recognition to, diversities of sex, ethnicity, and aboriginality that had not previously been represented in such exalted offices of state.

A corollary of the view that modern society is more like a television set with many channels than a contest to determine whose voice will triumph and silence the losers is the pressure to diversify the representational basis of political authority. Bureaucratically, the contemporary Canadian state is honey-combed with particularistic portfolios and commissions devoted to official-language minorities, the disabled, the young, the old, ethnic groups, women, Aboriginal peoples, and so on. Police forces across the country, especially in metropolitan centres, find their effectiveness and legitimacy challenged if their minority representation is inadequate. The insensitivity of legislatures is attributed to their lack of representativeness, leading to proposals for special guaranteed Aboriginal representation in the Senate and the House of Commons and for electoral systems that will produce roughly proportionate male and female representation.[56] This latter goal explains the tendency for contemporary feminist scholars in Canada to advocate proportional representation or dual-member constituencies, because of their capacity to enhance women's representation.

A recent advocate of special Aboriginal electoral districts described Parliament as "the exclusive domain of the settlers, a reflection no doubt, of the fact that the electoral system was designed by settlers, for settlers, and historically developed to exclude aboriginal peoples."[57] Aboriginal peoples are seriously underrepresented, with the 900,000 Aboriginal people south of the sixtieth parallel having only one MP of Aboriginal descent to represent them. Accordingly, "Aboriginal people question the legitimacy of the electoral system and the capacity of Parliament to deal effectively with Aboriginal issues."[58] A similar argument was used by Christine Boyle, who concluded that the existing electoral system "developed by men for use by men" grossly underrepresented women. She recommended "a form of benign segregation [some form of separate representation of women], at least on a temporary basis, in order to ensure representation of women by women and, I hope, in the interests of women."[59]

Courts are criticized for not proportionately representing minorities in their ranks, which allegedly results in limited empathy for or understanding of the concerns of the underrepresented. Hence the steady pressure from feminist groups for more women on the Supreme Court and from ethnic organizations for judges outside the French-English "founding" stock.[60] Growing pressures for a separate system of justice for Aboriginal peoples draw on the analogous assumption that cultural differences between Aboriginals and whites generate insensitivity, misunderstandings, and injustice, when those who hold judicial office are culturally different from those on the receiving end.

Public hearings on the Meech Lake Accord provided graphic evidence of distrust toward elites that lacked the appropriate ascriptive or acquired characteristics. Presentations by a host of groups defined by gender, ethnicity, race, disability, and indigenousness routinely and categorically denied that "eleven white able-bodied male" first ministers could or would represent the group's interests when they negotiated constitutional changes among themselves.

With suitable modifications to their own situation, most of the Meech Lake critics would agree with George Erasmus, then national chief of the Assembly of First Nations, who strongly repudiated the assertion that Aboriginal peoples were appropriately represented by the first ministers that Aboriginal voters had helped to elect. "This bland assertion that First Nations and their governments are represented by non-aboriginal politicians who have no interest, demonstrated or latent, in advocating our rights is bogus and is without foundation in fact or action."[61] Erasmus's thesis reflected the pervasive Aboriginal belief that the existing system essentially represents non-Aboriginal interests, either because Aboriginal peoples are too scattered and numerically weak to have electoral influence or because only direct, unmediated Aboriginal representation can effectively and sensitively represent Aboriginal interests. The suggestion that Aboriginal peoples should trust elected white leaders was scorned by two Aboriginal law professors: "Trust us: I mean what do you think we are, forgetful or just plain crazy?"[62]

Many social groups support the proposition that dissimilar others cannot speak for or represent them, that their concerns will be overlooked or given scant consideration if one of their own is not at the bargaining table or in the decision-making body. The extent of this phenomenon was lucidly revealed in the reactions of the Métis National Council (MNC) to the federal proposals in *Shaping Canada's Future Together: Proposals*. The MNC requested guaranteed participation in "all constitutional matters," guaranteed seats in the Senate and the House of Commons, appointment of a Métis to the Supreme Court "at the government's earliest opportunity," a requirement of consent by Métis to all future amendments affecting them, and specific representation in the proposed Council of the Federation.[63]

The pressures lying behind demands for more mirror-like practices of representation lead to more fundamental structural demands; hence advocacy by the elites of New Brunswick Acadians, Francophones outside Quebec, Indians, Inuit, and Métis for direct control over institutions explicitly sensitive to the groups concerned, and Quebec Anglophones' objective of retaining control of their own institutions and keeping them viable. Minorities use voice to demand a form of opting-out, or institutional exit, in a complex version of the voice-and-exit strategies brilliantly described by Hirschman.[64]

The impact of diversity on public life acquired a special dimension in Canada because it coincided with a constitutional crisis and the federal government's support for a Charter of Rights as one of the responses to the crisis. As a result, various groups became attached to the Charter at a time when Ottawa was seeking allies. The Charter's anti-majoritarian thrust added to its attractiveness for groups that had their own apprehensions about majority rule.

The Charter is more than an instrument that hands out abstract rights equally to all Canadians and is indifferent to their various statuses defined by gender, ethnicity, official-language status, and the presence or absence of disabilities. In fact, it specifically mobilizes Canadians in terms of these categories. It encourages Canadians to think of themselves for constitutional purposes as women, as official-language minorities, as disabled, or as ethnocultural Canadians. Particular Charter clauses and the high profile of the constitution in recent years engender constitutional discourses organized around gender, ethnicity, indigenousness, and so on, which join the historic constitutional languages of federalism and parliamentary government. Organizations, often publicly funded, have developed to enhance the potency of Charter clauses relevant to their clientele. These clauses generate constitutional identities, formerly lacking, in those to whom they apply. The elites of the social categories concerned may be said to occupy constitutional niches, or to possess constitutional clauses. They also think of themselves as constitutional somebodies. The public profile of the social categories accorded such recognition is markedly enhanced, as is their sense of distinctiveness.

Much public discussion of particular Charter clauses is dominated by the clientele with a strong interest in an expansive definition of their clause – for example, women and section 28, non-founding peoples and section 27, Aboriginals and section 25 of the Charter and section 35 of the Constitution Act, and section 15 and the groups mentioned in its equality provisions. This clustering of attention driven by self-interest largely reflects the normal gravitational pull that draws thirsty people to oases. In addition, however, there is a tendency to treat those who do not belong to the clientele group concerned as intruders or outsiders illegitimately entering into a discursive terrain that belongs to "insiders." This control by insiders and the cultural restraints inhibiting discussion by outsiders suggest that only those directly affected can understand or legitimately comment on a constitutional clause[65] – an assumption that lay behind much of the criticism of the Meech Lake process.

Charter clauses referring to "everyone," "every citizen," or "any person" are less likely to elicit political mobilization. From this perspective, the constitutional politics of the Charter responds to and mirrors the fragmentation of society. The Charter's diffuse contribution to a more democratic constitutional culture is supplemented, and perhaps undermined, by its stimulus to constitutional fragmentation. The Charter is a political battleground between supporters of competing clauses and between rival claimants to being the leading advocate for a particular clause.

The politicization and constitutionalization of diversity redefine groups previously excluded from the franchise on grounds of their difference – construed in the past as evidence of civic incapacity – as having unique voices, or vantage points, that justify their specific and explicit inclusion in public forums. The formerly excluded see their task as that of challenging a uniformity that is viewed as a mask for the hegemony variously of males, of whites, of non-Aboriginals, of the historically privileged, or of those who do not live with disabilities.

Our steady progress toward a universal franchise has led to a more heterogeneous electorate, more self-conscious of its own internal differences than was true of earlier, more exclusive electorates. Indeed, earlier franchise restrictions on Indians, Asians, and women produced a relatively homogeneous electorate and a narrow range of views to be considered in policy determination, at the price of excluding the carriers of difference. Homogeneity was a code word for coercion and marginalization. As the formerly marginalized emerge from what Chantal Maillé, writing of women, describes as "a long culture of exclusion from politics," [66] it is not surprising that they do not leave behind the sense of difference forged when they were left out as they enter political arenas shaped for less variegated electorates.

This politicized heterogeneity may pose problems for a representative system that presupposes that one representative can speak for the many who are different. The emergence from the audience or the background of the previously silenced or acquiescent female majority and of historical minorities, supplemented and invigorated by the ethnic diversity fostered by contemporary immigration patterns, alters the relationship between those who are represented and their representatives. It requires us to rethink citizenship.

## Conclusion

The past is another country. Yesterday's constitution was able to contain the less aggressive nationalism of Quebec by federalism and various accommodative practices at the centre. This is no longer so. Some significant recognition of distinctiveness, of special status, so that Quebec and its people will not be precise counterparts of other provinces and provincial populations appears unavoidable.

The indigenous peoples were relegated to the backwaters of Canadian life for most of our first century. The Inuit (then Eskimo) were isolated and ignored in northern Canada; Indians were mostly out of sight on reserves; and the Métis were technically Canadians like any others. The concepts of wardship, vanishing races, and assimilation conjured up various prospects for indigenous peoples but no recognition that they might develop unique constitutional voices in the service of distinctive constitutional futures. The rubric "Aboriginal" did not exist to generate shared constitutional concerns among indigenous peoples. Aboriginal peoples are no longer in the background. They do not aspire to be citizens like the rest of us. Their distrust of the federal and provincial governments is so high, and their sense of difference so profound, that they seek not to be accepted by the majority as individuals on the former's terms but to achieve institutional and constitutional recognition of a special status that will contribute to their ongoing survival as distinct nations.

The nationalism of Quebec and of the Aboriginal peoples induces the ROC to think of itself, reluctantly, as some kind of national people, if only because to be both a majority and defined as residual, as rest-of-Canada, is psychologically debilitating.

The struggles today of these three national communities undermine the pan-Canadianism that Anglophone Canadians, at least, thought of as a transcending identity. The norm of equal citizens' rights, crystallized by the Charter, and equality of provinces, as embodied in the amending formula and in the rhetoric of provincial ideologists of a federalism of principle, are both challenged by Aboriginal and Québécois nationalism. Differential support for the Charter from the three national communities exerts pressure for its differential application or, at a minimum, for a differential in the willingness to override some of its clauses – presupposing that the (or perhaps a special) override is available to Aboriginal governments. Both the special status sought by Quebec and the third order of government sought by Aboriginal peoples are outside the norms of basic, everyday provincehood. Even if a partial accommodation of Quebec takes place that appears, by obfuscating constitutional mechanisms, to preserve the illusion of provincial equality, the *de facto* reality of future decades will not be a Quebec indistinguishable from the other provinces.

This of course, may not be enough, and two or more successor Canadas may emerge by accident or design. Further, special status for Quebec, if it involves reduced roles for Quebec's MPs, reduced application of the Charter in Quebec, jurisdictions wielded by Quebec's government that are unavailable to the other provinces, and an asymmetrical citizenship, may be unstable and may not survive.

An additional fragmentation of citizens' consciousness occurs along the lines of such characteristics as sex, ethnicity, lifestyles, and disabilities. The modernity that was to make us one has led instead to an explosion of particularistic self-consciousness that denies, in Iris Young's words, the idea of a universal citizenship. [67] The mosaic label applies not only to our ethnicity but also to other diversities whose spokespersons insist on recognition. Many of the latter represent the formerly excluded – those who were late in getting the vote or who in other ways felt mistreated or defined as second-class citizens. These historical memories contribute to distrust, suspicion, and reluctance to have one's fate determined by others devoid of the appropriate signifying characteristics. In a word, we lack fraternity and sorority within each of the three nations as well as across them.

We also, as Michael Bliss recently observed, no longer have a unified vision of Canadian history with which citizens can identify. Historians, at least in English Canada, have become specialists in minutiae, with Donald Creighton's grand if somewhat arrogant visions replaced by studies of "the history of housemaid's knee in Belleville in the 1890s." [68]

We are not alone in our fragmentation and wonderment about whether the centre can hold, or if we are still capable, occasionally at least, of thinking and acting as a single people. Hugh Heclo portrays the American political system as "much more open, fragmented, self-critical, nondeferential, and fluid in its attachments" than formerly. He describes a factionalism that "has shaped itself around a governmental presence that is doing so much more in so many different areas of life. . . . Factions . . . now come to life across a huge spectrum of government activities touching almost everything about ourselves as a society." [69]

The crucial Canadian difference is that our most serious fragmentation is structured around competing nationalisms and is also entangled with the constitution. Hence our peril and our challenge are much greater.

This, then, is the fragmented human base we have to work with – the raw material of the variegated citizenship of the future that we must both respond to and then employ in the citizenship tasks of the twenty-first century. If we survive as one country, we must accommodate diversity without so destroying our interconnectedness that we shall be incapable of undertaking future civic tasks together. Since the latter will be more demanding than yesterday's challenges, we must hope that a citizen body lacking the bond of a standardized citizenship but nevertheless participating in common civic endeavours is not an oxymoron.

Chapter Seven

# The Case for Charter-Federalism

The ideal post-Meech constitutional package would both get the agreement of the relevant actors, including the public, whose support is necessary for implementation and legitimacy, and respond effectively to deep historical forces whose long-run accommodation is required if we are to get respite from our constitutional agonies. This article is devoted to the latter, particularly to the need for a constitutional *rapprochement* between federalism's geographic emphasis on community and alternative spatially diffuse civic identities, partly stimulated by the Canadian Charter of Rights and Freedoms. While the subject matter dictates its historical approach, this essay also reflects my apprehension that constitution-makers seeking agreement at one minute to midnight may privilege the momentary and the trivial and undervalue more enduring forces.

Government and citizens often see the constitution through different lenses. The immensely popular 1982 Charter was opposed by eight provincial governments. The Meech Lake Accord, repudiated by English-Canadian public opinion, initially had unanimous government support.

*This* constitutional divergence may lack the drama of the Quebec/rest-of-Canada confrontation, but its transcending is essential to future constitutional harmony. It reflects the tension between federalism's emphasis on territorial community and alternative transprovincial identities. Tension alleviation requires a recognition that no winner is possible in this unending game.

The goal is a creative constitutional symbiosis among the various identities that we all carry. Constitutional success will be measured by how we accommodate the historic territorial realities of federalism, reinforced by an emerging Aboriginal third order of government, and the contemporary reality of constitutionally recognized, transregional identities given sustenance by the Charter. For various reasons, the historic roots of these tensions have received inadequate attention. Even less has been devoted to their possible complementarity, the subject of this paper's closing paragraphs.

## Federalism and Territory

For decades, Canadians have been seeking a more sensitive constitutional expression for the regional dimension of their existence, particularly Quebec nationalism and other complementary centrifugal provincial pressures. The provincialism of the defeated Meech Lake Accord and the dynamics of the current constitutional round confirm that federalism and territorialism are still central to our identity. The 1982 amending formula, based on the assumed primacy of governments as constitutional players – constrained only by the requirement of legislative ratification – strengthens federalism's input at the constitutional bargaining table. Outside Quebec, the hitherto rare idea that federalism should reflect principles, such as provincial equality, rather than being viewed pragmatically further supports federalist definitions of who we are.

Territorialism is strengthened by Aboriginal self-government demands. Many Aboriginal peoples do not have discrete land bases. However, over 600 Indian bands do; the Inuit will be a majority when Nunavut achieves quasi-provincial status; future land claims settlements will give varying degrees of jurisdictional powers over defined land areas to Aboriginal peoples; some land may be allocated to the Métis. Thus Canada's future internal political borders will become much more complex. The third order of entrenched Aboriginal government will display vast jurisdictional asymmetries ranging from limited functions handled by urban Aboriginal peoples to possibly extensive powers for a handful of larger, wealthier Indian nations. As extensive financial assistance to Aboriginal governments will be required to alleviate the present anomic malaise of their peoples, the territorial complexities of governing Canada can only increase.

Canadians are heading toward a triple-decker federalism in which the different tiers will interact in various ways with ethnicity. Thus the third order of Aboriginal self-government is a response to indigenous ethnicity; an indigenous Inuit quasi-province is also imminent; and, of course, Quebec will have some enhanced recognition based on its distinct society. In some cases, the interaction between these tiers and ethnic pluralism will be staggeringly complex. For example, the citizens of Aboriginal communities will simultaneously be members of a provincial and the Canadian community. Their triple constitutional identities will vary from one Aboriginal community to another, depending on the particular mix of federal and provincial jurisdictions wielded by each Aboriginal government. Thus Aboriginal citizenship will not be uniform but will vary in accordance with the different jurisdictional packages wielded by hundreds of Aboriginal governments. While all self-governing Aboriginal peoples will have a unique relationship to either or both of their federal and provincial governments, the nature and degree of their difference from their non-Aboriginal citizen neighbours will display immense variations.

## The Proliferation of Non-territorial Identities

Paradoxically, the escalating constitutional significance of territory coincides with a parallel emergence, mobilization, and constitutionalization of non-territorial identities. The sources of this transformation, too complex to be more than noted here, include the universalization of the franchise as the formerly excluded women, various ethnic minorities, and status Indians were belatedly given the vote. As the social base of the constitution became more heterogeneous, provincial definitions of community were weakened. In the last forty years, an expanding recognition of our multicultural, multiracial character has emerged to supplement the historic stress on the two founding nations (French and English) view of Canada that reinforced federalism. Diefenbaker's prairie-based sensitivity to ethnic pluralism led him to attempt to transcend ethnic diversity by emphasizing the unhyphenated Canadian; the successful derailment of the terms of reference of the Royal Commission on Bilingualism and Biculturalism in fact led to a push toward multi- rather than biculturalism and, eventually, to the official policy of multiculturalism; the incorporation of s. 27 in the 1982 Charter recognized Canadians' multicultural heritage; and in 1984 the House of Commons Committee on Visible Minorities was created. All of these reveal the accelerated policy and constitutional attention devoted to those outside the charmed circle of European founding peoples.

## Rights and Federalism

Simultaneously, Canadians' definitions of themselves as a people have progressively incorporated a constitutional rhetoric of rights. Stimulated by the post-World War Two emerging international rights culture, symbolized by the 1948 United Nations Universal Declaration of Human Rights, Canada moved at the national level from the weak 1960 Diefenbaker Bill of Rights to the 1982 Charter, which profoundly changed the citizenry's relation to the constitutional order.

The blending of the Charter's transprovincial rights with the territorial communities of federalism is an unfinished task. From one perspective, their constitutional and societal coexistence can be viewed as a contradiction, as an incoherence, or as a damaging rivalry between the territorial identities of federalism and the competing non-territorial identities of the Charter. From a more positive perspective, the constitutional coexistence of overlapping lines of cleavage is simply an appropriate recognition of the multiple identities of a heterogeneous modern people. We live and think of ourselves in terms of spatial communities, but we are also men or women, disabled or not, perhaps a member of one or other official-language minority community, and a strong or lax identifier with one of the 100 plus national ethnic origin communities resident in Canada.

Rights-linked identities, applied to women and the disabled, for example, do not fit easily into the territorial concepts natural to federalism. Obviously, the pan-Canadian application of rights to citizen-government relations in the provinces limits the provincial diversity encouraged by provincial governments. From a provincial perspective, the Charter is an intruder injecting a Canadian dimension into the heart of provincialism. Although the pan-Canadian rights dimension overlaps Ottawa's jurisdiction, it does not coincide with it. The pan-Canadianism of rights applies to both orders of governments. Jurisdictional Canadianism and rights Canadianism, therefore, are not the same. The 1960 Diefenbaker Bill of Rights was relatively ineffectual because provincial government resistance restricted its application to federal government jurisdiction, a weakness compounded by the inclusion of a notwithstanding clause and the Bill's non-entrenched status. The accommodation between rights and federalism was fought out again in the 1980-82 struggle that produced the Charter. Eight provincial governments' opposition to the Charter was countered by the widespread support for a strong Charter from organizations speaking for women, for ethnic minorities, for the disabled, and for others for whom federalism and parliamentary supremacy were not sacred icons but arrangements that should give ground before the advance of rights. The federalism-Charter accommodation was reflected in the notwithstanding and reasonable limits clauses, both of which supported limited versions of the parliamentary supremacy that the Charter challenged.

## Federalism Is Not Enough

The arrival of an entrenched Charter transformed the historic debate about the Supreme Court's composition, which had hitherto focused on federalist criteria based on the Court's role as umpire of federalism. The Charter and Aboriginal constitutional clauses elicited a broader concern that the Court's composition should not only be sensitive to provinces, but also to women, to ethnocultural communities, to Aboriginal peoples, and to others who view the constitution through the focus of the Charter and Aboriginal rights. For the new constitutional players, sensitivity to federalism concerns is an insufficient criterion for Supreme Court (and other judicial) appointments.

Contemporary views about Senate reform also reflect the reduced priority attached to territory. Historically, criticism of the Senate focused on its ineffective representation and protection of provincial concerns. Indeed, the contemporary sponsors of a triple-E Senate assumed that to describe the Senate as an instrument of federalism verged on being a tautology that required no justification. However, at the federal Conference on Institutional Reform held in Calgary last spring, an exclusively territorial definition of the Senate was battered by demands from women's organizations, the disabled, and other marginalized groups arguing that its composition should reflect various non-territorial interests that are underrepresented in existing legislatures.

Here again, as for the Supreme Court, exclusively federalist criteria for representation are unacceptable to the new constitutional players. The latter's support for a proportional representation system that will give voice to the hitherto underrepresented has led to a little-noticed incoherence in the multiple demands now made for a reformed Senate. When Senate representation is argued in terms of non-territorial interests, the federalist rationale for equality of provincial representation disappears. If the Senate is to represent women, there is no reason why a representative of women's concerns from Ontario should require seventy times as much voter support as a like representative from P.E.I.

The amending formula in the 1982 Constitution Act is also affected by the relative decline in the salience of federalism. Drafted by provincial governments (the "Gang of Eight") for (especially provincial) governments, it assumed government domination of the formal amending process. Perhaps blinded by their opposition to the Charter, the Gang of Eight was oblivious to its potential impact on the country's constitutional culture. Hence the formal requirements of their amending formula were appropriate to the constitutional world they were leaving behind. When the country's first ministers employed the formula as literally as possible in an attempted executive federalism coup to drive through the Meech Lake Accord, they produced a procedural fiasco that left executive federalism – at least as far as constitutional matters are concerned – in ruins. The new non-governmental constitutional players, resentful of the attempt to relegate them to the audience, successfully orchestrated the vitriolic criticisms of the elitism of the Meech Lake process. The now widespread view that the constitution is not just a concern for politicians adjusting the instrumentalities of federalism, but also for the citizenry, reflects the transformative impact of the Charter on the Canadian sense of citizenship.

Thus the need to find a fruitful accommodation between the Charter and what had been thought of as instrumentalities of federalism is a major problem. The search for accommodation applies to the Charter itself; it is the central issue informing debates about the notwithstanding, reasonable limits, and distinct society clauses. The contemporary debate about the role and composition of the Supreme Court focuses on the relative judicial salience of federalism and the Charter. The Charter and Aboriginal constitutional concerns have undermined the legitimacy of government domination of the amending process by executive federalism. The constitutional identities triggered by the Charter have transformed the debate about Senate representation.

In Meech Lake, the Quebec government sought to soften the Charter's impact by filtering it through the interpretive lens of the distinct society clause. The Quebec/Charter debate is replayed in the debates about Aboriginal self-government, with the Native Women's Association strongly supporting the Charter's application to self-governing Aboriginal communities, against the Charter opposition of the male-dominated Assembly of First Nations. Both in Quebec and in Aboriginal communities, the strongest Charter support comes from groups fearful of majoritarianism – Anglophones and allophones in Quebec, and Native women who lack community influence proportionate to their numbers. Individuals and groups who doubt their political power in Aboriginal and provincial communities are prone to see the Charter and the rights it protects as a welcome Canadian opt-out against majoritarian community coercion.

## Charter-Federalism

Even a superficial analysis of our recent constitutional history confirms that federalism by itself cannot accommodate the multiple Canadian conceptions of community and identity. Canadian federalism is appropriately lauded for its capacity to alleviate ethnic tensions by reducing the points of contact, and hence of necessary agreement, between the territorially concentrated French-speaking majority and the country-wide English-speaking majority. While this contribution of federalism remains vital, the question of the appropriate relationship between the constitutional order and ethnicity now extends to the dramatic increase in Canada's ethnic and racial heterogeneity. Unlike Quebec's Francophone majority and some of the Aboriginal peoples, the rapidly growing, territorially dispersed ethnic minority communities cannot find constitutional salvation in self-government. According to a recent projection, by the turn of the century Metropolitan Toronto will have a population of 44.6 per cent visible minorities, Vancouver 39.3 per cent, and Edmonton and Calgary 25 per cent each. By 2001, visible minorities will constitute nearly 18 per cent of a projected Canadian population of 32.5 million.[1]

The two faces of ethnicity, territorial and non-territorial – those for whom provincehood or a third order of government does or can exist, and those for whom they are unavailable – suggest the need for federalism and a charter as separate, tailored constitutional responses. The double garb that ethnicity sports – concentrated or dispersed, capable of wielding majority power or subject to perpetual minority status – in fact illustrates a universal condition. Our abstract citizen status in provincial, territorial, and Canadian communities, in which in certain circumstances we can participate in a majority, does not exhaust our political identities and group memberships. On the contrary, if our territorial community memberships are considered exhaustive, we experience a sense of constitutional impoverishment. All of us either fear mistreatment as minorities where we live, or we escape from territorial identities to transprovincial identities as women, the disabled, and other statuses that generate particularistic fellow feeling across provincial boundaries. The explosion of particularistic identities characteristic of a post-modern era multiplies minority identities and weakens the legitimacy of territorially based majoritarianism in both province and country. The virtue of a charter of rights, accordingly, is the recognition it gives to individuals and groups for whom federalism's privileging of territory is experienced as narrow and confining. As Samuel LaSelva notes, "That is why a Bill of Rights is so important in a federal state. Through it, individuals and groups are given recognition in a federal system, and their interests are placed on the same footing as those of other constitutional actors."[2]

If the preceding analysis is roughly correct, we might then think of a new descriptive label for one of the constitutional packages suitable for a democratic people for whom federalism is necessary but not sufficient. The label Charter-federalism, with the words hyphenated to suggest a positive relationship, is appropriate for Canadians who need federalism to manage space and territorial senses of community, especially in Quebec, but for whom federalism bypasses important components of their identity, hopes, and apprehensions that a Charter addresses. Accordingly, when the post-Meech Lake package emerges, one way of assessing its quality and long-run utility is the success with which it balances territorial conceptions of community in provinces/territories and in the Aboriginal third order of government with trans-provincial/trans-third order conceptions of who we are, which are partly defined in terms of the enforceable rights that we possess. Does the package meet the requirements of Charter-federalism? Does it respond to the coexisting multiple, plural identities we carry?

In the light of our demographic, ethnic, national, and spatial characteristics as a complex, heterogeneous modern people it is misleading to assert that we have chosen Charter-federalism. We did not choose federalism in 1867. Inescapable realities chose it for us. Similarly, in light of the history of the previous third of a century, we did not choose a Charter in 1980-82. The Charter formally expressed what we were already becoming. It might, of course, have been delayed. Its contents might have been different. Even now its application to Quebec and Aboriginal peoples might respond to certain specific Quebec and Aboriginal cultural differences. Conceivably, there could be separate Aboriginal charters in the future whose contents overlap the Canadian Charter. Conceivably the Quebec Charter could monopolize the "rights territory" within Quebec jurisdiction. Theoretically, each of these versions can be thought of as Charter-federalism. The latter, as a composite genre of constitutional government, as a mixed constitution, has a logic appropriate to the multiple identities of a people for whom federalism is not enough, but equally for whom a Charter without federalism would not be enough.

Chapter Eight

# Reflections on the Political Purposes of the Charter: The First Decade

## Introduction: The Living Canadian Charter and the Evolving Canadian Society

Given the appropriate dominance of the legally trained at this conference – I believe I am the only person on the program without a law degree – I expect my role is analogous to that of "ordinary Canadians" at the January-March, 1992, public constitutional conferences; namely, to raise issues that the experts have screened out. [1] Be that as it may, I have interpreted my task as the provision of a vantage point that comes naturally to a political scientist, and that is rarely employed by practising lawyers and the legal professoriate. What were the political purposes of the Charter, and what have been its major political and constitutional consequences in its first decade?

An initial confession may clear the air. I realize that categorical statements about the Charter's original political purposes are subject to all the caveats about original understanding or intent. A policy such as the Charter that emerges from the interaction of a multitude of players, both governmental and private, is the product of the diverse purposes, often competing, of the many actors involved in its making. Most of the members of the "Gang of Eight," for example, grudgingly supported a Charter they did not like as the price they had to pay to get their amending formula accepted. Further, it strains credulity to assert that the various Charter-supporting constitutional lobby groups – civil liberties groups, feminist and ethnocultural organizations, for example – realized they were participating in a plan to transform the constitutional order by diluting provincialism, muting Quebec nationalism, and redistributing constituent power downwards to the people. Also, and somewhat surprisingly, some of the key legal officials in the federal government team in the late seventies were relatively oblivious to the political purposes that lay behind Prime Minister Trudeau's Charter advocacy. They did not transcend the legal perspective natural to their craft that saw the Charter in terms of rights, lawyers, and courts. Finally, of course, political purposes are not instructions to judges – but large, hoped-for constitutional consequences that are expected to emerge if the Charter experiment has been finely tuned and the socio-political theory behind it is valid.

The many changes in the constitutional culture of Canadians from 1982 to 1992 obviously cannot be defined as effects of the Charter. Such a succumbing to the imperialism of single causes would ride roughshod over the complex interaction of underlying forces and human choices that have moved Canadians in the past decade. Further, the Charter is not an unmoved mover, but is itself shaped by the environment of ideas, events, societal transformations, and, of special importance, the agonizing constitutional introspection Canadians seem unable to escape. Thus the 1992 Charter bears the indelible imprint of the constitutional turmoil of the eighties.

The Charter had the misfortune to be introduced at a time of intense and embittered constitutional controversy. Its origins in a conflict between two competing Quebec elites, symbolized by Trudeau and Lévesque, explain its rejection by the Parti Québécois government and its subsequent relative failure to "take" in Quebec. From the perspective of nationalist Quebec elites, the Charter is partly seen as a weapon of the victors rather than a liberating instrument for the citizenry. The Quebec nationalist interpretation of 1982 as a betrayal further weakens allegiance to the Charter among the Quebec political class. The Parti Québécois government's systematic use of the notwithstanding clause to exempt Quebec legislation from as much of the Charter as section 33 allowed symbolically cast the Charter as an anti-Quebec instrument. The specific use of the notwithstanding clause by the Bourassa government to sustain Bill 178, and the furore it caused, underlined the clash of views between the Charter's supporters outside of Quebec and the political imperative to protect Quebec's "deep diversity," in Charles Taylor's terms,[2] against Charter clauses that appeared to thwart its preservation and enhancement. The Charter featured prominently in the Meech Lake debate, as Charter supporters outside Quebec saw the interpretive lens of the distinct society as a threat to the universal availability of the Charter's rights. The result was summed up by one Québécois scholar as the rest of Canada's "'Charter of Rights against [Quebec's] distinct society'. The Charter won."[3]

Throughout the Charter's first decade, the notwithstanding clause was alternately vilified as an unseemly moral stain on the constitution and defended as an appropriate safeguard against judicial decisions that might be hostile to a desirable public purpose. This debate, in which Prime Minister Mulroney was a vigorous participant, revealed that the 1982 compromise between the Charter's rights and the notwithstanding clause was not an equilibrium position. The Charter is again on the agenda in the post-Meech round, with the notwithstanding clause challenged by the original 1991 federal proposals,[4] with the distinct society again introduced as an interpretive lens for the Charter,[5] and with visible minority groups seeking the removal of section 15(1), equality rights, from the ambit of the notwithstanding clause.[6] Finally, the applicability of the Charter to future Aboriginal self-government is a contentious issue, discussed below, with divisions between the federal government and some Aboriginal leaders, and with a tendency for Aboriginal men and women (in favour) to be on opposing sides. In sum, and not surprisingly, the defenders and opponents of this prominent new constitutional instrument struggled to bend its meaning and applications in preferred directions in its first decade.

The Charter is now encrusted with the experiences and events that buffeted it in its first decade. In 1982 Canadians saw the Charter as an experiment getting under way, one whose future pattern of coexistence with the historic tradition of parliamentary supremacy, given explicit but limited support in the section 33 notwithstanding clause, was unpredictable. Now, we see a Charter that has been tried in the judicial wars, that has figured prominently in the convulsive constitutional controversies of the past decade, and that has acquired a political constituency of its own, sometimes called Charter Canadians. Thus, the Charter's impact on Canadians cannot be divorced from the impact of the constitutional and other turbulence of the last decade on the Charter. If constitutions can be thought of as "living," so obviously can their key components, especially in the formative years following their introduction before jelling has occurred.

Thus, our quarry is elusive. The Charter itself is an unvarying name applied to an evolving instrument. The political actors that presided at its creation had varied and sometimes contradictory purposes. Its contribution to our present political condition and to the Canadian constitutional culture interacts with the impact of free trade, recession, demographic change, the shifting fortunes of political parties and their leaders, and the myriad host of deliberate efforts, random events, and deep social forces that unpredictably move societies away from whatever are arbitrarily defined as starting points. Fortunately, however, the limited space at my disposal precludes the nuance appropriate to a monograph and justifies the broad brush strokes whose bold colours can communicate a big picture only by a relative disregard of contradictory detail.

## The Political Purposes of the Charter

Four political purposes[7] provided the dynamic for Prime Minister Trudeau's unyielding Charter advocacy.

(1) The Charter's constitutional language policy, especially the section 23 minority-language educational rights, was the servant of a country-wide view of French Canada, in opposition to the Quebec-centred view of Quebec nationalists, who redefined French Canadians in Quebec as Québécois, a national people, whose real government wielded the lever of *l'etat du Québec.* If the former view could be kept alive by constitutional succouring, and if simultaneously the Anglophone minority could be sustained in Quebec to invalidate the dangerous (to Trudeau) equation of a French-speaking nation with the totality of the Quebec people, then the Quebec nationalist drive toward an assertive provincialism or an independent Quebec would be muted.

Clearly, as our present constitutional disarray testifies, the erosion of Quebec nationalism has not occurred. On the other hand, the Charter has definitely stimulated official minority-language rights holders to see themselves in Canadian terms and to see the constitution as their defender. However, the Charter's language regime provides constitutional support to a particular view of the appropriate relationship between the two official-language communities and thus impedes the development of an alternative territorial language policy that some scholars deem preferable.[8] The application of the Charter's language regime to Quebec is the focal point of Quebec nationalist criticism.

(2) More generally, the citizenry's possession of Charter rights was designed to transform the base of the constitutional order. A citizenry seized of the constitutional recognition accorded by the Charter would be drawn out of provincialism into a pan-Canadian sense of self. Viewed this way, the Charter would support a positive answer by Canadians to Renan's thesis that a nation is a plebiscite of every day. Put differently, the Charter was a nationalizing, Canadianizing constitutional instrument intended to shape the psyches and identities of Canadians. The Charter, accordingly, was a constitutional weapon analogous to disallowance, with its objective of constraining the diversities that federalism both reflects and sustains. At the time of its implementation, it was a rival to the constitutional definition of Canada as a community of communities espoused by Conservative leader Joe Clark, Brian Peckford of Newfoundland, and others.

The Charter was to be ubiquitous, monitoring Canadian presence within every province. That presence was not intended to be detached and impersonal, an esoteric subject in law faculties and pulled off the shelves in courtrooms, but a perpetual, embedded presence socialized into the psyches and identities of the citizenry. The latter, as bearers of Charter rights, were to evaluate provincial performance through the lens of a constitutional rights-defined Canadianism.

From the Diefenbaker Bill of Rights to the 1982 Charter, the federal government had led the drive for entrenched rights binding on both orders of government, with opposition or reluctance coming from most of the provincial governments. That the 1982 notwithstanding clause was a response to provincial demands and has been employed only by provincial governments, that successive federal governments either opposed its introduction, sought to make its application tougher, or advocated its elimination – these all reflect the self-interested, federalism-driven political logic of the competing government actors in the constitutional order. The strongest government support for the notwithstanding clause, therefore, logically should and does come from the Quebec government. Political understanding of the Charter, accordingly, begins with the recognition that it was not introduced as a neutral instrument, but as a weapon in the never-ending struggle of the competing governments of Canadian federalism for influence and survival. Federal government support via the Charter for intraprovincial minorities, for example, psychologically erodes the latter's attachment to the provincial community by inducing them to look outward to find their protection. In the conflict between rights and parliamentary supremacy, the tendency of the federal government to support the former and the provinces the latter is not fortuitous.

At a very general level, with important exceptions noted below, this political purpose has been achieved. The Charter has generated a powerful, vocal clientele of supporters who see themselves in Canadian terms and who tend to defend a strong federal government role, sometimes, as in Meech Lake, to the embarrassment of the federal government. The Charter, therefore, impedes constitutional changes that would markedly strengthen provincial jurisdiction. It also, along with the equality of the provinces norm, provides ammunition for opponents of special status for any province that might lead to province-specific differences in citizenship entitlements.

(3) Linked to the previous point, the Charter was an instrument to relocate sovereignty in the people rather than in the governments of Canadian federalism. The fact that the original federal proposals of 1980 combined the Charter and an amending formula with a referendum component underlines the coherence of the constitutional theory of the then federal government. To give rights against governments to citizens in normal politics and to deprive those same citizens of a role in the formal amending process by which those rights could be eliminated, enhanced, or reduced was simply illogical. However, that very illogic was embedded in the 1982 Constitution Act that brought together an amending formula designed by provincial governments according to federalism criteria and a Charter whose basic pan-Canadianizing and democratizing thrust presupposed that the constitution belonged to the Canadian people. This contradictory legacy of the 1982 Constitution Act, little noticed at the time, was played out in

the Meech Lake conflict between executive federalism and the participant con-stitutional culture stimulated by the Charter.

The post-Meech difficulty of finding a *modus vivendi* between the elitist assumptions of executive federalism and the participant dynamic unleashed by the Charter, and by Aboriginal constitutional ambitions, runs like a connecting thread through the hearings and reports of the Spicer Commission, the Beau-doin-Edwards Committee, and the Beaudoin-Dobbie Committee.[9] The six public constitutional conferences in the winter of 1992 provided tentative short-term answers to pressures for participation. More fundamental institutional answers are suggested by the ubiquitous proposals for referenda and constituent assemblies in the post-Meech era.[10]

(4) Finally, the prominence accorded to a Charter in federal proposals throughout the Trudeau period was a tactic to delay constitutional discussion of the division of powers until Ottawa's objectives had been achieved in terms of rights and the reform of central institutions. In the interim, the federal govern-ment could employ, as the Kirby memorandum of 1980 underlined, a rhetoric of a people's package versus a government package dealing with powers and insti-tutions.[11] This allowed the federal government to contrast its high-minded sup-port for the people's package of rights and patriation with the grubby, self-inter-ested provincial concern for more powers. The deeper federal strategy was to view constitutional reform in stages so that by the time the division of powers appeared on the agenda, the federal government's legitimacy would be so enhanced by the Charter's support for a Canadian versus provincial view of Can-ada that public support for provincial jurisdictional aggrandisement would be greatly reduced. The reform of central institutions, not yet achieved, of course, had the same objectives; if the federal government could successfully respond to provincial diversity by change internal to itself, the competing claim that accom-modation of a frustrated provincialism required more powers for provincial governments, and hence a weaker Ottawa, could be countered.[12]

While this federal tactic worked in the minimum sense that it delayed grap-pling with division of powers issues, the Charter's arrival has not reduced provincial government appetites for more jurisdiction. Centrifugal pressures for enhanced provincial jurisdiction were evident in the contents of the Meech Lake package, and are likely to be even more so in any post-Meech settlement. Never-theless, the pressures for decentralization are countered by the Charter Cana-dians who support a strong central government.

## The Charter as a Political Instrument:
## A Preliminary Judgement

It is almost certainly premature as we enter the Charter's second decade to come up with more than an interim and ambiguous verdict on its impact on Canada's social fabric and constitutional culture. Only a Panglossian optimist would expect the Charter to have fully met in its first decade the various purposes ascribed to it above. Macro constitutional change is even more of an experiment with the future than is garden-variety ordinary policy. No sooner is a major transformation such as the Charter formally in place than the various interests that supported and opposed its introduction reposition themselves to do further battles in the new constitutional order that the Charter creates. That battle takes place in many arenas – the appointment of judges, the language of politics, the socialization of the citizenry, and all the arenas for constitutional reform. The Charter's impact extends well beyond the tabulation of winners and losers in courtrooms, and the law journals' case commentary on "reasonable limits," to profound changes in constitutional culture and, indeed, in the very identities of many Canadians. My remarks in this section focus on a few major transformations in constitutional culture that appear to have significant Charter roots.

The drive for a more open, participatory process of constitutional reform is intimately linked to the Charter. The Charter was shaped and entrenched in the constitution by a *de facto* alliance between the federal government, supported by Ontario and New Brunswick, and a diverse group of Charter supporters – women's groups, the disabled, ethnocultural organizations, civil liberties groups, visible minorities, and others. The latter were essential allies for a federal government that threatened unilateral submission of a reform package to the United Kingdom Parliament despite strong opposition from most provincial governments. These Charter supporters were there at the creation, and the final product was significantly shaped by their vigilance and input before the 1980-81 Special Joint Committee hearings. Accordingly, their claimed entitlement to participate in later processes of constitutional reform is analogous to the compact theory claims of the original four founding provinces to be legitimate, indeed essential, actors in revisions of the 1867 constitutional instrument they had fashioned. In each case, the founding act generates a proprietary attitude to the constitution among the original participants. The constitution, or at least the parts of special concern to particular groups, becomes "theirs" in a way that had no counterpart for the citizenry when the BNA Act was primarily concerned with federalism and thus was thought of as an affair of governments.

The Charter gives the constitution a popular base. It bypasses governments and speaks directly to the citizenry. The Charter-driven entanglement of the constitution and Canadian society can be expressed either as: society has been constitutionalized, or the constitution has been socialized. Constitution and society now interact and influence each other in an unending series of exchanges. The tighter fusion of constitution and society through the vehicle of rights weakens federalism and parliamentary supremacy as constitutional ordering principles, diminishes the status of governments in the constitution, and erodes their historically assumed dominance in the formal process of constitutional reform.

The battering delivered to the elite-driven process of executive federalism in the agonizing demise of the Meech Lake Accord after its secretive birth was, therefore, in the nature of things. The governments' prevailing view that the constitution was theirs to amend in response to their definition of what needed to be done was effectively repudiated by the insistence of Charter groups and Aboriginal organizations that they, too, had constitutional interests, that part of the constitution belonged to them, and that they were unwilling to be treated as grateful, deferential subjects ready automatically to applaud what their constitutional betters, elected and appointed, had accomplished.

Meech Lake confirmed that the Charter has elevated citizenship as a constitutional category. Citizenship should now be thought of as one of the central institutions of the overall constitutional order in the same way as the judiciary, legislatures, executives, first ministers' conferences, and the mandarinate. Citizenship, accordingly, should be thought of as an office that requires appropriate, responsible behaviour of the office-holders, behaviour that has to be painfully learned, for it must require some restraint on the pursuit of narrow self-interest.

There is general agreement with the basic Meech Lake message that executive federalism, even if accompanied by what was conceived of as a perfunctory ratification of proposed amendments by legislatures, is no longer acceptable as the virtually exclusive instrument of constitutional change. The general direction of change is clear enough in the battery of proposals for referenda, constituent assemblies, Spicer Commission-type grassroots hearings, constitutional conferences with public participation, and so on. How these participatory vehicles can be integrated with the unavoidable leadership and orchestrating role of governments and the formal requirements of the amending process is, however, unclear.

Resolution will not be easy, for the consistent evidence from our constitutional agonies of the last decade and a half is that the constitutional agendas of governments and citizens diverge. This was true of the 1980 Quebec referendum, as the Parti Québécois discovered. The 1980-81 constitutional process pitted a Charter-supporting public against the Charter-opposing majority of provincial governments. Most provincial governments at the time also strongly opposed the referendum component of the Trudeau government's amending proposals because of their palpable fears that the provincial residents for whom they claimed to speak might speak with a different voice if given the opportunity. Meech Lake, of course, graphically revealed the gulf between the public's agenda and that of governments. Public hearings outside of Quebec consistently challenged government definitions of both the problem to be solved and the solution. The gap between the public and governments continues unabated in the post-Meech constitutional world. For example, Monahan, Covella, and Batty write:

> The most probable outcome of a ROC constituent assembly would be a set of proposals which either directly contradicted Quebec's stated agenda or, at best, was merely indifferent to it. Thus, a constituent assembly convened in the ROC would likely produce a list of proposals along the following lines: a strengthening of the *Canadian Charter of Rights and Freedoms* through the addition of social and economic rights, or the removal of the notwithstanding clause; a Triple-E Senate; enhancement of constitutional protections for multiculturalism, gender equality, environmental rights, and disabled rights; entrenchment, in the Constitution, of powers for municipal governments; recognition of the right to aboriginal self-government; and entrenchment of a Canada Clause in the Constitution.[13]

The most notable aspects of this list are its concentration on the Charter and on rights and its relative indifference to federalism concerns, with the exception of the triple-E Senate. Not surprisingly, the authors conclude that a constituent assembly for the ROC would drastically limit the negotiating flexibility of political leaders outside of Quebec.[14]

In addition to its diffuse contribution to empowering the citizenry, the Charter generates a host of focused constitutional interest groups that identify with particular clauses and see their task as the protection or strengthening of their niche in the constitution. Hence, feminist organizations identify with section 28, the Canadian Ethnocultural Council with section 27, official-language minorities with section 23, visible minorities and the disabled with section 15, and so on. The proliferation of constitutional interest groups and lobbyists stimulated by the Charter leads to a constitutional fragmentation. A multiplicity of competing public and private interests falsely acts as if there is a Smithian invisible hand that transforms the competitive pursuit of constitutional self-interest into the public good.

Superficially, at least, the Charter fosters a more principled constitutional discourse employing the language of rights. This discourse generally focuses on the citizen-state relationship. It inexorably leads to questions about the locus of sovereignty. "Rights" pushes university law faculties in the direction of legal theory and political philosophy. The Charter necessitates a rethinking of both parliamentary supremacy and federalism, the former because the notwithstanding and reasonable limits clauses require principled discussions on the place of majoritarianism and executive dominance in a regime of rights, the latter because the hitherto untrammelled provincial government capacity to create province-specific citizen rights and duties is now constrained by the Charter. In different language, the fundamental assumptions of both parliamentary government and federalism have to be rethought in the context of the rights challenge to the historic privileging of majoritarianism by responsible government and of territorial diversity by federalism. The master inherited institutions of parliamentary government and federalism have to adapt to the rival claims of the constitutionally enhanced rights-based institution of citizenship. This dramatically transforms the discourse of a constitutional order hitherto characterized by tradition, by incrementalism, by the slow broadening down of precedent, and by the dominance of tacit assumptions and understandings.

The virtue of clarity to which rights discourse leads and the mobilizing capacity of rights are purchased at the cost of a diminished capacity to compromise. Rights tell us who we are. They also threaten to tell us who is not one of us. As is noted below, if Canada is thought of as a multinational society of (1) Francophone Québécois, (2) Aboriginal nations, and (3) rest-of-Canada/English Canada, the allegiance to the Charter, especially among nationalist elites, falls off noticeably outside its constitutional stronghold in English Canada. For those who wish to escape its mandate, the Charter is viewed as an imperialist intervention in their affairs; for its believers it encourages the view that those who seek exemption from its coverage are unbelievers, outside the community.

Flexibility and sensitivity are central virtues of both parliamentary government and federalism. Parliamentary government, with its master principle of parliamentary supremacy, is designed for flexibility and sensitivity over time. Its elemental message is that the future is not to be a colony of the past, that tomorrows have the same rights of choice as yesterdays, and that we cannot bind our successors. Federalism is about diversity over space. It sanctions and facilitates policy divergence in the jurisdictional areas under provincial control. Federalism says we are not responsible for our neighbours' policy choices for matters that do not pertain to the common jurisdiction of the Canadian government of all of us.

The Charter, by contrast, gives an imperialist answer to the future by narrowing the range of allowable choice of generations not yet born. It is equally imperialistic over space with its limitation on the expression of provincial variations in taste that conflict with Charter norms.

The rigidities to which the Charter seems to lead are softened by various escape valves, including but not confined to the notwithstanding and reasonable limits clauses. [15] Further, its judicial interpretation may be sensitive to the territorial particularisms of federalism. The Charter's amendment, of course, is also possible. Nevertheless, the basic Charter message is to limit the policy discretion available to governing majorities over time and across space. The Charter's relation to diversity is paradoxical. On the one hand, it protects minority diversities against insensitive majority coercion. On the other hand, it impedes diversified policy responses to the diverse situations governments encounter over time and across space.

## Multicultural, Multiracial, and Multinational Canada

The suitability of a charter for a heterogeneous, multicultural, multiracial society verges on being a conventional wisdom. It was a driving rationale for F.R. Scott, one of our greatest civil libertarians.[16] It is repeated by Tom Berger, a contemporary who wears Scott's mantle.[17] It is reiterated in scholarly analysis. It is sustained by the support ethnic and racial minorities give to the Charter. It is reinforced by the pressure of various minority groups, especially visible minorities, to strengthen their Charter protection by exempting the section 15(1) equality clause from the notwithstanding clause.[18] The Charter, therefore, is widely seen as an ideal instrument for the protection of minorities scattered throughout a heterogeneous society, who distrust a majoritarianism from which they may be excluded.

On the other hand, Aboriginal peoples and Québécois define themselves not as dispersed minorities in the midst of majorities but as founding peoples or First Nations. Quebec's sense of nationhood has been evident for decades; that of Aboriginal peoples is more recent. In the last decade or so, however, it has become a routine self-description. The message from the consultations of the Assembly of First Nations parallel constitutional process was that the Indian peoples:

> ... are the First Nations, *the* founding people, because their ancestors were living here on Turtle Island, with their own laws and institutions, before the Celts swarmed over Britain and the Gauls invaded what is now France. They had municipal government, international agreements, sophisticated community structures, and an established justice system when Champlain's men were toughing it out [on] the St. Croix River.[19]

The Métis National Council describes the "Metis Nation [as] a distinct Aboriginal Nation . . . a Nation within a Nation."[20] The Inuit are "one of the founding nations of this country . . . distinct peoples."[21] While there clearly is no Aboriginal nation as such – the constitutional rubric "aboriginal" being an encompassing rubric rather than a defining identity – there are separate Aboriginal nations. Aboriginal and Quebec claims to unique identities and singular constitutional treatment are sanctioned by time immemorial, not by freshly minted citizenship papers.

Both resist inclusion in the multicultural/multiracial category. Both seek new or expanded powers of self-government. Both seek to perpetuate their peoples. Both see themselves as an ongoing community or communities, as a continuing collective presence that should vitally inform the values of future generations of their own kind. The Charter's appropriateness for a cultural, racial pluralism whose bearers do not speak the language of nationalism is challenged when it encounters minority nations within the larger Canadian whole.

The conflict between the Charter and the multinational character of the contemporary Canadian state is far from total, but is nevertheless significant. Overt Charter antipathy is disproportionately found among the nationalist elites of the Aboriginal peoples, especially the Assembly of First Nations, and of the Francophone majority in Quebec. The most powerful academic/political literature critical of the Charter no longer comes from the surviving believers in parliamentary supremacy, as it did in the 1980-82 constitutional battles. Their voices are muted, or are raised only to defend the section 33 notwithstanding clause against its many detractors. They fight a rearguard battle. The passion of contemporary Charter criticism is driven by territorially based minority nationalisms who see their present or prospective governments as their major weapons in the fight for survival.[22] According to Boldt and Long, writing in 1985, "the Charter's severest critics have been native Indians."[23] This migration of the grounds of Charter criticism from a defence of the historic British tradition to the defence of internal minority nationalism deserves a brief examination.

To some extent, charters of rights are nation-specific. They are blends of universal values and local adaptations. Thus scholars point out the Canadianness of the 1982 Charter and contrast it with the American Bill of Rights.[24] Section 27 (multiculturalism heritage), sections 16-22 (Official Languages of Canada), section 23 (minority-language educational rights), section 29 (constitutional rights or privileges of denominational, separate, or dissentient schools), and of course section 33 (notwithstanding clause) are all appropriately identified as Canadian adaptations or innovations.

The same logic that tailors the Charter to Canada as a distinct national political community, however, also stimulates internal national communities to query its appropriateness and sensitivity for their particular national circumstances. This questioning is especially likely if such communities have or seek governing powers to shape their people, as is assuredly true of French-speaking Québécois and Aboriginal peoples, both of whom unself-consciously apply the label "nation" to themselves.

It is not surprising, therefore, that the major political opposition to the

Canadian Charter comes from the two national communities that were minimally involved in its making and are least likely to be sympathetic to its political,
Canadianizing purposes. Both Québécois and Aboriginal peoples were successful, at the time of the Charter's creation, in restricting its full application to themselves. Quebec was exempted by section 59(1) of the Constitution Act, 1982, from
the application of section 23(1)(a) that would otherwise increase the number of
Quebec parents with a right to have their children receive primary and secondary
school instruction in the English language. Section 25 of the Charter protects
"aboriginal, treaty, or other rights or freedoms" from abrogation or derogation
by Charter rights and freedoms.

Not surprisingly, a prominent strand in some of the post-Charter nationalist
rhetoric of Québécois and Aboriginal elites portrays the Charter as hostile to the
political goals they have for their peoples. Their vantage point is not that of dispersed minorities seeking protection but of concentrated majorities (not true, of
course, of all Aboriginal peoples) who have or seek power to shape their peoples.
They view the Charter from the perspective of present or future political executives charged with the responsibility of nourishing their minority national communities in a threatening, assimilating environment. They see the Charter,
therefore, not as a liberation, but as a constraint. These elites see parliamentary
supremacy and executive power not from the vantage point of marginalized
minorities fearful of state power but as leaders of majorities seeking to use power
on behalf of their peoples.

Their opposition to the Charter is a stronger version of the arguments of the
provincial governments that opposed the Charter in 1980-82 because it would
interfere with their province-building activities for which parliamentary
supremacy was a positive instrument. The contemporary tension between federalism and the Charter is most pronounced when the nationalism of a culturally
distinct provincial (or Aboriginal) community conflicts with the Canadianizing
assumptions, incentives, and ambitions built into the Charter. The Charter's
goals of pan-Canadian unity, of political integration, of weakening centrifugal
pressures, and of linking individual citizens directly and emotionally to the Canadian community are not shared by those who seek to preserve minority
national differences within the state, who prefer their people to have instrumental, not emotional bonds to the larger Canadian whole, who, as Boldt and Long
assert of status Indians, do not define themselves as "fully participating Canadian citizens" and who appear little interested in becoming so.[25] Emotional
bonds are to be monopolized by the Québécois or Aboriginal governments as the
case may be.

The Charter becomes a battleground for competitive nation-building objectives as these tensions are played out. From the federal government's Canadian
perspective, the Charter's coast-to-coast undifferentiated application to both

orders of government and to a prospective third order of Aboriginal government is a potent statement of Canada's wholeness. Conversely, its patchwork application would suggest a defeat of the idea of Canada as a traditional nation-state with only one version of citizenship, and possibly portend an ongoing process of disintegration. From the perspective of internal minority nations, however, desirous of pushing Canada in the direction of a two-nation or multinational state, an antithetical logic may make more sense. In these circumstances, rival charters – existing or potential – can be instruments of rival nationalisms, weapons against the assimilating pressures of the Canadian Charter. Thus the Quebec Charter has a visibility and prominence accorded to none of its provincial counterparts elsewhere. Its role as a national symbol and the patriotic literature it stimulates, are, among provinces, unique to Quebec and are only paralleled by the role of the Canadian Charter for Canadians elsewhere. Although Aboriginal nationalism is at a much earlier stage, there is, at a minimum, widespread Aboriginal interest in one or more specific Aboriginal charters of rights.[26]

Some of the pressure for an Aboriginal Charter and Quebec nationalist support for the primacy of the Quebec Charter reflect the nationalist attachment to what K.C. Wheare labelled the "principle of constitutional *autochthony*, of being constitutionally rooted in their own native soil."[27] In different language, one political purpose for having a Charter of one's own is to attach a Charter's powerful symbolism to one's own nation and to weaken the symbolism of the rival, encompassing Canadian nation.

The resistance of the Assembly of First Nations to the application of the Canadian Charter is accompanied by a recommendation "that gender equality be formally established in formal Aboriginal Charters of Rights and Freedoms."[28] In various publications, the Native Council of Canada recommends that each Aboriginal nation address the issue of protecting individual civil rights, and suggests that one option would be to develop "a distinctly 'Aboriginal' Charter," building on section 35(4) that guarantees Aboriginal treaty rights equally to both males and females.[29] The Métis National Council appears to support the existing Charter, complemented by a separate Métis Charter.[30] The Inuit Tapirisat is willing to consider accepting the Canadian Charter as long as the override is available "to protect Inuit language or culture."[31]

Aboriginal public discussion of one or more Aboriginal charters is extremely weak. The Assembly of First Nations proposal is neither defended nor explained in its constitutional document, *To the Source*. The overlap or contradiction between the proposed constitutionally coexisting Métis Charter and the Canadian Charter is unclear. The Native Council of Canada position is undecided, with the existing Charter or an Aboriginal Charter as live options.

Although discussion of separate Aboriginal charters is at a very preliminary stage, several tentative observations may be useful. (1) The Charter issue cannot be avoided. Its strongest opponents, such as the AFN, have to propose an alternative Aboriginal Charter to retain credibility. The contagion of Charterism has deeply influenced Aboriginal constitutional rhetoric. The AFN's *To the Source* describes the debate about the role of the Canadian Charter as "perhaps the single most contentious issue among Aboriginal people concerning self-government."[32] At the federal government-supported conference on *First Peoples and the Constitution* "one of the most widely debated issues ... focused on whether or not the Charter ... would apply, fully or in part, to newly constituted Aboriginal governments."[33] (2) The Aboriginal pressure to keep the Charter issue on the Aboriginal constitutional agenda comes overwhelmingly from Aboriginal women. There is, accordingly, an implicit alliance between the federal government and Charter-supporting Aboriginal women. (3) Much of the push for Aboriginal charters comes from Aboriginal nationalism. Métis advocacy of a Métis Charter reflects, among other things, the desire for constitutional recognition of the Métis nation. Both the AFN rejection of the alien Canadian Charter and its support for separate Aboriginal charters are driven by Indian minority nationalism building on more than a century of separate treatment of status Indians. The striking contrast between the milder Inuit and Métis response to the Charter and the vehement AFN hostility presumably has historic roots. Of the three categories of Aboriginal peoples, status Indians had the closest approximation to a truly colonial experience. They were both administered and culturally assaulted. Consequently, their nationalism is much more likely to involve a nativist rejection of the colonizer's values. (4) The complexities of formulating and gaining Aboriginal and rest-of-Canada acceptance of Aboriginal charters have almost certainly been greatly underestimated. In particular, a multiplicity of separate charters would probably be constitutionally unmanageable. On the other hand, the idea of a single Aboriginal Charter acceptable to Indians, Inuit, and Métis is probably unrealistic.

Quebec nationalist opposition to the Charter is more fully developed than that of Aboriginal peoples. It is eloquently expressed in the Bélanger-Campeau Commission's documentation of the Charter's antipathy to the accommodation of Quebec's specificity. According to the Commission, the 1982 Constitution Act bolstered visions of the federal system and of a "national Canadian identity which are hard to reconcile with the effective recognition and political expression of Quebec's distinct identity."[34] One component of these visions is reflected in the theme of:

> *The equality of all Canadian citizens from coast to coast and the uniqueness of the society in which they live.* This political vision, based on the Canadian *Charter of Rights and Freedoms* enshrined in the 1982 Act, perceives equality as having a strictly individual scope and applying uniformly across

Canada: it does not make allowance for Quebec society to receive special constitutional recognition. The notion of a distinct Quebec society is thus understood as being a source of inequality and incompatible with the principle of equality of all Canadian citizens. [35]

Guy Laforest has amplified the Bélanger-Campeau thesis in recent papers. [36] He objects to the Charter from a Quebec nationalist perspective because its political goal of building a Canadian national identity, based on individual allegiance, leaves no room for a coexisting Quebec national identity. The Charter threatens all efforts to promote Quebec as a distinct society, as the Meech Lake experience testifies. To Laforest, the Charter's Canadian vision does not include an enduring Quebec community, a distinct Quebec people with a collective sense of itself, seeking its own perpetuation, but only individual Canadian citizens who happen to live in Quebec and who bear transportable Charter rights. The Charter, accordingly, as a political instrument of pan-Canadian nationalism, is an enemy of, and is designed to enfeeble, the rival Quebec political nationalism espoused by Laforest. Therefore, the primacy of the Quebec Charter on Quebec territory, interpreted by judges appointed by the Quebec government, is the first requirement of an acceptable Canada-Quebec partnership. [37]

That Laforest's critique, which sees the Charter as sickly and vitiated by its illegitimate political purposes, [38] is not directed at the Charter's rights *per se* bears underlining. His overall support for rights is evident in his support for the Quebec Charter. He also admits that it will not be easy to convince his fellow Québécois citizens, equally supportive of rights, of the dangers residing in the Charter. [39] The tension is not between supporters and opponents of rights, or parliamentary supremacists versus Charterphiles, but over whose Charter – with some variation in content mainly relating to language rights – will be dominant, and therefore which national community, Québécois or Canadian, will be strengthened. The Charter is embroiled in the struggle of rival political nationalisms that is much more salient to political elites than to the ordinary citizenry.

Discussions and analysis of potential tensions between Aboriginal nationhood and the Charter are at an early stage. The efforts to escape from the reach of the Charter, or at a minimum to make the (or a special) notwithstanding clause available to Aboriginal governments, or to have culturally specific charters are part of a broader process of differentiating Aboriginal peoples from other Canadians. Status Indians, of course, have been fashioned by more than a century of existence under a distinct legal regime. Inuit distinctiveness has been sheltered by isolation. The contemporary Métis, brought into the Constitution by section 35 of the Constitution Act, 1982, now seek to be brought under the federal government's jurisdiction of section 91(24) of the Constitution Act, 1867, to the end of further differentiating themselves from ordinary Canadian citizens.

After the successful repudiation by status Indians of the assimilation policy of the federal government's 1969 White Paper, Aboriginal constitutional politics has consistently been directed to fashioning a distinct Aboriginal status in Canada. Even a cryptic survey of the relevant developments is remarkably impressive: the rapid emergence of labels (First Nations) and ideologies of Aboriginal nationalism; the decade-long push for self-government; the pressures for a separate justice system; four constitutional conferences devoted exclusively to Aboriginal concerns; proposals for separate representation in both the Senate and the House of Commons; the partial exemption from the Charter already provided in section 25; the imminent emergence of a *de facto* Inuit jurisdiction, a quasi-province, in Nunavut; and the acceptance of separate Aboriginal representation at the 1992 constitutional bargaining table – a status accorded to no other non-governmental group.

The question of the applicability of the Canadian Charter to the self-governing Aboriginal peoples of the future must be put in the context of the host of differentiating factors described above. However, there is no consensus among Aboriginal peoples on the Charter issue. The strongest opposition to the Charter comes from the Assembly of First Nations. The Assembly's anti-Charter position flows directly from its basic socio-political philosophy. *To the Source*, the document derived from the Assembly's parallel constitutional inquiry, sees the revival and healing of the Indian nations in terms of a return to past values and practices. [40] The pre-European period is portrayed as little short of idyllic, contrasting very favourably with contemporaneous European conditions. This relative Eden was undermined by contact with Europeans. The post-Confederation Indian Act regime was paternalistic and insensitive, and was accompanied by an orchestrated onslaught against Indian values and identity. The resultant disorientation of Indian society led to the present malaise and social disintegration, and introduced destructive and inferior Euro-Canadian values – individualism, materialism, sexism, authoritarianism, and an ill-conceived domineering attitude to the environment. If Aboriginal communities are "an ungodly mess," the blame lies with Euro-Canadian values and methods. "White values, white institutions half-killed us and are killing us now." The restoration of tradition, "of balance, harmony and healing," is the solution. [41] The location of solutions in the past explains the current emphasis on the wisdom of the Elders (always capitalized). Four of the Assembly's first six constitutional recommendations refer to the Elders, while a fifth refers to "the principles and values inherited from our ancestors." [42]

The admitted mistreatment of First Nations women by men is due to the encroachment of European values that subordinated women to virtual chattel status and ended the equality of men and women in "traditional aboriginal cultures." [43] The recovery of sane, healthy, egalitarian relations between First

Nations men and women, therefore, is to come from the recovery of past traditions that will give "Aboriginal women . . . more power, more status, more respect
than their feminist white sisters."[44] The Charter, a "document which is foreign to
our people,"[45] is no solution, apparently because it values individualism, not
"the collective" as Aboriginal culture does. "If the right of the individual conflicts
with the right of the group," states the Assembly, "our tradition is clear. The
Charter is not an Aboriginal document."[46] Its acceptance would be an aggra-
vation, not a contribution to a solution. According to Boldt and Long, whose
analysis supports the AFN position, the Charter is a major challenge to Indian
cultural identity.[47] Indians, they report, see the Charter as a chosen instrument
of the federal government to assimilate them. More generally, they assert, the
Charter rests on the same ethnocentric denigration of Indian culture that led to
the imposition of Christianity, to the "racist" Indian Act, to the imposing of alien
forms of government, and to the overall legislative goal of assimilation.[48]

To apply the Charter, states the Assembly, would mean that:

> women would be asking the Canadian government to look after their
> interests, probably through litigation . . . litigation [is] a non-Aboriginal
> way of solving disputes. . . . In any event, real membership in the commun-
> ity cannot be litigated; it can only be earned, and insisting on 'my rights' is
> neither an Aboriginal custom nor a good way of winning a welcome from
> the community.[49]

*To the Source* recommends that the Charter not apply, "but that gender equality
be formally established in formal Aboriginal Charters of Rights and Freedoms,"[50] a proposal that is neither defended nor explained.

The strongest support for the Charter's application appears to come from the
Native Women's Association of Canada. Much of their clientele is drawn from
Aboriginal women who lost Indian status, regained it under Bill C-31, but are
very often unable to regain band membership and resume reserve life. As a result,
their literature pays negligible attention to Métis and Inuit, and directs its political attacks at the Assembly of First Nations and the reserve-based political
systems fostered by the Indian Act.[51]

Their case for the Charter is straightforward. They describe the reserve system
and band councils as male-dominated, leading to the continuing legal, political,
and social subordination of Aboriginal women. Patriarchal power structures,
established and supported by the federal government, help to explain the former
legal requirement that Indian women lost their Indian status when they married
non-Indians. They note that challenges to this practice were fought in court by
many Indian organizations and provincial associations of chiefs. Deliverance
came with the Charter, and "might have taken many more years" without it.[52]
Many of the reinstated women under Bill C-31, however, have been unable to gain

band membership and return to reserve life because, it is claimed, of the opposition of male leaders on reserves. In sum, "male privilege" is described "as the norm on reserve lands."[53] Anomie and social disorganization are rampant on many reserves, and physical and sexual abuse of women is widespread.[54] Accordingly, "it is asking a great deal to ask us as women to have confidence in the men in power in our communities."[55] As a result, the Native Women's Association categorically asserts that the Charter must apply and the notwithstanding clause should not be available as an escape clause for Aboriginal governments.[56] Interestingly, the claim that the Charter should apply tends to be justified by an appeal to international norms and instruments, not to Canadian citizenship.[57] Thus a recent paper by the Native Women's Association arguing for the application of the Charter referred glowingly to the Charter of the United Nations and the Universal Declaration of Human Rights, and described the Association's task as "to ensure women's enjoyment of all the rights granted to us by the United Nations."[58]

Their dependence on the Charter is based on a double sense of minority, outsider status. Historically, both Indian band council governments and the federal government have been seen as opponents rather than supporters of their interests and rights. Indeed, Ottawa is described as "a foreign government" that created an insensitive patriarchy in Indian communities.[59] Consequently, they appear as rootless and placeless in their own political literature, and hence especially attracted to rights and prone to passionate advocacy of their need to be personally heard in constitutional and other forums, because others cannot be trusted to speak for them.

Structurally, the support of Aboriginal women for the Charter is precisely analogous to the strong Charter support among Anglophones and allophones in Quebec. In each case, Charter supporters are found among those who expect to be on the receiving end of power – minorities in Quebec, and women in Aboriginal communities – not among those who expect to wield it.

Although we do not know how many Aboriginal women share the apprehensions of the Native Women's Association of Canada, the social disorganization the latter describes is not denied by the major Aboriginal organizations. Consequently, the Association has triggered a valuable debate on issues that might otherwise not have surfaced in the contemporary climate of opinion – namely, does the political sociology of Aboriginal (especially reserve) communities argue in favour of or against the application of the Charter. Analysis from this vantage point sidesteps the basic AFN contention that the Charter's conflict is with traditional Indian culture, to which a return is sought. Boldt and Long, strong supporters of Indian opposition to the Charter, agree that Indians are not "currently uniformly and consistently" adhering to traditional customs and admit that they have gone a "long way" toward more "modernized" institutions. Their traditions constitute a "charter myth" of the good society, not a description of the present situation. [60] Obviously, an answer to the question of whether the Charter should apply to Indian communities depends on whether the reality the Charter will confront is the contemporary reality of socially disorganized communities or a future reality in which Indian peoples will have recovered and live by traditions that are now enfeebled. The next few paragraphs presuppose the former is the reality test.

The following are among the more obviously relevant conditions that the Charter decision must confront. (1) The small populations of Aboriginal communities, coupled with pervasive kinship ties, are likely to generate a politics of factionalism in which the ins and the outs are sharply demarcated, to the benefit of the former when public goods are distributed. (2) Given the poverty of most Aboriginal communities, access to the public sector – its jobs, its contracts, and the possession of official political and bureaucratic power – will be one of the main routes to economic success. Further, office-holders will partly be protected from vigilant opposition by the absence of an independent entrepreneurial, employing class. (3) The relatively great extent of external public funding will have the side effect of reducing the constraints that otherwise apply to office-holders dependent on their own citizenry for funds. (4) The homogeneous ethnic base of Aboriginal political communities and the predictably periodic occurrence of tensions with their non-Aboriginal neighbours, or with federal and provincial governments, will, on such occasions, generate an in-group solidarity that may make dissent difficult. [61] (5) Finally, there is general agreement that many Aboriginal communities, victims of historical maltreatment by others, are home to social anomie, malaise, and a staggering array of ills indicative of major social breakdown. While self-government is admittedly designed to alleviate these conditions, they do not constitute a particularly auspicious starting point for unfettered majoritarian government.

The preceding conditions all strongly argue for application of the Charter or a functionally similar Aboriginal equivalent. [62] Attention needs also to be given to the context in which an Aboriginal government might apply the notwithstanding clause, if constitutionally empowered to do so. Resort to the notwithstanding clause by a government of the existing federal system takes place in a context of legal advisers, and of parliamentary politics, with vigilant opposition parties and inquisitive media. It is a public act that carries high risk, given the general popularity of the Charter and the existence of a professional class of Charter monitors. How many of these conditions will be duplicated in an Aboriginal nation of under a thousand people in northern Canada? Does the equality argument that the third order of Aboriginal government should have the notwithstanding clause because the federal and provincial governments have it also suggest that its use should be subject to the same controls of professional advice, high visibility, opposition challenges, etc.? If the answer is "yes," how can that similarity of context be achieved?

A concluding observation: Aboriginal self-government will not relieve the Canadian government from international responsibility for the rights record in Aboriginal communities. Aboriginal leaders have brilliantly exploited the international arena to embarrass the Canadian government. The same external monitoring will continue after self-government, but since an international presence and visibility attaches to Canada, not to each of the hundreds of self-governing Aboriginal peoples, it is the former that will be held accountable for the availability of rights among the latter. A Canadian government plea of cultural relativism, to justify the non-availability of Charter rights, for example, will fall on deaf ears.

The preceding arguments for the availability of Charter rights in Aboriginal communities are supported by an additional practical concern that appears, thus far, to have received inadequate attention. If self-governing Aboriginal peoples of the future manage to reject the Charter's application to their affairs while remaining heavily dependent on the larger society for funds, they risk defining themselves as strangers to those who control and disburse the funds and resources they need. Obligations owed to fellow-citizens carry a compulsion that philanthropy to needy quasi-strangers does not.

## Conclusion

Those who trivialized the 1982 Constitution Act, with its Charter, as a limited achievement, by contrasting it with the many remaining unmet constitutional demands, were mistaken. The Charter, as the first part of this paper argues, has profoundly transformed the Canadian constitutional order. Nevertheless, those who hoped that the Charter would reduce federal-provincial tensions and dampen Quebec nationalism by strengthening the pan-Canadian community are, ten years later, disappointed. The pan-Canadian community has been strengthened, but unevenly, as the Charter receives differential support from rest-of-Canada, Québécois, and Aboriginal peoples, especially from their elites.

Initially, students analysed the Charter in terms of its compatibility with federalism and parliamentary government. Ten years later, the defenders of parliamentary supremacy have admitted defeat, and struggle to keep the notwithstanding clause alive. While the integration of the Charter with federalism is not yet a settled issue, these two constitutional instruments no longer confront each other as rival crusading principles hoping for a knockout blow. The task now, engaged in by courts, governments, and scholars, is to work out an accommodation respectful of both.

The political task for the coming decade is to fit the Charter to what we increasingly see as the multinational reality of contemporary Canada. This is difficult precisely because the Charter's political purposes confront rival national ambitions, particularly among some of the nationalist Québécois and Aboriginal elites. In other words, the lack of consensus on the nature of the Canadian community, the very lack the Charter was intended to overcome, inevitably gets redefined as a debate on the Charter's role in a deeply divided society unable to agree on fundamentals.

These shortcomings might suggest to some that the introduction of the Charter was a regrettable and avoidable mistake in constitution-making, because lions and lambs do not yet cavort peaceably together. This would be the wrong conclusion to draw. The enthusiasm of those who fought for the Charter and who became Charter Canadians after its introduction clearly suggests that the combination of federalism and parliamentary government made insufficient contact with the values and identities of many Canadians to legitimate the overall constitutional order. Further, those who define the Charter as a failure because its achievements, thus far, fall short of the ambitious political goals of its sponsors are, perhaps without realizing it, advocates of a constitutional incrementalism restricted to marginal change. Who would found nations, create national health schemes, fashion charters, pursue Aboriginal self-government, or – as Newfoundland did in 1948 – vote to join Canada if such actions should only be pursued if the middle and long-range outcomes were clearly known in advance? To so argue is a recipe for paralysis and a denial of the right, often the necessity, to act in the face of uncertainty. The requirement to act in the face of uncertainty confronts us now, as we make decisions on the Charter's future role, as part of the larger, also risky decision to try and get our constitutional house in order so that we can get on with the task of living together as one or more peoples. We have been a constitutional Hamlet for too long.

Chapter Nine

# Constitutional Change and the Three Equalities

## Introduction

The impediments to a successful future round of constitutional change are many and varied. The long history of failed reform efforts, most recently Meech Lake, confirms that constitutional reform is not a casual game to be lightheartedly undertaken. While analysis of past failures would be instructive, the contemporary situation is *sui generis* for three fundamental reasons:

- In 1982, Canadians constitutionalized a comprehensive domestic amending formula based on the principle of equality of the provinces.
- Formal constitutional change since 1982 confronts a constitutional culture strongly influenced by the Charter.
- The post-Meech Lake Quebec demands will be couched in the language of nationhood. Quebec, according to Premier Bourassa, will negotiate only with Ottawa, one-on-one.

Whether Canadians emerge as one or more people from their contemporary constitutional malaise will be dictated by how they respond to the three equalities noted in the title of this chapter – of citizens, of provinces, and of two nations. The first equality, of citizens, is symbolized by the Charter, and addresses the citizen-state dimension of Canadian existence. The second equality, of provinces, articulated most explicitly in the amending formula, is a contemporary response to federalism, one of the historic pillars of the Canadian constitutional order.

The third equality of two national peoples is implicit in the possible shattering of Canada into two sovereign states. Each of the three equalities is imperialistic, unwilling to be restricted to a narrow sphere of Canada's constitutional life. Their coexistence is disharmonious. The constitutional task is to decide on their interrelationships, and on how and where each equality is to be favoured or sacrificed in whole or in part.

Meech Lake is inexplicable if the contribution of the first two equalities to its unravelling is not given analytical pride of place. The equality of provinces dictated that what was given to Quebec, the distinct society excepted, was extended to all provinces, transforming a Quebec round into a provincial round and antagonizing supporters of a strong central government. The equality of citizen norms stimulated by the Charter was the source of much of the opposition to Meech Lake, on the grounds that the "distinct society" clause would or could lead to unacceptable inequalities in citizenship between Québécois and other Canadians.

The constraining effect of these two equalities lies behind this paper's argument that an asymmetrical federalism profoundly sensitive to the particularity of Quebec, and that takes Quebec out of the conventional normative frameworks of equal provinces and equal citizens, is one of the few constitutional stopping points available short of Quebec sovereignty. If this is so, an asymmetrical status for Quebec should also be seen as a vehicle to salvage an admittedly uneven country-wide role for the federal government.

The impediment to a two independent nations solution is not the existence of equality norms that need to be bypassed, but the inchoate nature of the rest of Canada, one of the two imputed national entities that are to emerge from the debris of a failing federalism to confront each other as coexisting sovereign neighbours. That a Canada-without-Quebec might become a cohesive self-confident country is clear. However, that it does not now enjoy an institutional frame that shapes it and official leaders that speak to it and for it is also clear. As long as the Canadian Confederation continues, Canada-without-Quebec is officially headless and voiceless. One of the parties in the prospective third equality of two nations, therefore, is waiting to be born. In formal terms, it will only emerge after the breakup and thus too late to work out in advance the terms of its coexistence with a sovereign Quebec.

Discussion of if and how we can bypass two symbolically potent equalities is not the stuff of empirical social science. Even less so is a speculative appraisal of some complexities of moving toward a two-nations solution when only one of the two prospective polities now exists in corporeal form. Consequently, this paper is written as a reflective essay. Its purpose is to portray certain big constitutional features sharply rather than to linger lovingly over a nuanced portrait overflowing with detail.

# Renewed Federalism

### CONSTRAINING NORMS: THE CHARTER

There is general agreement that the Charter contributes to a more participant-oriented constitutional culture, and, in particular, that it has fostered constitutional interest groups devoted to the protection and enhancement of "their" constitutional clause: section 28 for women, section 27 for ethnocultural elites, section 23 for official-language minorities, and section 15 for the particular groups identified in that clause and for equality-seekers in general.[1] These orientations, when combined with the constitutional politics of the Aboriginal peoples, generate what might be called multiple constitutional particularisms, or, from a different perspective, a constitutional fragmentation, as discrete, self-interested social groups seek to monopolize particular constitutional (mainly Charter) clauses.[2] The multiplication of the cast of would-be actors in the constitutional reform process profoundly complicates the pursuit of formal constitutional change. Meech Lake confirms that governments can no longer control the process of constitutional reform and that Canadians lack agreement on the kind of amending process, including formal and informal aspects, able to accommodate both governments and relevant publics. To end the analysis of the Charter's impact at this point, however, would be to miss the more general constraint it injects into the constitutional process.

For its Anglophone supporters, the Charter fosters a conception of citizenship that defines Canadians as equal bearers of rights independent of provincial location. This legitimates a citizen concern for the treatment of fellow Canadians by other than one's own provincial government. By contrast, the working theory of federalism, especially in its classical version, had been that an individual's provincial concerns should be restricted to the fellow residents of his or her own province. Federalism presupposed high fences and uninquisitive neighbours.

Historically, this isolation of provincial domains has always been qualified by various constitutional instruments, often viewed as anti-federal devices – disallowance, the declaratory power, the spending power, etc. – that have been vehicles for federal government intervention in provincial affairs. While these traditional instruments have become weakened or obsolete, the Charter was deliberately designed as a new constraint on federalism; indeed, that was its purpose. The Charter may be thought of as a floor of rights, subject admittedly to the notwithstanding clause, that politicians are instructed to respect and courts to enforce. The Meech Lake debate, however, indicates that the Charter norm is also sustained by a citizenry that views the possibility of a distinct and weaker Charter regime in another province as a constitutional affront. It offends the norm of an equal rights-possessing citizenry uniformly present in the federal, ten provincial, and two territorial arenas.

The Charter generates a roving normative Canadianism oblivious to provincial boundaries, and thus hostile to constitutional stratagems such as the Meech Lake "distinct society" that might vary the Charter's availability in one province. Federalist and even stronger dualist justifications for constitutional recognition of Quebec as a distinct society clashed with a Canadian Charter norm applied to Quebec by those who lived elsewhere. The Quebec rationale for an asymmetrical Charter confronted a homogenizing Charter-derived rights-bearing Canadianism that applied not to Québécois but to Canadians who happened to live in Quebec. The psychological potency of the Charter was a recurrent theme in the New Brunswick Select Committee hearings and the Manitoba Task Force hearings. The former stated that "of all the Constitutional acts, the Charter is undoubtedly the most important for individual Canadians" and recommended including it in the Accord as a fundamental characteristic of Canada.[3] The latter reported that over half of its interveners were apprehensive about the Accord's impact on "Charter rights, particularly sex equality rights."[4] The Charter, in the words of a Francophone student of the reactions to Meech Lake, has virtually become an icon in English-speaking Canada, a symbolic appreciation it does not receive from the Quebec Francophone majority, especially from nationalist elites.[5]

Anglophone Charter support makes it difficult for the federal and other provincial governments to respond positively to Quebec demands for a distinctive constitutional recognition that might weaken the relative availability of Charter rights. This constraint is exacerbated by the fact that the Charter, as noted above, generates participant orientations in its Anglophone supporters that are hostile to the elitist practices of executive federalism.

The Charter's potency derives from its linkage with citizenship, a highly symbolic concept infused with elements of the sacred and a concept that by its very nature is country-wide in application. Federalists such as Clyde Wells objected to the Meech Lake "distinct society" clause for its violation of the equality of the provinces principle.[6] In marked contrast, women's groups and other Charter supporters objected to the distinct society on the ground that it violated the norms of equal citizenship. To Meech Lake's Charter-supporting opponents, the distinct society suggested an asymmetrical citizenship that was viewed as a self-contradiction. Accordingly, advocates of a Quebec constitutional status going beyond Meech Lake must think through the feasibility and consequences of an asymmetrical application of the Charter to Quebec and the asymmetrical citizenship that logically follows.

## CONSTRAINING NORMS: EQUALITY OF PROVINCES

One of the key issues in the long-lasting Canadian debate over a domestic amending formula as a prerequisite to patriation was whether province or region should be the basic unit for determining support for a constitutional amendment. The choice of region, as in the Victoria Charter proposals and in the federal government proposals in the 1980-81 unilateral package, necessarily entailed the inequality of the provinces. In each of the four-province regions of western and Atlantic Canada up to two provinces could find themselves on the losing side of a successful amendment. Ontario and Quebec, defined as regions, could not suffer a similar fate.

The provincial equality solution to this "inequity" was to devise an amending formula that repudiated the concept of region for amendment purposes and replaced it by province, as was done in the Constitution Act, 1982. The relevant formula, therefore, became two-thirds of the provinces with 50 per cent of the population plus the federal government; or for a select list of constitutional provisions, the unanimous approval of all governments. The equality of the provinces in the two-thirds plus 50 per cent amending category was supported, as well, by the opting-out provisions that allowed up to three provinces in a ten-province Canada to opt out of an amendment transferring legislative jurisdiction to the federal government, and in certain circumstances to receive financial compensation. The equality principle was further extended in the Meech Lake Accord, which enlarged the subject matters covered by the unanimity amending formula and also enriched the compensation requirement by extending it to all cases of provincial government opting out of an amendment transferring jurisdiction to the federal government.

The imperialist diffusion of the equality of the provinces principle to other realms is illustrated by its central status as one of the three principles of the proposed triple-E Senate (equal, elected, and effective). Further, the Meech Lake practice of giving to all ten provinces whatever was needed to respond to Quebec's five demands, with the exception of the distinct society interpretive principle, was justified by the federal government as a response to the "principle of the equality of all the provinces."[7] In this way, the Quebec round became a provincial round. What Quebec asked for, British Columbia received.

For Premier Wells, however, this was an insufficient accommodation to the equality of the provinces principle. He feared that the application of the "distinct society" clause to Quebec alone, in conjunction with the affirmation of the "role of the legislature and Government of Quebec to preserve and promote the distinct identity of Quebec," would give the Quebec government powers unavailable to any other provincial government.[8] Premier Vander Zalm responded to this apparent contradiction by releasing a British Columbia government position paper that proposed recognizing all provinces as distinct societies. [9]

The provincial equality principle is a potent constraint on constitutional responses that recognize Quebec's specificity by an asymmetrical federalism granting Quebec jurisdictional powers not possessed by other provincial governments. The ability of the rest of Canada to respond to Quebec is restricted by its reluctance to provincialize itself. Alternatively, the provincialization of the rest of Canada is to be driven by Quebec nationalism. In this case, the cost of accommodating Quebec is paid by those Anglophone Canadians who have no desire to strengthen their provincial against their Canadian selves. The equality of the provinces principle, like the Charter norm of citizen equality, therefore, greatly impedes a sensitive accommodation to Quebec's specificity by jurisdictional differentiation as long as Quebec is defined as a normal province.

### FINDING ROOM TO MANOEUVRE: ESCAPE FROM THE CONSTRAINTS OF MINIMUM CHANGE

One of the conventional post-Meech Lake wisdoms is that if "English Canada" rejected the limited Meech Lake package, it will be even more resistant to a larger package. As the proposals of the Bélanger-Campeau Commission, the Quebec Liberal Party, and the Quebec government will certainly go beyond Meech Lake, the possibility of an agreement with "English Canada" is considered minuscule. This logic, however, is not irresistible.

The equality of provinces and Charter constraints derive from the definition of Quebec as a province like the others, and of Quebec citizens as citizens like the others. In each case, the constraint flows from the placing of Quebec and its citizenry in the categories "province" and "citizen" from which certain constitutional consequences, in particular a rough uniformity of treatment, are deemed necessarily to follow. Further, as already noted, both equalities of provinces and of citizens have recently been fleshed out and made concrete by the amending formula and the Charter. They are ascending, not declining, constitutional norms. Hence, escape from their constricting assumptions in contexts where they fully apply has become more rather than less difficult in the last decade.

These restraints can most logically be avoided by removing Quebec from the category "province" and Quebec residents from the category of homogeneous, standardized rights-bearing Canadians. This requires devising conceptions of the relationships between Quebec and the rest of Canada that rupture the symmetry rationale flowing from the application of the equality of the provinces principle. Such a conception should simultaneously provide a rationale for the application of a greatly weakened Charter regime to the citizens of a jurisdiction that is not a jurisdiction like the others.

The political logic is straightforward. The Meech Lake lesson is that the flexibility and manoeuvrability of the rest of Canada in responding to Quebec are severely limited by the two equalities. However, a larger change can escape the constraints by redefining the Quebec/rest-of-Canada relationship as being unique, as involving neither a province nor a standardized version of Canadian citizenship. Such a redefinition must make it appear "natural" that the reception and applicability of the Charter change as it hits the Quebec border and that the criteria applicable to standardized provincehood are irrelevant to the prospectively unique Quebec situation. From this perspective, the difficulty with Meech Lake was that its accompanying rhetoric of returning Quebec with honour and enthusiasm to the Canadian family of governments and couching the Accord, distinct society excepted, in the language of the equality of the provinces immediately brought to the surface the two sets of equality constraints that contributed to the Accord's downfall. Accordingly, a small change may be less digestible than a larger one if it is subject to constraints from which a larger package escapes.

On the other hand, the larger package might generate other problems no less resistant to resolution. That discussion is taken up later. The limited purpose of this section has been only to suggest that some constraints can be avoided by redefining the situation to facilitate escape from a system of otherwise controlling comparisons. If, for example, constraint X is a consequence of being a Y, it may be avoided by transforming a Y into a Z. Meech Lake did not travel that route. It sought instead to make Quebec a special kind of Y, but the degree of differentiation sought did not lift it above the constraints that apply to a Y. While an independent Z is the most obvious escape route, an asymmetrical Z(I) may have an almost equal capacity, along with the added virtue of limiting disruptive discontinuities. This discussion is not tautological and it does not impute magic to changes in labelling. It suggests the need for a convincing argument that Quebec is a Z(I) rather than a Y, and hence not subject to the constraints of X.

### FINDING ROOM TO MANOEUVRE: CHARTER GROUPS, ABORIGINAL PEOPLES, AND QUÉBÉCOIS

The Constitution Act, 1982, has greatly increased the cast of constitutional stakeholders; they now extend beyond governments to include a variety of Charter constituencies and the Aboriginal peoples of Canada. The Charter gives constitutional recognition to a non-territorial pluralism of women, "multicultural" Canadians, official-language minorities, and section 15 equality-seekers, among others. That their recognition occurs via the Charter tempts them to employ the non-bargaining, non-compromising language of rights. That their constitutional status has only recently been achieved, and after struggles and reversals, makes them suspicious of constitutional change proposals fashioned in their absence. That their constitutional identities and ambitions have come to be bound up with "their" Charter clauses infuses their constitutional language with passion and emotion. The Charter groups are joined by the Aboriginal peoples – Indians, Inuit, and Métis – attached to a different set of constitutional clauses and driven by a different set of constitutional ambitions that, especially for status Indians, challenge Canadianism with rival nationalisms.

Thus, the constitution is now home for a counter-culture, for Canadians with a tendency to see themselves as marginal, as overlooked, or as the Métis are often described, as the "forgotten people." The avid response of these groups to the Aboriginal constitutional clauses and to the Charter suggests that federalism and the first ministers who speak for it make only limited contact with the multiple particularistic identities of a modern people. Further, the politics of the 1982 amending formula, with its requirement of legislative ratification, gives these new players access to make their case. Finally, they display little willingness to go to the end of the queue and await their constitutional turn.

From one perspective, Meech Lake was the site of a clash between the territorial pluralism of federalism and the homogenizing, universalizing thrust of the Charter. For its Anglophone supporters the Charter postulated a country-wide uniformity of rights-bearing citizens. These rights constituted a Canadian floor protected against provincial transgression, save by resort to the notwithstanding clause, whose use was fraught with political danger for its employers. A similar version of the Charter was held by its Quebec opponents, except they evaluated it negatively as a juggernaut of uniformity crushing justified provincial initiatives, most threateningly language policy, that challenged its writ. [10]

Is there an alternative view of the Charter that might soften its conflict with federalism in general and Québécois specificity in particular? Conceptually yes; politically maybe.

A minority tendency in Charter literature, illustrated by Tom Berger and David Elkins, views the Charter as a vehicle for particular groups to realize their objectives. For Berger, the Charter is an instrument for the recognition of indigenous, ethnic, and linguistic pluralism. [11] For Elkins, the Canadian Charter contrasts profoundly with the American Bill of Rights in its pervasive emphasis on collective and community rights. [12] Their view of the Charter as more than an instrument of liberal individualism is empirically, if indirectly, supported by the nature of the Charter's contribution to constitutional politics. Quite independently of how the tension between group and individual rights is adjudicated in courtrooms, the Charter enters the arena of constitutional reform under the banner of organizations speaking on behalf of particular groups – women's organizations on behalf of section 28, ethnic organizations on behalf of section 27, official-language minority organizations on behalf of section 23, and various equality-seeking groups on behalf of section 15. They, rather than the various civil liberties associations, were the defenders of the Charter against the Meech Lake Accord. When their numbers are swelled by the many Aboriginal organizations that press Aboriginal claims, it is evident that the new constitutional actors who advocate Charter and Aboriginal constitutional concerns are drawn from a handful of social categories defined by language, gender, race, indigenousness, ethnicity, disability, etc.; they are united by ascriptive or acquired characteristics. The members of each group share a certain fellow-feeling derived from some similarity of social condition and a shared constitutional fate. Whether their constitutional condition can best be described as group or collective rights is not germane to my argument here. What is relevant, however, is that when their constitutional situation, self-perceptions, and aspirations are approached sociologically it is evident that they share many traits with nationalist Québécois.

It is not unreasonable to see parallels between the desire of various named groups for affirmative action under section 15(2) and Quebec's desire to gain the constitutional leverage of being recognized as a distinct society. Section 25 of the Charter that protects "aboriginal, treaty or other rights or freedoms" from abrogation or derogation by the Charter is practically a constitutional replica of the Quebec desire to use the Meech Lake "distinct society" clause to mute the Charter's impact. Further, both Aboriginal peoples and Québécois share an historic sense of once having been masters of their collective fate in ancient times. Both, of course, fear engulfment, resist assimilation, and are apprehensive about the future of their language(s). The opposition of status Indians to the assimilation objectives of the federal government's 1969 White Paper was analogous to the Quebec nationalist concern that the Charter's language rights will weaken the linguistic measures needed to protect the Quebec Francophone community. The status Indian attack on the 1969 White Paper was mounted behind the banner of "citizen plus" to describe their unique position in Canada,[13] again a relatively clear functional equivalent of Quebec as not a province *comme les autres* but as a distinct society. Another supportive example is provided by feminist authors who assert that section 28 is not to be thought of as a simple equalizer of the rights of men and women, but rather as a vehicle for the attainment of substantive equality in that it contains an implicit directive to the judiciary to make the clause a vehicle for feminist affirmative action.[14]

Conceptually, therefore, there is considerable symmetry or congruity in the constitutional orientations of Aboriginal peoples, many Charter supporters, and Québécois. The non-territorial social pluralism of women, the disabled, and ethnocultural Canadians, the self-government aspirations of Aboriginal peoples, especially those with a land base, the private fears and the constitutional objectives of official-language minorities, and the territorially based desire of Francophone Québécois for a constitutional arrangement within which their individuality can flourish are all grounded in the belief that diversity may need special constitutional succouring. In some cases, this may require the support of the Charter; in other cases, escape from it.

None of the preceding suggests that the apparent conflict that pitted the Charter and Aboriginal constituencies against Quebec in the Meech Lake Accord was based on false consciousness. It does suggest, however, that the conflict can be recast as one in which the contestants are playing the same rather than a different game. The constitutional task, therefore, may be redefined as the need to reconcile coexisting solidarities, the search for a *modus vivendi* among territorial (Quebec, some Aboriginal peoples) and non-territorial social pluralisms (the many diffuse constituencies of Charter supporters and those Aboriginal peoples who are landless and dispersed).

While recognition of at least some affinity of group identity and aspiration among the above groups does not eliminate their conflicts, it may support mutual understanding and provide a limited common ground for a *rapprochement*. That *rapprochement*, of course, must occur within the Québécois community, which is internally plural, as well as between it and the others. Making constitutional sense of our territorial federalism and our social federalism, much of which is caught up in the Charter, requires a blending of affinities that are already intertwined, not a clash of light and darkness.

ASYMMETRICAL FEDERALISM: TWO QUEBEC ASYMMETRIES –
CHARTER AND JURISDICTION

Politically, the Charter was conceived as an instrument of Canadian unity. Its Quebec application, however, has been problematic. Initially it was seen by the nationalists as a central component of the "betrayal" of 1980-82. Conceptually, its claimed individual rights emphasis and its minority official-language rights were seen as threatening Quebec's attempt to shape its own linguistic future. Quebec political and scholarly analysis is replete with negative references to the homogenizing, universalizing thrust of the Charter.[15] Intellectually, the passionate Charter activists in Anglophone Canada have almost no counterparts in Francophone Quebec. In particular, the support of Anglophone academics for the political, nation-building purposes of the Charter is not duplicated in Quebec.

The notwithstanding clause was initially employed by the Parti Québécois government across the board to limit the Charter's impact on Quebec and to symbolize the Quebec government's opposition to the 1982 settlement. Subsequently, Premier Bourassa not only used the notwithstanding clause for

Quebec's language of signs legislation, but vigorously defended the clause as an essential instrument of Quebec protection against the Charter.[16] Among its other purposes, the Meech Lake "distinct society" clause was intended to constrain the impact of the Charter on Quebec.

If Quebec's moves toward greater autonomy are contained within a revised federalism, a fully applicable Charter will appear even more alien. It will be seen as an unwelcome tight ideological link contrasting strongly with the generally attenuated links with the rest of Canada characteristic of asymmetry. Asymmetry will strengthen the already well-developed tendency to see the Quebec Charter as the appropriate vehicle for rights protection in Quebec. Perhaps in anticipation, Francophone representations before the Bélanger-Campeau Commission have been virtually devoid of positive Charter references.

While there are competing political tendencies in Quebec, including strong Charter support from Anglophone and other minority communities and residual reminders that the Charter was conceived by Pierre Trudeau and Quebec federalists, there is little doubt that the overall tendency of Quebec evaluation is much more negative than elsewhere in Canada. Accordingly, the rest of Canada should be prepared to consider seriously an asymmetrical federalism in which the Charter has a more limited or even non-existent application to the enhanced jurisdictional powers that a future Quebec in Canada will wield.

In one sense, the generation of an asymmetrical Charter regime is an easier goal to achieve than is an asymmetrical jurisdictional status for Quebec. This is because the repercussions of the latter on the overall constitution, requiring an asymmetrical status for Quebec MPs at a minimum, would be much more pervasive and consequential than the impact of the former.

In relative terms, an asymmetrical Charter regime by itself would have limited ramifications for other institutions of government. Since it would not directly affect the division of powers, it would not, of itself, affect the status of Quebec MPs in the House of Commons. Federal legislation would apply to Quebec as to the rest of Canada and would, of course, be subject to the Canadian Charter in Quebec as elsewhere. It is true, of course, that an asymmetrical Charter regime for Quebec's domestic legislation has jurisdictional consequences as it subjects that legislation and administrative behaviour to less onerous restraints than are applied elsewhere. The restriction or non-application of the Charter to Quebec jurisdiction might involve a reshuffling of procedures and criteria for appointments to the Supreme Court and to the Quebec superior courts, but these pose a lesser order of complexity than the changes to House of Commons representation and to the practice of responsible government that would follow an asymmetrical enhancement of Quebec jurisdictional powers.

On the other hand, an asymmetrical Charter means an asymmetrical citizenship at a time when the Charter has immensely strengthened citizenship as a constitutional category in the rest of Canada. It provides the core constitutional identity for many English-speaking Canadians. It is a potent instrument of constitutional mobilization. The input from Charter groups to the various Meech Lake hearings was rivalled in extent and passion only by Aboriginal presentations.

Overt constitutional recognition of an asymmetrical Charter, therefore, is not a trivial constitutional adaptation. It is not tinkering. It may be institutionally straightforward, but it is morally complex. It is a profound admission of our constitutional divisions, a recognition of the fact that we are not now and have despaired of becoming a single people whose dualism is transcended by an allegiance to a common regime of rights.

None of this is to suggest that a significantly different Charter regime in Quebec should be automatically rejected. In the practical and psychological sense a different *de facto* regime already exists. To constitutionalize and build on the difference is to admit that the political purposes of the Charter project have not been met in Quebec and cannot be met in the future.

The second and more important asymmetry for Quebec involves jurisdiction. From the mid-sixties to the Constitution Act, 1982, the division of powers was a priority item on Quebec's constitutional agenda. The federal government under Trudeau sidetracked the issue by stressing the need to deal, first, with a Charter and, second, with the reform of central institutions before turning to the division of powers. Meech Lake addressed the division of powers only indirectly. In the coming round of constitutional negotiations extensive Quebec-strengthening changes to the division of powers are probably unavoidable.

A response to Quebec, which is controlled by the equality of the provinces principle, will at the extremes display one of the following tendencies: (a) the response to Quebec will be minimal as the rest of Canada tries to salvage significant responsibilities for the central government; (b) alternatively, a sensitive accommodation of Quebec will produce an extensive across-the-board decentralization that neither in extent nor possibly in substance would represent an optimum division of federal-provincial responsibilities outside Quebec. Moreover, the latter response would deny Quebec the symbolic good of differentiated treatment that its nationalism seeks.

In sum, the equality of the provinces principle in future Quebec-Canada relations within a revised federalism no longer appears tenable. Consequently, and at a minimum, there will have to be constitutional recognition that Quebec is not a province like the others; preferably, the status of Quebec should be cast in terminology other than provincehood. The magnitude of this change should not be underestimated; however, its serious consideration is necessary if a constitutional option within federalism and short of independence is to be kept alive.

In evaluating this option, and working out the terms of its implementation, it will be necessary to extend the discussion beyond its most recent focus – consideration of the equality of the provinces norm or its violation from the sole vantage point of equity among provincial governments. Significant jurisdictional inequalities among provincial governments are simultaneously inequalities of citizenship between the residents of those provinces with different jurisdictional powers. It necessarily follows that the significance and application of federal government jurisdiction will vary from province to province. Hence, citizens in different provinces will have structural inducements to differ in their evaluations of the relative importance of federal and provincial arenas. If province X is not to be a province like the others in terms of jurisdiction, its citizens will not be citizens like the others. Further, the lesser jurisdiction of the federal government in province X necessarily suggests a correspondingly diminished role for MPs from province X. Otherwise the citizens of that province will wield voting power that violates the norm of equality of the vote, and may even violate the Charter.

In other words, major asymmetries in jurisdictional status lead inexorably to inequalities or proportionate asymmetries in the role and responsibilities of Quebec MPs in the House of Commons, and probably of senators as well. While minor anomalies are ubiquitous in a functioning constitutional order of some vintage, major anomalies that offend fundamental constitutional principles are unacceptable. The one in four members of the House of Commons from Quebec cannot be full participants when the House deals with matters that are in federal government jurisdiction outside Quebec but in "provincial" government jurisdiction in Quebec. In the negotiation of an asymmetric federalism, this is the crucial issue. It requires a rethinking of the practice and theory of responsible government – no mean task.

### ASYMMETRICAL FEDERALISM: IS ASYMMETRY VIABLE?

A system of asymmetrical federalism presupposes that the Quebec government has jurisdictional responsibilities not held by other governments, probably a different set of rights and obligations of Quebec MPs, and possibly a less comprehensive or stringent application of the Charter to an enhanced Quebec jurisdiction. Assuming that asymmetry can be attained, is it likely to endure?

On the one hand, it might be assumed that a particular asymmetrical arrangement more responsive than provincial status to Québécois nationalist pressures would have a greater stability than the standard provincehood left behind. By inference, also, the constitutionalization of asymmetry would clearly indicate a rest-of-Canada recognition of the Quebec difference and thus facilitate a coexistence based on dignity and respect.

On the other hand, these positive features are countered by the inducements to instability seemingly inherent in the absence of an external reference standard for asymmetrical status as a control. A system in which "a province is a province is a province" provides visible external criteria for the status of provincehood in the form of neighbouring provincial jurisdictions belonging to the same system. By the same token, the virtue of independence is that we know in juridical terms what an independent nation-state is; analytically, it is evident that the evolving meaning of statehood is transmitted by the international state system to its component units. In each case, province and nation-state, behaviour is constrained by a system of norms and statuses that have a certain givenness/naturalness. Definitions and criteria are not idiosyncratic, and hence are neither contingent nor subject to constant challenge. They are products of a system of evolving meanings, widely understood, sustained by tradition, and upheld by the other actors.

By contrast, any particular version of asymmetrical federalism lacks the stabilizing influence of controlling external models. On the contrary, the influence of the two most powerful models in its environment – province and nation-state – are likely to be destabilizing. As the future attraction and repulsion of these two models waxes and wanes within Quebec and in the rest of Canada, Quebec will be alternately pushed and pulled in the direction of one or the other reference point. Within Quebec the attractions of nation-statehood are likely to be stimulated by the dynamics of nationalist competition. In the rest of Canada, the provincial equality imperative will be wielded by expansive provincial governments hoping to level-up and by others resistant to anomalies seeking to level-down.

Any particular asymmetrical position is likely, therefore, to appear contingent and arbitrary, for its justification does not come from a body of rules that apply to many actors. Thus, in the world of constructed political arrangements, significant asymmetrical status is likely to be highly unstable.

This instability will be exaggerated in Quebec because the dynamics of political competition will continue to be driven by nationalism. Further, the diminished pan-Canadianism that will flow from asymmetrical status with its relative enhancement of the status of Quebec politicians at home and the diminished status of Quebec politicians in Ottawa, along with the aggrandizement of Quebec citizenship at the expense of Canadian, will be a weak counterfoil to Quebec nationalism. The relative decline in the status of the MPs from Quebec and the truncated political careers they will experience, including barriers to holding at least some cabinet posts, will reduce the relative quality of Quebec representation in Ottawa and the visibility of the federal government in Quebec.

If the Charter's applicability to Quebec were limited, as the Parti Québécois suggested in 1985, to democratic rights (sections 3-5),[17] associational ties crossing the Quebec/rest-of-Canada borders would be weakened. Charter litigation interest groups such as LEAF would retreat to the rest of Canada, retaining only a tenuous Quebec connection because of the surviving federalist jurisdiction in Quebec still covered by the Charter. The constitutional discourse of Quebec and the rest of Canada would increasingly diverge. Outside Quebec, a Charter-influenced series of constitutional discourses would revolve around issues of gender, multiculturalism, the equality rights of section 15, etc. While Québécois might have analogous discourses directed to their own political existence and focusing on Quebec's own Charter, such rhetoric would develop its own rhythms, would be directed to a different polity, and would reinforce the psychological basis of the constitutional separateness of Quebec. Conceptions of community in Quebec and in the rest of Canada would respond to different cues. Each would appear as somewhat of a stranger to the other. Conceptions of a common citizenship, perhaps the most potent constitutional category in democratic politics, would be displaced by coexisting if overlapping civic identities. Obviously, the normative assumptions behind what Pepin-Robarts called "sharing," which included "the equitable distribution of benefits," [18] would be eroded. The sense of mutual obligation that is the moral basis of sharing by means of equalization payments and regional development programs would be weakened. The spirit of calculation, already widespread in federalism's accounting mentality, would be especially pronounced on both sides of the asymmetrical divide.

In such circumstances, would Canada outside Quebec, British Columbia for example, not be resistant to making equalization payments to a Quebec whose Canadianism was gravely attenuated? Conversely, would Quebec agree to be treated as a "have" province whose taxpayers contributed extensively to equalization payments distributed to Atlantic Canada and to one or more western provinces?

For Québécois, an asymmetrical federalism produces an asymmetrical psyche in which the balance of loyalties to and identifications with Quebec and Canada is strongly tilted to the former. The emotional connection to the latter exists, so to speak, on sufferance rather than as the balance appropriate to a federalism in equilibrium, with both orders of government applying significant jurisdictional powers to the Quebec citizenry. From the Quebec perspective, stability in such a situation would derive only from a consistency of will over time, ideally informed by an unvarying self-interest. But such an enduring consistency and unvarying self-interest would be highly problematic in a context riven with the passion of nationalism and the spirit of calculation.

In the transition period, the instability is likely to be aggravated by the learning and unlearning involved in making the new asymmetrical arrangements work. These new arrangements will clearly be complicated with a Quebec government enjoying powers not possessed by other governments, Quebec MPs presumably wielding lesser powers than other MPs, Quebec citizens relating to the Charter differently from other Canadians, and a host of arrangements particular to Quebec with respect to executive federalism, the Supreme Court, and to various boards and commissions.

Accordingly, the task of managing the settling-in process of asymmetrical federalism will be, to say the least, challenging. The difficulties of the task will be compounded if the rest of Canada is simultaneously rearranging the relationships between the central government and the other nine provinces and two territories. Concurrently, those Québécois who previously supported the Charter and other arrangements of a departed federalism from which they gained status and identity are likely to be less than fully allied to the new constitutional regime.

Even in the long run, an above-average degree of instability appears probable, as the disputes that will attend asymmetry will not be resolvable by appeals to general rules but will be responded to in particularistic terms specific to one relationship only. Such a system of dispute resolution appears uniquely prone to allegations of favouritism or unfairness because of the relative absence of more general criteria to which appeals can be made.

## Independence: The Rest of Canada in an Ambiguous Game

A central ambiguity of the pending round of constitutional change is the coexistence of two very different constitutional games. The first is the traditional federalism game – the refashioning of the constitutional system to reduce the tensions among dualism, provincialism, and Canadianism. This time around this game, if played out to a conclusion, will probably produce a drastically different federalism with Quebec breaking through the constraints of provincialism to attain an asymmetrical relationship to the other provinces and to the central government. Provincialism will no longer constrain the Quebec side of dualism. However, such an outcome will still be federal in some minimum sense. The federal government will retain some independent jurisdiction in Quebec and there will continue to be Quebec members in the federal Parliament. Consequently, there is an obvious bargaining role for the federal government in achieving such an outcome. It can speak for the modified pan-Canadian dimension that will survive in the next constitutional regime and for its own future role as a government of all Canadians. Thus, this constitutional game can possibly be handled, admittedly with difficulty, by an adaptation of the amending process to accommodate Premier Bourassa's assertion that from now on he will only negotiate one-on-one with the federal government.

The second game is the independence game in which Quebec seeks the status of an independent nation-state, even if it is one linked to a surviving, if shrunken, Canada by various agreements. This outcome necessarily implies the emergence of one or more parallel states alongside an independent Quebec. For the sake of simplicity I will assume that Canada-without-Quebec will survive as a single entity, initially at least as a country of nine provinces, two territories, and a central government.

If that is the direction in which we are headed, the second nation-state has no official spokesperson to articulate its concerns prior to the actual rupture. The provincial governments outside Quebec, acting either collectively or individually, are incompetent to speak for an English-speaking rest of Canada waiting eagerly or reluctantly to be born. Their concern is with the provincial jurisdictional dimension of our existence as a people. Further, each of them speaks only for a limited territorially restricted segment of a future Canada-without-Quebec. They are thus doubly incapacitated, by jurisdiction and territory, from assuming a Canadian leadership role. They are conditioned by tradition to be provincial and by electoral constraints not to deviate from tradition. At least some of them will be tempted to employ the equality of provinces principle as a vehicle to ride on the coattails of Quebec demands and thus strengthen (what might be) the misperception that Canadians are engaged in a federalism game. This will delay the recognition that Canadians are engaged in, if such it is, an independence game.

Occasional exceptions to the contrary, there is little recent evidence to encourage the belief that the premiers of the rest of Canada will rise above their provincial ambitions to speak for a Canadian constituency. A Canada-without-Quebec fashioned by provincial hands would not do justice to the Canadian dimension. In 1980-81 the Gang of Eight provincial governments opposed the Charter, fought successfully for a notwithstanding clause to weaken its impact when they realized they could not defeat it, and were the successful sponsors of an amending formula more sensitive to the provincial than to the Canadian dimension. Wielding the 1982 rules the provincial governments turned the Meech Lake Quebec round into a provincial round.

It is futile to deprecate their behaviour. They are simply doing their provincial job in response to the powerful shaping cues of federalism that make concern for the whole someone else's responsibility. Accordingly, to look to the provincial governments outside Quebec to speak for and to the national dimension of a Canada-without-Quebec is to be guilty of a constitutional oxymoron. It is also to subscribe to a modern version of the compact theory by which what the rest of Canada holds in common is attributed to provincial government generosity. Unfortunately, however, it is structurally easier for provincial governments to anticipate and prepare for their future in a Canada-without-Quebec than it is for the federal government. They lose only a partner. They continue as political, constitutional entities, with territory, jurisdiction, and population intact. In a Canada-without-Quebec, the federal government loses territory, citizens, an historic identity, some of its bureaucracy, and many of the political responsibilities that flowed from its former management of a linguistically dual people. Little preparation by the federal government for such an unsought goal is likely.

The federal government cannot speak or bargain for Canada-without-Quebec, for its mandate is Canada-with-Quebec. It cannot speak for Anglophone Canada in the nine provinces and two territories as a potentially separate people. It speaks for them only as they are part of a pan-Canadian people linked to their Francophone confreres in a common country. The pressure of institutional self-interest and the weight of the past drive the federal government to speak for a federal solution, for any other solution dismembers it along with the country that is breaking up. Political responsibility drives it in the same direction, for up until the final rupture there will still be Canadians within Quebec who seek a federal solution and who resist having a Québécois identity totally displace their Canadian identity. At least some Quebec Anglophones and members of other minorities will query the legitimacy of a constitutional change that removes them from a country they do not wish to leave. Aboriginal peoples will continue to assert a distinctiveness that is transprovincial and for status Indians is historically linked to the federal government. Some federal and federalist MPS from Quebec will express the surviving Canadian concerns among their Québécois constituents.

For all of these reasons, the federal government of all of Canada lacks the capacity and inclination to speak as the prospective federal government of a Canada bereft of Quebec. In fact, the federal government is inherently incapable of impartially assessing the relative advantages of Canada with and Canada without Quebec. Its self-interest as a government and its traditional identity will drive it to prefer even a slender thread of continuity to a complete rupture and its own dismemberment, even when the balance of advantages more judicially assessed from the perspective of the rest of Canada might deliver a verdict in favour of a breakup. In other words, a federal government leadership role treats the rest of Canada not as a prospective independent people, but as an integral component of a dualist pan-Canada. This will have deleterious consequences for the rest of Canada if the independence game is the real one.

Thus, if constitutional game number two displaces constitutional game number one, the cast of actors has to be reshuffled. The Canadian government speaking for a Canada that has been rejected by Quebec leaves the table to be replaced by what? Canada outside Quebec is headless and voiceless. It has no institutional or corporate existence. At this point, we leave the stage of normal constitutional politics and enter uncharted constitutional territory.

The difficulty is even more serious than has been suggested because the problem is not only who will be available, occupying what legitimate office, to speak for an emergent Canada-without-Quebec, but what preparation, what forethought, what anticipatory socialization of a new people has prepared Canada-without-Quebec for its truncated future.

At this stage, the contrast with Quebec will be chastening. A strain of *indépendantiste* thought has never been absent from Quebec political and intellectual life. Movements and parties seeking independence or sovereignty-association have flourished in the last thirty years. An independence-oriented party was in power for a decade and is now the official opposition. One referendum has already been held in 1980; the Bélanger-Campeau hearings are under way as I write (December, 1990); the governing Quebec Liberal Party is separately exploring constitutional options; and sometime in the next few months the Quebec government will announce the constitutional goal it seeks for Quebec. The Francophone majority in Quebec is further aided in its constitutional exploration by the self-consciousness that attends its historic minority status in Canada and North America.

Canada-without-Quebec lacks a lengthy preparation and conditioning for an independent existence. Anglophone Canada within and without Quebec has been attached to the whole from which it gained many benefits. The Anglophone majority in the rest of Canada is inevitably poorly prepared for an unchosen future. The expanded sense of identity that independence will produce for many Québécois is unlikely to be duplicated for the other partner, at least initially, painfully adjusting to a shrunken sense of self and identity.

The complexities of the situation are compounded by the fact that the federalism game and the independence game are being played simultaneously, not sequentially. This is much less of a problem for Quebec than for the rest of Canada. Although at any given time supporters of both games, and thus opponents of each other, will vie to control the content of Quebec's constitutional demands, the government of Quebec remains the official spokesperson for whatever constitutional objectives Quebec pursues. In fact, the Quebec government, relative to the other actors in federalism or to a prospective rest-of-Canada national partner, can flexibly move from one game to another. The rest of Canada is not so fortunate. It is extremely difficult for it to play both games at once and even more difficult to switch from one game to another, for the two games require different actors and they appeal to competing versions of identity and community. In the federalism game, the rest of Canada is submerged in all of Canada that is struggling to survive. Its sociological existence is implicit. Its political existence is imaginary. In the independence game, the rest of Canada acquires a potential sense of itself as a political people, but that sense still lacks institutional expression. For Canada outside Quebec the independence game prior to disruption has to be played by an inchoate cast of non-governmental actors, and they risk being accused of scuttling an historic people. Official Canada has to get ready for a federalism response to Quebec, while the unofficial rest of Canada should simultaneously be preparing for the possibility of its own independence.

The coexistence of two games, one actual and one potential, will be under-lined when the next round of official negotiations gets under way. The asym-metrical status that will be Quebec's minimum goal will explicitly define the rest of Canada as a discrete community. That definition will be strengthened by the recognition that Quebec independence is a serious viable alternative in Quebec. For the rest of Canada this period will be one of intense, rapid learning and a somewhat chaotic exploration of alternative futures. In functional terms, there-fore, the negotiation stage should be seen as a crucial forum for educating and preparing the rest of Canada for future choices that up until then it will have scarcely considered. Psychologically at least, negotiations will begin the process of separating out the Canadian and the rest-of-Canada dimensions. The former will be redefined to accommodate the weaker presence of Quebec if historic Canada survives, and the latter will commence to reshape itself from a leftover category to a potential people sharing an asymmetrical federalism with Quebec, or sharing as a separate people the northern portions of North America with an independent Quebec.

## Conclusion

The two most plausible constitutional options confronting Canadians – an asymmetrical federalism according unique status to Quebec or an independent Quebec coexisting with an independent, still federal, but diminished Canada – both require Canadians in and out of Quebec to manoeuvre through the minefield of three equalities: of provinces, of citizens, and of two national communities.

The first two equalities, of provinces and citizens, are emergent constitutional principles that have been hammered out and refined in the last two decades. The former dominates the amending formula and illustrates the contemporary ten-dency to subject the operation of federalism to federal principles. The latter is the powerful message of the Charter. Both equalities reduce flexibility in responding to a Quebec that seeks differential treatment, especially if the latter is highly visi-ble and highly symbolic. They remove the issue of asymmetry, either of govern-ment jurisdiction or of citizen rights, from the realm of pragmatism to the stratosphere of high constitutional principle. They are examples of constitu-tional rationalization, the application of principles to citizen-state relations and to the range of acceptable variations in the cluster of factors that comprise prov-incehood. The symmetry these principles bring is paid for by a diminished con-stitutional capacity to provide individualized responses to distinct societies and to distinct situations. They are more sympathetic to uniformity than to diversity in the domains to which they apply.

They obviously do not apply to an independent Quebec, and an asymmetrical Quebec by definition would not be a province like the others, and almost certainly would be subjected, at a minimum, to a lesser Charter regime. The first two equalities, therefore, have to be breached whether Quebec is accommodated inside or outside federalism. Escape from their reach within federalism appears essential if the enhancement of Quebec's powers is to stop short of sovereignty. The equality of provinces principle either constrains Quebec or becomes the vehicle for an unacceptable expansion of the jurisdiction of all provinces driven by Québécois nationalism. A relaxation of the Charter's application to Quebec, especially relating to minority-language education, would remove a chafing constraint and would give pride of place to the Quebec Charter.

The Canadian Charter is so clearly linked to conceptions of citizenship outside Quebec that it seems inappropriate to have it apply to the unique status of Quebec citizens in an asymmetrical federalism. Acceptance of this escape from the Charter may be eased by the recognition that the Quebec desire to give constitutional support to a language and a way of life has many similarities with other groups who see the Charter as a vehicle to enhance their objectives as women, the disabled, visible minorities, and others. Such recognition could also extend to Aboriginal peoples, whose as yet unrealized constitutional ambitions are driven by a nationalist rhetoric little different from that of Quebec nationalists.

Escape from the coverage of these two equalities would be a clear and symbolically potent affirmation of Quebec's specificity. Two of the central components of the Canadian constitutional order would have no or an incomplete application to Quebec. The big change of escape from these two equalities is cleaner and less troublesome than the small change of partial accommodations attempted by the Meech Lake distinct society. The stability of such an arrangement, however, is problematic. The dynamics of an asymmetrical federal relationship may make it only a way station on the road to a fuller independence.

The difficulty with the third equality, if our future is to be two independent peoples coexisting side by side, is that the rest-of-Canada partner has a potential rather than a contemporary existence. At the moment, while a federalism that includes Quebec still lingers, the "rest of Canada" is a mental construct only. Paradoxically, Québécois speak and write much more confidently of the rest of Canada than do those who belong to it. To Québécois nationalists, the rest of Canada is the "not us" to whom they attribute a collective self-consciousness akin to their own. Unfortunately, to look out from Quebec in the search for the other "nation" whose existence will confirm a pleasing symmetry, and thus facilitate one-on-one bargaining, is a recipe for failure. Outside Quebec are Canadians, Manitobans, Aboriginals, Charter supporters, and a society that is increasingly multicultural and multiracial. One does not, however, find the rest-of-Canadians. One does not find a community with a distinctive sense of self, with political institutions that shape it, with office-holders having a responsibility to educate that community in its needs and options, a community with a long history of trying to make the rest of Canada its very own country. On the contrary, the history has not been one of trying to get out, but rather of positive attachment to a coast-to-coast country built by all Canadians. Rotstein identifies the Anglophone attitude to Canada as "mappism";[19] Resnick correctly notes how allegiance to the government of Canada is central to the Anglophone political identity.[20] McNaught earlier referred to the increasingly non-national outlook of Anglophone Canadians;[21] more recently, for many Canadians outside Quebec and for Anglophones and other minorities within Quebec, the Charter's elevation of the status of a country-wide rights-possessing citizenship has stimulated a Canadian, not a rest-of-Canadian, identification with the constitutional order. These all speak to the Canadian dimension, not to the rest-of-Canada dimension.

For Quebec to get its act together has not been easy, and is not yet completed, but blessed with the focus of a single government to channel the politics of self-affirmation the Quebec task is simplicity itself compared to the task confronting the rest of Canada. The very labels employed – the "rest of Canada," "Canada-without-Quebec," or "Anglophone Canada" (which awkwardly includes Aboriginal peoples and Francophone minorities and excludes Quebec Anglophones) – attest to the institutional and psychological impediments to a coherent sense of self while traditional Canada remains alive.

The two-nations solution encounters the non- or at best incipient existence of one side of the prospective two-nation equality. This asymmetry of self-consciousness and self-identification is most serious, of course, in the preparatory stages leading to the possible rupture of Canada. As noted elsewhere in this essay, the difficulty is compounded because the rest of Canada is being asked to play two games at once, the save-federalism game and the two-nations game. The systemic bias of an existing federal system with a central government fighting for its country-wide survival favours the allocation of political and intellectual resources to the first game, and almost inevitably reduces the attention paid and the quality of effort devoted to the second game, which may well be the more important of the two. No such bias applies to the challenging Quebec government.

The likelihood of governments outside Quebec devoting adequate and appropriately directed intellectual, political, and bureaucratic resources to this urgent political task for the rest of Canada is minimal. The responsibility must be assumed by other than governmental actors, unless the ostrich is to be the emblem of the rest of Canada. The tendency of academics and others to line up behind governments must be tempered by the recognition that the rest of Canada is an empty chair at the constitutional bargaining table. Of all the constitutional players it is most in need of assistance to address its constitutional concerns.

Chapter Ten

# Aboriginal Canadians, Citizenship, and the Constitution

## Aboriginal Canadians and the Constitution

The present relationship of Aboriginal Canadians to the constitutional order and their future citizen status in it are both unclear. The contemporary situation is transitional, but the answer to the question – transition to what? – has no ready answer. One answer will come from the Royal Commission on Aboriginal Peoples. If it is not disabled by the kinds of internal controversies that have recently plagued several royal commissions, its Report will speak with the weighty authority characteristic of the genre. Its portrait and analysis of the desired future relationship between Aboriginal and other Canadians will carry a special legitimacy derived from its mixed and prestigious composition, including an Aboriginal majority among the commissioners. If its recommendations are unanimous, or if dissents are marginal to the core of its proposals, the Report will set the parameters for the subsequent debate. The many audiences that will respond to the Report – the Aboriginal peoples themselves, the organizations that speak for them, the governments of Canadian federalism, the intellectual classes, the political parties, the women's movement, and the heterogeneous Canadian electorate, in short, the diversity of interests and viewpoints character-istic of a complex modern society – will encounter the same difficulties that the commissioners presumably will have overcome. Simply put, the difficulty is that the direction in which we are going is uncharted territory, with few sign-posts. Since a high proportion of the research community with competence in

Aboriginal issues will have direct involvement with the Commission, there is a danger that the Report's proposals will not receive the independent public scrutiny merited by the exceptional significance of the Commission's mandate.

The history of the majority's relationships with Aboriginal peoples is not a guide for constitutional policy-makers, for it is escape from that history that is sought. Status Indians seek an escape from their experience as an administered people under a regime of internal colonialism. Métis seek escape from their previous status as ordinary Canadians to an explicit recognition of their Métis nationhood. Inuit, the forgotten people, who had minimal contact with Canadian society or the federal government only half a century ago, are now preparing to take over a public quasi-provincial government of their own in Nunavut, the eastern portion of the Northwest Territories, where most of them live.

The inclusion of Aboriginal Canadians in the Canadian community on the model of other formerly excluded groups – Asian Canadians, women, the disabled, for example – is unacceptable, for they are not seeking entry, membership, and participation on the same terms as those that are already in. On the contrary, they advocate a permanent constitutional and institutional recognition of difference in order to sustain and strengthen distinctive senses of peoplehood in the future.

Discernment of future Aboriginal status is further clouded because they have rejected provincehood as the appropriate vehicle for their self-realization (Nunavut being a partial exception). Provincial status would have immediately triggered a host of understandings, norms, and practices that would integrate their future with our federal inheritance. Admittedly, the alternative of a variegated third Aboriginal order of government based on an inherent right to self-government speaks a limited language of federalism with its assumption of an entrenched order of government. However, a federalism of three entrenched orders of government is very different from a federalism based on two orders of government. Further, the third Aboriginal order will not be like the second, as it will be characterized by extensive internal asymmetry; also, as its jurisdictions will be drawn from ones now wielded by both federal and provincial governments, its subjects will have a more limited involvement in federal and provincial communities than other Canadians. In addition, Nunavut excepted, full participatory civic membership in self-governing Aboriginal communities will presumably be restricted to individuals who meet the legal criteria for membership – who are Aboriginal in terms of each community's precise definition of membership. This is the presumption behind the Charlottetown Accord's proposal to enumerate and identify Métis. In other words, the self-governing Aboriginal communities encompassed under the third order of government will not be open communities as provinces are, communities that incoming individuals can easily join after meeting minimal residence criteria. The third order of

Aboriginal government will be unique in many ways. Consequently, the guidance to be derived from the second provincial order and from its relationships with the federal government is limited.

The language of nationalism wielded on behalf of, in many cases, small Indian reserve communities of several hundred people is an additional impediment to understanding. As is noted below, the discrepancy between the label – what is conventionally conjured up by the word "nation" – and the demographic reality contributes more to the emotional satisfaction of its users than to clarity of thought. Further, until recently there has been a principled Aboriginal unwillingness to discuss practical matters of jurisdiction, capacities, financing, etc. while the inherent right remains unrecognized. Significantly, even the Charlottetown Accord, with its hitherto unequalled recognition of a very highly differentiated Aboriginal constitutional status, was strong at the level of a general sense of direction but virtually devoid of specifics, which were left to future negotiating or judicial processes.

The remarkable diversity within the category "Aboriginal" also complicates constitutional policy discussion of Aboriginal futures. On the one hand, the very label "Aboriginal" invites us to think of responses applicable to all members of the category. On the other hand, the diversity within the category almost paralyses thought, as every generalization elicits a version of the anthropologist's response – "Not on Easter Island!" There is no Aboriginal people as such with a sense of Aboriginal selfhood. Métis, Inuit, and status Indian are very different ways of being Aboriginal that derive from distinct histories and particular interactions with Euro-Canadian society. The aboriginality of Métis, of course, only received official recognition in the 1982 Constitution Act. The Assembly of First Nations, the voice of (particularly reserve-based) status Indians and the most influential of the Aboriginal organizations, faces almost insurmountable problems in straddling the diversity of interests and nations within its imputed membership. Identity is very often local – by band, by treaty area, or by broader culture area. The contexts in which ambitions for self-government are played out are also immensely varied. Aboriginal peoples in metropolitan Toronto – numerically one of the largest "reserves" in Canada – cannot aspire to or achieve the type and extent of self-government that is possible for a wealthy Alberta band with oil revenues or for the Inuit in a prospective Nunavut.

This paper's objective, given the preceding considerations, is the comparatively modest one of clarifying some of the issues involved in deciding on the future relationships between Aboriginal and non-Aboriginal Canadians.[1] While history is essential to a full understanding of where we are, space limitations preclude the historical depth such understanding would require.[2] The novelty of the present situation can be adequately appreciated by contrast with the relatively recent past of half a century ago.

## The Situation at Mid-Century

By the mid-twentieth century, three basic patterns of Aboriginal/non-Aboriginal relations had developed. Only the status Indian community was explicitly treated as an Aboriginal people. The word "status" clearly indicates the official, legal nature of the Indian people over whom the federal government had assumed responsibility by virtue of s. 91(24), "Indians and Lands Reserved for the Indians." Individuals gained and lost status by intermarriage. An Indian woman who married a non-Indian lost status. A non-Indian woman who married a status Indian gained legal Indian status. Specific status Indian communities, therefore, were legal communities, not purely indigenous communities. Many of their members had no biological Indian background. Many others who thought of themselves as Indian and were so regarded by their acquaintances had no legal status. Nevertheless, in spite of the arbitrary legal boundaries, the members of individual reserve communities constituted a community of fate. They shared a common space and participated in the common experience of adapting to and resisting the administration of the local Indian Affairs officials. In other words, in the same way as Albertans became a particular provincial people after a straight line was drawn on the map in 1905 separating them from the simultaneously created Saskatchewan, particular Indian communities changed their conceptions of self in response to the legal definition of who they were.

Although the Inuit (then Eskimo) had been judicially interpreted as falling under s. 91(24) federal government jurisdiction by a 1939 Supreme Court decision, actual federal policy was virtually non-existent until the fifties. Limited Inuit contact with Canadian society largely came from the RCMP, missionaries, the Hudson's Bay Company, and a handful of other traders. There was no Eskimo Act to parallel the Indian Act, and no branch of Eskimo administration as a counterpart to the Indian Affairs Branch. Federal government authority was nominal, and federal policy, which could be described as *laissez-faire* or benign indifference, was facilitated by the isolation of the small Inuit population.

The situation changed in the mid-fifties as the Cold War underlined the strategic significance of the North and radar lines were constructed. The federal government also established the Department of Northern Affairs and National Resources in 1953. This, however, did not signal the development of policy for the Inuit as an Aboriginal people. The prevailing assumption was that Inuit were Canadian citizens who required transitional supplementary measures to facilitate their adaptation to "modern ways."

The Métis in western Canada, a people who combined Indian and European backgrounds, thought of themselves as a separate people or nation. On the other hand, they received no distinct constitutional treatment, apart from early dealings in scrip (certificates for land allowances). They had their own heroes/martyrs in Riel and Dumont, and, like Québécois with their memories of the Conquest, had memories of rebellions and defeats in their own past and revered locations such as Batoche where battles had been fought. However, the Métis identity and sense of nation had no constitutional consequences.[3] In general, the Métis had low status in western Canada, and given their mixed ancestry, there was considerable slippage as individual Métis passed for white by suppressing their Indian heritage. Until the recent emergence of Aboriginal nationalisms, the Métis were more likely to stress their European than their Aboriginal background.

So by the mid-twentieth century there was no Aboriginal policy as such, and no constitutional category "Aboriginal." Two of the three future sub-categories of Aboriginal peoples in the 1982 Constitution Act, Inuit and Métis, received no particular treatment. Indians with legal status, by contrast, were subject to a specific policy and administrative regime in the Indian Act, flowing from s. 91(24) of the BNA Act. The long-run goal of Indian policy, however, remained what it had always been, the eventual absorption of Indians into the general population.

## From the 1960 Extension of the Franchise to the Defeat of the White Paper

Given the coexistence of competing approaches to the constitutional position and policy treatment of what were to become the three components of the Aboriginal constitutional category of the future, there were three main possible constitutional policy packages for the Indian, Inuit, and Métis peoples. (1) The existing pattern could continue with differential treatment/recognition restricted to status Indians. (2) Differential treatment for status Indians might be phased out, thus placing Indians, Inuit, and Métis in the same category as ordinary Canadian citizens. Or (3), a greater uniformity of constitutional recognition and policy treatment could be achieved by placing Inuit and Métis alongside of status Indians in a special overarching constitutional category – the 1982 solution. In addition, there were various intermediate categories, but the above typology portrays the major choices.

The crucial variable determining which scenario would triumph was the future status of the legal Indian community. Its special significance derived from its size as the largest of the three and from its being singled out for special treatment even prior to Confederation. This meant, incidentally, that the limited thought Canadians devoted to Aboriginal constitutional issues was overwhelmingly directed to status Indians. Neither Inuit nor Métis, by contrast, had a branch of government devoted to their affairs, which weakened the incentive to think about their future in constitutional terms. Finally, it was easier for Indians to make themselves heard. They had organized band government, albeit under

Indian Act criteria; they had political organizations, albeit better organized at the provincial than at the pan-Canadian level. Their constitutional recognition generated a variety of public arenas, such as parliamentary committees, where they could make themselves heard.

In 1960, the Diefenbaker government extended the franchise to status Indians. This was less the result of Indian pressure to gain a civic right from which they had been excluded than Diefenbaker's response to a new international climate of opinion influenced by decolonization and the United Nations-led proselytization on behalf of rights. Diefenbaker assured status Indians that the franchise extension did not portend the erosion of treaty or other rights. Nevertheless, there was a Janus-faced aspect to the extension. On the one hand, the extension of the leading symbol of Canadian citizenship to status Indians, from whom it had formerly been withheld as incompatible with their wardship status, eliminated a differentiation that had symbolized inferiority. In that sense, it was an inclusive Canadianizing policy. On the other hand, it reinforced Indian special status with its message that penalties – such as suffrage deprivation – were not inherent consequences of legal status difference but were policy choices that might become increasingly difficult to defend.

In the sixties, the competing poles of policy toward status Indians were crystallized in the contrast between the Hawthorn-Tremblay proposals and the federal government's 1969 White Paper. The Hawthorn-Tremblay inquiry was commissioned by the federal government in 1964. Its Report in two unwieldy volumes in 1966 covered educational, economic, political, administrative, and constitutional concerns. Responding to terms of reference that restricted the inquiry to status Indians, the Report's constitutional philosophy was summed up by the phrase "citizens plus" as the appropriate label for the future status of Indians. By "citizens plus" Hawthorn-Tremblay argued that Indians should have all the normal entitlements of citizenship, but in addition they should be the beneficiaries of a "plus" category, drawn from treaties, from historical priority, and from the fact that the non-Aboriginal society had built a rich, flourishing civilization from lands and resources originally occupied and exploited by Indians. The contents of "plus" were to be worked out in a political process that accepted the fact that Indians were entitled to a positive special status. The Report noted that historically Indians' unique status had been used to deprive them of normal benefits. The Indian Act special status had in fact made Indians "citizens minus" in the past. Hawthorn-Tremblay also both assumed and advocated a continuing role for the Indian Affairs Branch, which, possibly optimistically, it hoped would act as a conscience arguing for Indian interests within government. The Report further recommended positive support for Indian political organizations as minority voices that required strengthening in a cacophonous public arena. In general, the Report followed the Diefenbaker philosophy on franchise extension – namely that Indian status was fully compatible with the receipt of the normal benefits of a Canadian citizen. In fact, of course, with its "plus" advocacy, it went beyond the Diefenbaker approach. The "plus," however, did not imply a parallel Indian community coexisting with but not part of the Canadian community of citizens. On the contrary, Indians were to be regular citizens with supplementary entitlements. Hawthorn-Tremblay strongly believed that Indians had suffered greatly from being kept outside of Canadian citizenship.[4]

The 1969 federal government White Paper on Indian policy took the diametrically opposite view to the "plus" aspect of Hawthorn-Tremblay.[5] Heavily influenced by Trudeau's liberal individualist values and his fear that special status for Indians might strengthen Quebec's special status claims, the White Paper espoused a straightforward assimilationist strategy/philosophy. Its underlying thesis was that separate status contributed to economic backwardness, social isolation, and retrogressive cultural enclaves. The White Paper, in fact, was a late twentieth-century version of the Durham Report of the previous century, with Indians substituted for the backward, unprogressive Quebec peasantry. In adopting and publicly defending an assimilationist philosophy that would see the end of a separate special Indian legal status, the White Paper explicitly repudiated the Hawthorn-Tremblay attempt to combine standard citizenship with benefits flowing from a unique legal status.

While the 1969 White Paper can be viewed as a direct reversal of previous Indian policy and philosophy, there is another sense in which it was no more than an attempt to accelerate history. The basic goal of Indian policy had historically been the assimilation of Indians and their eventual disappearance as a distinct people as they were absorbed into the basic Canadian community. The policy was vigorously enunciated on widely separated occasions by Sir John A. Macdonald in 1887, Duncan Campbell Scott, the Superintendent-General of Indian Affairs, in 1920, and Diamond Jenness, the noted anthropologist, in the 1940s.[6]

From the perspective of the three macro policy choices noted at the beginning of this section, Hawthorn-Tremblay recommended an amplified version of the status quo, with an enhanced Indian special status. The Report said nothing about Inuit and Métis, who were outside its terms of reference. The federal White Paper opted for scenario two, the phasing out of differential status so that Indians, Inuit, and Métis would be officially indistinguishable from ordinary Canadians, whose ranks the formerly status Indians would now join.

Status Indians vehemently opposed the elimination of their unique status and repudiated the White Paper. Significantly, the Indian Association of Alberta, which led the assault on the White Paper, fought under the banner of Citizens Plus.[7] The defeat of the White Paper, the most important development in Aboriginal constitutional politics since Confederation, meant that the long-standing official policy of assimilation for status Indians was foreclosed. The defeat reflected and stimulated Indian nationalism. It was a remarkable achievement given the historical passivity of Indians and the weakness of their political organizations. Further, it gravely weakened, indeed almost removed, the federal government leadership role in Indian policy. At a minimum, it suggested that policy-making pertaining to status Indians was no longer an affair of governments alone but must become a collaborative affair with Indian leaders playing central roles. This political victory by status Indians is a direct antecedent of the 1992 constitutional meetings with the leaders of the four main Aboriginal organizations sitting down and bargaining their constitutional future with first ministers.

The White Paper defeat was also a crucial event for the Inuit and Métis. They could not have carved out a future special status for themselves if the Indian people had lost theirs. In fact, the White Paper defeat stimulated the nationalist self-consciousness of all Aboriginal peoples. The policy decision of the early seventies to fund Aboriginal organizations ensured that when future discussions of indigenous peoples strayed beyond status Indians, a number of Aboriginal voices would be heard.

## From the 1982 Constitution Act to the Charlottetown Accord

The Aboriginal peoples made major constitutional advances in the 1982 Constitution Act. Section 35(1) of the Constitution Act recognized and affirmed "the existing aboriginal and treaty rights of the aboriginal peoples of Canada," while section 25 of the Charter protected "aboriginal, treaty or other rights or freedoms that pertain to the aboriginal peoples" from abrogation or derogation by the Charter. The phrase "aboriginal peoples of Canada," hitherto unknown in constitutional terminology, was newly coined and defined to include "the Indian, Inuit and Métis peoples of Canada." Their constitutional recognition was a remarkable achievement for the Métis. It added to the numbers and to the internal diversity of the now constitutionally recognized indigenous peoples. Section 37 obligated the federal government to hold a constitutional conference with the task, *inter alia*, of identifying and defining the Aboriginal rights recognized elsewhere in the 1982 Act. Ultimately, four constitutional conferences on Aboriginal issues were held from 1983 to 1987. Although they failed to reach agreement on the main Aboriginal goal of self-government, they confirmed that Aboriginal peoples were not as other Canadians, that they had a unique status that justified bargaining almost as equals, nation-to-nation, with the governing elites of Canadian federalism.

The attempt by Prime Minister Mulroney and the provincial premiers to treat the recently practised high-level Aboriginal participation as an aberration was a major factor in the Aboriginal contribution to the defeat of the Meech Lake Accord. The lesson that Aboriginal people could not be ignored, as had been attempted in the Meech Lake fiasco, contributed – as a reaction – to their extraordinary prominence in the process that led to the Charlottetown Accord and in the remarkable gains they achieved in the bargained outcome that was subsequently rejected by the Canadian people in the October, 1992, referendum.

## Aboriginal Peoples and the Charlottetown Accord: Reflections on the Direction of Constitutional Thought

The Charlottetown Accord is now an historical curiosity, repudiated by the referendum electorate and not even supported by reserve-based status Indians, whose votes were separately counted. It is nevertheless an extraordinarily revealing document. It is a bargained outcome from negotiations between the leaders of the four main Aboriginal organizations and the elected leaders and their bureaucratic advisers of the eleven governments of Canadian federalism and of the northern territories. In general, the drive for differential constitutional status embodied in the Accord comes from Aboriginal peoples, or at least from their organizations. The constraints or limits come from non-Aboriginal governments. The remarkable nature of the compromise that was struck between these contending forces is underlined when contrasted with the previous record of failures: (1) the status Indian repudiation of the 1969 federal government White Paper; (2) the inability to achieve agreement on the most important issue to Aboriginal leaders, the inherent right to self-government, in the four Aboriginal constitutional conferences from 1983 to 1987; (3) the sidelining of Aboriginal issues and advocates in the Meech Lake round, labelled the Quebec round, though in reality a provincial round led by Quebec.

The Charlottetown Accord agreement is especially significant because it was the first time that an attempt was made to accommodate Québécois and Aboriginal nationalisms in one constitutional package. As argued elsewhere,[8] perhaps the most striking feature of the Accord was the dramatically greater willingness to respond generously to Aboriginal than to Québécois nationalism. That contrast, indeed, is an extremely revealing indicator of the profoundly different assumptions that the rest of Canada applies to the question of Quebec's place within Canada and that Canada applies to the question of the place of Aboriginal peoples. Briefly, the rest of Canada sees Quebec and Québécois through Canadian eyes as integral parts of the Canadian community. By contrast, non-Aboriginal Canadians, or at least the elites that speak for them, see Aboriginal peoples as being in some kind of parallel relationship and not as a central component of their own sense of Canadian identity. There is, therefore, much more potential flexibility in relationships with Aboriginal Canadians than with Québécois because readjustments of the former seem to occur alongside of rather than within non-Aboriginal Canada's sense of its Canadian self.

The Aboriginal components of the Accord would have led to a very differentiated, constitutionally specific relation of Aboriginal peoples to the Canadian constitutional order. However, some of the plausible consequences of a constitutional settlement that distances Aboriginal peoples from the standard norms and practices of Canadian citizenship appear to have been overlooked.

The Charlottetown Accord proposed extensive changes in the relationship of Aboriginal peoples to the constitutional order. What was formerly rejected was accepted – constitutional recognition of an inherent right to self-government, the inclusion of Métis under s. 91(24) as being in federal jurisdiction, and, following on the 1983-87 Aboriginal constitutional conferences, the acceptance in the executive federalism negotiating process that produced the Accord of nation-to-nation bargaining, with its clear implication that non-Aboriginal governments do not speak for Aboriginal peoples in their electorates. Although the Charlottetown Accord was thin on details, the overall direction was clear and consistent. [9]

(1) The Accord proposed constitutionally entrenching a third order of Aboriginal government based on an inherent right of self-government. Aboriginal peoples, accordingly, would be removed from the jurisdiction of federal and provincial governments to the extent they assumed jurisdiction over themselves.

(2) Separate Aboriginal representation in the House of Commons was supported, with details to be proposed by a House of Commons committee reacting to the recommendations of the Royal Commission on Electoral Reform and Party Financing.

(3) Aboriginal peoples were to have guaranteed Senate representation. As their Senate seats were in addition to provincial seats, the clear implication was that they were not considered part of the provincial communities. Aboriginal senators might be given a "double majority power in relation to certain matters materially affecting Aboriginal people."

(4) Aboriginal peoples were to have a limited role in the preparation of lists of candidates for Supreme Court appointments and could offer advice on candidates proposed by provincial and territorial governments. Consideration was to be given to a proposed Aboriginal Council of Elders that could make submissions to the Supreme Court when it considered Aboriginal issues. In general, the Aboriginal role relating to the Supreme Court was to be on the agenda of a future first ministers' conference and was to be recorded in a political accord.

(5) Aboriginal consent would be required for constitutional amendments directly referring to Aboriginal peoples, by a mechanism to be determined.

(6) Aboriginal representatives were entitled to participate on any agenda item at first ministers' conferences "that directly affects the Aboriginal peoples."

(7) The Métis people were to be brought under the federal jurisdiction of s. 91(24), a goal for which they had long striven.

(8) A Métis Nation Accord was being prepared by the federal government, the five most westerly provinces (Ontario to B.C.), and the Métis National Council, which would commit governments to negotiate various issues related to Métis self-government. Further, the Métis were to be defined and members of the Métis nation were to be enumerated and registered.

(9) Aboriginal exemption from the Charter, already provided for in s. 25, was significantly extended by new language ensuring that nothing in the Charter "abrogates or derogates from . . . in particular any rights or freedoms relating to the exercise or protection of their languages, cultures or traditions."

(10) Aboriginal governments were specifically exempted from the Charter's democratic rights, which gave every citizen "the right to vote in an election of members . . . and to be qualified for membership" in federal and provincial legislatures, an exemption to allow traditional Aboriginal practices of leadership selection that would otherwise violate the Charter.

(11) The Charlottetown Accord proposed four first ministers' conferences on Aboriginal constitutional matters commencing no later than 1996 and following at two-year intervals.

(12) The philosophy lying behind the above-noted Aboriginal proposals was expressed in the *Consensus Report*'s description of Aboriginal governments' authority within their jurisdiction as being

(a) to safeguard and develop their languages, cultures, economies, identities, institutions and traditions; and,

(b) to develop, maintain and strengthen their relationship with their lands, waters and environment so as to determine and control their development as peoples according to their own values and priorities and ensure the integrity of their societies. [10]

The Accord's Aboriginal clauses elicited astonishment and enthusiasm from students of Aboriginal issues. Virtually every major institution of the Canadian state would in future have a distinctive Aboriginal input or presence – Senate, House of Commons, Supreme Court (tentatively), first ministers' conferences, and amending formula. The Charter, a crucial symbol of citizenship to many Canadians, would have a greatly weakened application to Aboriginal peoples; further, depending on the jurisdiction of Aboriginal governments, their peoples would have an attenuated relationship to either or both of the two traditional orders of Canadian government, federal and provincial. One of the implicit paradoxes of the Accord was the tension between its proposals to reduce the federal Parliament's jurisdiction over Aboriginal peoples by self-government

while simultaneously advocating an enhanced and explicit Aboriginal representation in both houses of Parliament.

## Explanation of Aboriginal Charlottetown Gains

The question that seeks an answer is not whether the Aboriginal components of
the Accord fully reflected Aboriginal aspirations. Presumably they fell short of
the perfect package from an Aboriginal perspective, although it can be assumed
that the pronounced stress on the uniqueness of the Aboriginal place in the constitutional order reflected Aboriginal pressures in the bargaining process. The
more interesting question is why the elites of the two territories and of the eleven
governments of Canadian federalism, backed by hundreds of advisers, supported the Aboriginal package.

There are three plausible major explanations for the acceptance by non-
Aboriginal negotiators of the magnitude and direction of Aboriginal gains in the
Accord. (1) Possibly acceptance was based on a clear understanding of the package sustained by a too-long-delayed generosity toward and empathy for Aboriginal peoples; or, (2) acceptance might be construed as indicating that non-
Aboriginal Canadians, or at least their governments, have few criteria to guide
and channel their response to Aboriginal aspirations, that they view Aboriginal
Canadians as on a constitutional path for which there are almost no rules of the
road, beyond preserving some minimum definition of the integrity of the Canadian state. (3) Finally, and with particular reference to the Accord's tendency to
treat Aboriginal Canadians as belonging to parallel communities, acceptance
might suggest that Aboriginal Canadians are not thought of as being part of the
same "we" community as the non-Aboriginal majority.

All of these have some plausible validity. At a very general level, there is considerable support for measures to improve the condition of Aboriginal peoples,
although it would be straining credulity to attribute a clear understanding of the
Aboriginal constitutional package to more than a small minority. My own
impression is that the second and third explanations carry special weight. The
defeat of the Meech Lake Accord, to which the "distinct society" clause was a
major contributor, and the limited concessions to Quebec in the Charlottetown
Accord, when contrasted with the wide-ranging response to the Aboriginal
peoples, clearly suggest that Aboriginal constitutional aspirations run into fewer
roadblocks than Quebec's. They are not affected by the equality of the provinces
norm and are less constrained by the Charter than is Quebec. Both Aboriginal
and non-Aboriginal Canadians see the former as on a separate, uncharted constitutional path. Stopping points emerge, therefore, less as the result of a previously agreed principle than through *ad hoc*, last-minute interventions. The

introduction in the final days of bargaining that Aboriginal laws or assertions of authority "may not be inconsistent with those laws which are essential to the preservation of peace, order and good government in Canada" (*Consensus Report*, p. 47) and the attempt by Bourassa to protect Quebec's territorial integrity by the provision that the self-government clauses "should not create new Aboriginal rights to land" (*Consensus Report*, p. 44) give the clear appearance of constitutional policy-making on the run.

The third explanation also has intuitive validity. In general, past theory and practice have defined Aboriginal peoples as outside the mainstream Canadian community, with the ambiguous exception of the Métis. Recently, Aboriginal peoples have bolstered this perception – the rhetoric of separate nations, the overt suspicions of white society, and the stress on Aboriginal "otherness" in constitutional advocacy. The vigorous exploitation of the constitutional process by Aboriginal leaders to underline the manner and extent of their profound difference from other Canadians was their key justification for separate constitutional and institutional recognition to strengthen that difference. This is clearly so for the Métis, whose essential goal is the constitutional recognition and protection of their distinct nationhood that has hitherto been denied.

In their recent advocacy of a separate Aboriginal justice system, Monture-Okanee and Turpel (constitutional adviser to the Assembly of First Nations) underline the specificity of the Aboriginal presence in Canada. "Aboriginal peoples, [who are] . . . both different and separate, simply cannot be considered as part of Canadian society. . . . We are not necessarily culturally, linguistically or historically part of Canada or Canadian legal and political institutions. We are . . . set apart by our cultures, languages, distance and histories." They continue by noting that the fact of being "First peoples distinguishes us from any other 'group' or 'minority' in Canada," and justifies special constitutional status.[11] Not surprisingly, the historical background and the reiteration of similar messages, although less frequently by the Inuit, induces other Canadians not to include Aboriginal peoples in their understanding of the "we" community when they describe themselves. This exclusionary tendency is strengthened by the absence of a prominent Aboriginal Trudeau who bridges the cleavage between the indigenous and non-Aboriginal peoples and defends positive links with the latter from a position of member of the former. Thus, the federalist presence within Quebec makes the Quebec-Canada debate both a debate within Quebec and a debate between Quebec and the rest of Canada. The Aboriginal-Canada debate, by contrast, appears as a debate between two actors, because overt advocacy of the Canadian dimension of future Aboriginal constitutional existence does not come from the elites of the Aboriginal community.[12] Canadianness appears as an externally imposed ceiling on Aboriginal aspirations, above which Aboriginal peoples are forbidden to go.[13]

## The Debate That Has Yet To Occur

Although the participation of Aboriginal peoples in constitutional reform processes and the developing acceptance of a unique Aboriginal constitutional status have both been characterized by extensive fluctuations, the general line of development is very clear.

(1) Some form of special positive status for Indians is increasingly recognized as either desirable or inevitable, or both.

(2) The original indigenous constitutional category "Indian" (judicially interpreted to include Inuit) has expanded to the enlarged category "Aboriginal peoples." This greatly enlarges the indigenous constitutional category – now approximately a million – seeking distinct treatment. Further, from two perspectives the diversity within the new "Aboriginal" category is markedly greater than the contents of the previous category "Indian" (including Inuit). First, the inclusion of Métis adds a new constitutional player. Second, Aboriginal constitutional policy now applies to non-land-based Aboriginal peoples, not only the Métis, but non-status Indians and off-reserve status Indians. Land-based Aboriginal peoples now constitute only about one-third of the total Aboriginal population.

(3) The Charlottetown Accord indicates that the differential constitutional and institutional treatment of Aboriginal peoples could be pronounced.

(4) The application of various equality norms, some of which are driven by the Charter and others by the coexistence of distinct indigenous peoples under the rubric of "Aboriginal peoples," is a major vehicle for change within the Aboriginal category. The equality provisions of the Charter are responsible for the Bill C-31 reinstatement of Indian status for nearly 90,000 Indian women and their families.[14] However, since very few of the reinstated have been able to regain band membership and thus the right to live in reserve-based Indian communities, the off-reserve category of status Indians has been greatly enlarged.

The inclusion of distinct peoples – Indian, Inuit, and Métis – under the same rubric stimulates the use of intra-Aboriginal comparisons as levers to advance the rights/recognitions of the relatively disadvantaged. The Métis have brilliantly exploited this possibility by asserting the need to level the playing field in the interest of justice, by which is meant increasing the status and treatment difference between Métis and ordinary Canadians by reducing the status and treatment difference between Métis and Inuit or Indian. The equality argument is employed in the service of increasing inequalities of treatment between Métis and non-Aboriginal peoples.

A special version of the equal treatment argument lies behind the claim of off-reserve Aboriginal peoples in urban settings for some self-governing powers.

(5) In general, the constitutional response to the Aboriginal presence has moved from the focused and narrow – the original s. 91(24), which indicated which order of government had authority over (some) Aboriginal peoples – to an increasingly comprehensive coverage. For example, in addition to defining Aboriginal peoples in s. 35 of the 1982 Constitution Act, other clauses exempted Aboriginal peoples from the Charter's application in certain circumstances (s. 25), recognized Aboriginal rights (s. 35), and laid out a constitutional conference process for determining what they were (s. 37). Although the Meech Lake Accord was not a response to Aboriginal constitutional aspirations, Aboriginal pressure was successful in exempting their constitutional clauses from the application of the distinct society (s. 16), an achievement the women's movement was unable to duplicate. As already noted, the Charlottetown Accord more or less proposed a separate Aboriginal constitution nestled within the overall written constitution.

These developments are dramatic – recognition of an enduring Indian special status; the extension of special status to an enlarged category of Aboriginal peoples; a far-reaching enhancement of the contents of special status; and the *de facto* emergence of an Aboriginal constitution.

The remarkable evolution, both achieved and prospective, of the constitutional status of Aboriginal peoples is in part the legacy of history, of a paradigm breakdown, skilful Aboriginal leadership, the opening up of the constitution for non-Aboriginal reasons, and several other factors. It was not, in other words, the result of a victory of one set of ideas over another in an academic-type setting. This is not surprising, as ideas always jostle with such other factors as inertia and power in determining policy. Nevertheless, it is deeply instructive to examine several striking characteristics of the debate about the future constitutional status of Aboriginal peoples.

(1) The quality and openness of the debate are both damaged by taboos that inhibit serious public examination of questions in ways that might challenge the feasibility or desirability of Aboriginal goals. This is widely recognized, commented on, and sometimes deplored by those subjected to its constraints.[15] The source of these constraints lies in some combination of liberal guilt and the inchoate acceptance of the voice appropriation thesis that disadvantaged "others" should be allowed to speak for themselves. It is at a minimum very clear that Aboriginal leaders occupy the high moral ground and advocates of alternative positions are on the defensive. Part of the explanation, of course, is that past policies have failed, the status quo is unacceptable, and the historic goal of absorption or assimilation has been rejected.

(2) A second crucial factor that informs the debate and the intellectual/cultural climate attending it is the relative absence of a rich store of constitutional thought we can ransack. In contrast to the Quebec-Canada situation, our intellectual capital in this new Aboriginal constitutional world is remarkably thin.

The contemporary Quebec-Canada debate occurs against the backdrop of a rich intellectual capital developed since Confederation, and more generally since the last half of the eighteenth century. This backdrop, with its varied contents – compact theory, the Durham Report, provincial autonomy, Tremblay Report, *les rois nègres*, B&B Commission – does not mean that the contemporary debate is only a reshuffling of old ideas. Clearly, the literature on Quebec independence, or sovereignty-association, or the rest of Canada as a separate political entity has advanced remarkably in recent decades. Nevertheless, the present debate builds on the past, and is informed by it. It is a grounded debate. It has moorings.

By contrast, while the Aboriginal-Canadian debate also has a history, its guiding norms, formerly wielded by governments, are now rejected. From the vantage point of the latter, who were the controlling actors up until the late sixties, the goal of Indian policy was assimilation, if disappearance from the shock of contact did not occur first. The Métis were not recognized as having any specific constitutional status, and basic policy for Inuit, to the extent that one existed, was to treat them as ordinary Canadians who might require transitional special treatment.

Clearly, this official intellectual legacy is in ruins, as the goal of disappearance or non-recognition that was its core value has been categorically rejected. To the extent that difference was historically recognized, as in the Indian Act, it was the difference of inferiors, of those who were less than full citizens, and of those whose culture was assaulted by official change agents of the Canadian state. Behind the attribution of inferiority to difference lay such labels as "wards" and "children" and the half-formed racist assumption that perhaps Indian people lacked the capacity to participate as equals in the majority Euro-Canadian society.

From these perspectives, the official past is the enemy, not a rich source of stimulating ideas that can inform contemporary debates. The political-intellectual counterattack that repudiated the above assumptions has produced a new hegemony in which positive distinctive recognition and special constitutional status are now conventional wisdoms. The counterattack on a tradition that denigrated difference, or practised non-recognition, has led to a supportive infrastructure of ideas, organizations, university programs, and a composite Aboriginal/non-Aboriginal intelligentsia that positively valorizes difference and that seeks constitutional recognition and institutional support for distinctiveness. (No doubt future research will elaborate the intellectual antecedents in the Aboriginal past that inform contemporary Aboriginal constitutional aspirations. That intellectual pedigree, however, has not yet successfully infiltrated contemporary constitutional discourse.)

(3) The logic of adversarial constitutional politics induces the advocates of differential treatment to stress their difference, not their sameness. That they will

feel little empathy with the majority society they view as the historical instrument of their oppression and discrimination is also to be expected.

(4) The obvious analogies to Aboriginal constitutional politics are the Third World nationalist movements – based on cultural revivalism and nationalist affirmation – seeking to displace alien imperialist elites by indigenous leaders. In the Canadian case, the language of nationalism, commonly employed by Aboriginal leaders, contributes much of the drive for an elaborate and distinctive Aboriginal constitutional status. Its emotional resonance comes from the politically reinforced memory of the equality of bargaining/recognition in early treaties, especially the Royal Proclamation of 1763, from the contrasting subsequent treatment of status Indians as an inferior administered people, from a sense of self born of geographical isolation for the Inuit and the very belated extension of the effective application of Canadian law, and from the Métis memory of the previous nationhood that lay behind two rebellions in the late nineteenth century.

In all cases, the sense of differentiation on which nationalism feeds is reinforced by memories of specific past maltreatment. The adversarial nature of nationalist rhetoric stresses the profound difference between Aboriginal and non-Aboriginal thoughtways and values. Mary Ellen Turpel, for example, postulates a fundamental radical incommensurability between the Canadian Charter and Aboriginal concepts of rights and justice.[16] Aboriginal political literature is replete with contrasts between Aboriginal and non-Aboriginal ways of life.[17] Relatedly, it is commonly argued that non-Aboriginals cannot represent Aboriginals. In other words, a powerful strain of Aboriginal political discourse challenges or discounts the possibility of Aboriginal and non-Aboriginal Canadians sharing a common membership in a single community.

More generally, the interaction of the language of nationalism with the analogy of colonialism to describe past treatment logically leads to the goal of independence, if the Third World from which the language of nationalist/imperialist struggle is taken is considered an appropriate model. The rhetorical definition of the situation in nationalist/colonialist terms therefore presupposes a goal that for the overwhelming majority of Aboriginal Canadians is neither sought nor practically attainable. The language of nationalism does not lead easily and naturally to a recognition of, let alone a stress on, what is shared with the former imperialist master with whom one wishes to go on living in an ongoing relationship. The real issue, in other words, is not how to break free, to which the language of nationalism leads, but how to become part of, while retaining concurrently a sense of separate selfhood. The difficult intellectual and emotional task is to employ a rhetoric of nationalism to forge new bonds of connection and positive interdependence with the society and polity that nationalism is reacting against.

The history of Aboriginal/non-Aboriginal relations structures the contemporary debate on their future relations in an extremely unfortunate way. Past failure leaves non-Aboriginal Canadians impotent before the challenge "What is to be done?" Guilt weakens their ability to resist Aboriginal claims, and taboos inhibit their willingness to ask questions that might appear to be negative. At the same time, the relative absence of a shared sense of community and citizenship facilitates acceptance of constitutional provisions that will constitutionalize and reinforce difference. From Aboriginal elites the overwhelming pressure is to make positive an historic separateness that has hitherto been negative, or for Métis to escape from a togetherness that appeared more as a suppression of difference than a sharing of community. The apartness of the past – legal for status Indians, psychological for Métis, and geographical for Inuit – sustains proposals for a future apartness that encounters weak resistance from non-Aboriginals because they, too, see future separate status as continuity, not as a sundering of a vibrant "we" community that encompasses Aboriginal peoples.

The question that gets left out by this structuring of the debate is whether a basis for sympathy, empathy, and sharing can survive the reinforcement of difference – difference between the powerful rich majority society and what for the most part will continue to be poor disadvantaged Aboriginal peoples.

A vision of "them" and "us" sees the past as a battleground in which bounded communities of Aboriginal peoples interacted with bounded Euro-Canadian societies. This billiard ball theory of society presupposes that Aboriginal and non-Aboriginal societies interact as wholes. This leads to constitutional statements describing the task of Aboriginal governments as using their jurisdictional authority "to determine and control their development as peoples according to their own values and priorities and ensure the integrity of their societies" (*Consensus Report*, p. 41). Similar assumptions lie behind the Charlottetown Accord's description of Quebec in the Canada clause as a "distinct society [with] a unique culture" that is to be preserved and promoted by the legislature and government of Quebec.

References to the integrity of societies and to distinct societies with unique cultures are misleading in the modern world. No realist student of international politics would accept "integrity," "distinct," or "unique" as accurate descriptions of the cultural condition of contemporary nation-states, viewing all such polities as massively penetrated by external forces. This must be even more the case with an open province such as Quebec within a federal system, and dramatically more so with smaller dependent local Aboriginal societies.

The most elementary data on the ratio of multiple to single origins (in the 1986 census) confirms the extensive Aboriginal/non-Aboriginal intermixture of Canadians reporting Aboriginal identities. Even among the Inuit, the most isolated Aboriginal people, one in four report multiple origins. Among

"Amerindians" slightly under one-half report multiple origins. The Métis, a mixed category from the beginning, reported about 60 percent multiple origins.[18] As already noted, the Indian community is a legal community that has received tens of thousands of white women "immigrants" who married status Indian males. In ten of the nineteen years from 1967 to 1985, 50 per cent or more of status Indian marriages were with non-Indians,[19] figures that suggest extremely high levels of cultural exchange and diminish the credibility of assertions of ineffable difference. Mixed ancestry is supplemented by more direct evidence of cultural transmission. An early 1969-70 study by Boldt indicated about a fifth of the then "Native Indian leaders" favoured integration.[20] The Native Women's Association of Canada is in the vanguard of contemporary Charter supporters. The rationale for self-government is frequently couched in terms of restoring Aboriginal values in societies that have been heavily influenced by the virus of Euro-Canadian materialism and individualism. Aboriginal leaders shrewdly and vigorously employ the Western rhetoric of nationalism, and the Aboriginal past is often described in ways that make contact with majority Canadian values. Some of this, no doubt, reflects what Mary Ellen Turpel describes as the regrettable necessity of having to use the oppressor's language in order to gain the master's attention,[21] but it is difficult not to believe that in many cases such use of language is more than instrumental, that it has become value-laden for those who use it as well as those who are in the intended audience.

This suggests that Aboriginal societies, like all other societies, are penetrated societies. Their members live in many worlds at once and relate to more than one community. Aboriginal societies, therefore, like Quebec and Canadian society, are partial societies. They do not exhaust the identities or community senses of their members. The constitutional question, accordingly, should be rephrased as one of finding the constitutional framework in which citizens can belong to several political communities at the same time, to each of which loyalty is given and from each of which components of multiple identities are fashioned.

For status Indian communities in particular, the demographic reality is even more complex than noted above. The new Bill c-31 criteria for inheriting Indian status mean that reserve Indian communities will have two categories of legal members with a differential capacity to transmit status to their children, resulting in children living on reserves who lack Indian status. Further, spouses from outside will no longer have Indian legal status, although they may spend their entire adult life in the reserve community. To further complicate the picture, Indian bands can now determine their own membership, which may encompass non-Aboriginals who will have political rights but not the rights – to education, for example – that go with legal status. Membership codes may also debar legal status reserve Indians from political membership. Membership codes had been adopted by 236 bands by May, 1992.[22]

Even more than in the past, First Nations communities are internally plural, with marked status differentials and with strong links with the surrounding non-Aboriginal society. Indeed, given existing criteria for legal status and anticipated intermarriage rates, projections are that the legal Indian population will decline in the next century.[23]

Many of the consequences of the preceding are unclear, and in any event are subject to modification by political intervention. However, the pervasive connections with the surrounding society and the ineradicable heterogeneity of values and identifies they foster are inescapable facts to which the theory and practice of future self-government must sensitively respond. Future policy for the Métis, intermingled with Euro-Canadian society, and for non-reserve-based Indians (both status and non-status) must also be sensitive to the demographic and cultural considerations that affect their reality even more profoundly. Conceptions of contemporary Aboriginality, therefore, must accommodate the non-Aboriginal influences that help to shape it.

For a federal people the issue of identity and community is inherently more complex than for a unitary people. To survive, federal regimes require divided loyalties, dual identities, and simultaneous senses of belonging to the overlapping federal and provincial communities in which the citizen exists. For Aboriginal peoples in a triple-decker federalism, the complexity is even greater for they will simultaneously be members of three communities – Aboriginal, provincial, and federal (although for most Inuit, as Nunavut emerges, the first two will be collapsed). Constitution-making that does not address the fact of multiple overlapping communities, but instead concentrates on one layer of community, misconceives the requirements for stability of the very complex federal society toward which the Charlottetown Accord was heading. Such a misconception exaggerates our differences and fosters constitutional policies, like the Charlottetown Accord, that stimulate the divisions they profess only to reflect.

## The Perils of Too Great a Degree of Differentiation

The most consistent tendency of the last two decades in the implicit and explicit constitutional theory applicable to Aboriginal peoples has been a continuing enlargement of the contents of successively proposed constitutional packages defining a unique Aboriginal relationship to the Canadian state and a progressive enhancement of the numbers of Aboriginal Canadians it will encompass. Turned on its head, this tendency can be described as the continuing erosion of the future Canadian content in the lives of Aboriginal peoples. This conclusion can be elided by redefining as Canadian content all of the ways in which the relation of Aboriginal Canadians to the Canadian state will differ from that of other Canadians and all of the ways in which they will live under different laws and policies than do other Canadians. However, this tautological obfuscation does not respond to the concern that the removal of Aboriginal peoples from the "we" group of the non-Aboriginal Canadian majority will tend to reduce the degree of concern and civic obligation held by the latter for the former. Simultaneously, it will tend to weaken the moral power behind the claims the former can make on the latter.

This suggests, as Tocqueville argued in *Democracy in America*,[24] that the principle of self-interest should not be narrowly understood, a maxim particularly appropriate for those who are engaged in working out an Aboriginal/non-Aboriginal constitutional *rapprochement*. Empathy and consideration for the other are reciprocal. They are undermined by the degree to which common bonds and shared conceptions of community are absent. In certain circumstances, obligation and a sense of responsibility can generate a paternalistic obligation of superiors to uplift inferiors. This is the mixture of altruism and aristocratic duty that lay behind the nobler aspects of "the white man's burden." The new relationship, however, is to be among equals – symbolized as nation to nation – to which hierarchical conceptions of duty and moral superiority will, quite properly, not apply. In relationships between equals, every weakening of the bonds of community attenuates the responsibility of the larger, wealthier party for the disadvantaged as the latter's relationship to the former becomes increasingly tangential.

This understanding is relatively absent from Aboriginal constitutional advocacy. The nationalist endeavour facilitates negative evaluations of the oppressor and hence undermines conceptions of a common, sharing "we" community. Further, the major objective of Aboriginal elites in the nineties is to gain recognition of the uniqueness of their situation and their special status. In addition, there is a widespread belief that the obligations of the larger society to provide services, funding, and other support for Aboriginal peoples can be sustained by guilt or by recognition that the wealth of the larger society is a product of the inequitable appropriation of lands and resources once occupied and used by Aboriginal peoples. Positive treatment now and into the indefinite future therefore is a kind of payment. However, to pin the security of future treatment on this assumption involves high risks.

Given the hundreds of experiments in Aboriginal self-government that will develop in coming decades, instances of corruption and abuse of power are inevitable. Their likelihood is magnified by the poverty of many Aboriginal communities, the prominence the public sector will enjoy, and kinship links that will strain against universalistic norms. It cannot be assumed that traditional consensual practices can survive, or be revived. The transition to self-government as an instrument of nationalist self-assertion for Aboriginal peoples is the domestic version of the move of Third World peoples to independence in recent decades.

Although the context is strikingly different, there are some common impediments to the emergence of political communities respectful of the dignity of their heterogeneous citizenry. If the Aboriginal communities are not considered to be integral parts of the Canadian community, every appearance of maladministration will reinforce an attenuation of non-Aboriginal concern for Aboriginal peoples that will already have been fostered by constitutional and institutional distancing.

In brief, excessive constitutional and institutional differentiation of Aboriginal from other Canadians may have adverse consequences that have been overlooked. Too little positive differentiation errs in the opposite direction by providing insufficient capacity to foster a continuing degree of distinctiveness. The momentum of the past two decades has been largely driven by the latter consideration. A more appropriate balance of concerns would pay equal attention to the former danger and perhaps lead to a constitutional package that accepts inescapable interdependencies and stresses connections to the Canadian community, and to the values of a common citizenship, as well as giving positive support to Aboriginality.

## Postscript

The preceding analysis focuses on what Dan Smith calls "the Great Game"[25] of constitutional politics and what my colleague Paul Tennant describes as the politics of "Big Men in Big Places," such as first ministers' conferences.[26] This contrasts with local community politics, which are often far removed from contests over abstract constitutional terminology. Smith's journalistic *tour de force* describes the extensive and positive grassroots move toward self-government in such areas as policing, education, child welfare, and "healing circles" where a community tries to re-establish its moral integrity and take responsibility for its own progress. These local advances are far removed from "the Great Game" and suggest a gap between leaders' aspirations and the community concerns of those they claim to represent.

The extent and nature of the gap between Aboriginal leaders and their people at the grassroots is a crucial question not directly addressed in this paper, and it requires further research. Finding ways of bridging the gap if and where it exists – and it will no doubt vary among Indian, Métis, and Inuit and within each category – will foster a more representative politics of constitution-making for Aboriginal peoples. Both the grassroots and "the Great Game" are real. Even if the latter may on occasion appear divorced from life in Old Crow in the Yukon or on the Kahnawake Reserve, it is not. After all, the 1867 decision to place jurisdiction over "Indians, and Lands reserved for the Indians" with the federal government generated a train of consequences all too real in the anomic state of many contemporary First Nation communities. Hence, while I agree that a comprehensive portrayal would go beyond the constitutional focus of the preceding pages, the division of academic labour assumes that the examination of a portion of an interdependent whole, in this case the constitutional arena, can help put one more piece in place in the jigsaw puzzle of understanding the real world that engages us.

PART V

CONSTITUTIONAL REFORM

Chapter Eleven

# The Charter, Interest Groups, Executive Federalism, and Constitutional Reform

Contemporary Canadians disagree on the role and function of the written constitution. To governments it remains what it always has been, an instrument of federalism. The division of powers, its interpretation by the courts, its management by intergovernmental machinery, and the process of its formal amendment comprise the vision of the written constitution that is natural to first ministers. From this governmental perspective, constitutional debate also focuses on intrastate federalism – the extent and nature of regional input at the centre and the continuing propriety of what might be called intrastate federalism in reverse, the various instruments by which the federal government can insert itself into matters of provincial jurisdiction – disallowance, reservation, the declaratory power, and the spending power. From the perspective of what may be called the governments' constitution, the community basis of the constitutional order is found in the pan-Canadian community and the ten provincial and two northern territorial communities. Canadians are to be thought of as Manitobans, Yukoners, or as citizens of a country-wide community.

Federalism provides rich constitutional fare. Until the arrival of the Charter, federalist discourse dominated our jurisprudence. Constitutional debate revolved around what the Fathers intended, generated the contested compact theory of Confederation, and praised or criticized the Judicial Committee of the Privy Council for its contribution to the evolution of Canadian federalism. It was natural in this tradition that such great state papers on the constitution as the Rowell-Sirois and Tremblay reports were, above all else, analyses of the past and future of federalism as a constitutional arrangement.

Federalism is no longer enough. It occupies a shrinking portion of our constitutional terrain. It is jostled by a rights discourse that preceded but was greatly stimulated by the 1982 Charter. Via the Charter the post-1982 constitution speaks directly to Canadians in terms of citizen-state relations. The Charter also triggers various specific constitutional discourses – an ethnic discourse that responds to section 27 of the Charter from the vantage point of a society that is increasingly multicultural and multiracial; a discrete focus on the consequences of the sex division in society for the constitution, and vice versa, that is driven by the feminist movement and focuses on sections 28 and 15 of the Charter; an equality debate given constitutional stimulation by section 15 of the Charter and kept alive by what have come to be called "equality seekers"[1]; and a debate about the role of the constitution in relation to linguistic duality that draws from sections 16 to 23 of the Charter.

Yet another focus on the constitution, only peripherally linked to the Charter, addresses the question of the role and recognition of Aboriginal peoples in Canadian society. What mix of special status and normal Canadian citizenship are they to enjoy? What differences, if any, should exist in the constitutional treatment of Indians, Inuit, and Métis? In one sense these are not new constitutional questions, as the appropriate relationship between Aboriginal peoples and other Canadians has been a constitutional policy issue since Confederation. Clearly, however, the constitutional politics of Aboriginal issues is now driven by a combination of numbers, self-confidence, indigenous nationalisms, a supportive international climate, and an enhanced degree of constitutional recognition since 1982 that no longer allows their relegation to the backwaters in which they formerly languished.

The written constitution has become, accordingly, a many splendoured and much more comprehensive arrangement than was true of its spare predecessor, the BNA Act. It is therefore not surprising that Canadians disagree on the process of formal constitutional change, on who should participate and who should be in the audience. In the post-Meech Lake era Canadians are clearly in a state of constitutional transition, not only in terms of the Quebec/rest-of-Canada relationship but also in terms of the relationship of the Charter and Aboriginal constitutional clauses to the traditional concerns of federalism. We disagree about the substance of the existing constitution and about the procedures we should employ in trying to move to a new constitutional equilibrium.

We are now paying a heavy price for the prolonged constitutional immaturity that left the formal power of constitutional amendment in crucial matters in British hands until 1982. We too-long avoided the basic question of where sovereignty resided by leaving, formally, large chunks of it in the Parliament of the former imperial mother country. This allowed us simultaneously to avoid the challenge of forming ourselves into a constitutional people, agreed on the fundamentals of our civic existence.[2] As a result, we now confront the issue of our constitutional future at a time when the Quebec challenge to the federal dimension of our identity is supplemented by an Aboriginal challenge to our Canadianism and by a non-territorial pluralism drawing on the social cleavages of sex, ethnicity, race, disability, etc.

The written constitution has become a symbolic document of great importance. It hands out differential status to Canadians in terms of sex, ethnicity, language, indigenous status, and other social categories singled out for explicit constitutional attention. Meech Lake makes it clear that such questions as who is to receive constitutional recognition as a distinct society and what are to be included in the constitution as fundamental characteristics of Canada are not dry technical matters but minefields of explosive emotions. Not surprisingly, the profound importance of our unanswered constitutional questions generates disagreement over the process we should follow in seeking answers. Our recent constitutional history confirms that constitutional process and constitutional outcome are closely linked.

## Hobson's Constitutional Reform Choice: Failure or a Pyrrhic Victory?

In the mid-sixties, when we began the constitutional soul-searching in which we have ever since been engaged, there was a tendency to assume that the task was relatively straightforward. In the midst of the counter-culture climate and the blossoming of new Third World nations as ancient empires crumbled, the "out with the old and in with the new" did not seem a daunting task. Paper constitutions flourished and otherwise sensible people delighted in mocking the decrepit BNA Act as an anachronism whose imminent destination was the graveyard.

We now know better. Enthusiasm for constitutional reform is restricted to masochists and those who derive pleasure from Sisyphean tasks. The most likely outcome of a constitutional reform effort is failure. The demise of Meech Lake is simply the latest in a long list of failed attempts to change constitutional direction in a fundamental way. The historical evidence is depressing – the Fulton-Favreau amending formula of the mid-sixties, the Victoria Charter of 1971, Bill c-60 of the late seventies, and the four unsuccessful Aboriginal constitutional conferences of the mid-eighties all join Meech Lake in testifying to the resilience of the discredited old order that so many would like to leave behind. Thus, defeat of reform efforts is the basic pattern.

The proposed federal government 1980-81 threat to proceed unilaterally to request an amendment from the British Parliament revealed an additional recurring pattern in the constitutional reform process – the tendency of those in charge to exclude, or try to exclude, other constitutional actors who stand in the way of agreement. The Trudeau unilateralism threat – a by-product of the unclear norms as to how much provincial government support was necessary for a "proper" request to Westminster – was designed to bypass provincial governments "unreasonably" opposing the proposed federal request. Further, the amending formula proposed by the federal government in the patriation package could have left up to four provincial governments in Atlantic Canada and western Canada on the losing side, or if the proposed referendum route were employed, theoretically ten provincial governments could have been opposed to an amendment that would nevertheless be implemented on the basis of receiving the requisite voter support in the regions of Canada.[3] Although the threatened unilateralism route was not followed, and the proposed referendum route to constitutional change was not implemented, the actual 1982 Constitution Act left an embittered Quebec government on the sidelines crying betrayal over its exclusion from the agreement.

That same 1982 constitutional outcome featured a last-minute erosion of the rights and recognitions that women and Aboriginal Canadians thought they had won, which were only restored by applying extreme political pressure on the recalcitrant provincial premiers. The Meech Lake strategy, of course, was based on the thesis that a unanimous collective intergovernmental unilateralism could safely ignore the vehement opposition of Charter supporters and Aboriginal elites who thought that their constitutional interests were being ignored or threatened. Had Meech Lake succeeded, accordingly, the vociferous cries of the aggrieved losers would have sullied the outcome in a manner analogous to the absence of the Quebec government from the winner's circle in 1982.

Losers remember. They nourish their loss. It may be turned into a rationale for a more sympathetic constitutional round next time, as the "betrayal" of 1982 became the justification for the special Quebec round called Meech Lake. It may feed a simmering politics of constitutional resentment, as among Aboriginal peoples, after the failure of four Aboriginal constitutional conferences was quickly followed by the seeming triumph of the Quebec-sensitive Meech Lake Accord, an historical context that makes Elijah Harper's behaviour understandable. Or, as among feminist groups, the memories of past constitutional struggles suggest that without unceasing vigilance one's constitutional interests will be forgotten, ignored, or trampled upon. Thus, the difference between a constitutional "success" and a constitutional "failure" is less than meets the eye. Triumphs are not seen as such by the wounded losers. Defeats are not seen as such by those who opposed a failed constitutional package. Thus, both the category "triumph" and the category "defeat" contain winners and losers, albeit probably in different proportions. As the number of would-be constitutional players increases, the number of losers is likely to increase more than proportionately.

The high probability of failure and the difficulty of including all of those whose interests might be affected account for the frequent resort to extraordinary stratagems to bring about constitutional change; hence the threatened unilateralism route of the Trudeau Liberals that would have required the British MPs to hold their collective noses and pass the federal government package in spite of the oppositionist tactics of some provincial governments and Aboriginal organizations in London; hence also the attempt in the weeks leading up to Meech Lake to throw the media and constitution watchers off the trail by describing the pending Meech Lake meeting as exploratory only, rather than the setting for an attempted constitutional *fait accompli.* [4] Another indication that desperate constitutional times might require extraordinary constitutional measures was the Parti Québécois strategy decision to hold a referendum to generate and confirm the popular support for a fundamental constitutional change in Quebec's status that could then be employed as a bargaining resource in the subsequent negotiations. For the nationalists, the referendum was a humiliating confirmation of the high risk of failure in constitutional reform efforts with which discussion in this section began.

Thus major constitutional reform is not to be undertaken by the fainthearted or by those who seek a guaranteed return on their investment of time and energy; it is not to be undertaken by those who cannot tolerate the possibility that at the end of the day they might both be exhausted and worse off than before they began (the Parti Québécois after the referendum and the 1982 Constitution Act), or by those who do not wish to risk the possibility that the constitutional order itself might be seriously damaged by a failure (as after Meech Lake).

Given these grim lessons, there are only three possible explanations for the quarter-of-a-century-long addiction of Canadians to constitutional reform: an overpowering necessity based on intolerable shortcomings of the existing constitutional order; an optimistic naiveté based on short memories; or the inability to stop a reform momentum that once begun can only be brought to a close by some kind of resolution. The last explanation is the most plausible, supplemented by intermittent doses of naiveté and, for a handful of the participants, the intolerable nature of the status quo.

# A Brief Revisionist Historical Digression

## CONSTITUTIONAL EXECUTIVE FEDERALISM:[5]
## THE GOLDEN AGE THAT NEVER WAS

The drama of Meech Lake is so recent and our emotional involvement with the roller-coaster of its fluctuating development was so intense that we are in danger of drawing lessons from it that are insufficiently steeped in history. One lesson that is true in one version but misleading in another is that Meech Lake was the occasion for the defeat of executive federalism in constitutional matters. The obvious truth of this assertion is that in intent Meech Lake was what Simeon calls a "textbook example of 'executive federalism,'"[6] and that it was administered a staggering rebuff by the varied constituencies of Charter supporters and Aboriginal peoples. The correct interpretation of Meech Lake as a repudiation of executive federalism is, however, misleading if it is taken further to imply that prior to Meech Lake Canadians had enjoyed a golden age of executive federalism in constitutional matters. Nothing could be further from the truth.

The successes of executive federalism are found in the normal intergovernmental politics of working an ongoing federal system,[7] not in formally amending the constitution. In fact, the need for a pragmatic executive federalism of everyday was justified by our collective inability to keep the constitution up-to-date by amendments. The First Ministers' Conference to deal with the Rowell-Sirois Report in 1941 provided great theatre but broke up in disorder without seriously considering the Rowell-Sirois proposals.[8] For half a century, the executive federalism meetings of first ministers were unable to agree on a domestic amending formula, including the high-profile failures of the Fulton-Favreau formula and the Victoria Charter.

The replacement of the Judicial Committee of the Privy Council by the Supreme Court, the admission of Newfoundland, and the adoption of the limited domestic 1949 amending formula were all undertaken unilaterally by the federal government against the opposition of one or more provinces. With respect to the elimination of appeals to the JCPC, St. Laurent simply refused even to consult with the provinces because he knew Duplessis would never agree to such a change.[9] Thus Trudeau's threatened unilateralism in 1980-81, although perhaps unique in the extent of the constitutional changes he proposed, had a distinguished pedigree behind it.

The 1982 Constitution Act, and particularly the Charter, as is noted below, can only be described as a triumph of executive federalism by stretching the truth. Meech Lake, of course, a classic example of an attempt to amend the constitution by the instrumentality of executive federalism, was a catastrophic failure. In sum, the non-trivial amendments achieved by executive federalism in the last half-century are limited to a handful of discrete changes in the welfare field dealing with unemployment insurance and old age and disability pensions.[10] Meech Lake, therefore, should not be thought of as the defeat of an established tradition of constitutional executive federalism sanctified by its positive achievements. Meech Lake is more accurately thought of as a confirmation of the very limited capacity of executive federalism to grapple successfully with constitutional issues, a conclusion in agreement with Dupré's pre-Meech Lake pessimistic assessment of what he labels the "'constitutional review model' of federal-provincial summitry."[11]

## A ROLE FOR THE PUBLIC IS NOT NEW

Meech Lake was defeated because it clashed with the competing constitutional visions of Aboriginal peoples, of English-speaking Canadians who identified strongly with the Charter, and of supporters of a strong central government. They made their views known before provincial legislative committees or task forces in New Brunswick, Ontario, and Manitoba, before the hearings of the Special Joint Committee of the Senate and of the House of Commons on the 1987 Constitutional Accord, and also before later separate Senate and House of Commons hearings. Provincial elections in Manitoba, New Brunswick, and Newfoundland replaced Meech Lake-supporting governments with successors who opposed Meech Lake. This legitimated opposition to the Accord by providing leadership to the anti-Meech Lake forces from within the political establishment. By the end of the three-year period in June, 1990, dating from the Accord's ratification by the Quebec National Assembly, the defeat of the Accord was in tune with public opinion.

As Lowell Murray and the Prime Minister ruefully observed, this was not at all what they had anticipated. They incorrectly thought that the agreement of eleven first ministers was an irresistible juggernaut that could easily deliver the goods of legislative ratification. As Mulroney reiterated, the first ministers gave their word, their word was their bond, and that was all there was to it.[12] This was, so to speak, an egregious error in understanding. The misunderstanding was many layered.

The first ministers failed to appreciate that the requirement of the 1982 Constitution Act amending formula for legislative ratification within a three-year period was not a simple formality, a mopping-up operation after the real business of getting the agreement of first ministers had been achieved. Under the 1982 Constitution Act amending formula the requirement for legislative ratification is a discrete second stage of hurdles that has to be overcome. As well, the organizers of Meech Lake failed to understand that the 1982 incorporation of a Charter of Rights into the constitution changed the constitutional culture of English-speaking Canada by giving various groups linked to the Charter a sense that they were legitimate constitutional actors with stakes in the constitution. More generally, the Meech Lake failure derived from an insensitivity to the potent new symbolic role of the constitution, especially the Charter, in English-speaking Canada. There was also a failure to appreciate the developing constitutional self-consciousness and constitutional ambitions of the Aboriginal people, which were partly a by-product of the limited recognitions they had achieved in the Constitution Act, 1982, and of their frustration over the failure of four constitutional conferences from 1983 to 1987 to clarify their rights.

In these ways, the Meech Lake failure was the consequence of an inadequate short-term historical understanding or, slightly differently phrased, of an outdated constitutional theory that had not caught up with post-1982 constitutional realities. In fact, however, the weak sense of history went beyond the inadequate appreciation of the consequences of the Constitution Act, 1982, to a larger failure to appreciate the varied manner in which the public has played a role in constitutional politics since the 1960s.

In the mid-sixties, the Fulton-Favreau formula for constitutional amendment, agreed to at a First Ministers' Conference, foundered on nationalist opposition in Quebec that saw the formula as a straitjacket hampering Quebec's future constitutional ambitions. A few years later, the Victoria Charter constitutional package, fashioned at a First Minister's Conference, also fell by the wayside – again because of Quebec nationalist opposition, this time directed *inter alia* to the package's failure to respond to Quebec's social policy goals.

In the late seventies, the Parti Québécois assumed that the major constitutional change of sovereignty-association that they sought was not simply a decision for the Quebec government to make but required the referendum approval of the Quebec people. The referendum campaign was passionate, the outcome deeply divisive, and the referendum question was not a model of clarity. However, the people spoke. Their verdict was negative, and it was respected by those who wished it otherwise.

The subsequent Constitution Act, 1982, and particularly the Charter, as previously noted, was only achieved because of the strong public support for the latter expressed in Special Joint Committee hearings and in poll results that overcame the opposition of most provincial governments to this un-British repudiation of parliamentary supremacy. So the Charter was achieved in spite of executive federalism, not because of it. Further, both Aboriginal organizations and women's groups engaged in massive political mobilization in order successfully to reinstate what they had lost in the final First Ministers' Conference. This explains the feminist phrase, "The Taking of Twenty-Eight," [13] used to describe how section 28, the sex equality clause, got into the constitution and was protected from the ambit of the notwithstanding clause.

The Constitution Act, 1982, sanctioned a further breach in executive federalism by its section 37 requirement to hold a First Ministers' Conference to discuss Aboriginal matters with representatives of the Aboriginal peoples. Although the four conferences that were in fact held failed to achieve their objective, they clearly confirmed that pure executive federalism was an insufficiently comprehensive vehicle for the resolution of Aboriginal issues that had a constitutional dimension.

These examples of public involvement and direct public influence on constitutional outcomes have been a recurring phenomenon, not an aberration. For thirty years Canadians have gone through a searing experience of constitutional consciousness-raising. Thousands of briefs have been prepared and presented to the succession of royal commissions and task forces, parliamentary hearings, and provincial legislative committees that proliferated as Canadians lived through a seemingly unending period of constitutional introspection. To put it differently, it is not only governments that have been involved and have improved their constitutional understanding, but also the citizenry, especially of course the elites of the various groups, such as women, ethnic groups, and Aboriginals, who have developed constitutional knowledge to sustain their constitutional ambitions.

The nature of the public role has varied. Frequently it has been a blocking role, but that is mainly because the initiating role has been played by governments. Governments have not always welcomed public participation, because it often thwarts their constitutional objectives. The public role is not always incorporated into the process but sometimes emerges in spite of it, as a reaction to what governments thought was a *fait accompli*. Occasionally, as in the making of the Charter, there is a clear alliance between one or more governments and an array of supportive interest groups. Normally, this is an attempt by governments to reach outside the circle of first ministers in order to increase their bargaining power in executive federalism. This, of course, was the object of the Parti Québécois referendum, although the assumption was that the subsequent bargaining would be one on one between Quebec and Ottawa.

Whatever the nature of the public role, whether solicited or unsought by governments, whether supportive or opposed to the agenda of governments, the public response in the reform process, as in Meech Lake, has been tenacious and influential in the past three decades. It is not, however, a routinized role. It has been expressed in a diversity of ways. That is partly why its extent and significance have not been adequately appreciated.

## The Charter and Executive Federalism: An Inevitable Conflict

Much of the opposition to Meech Lake came from the varied constituencies of Charter supporters. They objected not only to the substance of Meech Lake, but also emphatically and truculently to the executive federalism process by which it was to be brought about. While much of this opposition was to the particulars of Meech Lake, there was a naturalness, almost an inevitability to it, that derived from a larger opposition between Charter supporters and executive federalism that has roots in history and principle.

Initially, this opposition derives from the fact that the Charter is inherently an anti-federal instrument, while executive federalism is the classic vehicle for empowering governments to speak for Canadians in terms of their membership in the territorial communities of province and nation. The Charter confronts the territorial identities of federalism with, first, a stress on individual citizens, and, second, a stress on the varied social categories singled out for specific mention – women, multicultural Canadians, official-language minorities, the equality-seekers in section 15, and others. In other words, the Charter does not address Canadians in the language of federalism but in a mixed language of individual rights and non-territorial social pluralism.

The Charter's message is not, however, indifferent to the distinction between provincial communities and the coast-to-coast pan-Canadian community. The Charter's message is a Canadian message. The rights it enshrines are Canadian rights. The community of citizen membership that it fosters is the overall Canadian community. It is the Canadianism of the Charter that explains the continuing lesser sympathy for, and the previous opposition to, the Charter by provincial governments. This differential pattern of empathy for the (or a) Charter by the federal and provincial governments is the source of the consistent pattern that emerges from the encounter between the Charter idea and federalism over the past three decades.

### FEDERAL GOVERNMENT CHARTER LEADERSHIP

The drive for a Bill of Rights and subsequently for a Charter were both led by the federal government. For both Diefenbaker and Trudeau this leadership role was a product of the nation-building function they attributed to rights. The 1960 Bill of Rights was the product of Diefenbaker's pan-Canadian one-Canada vision. His political purpose was to reduce the status difference between the British and French founding peoples and other Canadians, those who came to be called "third-force" Canadians a few years later. The momentum that led to the 1982 Charter was consistently supplied by the federal government after Trudeau entered the Pearson cabinet. Its nation-building political purposes, to restrain centrifugal provincialism and to keep alive a conception of French Canada extending beyond Quebec, have been analysed by Peter Russell and others.[14] In the contemporary period, the federal government has generally seen rights as a constitutional bulwark against provincialism.

### PROVINCIAL GOVERNMENT CHARTER OPPOSITION

One of the weaknesses of Diefenbaker's Bill of Rights, its non-applicability to the provinces, reflected Diefenbaker's recognition that the provinces would not support a constitutional amendment that would apply the Bill of Rights to their jurisdiction. Trudeau encountered similar resistance from provincial governments. Bill c-60 in 1978 was a contorted attempt to have a Charter incrementally extend to the provinces as they individually opted in.[15] Provincial government support for the Charter from the dissenting provinces was only gained in a trade-off in which the Gang of Eight got their amending formula into the 1982 constitution package.

### PROVINCIAL GENESIS OF THE NOTWITHSTANDING CLAUSE

The pressure for a Charter-weakening notwithstanding clause came from provincial governments in western Canada and was reluctantly acceded to by the federal government. Thus far the use of the notwithstanding clause has been restricted to provincial governments. The pressure to eliminate the clause disproportionately comes from federal politicians.

### INTEREST GROUP CHARTER SUPPORT IN HEARINGS, PROVINCIAL GOVERNMENT OPPOSITION AMONG FIRST MINISTERS

In the making of the Charter, a clear pattern emerged as discussion moved back and forth from the intergovernmental executive federalism arena to the public world of parliamentary hearings and interest groups. The initial federal government version of the Charter, emerging out of the 1980 summer of intergovernmental constitutional talks, was weak, reflecting the impact of the recent provincial government antipathy to the Charter on federal thinking. Subsequent pressure in the public arena of parliamentary hearings strengthened the Charter as the federal government realized that it might be better and easier to get strong public support for a strong Charter than limited provincial government support for a weak Charter. When the Charter moved back into the executive federalism arena for the last time, provincial pressure led to the section 33 notwithstanding clause and to encroachments on the rights of women and Aboriginal peoples. The limited provincial government support for the Charter was reciprocated by the indifference of the interest groups that supported the Charter to provincial government concerns over the Charter's erosion of parliamentary supremacy.

This pattern of federal initiatives, public support, and the tendency of provincial governments to oppose the Charter sprang from the Charter's political purposes – clearly and specifically to set limits to the capacity of provincial governments to respond to their local situations in ways that offended against the constitutional norm of Canadianism enshrined in the Charter. The Charter was the Liberal government's answer to the Joe Clark definition of Canada as a community of communities. More fundamentally, it was an attack on the compact theory of Confederation that privileged provincial governments and provincial communities – especially the founding four of Ontario, Quebec, New Brunswick, and Nova Scotia – as the building blocks of Confederation. As Duplessis used to say, the provinces are the parents and the federal government is the child, and children should not devour their parents. From the perspective of the Charter, the basis of the polity was not provincial governments and provincial communities but Canadian citizens. In the rhetorical language of the Kirby memorandum, the competing positions in the 1980-81 constitutional discussion could be summed up as the federal government's "People's Package" versus the (provincial) "Powers and Institutions Package" in which the Charter was the key component of the "People's Package."[16] At the time, the federal government succeeded in aligning supportive interest groups behind the Charter and against the opposing provincial governments. By the time of Meech Lake, the next generation of Charter-supporting interest groups defended the Charter against both orders of government. The Meech Lake clash between Charter supporters and an executive federalism arena attuned to provincial government wishes was, given recent history, virtually inevitable.

## The Charter and Meech Lake

While as already noted, a public role in the constitutional reform process is not new, the public input in 1987-90 was qualitatively different for several reasons:

(1) The initial attempt to freeze out the public, that subsequently unravelled, occurred against the backdrop of the 1980-82 exercise in which citizens' groups had unquestionably contributed decisively to the final outcome. Not only did much of the precise wording of the Charter derive from interest group suggestions, but the very existence of the Charter would have been problematic in the absence of strong public support. To some extent, therefore, the Charter came to be seen as their Charter by the many groups involved in its creation, and particular clauses as their clauses.

(2) The positive group memories of having had an effect in the earlier process

were supplemented by the fact that the Charter made them constitutional stake-holders. Thus the attempt to exclude them in Meech Lake was a constitutional indignity in a way that had been less true of their attempted exclusion in pre-Charter days. In this sense, the Charter delegitimated an executive federalism first ministers' monopoly of the constitutional reform process and legitimated citizen input. These mutually supporting tendencies might have been weakened had it been widely believed that the Charter had powerful and faithful defenders among the first ministers, particularly the Prime Minister. However, evidence to support this belief was lacking. This failure was viewed as a breach of faith, possibly because it contrasted with federal government leadership in the introduction of the Charter. It was seen as a failure of the federal government to do its duty of speaking for, strengthening, and defending the overall Canadian community of Charter rights holders. The participant impulse, accordingly, was stimulated by a lack of trust in elites.

(3) The Charter structured the presentations of those who spoke on its behalf. This degree of consistency or appeal to a common document was much less possible in pre-Charter days when no such focal point existed around which citizen groups could coalesce and structure their constitutional thoughts. In 1980-81, the groups that appeared before the Special Joint Committee brought diffuse constitutional aspirations to their presentations. In 1987-90 they brought a Charter-inspired vision of Canadianism that was hostile to provincial variations in the availability of rights. Such variations were no longer the acceptable by-products of the territorial diversities that federalism reflects and nourishes. On the contrary, they had become violations of the rights of fellow citizens so that a simple appeal to federalism, or the assertion that the use of the notwithstanding clause was constitutionally legitimate, was an insufficient justification.

The everyday political or constitutional importance of the Charter, therefore, is that it gives citizens a Canadian constitutional norm to judge the behaviour of government in other jurisdictions. To put it differently, it psychologically involves all Canadians in the internal affairs of other jurisdictions when Charter rights are involved. Logically, this is more of a constraint on the provincial governments than on the federal government, for involvement in the affairs of fellow Canadians for matters under federal jurisdiction necessarily followed from the simple existence of the federal government and the Canadian community its policies served. For an individual provincial government, however, the Charter created critical external audiences who could now pass legitimate judgement as Canadians on government policies in other provinces. Thus Bourassa's use of the notwithstanding clause to pass his language of signs legislation was not just a Quebec matter but a constitutional issue for Canadians. In rights matters, therefore, provincial politics is not insulated from external judgements by the division of powers. When Charter concerns are at stake, the watertight compartments of federalism disappear. Accordingly, that the notwithstanding episode gravely weakened support for Meech Lake outside Quebec was to be expected.

The Charter's capacity to generate a roving Canadianism is not confined to normal politics, but inevitably inserts itself into the constitutional reform process if it appears that the Charter as such is threatened with a loss of constitutional status, or if particular rights appear to be weakened. The Meech Lake outcome, therefore, is explicable only if we appreciate how the Charter's taking root in English-speaking Canada has major consequences for the constitutional reform process.

The major source of opposition to Meech Lake in English-speaking Canada came from Charter supporters. Both the Manitoba Task Force Report and the New Brunswick Select Committee Report underlined the extent of Charter support in Anglophone Canada.[17] For many, it has become the focal point of their constitutional identity, providing a vision of a country whose citizens possess equal rights.

Consequently, the Charter restricts the range of acceptable constitutional variations in the treatment of the provinces. It sets constraints on what can be offered to Quebec by limiting the manoeuvrability of executive federalism in responding to Quebec demands for differential treatment. From the Quebec perspective, such demands are likely to involve the Charter, for it has not taken root among the Quebec Francophone majority in the way it has elsewhere.[18] For Quebec political elites, the Charter has an especially deleterious impact on Quebec's language regime by restricting the choice of policy instruments available to protect a beleaguered linguistic minority. Thus, for the Bourassa government, Meech Lake's distinct society clause was an attempt to escape from the chafing constraints of the Charter. However, the Charter's linkage with the English-Canadian conception of citizenship clearly makes it difficult for political leaders outside Quebec to convince their citizenry that an asymmetric application of the Charter to Quebec and the rest of Canada is sound constitutional policy. The Charter limits the constitutional policy flexibility of the federal government and the other provincial governments in the same way as Québécois nationalism does for Quebec premiers. Thus the Anglophone rejection of Meech Lake is simply the rest-of-Canada counterpart of Quebec nationalism's earlier rejection of Fulton-Favreau and the Victoria Charter. It is not a rejection of Quebec, but the projection of a competing Charter-infused vision of Canada.

## The Aboriginal Opposition to Meech Lake

A distinct category of opposition to Meech Lake came from what section 35 of the Constitution Act, 1982, calls the "aboriginal peoples of Canada," defined as including the Indian, Inuit, and Métis peoples of Canada. The complex history that lies behind this Aboriginal opposition can only be summarized here.

Six crucial historical developments or conditioning factors are central to the contemporary constitutional politics of the Aboriginal peoples:

(1) The defeat of the 1969 assimilationist White Paper on Indian policy by status Indians eliminated one of the historic options in federal government Indian policy, the erosion of special status and the merging of Indians in the general population.[19] Consequently, some kind of special status regime no longer characterized by inferior treatment became the vaguely defined goal of Indian policy.[20]

(2) The constitutional broadening of the indigenous community from status Indians in section 91(24) to "aboriginal peoples" significantly enlarged and diversified the population seeking some kind of distinctive constitutional response. Although Inuit (formerly "Eskimos") had been included in the BNA Act definition of Indian since a 1939 judicial decision,[21] the 1982 inclusion of Métis in the new constitutional category "aboriginal" was a major constitutional change. It inevitably meant that the demands of status Indians, possessed of a land base on reserves and with a long history of unique policy treatment, would spill over to the Métis. The Inuit, because of their small population, northern location, and historical separateness were clearly a discrete entity, although they, too, joined in the pressures for self-government.

(3) Throughout the seventies, Aboriginal organizations supported by federal funding improved their political skills and enhanced their visibility at a time when stalemate prevailed in federal policy toward status Indians and the larger category of Aboriginal policy was inchoate. Aboriginal organizations aggressively and successfully fought their way into the constitutional reform process and achieved considerable recognition. Section 25 of the Charter guaranteed that its "rights and freedoms shall not be construed so as to abrogate or derogate from any aboriginal, treaty or other rights or freedoms that pertain to the aboriginal peoples of Canada."[22] By section 35 of the Constitution Act, "the existing aboriginal and treaty rights of the aboriginal peoples of Canada are hereby recognized and affirmed," and Aboriginal peoples were defined in the way already noted. Section 37 of the Constitution Act also guaranteed the holding of a constitutional conference with an "agenda . . . item respecting constitutional matters that directly affect the aboriginal peoples of Canada, including the identification and definition of the rights of those peoples to be included in the Constitution of Canada, and the Prime Minister of Canada shall invite representatives of those peoples to participate in the discussions on that item." These were remarkable gains and recognitions for indigenous peoples who had long been relegated to the constitutional sidelines. Status Indians did not even get the vote until 1960.

(4) Instead of one, four constitutional conferences with Aboriginal leaders participating were held. While they failed to spell out Aboriginal rights, and in particular to agree on the issue of self-government, the simple fact that they were held confirmed that the Aboriginal peoples of Canada were not to be thought of as other Canadians. Their identity and present and future status did not and would not derive from the Charter,[23] but from their several unique historical backgrounds as the first Canadians, especially, of course, status Indians and Inuit.

The failure of the four conferences, the last of which just preceded the meeting of first ministers at which the Meech Lake deal was struck, angered Aboriginal leaders who concluded that their demands had not been taken seriously.

(5) Like other minorities, Aboriginal peoples are especially sensitive to the symbolism of constitutional documents and of the manner and extent of their recognition or lack of it by those who hold positions of authority in the state. Thus the symbolism of Meech Lake defining Quebec as a "distinct society," and "French-speaking Canadians . . . and English-speaking Canadians" as constituting "a fundamental characteristic of Canada," but handing out no similar recognition to Aboriginal peoples was received as an insult.

(6) Finally, Aboriginal peoples, especially their elites, are sustained in their political goals by their identification with an international movement of indigenous peoples and a supportive international climate. Canadian Aboriginal leaders, in fact, are remarkably assiduous in exploiting the international environment in support of their domestic goals.

The preceding can be summed up in the statement that one of the key sets of players in Canadian constitutional politics is now found in the Aboriginal peoples of Canada and the organizations that speak for them. Their language, like that of Quebec nationalists, is a collective language of nationalism, self-government, sovereignty, and independence, although its applicability to the Métis is problematic.

In the same fashion as the Anglophone supporters of the Charter, Aboriginal peoples used the various Meech Lake hearings as platforms to protect and advance their interests. By my calculations, approximately thirty organizations and individuals explicitly speaking for Aboriginal peoples appeared before the Special Joint Committee of the Senate and the House of Commons and the Charest Committee.[24]

## Conclusion

The contribution of executive federalism to successful constitutional reform is, at best, limited. Meech Lake, therefore, does not represent the repudiation of a long-established successful practice that has earned the status of a cherished tradition. Further, the involvement of the public in the constitutional reform process, although erratic, and varied in its manner and its impact, has been a recurrent factor in the reform efforts of the last three decades. What was unique about Meech Lake was not the impact of the public, but the tenacity of the unsuccessful effort by the leading governmental players to render the public role ineffectual.

Nevertheless, the public role in Meech Lake did have certain distinguishing characteristics that derived from the Constitution Act, 1982. The Charter and the Aboriginal constitutional clauses have generated a greatly increased cast of constitutional players. On the whole these new players, clothed with the legitimacy of constitutional clauses they identify with, express the social, ethnic, and gender cleavages of contemporary Canadian society. So accustomed have we become to seeing a parade of organizations representing women, Aboriginal Canadians, and ethnic communities dominate the organized expression of briefs before legislative committees that we are in danger of forgetting that they represent only a particular slice of Canadian society. For example, by my count, and employing the categories used by the New Brunswick Select Committee, the Charest Committee heard eighteen organizations speaking for Aboriginal peoples, eleven linguistic lobbies, nine for women, six for commercial interests, three for multicultural groups (one of which was the umbrella organization, the Canadian Ethnocultural Council), and two for trade unions. What is striking is the limited participation in this kind of arena of the big battalions of business and labour, at least in terms of numbers of presentations. [25]

These statistics underline the extent to which the challenge confronting the constitution recently has been how to accommodate the federal dimension of our existence – the priority agenda of executive federalism – with the cleavages of an increasingly heterogeneous society whose component parts have highly developed particularistic forms of self-consciousness. The task, succinctly, is to find a constitutional *modus vivendi* responsive to the territorial communities of federalism, represented by governments, to the non-territorial societal pluralism of the various groups that attach themselves to the Charter, and to the complexities of the Aboriginal peoples, not all of whom live in organized communities on a discrete land base. The task is compounded because the executive federalism arena and the public hearings process respond to different segments of the totality whose constitutional synthesis is sought. What Robert Campbell said of Meech Lake reflects the very different mobilization of bias within executive federalism and within the public world of parliamentary hearings. He noted that although provincial government concerns dominated in the closed first ministers' meetings of Meech Lake and the Langevin Building, "these provincial issues and concerns all but disappeared [in the ratification process], pushed to the side as new players finally entered the process and articulated a bewildering and eclectic array of issues: women's rights, multiculturalism, national social programs, native rights, the status of the territories, language issues, the efficacy of the federal government, and so on."[26]

For the student of constitutional politics, observing where we have come from and where we now are, several questions beg for discussion beyond the central issue of the relationship between Quebec and the rest of Canada:

(1) Is the existing constitutional mobilization of bias, outside of governments, an appropriate counterweight to governments' domination of executive federalism? In particular, is the minimal presence of capital and labour, business and unions, and the class division of society a deficiency that needs correcting? In the depression of the thirties, discussion flourished on the conflict between federalism and capitalism. In more recent constitutional discussions, concern for the economy has been little short of invisible with the exception of belated high-profile attempts by business organizations whose political bottom line is to favour whatever constitutional agreement will produce stability. The provincial government commission examining Quebec's constitutional future has strong business and union representation. A move in that direction by the rest of Canada would be salutary for the next round of constitutional debates.

(2) One of the biases revealed by the Meech Lake process is how the Charter and Aboriginal spokespersons have little sympathy for provincial governments. The provincial governments of English Canada, faced with this opposition, were unable to convince their provincial residents of the virtues of a province-strengthening constitutional package. Is the politics of constitutional discussion outside Quebec biased against provincialism by the Charter in a way that does an injustice to provincial orientations that are not being tapped?

(3) How good are the democratic and representative credentials of those who speak for women, Aboriginals, and others who feature so prominently in legislative forums? Can constitutional lobby groups develop the flexibility that allows some bargaining leeway or is the normal relation between leaders/officers and members such that their role is restricted to a rigid declamatory advocacy?

(4) Even if the answers to the preceding question are positive, what kind of constitution is likely to emerge from the clash of self-interested private organizational actors – who do not and cannot speak for the multiple constitutional concerns of a modern people – and equally self-interested governments? In this constitutional marketplace can we put our faith in an invisible hand that translates the competitive pursuit of constitutional profit into the public good?

(5) Can we continue with a constitutional reform process in which the presence or absence of non-governmental constitutional actors, the role they play, and the reception they receive seem to result from the tension between governing elites who seek to control and manipulate and the struggle of private groups to be heard and taken seriously? A degree of procedural predictability erring on the

side of openness would surely mute some of the rancour and ill-temper that now derive from attempted exclusion, insecurity, and uncertainty.

(6) Is there a role for referenda in our constitutional reform process of the future? An automatic Pavlovian rejection of such a proposal as not the Canadian way should be restrained while we ponder the dismal reality that there is no Canadian way and that referenda might be a salutary check on the competition between governments and organized interests that otherwise is likely to prevail.

I began this paper with the assertion that federalism is no longer enough. I conclude it with the thought that in the process of constitutional reform we may be driven to conclude that to add up those who speak for federalism, for the Charter, and for Aboriginal constitutional concerns does not satisfy the representational requirements of a legitimate process.

Whatever the answer to such questions, the student of the constitutional politics of the future must examine and analyse the new constitutional actors generated by the Charter and Aboriginal constitutional clauses with the same rigour that is applied to the study of governments. The constitutional politics of the Assembly of First Nations and of the National Action Committee on the Status of Women deserve some of the attention we have previously devoted to executive federalism, courts, and amending formulas. The organizers of Meech Lake ignored these new constitutional players to their serious detriment. It is an unhelpful form of flattery for scholars to imitate the errors of those temporary office-holders who are our servants.

Chapter Twelve

# The Charlottetown Accord: Multinational Canada versus Federalism

## The Battleground of Recent Constitutional History

Traumatic events, such as the recent constitutional referendum, heighten self-consciousness without generating agreement on what has transpired. Indeed, the reverse is more likely true, since the particularistic self-consciousness activated by the referendum process informs the subsequent competition to affix self-interested meaning to this latest Canadian constitutional episode. As rival interpretive claims battle for attention, the pre-referendum constitutional past also gets subtly redefined. Interpretations of the Charlottetown Accord and referendum are indirectly reinterpretations of Meech Lake, of the 1982 Constitution Act and the Trudeau legacy, of past relations between Aboriginal peoples and the Canadian state, and of historical patterns of relationship between Quebec and the rest of Canada (ROC). For the constitutional competitors, the intense constitutional conflict of recent decades makes the past a political resource that is too valuable to be left to one's opponents, or to the academics.

The unavoidable political uses of the past do not preclude the raising of larger and different questions of meaning and interpretation by academics. Indeed, the latter have an obligation to step back, to adopt a longer-run perspective, and to raise issues that the more directly involved may overlook or prefer to leave unexamined. A constitutional process dealing with issues of nationhood, survival, identity, and community at a time of crisis shakes the inertia and ongoingness characteristic of society in normal times. When the dust has settled on such existential episodes, they should receive intense academic scrutiny for the light they may throw on what normality conceals. This paper's contribution to that constitutional introspection analyses the Accord and the referendum from the perspective of the inchoate emergence of Canada as a multinational state[1] and the latter's entanglement with an inherited federalism.

## The Emergence of Multinational Canada

The process leading up to the Accord, its contents, and the verdict of the electorate reveal a multinational society struggling for constitutional expression in a federal constitutional order that defines Canadians in the traditional terms of province and country. Canadian identities, however, are no longer adequately accommodated by the coexisting provincial and countrywide identities natural to a federal people. They are supplemented and challenged by various internal national identities – Québécois, Aboriginal, and, haltingly, the ROC.

Québécois not only see themselves as a distinct people but also recognize two "others" – the ROC, or English Canada, and, somewhat ambivalently, the Aboriginal nation(s). The latter, in turn, seek recognition as a third founding nation.[2] They are also intensely cognizant of Quebec/ROC differences, fully appreciating that Quebec-Aboriginal relations could be bitter and acrimonious should Quebec leave Canada. The ROC is unhappily aware that its former hegemony over all of Canada is challenged by both Québécois and Aboriginal nationalisms. These reciprocal national recognitions and the struggles they precipitate are played out in the context of a still surviving, if retreating, pan-Canadian nationalism to which varying allegiance is given by the adherents of the other nationalisms. Described as above, Canada's multinational nature, in terms of each national community's recognizing and engaging in conflict with the others, is a commonplace, the appreciation of which, however, challenges federalism's traditional stranglehold over high constitutional politics.

These nationalisms do not confront one another as such. Québécois, Canadian, and ROC nationalisms confront one another in a federal system that reduces Quebec to the status of a province and muffles the voice of the rest of Canada, which lacks the jurisdictional clothing to shape its self-consciousness. The various Aboriginal nationalisms are given voice not by governments but by four Aboriginal organizations, which are challenged by a fifth representing Aboriginal women. Their presence at the bargaining table is, unlike the others (except for the northern territories), not accompanied by formal responsibilities in the amending process. They are, therefore, dependent on the governments of federalism to achieve constitutional objectives that will profoundly transform federalism and greatly complicate its future workings.

Indian, Inuit, and Métis identities have been fashioned by distinct political histories, which for status Indians and Inuit have involved idiosyncratic relations to the federal system. Only the Métis have experienced the garden-variety existence of ordinary Canadians subject to the normal application of the division of powers, until their recognition as an Aboriginal people in 1982.

Of the four nationalisms (viewing the various Aboriginal nationalisms as one), only the Canadian, with the federal government as its advocate, is harmonious with the constitutional assumptions of federalism. Its existence flows naturally from the federal facts of a central government and the countrywide community it serves. Now, however, it is a defensive nationalism, under attack and seeking to salvage what it can. Aboriginal nationalisms and Québécois nationalism work the constitutional machinery to strengthen their nationhood. Much of the complexity and confusion of the Canadian constitutional process is because Canadians are playing a multinational game by rules that presuppose that they are essentially a federal people. We find, therefore, much ambiguity and slippage of identity and terminology. Does the federal government speak for Canada or for the rest of Canada? If the former, who speaks for the latter? Does the *premier ministre* of Quebec represent a province or a nation? Do Aboriginal peoples participate as nations, as supplicants, or as provinces of the future?

At the level of ordinary social observation, Canadians outside Quebec recognize that in some sense Quebec is clearly a distinct society, nation, or people. Yet viewed through the constitutional lens of federalism, Quebec is simply a province. The Canadian constitutional model adhered to by the ROC allows only extremely limited official constitutional recognition to what is widely accepted as a social reality, the unique sociocultural, linguistic, historic aspects of the Quebec people. The natural assumption, however, that it is the ROC's sense of the Canadian nation that sets limits to the degree of constitutional diversity that can be officially sanctioned is, somewhat surprisingly, clearly erroneous. As discussed below, the Charlottetown Accord – largely fashioned by federal, provincial, territorial, and Aboriginal leaders before the Quebec government came to the bargaining table – was dramatically more responsive to Aboriginal nationalisms than to Quebec nationalism. Since in most ways the differences between Aboriginals and other Canadians are already much more pronounced than between Québécois and other Canadians, and since the Charlottetown Accord potentially constitutionalized a profoundly greater diversity of constitutional status and treatment for Aboriginal peoples than for Québécois, the limited response to Quebec cannot be explained by a generalized antipathy to recognizing cultural difference or by resistance to deviations from constitutional normality. Why it is apparently easier to give constitutional recognition to Aboriginal than to Québécois diversity, using the Charlottetown Accord as an example, is tentatively answered below.

The first major contemporary attempt to find a constitutional reconciliation among Quebec nationalism, Aboriginal nationalism, incipient ROC nationalism, and the inherited pan-Canadian nationalism occurred in the post-Meech process that led to Charlottetown. In the 1960s and 1970s the constitutional challenge came from Quebec, with Aboriginals only beginning to emerge from the shadows. Although Aboriginal Canadians made major gains in the Constitution Act, 1982, much of their achievement was a promissory note that has not yet been met.

By the 1980s, the constitutional status quo was challenged by both Quebec and Aboriginal nationalisms, but their challenge occurred in discrete arenas, which avoided the necessity of producing a synthesizing response. Aboriginal issues received constitutional attention, but minimal response, in the four special Aboriginal constitutional conferences, 1983-87, in which Quebec did not officially participate. In the subsequent Meech Lake constitutional round, dubbed the Quebec round, the other Canadian provinces made constitutional gains on Quebec's coattails by insisting that the equality of provinces principle had to be followed, so that what Quebec asked for – distinct society excepted – Prince Edward Island also received. Aboriginal organizations, lacking formal veto power and being absent from the intergovernmental negotiations, were unable to duplicate the gains of provincial governments outside Quebec. Although Aboriginal organizations successfully exempted Aboriginal constitutional clauses from the distinct society's application and although they played a key role in discrediting and defeating the Meech Lake Accord (in particular, by Elijah Harper's Manitoba role), their input is best described as constitutional guerrilla warfare.

Thus, until the post-Meech processes, responses to Quebec and Aboriginal nationalisms were separated. They came together for the first time in the Charlottetown Accord and in the events that preceded this failed effort at major constitutional reform. The four main Aboriginal organizations not only participated directly in the negotiation process but conducted their own consultations with their specific Aboriginal constituencies. Quebec, too, conducted itself as a separate actor, with the Allaire and Bélanger-Campeau inquiries, two National Assembly committees to examine sovereignty and offers of renewed federalism, and the planned Quebec referendum. As there was minimal input from Quebec and Aboriginal peoples to the Spicer Commission, the Beaudoin-Dobbie committee, and the winter, 1992, public constitutional conferences, these designedly Canadian processes unexpectedly developed into vehicles for the ROC to develop its own constitutional positions. There was, therefore, separate input from the three national communities before the federal dimension, including the federal government's version of Canadian nationalism, asserted itself in the final negotiation stage (with Aboriginal leaders and advisers, of course, also present).

The Charlottetown Accord, therefore, including its background and its electoral repudiation, is an historic event that illuminates the difficulties of responding to multinational realities through federalist amendment processes. It also illustrates the ambiguities and tension between Canada, as an official, constitutional actor speaking through the federal government, and the ROC, whose existential existence lacks constitutionally authoritative advocates.

## Quebec and the Rest of Canada: Recognition with Limited Response

At one level of behaviour and perception, Quebec and the ROC clearly see each other as separate entities and fully recognize that in constitutional politics they are responding to each other.[3] At this level, it is understood that Quebec has a national existence, that it is not a province like the others, and that it might opt for and attain independence. Simultaneously, the ROC understands that it may become the reluctant inheritor of a Canada without Quebec and begins, psychologically and gropingly, to adjust to that unwelcome but not implausible future.

At a different level, Quebec is a province trapped in the workings of federalism, and the ROC responds to the structure of federalism by putting on its Canada mask or losing itself in competing provincialisms. In recent decades, the inertia of federalism has triumphed over the two nations view that is especially congenial to Quebec, particularly when constitutional proposals are formulated and in the ratification process. Québécois nationalism chafes against the provincial constraints imposed by Canadian federalism. The equality of provinces norm is opposed as being incompatible with the preferred two nations view of Canada. Francophone Québécois, like Aboriginal peoples, also categorically resist any suggestion that they are part of multicultural Canada.

The powerful presence of nationalism is evident in numerous phenomena – the election of the Parti Québécois in 1976, the continuing presence of a major *indépendantiste* party, either in government or waiting in the wings to become the government, a nationalist intelligentsia, an extensive international presence, the tenacious search for formal constitutional recognition under the rubric of a distinct society, and the paraphernalia of statehood (National Assembly, "prime minister" rather than "premier") that evidence a degree of nationalist affirmation unrivalled in other provinces. These nationalist indicators are sustained by an unremitting concern for the survival of a distinctive people and language threatened by demographic weakness in an engulfing English-speaking continent. Quebec's sense of national distinctiveness is also fed by demographic trends – the significant decline in the Quebec Anglophone community as a result of extensive emigration, a consequent increase in the Francophone share of the total Quebec population, and, simultaneously, the increasing concentration of the Canadian Francophone population within Quebec.

Nationalist rhetoric is part of everyday political language and is uttered by federalist Liberals with a passion almost indistinguishable from that of their Parti Québécois opponents.[4] "Quebecers," in the words of the preamble to the Act establishing the Bélanger-Campeau Commission, "are free to assume their own destiny, to determine their political status and to assure their economic, social and cultural development."[5] Rhetoric is supplemented by distinctive political and constitutional behaviour that suggests a degree of self-perceived uniqueness that goes well beyond the provincial diversities in the ROC – behaviour that strains the limits of Quebec's jurisdictional status as a province. The very acronym ROC, which is used both inside and outside Quebec, imputes a singularity to Quebec's position that is implicitly recognized by Canadians outside Quebec. No one would refer to the nine provinces outside Manitoba or Nova Scotia as the ROC.

Quebec repeatedly conducts itself as a national rather than provincial actor, and engages in bouts of nationalist introspection about its past treatment or preferred futures. From 1976 to 1980, Quebec introspectively prepared for its pending referendum, designed to increase its constitutional bargaining power, while Canada, acting for the ROC, readied its response to Quebec by Bill C-60 and the Pepin-Robarts task force, in which the Parti Québécois government displayed minimal interest (especially in the former). The 1980 referendum was an inward-looking exercise in national choice, self-definition, and democratically based national self-determination. Significantly, there was general acceptance by Canadians outside Quebec of the right of Québécois democratically to choose their own future. The threat of using force to keep Quebec in a Canada that its citizens wished to leave was conspicuously absent from the responses of the rest of Canada.

Revealingly, Canadians outside Quebec were clearly defined as outsiders or unwelcome intruders in the referendum as Quebec engaged in agonizing constitutional introspection. Thus, the ROC was relegated to an apprehensive audience role while it awaited the referendum outcome. Later versions of constitutional introspection, the Allaire and Bélanger-Campeau reports, which examined alternative futures for Quebec, displayed monumental indifference to the Canadian dimension of the contemporary Quebec-Canadian reality. These powerful symbolic acts implicitly assumed that Québécois, defined in national terms, should decide on their future in their Québécois capacity, not their Canadian capacity. By eliminating the latter from consciousness, or at least from conscious attention, they induced Canadians elsewhere to think of themselves as the ROC.

The Quebec government has deliberately and shrewdly deployed nationalist symbolism in its confrontational encounters with the Canadian government and the ROC. It responded to the proclamation of the 1982 Constitution Act, following the isolation of the Quebec government in the closing days of its negotiations, by the symbolism of Quebec flags at half mast. Officially, the Quebec government rejected both the Act and its "bloody Charter" (as René Lévesque referred to it). The Quebec government subsequently wielded the notwithstanding clause across the board as a symbolic defiance of the Charter until the Parti Québécois defeat in 1985, turned inward and retreated from intergovernmental conferences from 1982 to 1985, and declined official participation in the 1983-87 Aboriginal constitutional conferences while Quebec's constitutional demands remained unmet.

In the Meech Lake constitutional drama, the Quebec government conducted itself as the aggrieved party that had been betrayed in 1982, established its minimum demands for a return to the constitutional family, quickly ratified the Meech Lake resolution after it had gained intergovernmental agreement, and then retreated to the sidelines until the closing weeks of the three-year ratification period, as a provincially fragmented ROC struggled without success to produce the requisite unanimous positive response.

After the Meech Lake fiasco, Quebec watched or participated only minimally in the various constitutional activities and processes that produced the Charlottetown Accord, until the final meetings in August, 1992. Robert Bourassa had previously asserted that he would bargain only one on one – "nation to nation" – with the federal government, thus attributing to the latter a responsibility it cannot assume, to be the representative and advocate of the interests of the ROC. In the interval between Meech Lake and the Charlottetown Accord, Quebec established two National Assembly committees to examine, respectively, renewed federalism offers and sovereignty; it established a deadline of October 26, 1992, for a Quebec vote on sovereignty if a reasonable offer of renewed federalism was not forthcoming; and, in general, it conducted itself as a nation – as one of two nations – capable of opting for sovereignty by a unilateral act, following an analysis of the advantages of staying and going according to the criterion of Quebec's self-interest.

Finally, although both the Canadian and Quebec referenda were held on the same day and asked the same question, the Quebec referendum campaign was essentially a separate campaign. It was governed by Quebec referendum legislation that structured the campaign under two umbrella organizations for Yes and No, headed, respectively, by Robert Bourassa and Jacques Parizeau, the leaders of the two main parties in Quebec. As far as the Accord's specifics were concerned, the Quebec campaign focused primarily on Quebec's gains and losses. The Quebec and ROC referendum debates, accordingly, were two inward-looking solitudes that did not engage each other. This absence of a common discourse, with few exceptions, was "the most important and significant single fact about the referendum debate of 1992." [6] To Guy Laforest, the very fact of Quebec's administering its own referendum confirmed the message of the earlier 1980 referendum, namely, that Quebec had a right to determine its own future by introspective actions that already indicated a psychological special status.[7] Throughout the whole period, from the Parti Québécois victory in 1976 to the present, nationalist rhetoric insistently defined Canada as English Canada or the rest of Canada and thus sought to deny the psychological presence of Canada in Quebec. The preceding are the visible manifestations of an aggressive, frustrated, underlying nationalism.

The reality and symbolism of Quebec nationalism have induced Canadians outside Quebec to think of themselves, at one level, as the ROC, and at crucial constitutional moments to realize that they are responding to Quebec in their ROC capacity. Admittedly, this recognition is muffled by the constitutional reality that the ROC acts through federalism and thus through a Canadian government that represents Quebec and has been led by a Quebecer for a quarter of a century, except for the Turner and Clark interludes. While this Canada/ROC split personality runs through the events cited below, this very ambiguity contains the premise that from one perspective the ROC exists and seeks to express itself in spite of its lack of constitutional clothing.

The range and diversity of ROC response to Quebec in the last decade include the following positions: (1) as the partner that concludes that an agreement is impossible and therefore goes its own way (Constitution Act, 1982); (2) as a divided party that fully recognizes that its response to the Meech Lake Accord is a response to Quebec but fails to muster a Yes response to Quebec's demands; (3) as a composite actor employing various means on multiple fronts to generate a set of offers that will entice Quebec back into the constitutional family (Spicer Commission to Charlottetown Accord); (4) as a referendum electorate that fails to support the Charlottetown Accord negotiated by its own leaders, a repudiation concurred in by the Quebec electorate for different reasons.

Widespread acceptance of a "two nations" view was evident in public discussion throughout the recent referendum campaign, in which the worst scenario was consistently portrayed as either Quebec votes Yes and the ROC votes No, or the reverse, a Quebec No and ROC Yes.[8] Implicit in this analysis was the assumption that behind the eleven governments, two separate national partners were deciding whether or not they could agree with the future terms of their coexistence as proposed in the Charlottetown Accord. That Quebec might react to various negative referendum outcomes as a frustrated nation rather than just a disgruntled province was taken for granted.

The above episodes indicate that, from one perspective, the ROC clearly sees itself as participating in a two-nation constitutional game. This, however, shades into the recognition that constitutionally it is both fragmented into provinces and incorporated in a pan-Canadian community that includes Quebec, and for which the federal government is the authoritative spokesperson. The latter speaks not for the ROC as such, but for the ROC as part of Canada. Unlike Quebec nationalism, whose encounter with Canadian nationalism is an encounter between governments, ROC nationalism neither encounters Canadian nationalism through a government of its own nor as a rival. Hence, ROC nationalism, the response of non-Québécois to Quebec nationalism, is muffled behind a Canadian nationalism that seeks to shore up the Canadian component of the Québécois psyche. When the ROC indulges its taste for complexity, it recognizes the existence of a third set of Aboriginal nationalisms that has to be accommodated (discussed below).

The triangular relationship between Quebec, Canada, and the ROC is immensely complicated by the ambiguities in the self-conceptions and identities of the major actors. The Quebec government acts as the voice of a nation from the constitutional vantage point of a province. It conducts itself in terms of what it hopes to become and thus denies what it constitutionally is. At first glance, the Canadian government acts straightforwardly as the senior government of a federal system containing ten provinces and two territories, and thus as the government of the coast-to-coast community of all Canadians. This self-definition, however, presupposes a reality that is contested by Quebec nationalists, who repudiate Quebec's provincial status and who seek escape from standard Canadian citizen status, either to some special national status or to independent statehood.

Quebec nationalism elicits an incipient counter-nationalism in the ROC, which exerts diffuse pressure on the federal government to see its conciliation task as applying not to a dozen provinces and territories but to two national peoples – Quebec and the ROC. To the extent that the Quebec government succeeds in monopolizing the Quebec nationalist voice, the federal government is pushed to become a spokesperson for the rest of Canada. The latter, defined by Quebec as the coexisting national partner, and defined by the official constitutional order as non-existent and in any event incapable of acting because it lacks an authoritative centre, is correctly diagnosed as having a split personality/identity that paralyses choice.

To a large extent, the difficulty of resolving Canada's constitutional problems results from the ambiguity that attends the behaviour, identity, and constitutional reality of these three major actors. The constitutional politics of "as if" mean that the standard rules of the constitutional game, which presuppose stable realities of identity and community that faithfully reflect the existing formal constitutional order, in fact apply to a Kafkaesque-Pirandello world of things that are not as they seem. This complexity is deepened, as noted below, when Aboriginal Canadians are brought into the constitutional picture.

The major ambiguity, or identity confusion, or location between two worlds that attaches to the ROC deserves further comment. To Philip Resnick, the ROC, or English Canada, is the nation "that too often dares not speak its name."[9] The ambiguity of identity in the absence of a positive label runs through a recent volume on the view from outside Quebec (for example, "So long as Quebec is an integral part of Canada, we lack a name"; "the mystery spouse – the counterpart to Quebec"; and "an entity – whatever we call it – that has no institutional form without Quebec").[10]

ROC self-consciousness is reactive. The labels and acronyms under which it operates – rest of Canada and Canada-without-Quebec (CWOQ) – have little capacity to stir nationalist passion. They appear not as goals but as by-products of someone else's activism. The development of a positive nationalist ROC self-consciousness is impeded by the absence of an official leadership that can speak for and to the ROC. The holders of official office in the federal system address their citizens as Canadians and as members of provincial communities or of northern territories, but not as rest-of-Canadians. Prime Minister Brian Mulroney explicitly and correctly denied the capacity and propriety of the federal government's speaking for "English Canada" as such, because the federal government speaks for all Canadians.[11] As Reg Whitaker asserts, federal politicians, especially from Quebec, "have a vested interest in stifling the development of an authentic English-Canadian voice."[12] Thus, it was only to be expected that asymmetrical federalism, which received considerable support at the Halifax public constitutional conference – suggesting special powers for Quebec and a strong central/national government in Ottawa for "English Canada" – disappeared when the "provincial powerbrokers" took charge in the final negotiations.[13] "English Canada" has a much stronger existence at the level of the citizenry than in the minds of the leaders of the non-Quebec governments of federalism.

In spite of these structural impediments, ROC self-consciousness receives stimulation with every failure to reach an accommodation with Quebec and with each renewed effort to try one more time.[14] Barbara Cameron correctly notes the "remarkable" development in the post-Meech round of "distinctly English-Canadian views of constitutional arrangements." This was partly stimulated by the contagion of Quebec and Aboriginal nationalisms that "forced English Canadians to act like a national community, too."[15] A nationalist intelligentsia in the ROC now openly canvasses and sometimes supports a two- or three-nation definition of Canada, or unflinchingly faces the prospect of a Canadian breakup as being advantageous for the two national communities of European origin.[16] Indeed, the slow and grudging but steady, reactive development of a separate, incipiently nationalist self-consciousness in the ROC is the ultimate testimony to the powerful impact of Quebec nationalism on how Canadians outside Quebec see themselves.

ROC self-consciousness is anticipatory. It is held in reserve. It is an insurance consciousness. In a period of constitutional uncertainty, the ROC citizen lives in two worlds. The first is the inertial world of the status quo, in which Canada still exists and receives loyalty and civic attachment from its ROC citizens. It is the everyday world with deep historical roots. Yet attachment to it is no longer habitual and unthinking, for its solidity can no longer be assumed. The second world is a plausible tomorrow world, in which Quebec has departed and the ROC takes ownership of the name Canada and applies it to the diminished, geographically bifurcated, but more homogeneous survivor that it has become. For the ROC, this world is an imagined if largely unsought future, which might emerge because continuity with the past has been broken by the Quebec national partner. Simply put, the ROC exists psychologically because human beings live in the future as well as the present. Citizens naturally prepare themselves psychologically for plausible futures, both sought and unsought. At the moment, the relative balance between these two worlds is unclear, although the second future world is gaining ground.

The ROC, however, is incapable of responding directly to Quebec. Nobody acts for it. It speaks through the multiple outlets of the governments of Canadian federalism outside Quebec. These governments submerge and conceal the ROC's identity and sense of self behind the normative and institutional realities of a federal system with a Charter. The "ten equal provinces" view overpowers the "two nations" view when office-holding incumbents take charge. The Charter imposes a standard version of Canadian citizenship that limits deviations from the norm of equal rights. The amending formula, especially when the unanimity requirement is relevant, provincializes both the making and the evaluation of proposed amendments. When a referendum is added, as for the Charlottetown Accord, unanimity makes provincial self-interest one of the dominating criteria for the electorate.

While it was clear, following the demise of Meech Lake, that a positive response to Quebec was the core requirement of the next constitutional round, the actual response was restrained, especially given the constitutional demands of the Allaire Report and the knowledge that a referendum on sovereignty was required under Quebec legislation. The reasons for this restrained response become apparent when it is contrasted with the much more far-reaching set of proposals offered to the Aboriginal peoples of Canada. The response to Quebec was constrained by the reality that Quebec is now a province – and thus caught up in a network of norms and assumptions that derive from contemporary federalism and have countrywide application – and that its people are an integral part of the Canadian community of citizens to whom it is assumed, especially since the Charter, that a common set of rights should apply. Significant constitutional advances for Quebec in the direction of special status are constrained by the perception that it is part of a system of provinces and that its people are part of a Canadian community of citizens. Aboriginal peoples, by contrast, are not thought of in federal terms – the constraints of provincial equality do not limit responses to their aspirations – and in some sense they already have a recognized status of being apart, which sustains policy responses that further institutionalize their apartness. The contrast between the limited response to Quebec, described immediately below, and the elaborate response to Aboriginal peoples, described later in this essay, can be understood only in the light of the profound difference in their starting points.

The Charlottetown Accord was a limited response to the heightened Quebec constitutional aspirations that developed following the defeat of the Meech Lake Accord, which had been based on Quebec's minimal demands.[17] Quebec received an initial allocation of an additional eighteen seats in the House of Commons; the guarantee of a minimum 25 per cent of the seats in the House of Commons in the future; a weak reference to the distinct society in the Canada clause, which also affirmed the "role of the legislature and Government of Quebec to preserve and promote the distinct society of Quebec" (*Consensus Report*, s. 1(2)(2)); a double-majority Senate voting rule that would require there to be both a majority of all senators voting and of Francophone senators voting for bills "that materially affect French language or French culture" (*Consensus Report*, s. 12); a concession to Bourassa that provincial senators could be selected by the Quebec National Assembly; a guarantee of three Quebec seats on the Supreme Court, to be filled from a list of candidates submitted by the Quebec government; a veto on future changes to central institutions; controls on the future use of the federal spending power; provincial control over culture within the province; a significantly enhanced provincial role in manpower training; a federal commitment to negotiate an immigration agreement; a federal commitment to withdraw from a number of areas already clearly within provincial jurisdiction (*Consensus Report*, s. 30-5); and various constitutional instrumentalities that might be beneficial to future Quebec governments. In addition, the federal powers of disallowance and reservation were to be repealed, future use of the federal declaratory power would require explicit provincial consent, designated future intergovernmental agreements were to be constitutionally protected from unilateral change for periods of up to five years, and new agreements were to be negotiated with provincial governments concerning regional development and telecommunications.

Most of the proposed changes applied to all provincial governments, including all division of powers proposals and the enlargement of the category of amendments requiring unanimity. While the overall package was far from trivial, it was very limited in the area of division of powers, the core of Quebec's constitutional demands and the centrepiece of the Allaire Report.[18] Further, the pervasive tendency to generalize changes to all provinces, thus repeating the Meech Lake practice, suggested that in the conflict between recognition of formal asymmetry or explicit special status versus equality of the provinces, the latter principle had once again triumphed. Even the Reform Party of Canada was struck by the very limited nature of Quebec's gains in terms of its major demand for more power at the provincial level, suggesting that the distinct society clause had been "effectively gutted" and that gains in the division of powers were "marginal." The Reform Party also noted what many other analysts commented on, the fact that Quebec's greatest gains were in central institutions – the Supreme Court, the House of Commons, a double majority in the Senate with Quebec members in effect nominated by the Quebec government, and a veto with other provinces on constitutional changes to central institutions. "The net effect," according to the Reform Party, "instead of granting Quebec more provincial autonomy, is to involve it more deeply in national affairs."[19] The limited nature of Quebec's gains was underlined by the much more generous response to the Aboriginal peoples.

## Canada and Aboriginal Peoples: Recognition and Response

After the Aboriginal contribution to the defeat of the Meech Lake Accord, and after the serious Oka disturbances, it was widely understood that the next constitutional agreement would have to respond to Aboriginal demands for a constitutional recognition that would differentiate them from standard versions of Canadian citizenship.[20] The understanding that there were two sides – non-Aboriginal and Aboriginal – and that the former, the historical Canadian community, had to respond to the separate Aboriginal nations in its midst, and to do so from a basis of rough equality, was little short of revolutionary in the light of the Canadian past.

Although the Charlottetown Accord containing the agreement that had been struck between Aboriginal and non-Aboriginal leaders failed to pass in the referendum, the Aboriginal components of the Accord remain instructive. They indicate how far the leaders of the existing eleven governments were prepared to go and what Aboriginal leaders were prepared to accept. Further, the ongoing research and the hearings of the Royal Commission on Aboriginal Peoples will likely inject many of the Accord's Aboriginal proposals into the Commission's report. The Charlottetown Accord proposed a remarkable battery of recognitions and constitutional accommodations for the Aboriginal peoples of Canada. At mid-century, status Indians lacked the vote; the Inuit (then known as Eskimo) were politically voiceless and enjoyed only a superficial, romantic, postcard existence in Canadian consciousness; the Métis were, at least officially, considered to be ordinary Canadians with a somewhat unique background. No constitutional category "Aboriginal" then existed to give these three contemporary sub-categories of indigenous peoples a common label and a shared constitutional identity. Further, the off-reserve status Indian population was then absolutely and proportionately much smaller than it is now (30-40 per cent of the status Indian population). The distance between the isolation and virtual invisibility of Aboriginal peoples at mid-century and their position during the Charlottetown Accord proposals of 1992 is truly breathtaking.

The extent and openness of the Accord's response to Aboriginal peoples, contrasted with past treatment, both astonished and gratified academic students of Aboriginal issues. According to Radha Jhappan, a sympathetic student of Aboriginal issues, the self-government provisions "represent a historic (though imperfect) achievement for the First Nations of Canada" and "far exceed the expectations and even imaginations of most informed observers of aboriginal politics. . . . The accord is a magnificent coup for the aboriginal leaders."[21] According to Tony Hall, another shrewd scholar of Aboriginal affairs, the top leaders of no other country had ever before lavished so much attention on the accommodation of "Aboriginal aspirations" within the governing arrangements of a contemporary "New World State." The Charlottetown Accord, he continued, gave "concrete political form to the new thinking" associated with the re-evaluation of the "horrific legacy" of Christopher Columbus.[22] Two of the most prolific legal writers on Aboriginal matters were equally laudatory of the Accord. To law professor Douglas Sanders, the Accord's "Aboriginal Provisions . . . [were] a hallmark of tolerance and generosity."[23] Bradford Morse asserted that the "changes [proposed in the Accord] . . . would truly represent a major departure from our colonial history and set us on the path of restoring the mutual respect and partnership that was the foundation of our initial relationship."[24] "For off-reserve Indians and Métis in Canada," stated Ron George, president of the Native Council of Canada, "the acceptance of these provisions represents an historic breakthrough that is comparable to the bringing down of the Berlin Wall."[25]

The Accord's Aboriginal proposals sanctioned an extraordinary degree of institutional and constitutional separateness. Most important was the proposed constitutional recognition of "the inherent right of self-government within Canada," to be exercised as "one of three orders of government in Canada" (*Consensus Report*, s. 41). Within their jurisdictions, Aboriginal governments were to have the authority:

(a) to safeguard and develop their languages, cultures, economies, identities, institutions and traditions; and,

(b) to develop, maintain and strengthen their relationship with their lands, waters and environment

so as to determine and control their development as peoples according to their own values and priorities and ensure the integrity of their societies. (*Consensus Report*, s. 41)

Significantly, off-reserve urban Aboriginal populations were not to be denied versions of self-government, which would probably provide services to mixed Aboriginal urban peoples, even though they lacked a land base.

The third order of Aboriginal government was to be accompanied by separate Aboriginal representation in the House of Commons and in the revised Senate, the details to be worked out by Aboriginal peoples, their leaders, and relevant governments. Both proposals, with that for the Commons being tentative rather than definite, implied that Aboriginal peoples should be represented by their own kind, and the latter carried the additional implication that Aboriginal peoples were not part of provincial or territorial communities, since Aboriginal seats were to "be additional to provincial and territorial seats" (*Consensus Report*, s. 9). Aboriginal senators, in addition to the standard senatorial responsibilities, might have received a "double majority power in relation to certain matters materially affecting Aboriginal people" (*Consensus Report*, s. 9), thus paralleling the proposed double majority role of Francophone senators with respect to bills that "materially affect French language or French culture" (*Consensus Report*, s. 12). In addition, various proposals held out the possibility of a distinctive Aboriginal relationship to the Supreme Court and potential roles in nominating candidates for the Court. The federal government and Aboriginal groups were to consider "the proposal that an Aboriginal Council of Elders be entitled to make submissions to the Supreme Court when the court considers Aboriginal issues" (*Consensus Report*, s. 20). Section 53 proposed four first ministers' conferences on Aboriginal constitutional matters, commencing no later than 1996 and following at two-year intervals. In the future, specific Aboriginal consent to constitutional amendments that directly referred to Aboriginal peoples would be required (by a mechanism not yet determined). Aboriginal representatives were to participate on any agenda item at first ministers' conferences "that directly affects the Aboriginal peoples" (*Consensus Report*, s. 23). The Canada clause required the constitution to be interpreted in a manner consistent with various fundamental characteristics of Canada, one of which was that

the Aboriginal peoples of Canada, being the first peoples to govern this land, have the right to promote their languages, cultures and traditions and to ensure the integrity of their societies, and their governments constitute one of three orders of government in Canada. (*Consensus Report*, 1(2)(1)(b))

Finally, the original 1982 exemption of certain Aboriginal rights from the Charter's application by section 25 of the Charter was strengthened to ensure that nothing in the Charter "abrogates or derogates from . . . in particular any rights or freedoms relating to the exercise or protection of their languages, cultures or traditions" (*Consensus Report*, s. 2). Further, Aboriginal governments were exempted from the Charter's democratic rights, which gave every citizen "the right to vote in an election of members . . . and to be qualified for membership" in federal and provincial legislatures (*Draft Legal Text*, s. 24). The purpose of this exemption was to facilitate traditional practices for determining leaders – practices that would otherwise violate Charter requirements. Aboriginal legislatures were given access to the notwithstanding clause, and Aboriginal governments were to have authority to "undertake affirmative action programs for socially and economically disadvantaged individuals or groups and programs for the advancement of Aboriginal languages and cultures" (*Consensus Report*, s. 51).

The importance of these constitutional proposals was magnified by the extended coverage of the new constitutional concept "Aboriginal" in section 35 of the Constitution Act, 1982, to include Indian, Inuit, and Métis. The inclusion of the last of these was a signal political triumph for the Métis, who were thereby given constitutional leverage to press for whatever positive treatment was available to the Inuit and Indians with whom they now shared a common constitutional clause. This leverage was used to good effect in the Charlottetown Accord Canada round, under which "for greater certainty" Métis were explicitly to be brought under the federal jurisdiction of section 91(24), a recognition that would have constituted yet another lever behind Métis demands for equal treatment in terms of perquisites and services available to Indians. Section 56 of the *Consensus Report* noted that a Métis Nation Accord was being prepared by the federal government, the five most westerly provinces (Ontario to British Columbia), and the Métis National Council, and that it would commit governments to negotiate various issues related to Métis self-government. As part of this development, the Métis were to be defined and members of the Métis Nation were to be enumerated and registered.[26] Had the Charlottetown Accord been implemented, the Métis, who lacked explicit constitutional recognition until 1982, would by 1992 have taken several large steps to differentiate themselves from the general mass of Canadian citizens. According to Radha Jhappan, the Accord signalled "great progress for the Métis peoples' claims and aspirations."[27]

To summarize, although many of the details were left to the future, the Accord very clearly proposed a unique Aboriginal relation to the Canadian state. The proposed changes were to apply to an enlarged category of Aboriginal peoples – approximately one million – and they were to apply, albeit differentially, to Aboriginal peoples without a land base. Hence, different versions of this special Aboriginal constitutional regime would extend to a population larger than that of five, possibly six, of the ten Canadian provinces. This massive proposed enhancement of the constitutional/institutional accommodation and expression of indigenousness occurred in a supportive climate of guilt, diffuse support, and despair over the failure of past policies. However, the cumulative consequences of all the specific changes proposed in the Charlottetown Accord were neither publicly examined nor discussed, at least not in non-Aboriginal communities.

## Constitutional Theory in the Negotiation Process and in the Aboriginal Package

To step back from the particulars and cast a synoptic glance at the total Aboriginal package is to realize that the implementation of the Charlottetown Accord would have fostered and powerfully reinforced the aboriginality of Aboriginal Canadians. Just as children in Red Deer become Albertans by the reinforcing cues they receive from their provincial environment, and just as the experience of living under the Indian Act regime has fashioned status Indians into a distinct people who are apart from other indigenous Canadians, so the Aboriginal peoples of the future, as a whole, would constantly have been reminded of their separate status by their particularistic interactions with institutions specific to themselves. Equally, non-Aboriginal Canadians would constantly have been reminded of the unique status of the various Aboriginal peoples.

The distinctive treatment of Aboriginal peoples that would have emerged if the Accord had been implemented was foreshadowed by, and indeed developed from, the unique and innovative manner of Aboriginal participation in the post-Meech constitutional reform process. The Accord's elaborate recognition of Aboriginal particularity emerged from a bargaining context in which leaders of the four Aboriginal organizations were the only non-governmental participants at executive federalism meetings that were devoted to comprehensive constitutional change and that had hitherto been the preserve of elected politicians and their advisers. In an earlier breakthrough, from 1983 to 1987 Aboriginal representatives had participated in four constitutional conferences devoted to Aboriginal constitutional concerns. In the Canada round, however, Aboriginal participation extended to the whole range of constitutional issues on the table. This Aboriginal presence suggested, if only implicitly, that existing governments and their elected political leaders lacked the legitimacy to speak authoritatively for the Aboriginal peoples in their electorates on constitutional issues. Non-

Aboriginal leaders, accordingly, were implicitly defined as representing only non-Aboriginal Canadians in constitutional policy-making, in spite of the Aboriginal voters in their electorates.

The significance of Aboriginal possession and exercise of the federal and provincial franchise was proportionately reduced by this excision. The inference that Aboriginal advocacy and representation, at least in constitutional matters, were the responsibility of the four major Aboriginal organizations then shifted the question of representative legitimacy to the latter's right to speak for their imputed membership. The answer was not self-evident, since the Native Women's Association of Canada (NWAC) categorically denied the capacity of the Assembly of First Nations leadership to speak for NWAC members, an interpretation supported by the Federal Court of Appeal. [28]

This remarkable act of representational affirmation by government-funded Aboriginal organizations underlined Aboriginal alienation from the conventional practices of the Canadian state. Its accommodation by the first ministers leaves the conventional theory of parliamentary representation in disarray, a consequence that received virtually no attention. If Aboriginal organizations are to displace the representational role of elected legislators and ministers, even if only in constitutional matters, then the role of Aboriginal voters in federal and provincial elections becomes problematic. What logic restricts the delegitimation of non-Aboriginal representatives acting on behalf of Aboriginal constituents to constitutional matters? Further, if Aboriginal organizations become public bodies performing crucial representational roles within the state, irresistible pressure will develop to subject their internal procedures to public scrutiny and regulation. If there is to be an ongoing division of representative labour between Aboriginal organizations and elected politicians in constitutional or other matters, the boundaries should be clearly drawn and publicly known, rather than being overlooked, as in the recent constitutional negotiations.

The contemporary origins of separate Aboriginal representation at the first ministers' constitutional bargaining table date from Elijah Harper's contribution to the blocking of the Meech Lake Accord. Harper's role was jubilantly seen by Aboriginal peoples as a decisive and positive Aboriginal assertion of constitutional power. The basic post-Meech Aboriginal strategy was to minimize participation that threatened to reduce the status of Aboriginals to that of an ordinary interest group and to fight for participatory roles that recognized their status as First Nations. This meant either being treated as the equal of governments or being treated separately from other Canadians, or both.

From Meech Lake to the Charlottetown Accord, Aboriginal peoples participated only minimally in the grand national inquests by the Spicer Commission and the Beaudoin-Dobbie parliamentary committee. Their more extensive participation in the Beaudoin-Edwards committee's examination of the amending process was largely devoted to obtaining an Aboriginal right of consent, and hence of veto, to constitutional change directly affecting Aboriginal treaties, status, and rights. As the committee's report phrased it, "The underlying concept here is that of sovereign nations and government-to-government relations."[29]

The four main Aboriginal organizations held separate, publicly funded, officially recognized Aboriginal consultations with their respective constituencies that paralleled the Beaudoin-Dobbie inquiries. A separate Aboriginal public constitutional conference on Aboriginal constitutional issues was held in the winter of 1992.[30] Although these separate Aboriginal inquiries attracted little public attention, they were Aboriginal equivalents of Quebec's Bélanger-Campeau inquiry. The fact that they were undertaken as federally recognized inquiries was an advance intimation that Aboriginal peoples, by virtue of their aboriginality, had both an existing and a prospectively unique constitutional status that the consultative inquiries were to explore. Consequently, while the status of the major Aboriginal organizations was less than that of governments in the post-Meech constitutional process, it was clearly superior to that of ordinary constitutional interest groups.

*To the Source*,[31] the report of the parallel Assembly of First Nations' constitutional consultation of its status peoples, is the most elaborate and uncompromising of the Aboriginal reports that developed alongside the Beaudoin-Dobbie inquiry. In attributing a profound sense of cultural singularity to its people (while portraying Euro-Canadians in terms of diametrically opposed values), it is an Aboriginal version of Quebec's Tremblay Report of the mid-fifties, which portrayed French and English Canada as polar opposites.[32]

*To the Source* attributes virtually all the ills of contemporary Indian societies to the contaminating intrusion of Euro-Canadian values. Hence, the application of the Charter to Aboriginal self-government is considered unacceptable, because it is an instrument of an individualistic Euro-Canadian culture, whose acceptance would further the disintegration of Indian society and conflict with the desired recovery of tradition. *To the Source*, a classic example of the nativistic revivalism that is a common feature of nationalist movements, suggests that status Indians identify only minimally with the surrounding Canadian society. If future Aboriginal governments are to be informed by the philosophy of *To the Source*, they will be bastions of "otherness" conducting foreign relations with their Canadian neighbours.

The Assembly of First Nations' request to have the reserve votes of status Indians counted separately – a request granted by the chief electoral officer – further underlined the apartness of status Indians from the Canadian community. It suggested that the status Indian vote would be a response not to the whole package but to its Aboriginal components. It implied that if the status Indian vote and the Canadian vote went in opposite directions, the latter results might not be conclusive with respect to the Aboriginal package. According to Ovide Mercredi, chief of the Assembly of First Nations, an Indian rejection should trigger further negotiations. The same thesis of the need for a double majority or a separate Aboriginal vote count was advocated for the proposed Quebec referendum on sovereignty.[33]

The desire for a separate status Indian vote was a logical response to a constitutional package whose Aboriginal contents had been shaped by Aboriginal inputs and that proposed a very high degree of institutional differentiation of Aboriginal peoples from other Canadians.

A number of Indian First Nations carried the logic of separate status further by boycotting the referendum, which they saw as incompatible with their treaty relations with the Crown. For them, the Accord's goal of resolving Aboriginal/non-Aboriginal constitutional differences foundered on a referendum process that presupposed a commonality of Canadian and First Nations citizenship, which they denied.[34] Professor Tony Hall, noting the number of band governments that prevented the setting up of polling stations, stated: "This decision reflects a strong current of opinion among many First Nations people that their participation in the vote, no matter which side of the question they took, would be inconsistent with the distinct constitutional status of Indian societies in Canada."[35] The same logic lay behind the suspicions many status Indians had earlier held about Prime Minister Diefenbaker's 1960 extension of the franchise to their people – the fear that acceptance would be a form of assimilation that would eat away at their distinct status.

Had the Accord been fully implemented, Aboriginal peoples would have experienced a profound degree of institutional and constitutional separateness. They would probably have voted separately from other Canadians on separate Aboriginal rolls for Aboriginal candidates for the House of Commons. They would have had separate Aboriginal representation in the Senate, clearly indicating that they were not thought of as members of the provincial communities. To varying degrees (the Inuit in Nunavut excepted), they would have been directly linked to a third order of government responsive to Aboriginal citizens separated out from the general community. Accordingly, they would have experienced the jurisdictional impact of federalism in a markedly different fashion from other Canadians; the impact of the Charter – a key symbol of citizenship for many Canadians – would have been greatly attenuated; the Métis would have been brought under the section 91(24) jurisdiction of the federal government and, like status Indians, would have become a legally defined community with specific criteria for inclusion in and exclusion from its official membership roster. Consequently, a new category of non- or unrecognized Métis would have emerged to trouble future policy-makers.

The extensive differential constitutional and policy treatment proposed for about one million Aboriginal Canadians received negligible public discussion in the non-Aboriginal community. Discussion concentrated on Aboriginal self-government, for which details were sparse, at the expense of a larger focus on the potential cumulative consequences of the overall battery of proposed changes. The following concerns do not appear to have been addressed.

(1) If Aboriginal peoples are progressively differentiated from other Canadians by a spate of reinforcing specific constitutional arrangements, what sense of shared Canadian citizenship will develop within the Aboriginal and the larger Canadian community? If a sense of shared citizenship is severely attenuated, will the governments of Canadian federalism, responsive and responsible to non-Aboriginal majorities, be willing to support the flow of funds that impoverished Aboriginal peoples and their governments will require for decades to come? Can generous financial arrangements be sustained for an indefinite future simply as entitlements, unsupported by a fellow feeling of shared citizenship?

(2) What theory of representation lies behind the following proposals? (a) Representation of Aboriginal peoples will be specifically provided in both houses of the federal Parliament.[36] The Aboriginal senators are to have the "same role and powers as other Senators, plus a possible double majority power in relation to certain matters materially affecting Aboriginal people" (*Consensus Report*, s. 9). The specification and strengthening of Aboriginal parliamentary representation, however, coincides with a prospective reduction in the application of federal (and provincial) legislation to Aboriginal peoples when the constitutionally entrenched third Aboriginal order of government takes shape. Thus, Aboriginal peoples, to varying degrees, were to be progressively removed from federal government jurisdiction at the same time as their representation in the federal Parliament was to be enhanced. (b) "Representatives of the Aboriginal peoples of Canada should be invited to participate in discussions on any item on the agenda of a First Ministers' Conference that directly affects the Aboriginal peoples" (*Consensus Report*, s. 23). Does this imply that the federal government – with specified Aboriginal representation in both houses, possibly with Aboriginal members on the government side of the House, and conceivably with Aboriginal members of the cabinet – has no legitimacy on issues that directly affect Aboriginal peoples? (c) There should be "Aboriginal consent to future constitutional amendments that directly refer to the Aboriginal peoples" by means of an Aboriginal consent mechanism to be worked out (*Consensus Report*, s. 60). Does this imply that non-Aboriginal governments do not speak for Aboriginal peoples on these issues? Or perhaps that they speak for the Canadian component of Aboriginal Canadians? If the latter, what is this Canadian component? Is it the residual and varying federal and provincial jurisdictions that will continue to apply to Aboriginal peoples in matters that have not been taken over by Aboriginal governments?

Are Canadians to assume that in the same way as non-Aboriginal Canadians have federal and provincial identities, Aboriginal Canadians are to have three constitutional identities derived from their coexisting membership in three constitutionally recognized communities? If this is the case, each of the three orders of government will represent a distinct component of the multiple identities and community memberships of Aboriginal Canadians, who are simultaneously members of Canadian and provincial communities, as well as being an Aboriginal people. Contemporary Aboriginal nationalists pay little attention to this criterion for a well-functioning constitutional order with three levels of entrenched government, each of which will have some jurisdiction over Aboriginal Canadians.

The multiplication of what appear to be *ad hoc* responses to the question of Aboriginal representation in Parliament, in the amendment process, and at first ministers' conferences at the same time as the Accord was giving birth to a triple-decker federalism produced disconnected, confusing, and contradictory representation proposals. The failure to confront these apparent contradictions would doubtless have damaged future Aboriginal/non-Aboriginal relations had the Accord's various loose ends been worked out and implemented in terms of their varying intents. Perhaps the incoherence in Aboriginal representation that would follow from the combined third order of government, representation in both houses of Parliament, and executive federalism roles would have been viewed as an endearing anomaly, justified by the legacy of injustice it sought to rectify. Anomalies, however, are not self-explanatory. They, too, must be defended by rationales that can be contested. The basic contradiction is between the view that Aboriginal nations as such are to have direct access to and/or membership in the representative institutions of the Canadian state, including first ministers' conferences and amending processes, and the traditional assumptions of a parliamentary federalism based on countrywide and provincial communities of individual citizens, whose representation springs from federal and provincial electoral competition based on a virtually universal franchise.

## Why the Quebec-Aboriginal Difference?

The possibility of there being a more broad-ranging, sensitive, and far-reaching response to Aboriginal nationalism than to Québécois nationalism was indirectly signalled by the initial federal government proposals, *Shaping Canada's Future Together: Proposals*. In the introduction, the need to respond to Aboriginal Canadians was cited ahead of the need to respond to Quebec, and the opening chapter devoted nearly twice as much space to Aboriginal as to Quebec's constitutional requirements.[37] Senior Quebec civil servants were frustrated, annoyed, and disbelieving when the realities in the Accord confirmed these anticipations that Aboriginal gains would be markedly superior to those offered to Quebec, a comparison that was doubly wounding because Quebec poll respondents were twice as likely as Canadians in general to dislike the Aboriginal self-government proposals (19 per cent to 10 per cent). [38]

According to Quebec officials, the Aboriginal peoples were the "big winners," making gains they could not have hoped for only a few months earlier. Their inherent right to self-government surpassed in significance and impact Quebec's distinct society recognition. Their achievement of a third order of government underlined the failure of Quebec, constrained by the equality of the provinces principle, to attain asymmetrical status. The Aboriginal peoples' future right of veto on amendments referring directly to Aboriginal peoples was described as an important power that Quebec had never been able to obtain. Finally, Quebec officials feared that the implementation of the Aboriginal gains, most of which were general agreements in principle, would monopolize government attention for years to come and thus make it difficult for Quebec to achieve additional constitutional changes. [39] Nationalist academics were equally disturbed and irate. Guy Laforest, for example, bitingly contrasted the Accord's generous response to Aboriginal nationalism with its insensitivity, as in previous constitutional debacles, to Quebec's national aspirations. [40] While official explanations for this differential response to Quebec and Aboriginal demands are lacking, the phenomenon is so remarkable that speculation on its causes is worthwhile.

Some of the differences can be attributed to the presence of Aboriginal negotiators at the bargaining table that produced the Charlottetown Accord, contrasted with Quebec's absence prior to the penultimate stage. Further, Aboriginal negotiators were able and effective, and had positive public images, especially Ovide Mercredi. The contrast between the Charlottetown Aboriginal package and the minimal Aboriginal Meech Lake gains – protection of their constitutional clauses from the distinct society – when they were not part of the bargaining group provides supporting evidence that presence is better than absence. On the other hand, Quebec was not only present in the bargaining that led to Meech Lake, but it set the agenda in what was described as the Quebec round – and still received less than Aboriginal peoples gained in the 1992 Accord. Further, although physically absent, Quebec was a brooding presence throughout the post-Meech Lake constitutional process, either through the proxy of the federal government or by covert communications, or simply because the urgency that drove the entire process came from the looming Quebec referendum. The presence of Aboriginal negotiators in the pre-Charlottetown process partly explains why they did better than they had at Meech Lake, but it has only limited relevance to why their Charlottetown gains were greater than those offered to Quebec either at Meech Lake, with the Quebec government present, or in the Charlottetown package, with the Quebec government largely absent. Whether Quebec's physical absence throughout most of the post-Meech process diminished Quebec's gains is a moot point. It is, however, clear that by the time Quebec explicitly joined the negotiations in August, 1992, further Quebec gains were inhibited by the complex interdependence of the deals that had already been struck.

An easily overlooked explanation for the public's acceptance of the Aboriginal-Quebec difference is ignorance. The components of the Aboriginal package were not brought together for easy examination of their likely overall impact. Attention was directed almost exclusively to Aboriginal self-government, which was relatively undefined and thus not amenable to rigorous examination. The potential cumulative impact of the Aboriginal components was not only ignored in the public debate but does not appear to have been considered seriously in the private discussions that led to the Accord. In some part, this was due to the frantic pace dictated by the looming Quebec referendum, supplemented by the fragmentation of the 1992 spring and summer bargaining process into sub-groups – factors that concealed the big picture. In addition, first ministers and their advisers could put off asking the big questions because the details of virtually every part of the Aboriginal package were to be worked out in the future. The direction, however, was clear – toward a third order of Aboriginal government and a distinct Aboriginal role in or in relation to virtually every major institution of the Canadian state: Senate, House of Commons, amending formula, first ministers' conferences, the Charter, and, somewhat less clearly, the Supreme Court.

The logical question to which these parallel relationships led – what degree of institutional differentiation of a people is compatible with the nation-state form? – was never asked. Would the consistent departures from a common citizenship and from a common relationship to the Canadian constitutional order that would flow from implementation of the Aboriginal proposals be threatening to the flow of sympathy and empathy that should exist between members of the same political community? At what point do good fences cease to make good neighbours and instead make strangers of fellow citizens? Analogous questions, of course, also applied to Quebec, but here the questions were not new. A well-developed discourse was at hand to address them, which Pierre Trudeau ensured was vigorously employed.[41] By contrast, the developing Aboriginal constitutional discourse drove inexorably toward enhanced, positive differential treatment for Aboriginal peoples,[42] for which self-government was an encompassing code word. Fifty years ago, such aspirations would have been routinely scorned by non-Aboriginals as both unattainable and undesirable because of a taken-for-granted cultural backwardness or low levels of civilization of Aboriginal peoples. Even the issue of size has virtually disappeared as an acceptable rationale for non-Aboriginal opposition to self-government. "Nation" is now routinely employed as a self-description by small Indian bands of several hundred people.

Five of nine recent Indian band name changes added "nation" to the band's self-description.[43]

Additional backing for the more positive response to Aboriginal Canadians came from liberal guilt and, among the intelligentsia, from the political correctness imperative. According to Richard Gwyn, with the exception of Quebecers, who were introspectively obsessed with their own minority status, "all Canadians appear to agree . . . that a debt of guilt is overdue to be paid to Indians and Inuit."[44] By 1991-92, this was supplemented by memories of Elijah Harper and Oka and the recognition that Aboriginal support for the overall Canada package was politically essential. Douglas Sanders has noted the extreme reluctance of political leaders to appear to oppose – or even to ask tough questions about – Aboriginal self-government, an inhibition that Bryan Schwartz had previously observed at the four Aboriginal constitutional conferences from 1983 to 1987.[45] Recurring assertions by the Accord's non-Aboriginal opponents, such as Judy Rebick of the National Action Committee on the Status of Women and Sharon Carstairs, the then leader of the Manitoba Liberal Party, of their strong support for Aboriginal self-government confirm the Sanders and Schwartz thesis.[46]

In any event, from the ROC perspective, Quebec and French Canada have already been accorded a generous response – by federalism, by the Official Languages Act, by the language clauses of the Charter, by the virtual monopolization of the office of Prime Minister in all but one of the past twenty-four years, and by the perception that Quebec has been an excessively favoured recipient of federal bounty. The ROC did not view Quebec as an exploited, impoverished community whose plight elicited sympathy, but saw it as a fully integrated, thriving provincial member of the established system.

The Aboriginal status quo, however, was not defensible, with its ubiquitous indications of social malaise, poverty, and marginality. The impetus this provided for the acceptance of radical change was the basic premise behind Thomas Courchene and Lisa Powell's advocacy of a First Nations province: "The time for self-determination and self-government is clearly at hand. The old ways have not worked. [A First Nations province] . . . would clearly be a quantum leap, for both aboriginals and non aboriginal Canadians. There are no guarantees . . . [but] we have no choice but to vere [*sic*] boldly in a new direction."[47]

Further, in a constitutional sense, Aboriginal Canadians, unlike Quebec, have not been full members of the Canadian community; they have been on the periphery of the Canadian sense of self. A long history of neglect of the forgotten people, as Métis and Inuit were often called, and of exclusion from the franchise, the symbol of citizenship, as was true of status Indians until 1960, meant that Aboriginal peoples were not part of the "we" community of Canadian citizens; rather, they lived alongside it or, in the case of status Indians, were subject to it. Aboriginal peoples have been in waiting and thus are logically thought of as being in transition. This was most explicitly the case for status Indians, historically viewed as wards or children who were being prepared for citizenship in some distant tomorrow by the residential schools and the tutelary administration of the Indian Affairs Branch. Given this context of understanding, it was not irrational for voters outside Quebec to be seven times more likely to cite "Quebec got too much" as their main reason for voting No than to cite "Too much was given to aboriginals" (27 to 4 per cent), even though the latter were treated much more generously than the former.[48]

The contemporary momentum behind having an Indian status that is permanently differentiated from that of other Canadians derives from the vehement rejection by the Indian people of the assimilationist philosophy of the 1969 federal government White Paper on Indian policy. Indianness was not to be a transitional status or a way station on the path to undifferentiated Canadianness; from the time of the rejection of the White Paper, it was a presumptively permanent condition. This change of constitutional goal for the status Indian community inevitably spilled over to the Inuit, who, constitutionally if not legislatively, were Indians, and to the Métis, who had long struggled to catch up to the constitutional recognition accorded their indigenous brethren. The defeat of the White Paper is therefore a seminal event, because it blocked one line of development – the non-recognition of difference and of historical priority – and virtually ensured that differential status for Indians, logically extended to all Aboriginals, would survive in new forms that would evolve from future constitutional politics.

From the Aboriginal perspective, a constitutional and institutional recognition of difference represented continuity. As Monture-Okanee and Turpel argue in their advocacy of a separate Aboriginal justice system, "Aboriginal peoples, [who are] both different and separate, simply cannot be considered as part of Canadian society. . . . We are not necessarily culturally, linguistically or historically part of Canada or Canadian legal and political institutions. We are . . . set apart by our cultures, languages, distance and histories." This Aboriginal difference merits recognition because the fact of being "First Peoples distinguishes us from any other 'group' or 'minority' in Canada" and justifies special constitutional status. The Aboriginal desire for separate treatment is given further impetus by "centuries of mistrust . . . [based] . . . upon the centuries of ill-founded approaches to aboriginal-Canadian relations."[49]

Accordingly, from both Aboriginal and non-Aboriginal perspectives a separate Aboriginal institutional and constitutional path appeared more as a given than as a departure from a hitherto applicable norm or practice. For non-Aboriginals, a proposed third order of government and the battery of additional differentiating arrangements noted above were intellectually and psychologically less threatening and easier to digest when viewed as continuing, albeit updated, expressions of an historical pattern of different treatment. Recognition of separate Aboriginal roles and governments does not tear asunder an established relationship among equals. It can be viewed as a progressive revision of a parallel relationship, or the ending of paternalism, or as incorporating Aboriginal peoples as full participants in the Canadian polity, or as derived from unique histories and ancient legal entitlements. For example, David Bercuson and Barry Cooper – who advocate a parting of the ways between Quebec and the ROC because of the harm they consider the former's presence in Canada does to liberal principles – identify Aboriginal Canadians as "one exception to our general principle of citizen equality ... [for] they were Canada's first inhabitants and they entered into direct legal relationships with the Crown under the terms of which they surrendered their aboriginal title to the land in exchange for reserves, cash, and other considerations. Thus, it would be a violation of both law and moral standards to apply the same legal and constitutional status to them as to other Canadians."[50]

To some degree, also, the extent of the unique future constitutional status of Aboriginal peoples was concealed by the concept of a third order of government, with its reassuring implication that Aboriginal peoples were to become part of the Canadian constitutional system, in harmony with traditional, characteristic, federal ways. Thus, dramatic change was veiled behind the skilful use of common terms. It was, therefore, misleadingly easy to view a third order of government as a straightforward add-on and thus to pay negligible attention to its actual departure from Canadian constitutional traditions. A third order of entrenched Aboriginal government is not simply more of the traditional federalism game; it is the onset of a different game, in the same way that a three-team hockey game is qualitatively different from the traditional two-team game.

Not only is a three-order federal system qualitatively different from the traditional two-order system by virtue of its complexity, but the Aboriginal third order would be qualitatively different from the provincial second order. The third order of government was to apply to specific, listed populations of legally defined individuals (Nunavut excepted), in marked contrast to open provincial communities subject to pervasive mobility into and out of their ranks. Even had this significant difference been publicly noted and discussed, the non-Aboriginal reaction might have been supportive. Psychologically, an elaborate constitutional recognition of Aboriginal difference is much less disturbing to the non-Aboriginal ROC sense of Canadian peoplehood, which historically marginalized Aboriginal people, than a much smaller response to Quebec, which is viewed as a full member of the Canadian community. (Within Quebec, however, the tension between Québécois and Aboriginal nationalisms, with the former fearing that the latter might successfully appeal to the same principles of national self-determination that the Québécois French-speaking majority employs, is deep and serious. The presence of rival nations on Quebec soil is not only an unwelcome, unassimilable alien presence, but it is a potential threat to Quebec's territorial integrity.[51] Space limitations prevent the fuller exploration of this issue beyond footnote references.)[52]

Since ROC nationalism dresses itself in the guise of pan-Canadian nationalism, its sense of self includes Quebec. As long as this correlation continues, the ROC cannot act as an independent constitutional participant and cannot extricate itself from its pan-Canadian, countrywide sense of community; accordingly, in officially responding to Quebec from a Canadian rather than ROC perspective, it is responding to itself rather than to a discrete external party that is detached from its own sense of community identity and membership. Consequently, the ROC, speaking through the other governments of Canadian federalism and wearing its Canadian hat, seeks to minimize differential treatment for Quebec, for that would necessarily rearrange the ROC's sense of its Canadian self. Further, the Quebec goal of asymmetrical status, with its corollary of a weaker federal government presence in Quebec and a weaker Québécois attachment to a pan-Canadian nation, is viewed by the ROC as an undesirable diminution and weakening of the Canadianism of Québécois, not as a liberation from a constraint that prevents Québécois from being truly themselves. By contrast, the historical outsider status of Aboriginal peoples, who have not been part of the "we" Canadian community, allows a more flexible range of policy responses.

The response to Quebec in both Meech Lake and the subsequent Charlottetown Accord was constrained by the equality of the provinces principle. In the former, it meant that what Quebec received (distinct society excepted) had also to be given to the other provinces. This equality principle was the most important factor in the opposition of Clyde Wells to the Meech Lake Accord. In the *Consensus Report on the Constitution* (the Charlottetown Accord), with Meech Lake in mind, respect for the equality of the provinces principle is reiterated like a reassuring mantra on page after page. According to Roger Tassé, former Deputy Minister of Justice and participating constitutional consultant in the pre-Charlottetown negotiations, it "is a theme that weaves its way through the entire set of proposals. . . . Of the current proposals on the division of powers, none singles out Quebec for special powers or a unique authority. In every case, the proposed transfer of power has been made available to all the provinces."[53] The equality of the provinces principle is explicitly affirmed in the Canada clause and in the composition of the reformed Senate. The provincial equality principle, however, had no application to the third, Aboriginal order of government.

A version of the equality of provinces norm could have applied to the proposed third order of Aboriginal governments in two separate ways. Their anticipated jurisdiction could have been modelled on the existing provinces. Instead, however, it was understood that the jurisdictional powers of self-governing

Aboriginal peoples could be drawn from jurisdictions normally possessed by either federal or provincial governments, thus differentiating them from existing provinces. Second, in spite of the difference in the content of their jurisdiction from that of provinces, an equality norm could have been applied to prospective Aboriginal governments within the third order. This, however, was not even considered. In the language of the Accord, "self-government negotiations should take into consideration the different circumstances of the various Aboriginal peoples" (*Consensus Report*, s. 46).

Even to describe the probable variations within the Aboriginal order of government as asymmetrical is misleading, for the concept implies a norm from which there are isolated departures. However, the variation in the jurisdictional powers wielded by Nunavut, as a future quasi-province with an overwhelming Inuit majority, compared with the limited powers to be wielded by Aboriginal people in metropolitan Winnipeg is sufficiently profound to become a difference in kind. In practical terms, these variations are appropriate responses to the diversity of situations in which Aboriginal people are located. Theoretically, however, they nevertheless raise constitutional questions. Logically, the potential variations of jurisdiction that will occur among the diversely situated Aboriginal communities raise the same constitutional issues that concern opponents of significant asymmetry within the second order of government – such as the role and status of MPs from provincial communities whose governments wield powers that for other Canadians are handled by the federal government. Analogously, the propriety of Aboriginal MPs representing Aboriginal people influencing policy and legislation that would not apply to their Aboriginal constituents raised the same constitutional issue, but it was not addressed.

The proposal by several non-Aboriginal scholars that the diverse aggregation of self-governing Aboriginal peoples be constituted as one province would overcome these concerns (assuming that such a province did not have "special status") and would have the tremendous virtue of familiarity and continuity.[54] This provincial proposal, however, appears to lack even minimal support from Aboriginal peoples.[55]

Analysis of the Canada round suggests that the equality of the provinces norm is a very specific norm of club membership that applies only to existing provinces. Hence, no version of the provincial equality norm had any application to, or was even considered for, future Aboriginal governments. Further, the Accord was explicit that equal provincial rights would not automatically be available to future new northern provinces, which accordingly would lack some of the basic attributes of provincehood held by the other ten. Although the provisions for the creation of new provinces were significantly eased, such provinces could only become full participants in the amending formula with the unanimous consent of the other eleven governments, and they would only be entitled to equal provincial representation in the revised Senate with unanimous agreement.

The equality of the provinces norm, which applies to existing club members, is perfectly compatible with the visiting of negative inequalities on future members. That new members should be lesser members can be accepted with equanimity by old members. The same principle of privileging first arrivals was used when Manitoba (1870) and, later, Saskatchewan and Alberta (both 1905) became provinces. The federal government retained control of their natural resources for nation-building and development purposes until they were given to the provinces in 1930. What is rejected by those already in the club is granting an existing member more status or powers than other club members have and admitting new members on equality terms if this might disadvantage those who are already full members. Had Aboriginal peoples sought province status both by name and in terms of jurisdictional powers and other standard perquisites, they would doubtless have encountered much greater resistance than they did when setting up their own third-order club. Conversely, had Quebec been seen as a political unit other than a province, with a distinctive constitutional designation, and had it been viewed as existing alongside rather than as a standard member of the provincial order, the response to its constitutional aspirations might have been more generous.

The flexible response to Aboriginal peoples derived from the perception that neither historically nor prospectively (a future Nunavut excepted) should they be thought of in provincial terms. Indicative of the Quebec/Aboriginal difference is the fact that the limits imposed on Aboriginal self-government appear to have been *ad hoc* responses developed hastily by policy-makers who lacked guidance and historical precedents in their novel situation. The Canada clause statement that the third order of Aboriginal government was "in Canada" (*Consensus Report*, s. 1(2)(1)(b)); the provision that Aboriginal laws or assertions of authority "may not be inconsistent with those laws which are essential to the preservation of peace, order and good government in Canada" (*Consensus Report*, s. 47) (this, incidentally, was not the traditional s. 91 POGG); the attempt by Bourassa to protect Quebec's territorial integrity by the provision that the self-government clauses "should not create new Aboriginal rights to land" (*Consensus Report*, s. 44); and the convoluted attempts to deal with the Charter issue – all these suggest policy-making on the run.

The seeming irrelevance of the equality of the provinces norm for Aboriginal peoples contrasted markedly with the salience of the issue of the equality of citizens, which generated a vigorous debate about the Charter's application to Aboriginal self-government. Once the concept of inherent rights had been accepted, the controversy over Aboriginal self-government concentrated on the

Charter of Rights and Freedoms. The negotiating governments and non-Aboriginal public opinion were advocates of the Charter's application to Aboriginal governments, a demand powerfully supported by the Native Women's Association of Canada.[56] The main resistance came from the Assembly of First Nations, whose constitutional document, *To the Source*,[57] was unrelentingly hostile to the Charter and whose constitutional adviser, Mary Ellen Turpel, had previously written a passionate critique of the Charter's application to Aboriginal peoples.[58]

The sensitivity of the issue was evident in the obfuscating ambiguity of its treatment in the Aboriginal package. Non-Aboriginal defenders of the Accord reiterated the Charlottetown Accord statement that "the Canadian Charter of Rights and Freedoms should apply immediately to governments of Aboriginal peoples" (*Consensus Report*, s. 43). This apparently wholehearted allegiance to the full application of the Charter norm to all Canadians presumably reflected the remarkable Charter support in Canadian constitutional culture, especially in English Canada, where the Charter has become a key symbol of civic identity. As already noted, the Charter's application was significantly eroded by various exemptions that were available only to Aboriginal peoples, along with the standard availability of the notwithstanding clause to legislatures. Had the Accord been implemented, the precise effect of these Charter-weakening constitutional clauses would only have become clear in future jurisprudence. Some legal scholars, however, were convinced that they would have severely reduced the applicability of the Charter.[59] That, after all, was their intent.

The difference in the Accord's treatment of the prospective application of the Charter in Quebec and to Aboriginal self-government is again instructive of the differential application of constitutional norms to the two aggressive nationalisms. For Quebec, the Charter – and indeed the whole constitution – was to be filtered through the interpretive lens of the specifications for a distinct society (which "includes a French-speaking majority, a unique culture and a civil law tradition"). These specifications were not in the Meech Lake Accord, and they are generally considered to have weakened the clause. The original section 25 Aboriginal non-derogation clause in the 1982 Charter, by contrast, is not simply an interpretive clause but is a categorical protection: in its pre-Charlottetown Accord form, Charter rights and freedoms "shall not be construed so as to abrogate or derogate from any aboriginal, treaty or other rights or freedoms that pertain to the aboriginal peoples of Canada." The Charlottetown Accord would have strengthened this protection. Thus, had the Accord been implemented, Quebec's protection from the Charter would have been slightly enhanced by the addition of a weak interpretive clause, while the protection of Aboriginal peoples, already stronger than Quebec's, would have been significantly supplemented by the strengthening of what was already a broadly worded imperative statement.

Thus, the Charter would have had much less applicability to Aboriginal governments than to Quebec. Again (although perhaps not so dramatically as with the equality of the provinces norm), Aboriginal peoples were defined as being on the periphery of a fundamental constitutional norm for other Canadians. Thus, it was apparently assumed that the ROC would accept the non-application of the Charter's democratic rights to Aboriginal governments (the right to vote and to be qualified for membership in a legislative body), when these same Canadians outside Quebec had reacted viscerally to Quebec's use of the notwithstanding clause to protect French-only outside commercial signs – presumably, a far smaller violation of Charter rights. By inference, the historic outsiderness of Aboriginals facilitated a continuing differentiation. The Accord's philosophy suggested that Aboriginal constitutional evolution should appropriately foster and even strengthen the original separateness that Aboriginals brought to the bargaining table.

To sum up, why was there this differential response to Québécois and Aboriginal nationalisms? The response to Quebec was constrained by the provincial equality principle, by the fact that Quebec was viewed as a fully functioning member of an ongoing system with its own norms, by the corollary that Quebecers were included in the ROC's Canadian sense of self – the disruption of which would be psychologically destabilizing – and by the fact that opposition to any extensive special status could draw sustenance from the existing, theoretically developed federalist discourse, which was championed by former Prime Minister Trudeau and widely held outside Quebec, and which pervades much of the 1982 Constitution Act.

In contrast, a third order of Aboriginal government, viewed as existing outside or alongside the norm of provincial equality, and the various supplementary recognitions of aboriginality did not require the ROC to retreat to a diminished sense of self.[60] The geographical isolation of the Inuit, the distinct constitutional, administrative, and policy regime that has historically been applied to status Indians, and the incorporation of Métis into a category given its meaning by Indians and Inuit psychologically distanced Aboriginal and other Canadians from each other. Thus, the historical civic marginality of Aboriginal peoples facilitated the further elaboration of differential treatment that was proposed in the Charlottetown Accord. Indeed, the new differentiation could be described, in a phrase of the Assembly of First Nations, as "closing the circle," as bringing Aboriginal peoples as such into the constitutional family. This definition of "closing the circle" by constitutionally sanctioning difference rested on the tacit acceptance that the most powerful discourse opposed to continuing differential treatment had been repudiated with the demise of the assimilationist 1969 White Paper. By contrast, in the case of Quebec, a province and people viewed as already being in the system, the constitutional recognition of extensive additional differentiation was once again resisted, on the grounds that the circle had already been closed.

The perceived direction of movement, therefore, which depends on what is considered to be the starting point, is crucial. As historical outsiders, Aboriginal peoples can be allowed a continuing degree of differentiation that is not available to the Quebec partner, which is already viewed as in the system by those who ultimately determine the permissible limits of change. Given the opposition of Premier Clyde Wells to the Meech Lake package, it is perhaps appropriate that the Quebec experience confirms the Newfoundland aphorism that you can't get there from here – where "here" is provincial status, and "there" is special constitutional recognition of Quebec as a nation within Canadian federalism. Aboriginal peoples, starting from a different and more distant "here," encountered less resistance on a longer journey to their "there."

## Conclusion

The preceding analysis of the Charlottetown Accord as the setting for an encounter between the multinational nature of contemporary Canada and federalism supports, without confirming, the following generalizations.

Federalism and a multinational definition of Canada are a poor fit. The sociological reality and self-perceptions of the Québécois as a nation can receive only limited constitutional expression as long as, constitutionally, Quebec is a province. The limited manoeuvrability available in responding to Quebec is a by-product of its provincial status and the contemporary federalism norms that attach to that status. These norms are powerfully embedded in the mentalities of all other government leaders. The central cue transmitted by the formal amending process to governments and citizens outside Quebec is that any proposed constitutional response to Quebec's aspirations is to be evaluated by federalist criteria. Accordingly, an inflexible response is, in a sense, routinized by the provincial equality principle.

If federalism makes it virtually impossible to treat Quebec as a nation entitled to jurisdictional and status perquisites not available to other provinces, it also muffles the voice of the rest of Canada, or English Canada. Officially, the ROC has no existence. Its sense of self as a distinct people, as a legitimate constitutionally recognized community, is not constantly reinforced, as provincial peoples are, by institutions that confirm its existence. Its identity, therefore, is diffuse, incoherent, ambiguous, and unstructured. Although an intelligentsia now addresses the ROC as a prospective national actor, the routinized messages that daily bombard the potential citizenry of the ROC either fragment it into competing provincialisms (and territorialisms) or submerge it in the pan-Canadian community that includes Quebec and is served on a countrywide basis by the federal government.

The inability of the rest of Canada to conduct itself officially as a nation undermines the possibility of treating Quebec as a nation. Bourassa hoped to bargain with Canada one on one, nation to nation. Instead, the constitutional politics of federalism reduced Quebec to the status of a province, to the extent that the Charlottetown Accord, particularly the area of the division of powers, was governed by the equality of the provinces principle. The logical dynamics of federalism, which muffle and suppress nationalist behaviour by the ROC, necessarily denationalize Quebec. It is easier for the provincialism of the ROC to force Quebec back into a provincial mould than for the nationalism of Quebec to extricate the ROC from its provincialism and pan-Canadianism and make it a national partner with whom nation-to-nation bargaining can take place. This is so even though at one level ROC citizens do see themselves as a nation, and specifically see themselves as the nationalist inheritors of what remains if Quebec should leave. This recognition, however, is frozen out or left behind when federalism's office-holders confront Quebec wielding an amending formula that is an instrument and reflection of federalism.

In dramatic contrast to Quebec and the ROC, constrained by federalism's norms, Aboriginal nationalism has much more latitude to express itself in highly particularistic constitutional and institutional arrangements. The control by comparison with other provincial realities that limits what Quebec can achieve does not apply to Aboriginal peoples. They are in a sense outside federalism as long as they do not conceive their future in provincial terms. Thus, the norms that automatically apply to provinces do not apply to the prospective units in a variegated Aboriginal third order of government. In addition, psychologically Aboriginal peoples are not viewed as standardized members of the Canadian community. Historically, they have been outside it – isolated by geography as the Inuit were or by distinctive constitutional and policy treatment as status Indians were, including exclusion from the franchise until 1960, or by marginalization as the "forgotten people," as Métis were. Consequently, positive differential treatment for Aboriginal peoples in the future rests on negative differential treatment in the past.

If, therefore, Aboriginal and Québécois nationalisms are judged by their capacity to achieve constitutional special status, a clear advantage resides with the former. This advantage, however, comes at a price – the troubling message that, from a Canadian perspective, Aboriginal Canadians are not fully "one of us." The willingness to sanction special constitutional and institutional treatment derives from an absence of fellow feeling. A little special status for Quebec is much more disturbing to the ROC's Canadian sense of self than a much more potent special status for Aboriginal peoples is. A sympathetic willingness to accord a special place for Aboriginal peoples may be the positive side of a Janus-faced reality, whose negative side is a relative indifference to the fate of peoples who are "them," not "us."

The process leading up to the Charlottetown Accord, the Accord itself, and the referendum that was its downfall were separately, and even more so jointly, unique phenomena. Possibly this paper has extracted more meaning, messages, and lessons from Charlottetown than that complex event, no matter how rich, can sustain. After all, the Meech Lake fiasco was a response to the "lessons" of the flaws in the substance and the making of the 1982 Constitution Act. The Charlottetown Accord, consigned by the referendum electorate to the overflowing graveyard of failed efforts at constitutional reform, was, in its turn, both in process and substance a response to the "lessons" of why Meech Lake went wrong. Since the lesson of the attempt to find lessons from 1980-82 and from Meech Lake is that real lessons are elusive, this paper and its author may join the distinguished company of past interpreters who have been outfoxed by a murky reality. The reader and the unfolding future can and will decide.

# PART VI

## THE CONSTITUTIONAL FUTURE

### Chapter Thirteen

# *Dreams versus Reality in "Our" Constitutional Future: How Many Communities?*

*Canada rated "best place to live" in world.* [1]

*The people of Canada, the people of Quebec included, are fed up with talking about the Constitution. . . . It is not as exciting to talk about asphalt as it is to have those professors of universities debating the Constitution. That is fun. Some have made a career "of it."* [2]

– Jean Chrétien

*Everybody who speaks with great confidence on how the future will unroll . . . is really writing fiction.* [3]

– Desmond Morton

This concluding chapter, written immediately after the Quebec provincial election in September, 1994, will be read by most readers after the date of the Quebec referendum. This is not a happy situation for a writer committed to explore the themes in the chapter's title. The daily journalist, whose words are read almost as soon as they are written, is much to be envied, as is the medieval historian who analyses a past whose future – a less distant past – will not disconfirm what she writes.

It is not only the inherent unknowability of the future that explains the difficulty of addressing the theme of this final chapter. Special factors compound the trepidation normal to all who leave the relative security of post-diction – the historian's task – for the perils of prediction, for which soothsayers and astrologists may be nearly as reliable guides as social scientists.

Canadians are in the grip of competing nationalisms driven by pride, resentment, humiliation, and anger – emotions that can easily get out of control when exploited by unscrupulous politicians, as they undoubtedly will be by some. Indeed, in the crisis atmosphere of contemporary Canada the crucial role of leading politicians contributes a special unpredictability. Analysts accustomed to writing of social and economic forces being in the saddle nevertheless unblushingly assume that the presence or absence of Pierre Trudeau in the coming referendum debate, the resignation of Robert Bourassa, the oratorical skills and charisma of Lucien Bouchard, the arrogance of Jacques Parizeau, and the canniness of Jean Chrétien will significantly influence the Quebec-Canada outcome. The skill or ineptitude of the key players will have major effects, as will the wisdom or folly of the strategies they follow. The wording of the referendum question, to be decided by the Quebec government, will have a marked effect on voter choice. "Separation" as the key word is the least and "sovereignty" the most attractive to Quebec voters, with "independence" in between.[4] The confusion about the meaning of these terms is so dramatic that the real intent of the referendum electorate will not be easily discerned. Thirty-one per cent of respondents in a 1992 poll believed a sovereign Quebec "would still be part of Canada," and 20 per cent thought Quebecers "would still elect members of Parliament to Ottawa," while another 1992 survey indicated that one-quarter of the supporters of "Quebec sovereignty" wished Quebec "to remain a province of Canada" rather than "to become an independent country."[5]

The salience of these personal factors and elite strategies is exaggerated because the rules of the constitutional contest Canadians are now engaged in prior to the referendum are unclear. The lack of an agreed-on recipe for the breakup of Canada means that the skill of the actors in defining the nature and rules of the game is just as important as how they then play the game. In fact, even this is an over-simplification, for Canadians are playing three kinds of federalism/constitutional games simultaneously: (1) the normal game of federal politics, working an ongoing system; (2) the renewed federalism game of keeping Quebec in Canada by formal constitutional change, as attempted in the failed Meech Lake and Charlottetown Accords; this game is on temporary hold; and (3) the breakup of Canada game, the goal of the Bloc Québécois and the Parti Québécois. These games shade into each other, and the leading players understand that their performance in one game may determine the outcome in a different game. For example, since its 1993 election the federal Liberal government has acted on the premise that good government and a shrewd playing of the politics of federalism can undercut support for separation (Ottawa's preferred word) in the independence game. By contrast, the Parti Québécois government elected in September, 1994, will exploit every opportunity in the federalism game, some of which it will have deliberately created, to persuade Québécois that federalism is a rigid, inefficient arrangement that should be rejected in favour of independence.

These games, dominated by French-English, Quebec-Canada, and federal-provincial concerns may be derailed, or have their hegemony challenged, by the unfinished business of responding to Aboriginal peoples in a way appropriate to their status as First Nations. The report of the Royal Commission on Aboriginal Peoples, expected in 1995, is a likely instrument of that challenge.

Confident future-oriented analysis is further clouded by the fact that the "our" of the chapter title is in quotation marks, correctly implying that its reality is somewhat notional. It is not only the Canadian "we," under attack from Quebec and Aboriginal nationalisms, that is fragile. The Quebec "we," the Aboriginal "we," and the rest of Canada "we" are also unstable. The social base behind these community labels employed to mobilize competing definitions of who we are is fluid and shifting. Quebec is a heterogeneous society with Aboriginal nations in its midst, and Montreal, its largest metropolis, is a cosmopolitan, multicultural, multiracial city. Support for the independence goal is overwhelmingly concentrated in the Francophone majority, on whose behalf it is sought, and overwhelmingly opposed by Anglophones, allophones, and Aboriginal peoples, a fact with serious post-independence repercussions. Should the Quebec referendum pass, the unity of the rest of Canada (ROC) is problematic. The ROC is likely to be reduced to competing provincial voices as provincial governments occupy the stage vacated by a defeated and demoralized federal government. Further, the Aboriginal category is not homogeneous. It encompasses three distinct sub-categories of indigenous peoples – Indian, Inuit, and Métis – whose interests often conflict, and the largest of which, the status Indian community, is further fragmented into hundreds of bands that differ in size, wealth, and treaty status. Given these realities, how yesterday's "Canadians" define who they are and their community membership in the volatile circumstances following a positive referendum vote may display marked and unexpected departures from identities no longer stabilized by the security of habitual constitutional arrangements.

The complexity of the identity transformations that may occur is both misconceived and too easily underestimated. The issue is not how discrete peoples with dissimilar identities are to fashion a future side-by-side coexistence on half a continent. With the few exceptions of the purist Québécois and Aboriginal nationalists, most Canadians carry several civic identities simultaneously – as a Canadian, as a possessor of Charter rights, as a provincial resident, and for about a million Canadians, as an Aboriginal, as well as other particularistic identities defined by ethnicity, gender, language, etc. The debate on our future is about how each of us as individuals should rearrange the various identities we separately carry. The task of Parizeau and Bouchard is to persuade Québécois that the Canadian identity is a burden, whose shedding will free their psyche from hampering restraints. Should they succeed, many non-Québécois will for decades nostalgically nurse an obsolete pan-Canadian identity no longer sustained by constitutional arrangements.

Given the indeterminacy and complexity of our future at the time of writing, I will simplify the chapter's theme by portraying what I consider to be the two most probable scenarios – the triumph of the status quo or a somewhat disorderly retreat into a transitional instability for the fragmenting components of the former Canada. While these two extremes are ideal types, unlikely to be mirrored in detail in the future, they represent more likely outcomes than the middle ground of the Panglossian optimists. The latter visualize a clean break, unaccompanied by domestic instability in either of what they view as the two main players in a constitutional rearrangement – Quebec and the rest of Canada – followed by a relatively amicable settlement of the host of issues that will attend the splitting of Canada into two new states. This is too implausible to merit serious discussion. The stridency and anger in the voices coming from outside Quebec in the pre-referendum period[6] suggest the much greater passions likely to be unleashed as the campaign gets under way. Further, non-Quebec analysts predict a difficult, divisive transition following a "yes" vote.[7]

The Parti Québécois perspective simplistically constructs English Canada (or Canada outside of Quebec) as a mirror image of itself – as a unitary actor, one of the two national peoples that will emerge with a coherent sense of self when Quebec departs. The understandable *indépendantiste* insistence on seeing Quebec as a nation rather than a province produces an inability to accept the reality that the ROC nation is provincialized, and that provincialism is likely to come to the fore at a time when the federal government is in disarray following a Quebec referendum "yes" vote. The second fallacious Parti Québécois assumption is that the responses of Canadians elsewhere to Quebec independence would be those of calculating "economic man" guided by an exclusive economic self-interest that would facilitate the undisturbed continuation of economic and trade patterns.[8] This blindness to the possibility that a rejected ROC might respond on the basis of wounded nationalist *amour-propre* confirms the superficiality of the Parti Québécois understanding of their Canadian neighbours.

In this essay I have not concentrated on the many practical issues of currency, division of the debt, the St. Lawrence Seaway, the National Capital Region, trading relationships, and an infinity of other urgent issues that will attend the initial disentanglement and the subsequent attempt to re-establish a new co-operative arrangement between the two or more successor states. My concentration on the social, community aspects of the breakup (if that is to be our fate) reflects my belief that a focus on the hard bread-and-butter issues deflects our attention from the much more disruptive prospect that how we define ourselves as peoples is far less stable than the clean-break optimists assume. Indeed, my reasons for not exploring the clean-break scenario are to be found in the serious instabilities that I expect to emerge should the independence of Quebec appear to be a certainty. Further, the deletion of the hard issues does not weaken my argument, for their inclusion would add to the post-independence strains, which from the community/identity perspective that I examine are already at the breaking point. The possibility of serious conflict, particularly between Quebec and some of the Aboriginal nations, cannot be discounted.

## The Tenacity of the Status Quo

When assessing the future of an historic constitutional order such as Canada's, a realist would probably assert that the future will repeat the past. Previous challenges to our territorial and constitutional integrity have been defeated or have faded away, from the threatened secession of Nova Scotia in the 1880s to the Quebec referendum of 1980, a century later.

The status quo has immense advantages, in spite of the reiterated assertions that it is dead[9] or that something "snapped" in Quebec after the failure of Meech Lake.[10] The status quo exists. Inertia, the comfort of the known (even if imperfect), the many interests that attach themselves to any ongoing regime, and the fact that most Québécois retain a residual affection for and identification with Canada support continuity over disruptive change.

The survival of the status quo does not mean immobility, but simply the continuation of the incremental changes that are characteristic of a living constitution. In our first century and a quarter this pattern of adaptive change was of immensely greater significance than formal amendment in generating flexibility and sensitivity to new conditions. The constitutional theory of the thirties, which viewed Canadians as imprisoned in a rigid constitutional arrangement that inhibited the implementation of needed policies, was rejected after World War Two by politicians who learned to work the system by intergovernmental agreements, various imaginative expedients, and the adroit use of the federal spending power. This "working the system" approach is what Chrétien, Daniel Johnson, and other advocates of pragmatic flexibility and staying away from the constitutional lever have in mind.

It is true that a modern version of this degree and pace of change will not satisfy those Quebec nationalists who long for a new country, who say with Lucien Bouchard, "*nous sommes une nation à la recherche d'un État.*"[11] It is also true that the impediments to an extensive constitutionalized special jurisdictional status for Quebec within federalism increase the relative attraction of the complete break of independence. The achievement of the latter, however, remains a formidable task. The fact that formally renewed federalism is difficult to achieve does not mean that Quebec independence will be easily attained and implemented. The move to independence is uncharted. There are no constitutional provisions that provide for the breakup of Canada. Further, the democratization of Canadian (including Quebec) constitutional culture, the precedents of past referenda – 1992 (Charlottetown Accord), 1980 (Quebec), 1948 (Newfoundland) – and the explicit undertakings of the Parti Québécois require the referendum approval of the Quebec electorate before independence machinery can be set in motion. That electorate is less enamoured of independence than is the *indépendantiste* elite. Hence, a "yes" referendum vote will not be easily achieved. Further, as elaborated below, there are inherent ambiguities both inside and outside of Quebec concerning the appropriate extent and composition of a "yes" vote before its legitimacy will be considered unquestionable. In the competition between the constitutional status quo and the alternative of an independent Quebec, the victory of the latter will require Herculean efforts successfully carried out against massive opposition that will have the support of inertia. In the other competition between the constitutional status quo and fundamental constitutional reform within federalism, the basic support for the former comes from the difficulty of departing from it and from the *de facto* flexibility that is compatible with formal stability.

Canadians have tried for a third of a century to find constitutional answers within federalism to perceived shortcomings in their civic living arrangements. Now, in a remarkable *volte face*, it is widely accepted that a federalist constitutional answer is unavailable. Hirschman's theory of why peoples oscillate between passionate commitment to public goals and a retreat to private goals provides one explanation.[12] Simply stated, the heady involvement in the public arena of constitutional politics has been a disillusioning experience for many, bringing more heartache than satisfying successes. Cultivating one's garden appears increasingly attractive in the aftermath of such public misadventures. The same phenomenon of constitutional exhaustion previously occurred in Quebec after the referendum loss of 1980 and the subsequent implementation of the 1982 Constitution Act against the opposition of the Quebec government. Remarkably, and confirming the recurring presence of boredom and constitutional fatigue, the election campaign that produced a Parti Québécois government in September, 1994, generated minimal passion or nationalist enthusiasm.[13] At the moment (October, 1994), we are in the paradoxical situation that even those who are in the *indépendantiste* camp pursue their goal with minimal zest.

The view that major, formal constitutional change directed to the revision of federalism to accommodate Quebec is not an available option is now almost a conventional wisdom. Bouchard, Claude Castonguay, Chrétien, Claude Ryan, Parizeau, Roy Romanow, and a host of academics and other constitutional observers are in broad agreement that we either stick with what we have or we move to a complete rupture between Quebec and the ROC.[14] In B.C. Premier Michael Harcourt's blunt formulation, "you're in or you're out."[15] Further, although this may be challenged when the Report of the Royal Commission on Aboriginal Peoples appears, the present federal government's Aboriginal policy also appears to be a step-by-step incrementalism,[16] and thus a retreat from the constitutional approach of recent years. Surrounded by the debris of recent constitutional failures, the political class has largely come to agree with Stefan Dupré and Paul Weiler[17] that reaching for the constitutional lever should be the last resort of those seeking to keep the constitution in tune with the times.

The sources of this pessimism about the possibilities of what Peter Russell calls mega-constitutional change[18] are not obscure. Three decades of constitutional introspection and proposals – including three major efforts, the post-1980 Quebec referendum process leading to the 1982 Constitution Act, Meech Lake (1987-90), and the Charlottetown Accord (1992) – have contributed to the divisions they were intended to heal. Memories of failure, of humiliation, of betrayal, and of hopes dashed are widespread among many who look back. The one major success, the 1982 Constitution Act, was deeply flawed by the Quebec government's repudiation of its contents and the process that generated it.

Further, both the law and the ideological spillover of the 1982 Constitution Act erect barriers to formal change. The provincialist amending formula in the 1982 Act has turned out to be an instrument of conservatism when mega-constitutional change is pursued. The Charter and Aboriginal constitutional clauses have generated a host of new constitutional stakeholders clamouring for a role in the revision of a constitution that now speaks directly to them. Their inclusion multiplies and diversifies the interests to be conciliated, thus reducing the possibility of getting agreement. More generally, the Charter fosters a diffuse participatory constitutional culture that contributed to the decision to hold a referendum on the 1992 Charlottetown Accord package. The results indicated that we have not worked out a theory and practice of constitutional reform that effectively blends the interests of citizens and governments.

The post-1982 constitutional culture outside of Quebec erects additional barriers to the accommodation of Quebec within a renewed federalism. The equality of the provinces doctrine has attained the status of a constitutional dogma,[19] thus inhibiting overt moves to special status for Quebec or, in contemporary parlance, asymmetrical status. To Lucien Bouchard, the doctrine is "*la répudiation de toute l'histoire du Québec et de ses aspirations.*"[20] The Charter fosters the belief that a right is a right regardless of provincial context, and more generally supports a conception of a uniform citizenship that is logically hostile to any markedly distinct status the people of Quebec would have under a Quebec government wielding powers unavailable to other provincial governments. To Reform Party leader Preston Manning, the principles of equality of provinces and of all citizens are fundamental.[21] To Lucien Bouchard, these two equalities erect insuperable barriers in the way of any recognition of Quebec as a distinct society.[22] Hence, the realism in the message of Robert Sheppard of the *Globe and Mail*: "There is no constitutional solution to the problems of Quebec and Canada. We have wasted 25 years on that course and it has got us only deeper into the muck."[23]

If there were no imaginable alternative to a federalism specifically reformed by new constitutional texts to accommodate Quebec, the above analysis might be accepted as conclusive, and our constitutional politics would drift toward quiescence. The possibility of independence, however, encourages its advocates to see the rigidities of federalism as strengthening the logic of their choice, which, it is thought, can be attained outside of the procedural impediments of the constitution's amending formula.

## Escape to a Simpler World

Living with difference is stimulating and frustrating, the relative significance of which is an indicator of the appropriateness of constitutional arrangements. For multinational, heterogeneous polities, the purpose of such arrangements is to diminish frustration either by providing protective, self-governing enclaves where minorities can be themselves or by providing a shield of rights to protect scattered minorities against majoritarian insensitivity, or by both. Such arrangements necessarily limit the autonomy of the majority community by reducing the powers it can exercise. When concentrated minority national communities, chafing against restrictions on their capacity to shape their own future, incessantly seek more provincial jurisdiction within a federal system, or the establishment of a third order of Aboriginal governments, they are asking the country wide majority community to diminish its own power. Where complete disentanglement is technically possible because a large minority is spatially concentrated and potentially viable, the majority itself may come to agree that maximally separate constitutional living arrangements (up to separate statehood) are preferable to a fractious togetherness. This process of contagious frustration is now playing itself out with respect to Quebec/ROC relations.

The desires of Aboriginal peoples and ardent Québécois nationalists for the enhanced governing capacities associated respectively with the inherent right to self-government and with the independence option are reactions against minority status. They are based on a wish to minimize or gain more control over an interdependence seen as threatening, and thus to increase Aboriginal and Québécois capacity to resist or manage exogenous pressures. The guiding assumption is that a simpler, more manageable world is within reach, whereby Québécois and Aboriginal peoples will have the dignity of complete or partial statehood as their own instrument. The resulting increased powers will enhance their capacities to be more fully themselves and to shape their "distinct society" (Quebec) or "to determine and control their development as peoples according to their own values and priorities and ensure the integrity of their societies."[24]

According to the Parti Québécois, escape from the paralysis of contemporary stalemated federalism would also be liberating for the ROC, viewed as a national people, straining like Francophone Quebec for an enhanced freedom of manoeuvre. The rhetoric of Bouchard and Parizeau returns again and again to that eagerly sought future of greater freedom when Quebec will be a "normal" society, and Québécois a "normal" people living in a "normal" country that "belongs to us."[25] Further, according to Bouchard, the federalist practice of sending Quebec MPs to Ottawa, at least prior to the Bloc, distorted and concealed Quebec's "true reality from English-speaking Canadians."[26] This particular aversion to the ambiguities of federalism shades into the pervasive *indépendantiste* thesis that the federal citizen with her divided allegiances and divided civic identities has an unhealthy, fractured personality. Such a person, tugged in contradictory directions, is the psychic counterpart of an unhealthy body immobilized by physical ailments. Federalism, it is argued, inhibits the flourishing of the healthy, single-dimensional identity Québécois could enjoy as citizens of an independent state.

While much Aboriginal rhetoric shares the Quebec *indépendantiste* aversion to divided civic identities, the lack of viability for nearly all Aboriginal nations limits the possible degree of escape from a shared constitutional co-existence with non-Aboriginal Canadians. Nevertheless, many status Indians do not consider themselves Canadian citizens.[27] Many have a strong antipathy to provincial involvement in their affairs, which they see as a threat to their special link with the federal government and the unique constitutional status it provides. Both minority nationalisms, Québécois and Aboriginal, seek escape to a simpler (the PQ would say "normal") state of affairs in which the formal power of other governments over their lives is either greatly reduced or eliminated, at least in a *de jure* sense.

In the interim, the advocates of nationalisms directed to more autonomous futures try to weaken the impact of rival identities on their people. Thus, in the recent Charlottetown constitutional round, Aboriginal organizations and the

Bourassa government both insisted on bargaining nation-to-nation with the federal government. This implicitly denied the Canadian component of those they spoke for and thus repudiated a role for the federal government in representing it.

The most striking example of a successful effort by Quebec nationalists to delegitimize the Canadian component of the composite Canadian/Quebec identity occurred in the 1980 Quebec referendum and no doubt will be repeated in the coming referendum.[28] Past and future Quebec referenda ask Quebec residents to choose their constitutional future in their provincial capacity as Québécois after a campaign dominated by provincial politicians. To redefine the context as one in which Canadians living in Quebec might be asked in a federal government-administered referendum to choose their constitutional future following a campaign dominated by Canadian federal politicians, a campaign in which provincial politicians both play a minimal role and are viewed as intruders, would be considered outrageous by Quebec nationalists. According to Guy Laforest, the Laval political scientist, "A referendum run by the federal government in Quebec [would be] . . . an illegitimate act, and I for one suggest it would bring massive civil disobedience."[29]

In startling contrast, a provincial campaign leading up to a provincial referendum on the question of whether the federal dimension should be extinguished appears as normality itself. While the admittedly incomplete exclusion of outsiders from Quebec constitutional debates is frequently noted and is now almost taken for granted, the fact that it marginalizes and distorts the Canadian dimension of the debate is often overlooked. The exclusion presupposes that Québécois do not share a community of constitutional discussion with Canadians elsewhere.

The contemporary assumption that the federalist/Canadian identity and option in the coming Quebec referendum should be presented by provincial politicians underlines the provincialization of the federal/Canadian side of the dual identity of Québécois. The Bloc's monopolization of Quebec's federal representation in the Commons goes even further by transforming the fifty-four Quebec MPs in the loyal opposition into delegates of the Quebec nation whose task is not to represent the Canadian dimension of Québécois in the federal House of Commons but to completely displace it. These developments confirm Lysiane Gagnon's observation that Quebec's political language focuses almost exclusively on Quebec and views Canada as a separate, distinct entity.[30]

While non-Aboriginal Canadians outside of Quebec find the ambiguities of federalism more tolerable than do Québécois, the frustrations of living in a constitutionally fractious, heterogeneous society are undoubtedly experienced by many as burdensome. This fosters a nostalgia for a vanished past when their sleep was not disturbed by unending threats to break up the country. It contributes to a growing acceptance of the René Lévesque thesis that a desirable simplification might come from the disentanglement of (rest of) Canada and Quebec that would accompany Quebec independence. Compared to the lead-up to the 1980 Quebec referendum, when talk of Canada without Quebec was a taboo subject, the literature on *Thinking English Canada*,[31] as one example, is now respectable in quantity, if often polemical in quality.[32] These books and articles are the early building blocks, the beginnings of an intellectual infrastructure designed to give a constitutionally shapeless people a better sense of itself.

An additional elusive psychological factor lies behind the only partially formed desire of Canadians outside of Quebec to be on their own, a feeling so obvious that its existence is often overlooked. The recurring frustration of being a bystander while Québécois decide to go or stay offends the idea of what a country is. For Canadians in the other provinces and territories to be told that their citizenship should be put on hold while others decide if their country is to continue generates an unwelcome sense of powerlessness. To be relegated to the audience while Québécois introspectively decide Canada's as well as Quebec's future inevitably induces the ROC to begin thinking of a future that excludes Quebec.[33]

The aspirations of Aboriginal peoples, Québécois, and non-Aboriginal Canadians outside of Quebec to increase their constitutional distance from each other are mutually reinforcing. The ROC's growing self-consciousness is a by-product of Quebec's threatened exit. That same possible exit strengthens the sense of distinct nationhood among Quebec Aboriginal nations to the extent that the territorial integrity of a seceding Quebec can no longer be assumed. The possibility that the pan-Canadian responsibilities of the federal government might be shattered by Quebec's departure encourages provincial governments other than Quebec to examine alternative ROC futures from a provincial perspective. Centrifugal trends are in the saddle, feeding on each other, driven in the first instance by the search for a simpler, more manageable world, and for later entrants in the reconstitution game by imitation, fear, and necessity.

The desire to reduce complexity and reinforce certainty is just as understandable and even praiseworthy in constitutional matters as in life. However, the cumulative effect of the galloping centrifugalisms already visible threatens to increase complexity and reduce certainty. The lessons from our recent constitutional past suggest without confirming that the constitutional route to a better world seldom takes us to where we would like to go.

## Lessons from Our Recent Constitutional History:
## Toward a More Complex Constitutional World

Our encounters with the constitution are far more likely to add complexity than simplicity to our lives. Our attempts to employ the constitution as the lever to sort out our difficulties of living together have steadily enlarged the constitutional reform agenda and increased the number of constitutional actors deemed to have a right to influence constitutional outcomes. A simple illustrative listing underlines the dynamic process at work:

(1) *From a limited to an unmanageable constitutional agenda.* In the early 1960s, the formal constitutional agenda was restricted to the search for an amending formula, with patriation as a by-product. By the eighties and nineties, the agenda included, variously but not exhaustively, the amending formula, a Charter, Aboriginal rights, institutional (especially Senate) reform, the division of powers, and a symbolic preamble.

(2) *From government control to citizen participation.* In the 1960s, formal amendment of the constitution was assumed to be an affair of governments. Now, extensive and influential public participation in constitutional hearings has become the norm. For major changes, referenda are now probably unavoidable.

(3) *From the attempt to eliminate Indian status to enhanced status for all Aboriginal peoples.* In 1969, the Trudeau government sought to end differential Indian status and thus the substantive significance of s. 91(24) of the BNA Act, which it saw as an apartheid-like impediment to Indian advancement. That effort failed, and the constitutional category "Indians" (subsuming Inuit) has been expanded to "Aboriginal peoples," including Métis. The word "nation" is now commonly applied to Aboriginal peoples, and their separate, possibly constitutionally based, future civic existence is taken for granted. Further, indigenous peoples, once considered constitutional outsiders or bystanders, participated almost as the equals of governments in the bargaining that led to the Charlottetown Accord.

(4) *From two nations to multinationalism.* The two nations view of Canada, stimulated by the Royal Commission on Bilingualism and Biculturalism, is now challenged, if not displaced, by a multinational interpretation of Canada, as the nationhood of Aboriginal peoples is widely accepted. We do not know how to reconcile newer multinational views of who we are with the federalist vision of Canada as a country of ten provinces and two territories, capped with a central government.

(5) *From unhyphenated to hyphenated Canadians.* The 1960 Diefenbaker Bill of Rights, reflecting the Prime Minister's preference for unhyphenated Canadians, made no mention of our multicultural population (or of Aboriginal

peoples). Now multiculturalism and hyphenated Canadians are official state policies, sustained by legislation, by state funding, and by constitutional recognition.

(6) *From a Quebec round to a provincial round to everybody's round.* In the Meech Lake "Quebec round," the equality of the provinces principle led to a constitutional package in which, distinct society excepted, everything that Quebec gained had also to be granted to all the other provinces. This provincial package was then attacked by non-governmental groups too numerous to mention for overlooking their constitutional concerns. The next Charlottetown Accord round was marketed as the Canada round, a label that indicated the attempt of the constitution-makers to include everyone in a comprehensive package of constitutional reform. This was especially evident in the preamble.

(7) *From a parsimonious preamble to a smorgasbord.* Proposals to modify the original spartan preamble to the 1867 BNA Act, of which the most salient phrase was "a Constitution similar in Principle to that of the United Kingdom," have become progressively more ambitious and comprehensive, culminating in the interpretive clause of the Charlottetown Accord. Its Canada clause was a singularly unpoetic listing of a cluster of "fundamental characteristics" of Canada ranging from constitutional principles to rights and institutions of government, to various equalities (racial and ethnic, male and female, and of the provinces), and to particular ethnocultural and linguistic rights and attributes of Aboriginal peoples, Quebec, and official-language minority communities. The search for a comprehensive definition of Canada's "fundamental characteristics" produced a grab bag of unrelated particulars – a snapshot of a moving target that would have been different five years earlier and a few years later.

The momentum of three decades has consistently moved Canadians toward a more complex, less manageable constitutional politics. The 1982 Constitution Act, our only major success, albeit rejected by the Quebec government, was only possible because the absence of a domestic amending formula gave the Trudeau government the leverage to threaten a unilateral request to Westminster for a package of formal amendments. Apart from that 1982 achievement, our record is bleak. We have greatly enlarged the constitutional agenda, increased the number of constitutional actors and hence of vetos in law or practice, reduced constitutional flexibility by distributing rights to all Canadians, added to the number of nations within Canada, stimulated ethnocultural particularisms, and defined our fundamental characteristics as a fragmented hodgepodge.

The cumulative consequence of our almost obsessive devotion to constitutional reform as the instrument of our salvation has been to stimulate and multiply our diversities and virtually paralyse our ability to achieve major constitutional change by means of the formal amending process. Who and where we now are is the result of a constitutional juggernaut we can neither control nor stop, which transforms us without taking us to our constitutional destinations. We have learned, perhaps too late, that there are limits to what the constitution can do for us, and that some constitutional issues are better left in darkness than subjected to partisan controversy that never attains closure.

Conceivably, the crisis of Quebec's departure would transform constitutional behaviour in the ROC. Self-seeking partisanship might be displaced by a concern for the whole. That result, however, presupposes a common objective capable of eliciting the sacrifice of particularistic interests. It falsely assumes that the momentum behind our recent constitutional evolution is shallow and can be fruitfully redirected. A more plausible prediction is the continued dominance of centrifugal forces.

## Implicit Constitutional Change

These dramatic developments in our constitutional culture did not occur because we had decided to proceed as if the constitution were a blank slate on which we could write our own desires. Indeed, Quebec *indépendantistes* apart, the governing classes believed that by confining change to the margins they were servants of constitutional continuity. Further, with the major exception of the 1982 Constitution Act, the opening up of the constitution has left the written text virtually unscathed. It is, however, shortsighted to assume that the only kind of constitutional change that exists, or matters, is explicit change by formal amendment. We need to think as well of implicit or indirect constitutional change that may not have been sought by the would-be elite engineers of our future, but that occurs as a by-product of the socialization process that a democratic people experiences when prolonged bouts of participatory constitutional introspection occur. The "lessons" of our recent past resulted from the practical seminar on constitutional politics Canadians have lived through. Some of those lessons, or new definitions, that have entered into our constitutional consciousness are properly to be regarded as constitutional changes. This developing constitutional public opinion, as it may be called, lacks the enforceability of the written text and the degree of acceptance of historic constitutional traditions. Nevertheless, in spite of its inchoate nature, its existence underlines what we know, and too often forget – that constitutions exist in the evolving mentalities of peoples, as well as in formal constitutional documents. Selective illustrations of these emergent constitutional understandings indicate the extent of *de facto* constitutional change that escapes codification in written documents.

• Representation in legislative bodies, on courts, in the bureaucracy, among the appointed personnel of various agencies, and among those who bargain constitutional change should more accurately reflect the variegated composition of the Canadian people than has historically been the case. This reformulated understanding of representation responds to the emergence of identity politics and its accompaniment, the thesis that membership in a social category, if not a prerequisite to understanding and empathizing with the sensitivities of its members, is at least a powerful asset. At the extreme, the absence of such membership leads to accusations of appropriation of voice, the denial that an "A" has the capacity to, and should be allowed to, represent/speak for a "B." This set of beliefs is more of an emotional-intellectual tendency that assaulted the status quo than a newly triumphant constitutional paradigm of representation that has carried the day. While its full-fledged acceptance would have paralysing consequences, tending to a destructive solipsism that would make representation impossible, it has, in milder versions, transformed how we think of the composition of all political institutions with a representative component. Its theoretical constitutional significance is simply that it addresses the fundamental citizen-state dimension of our existence. Empirically, the assumptions of the new understanding led to the devastating critique of the eleven white able-bodied males at the pinnacle of the Meech Lake executive federalism process.

• Whether Quebec remains in or leaves Canada is a decision for the Quebec people to make, subject to various conditions about the fairness of the question and the uncertainty about the legalities that would bring independence about. Force will not be used to keep an unwilling Quebec in a country that an acceptable Québécois majority wishes to leave. This democratic assumption of respect for Quebec's popular will was strongly supported by the Pepin-Robarts Task Force Report on Canadian Unity in 1979.[34] The subsequent participation of Trudeau and other federal ministers in the 1980 referendum campaign established an "unwritten convention . . . that separation was a valid objective . . . that separatist efforts are completely legitimate."[35]

• Adherence to the principle of "yes" to democratic self-determination and "no" to the use of force to prevent it is easy as long as independence is visualized in terms of a surgical excision undertaken as a single act. However, as our thinking about independence has evolved, the principle is seen to encounter practical obstacles. Independence is now seen not as a single act but as a sequence of acts extending over time, most of which relate to the distribution of advantages and disadvantages between Quebec and the successor state(s) of the ROC – debt, deficit, all the economic concerns, etc. The recognition now that there is more than one nation in Quebec – which was overlooked in 1980 – and the virtual certainty of opposition from most of Quebec's Native peoples mean that both the boundaries of the Quebec nation, who is of it and who is not, and of Quebec territory are now contested. That the resultant disagreements might lead to conflicts and the use of force can no longer be cavalierly dismissed. Further, as Stanley Hartt observed, even if the relevant actors outside of Quebec agree that Quebec has a right to secede after a democratic consultation of the Quebec electorate, the parting could still be hostile – "an amicable parting could easily break down in anger and aggression if negotiations on terms and means failed."[36] As long as the issue of independence cannot be entirely separated from the related issue of the terms that will accompany it, the response to the cluster of independence issues cannot be resolved by adherence to an abstract principle.[37] This is a constitutional policy area where first thoughts are re-examined as sober second thoughts are voiced.

• Major constitutional change dealing with the essentials of our existence must be legitimated by appropriate referendum support. The resulting relative displacement of governing elites in constitutional reform repudiates elite constitutional theory and practice taken for granted only a few years ago. An enhanced status for citizenship is the other face of the diminished status of elites.[38]

• Aboriginal peoples have a particular status in the politics of constitutional reform that takes them out of the category of ordinary Canadians. This was evident in Elijah Harper's role in the defeat of the Meech Lake Accord, in the participation of the leaders of Aboriginal organizations in the enhanced executive federalism process that led to the Charlottetown Accord, in the implicit assumption that even if the Charlottetown Accord had passed, the application of its Aboriginal provisions required the separate support of Aboriginal voters, and in the developing belief that Aboriginal peoples in Quebec are not automatically bound by a majority Québécois decision to leave Canada if they wish to remain part of Canada.

• Conceptually, Canada is to be thought of as a multinational as well as a federal community, the practical implications of which have not been worked out. This is a response to the emergence of Aboriginal nationalisms and the escalating constitutional ambitions of Québécois.

• The preceding point may be rephrased in terms of community and identity. In the last quarter-century, Canadians have been refashioning themselves into new peoples. The self-conceptions of Québécois and Aboriginal peoples have been transformed in recent decades. All Québécois (itself a new label) now live in two constitutional worlds, that of the status quo they may cherish or deplore and that of a post-Canada world of independence sought by many and opposed by many, but understood as a possibility by all. Aboriginal peoples have also changed the labels for their self-description – with "nation" being the preferred rubric – have articulated constitutional ambitions that would have been unthinkable only a few decades ago, and have thus transformed their orientation to the constitutional order to an extent that has achieved only limited recognition in written constitutional texts. They also live in two constitutional worlds, an historic status quo from which escape is sought and imagined futures in which they will have more control of their destinies.

In halcyon constitutional times, we overlook the futuristic components of individual and community identity because they appear as simple continuations or repetitions of past identities. Such confident, unreflective views of the future held by citizens are sustained by inertia and presuppose a stable present. At such times, the question, "To what community of tomorrow will we owe allegiance?" does not have to be asked. However, when stability is absent and continuity is threatened, exploring alternative futures is a psychological necessity.

The constitutional ambitions of Québécois *indépendantistes* and of Aboriginal nationalists, particularly the former, have inevitably induced other Canadians to visualize their own discontinuous futures. These reactive anticipatory communities in the ROC are responses to the recognized fragility of the present constitutional order. They lie behind the noticeable hardening of opinion outside Quebec to compromising with or making concessions to Quebec, even if such a hard-line posture leads to Quebec's separation.[39]

These formulations of what the ROC might become are constitutional in the elementary sense that they are preparations at the level of identity for constitutional arrangements often only dimly perceived. Their existence simultaneously reveals the contingent nature of the existing constitutional order and psychological preparation for membership in communities yet to be born – as citizens of the ROC, of an independent British Columbia, or of an Atlantic Canada cut adrift.

The evolution of our identities, the two constitutional worlds in which most of us live, and, among other things, the evolving understanding of how we will respond to such contingencies as a "yes" Quebec referendum vote join the written text as the available constitutional materials with which we approach the future. The radicalism and extent of this implicit constitutional change, which occurred while Canada remained formally still intact, anticipate the much greater crumbling of historic understandings and practices that may be expected if Canada does not survive as a single country. Quebec's departure would shatter our existing definition as a people and would trigger the examination of hitherto uncanvassed futures. If the "no" forces triumph in the referendum, the analysis that follows will still be of utility, for then the following speculations will serve the indirect purpose of underlining the stabilizing capacity of the existing constitutional order to constrain the centrifugal forces that would be unleashed by overt constitutional breakdown. Our understanding of peace is greatly sharpened by the experience of war. Our appreciation of constitutional stability will be likewise greatly enhanced by exploring the scenario of constitutional breakdown.

## After a Referendum "Yes"

A Quebec referendum "yes" vote will precipitate a significant rearrangement of the relations among the peoples, nations, and governments north of the United States. A particular constitutional accommodation more than a century old between the two European founding peoples will end. A particular federal experiment that began with four provinces and ended with ten, plus two northern territories – soon to have become three – will also be left to the historians. While "accommodation" cannot be used to describe the historical position and treatment of Aboriginal peoples, kept in the constitutional shadows until recent decades, their world, too, will be transformed in unpredictable ways.

The likely consequence of a constitutional collapse can be best anticipated by understanding where we have come from. The togetherness of the pre-referendum Canadian community is a constitutional creation. We have never been a "natural" people, a homogeneous ethnic people united by common descent and sharing a common history. We have been held together by constitutional arrangements, and up until the Charter the most we could hope for was to be a political nationality, alongside which our federal and other evolving diversities flourished. To put it differently, our constitutional clothing was not designed to fit a pre-existing "we" but rather to foster a limited "we" out of the diversities huddled north of the United States. Recently, as previous chapters have emphasized, centrifugal tendencies in both polity and society, although somewhat mitigated by the Charter, have been strengthened.

If Quebec nationalism breaks the constitutional container that mutes our particularisms, the major constraint on the always present centrifugal threats to our limited togetherness will be gone. How we, inside or outside Quebec, put ourselves together after Quebec independence will not be inherent in our condition at that time; rather, as in the mid-nineteenth century, as we regrouped in the process that led to Confederation, it will result from the play of political forces and the creativity of elites.

The first question to be addressed in a disintegrating Canada will be, "In what constitutionally recognized communities will we live out our future lives?" The obvious candidates clamouring for our attention will be the provincial communities, the two northern territories, the former province (now state) of Quebec, the Aboriginal communities in the provinces and northern territories and in Quebec, especially those with a land base, and the overarching transcending community of the rest of Canada. In the following pages, I will focus on the rest of Canada, Quebec, and Aboriginal peoples.

### THE REST OF CANADA

Quebec's departure will be seriously destabilizing for a residual Canada seeking to redefine itself in the turmoil following the dismemberment of the central government and the Canadian people. Many of the constitutional practices and public policies long accepted as part of what it means to be a Canadian rest on momentum – the end product of more than a century of nation-building bargains. They developed incrementally as adjustments to an evolving package that presupposed and was aimed at the continued existence of Canada.

A profusion of citizenship and identity issues will require resolution. The constitutional and policy significance of the diversities and cleavages within the ROC – provincial, social, linguistic, and national – will be reconsidered when the ROC no longer shares a country with Quebec. Federal policies over the past thirty years have been extraordinarily sensitive to the threat to Canadian unity posed by Quebec nationalism. A steady stream of policies directed to keeping Quebec in Canada and to fostering Canadian unity has issued from successive federal governments. Official language policy, the future status of the Francophone and Acadian minorities, now a much smaller percentage of the total ROC population, the willingness of Canada west of Quebec to continue the financial support for Atlantic Canada at a time of grave fiscal crisis, and the future of multiculturalism will all be re-examined in a Canada without Quebec. The constitutional position of the Aboriginal peoples, the lingering United Kingdom connection via the Crown, and the meaning of citizenship in one or more successor countries outside Quebec will be re-evaluated.

These constitutional, cultural, social, and policy redefinitions will be worked out in a context of centrifugal pressures as provincial governments will, in organizational terms, emerge relatively unscathed from Quebec's departure. The provinces and the territories will have the advantage of possessing governments and populations habituated to living together. Governments outside of Quebec will come to the constitution-making table speaking for peoples that already exist, and their leaders will speak with the authority derived from the possession of traditional office. They will be the component parts of the emergent but still amorphous (rest of) Canada entity whose future they will shape. The governments and peoples of the provinces and territories are likely to have a stronger sense of themselves than will the inchoate federal centre retreating to the residual ROC community, on whose behalf it formerly would not and could not speak. Provincial premiers will have already begun to position their people for a Canada without Quebec before the referendum votes are counted. The dominating presence of provincial voices in the ROC following a Quebec referendum "yes" will be strengthened by the weakening of economic linkages between the provinces. The common Canadian interests based on east-west trade, and formerly sustained by the now defunct National Policy, have been eroded by north-south and transpacific linkages. The weakening of the national basis of the Canadian economy has been accompanied by increased provincial autonomy in economic policy-making. Simultaneously, and closely connected, the willingness of the have provinces to see Canada as a regionally redistributive community of sharers is already eroding.[40] According to Premier Harcourt of British Columbia, Quebec's departure would lead to "an end to equalization payments to poorer provinces from the wealthier partners in the Confederation."[41] Quebec's departure will strengthen balkanizing tendencies that already have considerable momentum.

At the time of breakup, the government in Ottawa will probably look less like the confident government of a new people, albeit in a shrunken Canada, than like a battered survivor that has lost its traditional role and has not been restructured to assume its new one. The sorry condition of the federal government – bereft of one-quarter of its population, humiliated and wounded by the departure of Quebec, deprived of its *raison d'être* as an instrument of Canadian unity transcending and accommodating French-English and Quebec-Canada differences, and with the remnants of the Canadian party system in probable disarray – will greatly weaken its capacity to exercise leadership. Federal government weakness will be exacerbated by the unacceptably dominant position of Ontario, with over two-fifths of the seats in the House of Commons the day after Quebec's departure. This political, psychological, and structural weakness will undermine the role of the central government in bargaining with Quebec and in the reconstruction of residual Canada. In sum, the ROC will enter the Canada-without-Quebec debate with centrifugal forces ascendant.

The post-breakup strength of provincialism will be based not only on the fact that provincial governments will be intact while the federal government will be on the ropes following Quebec's departure, but on the additional consideration that both the governmental and community focal points for a sense of Canadianism will be gone. Their replacement in the service of rest-of-Canadianism will take time. A demoralized Ottawa will not be a strong political centre with a capacity to focus allegiance, and the uninterrupted coast-to-coast community of belonging will no longer exist – indeed, will have a huge gaping emptiness in its midst, an image with a weak capacity to stimulate citizen identification. The post-breakup transitional environment will offer far more support to a provincial than to a rest-of-Canada sense of belonging and identity. These centrifugal tendencies will be only marginally constrained by the weak voices of the premiers of Atlantic Canada, governing provinces physically separated from Ontario and fearful that their financial lifeline from Ottawa will not survive. While a self-interested provincialism will not lead to a new state for each old province, as various interprovincial allegiances will emerge, it is unlikely to lead to a strong centre and may not produce a united ROC.[42]

From the Parti Québécois perspective, Quebec's departure will free a second nation, English Canada, from a constitutional marriage that muffled its identity and inhibited its mature self-expression. On the contrary, the reality will be one of profound ambiguity and uncertainty. The constitutional situation will be without precedent, and hence without agreed-on rules on how to proceed. The intergovernmental bargaining with Quebec that will have to take place to settle the terms of breakup will be frustrated by disagreement on who the relevant ROC participants in the process should be and what weights should be assigned to their roles. It cannot be assumed that the shrunken federal government and the nine remaining provincial and two territorial governments can simply treat each other and the surviving rules for constitutional amendment as if nothing has happened to their legitimacy – as if the absence of Quebec was the absence of a marginal player leaving the old order in perfect working order. The reverse will be the case – the survival and shape of a Canada outside Quebec will immediately become a question mark. Its capacity to bargain with Quebec will be severely impaired. Further, since the rest of Canada will be rearranging its own future at the same time as negotiations with Quebec are under way, it will be impossible to exclude the citizenry from a process aimed at the creation of new states and nations.

The crucial variable here, which could weaken provincialist tendencies in the reconstruction period, is the influence of public opinion, how it is mobilized, and what arenas are available for its expression. Some versions of a constituent assembly with a membership that expressed more than provincial cleavages would increase the chances for the survival of a strong centre and a united Canada-without-Quebec. How, if, and by whom such a body could be established, however, are so much the products of particular circumstances that advance speculation can have only entertainment value.

## QUEBEC

Unless the federal government, the "no" forces in Quebec, and the rest of Canada misplay their hands catastrophically in the lead-up to the Quebec referendum, the best the "yes" forces can hope for is a narrow majority. While this will give a minimum legitimacy to the independence option, it will nevertheless be a precarious beginning for a new state. Lucien Bouchard admitted that a narrow referendum victory could put "the political solidarity of Quebecers in question" and challenge Quebec's "political cohesion."[43]

The acquiescence of losing minorities in the narrow victories of their opponents normally assumes that both majority and minority agree on the basis of the ongoing system, that together they constitute a people, and that the former will not irrevocably change the basic conditions of existence of the latter. When that happens, as in a completed move to independence, the losers lack the consolation of knowing that should they win the next election they can reverse the consequences of the referendum vote. By that time, they will be living in a new country.

The permanent nature of formal constitutional change usually requires extraordinary majorities. Within federal systems, the requirements normally include the support of the central government and a majority of the governments of the state units, or if referenda are employed, both national and regional majorities of the voters are required. Federalism necessarily imposes limits on majoritarianism.

The constitutional logic that suggests that a federally organized people cannot proceed by simple majority on fundamental constitutional issues has a functionally equivalent applicability to a nationally, culturally, and linguistically heterogeneous society such as Quebec. No fanciful interpretation of the facts is required to state that Quebec is internally a federal society with Anglophone and allophone minorities and eleven Aboriginal nations within its borders. It is also undeniable that the drive for an independent Quebec comes overwhelmingly from the majority Francophone community and that its purpose is to solidify the French language and culture. Not surprisingly, Anglophone, allophone, and Aboriginal peoples in Quebec are overwhelmingly opposed to, and often apprehensive about, an independent Quebec. A May, 1994, poll indicated that 80 per cent of non-Francophones in Quebec rejected independence.[44] That a large majority of Aboriginal Québécois oppose independence is conventional wisdom. Voting intentions before the Quebec provincial election tell the same story, with only 4 per cent of non-Francophones supporting the PQ and 90 per cent supporting the Liberals.[45] The subsequent PQ election victory "was achieved almost solely by 'French Quebec,' with the anglos and 'the others' . . . tending to stay with the Liberals."[46]

Given the divisions in the Quebec electorate, the magnitude of the constitutional issue to be addressed in a referendum, and the clustering of the minorities on the "no" side, the legitimacy of a bare majority will be challenged by some of the losers and by Canadians outside of Quebec. Accordingly, the likelihood of contested interpretations of the meaning of a slim "yes" victory is very high. Amazingly, only one in five Quebecers believes that a bare majority would be adequate to take Quebec out of Canada, with 73 per cent believing a larger majority would be necessary and 36 per cent asserting that two-thirds of the voters or more would be necessary for a "separatist victory."[47] Given the overwhelming Francophone majority of the Quebec population, a bare majority "yes" based almost exclusively on Francophones is achievable. A large majority is extremely unlikely. While a narrow majority may not qualify as a Pyrrhic victory, it almost guarantees that even within Quebec – leaving aside the reaction of the ROC – the post-referendum path to independence will not be harmonious.

The 1980 Quebec referendum was deeply divisive. Even in Newfoundland, with its remarkably homogeneous population, the 1948 referenda left bitter memories and disgruntled losers whose anger took decades to subside. Since the losing "no" forces in Quebec will be disproportionately composed of Canadian citizens with especially strong attachments to the central government and to Canada, the divisions will be deep and bitter. The election of the Parti Québécois in 1976 and the enactment of Bill 101 contributed to a huge increase in the annual net loss of Anglophones from Quebec by interprovincial migration, from an average per year of 12,600 from 1965 to 1976 to the much larger annual net loss averaging 21,300 from 1976 to 1981.[48] A referendum victory would almost certainly precipitate another exodus of Anglophones and, to a lesser extent, allophones. While Aboriginal peoples are much less mobile, many of them will be even more embittered, and some will resist incorporation in an independent Quebec. The most plausible outcome following a referendum victory is of an independent Quebec commencing its new life with a bitterly divided society within its borders, a sizable and serious exodus of non-Francophones, and serious tensions and possible confrontations between some Aboriginal nations and the Quebec government.

The possibility that some 60,000 Aboriginal peoples, about 10 per cent of whom are Inuit, grouped into eleven Aboriginal nations could opt out of a seceding Quebec and take their territory with them appears far-fetched. In 1980, it was assumed that the separation of Quebec with its territory intact would be peacefully achieved and that Aboriginal concerns were an irrelevant sideshow. In the mid-nineties this belief is challenged by two political developments. The first one, and of lesser importance, is the argument that the two major Quebec boundary extensions in 1898 and 1912 were granted to Quebec as a Canadian province and are accordingly severable from Quebec should it cease to be a Canadian province. Clyde Wells, for example, argues that if Quebec has a right to leave Confederation, it "could apply only to the same Quebec that entered Confederation, which is to say a Quebec much smaller than it now is."[49] Chrétien has delicately linked Quebec's territorial integrity with its continued membership in Canada,[50] while Preston Manning has labelled the PQ thesis that Quebec's boundaries are inviolate, but Canada's are not, as "nonsensical."[51] As a stand-alone argument, however, the boundaries-extension challenge to Quebec's territorial integrity would probably have little political weight.[52]

The linkage of the territorial argument with Native issues, especially in northern Quebec but with relevance elsewhere, greatly strengthens the territorial threat to Quebec's boundaries and gives the territorial issue an explosive

salience. The factors that come together to support the linked Native and territorial threat to Quebec leaving with its present boundaries are impressive.[53]

The fundamental factor is the mobilization of Quebec's Aboriginal people
behind the thesis that they, not a Quebec referendum majority, will determine
their own future. According to Rosemary Kuptana, president of the Inuit Tapirisat, the approximately 7,000 Inuit in northern Quebec, who are "a nation," will
decide their own future.[54] The Kahnawake Mohawks are unwilling to go along
with Quebec independence,[55] a position repeated by the Grand Chief of the
Akwesasne Mohawks.[56] The James Bay Cree plan a parallel referendum on their
future when the Quebec referendum is held.[57] Matthew Coon Come, grand
chief of the Quebec Cree, has taken his case to American audiences and stated the
Cree would ignore a Quebec secession vote and "request protection from the
Canadian military."[58] From a broader perspective, the Quebec branch of the
Assembly of First Nations passed a declaration that Native groups, not the Quebec government, would decide what country they will belong to.[59] These
Aboriginal declarations are supported by the federal Minister of Indian Affairs,
Ron Irwin, who promised Quebec Aboriginal peoples that they have a right to
stay with Canada should Quebec separate.[60] The most remarkable support for
the Aboriginal position came from a 54 per cent majority of Quebecers who
stated that Aboriginal peoples should have the right to their own referendum to
determine whether to stay with Quebec or Canada should Quebecers vote "yes."
Outside of Quebec, 81 per cent supported such an Aboriginal referendum.[61]

The Aboriginal position, which may have more support from the English-
speaking Cree and Mohawks than from the Montagnais and other French-
speaking Aboriginal nations, is reinforced by a measure of legal support, most
influentially presented by Daniel Turp, a legal adviser to the Parti Québécois.
According to Turp, the Native nations of Quebec have the same right to self-
determination under international law as the Québécois, including attaining
sovereignty, staying with Quebec, or remaining with Canada if Quebec leaves.
According to Turp, this right can be most justifiably exercised in northern Quebec, "where the Inuit, Cree, and Naskapi peoples, despite their small numbers,
are in the majority on the lands they identify as theirs, [so that] the choice of the
native majority as to the future of the territory could be decisive."[62]

The Aboriginal issue is the most crucial, but not the only, reminder that Quebec, in spite of its overwhelming Francophone majority, is nevertheless a federal
society containing distinct communities, especially the Anglophones and the
Aboriginal peoples. That "otherness" of historically derived identities for these
minority populations lies behind their minimal support for the PQ independence objective, which they see as a straightforward appeal to strengthen the
political power of the Francophone majority. Recognition of the multiple communities in the Quebec population is the source of the surprising number of

partition proposals that have surfaced in recent years.[63] Partition proposals are obvious responses to the heterogeneity of the Quebec population, especially where it is manifest in spatial clustering. The hostility to the idea that a bare majority would be sufficient to move to independence is also based, in considerable part, on the thesis that a simple majority is inadequate for a federal society, although whether that critique leads logically to the need for simultaneous majorities in at least the main Aboriginal and Anglophone communities is an unanswered question. Quebec's Aboriginal nations have given their own answer to the legitimacy question with the decision to conduct their own votes and be guided by their own majorities.

Partition proposals and the challenges to simple majoritarianism are alternative responses to the protection of the rights of the established Anglophone minority and the Aboriginal nations should they be on the losing side of a referendum that would remove them from Canada. The mere appearance of such arguments reveals the potential for tension, and at least isolated civil disorder, should a Quebec move to independence be based on a slim majority following a campaign in which ethno-national appeals are frequent and strident.

### ABORIGINAL PEOPLES

The impact of a "yes" vote on the future of Aboriginal peoples is shrouded in an even greater obscurity. Their numerical weakness and the diversities in their status, identity, and location limit their capacity to control events. Should Canada break up, they will be caught up in convulsions precipitated by others. At about the same time, however, the report of the Royal Commission on Aboriginal Peoples, scheduled to appear in the pre-referendum period, will be an important resource for Aboriginal peoples and the organizations that speak for them. At a minimum, the report will espouse the claims of Aboriginal nations in a vigorous way, underline the socio-economic malaise afflicting many Aboriginal communities, and support a significant degree of positive differential treatment or constitutional affirmative action for the First Nations. This will be a reminder, awkwardly so for Québécois nationalists, that they are not the only national community seeking to gain more control of their future by constitutional recognition, and that there is more than one nation on Quebec territory. At the same time, the presumably far-reaching recommendations of the report will emerge at a remarkably inauspicious time to elicit positive government responses. At the time of writing this essay, months before the report's analysis and proposals are known, it is difficult to go beyond the elementary proposition that the report will be a complicating reminder that the national question in Canada is not restricted to the French/English, Quebec/rest-of-Canada dimension.

The report will take its place alongside recent developments, too numerous to discuss in detail here, that reinforce the belief that Aboriginal peoples are in a distinct category as constitutional actors. They will therefore enter the arena of post-referendum constitutional politics with a symbolic status unavailable to any other non-governmental actors. In the recent Charlottetown Accord referendum, the Assembly of First Nations was successful in having a separate count of the on-reserve vote of status Indians. The clear assumption was that the Aboriginal components of the Accord required explicit Indian voting support before they could be applied to Indian nations. Further, the Consensus Report on the Constitution, which led to the legal text of the Charlottetown Accord, asserted the necessity of "Aboriginal consent to future constitutional amendments that directly refer to the Aboriginal peoples."[64] Although the Accord was not implemented, the intergovernmental agreement that lay behind it clearly suggested that Aboriginal peoples were not to be thought of as only ordinary voters in referendum processes, or that federal and provincial legislatures could ratify constitutional amendments applicable to and opposed by Aboriginal peoples as if their opposition was no different from that of any disgruntled minority. Their constitutional futures cannot legitimately be decided by majorities with whom they disagree. These emergent constitutional norms, even if they have not acquired the sanctity of enforceable written constitutional texts, support claims by Quebec Aboriginals that changes to their constitutional status, such as Quebec independence would involve, require their separate affirmative support.

More generally, in the overall reconstitution scenario that will follow the breakup of Canada, Aboriginal peoples have advantages and disadvantages. Their sense of differentiation, now clothed in the language of nationalism, is strong. Their participation in the closed sessions of the expanded executive federalism process that produced the Charlottetown Accord will support future claims for similar participation in the constitutional politics that shape the rest of Canada's and Quebec's separate constitutional futures. On the other hand, their effective constitutional voice has come from umbrella Aboriginal organizations whose funding comes almost entirely from the federal government. The extent to which this will continue following the departure of Quebec is unclear.

Psychologically, Aboriginal peoples will be profoundly affected if Canada breaks up. This explains Ovide Mercredi's strong support for a united Canada in the interest of Aboriginal peoples and his fear of Quebec's departure. "As difficult as it is right now to get our rights protected within a united country," he asserted, "can you imagine what it's going to be like when you're trying to protect your rights in one country that's forming and another country that's trying to organize?"[65]

Some Quebec Aboriginal peoples are likely to be caught up in a struggle against a government leading them to an independence they reject. Aboriginal peoples outside Quebec, especially those with tribal links to Quebec kin, will be vicariously involved in these Quebec tensions. Non-Quebec Aboriginals will be apprehensive about constitutional developments in the ROC that may frustrate their own constitutional ambitions. Status Indians in particular have long combined a positive identification with the central government with a mixture of suspicion and hostility toward the provinces. If the reconstitution of the ROC weakens the former and strengthens the latter, or leads to the ROC's fragmentation into two or more states, the relations between Aboriginal and non-Aboriginal peoples may seriously deteriorate. Aboriginal peoples in British Columbia, for example, will not happily accept the sundering of their ties with Ottawa and their enclosure within a newly minted independent state of British Columbia. Aboriginal reactions will be especially embittered if their aspirations following a quarter of a century of symbolic advances have to be put on hold one more time.

Aboriginal peoples will possess what they already possess – their disruptive capacity, and the recent acquisition of a supportive public opinion. Most of the Aboriginal peoples with a territorial base will, however, remain weak and impoverished communities with negligible capacity to go it alone if Canada does not survive. For redistributive reasons, they are likely to be one of the strongest defenders of a powerful central government and advocates of a rest of Canada that remains intact. Their voice, however, while influential, will not be decisive.

The prospects are even bleaker for the two-thirds of Aboriginal peoples who do not live on reserves or in a prospective Nunavut. If, as is plausible, the one or more polities that emerge out of the rest of Canada stress a homogeneous citizenship, the pressures to assimilate on Aboriginal peoples lacking a community concentration or a land base will be very powerful.

## Conclusion

To step back from the immediacies of the Canadian constitutional fray is to recognize the enduring reality that the lack of fit between states and nations is close to being the universal human condition. So, too, is the recurring desire of nationalist elites to escape from the ambiguities of identities that are by-products of the state-nation disjuncture, and which are compounded in Canada by federalism. For nationalist elites enamoured of the ideal fit, rarely seen in the modern world, between some future state and some future nation, Canada has more the appearance of an airport than of a country. Literally hundreds of communities, ranging from the Québécois to small Indian villages, proudly wear the label of nation.

What kind of country is it? – with over a million Aboriginal peoples internally divided into Inuit, Métis, and Indian in its midst, with hundreds of additional divisions within the latter category, with two main official language groups whose territorial distribution leaves significant numbers of each existing insecurely in areas where the other is politically dominant, with a rapidly growing and increasingly diverse population outside the founding (French and English and Aboriginal) peoples category, as immigration from non-traditional source countries in Asia, Latin America, the Caribbean, and Africa enlarges the visible minority population. The latter in turn is divided into high-achieving groups and marginalized others with high unemployment, low educational achievement, and poverty. Hostilities in faraway homelands on the Indian subcontinent and in the former Yugoslavia resurface on Canadian soil. In the major metropolitan centres of Vancouver, Toronto, and Montreal, with others to follow, "old Canada" in demographic terms is on the defensive.

The desire to escape from what might seem a tower of Babel is easily understood. Those who require certainty as to who they are, and how their grandchildren will define themselves, will find only limited sure footing in multinational, multicultural, federal Canada. For those who seek it, however, only a partial escape from these realities is available, and then only to concentrated minorities with some capacity to opt out. Even for them, the breakup of an historic constitutional order is fraught with high risks. The stability of past practices and understandings cannot be taken for granted once the moorings of the established order are left behind. Even in a united Canada untroubled by questions about the nature of its peoplehood, those moorings are insecure. Canada, as Simeon argues, is in the midst of a sea-change because the post-World War Two consensus on the role of governments, on citizen-state relations, and on how Canada should fit into the international economy have all been undermined by, among other forces, globalization, identity politics, and out-of-control public debt.[66] To add the breakup of a country to these already intimidating challenges to our capacity for worthwhile survival in a Darwinian world is a high-risk gamble with our future. If one accepts Bourassa's assessment of the Quebec reality – "We are not a martyred people" – then his conclusion seems unassailable. "If we were in an unbearable situation, the risk could be justified to break up the federation. But we are not in that situation. . . . It would not be justified to break up the federation for additional powers that we need."[67]

The Francophone majority in an independent Quebec will have escaped from its minority status within Canada to majority status in the new state, but its citizenry will be ethnically diverse. At least initially, Aboriginal nations and Anglophone and allophone minorities will be unhappy participants in the venture of building a Quebec nation. Many Anglophones and some allophones will vote with their feet, adding to the dramatic exodus that has already taken place in the last two decades. That some Aboriginal peoples will resist their inclusion in an independent Quebec established to satisfy a Francophone majority seems inevitable. Their urgent calls on the battered and shrunken central government of Canada for support will be reinforced by the political pressure of at least some Aboriginal peoples outside Quebec for "Canada" to assist their kinfolk.[68] To predict how this Aboriginal-Quebec scenario might unfold is impossible, but that it will have a destabilizing effect in both an independent Quebec and a neighbouring ROC, and will exacerbate the relations between them, is a virtual certainty.

The degree of escape from complexity and interdependence that is possible for Aboriginal peoples is limited, even if Canada remains united. Most of the Aboriginal nations are villages. Most Aboriginal peoples, including 30-40 per cent of status Indians, live off reserves and are intermingled with other Canadians. Unlike Québécois, they do not possess a modern state structure. On virtually every socio-economic indicator, their situation is deeply distressing. Where a land base does exist, economic resources are limited. Accordingly, self-governing Aboriginal peoples will unavoidably continue to be deeply dependent on the surrounding society for financial transfers to fund their self-government. In most cases, with the Inuit majority control of Nunavut being a partial exception, most of the services and programs they need will continue to be supplied by the federal and provincial governments that act for other Canadians. In addition, Aboriginal nations, small though most of them are, are riven with internal tensions. Reserve-based status Indian communities are internally heterogeneous and troubled by serious male-female tensions. "Violence against Aboriginal women has reached epidemic proportions" in recent years, according to one author.[69] Many status Indian communities are beset with the paralysing complexities of dramatically varied legal and citizenship statuses of those within their boundaries. Intermarriage rates are high, with estimates ranging from about 50 per cent for status Indians from 1967 to 1985,[70] to 34 per cent at the present.[71] The Bill C-31 amendments of 1985 result in marriages in which only one partner has Indian status, and whose children may also lack it. Further, depending on band membership rules, some reserve residents, even if they have Indian status or are otherwise legally on the reserve through marriage, may lack political rights. A recent report for the Assembly of First Nations portrayed many Indian communities as now, and even more so in the future, riven with deep cleavages between full-status Indians versus half-status Indians, Indians versus non-Indians, and members versus non-members.[72]

The situation of the Inuit is equally troubled. A recent report on the Inuit described depressing prospects, summed up in the title, "Lords of the Arctic: Wards of the State." According to Dr. Colin Irwin, the continuation of current trends will result in a situation in which "most of the Inuit living in the Arctic in the year 2025 will be second generation wards of the state whose society, economy and culture may have more in common with an urban slum than with the life their grandparents knew." Inuit youth, he continued, are "a lost generation whose education and enculturation provides most of them with little more than the skills required to live out their lives as wards of the state."[73]

While an independent Quebec can escape the limitations of provincehood and the frustrating intergovernmental interdependence of federalism, they will be replaced by the difficulty of initially working out and then managing the complexities of intergovernmental coexistence with whatever replaces Canada to its west and east and with the United States. In the best of circumstances, even the most civil severing of Quebec-Canada relations will generate an almost paralysing agenda of practical issues to be resolved. The likelihood that their resolution will be easy, quick, and painless is minimal. In the worst, but not improbable, circumstances of both residual Canada and Quebec deeply troubled by domestic tension and turmoil, it will be extremely difficult to strike any deals at all. The ROC is likely to be in a state of shock and instability as it comes to terms with its shrunken and transformed identity and with the fact that its inherited institutional arrangements will have lost the aura of naturalness and appropriateness linked to history and a united Canada. Who will bargain for the ROC will be controversial while it remains unclear whether Canada outside of Quebec will survive as a single political people. In the absence of agreement on the future of Canadians outside of Quebec, the credentials of the federal government, now dominated by Ontario, to bargain with Quebec will be challenged from within the ROC. As already noted, if the ROC's internal questioning appears to be leading to its possible breakup, or simply to a greatly weakened central government, Aboriginal peoples, especially status Indians, will be deeply disturbed, possibly leading to deteriorating and volatile relations between Aboriginal and non-Aboriginal peoples in the ROC.

The difficulties and problems just discussed can easily be exaggerated in the arguments of opponents of major change. While the problems should be recognized, they need to be balanced against positive gains. Further, many of the problems are transitional. Outcomes after Quebec independence will probably be much more reassuring in the long run than in the troubled early stages.

For those Québécois who welcome the change to independent statehood, presumably a referendum majority, a proud sense of being a people in control of its own destiny will surely develop. Further, more of the levers to manage interdependence and to steer the Quebec people in preferred directions will be under the control of democratically elected local politicians. Even if the net increase in real autonomy, in the capacity to control one's fate, were small, there would still be the satisfaction of being in charge, to the extent that remains possible in the contemporary international state system. For those who find it galling, the frustrations of a double identity as Canadians and as Québécois will also be ended.[74]

The gain in self-esteem and in recognition for Aboriginal peoples following the arrival of self-government will also be beneficial. As more services flow through Aboriginal channels, cultural sensitivity will be enhanced. Further, a cadre of Aboriginal political leaders and administrators performing government functions will acquire higher and more prestigious profiles. The culture of dependency may be eroded at least in those circumstances where success stories occur, and the status of victim may be shed as the psychology of nation-to-nation relations gets more established in the minds of Aboriginal and non-Aboriginal Canadians.

Given the considerable weighting these positive consequences merit, they will, nevertheless, not be based on a one-to-one fusion of cultural nationality with Quebec statehood or with Aboriginal governments. All of the conventional communities by which we define our membership now and prospectively are, and will be, internally plural. The largest group, whether or not it is a majority, will not escape frequent contact with different others. This is true of Canadian, Québécois, rest-of-Canada, provincial, territorial, and Aboriginal communities. The rest of Canada, if it remains united, will not only be a staggeringly complex multicultural and multiracial society, but will contain sizable Francophone and Acadian minorities and nearly a million Aboriginal citizens in its midst. Assertions of an ineffable cultural otherness in much status Indian rhetoric, and accompanying claims of an incommensurability of rights, lack plausibility, at least in their more extreme formulations. Even the Inuit, more isolated than most, and whose experience of contact is both more recent and less intensive than that of other Aboriginal peoples, are far removed from any reality of an all-encompassing cultural distinctiveness. Irwin writes of "an abandonment of the aboriginal [Inuit] life style" in the past half-century, and asserts that "Inuit language, culture and traditional skills are being lost at an alarming rate."[75] In general, Aboriginal communities are massively penetrated by the values of the surrounding Euro-Canadian society and by global culture.

The women's movement has recently come to grips with the reality that there is no universal woman, but only a multiplicity of particular versions, many of which are composite categories – disabled women, black women, Métis women, middle-class women, gay women, and so on – that link them with men who partake of the same categories of experience or identity. It is equally true that there is no universal Canadian, no universal Quebecer, and no universal Aboriginal. As a result, each of the many identities we carry separates us from some and unites us with others of our neighbours. In the great game of politics we privilege some and downgrade other of our identities. Ethnic, cultural, linguistic, and national identities, especially if linked with territory, are powerful tools of political mobilization in the service of statehood, of drawing lines and saying, "This is a people."

When, however, we cease being hypnotized by the political and nationalist labels that dominate so much of our elite constitutional discourse, when we remind ourselves that none of us has a single dominating identity behind which all our other identities cower or fade into nothingness, when we look out on the streets where we live, or at the immigration figures – then, the rest-of-Canadian, Québécois, and Aboriginal realities do not appear as coexisting insularities but as composite categories, as is the Canadian. When we hold all the identities each of us individually carries up to the light, the initial reaction may be of bewilderment at the juggling act by which we shiftingly manage who we are. Then, a more considered appraisal will be struck by how much we are linked to each other, even as we are in the process of distancing ourselves from each other.

Although the particulars vary from one situation and one group to another, the overall reality is of a Canadian people in flux, of a heterogeneous society whether our vantage point is Canada or Quebec or Aboriginal communities, of the incessant crossing of ethnic boundaries by intermarriage, of individual cultures powerfully influenced by exogenous factors, and of a never-ending intermixture of cultures. These consequences flow from proximity to different others in our midst, and from the modern premise that life is to be made and chosen, not simply handed down from the past.

Given the scattering of peoples in our midst and immigration flows that can perhaps be moderated but not reversed, the search for the holy grail of the state with coterminous political and ethnic or national boundaries will not succeed. None of us in this country has the choice between living in a heterogeneous, polyglot community or on a cultural island protected against outsiders by political boundaries. Ethnic diversity and intercultural encounters are ubiquitous. As a consequence, there are minorities everywhere, most of whom have zero possibility of any kind of meaningful self-rule whereby they will be a majority. We can reshuffle the arrangements between peoples and governments, between nations and states, so that the Quebec majority can gain more power over its own future and over the minorities in its midst, and various Aboriginal majorities in much smaller communities can gain more power over their communities' future, and also over the minorities within their territories. Francophone and Aboriginal majorities in charge of Quebec and Aboriginal governments will have to realize, however, that they are not alone, even at home. Self-government and independence may satisfy majorities. Minorities need the protection of rights. In the interchange between majorities and minorities, creative cultural syntheses emerge, but they are best served by a prior creative constitutional synthesis that limits the nationalism of the majority in the interest of minority security. These arrangements for majority/minority relations are often misunderstood as ways of protecting cultural differences. They are more than that. In the modern world they should be thought of as establishing the rules for the interactions through which we engage in mutual efforts to persuade each other of the virtue of our way of being. This requires paying attention to the size of the communities involved, their economic power, their membership in a global language community or not, and numerous other factors that cannot be considered in these closing paragraphs. If we remember that we cannot escape the reality that we are always recreating ourselves, and others provide much of the raw materials we employ in our very personal reconstitutions, there is a good chance that we will gropingly move in the direction of choosing the right rules and institutions. Should Canada break up, that will be a reproach against the failure in majoritarian sensitivity of the generations that preceded us, and of ourselves. Whether we split or separate, may our successors exceed us in wisdom and virtue.

It should be clear by now that the vision that animates this concluding chapter is not a paean to nationalism. Its vision is captured by Edward Said and Salman Rushdie. For Said: "All cultures are involved in one another; none is single and pure, all are hybrid, heterogeneous, extraordinarily differentiated, and unmonolithic." And:

we have never been as aware as we now are of how oddly hybrid historical and cultural experiences are, of how they partake of many often contradictory experiences and domains, cross national boundaries, defy the *police* action of simple dogma and loud patriotism. Far from being unitary or monolithic or autonomous things, cultures actually assume more 'foreign' elements, alterities, differences, than they consciously exclude.[76]

Salman Rushdie:

Those who oppose [*The Satanic Verses*] most vociferously today are of the opinion that intermingling with a different culture will inevitably weaken and ruin their own. I am of the opposite opinion. *The Satanic Verses* celebrates hybridity, impurity, intermingling, the transformation that comes of new and unexpected combinations of human beings, cultures, ideas, politics, movies, songs. It rejoices in mongrelization and fears the absolutism of the Pure. *Mélange*, hotchpotch, a bit of this and a bit of that is *how newness enters the world*. It is the great possibility that mass migration gives the world, and I have tried to embrace it. *The Satanic Verses* is for change-by-fusion, change-by-conjoining. It is a love-song to our mongrel selves.[77]

\*   \*   \*

The constitutional task that confronts Canada and humanity is to construct constitutional orders that (1) are responsive to the demands of territorial minorities that seek some degree of self-rule in the service of cultural distinctiveness or linguistic preservation; (2) protect dispersed minorities characterized by "otherness" against majority oppression; (3) appreciate the powerful reality that no culture is an island, and that individual choice leads to cultural exchange, and often to high intermarriage rates when intercultural contact is extensive, thus unceasingly transforming the substance of the cultural distinctiveness behind claims for limited self-rule or independence; (4) accept the reality of multiple identities, including the multiple civic identities of the citizens of federal polities, and resist the tendency to define individuals and communities by one (allegedly dominating) characteristic; (5) understand both the creative impact of constitutional change and the absence of a clean slate on which we can freely write our future.

No matter how Canada is reconstituted, these considerations are relevant to every jurisdiction we can postulate – Quebec, an integrated or fragmented rest of Canada, self-governing Aboriginal communities, and a surviving, transformed Canada that stays together. In an era of passionate claims for independence and self-government, the first self-rule criterion above dominates our discussions, at least somewhat to the detriment of the other relevant criteria to which more importance should be attributed. To accept and respond to all of these criteria is the beginning of constitutional common sense. To deny them is comparable to denying the laws of gravity – and equally likely to produce unfortunate results.

# Notes

## Editor's Preface:
## In Praise of Hedgefoxes

1. Delivered at the Memorial Service, Bloor Street United Church, Toronto, May 7, 1990.
2. Cited in Stefan Collini, Donald Winch, and John Burrow, *That Noble Science of Politics* (Cambridge, 1983), p. 183.
3. See Alan C. Cairns, *Constitution, Government, and Society in Canada* (Toronto, 1988), and Cairns, *Disruptions: Constitutional Struggles, from the Charter to Meech Lake* (Toronto, 1991).
4. Donald V. Smiley, *Canada in Question: Federalism in the Eighties*, Third Edition (Toronto, 1980), p. 332.
5. Isaiah Berlin, *The Hedgehog and the Fox* (New York, n.d.; originally published in the second volume of *Oxford Slavonic Papers*, 1951), p. 1.
6. *Ibid.*, pp. 1-2.
7. For those unfamiliar with Macpherson's thought, compare *Democratic Theory: Essays in Retrieval* (London, 1973), especially chs. 1-3, and his "Humanist Democracy and Elusive Marxism: A Response to Minogue and Svacek," *Canadian Journal of Political Science*, IX (1976), pp. 423-30. A number of Taylor's more important essays have recently appeared as *Reconciling the Solitudes*, Guy Laforest, ed. (Montreal and Kingston, 1993). Other works of importance include his 1991 CBC Massey Lectures, *Malaise of Modernity* (Toronto, 1991), his massive study in philosophical anthropology, *Sources of the Self: The Making of the Modern Identity* (Cambridge, Mass., 1989), and the second volume of his philosophical papers, *Philosophy and the Human Sciences* (Cambridge, 1985), especially chs. 9-10.
8. This was an aspect of Alan Cairns's teaching at least twenty years ago. The author recalls discussions with Cairns of Berlin's distinction in the context of federalism, Canadian politics, and the evolution of political science itself as far back as the winter of 1975, when he was a recently arrived foreign-born doctoral student in Cairns's graduate seminar at the University of British Columbia.
9. Cairns, *Constitution, Government, and Society*, p. 13.
10. Cairns, *Charter versus Federalism: The Dilemmas of Constitutional Reform* (Montreal and Kingston, 1992). The review in question by Ian Urquhart

appeared in the *Review of Constitutional Studies*, 1, 1 (1993), pp. 171-79.

11. *Ibid.*, p. 172.

12. Robert C. Vipond, "Reflections on Federalism," *Queen's Quarterly*, 101, 1 (Spring, 1994), p. 226.

13. A further example of the misleading tendency to read Cairns's work in a dichotomous way can be found in another review of *Charter versus Federalism* that appeared in the *Winnipeg Free Press*, August 8, 1992, by Alan Mills, "Constitutional Dichotomy," p. B-31.

14. Cairns, *Constitution, Government, and Society*, p. 14.

15. Cairns, "The Canadian Constitutional Experiment: The View from Below," Killam Lecture, November 24, 1983, p. 6

16. *Ibid.*

17. For example, see "Citizens (Outsiders) and Governments (Insiders) in Constitution-Making: The Case of Meech Lake," first published in *Canadian Public Policy*, Special Supplement, xiv (1979), reprinted as Chapter Four of *Disruptions*. In a related vein, after completing his doctoral thesis research on early British pioneers in pre-imperial east and central Africa, published as *Prelude to Imperialism* (London, 1965), Cairns recalls that his next major research, on the politics and administration of Canadian Indian policy, convinced him that it was "a sociological absurdity to deny the shaping power of the law and a distinctive system of Indian administration on the behaviour and identity of the status Indian population of Canada." He continues, "it reinforced my inability to believe that institutions, law, and government were somehow inferior, secondary phenomena compared to socio-economic forces or 'real' behaviour of individuals." In one of the clearest expressions of Cairns's neo-institutionalism and overall dialectical approach, he concludes this recollection by noting, "I have always found incomprehensible any suggestion that a society has an existence distinct from the heritage of political and other institutions, which give it contours and a sense of direction. Without institutions there is no society, only a bunch of strangers milling around on top of the ground sharing propinquity." *Constitution, Government, and Society*, pp. 14-15.

18. See Robert K. Merton, *Social Theory and Social Structure* (Glencoe, Illinois, 1957). Merton's sociological approach to the analysis of institutions, as well as his contributions to the sociology of knowledge and academic disciplines, has played an important role in a number of Cairns's writings. For example, see "Political Science in Canada and the Americanization Issue," *Canadian Journal of Political Science*, vii, 2 (1975), pp. 192-234.

19. Cairns, "Constitutional Government and the Two Faces of Ethnicity: Federalism is Not Enough," in Karen Knop, Sylvia Ostry, Richard Simeon, and Katherine Swinton, eds., *Rethinking Federalism: Citizens, Markets, and*

*Governments in a Changing World* (Vancouver, forthcoming), mimeo, p. 2.

20. *Ibid.*, p. 5.

21. *Ibid.*, p. 11.

22. "The Living Canadian Constitution" first appeared in the *Queen's Quarterly*, LXXVII, 4 (1970), and is reprinted as Chapter One of *Constitution, Government, and Society*. "The Ambiguities of Citizenship" were outlined in three public lectures delivered in March, 1994, by Professor Cairns in his capacity as the first Brenda and David McLean Professor of Canadian Studies at the University of British Columbia, a recognition of the interdisciplinary nature of much of his work. These lectures tentatively are to be published by UBC Press in 1995.

23. Cairns, "Alternative Styles in the Study of Canadian Politics," *Canadian Journal of Political Science*, 7 (1974), p. 126.

24. Alan C. Cairns, F.R.S.C., "Donald Victor Smiley, 1921-1990," *Transactions of the Royal Society of Canada*, Series VI, Volume I (1990), p. 569.

25. See, respectively, Alan C. Cairns and Edwin R. Black, "A Different Perspective on Canadian Federalism," *Canadian Public Administration*, IX, 1 (1966), pp. 27-44; Cairns, "The Embedded State: State-Society Relations in Canada," in Keith Banting, ed., *State and Society: Canada in Comparative Perspective*, Vol. 31, prepared for the Royal Commission on the Economic Union and Development Prospects of Canada (Toronto, 1986), pp. 53-86, reprinted below as Chapter One; *Disruptions*, Chapter Four; "Constitutional Minoritarianism in Canada," in Ronald Watts and Douglas Brown, eds., *Canada: The State of the Federation, 1990* (Kingston, 1990), pp. 71-96, reprinted below as Chapter Four; "The Limited Constitutional Vision of Meech Lake," in Carol Rogerson and Katherine Swinton, eds., *Competing Constitutional Visions: The Meech Lake Accord* (Toronto, 1988), p. 248; and H.B. Hawthorn, *A Survey of the Contemporary Indians of Canada* (Ottawa, 1966), Vol. 1, pp. 396-98.

26. For a fuller discussion of Kant's thought along these lines, see Doug Williams, "Masons, Evangelists and Heretics in Karl Popper's Cathedral," *Queen's Quarterly*, 91 (1984), pp. 679-92; and Williams, *Truth, Hope and Power: The Thought of Karl Popper* (Toronto, 1989), ch. 3.

27. Compare Frederick Vaughan, "Critics of the Judicial Committee of the Privy Council: The New Orthodoxy and an Alternative Explanation," *Canadian Journal of Political Science*, 19, 3 (September, 1985), pp. 495-520, with responses by Peter Russell and Cairns, pp. 521-39; J.A.A. Lovink, "On Analysing the Impact of the Electoral System on the Party System," *CJPS*, 3, 4 (December, 1970), pp. 497-517, with Cairns's reply, pp. 517-21; Herman Bakvis and Laura G. Macpherson, "Quebec Block Voting and the Canadian Electoral System," paper presented at the annual meeting of the Canadian

Political Science Association, University of Calgary, June, 1994; Michael
Swayze, "Continuity and Change in the 1993 General Elections: Cairns and
Wiseman Revisited," paper presented at the annual meeting of the Canadian
Political Science Association, University of Calgary, June, 1994; R.A. Young,
Phillipe Faucher, and Andre Blais, "The Concept of Province-Building: A
Critique," *CJPS*, 17, 4 (December, 1984); Alan C. Cairns, "Alternative Styles
in the Study of Canadian Politics," *CJPS*, vii, 1 (March, 1974), pp. 101-28,
with replies from Norman Ward, J.R. Mallory, and Richard Van Loon and
Michael S. Whittington, pp. 128-34; Christopher T.R. McKee, "Constitutional Minoritarianism Revisited: The Two Faces of Constitutional Power
and Aboriginal Self-Autonomy Under the Constitution Act, 1867," paper
presented at the annual meeting of the Canadian Political Science Association, University of Prince Edward Island, June, 1992; Rainer Knopff and F.L.
Morton, *Charter Politics* (Scarborough, Ont., 1992), pp. 67-90; Ian Brodie
and Neil Nevitte, "Evaluating the Citizens' Constitution Theory," pp. 235-59,
Cairns, "A Defence of the Citizens' Constitution Theory: A Response to Ian
Brodie and Neil Nevitte," pp. 261-67, and Brodie and Nevitte, "Clarifying
Differences: A Rejoinder to Alan Cairns's Defence of the Citizens' Constitu-
tion Theory," pp. 269-72, all in *CJPS*, xxvi, 2 (June, 1993); F.L. Morton, "The
Charter of Rights and English Canada," paper presented at "The Rest of the
Country: Canada Outside Quebec" Conference, Robarts Centre for Cana-
dian Studies, York University, April 29-May 1, 1994; and T. Catherine Christopher, "Alan Cairns and the Constitutional Refashioning of Community,"
paper presented to the annual meeting of the Canadian Political Science
Association, University of Calgary, June, 1994. See also Serge Denis, *Le Long
Malentendu: Le Québec vu par les intellectuals progressistes au Canada anglais
1970-1991* (Montreal, 1992), pp. 93-98, 103-14, for a critical Québécois perspective on Cairns's constitutional writings.

28. For a fuller elaboration of this contrast, see C. Wright Mills, *The Sociological
    Imagination* (New York and Oxford, 1959), chs. 2-3.

29. Compare, for example, "Ritual, Taboo, and Bias in Constitutional Contro-
    versies in Canada, or Constitutional Talk Canadian Style," *Saskatchewan
    Law Review*, 54 (1990), and reprinted as Chapter Nine of *Disruptions*; and
    "Aboriginal Canadians, Citizenship and the Constitution," Chapter Ten of
    this volume.

30. Cairns, "Representation and the Electoral System: Some Possible Questions
    for Research," mimeo, March 28, 1990, p. 14.

31. See J.A. Corry, "The Uses of a Constitution," in Law Society of Upper Can-
    ada, Special Lectures, *The Constitution and the Future of Canada* (Toronto,
    1978). More generally, see Corry's memoir, *My Life and Work: A Happy Part-
    nership* (Kingston, 1981), especially chs. 3, 9, 10.

32. J.A. Corry, *The Power of Law* (Toronto, 1971), p. 62. Compare Cairns's recent Convocation Address at Carleton University, June 16, 1994, on the occasion of receiving an honorary doctorate, where he observed, "we haven't worked out how we will live together as a people. There is more to who we are than difference. We need empathy, sharing, the transcendence of difference." With characteristic humour, he concluded, "I dare not ask you to go forth and multiply, for the population pressures on our fragile planet preclude that option. My wish and hope is that you will go forth as happy citizen warriors – humble, knowledgeable, and courageous." Mimeo, pp. 7-8.

33. Cairns, *Constitution, Government, and Society in Canada*, p. 18.

34. In Jean Laponce and John Meisel, eds., *Debating the Constitution*, Proceedings of a Conference held in May, 1993, under the auspices of the Royal Society of Canada (Ottawa, 1994), pp. 85, 87.

35. Michael Oakeshott, "Political Education," reprinted in Timothy Fuller, ed., *Michael Oakeshott on Education: The Voice of Learning* (New Haven, 1989), p. 147.

36. Cairns, "The Embedded State: State-Society Relations in Canada," reprinted below as Chapter One.


# Author's Introduction: Whose Side Is the Past On?

1. Edward W. Said, *Culture and Imperialism* (New York, 1993), p. 3.

2. Daniel Tarschys, "Public Policy Innovation in a Zero-Growth Economy: A Scandinavian Perspective," in Peter R. Baehr and Bjorn Wittrock, eds., *Policy Analysis and Policy Innovation* (London, 1981), p. 11, cited in Richard Rose, *Understanding Big Government: The Programme Approach* (London, 1984), p. 29.

3. Mancur Olson, *The Rise and Decline of Nations* (New Haven, 1982), esp. chs. 3 and 4.

4. J.R. Mallory, *The Structure of Canadian Government* (Toronto, 1971), p. xi.

5. T.J.J. Loranger, *Letters Upon the Interpretation of the Federal Constitution known as the British North America Act (1867)* (Quebec, 1884).

6. D.G. Creighton, *John A. Macdonald*, 2 vols. (Toronto, 1952-55).

7. *Report of the Royal Commission on Dominion-Provincial Relations* (Ottawa, 1940) (Rowell-Sirois Report).

8. *Report of the Royal Commission of Inquiry on Constitutional Problems* (Quebec, 1956) (Tremblay Report).

9. W.A. Mackintosh, *The Economic Background of Dominion-Provincial Relations*, ed. and introduced by J.H. Dales (Toronto, 1964), p. 2.

10. See Ramsay Cook, *Provincial Autonomy, Minority Rights and the Compact*

*Theory, 1867-1921* (Studies of the Royal Commission on Bilingualism and Biculturalism) (Ottawa, 1969), for an analysis of the debate.

11. *Report of the Royal Commission on National Development in the Arts, Letters and Sciences* (Ottawa, 1951) (the Massey-Lévesque Commission, commonly cited as the Massey Commission), pp. xi, 4, 6, 8, 132-36.

12. The Massey-Tremblay controversy is helpfully explored in William D. Coleman, *The Independence Movement in Quebec 1945-1980* (Toronto, 1984), ch. 3.

13. For a discussion, see Alan C. Cairns, "The Judicial Committee and its Critics," *Canadian Journal of Political Science*, 4 (September, 1971), pp. 301-45.

14. Theda Skocpol, "Bringing the State Back In," in Peter B. Evans, Dietrich Rueschemeyer, and Theda Skocpol, eds., *Bringing the State Back In* (Cambridge, 1985).

15. V. Seymour Wilson, "The Tapestry Vision of Canadian Multiculturalism," *Canadian Journal of Political Science*, 26 (December, 1993), pp. 657, 667.

16. Penney Kome, *The Taking of Twenty-Eight: Women Challenge the Constitution* (Toronto, 1983).

17. Royal Commission on Aboriginal Peoples, *Partners in Confederation: Aboriginal Peoples, Self-Government and the Constitution* (Ottawa, 1993), p. 36. This discussion paper very closely follows Brian Slattery, "First Nations and the Constitution: A Question of Trust," *Canadian Bar Review*, 71 (1992), p. 281, who states that "the Aboriginal right of self-government under section 35 . . . is *inherent*, in the sense that it originates from within Aboriginal communities as a residue of the powers they originally held as independent nations prior to European settlement."

18. For the Japanese-Canadian redress issue, see Government of Canada, news release, "Historic Agreement Reached on Japanese Canadian Redress," September 22, 1988; National Association of Japanese Canadians, *Justice in Our Time: Redress for Japanese Canadians* (Vancouver, 1988); Roy Miki and Cassandra Kobayashi, *Justice in Our Time: The Japanese Canadian Redress Settlement* (Vancouver, 1991); Maryka Omatsu, *Bittersweet Passage: Redress and the Japanese Canadian Experience* (Toronto, 1992).

19. For the Chinese-Canadian redress issue, see Chinese Canadian National Council, *It is Only Fair: Redress for the Head Tax and Chinese Exclusion Act* (Toronto, 1988).

20. For the Ukrainian-Canadian redress issue, the following are helpful. See Lubomyr Luciuk, *A Time for Atonement: Canada's First National Internment Operations and the Ukrainian Canadians 1914-1920* (Kingston, 1988), for an analysis of the approximately 5,000 internees of Ukrainian origin placed in detention camps across the country (1914-20), their arduous existence, the frequent suicides and attempts by the demoralized and embittered "enemy

aliens" to escape, and the plea for an apology and compensation. Ukrainian experience in one internment camp is documented in Bohdan S. Kordan and Peter Melynycky, eds., *In the Shadow of the Rockies: Diary of the Castle Mountain Internment Camp 1915-1917* (Edmonton, 1991). Desmond Morton, "Sir William Otter and Internment Operations in Canada during the First World War," *Canadian Historical Review*, LV, 1 (March, 1974), is an excellent analysis of the politics of internment and of the administration of the camps. A minority of the internees were German Canadians, whose internment conditions were much less severe. Frances Swyripa and John Herd Thompson, eds., *Loyalties in Conflict: Ukrainians in Canada During the Great War* (Edmonton, 1983), is the best overall survey dealing with both internment and Ukrainian disenfranchisement in the 1917 election, *inter alia*. See also the testimony of Dr. Lubomyr Luciuk (Civil Liberties Commission, Ukrainian Canadian Committee) in *Minutes of Proceedings and Evidence of the Standing Committee on Multiculturalism*, House of Commons, No. 11, December 7-8, 1987.

21. For the Italian-Canadian redress issue, see Bruno Ramirez, "Ethnicity on Trial: The Italians of Montreal and the Second World War," in Norman Hillmer *et al.*, eds., *On Guard for Thee: War, Ethnicity, and the Canadian State* (Ottawa, 1988); National Congress of Italian Canadians, "A National Shame: The Internment of Italian Canadians," mimeo (January, 1990); and Lana Michelin, "Italian Canadians seek redress for internment," *Globe and Mail*, January 8, 1990.

   For German Canadians, see Robert H. Keyserlingk, "Breaking the Nazi Plot: Canadian Government Attitudes Towards German Canadians, 1939-1945," in Hillmer *et al.*, eds., *On Guard for Thee*.

22. For the Inuit redress issue, see Alan R. Marcus, *Out in the Cold: The Legacy of Canada's Relocation Experiment in the High Arctic* (Copenhagen, 1992). The Royal Commission on Aboriginal Peoples has held special hearings on the High Arctic relocation and will report on the issue.

23. The House of Commons resolution, also passed by the Senate, "recognize[d] the unique and historic role of Louis Riel as a founder of Manitoba and his contribution in the development of Confederation." House of Commons, *Debates*, March 10, 1992, p. 7879; Senate, *Debates*, March 17, 1992, p. 1043.

24. National Association of Japanese Canadians, *Justice in Our Time*, p. 5.

25. "Ukraine: In the Shadow of Lenin: 'Enemy aliens' remember," *Edmonton Journal*, October 8, 1988.

26. Ukrainian Canadian Committee, Civil Liberties Commission, "A Time for Atonement: Canada's First National Internment Operations and the Ukrainian Canadians 1914-1920" (Toronto, 1989).

27. Ramirez, "Ethnicity on Trial," p. 71.

28. Chinese Canadian National Council, *It is Only Fair*, p. 23.

29. Chinese Canadian National Council, Ottawa Chapter, "Then, Now, and Tomorrow, 1988 Mid-Autumn Festival Edition September 1988" (Ottawa, 1988), p. 11.

30. Government of Canada, news release, "Historic Agreement Reached on Japanese Canadian Redress," September 22, 1988.

31. "Notes for an Address by Prime Minister Brian Mulroney, National Congress of Italian Canadians and the Canadian Italian Business Professional Association, Toronto, November 4, 1990," mimeo, p. 5.

32. John Herd Thompson, "The Enemy Alien and the Canadian General Election of 1917," in Swyripa and Thompson, eds., *Loyalties in Conflict*, p. 26.

33. Ramirez, "Ethnicity on Trial," p. 75. This is equally clear with the internment of Japanese Canadians. As the policy unfolded, "their Canadian birthright became meaningless, and henceforth they were to be judged solely on the basis of their racial ancestry not on their citizenship, or even the country of their birth." Miki and Kobayashi, *Justice in Our Time*, p. 24.

34. "Ukraine: In the Shadow of Lenin: 'Enemy aliens' remember," *Edmonton Journal*, October 8, 1988.

35. See Ramirez, "Ethnicity on Trial," p. 71, for the "thick veil of self-imposed censure . . . on [the] memory" of surviving Italian internees in Montreal. Joy Kogawa, who wrote *Obasan* (Markham, 1983), stated in 1984, "forty years later, most of the people of my generation are still hiding in the woodwork and not wanting to speak. As Aunt Emily says in *Obasan*, 'Our tongues were cut off. It takes a while for the nerves to grow back.'" National Association of Japanese Canadians, *Justice in Our Time*, p. 104. See also Omatsu, *Bittersweet Passage*, pp. 67, 69, 150.

36. House of Commons, *Debates*, March 10, 1992, p. 7880.

37. Omatsu, *Bittersweet Passage*, pp. 9, 13, 30.

38. It is not unique to Canada. Said writes: "Today . . . discussions of American history are increasingly interrogations of the history for what it did to native peoples, immigrant populations, oppressed minorities. . . . only recently have Westerners become aware that what they have to say about the history and the cultures of 'subordinate' peoples is challenged by the people themselves, people who a few years back were simply incorporated, culture, land, history, and all, into the great Western empires, and their disciplinary discourses. . . . An immense wave of anti-colonial and ultimately anti-imperial activity, thought, and revision has overtaken the massive edifice of Western empire, challenging it, to use Gramsci's vivid metaphor, in a mutual siege. For the first time Westerners have been required to confront themselves not simply as the Raj but as representatives of a culture and even

of races accused of crimes – crimes of violence, crimes of suppression, crimes of conscience." *Culture and Imperialism*, p. 195.

39. The latter thesis is argued by Donald A. Grinde, Jr., and Bruce E. Johansen in *Exemplar of Liberty: Native America and the Evolution of Democracy* (Los Angeles, 1991), and challenged in a review by J.A. Brandao in *Canadian Historical Review*, 74 (September, 1993), pp. 436-37. The discussion paper, *Partners in Confederation*, pp. 40, 65, n. 142, of the Royal Commission on Aboriginal Peoples approvingly cites the thesis without explicitly supporting it, but then appears to retreat slightly in a footnote.

The controversy was joined prior to *Exemplar of Liberty* in an exchange between Elisabeth Tooker, "The United States Constitution and the Iroquois League," *Ethnohistory*, 35, 4 (Fall, 1988), and Bruce E. Johansen, "Native American Societies and the Evolution of Democracy in America, 1600-1800," *Ethnohistory*, 37, 3 (Summer, 1990), followed by a "Rejoinder to Johansen" by Tooker.

40. Said, *Culture and Imperialism*, p. 30.

41. Bill Ashcroft, Gareth Griffiths, and Helen Tiffin, *The Empire Writes Back: Theory and Practice in Post-Colonial Literatures* (London, 1989). Grinde and Johansen, *Exemplar of Liberty*, is a good example of "writing back." "A fundamental purpose of this book is to let American Indian voices be heard on the issue of Iroquois political theory and its role in the development of American governmental structures" (p. xxiv).

42. Peter Novick, *That Noble Dream: The 'Objectivity Question' and the American Historical Profession* (New York, 1988), cited in David A. Hollinger, "How Wide the Circle of the 'We'? American Intellectuals and the Problem of the Ethnos since World War II," *American Historical Review*, 98, 2 (April, 1993), p. 324. Carl Becker's "Everyman His Own Historian" is reprinted in a volume of his essays under that title (Chicago, 1966; originally published 1935). I thank Allan Smith for drawing the Hollinger article to my attention.

43. Rosella Melanson, "Citizenship and Acadie: The Art of the Possible," in William Kaplan, ed., *Belonging: The Meaning and Future of Canadian Citizenship* (Montreal and Kingston, 1993).

44. Marc Cousineau, "Belonging: An Essential Element of Citizenship – A Franco-Ontarian Perspective," in Kaplan, ed., *Belonging*, pp. 143-44.

45. Glenda P. Simms, "Racism as a Barrier to Canadian Citizenship," in Kaplan, ed., *Belonging*.

46. Darlene Johnston, "First Nations and Canadian Citizenship," in Kaplan, ed., *Belonging*, p. 349.

47. *Report of the Royal Commission on the Status of Women* (Ottawa, 1970).

48. Marcel Trudel and Geneviève Jain, *Canadian History Textbooks: A Comparative Study* (Ottawa, 1970), p. 133.

49. Said, *Culture and Imperialism*.

50. Frantz Fanon, *The Wretched of the Earth* (New York, 1964).

51. Anne Norton, "Ruling Memory," *Political Theory*, 2 (August, 1993), pp. 457, 459.

52. *Ibid.*, pp. 455-56.

53. First Nations Circle on the Constitution, *To the Source: Commissioners' Report, Assembly of First Nations*, mimeo (Ottawa, 1992).

54. Admittedly, this formulation is far from providing concrete guidance to policy-makers. In the complexities of actual societies, equality quickly becomes equalities in competition with each other, not all of which can be satisfied at the same time. See Douglas Rae *et al.*, *Equalities* (Cambridge, Mass., 1981), ch. 1, "Tocqueville's Dread."

55. Antonio Gramsci, *Selections from the Prison Notebooks*, trans. and eds. Quintin Hoare and Geoffrey N. Smith (New York, 1992), p. 266, cited in Gerald P. Kernerman, "Who Can Speak for Whom? Struggles Over Representation During the Charlottetown Referendum Campaign" (M.A. thesis, University of British Columbia, 1994), p. 12.

56. Edward Shils, *The Constitution of Society* (Chicago and London, 1982), p. vii.

57. For a bitter critique of the Canada clause, see Errol P. Mendes, "Sinking Again into the Quagmire of Conflicting Visions, Groups, Underinclusion, and Death by Referendum," in Kenneth McRoberts and Patrick J. Monahan, eds., *The Charlottetown Accord, the Referendum, and the Future of Canada* (Toronto, 1993).

## The Embedded State

I should like to thank Keith Banting, Peter Hall, Karen Jackson, Philip Resnick, Ian Urquhart, Cynthia Williams, Doug Williams, and David Wolfe for comments on earlier drafts of this paper, which was completed in May, 1985.

1. B. Guy Peters and Marten O. Heisler, "Thinking About Public Sector Growth," in Charles L. Taylor, ed., *Why Governments Grow: Measuring Public Sector Size* (Beverly Hills, 1983), p. 186.

2. Daniel Tarschys, in Richard Rose, ed., *Understanding Big Government: The Programme Approach* (London, 1984), p. 29.

3. See Rose, *Understanding Big Government*, for an impressive discussion of the momentum and inertia behind existing programs.

4. Clauss Offe, "Political Authority and Class Structures – An Analysis of Late Capitalist Societies," *International Journal of Sociology*, 2, 1 (1972), p. 78.

5. Fred W. Gibson, "Conclusions," in his *Cabinet Formation and Bicultural*

*Relations: Seven Case Studies*, Studies of the Royal Commission on Bilingualism and Bilculturalism (Ottawa, 1970), p. 171, citing O.D. Skelton.

6. John L. Howard and W.T. Stanbury, "Appendix to Measuring Leviathan: The Size, Scope, and Growth of Government in Canada," in George Lermer, ed., *Probing Leviathan* (Vancouver, 1984), pp. 129, 132, 140.

7. Quebec, Royal Commission of Inquiry on Constitutional Problems, *Report* (Quebec, 1956); William D. Coleman, *The Independence Movement in Quebec 1945-1980* (Toronto, 1984).

8. Richard Simeon and Donald Blake, "Regional Preferences: Citizens' Views of Public Policy," in David Elkins and Richard Simeon, eds., *Small Worlds: Provinces and Parties in Canadian Political Life* (Toronto, 1980); Keith G. Banting, *The Welfare State and Canadian Federalism* (Montreal, 1982), ch. 8.

9. See Thomas Peterson, "Manitoba: Ethnic and Class Politics," in Martin Robin, ed., *Canadian Provincial Politics*, 2nd ed. (Scarborough, 1978).

10. See Keith Banting and Richard Simeon, eds., *And No One Cheered* (Toronto, 1983), for various analyses.

11. Stephen R. Graubard, "Preface," *Daedalus* (Fall, 1979), p. x.

12. Thomas Flanagan, "The Manufacture of Minorities," paper presented to the Conference on Minorities in Canada, Banff, May 21-24, 1984, p. 28 and *passim*.

13. For some of the dilemmas of affirmative action, see Conrad Winn, "Affirmative Action and Visible Minorities: Eight Premises in Quest of Evidence," *Canadian Public Policy*, 11, 4 (December, 1985).

14. Léon Dion, *Québec: The Unfinished Revolution* (Montreal, 1976), p. 86.

15. H. Laframboise, "The Future of Public Administration in Canada," *Canadian Public Administration*, 25, 4 (Winter, 1982), p. 513.

16. William D. Coleman, "Canadian Business and the State," in *The State and Economic Interests*, volume 32 of the research studies prepared for the Royal Commission on the Economic Union and Development Prospects for Canada (Toronto, 1985). See Coleman's appendix for the methodology of his study and the criteria for nationally relevant associations.

17. Rolf Mirus, "The Invisible Economy: Its Dimensions and Implications," in Lermer, ed., *Probing Leviathan*, p. 123. Toronto lawyer and law school lecturer Robert Couzin described the logic of non-compliance with the Income Tax Act as follows: "On a simple application of games theory, the probability of getting caught multiplied by the costs of getting caught is found to be less than the probability of not getting caught multiplied by the benefit of winning." *Globe and Mail*, July 12, 1983, p. B18.

18. S.M. Lipset, *Agrarian Socialism*, rev. ed. (Garden City, N.Y., 1968), p. 57.

19. William J. Goode, "Why Men Resist," in Barrie Thorne and Marilyn Yalom, eds., *Rethinking the Family* (New York, 1982), p. 146.

20. For a helpful discussion, see Roger Gibbins and J. Rick Ponting, "An Assessment of the Probable Impact of Aboriginal Self-Government in Canada," in Alan Cairns and Cynthia Williams, eds., *The Politics of Gender, Ethnicity and Language in Canada*, volume 34 of the research studies prepared for the Royal Commission on the Economic Union and Development Prospects for Canada (Toronto, 1985).

21. Raymond Breton, "The Production and Allocation of Symbolic Resources: An Analysis of the Linguistic and Ethnocultural Fields in Canada," *Canadian Review of Anthropology and Sociology*, 21 (May, 1984).

22. The many brilliant works of Erving Goffman on how we present the "self" in response to various cues are relevant here. See also F.G. Bailey, *The Tactical Uses of Passion: An Essay on Power, Reason, and Reality* (Ithaca, N.Y., 1983), for an illuminating discussion, particularly ch. 2, which explores "The Colony of Selves" that exists in each of us.

23. In another case, the business community complained that "older relationships with government were being cavalierly swept aside" by the 1982 reorganization of External Affairs. Robert Boardman, "The Foreign Service and the Organization of the Foreign Policy Community: Views from Canada and Abroad," in Denis Stairs and Gilbert R. Winham, eds., *Selected Problems in Formulating Foreign Economic Policy*, volume 30 of the research studies prepared for the Royal Commission on the Economic Union and Development Prospects for Canada (Toronto, 1985).

24. J.A. Corry, "The Fusion of Government and Business," *Canadian Journal of Economics and Political Science*, 2, 3 (August, 1936).

25. Karl Polanyi, *The Great Transformation* (Boston, 1957).

26. John Boli-Bennett, "The Ideology of Expanding State Authority in National Constitutions, 1870-1970," in John W. Meyer and Michael T. Hannan, eds., *National Development and the World System* (Chicago, 1979), pp. 223, 224.

27. Eric A. Nordlinger, *On the Autonomy of the Democratic State* (Cambridge, Mass., 1981).

28. The abstract nature of the analysis of this paragraph, and more generally of the whole paper, unfortunately precludes any attempt to construct typologies of the varying relations among the public and private players and to relate these to different policy areas. For some provocative insights, see Theodore J. Lowi, "Distribution, Regulation, Redistribution: The Functions of Government," in R.R. Ripley, ed., *Public Policies and their Politics* (New York, 1966).

29. Cited in David Held and Joel Kruger, "Accumulation, Legitimation and the State: the Ideas of Claus Offe and Jurgen Habermas," in David Held *et al.*, eds., *States and Societies* (Oxford, 1983), pp. 490-91.

30. Rick Van Loon, "Reforming Welfare in Canada," *Public Policy*, 27, 4 (Fall, 1979), p. 503.

31. Peters and Heisler, "Thinking About Public Sector Growth," p. 192. Pages 191-94 are especially valuable.

32. See Hugh G. Thorburn, *Group Representation in the Federal State: The Relationships between Canadian Governments and Interest Groups*, volume 69 of the research studies prepared for the Royal Commission on the Economic Union and Development Prospects for Canada (Toronto, 1985), pp. 60-62, for discussion of recent federal government unilateral initiatives.

33. Max Kaase, "The Challenge of the 'Participatory Revolution' in Pluralistic Democracies," *International Political Science Review*, 5, 3 (1984), pp. 303-04.

34. Robert Bothwell, Ian Drummond, and John English, *Canada Since 1945: Power, Politics and Provincialism* (Toronto, 1981), p. 4.

35. See Tim Luke *et al.*, "Review Symposium on Soviet-Type Societies," *Telos*, 60 (Summer, 1984), for discussion of social atomization and the virtual destruction of civil society in Soviet-type societies.

36. I thank Peter Hall and Philip Resnick for observing that in an earlier draft I paid inadequate attention to the qualitative distinction between the mildness of the fusion of state and society in democratic contexts and its Orwellian rigour in totalitarian systems.

## The Past and Future of the Canadian Administrative State

1. Albert O. Hirschman, *Essays in Trespassing: Economics to Politics and Beyond* (Cambridge, 1981).

2. See the seminal volumes by Eric Nordlinger, *On the Autonomy of the Democratic State* (Cambridge, Mass., 1981), and Peter B. Evans, Dietrich Rueschemeyer, and Theda Skocpol, eds. *Bringing the State Back In* (Cambridge, 1985), and the excellent review article by Stephen D. Krasner, "Approaches to the State: Alternative Conceptions and Historical Dynamics," *Comparative Politics* (January, 1984).

3. Hartle refers to "the vital role of the state as the ultimate rule maker and rule enforcer that can and does, by changing the rules, affect all of the sources of well-being of all individuals directly or indirectly, for good or for ill." Douglas G. Hartle, *Public Policy, Decision-Making and Regulation* (Toronto, 1979), p. 44.

4. Keith G. Banting, "Images of the Modern State: An Introduction," in Banting, ed., *State and Society: Canada in Comparative Perspective* (Toronto, 1986), p. 2.

5. As Peter Hall has noted, "the consequences of policy can gradually alter the societal organization of a nation." *Governing the Economy: The Politics of State Intervention in Britain and France* (New York, 1986), p. 267. "In advanced-industrial society," according to Benjamin and Duvall, "the state/society distinction blurs, and the state may be said virtually to merge with society. It is very difficult to tell where the private domain ends and the public one begins." Roger Benjamin and Raymond Duvall, "The Capitalist State in Context," in Roger Benjamin and Stephen L. Elkin, eds. *The Democratic State* (Lawrence, Kansas, 1985), pp. 45-47.

6. *Report of the Royal Commission on the Economic Union and Development Prospects for Canada* (Macdonald Commission report) (Ottawa, 1985), vol. 1, p. 24.

7. "Introduction" in O.P. Dwivedi, ed., *The Administrative State in Canada: Essays in Honour of J.E. Hodgetts* (Toronto, 1982), p. 5.

8. John L. Howard and W.T. Stanbury, "Appendix to Measuring Leviathan: The Size, Scope, and Growth of Governments in Canada," in George Lermer, ed., *Probing Leviathan: An Investigation of Government in the Economy* (Vancouver, 1984), p. 188.

9. Claus Offe, "Political Authority and Class Structures – An Analysis of Late Capitalist Societies," *International Journal of Sociology*, 2 (1972), p. 78.

10. W.H. Auden and Louis Kronenberger, eds., *The Faber Book of Aphorisms: A Personal Selection* (London, 1970), p. 231.

11. Cited in Howard and Stanbury, "Measuring Leviathan," p. 90.

12. Banting, "Images of the Modern State," pp. 2-3.

13. Howard and Stanbury, "Measuring Leviathan," p. 91.

14. A mass of statistical material supplementary to the data in the following paragraphs is available in the three volumes of the Macdonald Commission report and in the seventy volumes of its supporting research studies, in Canadian Tax Foundation publications dealing with national and provincial finances, in Howard and Stanbury, "Measuring Leviathan," and in W.T. Stanbury, *Business-Government Relations in Canada* (Toronto, 1986).

15. Stanbury, *Business-Government Relations*, p. 51.

16. J.W. Langford and K.J. Huffman, cited in Howard and Stanbury, "Measuring Leviathan," p. 164.

17. Macdonald Commission report, vol. 1, p. 26.

18. Stanbury, *Business-Government Relations*, p. 65.

19. Macdonald Commission report, vol. 1, p. 26.

20. *Ibid.*

21. Stanbury, *Business-Government Relations*, p. 59.

22. Richard Schultz, "Regulatory Agencies and the Dilemmas of Delegation," in Dwivedi, ed., *The Administrative State in Canada*, p. 91.

23. Economic Council of Canada, *Responsible Regulation: An Interim Report* (Ottawa, 1979), p. xi.

24. Macdonald Commission report, vol. 1, p. 26. For a helpful discussion and data, see Stanbury, *Business-Government Relations*, pp. 68-73.

25. Stanbury, *Business-Government Relations*, pp. 54-57. See also David A. Wolfe, "The Politics of the Deficit," in G. Bruce Doern, ed., *The Politics of Economic Policy* (Toronto, 1985).

26. Stanbury, *Business-Government Relations*, p. 77.

27. Macdonald Commission report, vol. 2, p. 550.

28. Banting, "Images of the Modern State," p. 3. Percentages refer to 1980-81.

29. Discussed *ibid.*, pp. 4-5.

30. M. Schmidt, "The Role of Parties in Shaping Macroeconomic Policy," in F. Castles, ed., *The Impact of Parties: Politics and Policies in Democratic Capitalist States* (London, 1982), p. 98.

31. Alex Inkeles, "The Emerging Social Structure of the World," *World Politics*, 27 (July, 1975), p. 495.

32. Banting, "Images of the Modern State," p. 9.

33. Doug Owram, *The Government Generation: Canadian Intellectuals and the State, 1900-1945* (Toronto, 1986).

34. Ramesh Mishra, *The Welfare State in Crisis* (Brighton, 1984).

35. Albert O. Hirschman, *Shifting Involvements: Private Interest and Public Action* (Princeton, N.J., 1982).

36. Personal communication.

37. Jacques Parizeau, "Transition," *Canadian Public Administration*, 31 (1988), p. 5.

38. Mishra, *The Welfare State in Crisis*, pp. 98-99.

39. Hartle, *Public Policy*, p. 18.

40. Stanbury, *Business-Government Relations*, p. 57.

41. Alan Cairns, "The Embedded State: State-Society Relations in Canada," in Banting, ed., *State and Society*, p. 72.

42. Law Reform Commission of Canada, *Report on Independent Administrative Agencies: A Framework for Decision-Making* (Ottawa, 1985), p. 76.

43. R.A. Macdonald, "Postscript and Prelude – The Jurisprudence of the Charter: Eight Theses," in E.P. Belobaba and E. Gertner, eds., *The New Constitution and the Charter of Rights* (Toronto, 1983), p. 341.

44. Law Reform Commission of Canada, *The Legal Status of the Federal Administration*, Working Paper 40 (Ottawa, 1985), p. 34.

45. *Hunter v. Southam Inc.* [1984] 2 SCR 145, at 146.

46. Law Reform Commission of Canada, *Towards a Modern Federal Administrative Law* (Ottawa, 1987), p. 16; Macdonald, "Postscript and Prelude," pp. 344-46; and Andrew Petter, "The Politics of the Charter," *Supreme Court Law Review*, 8 (1986), pp. 493-98.

47. Peter H. Russell, "The Political Purposes of the Canadian Charter of Rights and Freedoms," in R.S. Blair and J.T. McLeod, eds., *The Canadian Political Tradition: Basic Readings* (Toronto, 1987). See also Rainer Knopff and F.L. Morton, "Nation-Building and the Canadian Charter of Rights and Freedoms," in Alan Cairns and Cynthia Williams, eds., *Constitutionalism, Citizenship, and Society in Canada* (Toronto, 1985); and Alan Cairns, "The Canadian Constitutional Experiment," *Dalhousie Law Journal*, 9 (1984).

48. John Boli's language may founder on the particularities of the expansion of rights and the diffusion of charters in specific cases, but his general point is worth pondering: "The ideology of the expanding state while freeing individuals from traditional authority constantly co-opts the ideology of individualism by defining individuals in terms of citizenship and by translating human rights into citizen rights. This process of constructing citizenship, along with the inventory of citizen rights and national institutions, defines the individual as a member of the nation. Citizen rights are incorporative, serving not so much to strengthen the possibility of individual choice as to expand state jurisdiction over the lives of citizens, bringing individuals fully into the arena of state action and control." "Human Rights or State Expansion? Cross-National Definitions of Constitutional Rights, 1870-1970," in George M. Thomas et al., *Institutional Structure: Constituting State, Society, and the Individual* (Beverly Hills, 1987), pp. 133-34.

49. Alan C. Cairns, "Political Science, Ethnicity and the Canadian Constitution," mimeo, prepared for "Federalism and the Quest for Political Community," a conference held at York University, May 6-8, 1988, pp. 4-9.

50. F.L. Morton, "The Political Impact of the Canadian Charter of Rights and Freedoms," *Canadian Journal of Political Science*, 20 (1987), pp. 39-43.

51. *Ibid.*

52. Alan C. Cairns, "The Politics of Constitutional Conservatism," in Keith Banting and Richard Simeon, eds., *And No One Cheered: Federalism, Democracy and the Constitution Act* (Toronto, 1983), p. 42.

53. Macdonald, "Postscript and Prelude," p. 326. See also Morton, "The Political Impact of the Canadian Charter," p. 32: "The Charter was not brought into being to end tyranny. To the contrary, Canadians have always enjoyed a full measure of freedom and security from arbitrary and oppressive government."

54. See Cynthia Williams, "The Changing Nature of Citizen Rights," in Cairns and Williams, eds., *Constitutionalism*, for the historical background.

55. Thomas Flanagan, "The Manufacture of Minorities," in Neil Nevitte and Allan Kornberg, eds., *Minorities and the Canadian State* (Oakville, Ont., 1985).

56. Ian Hunter, "Liberty and Equality: A Tale of Two Codes," *McGill Law Journal*, 29, 6 (1983), p. 3.

57. Law Reform Commission of Canada, *The Legal Status of the Federal Administration*, p. 53.

58. Peter H. Russell, "The Effect of a Charter of Rights on the Policy-Making Role of Canadian Courts," *Canadian Public Administration*, 25 (1982), p. 32.

59. F.L. Morton and Leslie A. Pal, "The Impact of the Charter of Rights on Public Administration: A Case Study of Sex Discrimination in the Unemployment Insurance Act," *Canadian Public Administration*, 28 (1985), pp. 233-34.

60. Cited in Williams, "The Changing Nature of Citizen Rights," p. 99.

61. Albert Breton, Senate *Debates*, February 10, 1988, pp. 2731-34.

62. Alan C. Cairns, "Citizens (Outsiders) and Governments (Insiders) in Constitution-Making: The Case of Meech Lake," *Canadian Public Policy*, 14 (supp.) (1988), p. 129.

63. Allen M. Linden, *Taking Law Reform Seriously: Selected Addresses by the Honourable Allen M. Linden, President, Law Reform Commission of Canada, 1983-1986* (n.d., n.p.), p. 705. The developing research focus of the Law Reform Commission on "human rights" as of 1986 is described at pp. 705-14.

64. *Report on Independent Administrative Agencies*, p. 52. The commission has observed that as a result of the Charter, "minimum control of the ordering function is being replaced by a more encompassing judicial surveillance of government action." *Towards a Modern Federal Administrative Law*, p. 17. The Charter makes the question "of the rights of individuals . . . a central concern of administrative law. This area of the law is currently going through an important process of development, attempting to foster the attachment of rights directly to individuals through legislative reform, rather than limiting itself to its traditional concern with judicial review." Law Reform Commission of Canada, *The Legal Status of the Federal Administration*, pp. 34-35. For a recommended procedural framework to bring independent administrative agencies more into line with the Charter while paying appropriate regard to public administration values, see Law Reform Commission of Canada, *Report on Independent Administrative Agencies*, pp. 52-73.

65. J.M. Evans, "Developments in Administrative Law: The 1984-85 Term," *Supreme Court Law Review*, 8 (1986), p. 22.

66. *Ibid.*, p. 4, n. 9. See pages 4-7 for elaboration and additional observations.

67. Fergus O'Connor, "The Impact of the Canadian Charter of Rights and Freedoms on Parole in Canada," *Queen's Law Journal*, 10 (1985), p. 389.

68. Alan D. Reid and Alison Harvison Young, "Administrative Search and Seizure under the Charter," *Queen's Law Journal*, 10 (1985), pp. 393, 402. This

theme issue of the *Queen's Law Journal* on administrative law and the Charter is a valuable collection.

69. F.L. Morton and M.J. Withey, *Charting the Charter, 1982-1985: A Statistical Analysis*, Occasional Papers Series Research Study 2.1 (Calgary, September, 1986), p. 8. Of course, the section 15 equality rights section had been in effect only for nine months of the period covered. The methodology produced nearly twice as many Charter arguments (3,532) as Charter cases. See p. 31, n. 11.

70. Morton, "The Political Impact," pp. 37, 52.

71. Evans, "Developments in Administrative Law," p. 6.

72. Macdonald Commission report, vol. 3, p. 30.

73. "Countries with a British tradition recognize by implication what is elsewhere the subject of express proclamations . . . the Canadian authorities wished to break with the British tradition and use a charter of rights and freedoms, with the result that the latter were given appreciable force and effect. This has had certain consequences. By specifying certain rights rather than others, the drafters of the Charter conferred on them a primacy and pre-eminence over any other document. Accordingly, the Canadian approach to civil liberties is primarily the result of the rights contained in the Charter, which must now be regarded as a document of prime importance acting as a foundation. What this document says, or fails to say, thus becomes particularly significant." Law Reform Commission of Canada, *The Legal Status of the Federal Administration*, pp. 43-44.

74. For a discussion, see Alan C. Cairns, "The Limited Constitutional Vision of Meech Lake," in Katherine E. Swinton and Carol J. Rogerson, eds., *Competing Constitutional Visions: The Meech Lake Accord* (Toronto, 1988).

75. Raymond Breton, "The Production and Allocation of Symbolic Resources: An Analysis of the Linguistic and Ethnocultural Fields in Canada," *Canadian Review of Sociology and Anthropology*, 21 (1984), p. 124.

76. *Ibid.*, p. 125.

77. Elliot L. Tepper, "Demographic Change and Pluralism," and T. John Samuel, "Immigration, Visible Minorities and the Labour Force in Canada: Vision 2000," papers presented at the Conference on Canada 2000: Race Relations and Public Policy, Carleton University, Ottawa, October 30-November 1, 1987.

78. L.S. Lustgarten, "Liberty in a Culturally Plural Society," in A. Phillips Griffiths, ed., *Of Liberty* (Cambridge, 1983), pp. 97-98.

79. *Ibid.*, p. 101.

80. Ian Hunter, "Liberty and Equality: A Tale of Two Codes," *McGill Law Journal*, 29 (1983).

81. Krasner, "Approaches to the State," p. 228.
82. Vincent Del Buono, quoted in Law Reform Commission of Canada, *Recodifying Criminal Law*, vol. 1 (Ottawa, 1986), p. 2.
83. Economic Council of Canada, *Responsible Regulation*, p. 15.
84. Cairns, "The Politics of Constitutional Conservatism," pp. 31-45.
85. Roger Gibbins, "Federal Societies, Institutions, and Politics," in Herman Bakvis and William M. Chandler, eds., *Federalism and the Role of the State* (Toronto, 1987), pp. 28-29.
86. Krasner, "Approaches to the State," pp. 234-35.
87. Claus Offe, *Contradictions of the Welfare State*, edited by John Keane (Cambridge, Mass., 1984), pp. 166-67.
88. Krasner, "Approaches to the State," p. 228.
89. Douglas M. Johnston, *Canada and the New International Law of the Sea* (Toronto, 1985), pp. 52-53.
90. Daniel Tarschys, "Public Policy Innovation in a Zero-Growth Economy: A Scandinavian Perspective," in Peter R. Baehr and Bjorn Wittrock, eds., *Policy Analysis and Policy Innovation* (London, 1981), p. 11, cited in Richard Rose, *Understanding Big Government: The Programme Approach* (London, 1984), p. 29.
91. Krasner, "Approaches to the State," p. 240.
92. Alan C. Cairns, "The Embedded State: State-Society Relations in Canada," in Banting, ed., *State and Society*, pp. 55-58.
93. Leslie A. Pal, "Sense and Sensibility: Comments on Forget," *Canadian Public Policy*, 14 (1988), p. 11.
94. Macdonald Commission report, vol. 1, p. 28.
95. Frederick J. Fletcher and Donald C. Wallace, "Federal-Provincial Relations and the Making of Public Policy in Canada: A Review of Case Studies," in Richard Simeon, ed., *Division of Powers and Public Policy* (Toronto, 1985), pp. 128-29.
96. Colin Campbell, *Governments under Stress: Political Executives and Key Bureaucrats in Washington, London, and Ottawa* (Toronto, 1983).
97. J. Stefan Dupré, "The Workability of Executive Federalism in Canada," in Bakvis and Chandler, eds., *Federalism and the Role of the State*.
98. Donald V. Smiley, *Conditional Grants and Canadian Federalism* (Toronto, 1963).
99. Dupré, "The Workability of Executive Federalism," p. 238.
100. Gerald Wright, "Bureaucratic Politics and Canada's Foreign Economic Policy," in Denis Stairs and Gilbert R. Winham, eds., *Selected Problems in Formulating Foreign Economic Policy* (Toronto, 1985), p. 14. See also Richard J. Van Loon on the resistance of ministers, who "thrive on individual

recognition," to central agency controls. "Kaleidoscope in Grey: The Policy Process in Ottawa," in Michael S. Whittington and Glen Williams, eds., *Canadian Politics in the 1980s*, 2nd ed. (Toronto, 1984), p. 432.

101. Flanagan, "The Manufacture of Minorities," p. 109.

102. Cairns, "The Embedded State," pp. 76-77.

103. As noted in David Held and Joel Kruger, "Accumulation, Legitimation and the State: The Ideas of Claus Offe and Jurgen Habermas," in David Held *et al.*, *States and Societies* (Oxford, 1983), pp. 490-91.

104. *Report of the Royal Commission on Dominion-Provincial Relations* (Ottawa, 1954), p. 27, n. 17.

105. Léon Dion, *Québec: The Unfinished Revolution* (Montreal, 1976), p. 86.

106. Kenneth Bryden, *Old Age Pensions and Policy-Making in Canada* (Montreal, 1974), p. 194.

107. The author classified the 14,885 powers he discovered as 5,938 judicial, 2,933 administrative, 1,298 investigative, and 3,467 rule-making; this represented "only the tip of the iceberg." Philip Anisman, *A Catalogue of Discretionary Powers in the Revised Statutes of Canada 1970* (Ottawa, 1975), p. 23.

108. Robert J. Jackson *et al.*, *Politics in Canada* (Scarborough, Ont., 1986), pp. 333-35.

109. Macdonald Commission report, vol. 2, p. 551.

110. Keith G. Banting, *The Welfare State and Canadian Federalism*, 2nd ed. (Montreal, 1987), p. 101.

111. Leslie A. Pal, *State, Class, and Bureaucracy: Canadian Unemployment Insurance and Public Policy* (Montreal, 1988), pp. 161-68.

112. *Building on Our Strengths: Report of the Royal Commission on Employment and Unemployment* (St. John's, 1986), pp. 283-84.

113. Stanbury, *Business-Government Relations*.

114. *Ibid.*, p. 210.

115. *Ibid.*, pp. 77-80.

116. Hartle, *Public Policy*, p. 62.

117. For the growth of business associations, see William D. Coleman, "Canadian Business and the State," in Keith Banting, ed., *The State and Economic Interests* (Toronto, 1986).

118. Mishra, *The Welfare State in Crisis*, p. 36.

119. Stanbury, *Business-Government Relations*, p. 306.

120. Coleman, "Canadian Business and the State," pp. 260-61; Stanbury, *Business-Government Relations*, p. 306.

121. Macdonald Commission report, vol. 1, p. 43.

122. John Keane, "Introduction," in Offe, *Contradictions of the Welfare State*, pp. 18, 24.

123. *Ibid.*, p. 24.

124. Cited in Anthony H. Birch, "Political Authority and Crisis in Comparative Perspective," in Banting, ed., *State and Society*, p. 100.

125. Karl W. Deutsch, *The Nerves of Government* (New York, 1963), ch. 11.

126. Subject, of course, to the utilization of the section 33 override with respect to section 2 or sections 7 through 15 of the Charter.

## The Constitutional World We Have Lost

This is a revised version of a paper originally presented at the annual meeting of the Canadian Political Science Association, University of Prince Edward Island, June 1, 1992. Any improvements reflect helpful suggestions by Ned Franks, Ted Hodgetts, Les Jacobs, Richard Johnston, David Milne, Max Nemni, Paul Tennant, and Doug Williams. Stephen Phillips provided excellent research assistance.

1. "Notes for a Speech by the Right Honourable Joe Clark, PC, MP, President of the Privy Council and Minister Responsible for Constitutional Affairs to the Business Council on National Issues at the Four Seasons Hotel (Yorkville), Toronto, October 6, 1992," mimeo.

2. Judge Rosalie Silberman Abella, Commissioner, *Report of the Commission on Equality in Employment* (Ottawa, 1984), p. 1.

3. R.M. Dawson, *The Government of Canada* (Toronto, 1947).

4. *Report of the Royal Commission on Dominion-Provincial Relations* (Ottawa, 1940).

5. Quebec, *Report of the Royal Commission of Inquiry on Constitutional Problems* (Quebec, 1956).

6. W.F. O'Connor, *Report Pursuant to Resolution of the Senate to the Honourable the Speaker by the Parliamentary Counsel Relating to the Enactment of the British North America Act, 1867, any lack of consonance between its terms and judicial construction of them and cognate matters* (Ottawa, 1939).

7. In the mid-eighties, Mallory referred to "the once evocative term 'responsible government'. . . . For nearly a century, the concept of responsible government was the pivot around which English-Canadian historians developed the theme of evolving Canadian autonomy and the building of a Canadian nation. It was one of the few concepts about Canadian politics that stuck in the minds of generations of Canadian schoolchildren. It became a central part of the mythology of Canadian history, an outstanding example of the use of the past to create a sense of national identity in a colonial people." J.R. Mallory, "The Continuing Evolution of Canadian Constitutionalism," in Alan Cairns and Cynthia Williams, eds., *Constitutionalism, Citizenship, and Society in Canada*, volume 33 of the research studies prepared for the Royal

Commission on the Economic Union and Development Prospects for Canada (Toronto, 1985), p. 55.

8. See the discussion by H. McD. Clokie, *Canadian Government and Politics* (Toronto, 1944), pp. 54-66. See also S.M. Lipset, "Democracy in Alberta," *Canadian Forum*, 34 (1954-55), pp. 175-77, 196-98.

9. See, for example, Bora Laskin, *Canadian Constitutional Law: Cases, Text and Notes on Distribution of Legislative Power*, 3rd ed. (Toronto, 1966). The subtitle communicates the essence of the text.

10. Pierre Elliott Trudeau, *Federalism and the French Canadians* (Toronto, 1968), p. 120.

11. *A Preliminary Report of the Royal Commission on Bilingualism and Biculturalism* (Ottawa, 1965), p. 125.

12. *Ibid.*, p. 28.

13. For a good example, see Alexander Brady, "Canada and the Model of Westminster," in William B. Hamilton, ed., *The Transfer of Institutions* (Durham, N.C., 1964), pp. 67-68.

14. There were, of course, counter-trends. For western agrarian populists, House of Commons majoritarianism backed by the instrument of party discipline was seen as a vehicle for the domination of central over western Canada.

15. Reshaping the monarchical role and image also required enhancing Canadian control over the appointing process for Governors General, and ultimately appointing Canadians to that office.

16. See Mallory, "Continuing Evolution of Canadian Constitutionalism," for a general discussion of the decline of checks and balances in the Canadian constitutional system prior to the Charter.

17. Rogers M. Smith has written two excellent articles on the American exclusion strategy derived from the tensions between three citizenship discourses – classical liberalism, classical republicanism, and Americanism. "The 'American Creed' and American Identity: The Limits of Liberal Citizenship in the United States," *Western Political Quarterly*, 41, 2 (June, 1988), and "'One United People': Second-Class Female Citizenship and the American Quest for Community," *Yale Journal of Law and the Humanities*, 1, 2 (May, 1989). See also Judith N. Shklar, *American Citizenship: The Quest for Inclusion* (Cambridge, Mass., 1991).

18. Canada, *Final Report: Royal Commission on Electoral Reform and Party Financing*, vol. 1 (Ottawa, 1991), pp. 169, 176.

19. Richard Diubaldo, "The Government of Canada and the Inuit 1900-1967," Research Branch, Corporate Policy, Indian and Northern Affairs, 1985, mimeo, pp. 93, 113.

20. H.B. Hawthorn and M.-A. Tremblay, eds., *A Survey of the Contemporary Indians of Canada: Economic, Political, Educational Needs and Policies*, Part 1 (Ottawa, 1966), p. 345.

21. Quoted in Augie Fleras and Jean Leonard Elliott, *The 'Nations Within': Aboriginal-State Relations in Canada, the United States, and New Zealand* (Toronto, 1992), p. 40. Sir John A. Macdonald agreed, stating in 1887: "The great aim of our civilization has been to do away with the tribal system and assimilate the Indian people in all respects with the inhabitants of the Dominion, as speedily as they are fit for the change." Quoted *ibid.*, p. 39.

22. Noel Dyck, *What is the Indian 'Problem': Tutelage and Resistance in Canadian Indian Administration* (St. John's, Newfoundland, 1991), p. 3.

23. *Ibid.*, pp. 24, 27.

24. As Mallory stated in 1985, "the place of native peoples in the constitutional order [was] a non-issue for a century because the group involved was politically invisible . . . [in any event], it was the common, and, in modern eyes, arrogant nineteenth century belief that Indians (and later Inuit) were part of an inferior culture, and that conversion to Christianity and assimilation would lead to their disappearance as a distinct group." "Continuing Evolution of Canadian Constitutionalism," p. 84.

25. Hawthorn and Tremblay, eds., *Survey of Contemporary Indians*, p. 349.

26. *Report on the Metis Nation's Constitutional Parallel Process, The Metis Nation on the Move* (Métis National Council, March 31, 1992), p. 12.

27. Hawthorn and Tremblay, eds., *Survey of Contemporary Indians*, p. 346.

28. *Report of the Royal Commission on the Status of Women in Canada* (Ottawa, 1970), pp. 339, 340, 342.

29. *Ibid.*, p. 355.

30. André Siegfried, *The Race Question in Canada*, ed. Frank H. Underhill (Toronto, 1966; original French edition, 1906).

31. Alexander Brady, *Democracy in the Dominions: A Comparative Study in Institutions* (Toronto, 1947); Clokie, *Canadian Government and Politics*; J.A. Corry, *Democratic Government and Politics* (Toronto, 1946); Dawson, *Government of Canada*.

32. John Herd Thompson, *Ethnic Minorities During Two World Wars* (Ottawa, 1991).

33. John Porter, *The Vertical Mosaic* (Toronto, 1965).

34. *Report: Royal Commission on Electoral Reform*, 1, pp. 100-01.

35. *Ibid.*, p. 170.

36. Two referenda were held in Newfoundland in 1948 to determine its constitutional future, leading to union with Canada in 1949. See S.J.R. Noel, *Politics in Newfoundland* (Toronto, 1971), pp. 255-60, for an analysis. Reg Whitaker,

*A Sovereign Idea: Essays on Canada as a Democratic Community* (Montreal and Kingston, 1992), esp. chs. 6, 7, 8, is an incisive analysis of democracy and the constitution in Canada.

37. In his study of the Fulton-Favreau formula, Agar Adamson concluded that "many of the reasons for agreement in October 1964 were also causes of the formula's ultimate failure. The conferences were held in isolation and the public was not sufficiently informed of their deliberations. . . . The failure . . . should be a warning to Canadian politicians to take a greater interest in the 'demands' of society. . . . A greater effort must be made by those participating in the review of the Constitution to involve the public in their deliberations . . . they must explain their decisions to Canadians in order that this study of the Constitution can initiate the social changes necessary in the political system for its acceptance." Agar Adamson, "The Fulton-Favreau Formula: a study of its development 1960 to 1966," *Journal of Canadian Studies*, 6, 1 (February, 1971), p. 54.

38. Justice W.R. Riddell, "The Judicial Committee of the Privy Council," *Canadian Law Times*, 30 (1910), p. 304.

39. Alexander Brady, *Democracy in the Dominions: A Comparative Study of Institutions*, 2nd ed. (Toronto, 1952), p. 7.

40. See Carl Berger, *The Sense of Power: Studies in the Ideas of Canadian Imperialism 1867-1914* (Toronto, 1970), for a brilliant analysis of the imperial mentality of the British Canadian.

41. Robert M. Belliveau questions the thesis that Diefenbaker would have preferred an entrenched bill binding on both orders of government and asserts that Diefenbaker, a defender of provincial rights and a devoted supporter of parliamentary government, was happy with a declaratory bill applicable only to Ottawa. It would strengthen Parliament's respect for rights, while retaining parliamentary supremacy. Robert M. Belliveau, "Mr. Diefenbaker, Parliamentary Democracy, and the Canadian Bill of Rights" (M.A. thesis, Political Studies, University of Saskatchewan, May, 1992).

42. Peter C. Newman, *Renegade in Power: The Diefenbaker Years* (Toronto, 1964), p. 188. "Being of mixed origin myself," he stated to a meeting of eighty-five ethnic editors in 1961, "I knew something, in my boyhood days in Saskatchewan, of the feeling that was all too apparent in many parts of Canada, that citizenship depended upon surnames, or even upon blood counts." *Ibid.*, p. 187. See also J.L. Granatstein, *Canada 1957-1967: The Years of Uncertainty and Innovation* (Toronto, 1986), pp. 16-17, for Diefenbaker's desire for a "Canadian citizenship that knew no hyphenated consideration . . . 'I never deviated from this purpose,' Diefenbaker said. 'It's the reason I went into public life.'"

43. J.R. Mallory, *The Structure of Canadian Government* (Toronto, 1971), p. 395.

44. Donald V. Smiley, *Constitutional Adaptation and Canadian Federalism since 1945* (Ottawa, 1970), p. 25.

45. *The Task Force on Canadian Unity: A Future Together: Observations and Recommendations* (Ottawa, 1979), p. 21.

46. In different language, we no longer have the luxury of employing "constitutional abeyances" to keep insolvable, divisive issues in the constitutional shadows, one of the secrets of our former constitutional success. See David Thomas, "Turning a Blind Eye: Constitutional Abeyances and the Canadian Experience," mimeo, presented at annual meeting of the Canadian Political Science Association, Charlottetown, P.E.I., June 1, 1992. The legacy of this, of course, is a central reason for our present constitutional impasse.

47. Dyck, *What is the Indian 'Problem'*, pp. 142, 54, 103.


## Constitutional Minoritarianism in Canada

The J.A. Corry Lecture delivered at Queen's University, March 6, 1990.

1. Bruce Lincoln, *Discourse and the Construction of Society: Comparative Studies of Myth, Ritual, and Classification* (New York, 1989), p. 11.

2. Adrienne Rich, cited in Renato Rosaldo, *Culture and Truth: The Remaking of Social Analysis* (Boston, 1989), p. ix.

3. J.A. Corry, *My Life and Work, a happy partnership: Memoirs of J.A. Corry* (Kingston, Ont., 1981).

4. For a preliminary discussion, see Alan C. Cairns, "Political Science, Ethnicity, and the Canadian Constitution," in David P. Shugarman and Reg Whitaker, eds., *Federalism and Political Community: Essays in Honour of Donald Smiley* (Peterborough, Ont., 1989).

5. Robert C. Vipond, "Whatever Became of the Compact Theory? Meech Lake and the New Politics of Constitutional Amendment in Canada," *Queen's Quarterly*, 96, 4 (Winter, 1989).

6. Victor G. Kiernan, *The Lords of Human Kind* (New York, 1986).

7. Gwen Brodsky and Shelagh Day, *Canadian Charter Equality Rights for Women: One Step Forward or Two Steps Back?* (Ottawa, 1989), p. 149.

8. Lorenne M.G. Clark, "Liberalism and the Living-Tree: Women, Equality, and the Charter," *Alberta Law Review*, XXVIII, 2 (1990), p. 392.

9. For the Aboriginal challenge, see Mary Ellen Turpel, "Aboriginal Peoples and the Canadian *Charter*: Interpretive Monopolies, Cultural Differences," in Michelle Boivin *et al.*, eds., *Canadian Human Rights Yearbook* (Ottawa, 1990). For an analysis of what "real women's distinctive view of human interaction [could] do for the Constitution and thus for all of us," with respect to the American constitution, see Kenneth L. Karst, "Woman's

Constitution," *Duke Law Journal*, no. 3 (June, 1984). For a basic overview of feminist orientations to law in Canada, see Susan B. Boyd and Elizabeth A. Sheehy, "Canadian Feminist Perspectives on Law," *Journal of Law and Society*, 13, 3 (Autumn, 1986). See also the various bibliographies produced by Resources for Feminist Research.

10. Lincoln, *Discourse and the Construction of Society*, p. 7.
11. Alan C. Cairns, "Ritual, Taboo, and Bias in Constitutional Controversies in Canada, or Constitutional Talk Canadian Style," The Timlin Lecture, Saskatoon, University of Saskatchewan, 1989.
12. Subsequently, I encountered the criticism of Christine Boyle of "writing that embodies a male perspective on the world masquerading as an objective non-gendered perspective. This masquerade embodies an extravagantly polemical statement that the male equals the human and that it is not worth inquiring about the existence of a female perspective." "Criminal Law and Procedure: Who Needs Tenure?" *Osgoode Hall Law Journal*, 23, 3 (1985), p. 428.
13. Turpel, "Aboriginal Peoples and the Canadian *Charter*," p. 7.
14. Jim Sinclair, AMNSIS president, cited in *New Breed* (August/September, 1987), p. 4.
15. Edwin R. Black, *Divided Loyalties: Canadian Concepts of Federalism* (Montreal, 1975).
16. Alpheus Todd, *Parliamentary Government in the British Colonies* (Boston, 1880).
17. C.E.S. Franks, *The Parliament of Canada* (Toronto, 1987).
18. J.R. Mallory, *The Structure of Canadian Government* (Toronto, 1971), p. xi. Mallory's use of habitat specifically refers to "Parliament, the Cabinet, and the institutions related to them," to which I have added federalism.
19. Eric J. Hobsbawm and Terence Ranger, eds., *The Invention of Tradition* (New York, 1983).
20. "Equality-seekers have historically had the least access to the levers of power and the least experience with traditional venues of decision-making. They continue to operate from a disadvantaged position. Their 'partnership' in the community of persons concerned with the Charter remains unequal." Magda Seydegart, "Introduction," in Lynn Smith, ed., *Righting the Balance: Canada's New Equality Rights* (Saskatoon, 1986), pp. viii-ix.
21. Simone de Beauvoir, *The Second Sex*, trans. and ed. by H.M. Parshley (New York, 1974).
22. George Manuel and Michael Posluns, *The Fourth World: an Indian Reality* (Don Mills, Ont., 1974).
23. Harry W. Daniels, ed., *The Forgotten People: Métis and non-status Indian Land Claims* (Ottawa, 1979).

24. Dave McKay, "The Non-People," mimeo, 1972, Indian Claims Commission collection, National Library of Canada.

25. James Arvaluk, "Canada's Forgotten Colony," address to the Rotary Club of Ottawa, January 5, 1976, mimeo, p. 10.

26. Kathleen Jamieson, *Indian Women and the Law in Canada: Citizens Minus* (Ottawa, 1978).

27. Winnie Ng, "Immigrant Women: The Silent Partners of the Women's Movement," in Maureen Fitzgerald *et al.*, *Still Ain't Satisfied! Canadian Feminism Today* (Toronto, 1982), p. 250.

28. Federation of Francophones outside Quebec, *The Heirs of Lord Durham: Manifesto of a Vanishing People* (Ottawa, 1978).

29. P.E. Trudeau, "Transcript of the Prime Minister's Remarks at the Vancouver Liberal Association Dinner, Seaforth Armories, Vancouver, B.C.," August, 1969, mimeo, p. 8.

30. Women, of course, are not a numerical minority, nor are men a numerical majority. In terms of status, power, and self-perception, however, women are a minority and men a majority, rather in the same way that Quebec Francophones used to see themselves as a majority-minority and Quebec Anglophones as a minority-majority.

31. J. Stefan Dupré, "Canadian Constitutionalism and the Sequel to the Meech Lake/Langevin Accord," in Shugarman and Whitaker, eds., *Federalism and Political Community*, p. 245.

32. Turpel, "Aboriginal Peoples and the Canadian *Charter*," p. 23.

33. Cited in Jeremy Webber, "The Adjudication of Contested Social Values: Implications of Attitudinal Bias for the Appointment of Judges," September 14-15, 1989, mimeo, p. 4.

34. Madame Justice Bertha Wilson, "Will Women Judges Really Make a Difference?" the Fourth Annual Barbara Betcherman Memorial Lecture, Osgoode Hall Law School, February 8, 1990, mimeo, p. 19.

35. Sheilah L. Martin and Kathleen E. Mahoney, eds., *Equality and Judicial Neutrality* (Toronto, 1987), p. iii.

36. For example, a prominent and prolific feminist law professor recently argued that "the debate over feminist scholarship is about who may speak for other people and how the appropriation of experience can be legitimated in the process of constructing knowledge." Kathleen A. Lahey, ". . . Until Women Themselves have told all that they have to tell . . .," *Osgoode Hall Law Journal*, 23, 3 (1985), p. 525.

37. The literature is voluminous. An excellent survey of the issues is Bill Ashcroft, Gareth Griffiths, and Helen Tiffin, *The Empire Writes Back: Theory and Practice in Post-Colonial Literatures* (London, 1989). For a good case study, see Margery Fee, "Why C.K. Stead didn't like Keri Hulme's *the bone*

*people*: Who can write as Other?" *Australian and New Zealand Studies in Canada*, 1 (1989), pp. 11-32, for a discussion of whether "majority group members [can] speak as minority members, Whites as people of colour, men as women, intellectuals as working people." For a Canadian contribution to the debate, see Lenore Keeshig-Tobias, "Stop stealing native stories," *Globe and Mail*, January 26, 1990. Keeshig-Tobias, an Ojibway poet, asserts that Native stories written by whites or films produced by whites "amount to culture theft, the theft of voice."

38. James Clifford, *The Predicament of Culture: Twentieth-Century Ethnography, Literature, and Art* (Cambridge, Mass., 1988), p. 256.

39. *Ibid.*, p. 7.

40. Clifford Geertz, *Works and Lives: The Anthropologist as Author* (Stanford, Calif., 1988), p. 133.

41. *Ibid.*, p. 131.

42. John Claydon, "International Human Rights Law and the Interpretation of the Canadian Charter of Rights and Freedoms," *Supreme Court Law Review*, 4 (1982); Anne F. Bayefsky, "The Principle of Equality or Non-Discrimination in International Law: Implications for Equality Rights in the Charter," in Smith, ed., *Righting the Balance.*

43. Centre for Human Rights, *Human Rights: Status of International Instruments* (New York, 1987), p. 139.

44. David R. Cameron, "Lord Durham Then and Now, 1989 Morton Lecture," delivered at Trent University, May 17, 1989, mimeo, p. 30.

45. Mary Douglas, *How Institutions Think* (Syracuse, 1986), p. 100.

46. Quoted in George F. Kennan, "Witness" (review of Timothy Garton Ash, *The Uses of Adversity: Essays on the Fate of Central Europe*), *The New York Review of Books*, March 1, 1990, p. 4.

47. Lincoln, *Discourse and the Construction of Society*, p. 105.

48. Samuel LaSelva, "Does the Canadian Charter of Rights and Freedoms Rest on a Mistake?" *Windsor Yearbook of Access to Justice*, 8 (1988), p. 223.

49. Unfortunately, I have been unable to trace this statement to a source more reliable than my own memory.

50. J.A. Corry, *The Changing Conditions of Politics* (Toronto, 1963).

51. Jim MacPherson, "Litigating Equality Rights," in Smith, ed., *Righting the Balance*, p. 232.

52. Lowell Murray, "The Process of Constitutional Change in Canada: The Lessons of Meech Lake," *Choices* (Halifax, February, 1988).

53. See John W. Chapman and Alan Wertheimer, eds., *Majorities and Minorities* (New York, 1990), for a valuable discussion, primarily from an American perspective.

## Barriers to Constitutional Renewal in Canada

1. Some of the material in this lecture draws on an earlier lecture, the McDonald Currie Lecture, "Why is Constitutional Reform so Difficult?" delivered at McGill University, November 22, 1990.

2. Michael Kammen, *A Machine That Would Go of Itself: the Constitution in American Culture* (New York, 1987), p. xi.

3. An abridgement of the five volumes of the Tremblay Report is available. See David Kwavnick, ed., *The Tremblay Report: Report of the Royal Commission of Inquiry on Constitutional Problems*, Carleton Library No. 64 (Toronto, 1973).

4. *Report of the Royal Commission on Bilingualism and Biculturalism* (Ottawa, 1967-70).

5. Constitution Act, 1982, s. 35(2). "In this Act, 'aboriginal peoples of Canada' includes the Indian, Inuit and Métis peoples of Canada."

6. See Shiva S. Halli *et al.*, eds., *Ethnic Demography: Canadian Immigrant, Racial and Cultural Variations* (Ottawa, 1990), for up-to-date data and analysis.

7. In a Globe and Mail – CBC News/Poll, *Globe and Mail,* July 9, 1990, two out of three Quebec residents, and an even higher ratio outside of Quebec, believe that "Changes to the constitution should only be decided by the people voting directly in a referendum." In a slightly earlier poll, 71 per cent of Canadians supported having a referendum on Meech Lake, including 58 per cent Quebec support. Julian Beltrame, "Canadians want Meech referendum, poll finds," *Globe and Mail*, April 7, 1990.

8. First Ministers' Conference on the Constitution, verbatim transcript, Ottawa, June 9-10, 1990 (Document: 800-029/004 Canadian Intergovernmental Conference Secretariat), pp. 3, 9, 24, 33, 44.

9. Canada, Federal-Provincial Relations Office, *Amending the Constitution of Canada: A Discussion Paper* (Ottawa, 1990), pp. 1, 13, 20.

10. PC 1990-2347, Privy Council Minute of November 1, 1990, establishing the Forum, instructed the Chairman and Advisory Group "to lead a process of public discussion and dialogue," and to ensure "the participation of a broad spectrum of Canadians of all ages, backgrounds, regions, and walks of life. . . ."

11. Citizens' Forum on Canada's Future, "Getting Under Way, Mandate and Consultative Process," December 5, 1990, pp. 5-6.

12. "You will not be able to get me to ever cut off debate on a constitutional resolution. They can go on for as long as they want, years. I want to hear everybody. I want them recorded. I want them filmed. I want documents. I want (pause) and if I've missed anybody I'm going to reopen it." Robert

Sheppard, "Searching for a card Mulroney can play," *Globe and Mail*,
November 5, 1990, reporting an earlier June 11, 1990, *Globe and Mail* parliamentary bureau interview with Brian Mulroney.

13. Alan C. Cairns, "The Limited Constitutional Vision of Meech Lake," in
Katherine E. Swinton and Carol J. Rogerson, eds., *Competing Constitutional
Visions: The Meech Lake Accord* (Toronto, 1988), p. 248.

14. Immediately after the demise of Meech Lake, Premier Bourassa stated, in a
television address: "it is the position of my government to negotiate henceforth with two, not 11, to negotiate with the Canadian government, which
represents the whole of the population of Canada, bilateral negotiations
between the government of Quebec and the federal government . . . we can
decide to participate in certain conferences in which Quebec's interests are
involved, but never at the constitutional level." "A critical moment in Quebec's history," *Globe and Mail*, June 15, 1990.

15. For a discussion, see Alan C. Cairns, "Constitutional Change and the Three
Equalities," in Ronald L. Watts and Douglas M. Brown, eds., *Options for a
New Canada* (Toronto, 1991), pp. 93-97.

16. The raw materials for the debate are available in the exchanges in Annex A of
Donald Johnston, ed., *Lac Meech: Trudeau parle . . . Textes réunis et présentés
par Donald Johnston* (Ville LaSalle, Quebec, 1989).

17. I have explored this and related issues in "Constitutional Minoritarianism
in Canada," in Ronald L. Watts and Douglas M. Brown, eds., *Canada: The
State of the Federation 1990* (Kingston, 1990).

18. "My unease . . . springs from the fact that the Accord fails to embody any
vision of the national community, of Canada. It appears to be a document
drawn up by provincial governments for provincial governments, the result
of a constitutional contest in which the federal government was a referee but
not a player aggressively pursuing its own interest and vision." Roger Gibbins, "A Sense of Unease: The Meech Lake Accord and Constitution-Making
in Canada," in Roger Gibbins *et al.*, eds., *Meech Lake and Canada: Perspectives from the West* (Edmonton, 1988), p. 129.

19. Section 28: "Notwithstanding anything in this Charter, the rights and freedoms referred to in it are guaranteed equally to male and female persons."

20. Section 33: "(1) Parliament or the legislature of a province may expressly
declare in an Act of Parliament or of the legislature, as the case may be, that
the Act or a provision thereof shall operate notwithstanding a provision
included in section 2 or sections 7 to 15 of this Charter. . . . (3) A declaration
made under subsection (1) shall cease to have effect five years after it comes
into force or on such earlier date as may be specified in the declaration. (4)
Parliament or a legislature of a province may re-enact a declaration made
under subsection (1)."

21. Section 27: "This Charter shall be interpreted in a manner consistent with the preservation and enhancement of the multicultural heritage of Canadians."

22. Section 15: "(1) Every individual is equal before and under the law and has the right to the equal protection and equal benefit of the law without discrimination and, in particular, without discrimination based on race, national or ethnic origin, colour, religion, sex, age or mental or physical disability. (2) Subsection (1) does not preclude any law, program or activity that has as its object the amelioration of conditions of disadvantaged individuals or groups including those that are disadvantaged because of race, national or ethnic origin, colour, religion, sex, age, or mental or physical disability."

23. Section 16: "Nothing in section 2 of the *Constitution Act, 1867* affects section 25 or 27 of the *Canadian Charter of Rights and Freedoms*, section 35 of the *Constitution Act, 1982* or class 24 of section 91 of the *Constitution Act, 1867.*"

24. Section 25: "The guarantee in this Charter of certain rights and freedoms shall not be construed so as to abrogate or derogate from any aboriginal, treaty or other rights or freedoms that pertain to the aboriginal peoples of Canada including: (a) any rights or freedoms that have been recognized by the Royal Proclamation of October 7, 1763; and, (b) any rights or freedoms that may be acquired by the aboriginal peoples of Canada by way of land claims settlement."

25. See Bryan Schwartz, *First Principles, Second Thoughts: Aboriginal Peoples, Constitutional Reform and Canadian Statecraft* (Montreal, 1986), ch. vi, "Consent to Constitutional Amendments," for the complexities of the veto proposal and of a parallel opting-out proposal.

26. Cairns, "Constitutional Minoritarianism in Canada."

## The Fragmentation of Canadian Citizenship

1. The Report of the Special Joint Committee of the Senate and the House of Commons (Beaudoin-Edwards Committee), *The Process for Amending the Constitution of Canada* (Ottawa, June 20, 1991).

2. *Citizen's Forum on Canada's Future: Report to the People and Government of Canada* (Spicer Report) (Ottawa, 1991).

3. The "political vision, based on the Canadian Charter of Rights and Freedoms enshrined in the 1982 Act, perceives equality as having a strictly individual scope and applying uniformly across Canada: it does not make allowance for Quebec society to receive special constitutional recognition. The notion of a distinct Quebec society is thus understood as being a source of inequality and incompatible with the principle of equality of all Canadian

citizens." Bélanger-Campeau Commission, *Report of the Commission on the Political and Constitutional Future of Québec* (Quebec, 1991), p. 34.

4. For analysis of Canada from a three-nations perspective, see Peter G. White, "Understanding Canada's Cultural Reality: Accommodating Canada's Three Established Cultural-Linguistic Groups within the Canadian Federal System," submission to the Special Joint Committee on a Renewed Canada, January, 1992, mimeo. For recent advocacy of a three-nations view of Canada and a "National Covenant" negotiated and signed by their representatives, see "Speaking Notes by Ron George, President, NCC, to the Policy Conference on 'Identity, Rights and Values,'" February 6-9, 1992, Toronto. Ten academics from the University of Toronto and York University and the writer Christina McCall have also supported a three-nations approach. See "Three Nations in a Delicate State," *Toronto Star*, February 4, 1992.

5. See Sally M. Weaver, *Making Canadian Indian Policy: The Hidden Agenda 1968-1970* (Toronto, 1981), for an excellent analysis.

6. White, "Understanding Canada's Cultural Reality," p. 6.

7. André Siegfried, *The Race Question in Canada*, ed. Frank H. Underhill (Toronto, 1966; original French edition published in 1906).

8. René Lévesque, "For an Independent Quebec," in J. Peter Meekison, ed., *Canadian Federalism: Myth or Reality*, 3rd ed. (Toronto, 1977), p. 491.

9. M.E. Turpel and P.A. (Trisha) Monture, "Ode to Elijah: Reflections of Two First Nations Women on the Rekindling of Spirit at the Wake for the Meech Lake Accord," *Queen's Law Journal*, 15, 2 (1990), p. 345, and "The Myth of Canada's Dual Nationhood Was Stopped Dead in Its Tracks," p. 348.

10. For example, even the suggestion "that all of the Aboriginal people in Atlantic Canada could participate in one Aboriginal Electoral District" was described by a New Brunswick chief as a "non-Indian thought process." The Committee for Aboriginal Electoral Reform, *The Path to Electoral Equality* (Ottawa, 1991), p. 31.

11. *Sparrow v. The Queen* [1990] 1 SCR 1075 at 1108.

12. *Report of the Aboriginal Justice Inquiry of Manitoba*, Vol. 1, *The Justice System and Aboriginal People* (Winnipeg, 1991); Law Reform Commission, *Report on Aboriginal Peoples and Criminal Justice: Equality, Respect and the Search for Justice* (Ottawa, 1991).

13. Government of Canada, *Shaping Canada's Future Together: Proposals* (Ottawa, 1991), pp. 8-9.

14. Committee for Aboriginal Electoral Reform, *The Path to Electoral Equality*.

15. Deborah Wilson, "Loud, Clear Voice of the 'Other' Indians," *Globe and Mail*, December 17, 1991, citing Ron George, president of the Native Council of Canada. The Native Council describes the unacceptable divisions among Aboriginal peoples as follows: "Ottawa has created separate classes of

Aboriginal Peoples in a system of apartheid that presents little more than a choice of the form of cultural genocide: complete segregation or complete assimilation." Native Council of Canada, *Towards a New Covenant* (Ottawa, 1992), n.p. The Métis National Council also supports the interpretation that the federal government has, and should exercise, jurisdictional responsibility for Métis under section 91(24). "MNC Response to the Federal Proposal," mimeo, n.d., p. 3.

This goal may not be easily attained for the Métis. In a 1986 national survey, "even after pointed prompting in the interview only a small majority (55.5%) of the Canadian population classified the Métis as aboriginal people. Hence, it is difficult for the Métis to ride the political coattails of status Indians, if Métis leaders were so inclined." J. Rick Ponting, "Aboriginal Dilemmas of the Federal State in Canada," paper presented to the annual meetings of the Association for Canadian Studies in the Netherlands, Hilversum, The Netherlands, November 29, 1991, mimeo, p. 6.

16. Joe Clark, Minister Responsible for Constitutional Affairs, "Notes for a Speech . . . at a Luncheon Hosted by the Saskatchewan Métis Assembly at the Saskatoon Inn," Saskatoon, September 28, 1991, mimeo, p. 5.

17. Kim Campbell, Minister of Justice, "Aboriginal Constitutional Matters, Speech . . . at University of Ottawa, Faculty of Law, Ottawa, November 1, 1991," mimeo, pp. 8-9.

18. A recent paper by Robert K. Groves and Jean-Yves Assiniwi, "Aboriginal Peoples and the Division of Powers in a Reformed Federalism," January 10, 1992, mimeo, p. 5, citing what are viewed as conservative figures from Statistics Canada, gave a total of 950,000 Aboriginal people as of 1991 – 247,000 non-status Indians, 148,000 Métis without lands, 5,000 Métis with lands, 35,000 Inuit, 311,000 status Indians on reserve, and 205,000 status Indians off reserve.

19. When the Mohawk warriors were asked to surrender their weapons to facilitate a negotiated solution to the 1990 Oka crisis, Ellen Gabriel, Mohawk spokesperson, stated: "One sovereign country does not surrender its weapons to another sovereign country."

A history textbook, used in Mohawk schools, teaches the students that "they are the original inhabitants of North America, and because of their aboriginal occupation of this hemisphere, have a special status above all of the European, Asian and African immigrants to North America." Stanley G. French, "Native Peoples and Quebec Sovereignty," Montreal, December, 1990, mimeo, p. 4.

Although the main Aboriginal organizations have insisted that they are not pursuing complete independence, but self-government within Canada, "various aboriginal groups have argued that they are sovereign nations beyond the jurisdiction of Canadian governments." C. Radha Jhappan, "Aboriginal People and the Right to Self-Government: Response to the Government of Canada's proposals on Aboriginal Self-Government," Ottawa, November 6, 1991, mimeo, pp. 13-14.

20. Ponting recently noted the "Indians' demonstrated tendency to play the game of political embarrassment on the international stage" and that "Canadian aboriginals appear to have world public opinion on their side." Ponting, "Aboriginal Dilemmas," pp. 4, 3. See also J. Rick Ponting, "Internationalization: Perspectives on an Emerging Direction in Aboriginal Affairs," *Canadian Ethnic Studies*, 22, 3 (1990), pp. 85-109.

21. Report of the Canadian Bar Association, *Rebuilding a Canadian Consensus: An Analysis of the Federal Government's Proposals for a Renewed Canada* (Ottawa, 1991), p. 168. See Inuit Tapirisat of Canada, "Constitutional Position Paper – Inuit in Canada: Striving for Equality," Ottawa, February 6, 1992, mimeo, pp. 7-8, for elaboration of the Inuit demands for participation in the constitutional reform process, including a requirement for Aboriginal consent to amendments in key areas of concern to Aboriginal peoples.

22. Susan Delacourt, "Clark Offered Unity Plan Advice," *Globe and Mail*, October 3, 1991.

23. Government of Canada, *Shaping Canada's Future Together*, pp. 4-9.

24. The First Peoples Constitutional Review Commission, *Aboriginal Directions for Coexistence in Canada*, NCC Constitutional Review Commission Working Paper No. 1 (Ottawa, August, 1991), p. 3.

25. Frank Cassidy and Robert L. Bish, *Indian Government: Its Meaning in Practice* (Halifax, 1989), p. 56.

26. See French, "Native Peoples and Quebec Sovereignty," for a discussion. The conflict was clearly enunciated by national chief Ovide Mercredi of the Assembly of First Nations. See his "Speaking Notes for . . . Constituent Assembly on the Renewal of Canada: Identity, Rights and Values," Toronto, February 7, 1992, mimeo, p. 4, dealing with the tension between the proposed designation of Quebec as a distinct society and the "10 First Nations in the provincial boundaries of Quebec who do not have a tradition of French language, culture and civil law . . . [They] . . . cannot be made subject to French language, culture and civil law without their freely informed consent."

The Inuit Tapirisat proposed that section 25 of the Charter protecting Aboriginal, treaty, or other rights from other Charter guarantees of rights and freedoms be amended to ensure that the federal government's 1991 distinct society constitutional proposals also do not abrogate or derogate from Aboriginal rights. "Inuit in Canada: Striving for Equality," p. 7.

27. *Citizens' Forum on Canada's Future*, pp. 4, 16, 24-25.

28. *Ibid.*, pp. 3, 53-54, 64.

29. Government of Canada, *Shaping Canada's Future Together*, p. vi.

30. Jean Chrétien, of course, now (1992) holds a seat from New Brunswick.

31. Charles Taylor, "Shared and Divergent Values," in Ronald L. Watts and Douglas M. Brown, eds., *Options for a New Canada* (Toronto, 1991), pp. 74-76.

32. See Alan C. Cairns, *Charter versus Federalism: The Dilemmas of Constitutional Reform* (Montreal, 1992), pp. 120-22, for a discussion of the Charter's reception in Quebec. Mary Ellen Turpel's "Aboriginal Peoples and the Canadian *Charter*: Interpretive Monopolies, Cultural Differences," *Canadian Human Rights Yearbook*, 6 (1989-90), pp. 3-45, is a passionate critique of the Charter's appropriateness for Aboriginal peoples.

    The Law Reform Commission's *Report on Aboriginal Peoples and Criminal Justice* observed (p. 20): "The question of determining to what extent *Charter* rights are negotiable can hardly be avoided." As the *Globe and Mail* pointed out in a biting editorial, the Law Reform Commission ducked most of the tough issues that would attend Aboriginal justice systems. *Globe and Mail*, "Defining the Terms of Native Justice," December 26, 1991.

33. Justice Minister Kim Campbell stated recently: "I know Aboriginal women are pleased to see that the Federal Proposal provides for the protection of the Charter. There are traditional values in every society that should be sacred and there are traditional values in every society that should be held up to the light every now and then." "Aboriginal Constitutional Matters," p. 8. See also *Globe and Mail*, "Canada Reconsidered: Aboriginal Rights," January 11, 1992, for the preference of the Native Women's Association of Canada to subject Aboriginal governments to the Charter.

34. Inuit Tapirisat of Canada, "Inuit in Canada," p. 6. The Native Council of Canada also asserts that the Charter's sexual equality rights must apply to "any form of aboriginal self-government." This Charter support appears to extend only to sections 15 and 28, not to the whole document. Support is further qualified by the additional phrase "unless and until something more appropriate than the Charter is in place." Ron George, "Speaking Notes . . . Feb. 6-9, Toronto, 1992," mimeo, pp. 10-11.

35. Tony Hall, "Aboriginal Issues and the New Political Map of Canada," n.d., mimeo, p. 7.

36. *Indian Self-Government in Canada, Report of the Special Committee* (Penner Report), Minutes of Proceedings of the Special Committee on Indian Self-Government, No. 40, 12, October 20, 1983, p. 63.

37. *Ibid.*, p. 59. "The Committee recommends . . . Legislation under the authority of Section 91 (24) of the *Constitution Act, 1867* designed to occupy all areas of competence necessary to permit Indian First Nations to govern them-

selves effectively and to ensure that provincial laws would not apply on Indian lands except by agreement of the Indian First Nation government."

38. Noel Lyon, *Aboriginal Self-Government: Rights of Citizenship and Access to Governmental Services* (Kingston, 1984), p. 5.

39. Hence, as Philip Resnick argues, "Quebec, I am convinced, is going to have to choose. It can have new powers – substantially more than the current federal proposals would allow, something a good deal closer, in fact, to Allaire – but on one condition. For every transfer of power to Quebec, there must be a corresponding reduction in the power of M.P.s, ministers, indeed civil servants from Quebec, where the rest of Canada is concerned. Quebec cannot have it both ways. It can have increased power, if it is prepared to pay the price with drastically reduced influence over central institutions and, thereby, over the rest of Canada. It cannot have its cake and eat it too." "Brief to the Special Joint Parliamentary Committee on a Renewed Canada," mimeo, n.d., p. 9.

A.W. (Al) Johnson makes a similar proposal, employing the same reasoning, in "The Constitutional Proposals and the Canada-Quebec Dilemma, A Description, Analysis and Critique of the Government of Canada's Constitutional Proposals," November 12, 1991, mimeo.

40. Canadian Bar Association, *Rebuilding a Canadian Consensus*, p. 142.

41. The "problem" of special Aboriginal representation in the federal Parliament will be alleviated to the extent that Aboriginal self-governing powers are modelled on provincial jurisdiction, as is likely to be the case for Nunavut. If, however, Aboriginal provinces are carved out of the existing provinces, the issue of Aboriginal voters and representatives in provincial politics will arise.

42. The future reliance of Aboriginal governments on financial resources from federal and provincial governments is conceded by Ovide Mercredi. "We do not like it, but we are dependent on the rest of Canada for improving our socio-economic conditions. The right to self-government is only a means to an end." Rudy Platiel, "Mercredi Denies Grab for Power," *Globe and Mail*, November 7, 1991.

43. Much of the material, including statistics, in this section is taken, with minor modifications, from an unpublished paper by the author, "Representation and the Electoral System: Some Possible Questions for Research," an "Issues Paper" for the Royal Commission on Electoral Reform and Party Financing, March 28, 1990, mimeo.

44. David R. Cameron, "Lord Durham Then and Now," *Journal of Canadian Studies*, 25, 1 (Spring, 1990), p. 17.

45. L.S. Lustgarten, "Liberty in a Culturally Plural Society," in A. Philipps Griffiths, ed., *Of Liberty* (Cambridge, 1983), p. 98.

46. Jill Vickers, "Why Should Women Care about Constitutional Reforms?" October, 1991, mimeo, p. 3.

47. Turpel and Monture, "Ode to Elijah," p. 358.

48. Mercredi, "Speaking Notes . . . Constituent Assembly on the Renewal of Canada: Identity, Rights and Values," *passim.*

49. Sylvia B. Bashevkin, *Toeing the Lines: Women and Party Politics in English Canada* (Toronto, 1985), p. 55.

50. *Ibid.,* p. 76.

51. Chantal Maillé, *Primed for Power: Women in Canadian Politics* (Ottawa, 1990), pp. 6-12.

52. Christine Boyle, "Home Rule for Women: Power-Sharing between Men and Women," *Dalhousie Law Journal,* 7, 3 (October, 1983), p. 795.

53. Jennifer Jackson, "The Symbolic Politics of Multiculturalism," graduate course essay, December 16, 1991, University of British Columbia, pp. 12-13.

54. Turpel and Monture, "Ode to Elijah," p. 346.

55. Iris M. Young, "Polity and Group Differences: A Critique of the Ideal of Universal Citizenship," in Cass R. Sunstein, ed., *Feminism and Political Theory* (Chicago and London, 1990), pp. 250-74.

56. The National Action Committee on the Status of Women recently advocated putting mechanisms in place for a revised Senate to "ensure that women are represented politically in proportion to our presence in the population." Judy Rebick, Barbara Cameron, and Sandra Delaronde, "Why We Want Half the Senate Seats," *Globe and Mail,* October 28, 1991.

Another feminist scholar argues that Canada, like other nations, is "composed of two sexual groups which have different traditions and interests," that the strategy of electoral assimilation via single-member territorial constituencies has not really worked to represent women adequately, that at the present time men cannot represent women, and that accordingly the time has come to consider "some form of separate representation of women . . . in our electoral system." Boyle, "Home Rule for Women," pp. 790, 797, 808.

See also Susan Jackel's support for "post-modernist and post-colonial arguments against the coercive homogeneity of liberal democratic citizenship and legal regimes," leading her to recommend a complex but ingenious proposal to ensure 50 per cent representation of women in the total membership of both houses of a renewed Parliament. "Rethinking Equality and Citizenship," text of presentation at "Conversations among Friends," October 25, 1991, mimeo, November 13, 1991, pp. 6-9. See also Jill Vickers, "Brief Submitted to the Royal Commission on Electoral Reform and Party Financing," Ottawa, June 13, 1990, mimeo, pp. 4, 5, 6, 11, for advocacy of proportional representation (PR) or of designating half of each province's seats for women. She also suggests that "many Canadian women" support

"descriptive representation theories which require an accurate correspondence between the characteristics of the people to be represented and the
characteristics of the representatives." Maillé, *Primed for Power*, p. 33, recommends either PR or dual ridings, each electing one man and one woman.

57. Presentation by Senator Len Marchand to the Royal Commission on Elec-
    toral Reform and Party Financing, March 13, 1990, p. 3.
58. Committee for Aboriginal Electoral Reform, *The Path to Electoral Equality*,
    p. 10.
59. Boyle, "Home Rule for Women," pp. 791, 809.
60. The relevant issues are helpfully discussed in Ontario Law Reform Commis-
    sion, *Appointing Judges: Philosophy, Politics and Practice* (Toronto, 1991).
61. Cited in Alan C. Cairns, "Citizens (Outsiders) and Governments (Insiders)
    in Constitution-Making: The Case of Meech Lake," in Alan C. Cairns,
    *Disruptions: Constitutional Struggles, from the Charter to Meech Lake*, ed.
    Douglas E. Williams (Toronto, 1991), p. 113. See pp. 113-15 for a litany of such
    complaints. A weaker version of the same point was recently made by the
    Committee for Aboriginal Electoral Reform. It advocated separate Aborigi-
    nal electoral districts so that Aboriginal MPs "could pursue the concerns and
    interests of Aboriginal people with concentrated attention and vigour. . . .
    They could do so without fear of alienating non-Aboriginal constituents, a
    problem that sometimes arises for Aboriginal people elected under the cur-
    rent system." *The Path to Electoral Equality*, p. 14.
62. Turpel and Monture, "Ode to Elijah," p. 350.
63. Métis National Council, "MNC Response to the Federal Proposal," pp. 1, 3, 4,
    5, 7.
64. Albert O. Hirschman, *Exit, Voice, and Loyalty* (Cambridge, Mass., 1970).
65. I have discussed these and related "taboo" issues in "Ritual, Taboo, and Bias
    in Constitutional Controversies in Canada, or Constitutional Talk Cana-
    dian Style," in Cairns, *Disruptions*, pp. 199-222.
66. Maillé, *Primed for Power*, p. 3.
67. Young, "Polity and Group Differences." See also Jackel, "Rethinking Equal-
    ity and Citizenship," pp. 6-7, for a linking of the idea of asymmetrical
    citizenship postulated for Québécois with the idea of "*coexisting but not
    identical* citizen statuses [for the] . . . oppressed or disadvantaged citizens in
    Canada, if that differential were explicitly designed . . . to reduce oppression
    and move in the direction of equality."
68. J.L. Granatstein, quoted in Michael Bliss, "Privatizing the Mind: The
    Sundering of Canadian History, The Sundering of Canada," Creighton Cen-
    tennial Lecture, delivered as part of the University of Toronto History
    Department's 100th Anniversary Celebrations, October 18, 1991, mimeo,
    p. 12.

69. Hugh Heclo, "The Emerging Regime," in Richard A. Harris and Sidney M. Milkis, eds., *Remaking American Politics* (Boulder, Col., 1989), pp. 309-10.

## The Case for Charter-Federalism

1. T. John Samuel, "Visible Minorities in Canada: A Projection," mimeo, pp. 17, 35. Distributed as part of a "News Release, Canadian Advertising Foundation, 'Race Relations Advisory Council on Advertising,'" May 30, 1992. Figures include non-permanent residents.
2. Samuel LaSelva, "Does the Canadian Charter of Rights and Freedoms Rest on a Mistake?" *Windsor Yearbook of Access to Justice*, 8 (1988), p. 223.

## The Political Purposes of the Charter

1. For a report on these constitutional conferences, attended by a sprinkling of "ordinary Canadians" amidst batteries of experts, representatives of constitutional interest groups, and government officials, see A. Kroeger, "The Constitutional Conferences of January-March 1992: A View from Within," speech to IPAC/University of Victoria Conference, April 23, 1992, mimeo. Kroeger uses the phrase "informed public" (p. 4) rather than "ordinary Canadians" widely used at the time.
2. C. Taylor, "Shared and Divergent Values," in R.L. Watts and D.M. Brown, eds., *Options for a New Canada* (Toronto, 1991), p. 75.
3. P. Fortin, "Quebec's Forced Choice," mimeo, in *Conference on the Future of Quebec and Canada*, Faculty of Law, McGill University, Montreal, November 16-18, 1990.
4. *Shaping Canada's Future Together: Proposals* (Ottawa, 1991), p. 4, proposed subjecting use of the override "to stricter conditions" by requiring the support of 60 per cent of the votes of the members of a provincial legislature or Parliament rather than a simple majority.
5. *Ibid.*, p. 11. In the Meech Lake Accord the distinct society interpretive clause applied to the constitution of Canada, not just to the Charter.
6. A proposal supported by the New Democratic Party members of the Beaudoin-Dobbie committee. See *Report of the Special Joint Committee on a Renewed Canada* (Ottawa, 1992), p. 36.
7. For a nuanced discussion of many of the points in this section, and indeed of much of the rest of this chapter, see R. Knopff and F.L. Morton, *Charter Politics* (Scarborough, Ont., 1992).
8. See K. McRoberts, "Making Canada Bilingual: Illusions and Delusions of

Federal Language Policy," in D.P. Shugarman and R. Whitaker, eds., *Federalism and Political Community: Essays in Honour of Donald Smiley* (Peterborough, Ont., 1989), for strong advocacy of the territorial principle.

9. *Citizens' Forum on Canada's Future: Report to the People and Government of Canada* (Ottawa, 1991); *Report of the Special Joint Committee on a Renewed Canada* (Ottawa, 1991); *The Process for Amending the Constitution of Canada: The Report of the Special Joint Committee of the Senate and the House of Commons* (Ottawa, 1991).

10. See P. Monahan *et al.*, *Constituent Assemblies: The Canadian Debate in Comparative and Historical Context: Background Studies of the York University Constitutional Reform Project, Study no. 4* (North York, Ont., 1992), for an assessment of the Canadian debate on constituent assemblies. A national referendum is advocated by Patrick J. Monahan, "Closing a Constitutional Deal in 1992: A Scenario," in D.M. Brown *et al.*, eds., *Constitutional Commentaries: An Assessment of the 1991 Federal Proposals* (Kingston, 1992), p. 105-06.

11. "Report to Cabinet on Constitutional Discussions, Summer 1980, and the Outlook for the First Ministers Conference and Beyond," Ministers' Eyes Only, August 30, 1980.

12. See D.V. Smiley and R.L. Watts, *Intrastate Federalism in Canada* (Toronto, 1985), for a helpful discussion.

13. Monahan *et al.*, *Constituent Assemblies*, p. 48. A footnote adds: "The list reproduced in the text is not fanciful, but represents a summary of the views which have been expressed before the Ontario Select Committee on Confederation during its hearings over the spring and summer of 1991."

14. *Ibid.*

15. In particular, section 6(4), exemption from mobility rights; section 15(2), allowing affirmative action programs to ameliorate "conditions of disadvantaged individuals or groups . . ."; section 23(3), where numbers warrant provision for minority-language educational rights; section 25, exemption of certain Aboriginal rights from abrogation or derogation by the Charter; section 59(1), delaying the coming into effect of section 23(1)(a) of the minority-language educational rights in Quebec until authorized by the legislative assembly or government of Quebec.

16. See S. Djwa and R. St.J. MacDonald, *On F.R. Scott: Essays on His Contributions to Law, Literature and Politics* (Kingston and Montreal, 1983), for various assessments of Scott's diverse contributions to Canadian life.

17. T.R. Berger, *Fragile Freedoms: Human Rights and Dissent in Canada* (Toronto, 1981).

18. *Report of the Special Joint Committee on a Renewed Canada.*

*Notes* 389

19. Commissioners' Report, Assembly of First Nations, *To the Source: First Nations Circle on the Constitution* (Ottawa, 1992), p. 1.
20. Presentation by the Metis National Council to the Parliamentary Committee, Edmonton, Alberta, January 22, 1992, p. 1.
21. Background Notes to a Presentation by Rosemarie Kuptana, president of the Inuit Tapirisat of Canada, 32nd Premiers' Conference, Whistler, B.C., August 26, 1991, p. 4.
22. See Un Dossier du *Devoir, Le Québec et le Lac Meech* (Montréal, 1987), pp. 109-10, 123, 152-54, 157, 158-61, 180-81, 196, 252, 256, for critiques of the Charter as a homogenizing threat to Quebec and support for the distinct society as a defence against it. D. Robert, "La signification de l'Accord du lac Meech au Canada anglais et au Québec francophone: un tour d'horizon du débat public," in P.M. Leslie and R.L. Watts, eds., *Canada: The State of the Federation 1987-88* (Kingston, 1988), is a valuable discussion of differences in attitudes in English Canada and Francophone Quebec to the constitution in general and to the Charter in particular. See also A.C. Cairns, *Charter versus Federalism: The Dilemmas of Constitutional Reform* (Montreal, 1992), pp. 118-23, for the differential reception of the Charter in English-speaking Canada and Francophone Quebec, indicating the nationalist basis of Quebec's opposition.

   For strong Charter criticism from an Aboriginal perspective, see M.E. Turpel, "Aboriginal Peoples and the Canadian Charter: Interpretive Monopolies, Cultural Differences," *Canadian Human Rights Yearbook* (1989-1990), and M. Boldt and J.A. Long, eds., *The Quest for Justice: Aboriginal Peoples and Aboriginal Rights* (Toronto, 1985).
23. M. Boldt and J.A. Long, "Tribal Philosophies and the Canadian Charter of Rights and Freedoms," in Boldt and Long, eds., *The Quest for Justice*, p. 165.
24. D.J. Elkins, "Facing our Destiny: Rights and Canadian Distinctiveness," *Canadian Journal of Political Science*, 22 (1989).
25. Boldt and Long, "Tribal Philosophies and the Canadian Charter," p. 177.
26. Conference Report of Co-Chairs, *First Peoples and the Constitution, Ottawa*, March 13-15, 1992 (Ottawa, 1992), pp. 11-12.
27. K.C. Wheare, *The Constitutional Structure of the Commonwealth* (London, 1960), p. 89. Wheare was referring, of course, not to internal nationalisms, but to the nationalism of the independent members of the Commonwealth, especially the newer members.
28. Commissioners' Report, Assembly of First Nations, *To the Source*, p. 78.
29. *A Report of the NCC Constitutional Review Commission to the First Peoples' Congress*, Hull, Quebec, March 29, 1992, p. 14 (a committee recommendation only); Native Council of Canada, *Background and Discussion Points,*

Aboriginal-Federal Policy Conference, *First Peoples and the Constitution*, March 13-15, 1992, p. 3.

30. Métis National Council, *The Metis Nation on the Move: Report on the Metis Nation's Constitutional Parallel Process*, March 31, 1992, p. 27.

31. Inuit Tapirisat of Canada, *Analysis of the September 1991 Federal Proposal for Constitutional Reform, Shaping Canada's Future Together*, November 7, 1991, p. 28.

32. Commissioners' Report, Assembly of First Nations, *To the Source*, p. 61.

33. Conference Report of Co-Chairs, *First Peoples and the Constitution*, p. 11.

34. *Report of the Commission on the Political and Constitutional Future of Québec* (Québec, 1991), p. 33.

35. *Ibid.*, p 34.

36. G. Laforest, "La culture politique canadienne à l'heure de la Charte des droits et libertés," analyse préparée pour les Commissions sur le processus de détermination de l'avenir politique et constitutionnel du Québec mises sur pied par l'Assemblée nationale du Québec par l'entremise de la *Loi 150*, mimeo, 13 décembre 1991; "La Charte canadienne des droits et libertés au Québec: nationaliste, injuste et illégitime," mimeo, forthcoming; L.M. Imbeau, "Quebec's Distinct Society and the Sense of Nationhood in Canada," *Quebec Studies*, 13 (1991/92).

37. Laforest, "La culture politique canadienne," p. 47. He further states that "La Cour suprême canadienne ne devrait avoir aucune autorité sur le territoire du Québec." Taken literally, his proposals suggest that the Quebec Charter also applies to federal legislation in Quebec and that the entire constitution in its application to Quebec is to be interpreted by Quebec-appointed judges.

38. Laforest, "La Charte canadienne . . . nationaliste, injuste et illégitime," p. 4.

39. *Ibid.*

40. "There is a strong cultural nationalist movement among Indians today that has as its objective the reinstitution of many traditional values and customs." M. Boldt and J.A. Long, "Tribal Traditions and European-Western Political Ideologies: The Dilemma of Canada's Native Indians," in Boldt and Long, eds., *The Quest for Justice*, p. 334.

41. Commissioners' Report, Assembly of First Nations, *To the Source*, pp. 4, 18.

42. *Ibid.*, p. 78.

43. *Ibid.*, p. 59. "What changed? Very simply, the European view of women as subordinate to and owned by their menfolk infected the First Nations of Canada. It did so directly through the Indian Act, which tied women's identity and rights as Aboriginal people to those of their husbands, through government policies that reinforced women's status as dependents, and through its deliberate disruption of traditional life. . . . But sexism is not

merely imposed on First Nations from outside; it has entered our soul. To be blunt, a great many First Nations males need to have their consciousness raised. The women see leaders in particular as being sexist and discriminatory." *Ibid.*, pp. 59-60.

44. *Ibid.*, p. 62.
45. *Ibid.*, p. 64.
46. *Ibid.*, pp. 62-63.
47. Boldt and Long, "Tribal Philosophies and the Charter," p. 165.
48. *Ibid.*, pp. 172, 174.
49. Commissioners' Report, Assembly of First Nations, *To the Source*, p. 63.
50. *Ibid.*, p. 78.
51. Material in the next few paragraphs is taken from the following undated publications of the Native Women's Association of Canada: *Native Women and the Charter: A Discussion Paper; Native Women and Self-Government: A Discussion Paper; Statement on the "Canada Package"; Native Women and the Canada Package: A Discussion Paper*; with the Canadian Council on Social Development, *Voices of Aboriginal Women: Aboriginal Women Speak out about Violence*; "Aboriginal Women and the Constitutional Debates: Continuing Discrimination," *Canadian Women Studies*, 12, 3 (Summer, 1992); and the presentation by Gail Stacey-Moore, president, Native Women's Association of Canada, in Conference Report of Co-Chairs, *First Peoples and the Constitution*, pp. 31-33. See Turpel, "Aboriginal Peoples and the Canadian *Charter*," for strong opposition to the Charter from an Aboriginal woman law professor.
52. Native Women's Association, *Native Women and the Charter*, p. 3.
53. Native Women's Association, *Statement on the "Canada Package,"* p. 11.
54. "We are living in chaos in our communities. We have a disproportionately high rate of child sexual abuse and incest. We have wife battering, gang rapes, drug and alcohol abuse and every kind of perversion imaginable has been imported into our daily lives." Native Women's Association, *Statement on the "Canada Package,"* p. 14. See also Native Women's Association and Canadian Council on Social Development, *Voices of Aboriginal Women: Aboriginal Women Speak out about Violence*.
55. Native Women's Association, *Statement on the "Canada Package,"* p. 7.
56. Native Women's Association, *Native Women and Self-Government: A Discussion Paper*, pp. 4, 10, 14.
57. Native Women's Association, *Native Women and Self-Government: A Discussion Paper*, pp. 11-12; Native Women's Association, *Native Women and the Charter: A Discussion Paper*, pp. 3-4.
58. Native Women's Association, "Aboriginal Women and the Constitutional Debates," p. 16.

59. Native Women's Association, *Statement on the "Canada Package,"* p. 7. Male-dominated reserve governments are revealingly described as "Aboriginal government with white powers and white philosophies in our communities." Native Women's Association, "Aboriginal Women and the Constitutional Debates," p. 15.

60. Boldt and Long, "Tribal Philosophies and the Charter," p. 169.

61. The preceding four points are adapted from B. Schwartz, *First Principles, Second Thoughts: Aboriginal Peoples, Constitutional Reform and Canadian Statecraft* (Montreal, 1986), pp. 393-97.

62. It is significant that former Chief Justice Brian Dickson, universally recognized as highly sympathetic to Aboriginal peoples, eulogized the Charter in his overview presentation to the First Peoples and the Constitution conference, stating, "I must say that I am concerned that any new constitutional arrangements take due cognizance of the important values enshrined in the *Charter.*" Conference Report of Co-Chairs, *First Peoples and the Constitution*, p. 61.

## Constitutional Change and the Three Equalities

1. All references to Constitution Act, 1982.

2. I have discussed these and related issues in "Constitutional Minoritarianism in Canada," in Ronald L. Watts and Douglas M. Brown, eds., *Canada: The State of the Federation 1990* (Kingston, Ont., 1990), and in "Ritual, Taboo, and Bias in Constitutional Controversies in Canada, or Constitutional Talk Canadian Style," *Saskatchewan Law Review*, 54 (1990).

3. Legislative Assembly of New Brunswick, Select Committee on the 1987 Constitutional Accord, *Final Report on the Constitutional Amendment 1987* (Fredericton, 1989), p. 44.

4. Manitoba Task Force on Meech Lake, *Report on the 1987 Constitutional Accord* (Winnipeg, 1989), p. 25.

5. Denis Robert, "La signification de l'Accord du lac Meech au Canada anglais et au Québec francophone: un tour d'horizon du débat public," in Peter M. Leslie and Ronald L. Watts, eds., *Canada: The State of the Federation 1987-88* (Kingston, Ont., 1988), pp. 121, 153.

6. "Clearly . . . the Meech Lake Accord creates a special legislative status for one province. No federation is likely to survive for very long if one of its supposedly equal provinces has a legislative jurisdiction in excess of that of the other provinces." Clyde K. Wells, "The Meech Lake Accord: An Address to the Vancouver Board of Trade," February 12, 1990, mimeo, p. 6.

7. *1987 Constitutional Accord, 3 June 1987* reproduced in Anne F. Bayefsky, *Canada's Constitution Act 1982 and Amendments: A Documentary History*, Vol. 11 (Toronto, 1990), p. 955.

8. Section 2(3) of the Meech Lake Accord, *ibid.*

9. Premier William N. Vander Zalm to Prime Minister Brian Mulroney, January 19, 1990, attached to a news release, January 23, 1990, from the Office of Premier Vander Zalm, justified recognizing each province and territory as distinct as this would *"balance recognition of our distinction while clearly upholding the principle of equality. . . ."* (Italics in original.)

10. See the many negative references in Un Dossier du *Devoir, Le Québec et le Lac Meech* (Montréal, 1987), pp. 109-10, 123, 152-54, 157, 158-61, 180-81, 196, 252, 256. See also Robert, "La signification de l'Accord du lac Meech," pp. 121, 141-42, 149, 153.

11. Thomas R. Berger, "Towards the Regime of Tolerance," in Stephen Brooks, ed., *Political Thought in Canada: Contemporary Perspectives* (Toronto, 1984).

12. David J. Elkins, "Facing our Destiny: Rights and Canadian Distinctiveness," *Canadian Journal of Political Science*, 22 (December, 1989), pp. 699-716.

13. Sally M. Weaver, *Making Canadian Indian Policy: The Hidden Agenda 1968-1970* (Toronto, 1981), ch. vii.

14. Gwen Brodsky and Shelagh Day, *Canadian Charter Equality Rights for Women: One Step Forward or Two Steps Back?* (Ottawa, 1989), p. 37.

15. See the references in note 10.

16. Benoit Aubin, "Fight looms over opting-out clause," *Globe and Mail*, April 7, 1989.

17. "Draft Agreement on the Constitution: Proposals by the Government of Quebec," in Peter M. Leslie, ed., *Canada: The State of the Federation 1985* (Kingston, 1985), pp. 64-68.

18. The Task Force on Canadian Unity, *A Future Together: Observations and Recommendations* (Ottawa, 1979), p. 36.

19. Abraham Rotstein, "Is there an English-Canadian Nationalism?" *Journal of Canadian Studies*, 13 (Summer, 1978), p. 114.

20. Philip Resnick, *Letters to a Québécois Friend, with a reply by Daniel Latouche* (Montreal and Kingston, 1990), p. 15.

21. Kenneth McNaught, "The National Outlook of English-speaking Canadians," in Peter Russell, ed., *Nationalism in Canada* (Toronto, 1966).

## Aboriginal Canadians, Citizenship, and the Constitution

1. Earlier versions of this paper were presented at a conference on "Ethnicity and the Constitution," March 20, 1993, organized by the Royal Society, and at the 65th annual meeting of the Canadian Political Science Association, Ottawa, June 6-8, 1993.
2. Helpful historical background is provided by J.R. Miller, *Skyscrapers Hide the Heavens: A History of Indian-White Relations in Canada*, rev. ed. (Toronto, 1991); J. Rick Ponting and Roger Gibbins, *Out of Irrelevance: A sociopolitical introduction to Indian affairs in Canada* (Toronto, 1980); Richard Diubaldo, "The Government of Canada and the Inuit 1900-1967," Research Branch, Indian and Northern Affairs Canada (1985), mimeo; Diamond Jenness, *Eskimo Administration: Canada* (Montreal, 1964); Donald Purich, *The Métis* (Toronto, 1988).
3. There are, however, eight Métis settlements in Alberta, established under the authority of the Métis Population Betterment Act (1938). For a brief history, see "Background Paper No. 6, the Métis Betterment Act: History and Current Status," Policy and Planning Branch, Native Affairs Secretariat, Government of Alberta (March, 1985).
4. H.B. Hawthorn and M.-A. Tremblay, *A Survey of the Contemporary Indians of Canada: Economic, Political, Educational Needs and Policies, Part I* (Ottawa, 1966).
5. See Sally M. Weaver, *Making Canadian Indian Policy: The Hidden Agenda 1968-1970* (Toronto, 1981), for a superb analysis of the rise and fall of the White Paper.
6. See Augie Fleras and Jean Leonard Elliott, *The 'Nations Within': Aboriginal-State Relations in Canada, the United States, and New Zealand* (Toronto, 1992), pp. 39-40, for relevant statements by Macdonald and Scott. For the views of Diamond Jenness, see his "Plan for Liquidating Canada's Indian Problem Within 25 Years," in *Minutes of Proceedings and Evidence, No. 7, Special Joint Committee of the Senate and the House of Commons Appointed to Continue and Complete the Examination and Consideration of the Indian Act,* March 25, 1947 pp. 310-11.
7. Weaver, *Making Canadian Indian Policy*, p. 183.
8. Alan C. Cairns, "The Charlottetown Accord: Multinational Canada vs. Federalism," mimeo, presented at the Colorado College Colloquium, November 13-14, 1992.
9. The following points are taken from the *Consensus Report on the Constitution, Charlottetown, August 28, 1992, Final Text,* and *Draft Legal Text, October 9, 1992.*
10. Slightly different language and a more abbreviated description were used in

the Canada clause description of Aboriginal peoples as one of the "fundamental characteristics" of Canada. *Consensus Report*, 1. 2(1)(b).

11. P.A. Monture-Okanee and M.E. Turpel, "Aboriginal Peoples and Canadian Criminal Law: Rethinking Justice," *University of British Columbia Law Review*, Special Edition (1992), pp. 256, 258.

12. This perception may be an artifact of the tendency of Aboriginal leaders to stress a degree of difference that is not shared at the grassroots level. I am grateful to Paul Tennant for this suggestion.

13. The support of the Native Women's Association of Canada for the Charter is not really an exception, for NWAC tends to define the Charter in terms of its international, United Nations, origins, rather than as a specifically Canadian rights-protecting instrument. See Native Women's Association of Canada, *Native Women and Self-Government: A Discussion Paper*, pp. 11-12, and *Native Women and the Charter: A Discussion Paper* (n.d.), pp. 3-4.

14. Stewart Clatworthy and Anthony H. Smith give a figure of 87,274 reinstatements, resulting from Bill C-31, by April 30, 1992. "Population Implications of the 1985 Amendments to the Indian Act: Final Report," mimeo (December, 1992), p. 1. (Prepared for the Assembly of First Nations.)

15. See Alan Cairns, "Ritual, Taboo, and Bias in Constitutional Controversies in Canada, or Constitutional Talk Canadian Style," *Saskatchewan Law Review*, 54 (1990), pp. 132-39, for appropriate references and an analysis. In a recent lecture raising certain practical concerns about Aboriginal self-government, Ian Scott noted, but disagreed with, the suggestion his subject "is not, some will say, a matter about which non-aboriginals have a right to speak." "Facing up to Aboriginal Self-Government: Three Practical Suggestions," The Laskin Lecture 1992, York University, March 11, 1992, mimeo, p. 14.

16. Mary Ellen Turpel, "Aboriginal Peoples and the Canadian *Charter*: Interpretive Monopolies, Cultural Differences," *Canadian Human Rights Yearbook*, 6 (1989-90), pp. 3-45.

17. Commissioners' Report, Assembly of First Nations, *To the Source: First Nations Circle on the Constitution* (Ottawa, 1992), is a good example.

18. Karol J. Krotki and Dave Odynak, "The Emergence of Multiethnicities in the Eighties," in Shiva S. Halli *et al.*, eds., *Ethnic Demography: Canadian Immigrant, Racial and Cultural Variations* (Ottawa, 1990), p. 419.

19. R. Pierre Gauvin and Diane Fournier, "Marriages of Registered Indians: Canada and Four Selected Bands, 1967 to 1990," Technical Paper 92-1, Department of Indian Affairs and Northern Development (July, 1992), p. 8.

20. "That is, they proposed to do away with the present special status of Indians, eliminate all elements of separate political and legal administration and have Indians become as any other ethnic group." Menno Boldt, "Social Correlates of Nationalism: A Study of Native Indian leaders in a Canadian

Internal Colony," *Comparative Political Studies*, 14, 2 (July, 1981), pp. 214-15. Both Indian and Métis leaders are included in Boldt's sample.

21. Turpel, "Aboriginal Peoples and the Canadian *Charter*."

22. See Clatworthy and Smith, "Population Implications," ch. 3, for an elaboration and analysis.

23. See Clatworthy and Smith, "Population Implications," ch. 4, for an analysis.

24. Alexis de Tocqueville, *Democracy in America*, Vol. II (New York, 1954), ch. 8.

25. Dan Smith, *The Seventh Fire: The Struggle for Aboriginal Government* (Toronto, 1993), p. 76.

26. Paul Tennant, personal communication.


## The Charter, Interest Groups, Executive Federalism, and Constitutional Reform

1. Jill M. Vickers, "Majority Equality Issues of the Eighties," *Canadian Human Rights Yearbook 1983* (Toronto, 1983), p. 67.

2. Peter H. Russell, "The Politics of Frustration: The Pursuit of Formal Constitutional Change in Australia and Canada," *Australian Canadian Studies*, 6 (1988), p. 14.

3. The details of the proposed federal amending formula, the changes as it evolved, and the complex process by which it would become part of the constitution are discussed in Alan C. Cairns, "Constitution-Making, Government Self-Interest, and the Problem of Legitimacy," in Allan Kornberg and Harold D. Clarke, eds., *Political Support in Canada: The Crisis Years* (Durham, N.C., 1983), pp. 423-28.

4. "PM invites 10 premiers to discuss Quebec constitutional proposals," *Globe and Mail*, March 18, 1987.

5. By constitutional executive federalism I mean the application of the practice of executive federalism to the constitutional reform process, known as first ministers' conferences on the constitution. Donald Smiley, who coined the phrase, defined executive federalism as "the relations between elected and appointed officials of the two orders of government in federal-provincial interactions and among the executives of the provinces in inter-provincial interactions." *Canada in Question: Federalism in the Eighties*, 3rd ed. (Toronto, 1980), p. 91. In the following discussion, I apply the phrase "executive federalism" to first ministers' conferences on the constitution held before the phrase became part of the working terminology of Canadian federalism.

6. Richard Simeon, "Meech Lake and Shifting Conceptions of Canadian Federalism," *Canadian Public Policy*, 14 (supp.) (September, 1988), p. 522.

7. Although even here the record is mixed. "In summary," wrote Donald Smiley a decade ago, "the institutions and processes of executive federalism are disposed towards conflict rather than harmony." *Canada in Question*, p. 116. An excellent discussion based on case studies is provided by Frederick J. Fletcher and Donald C. Wallace, "Federal-Provincial Relations and the Making of Public Policy in Canada: A Review of Case Studies," in Richard Simeon, ed., *Division of Power and Public Policy* (Toronto, 1985), volume 61 of the research studies prepared for the Royal Commission on the Economic Union and Development Prospects for Canada. Ronald Watts provides a valuable comparative perspective in "Executive Federalism: The Comparative Perspective," in David P. Shugarman and Reg Whitaker, eds., *Federalism and Political Community: Essays in Honour of Donald Smiley* (Peterborough, Ont., 1989).

8. Dominion-Provincial Conference, January 14-15, 1941 (Ottawa, 1941).

9. Keith G. Banting, "Federalism and the Supreme Court of Canada: The Competing Bases of Legitimation," mimeo, revised, p. 21 (to appear in a forthcoming Ontario Law Reform Commission volume.)

10. Technically, the 1940 unemployment insurance amendment was not a product of executive federalism, strictly defined, as agreement was reached by correspondence. Paul Gérin-Lajoie, *Constitutional Amendment in Canada* (Toronto, 1950), p. 107.

A brief flurry of amendments emerged from the 1983 First Ministers' Conference on Aboriginal matters. The Prime Minister, provincial first ministers, and Aboriginal representatives agreed in 1983 to a constitutional amendment requiring "at least two [additional] constitutional conferences" (s 37.1 (1 & 2)) on Aboriginal matters. Two additional clauses were added to section 35 by constitutional amendment, clause (3) providing greater certainty to the definition of treaty rights, and (4) guaranteeing Aboriginal and treaty rights equally to both sexes. A new section 35.1 committed governments to giving Aboriginal representatives the right to participate in the discussion at future constitutional conferences of constitutional amendments made to Aboriginal constitutional clauses. Paragraph 25 (b) of the Charter protecting Aboriginal, treaty, or other rights and freedoms against derogation or abrogation by the Charter was also strengthened. See Bryan Schwartz, *First Principles, Second Thoughts: Aboriginal Peoples, Constitutional Reform and Canadian Statecraft* (Montreal, 1986), *passim*, for a detailed discussion. With Aboriginal representatives present and participating, this was clearly executive federalism with a difference.

Various tidying-up amendments since World War Two can be traced in the footnotes to the Constitution Acts, 1867 to 1982, reproduced in Richard J. Van Loon and Michael S. Whittington, *The Canadian Political System: Environment, Structure and Process*, 4th ed. (Toronto, 1987), Appendix. Without exhaustive research, it is not possible to tell how many of these were preceded by provincial consultation or were discussed (and agreed to) at first ministers' conferences. Russell identifies five minor amendments dealing with Parliament undertaken by the federal government on the authority of the unilateral federal amending power assumed in 1949. "The Politics of Frustration," pp. 7, 25 n. 13.

11. J. Stefan Dupré, "Reflections on the Workability of Executive Federalism," in R.D. Olling and M.W. Westmacott, eds., *Perspectives on Canadian Federalism* (Scarborough, Ont., 1988), p. 247. The components of the "constitutional review model" that impede agreement are succinctly described on pp. 247-48.

12. Graham Fraser, "Premiers who oppose accord 'desire a solution,' minister says," *Globe and Mail*, January 8, 1990; "Meech discord report rouses PM," *Vancouver Sun*, March 8, 1988; Graham Fraser, "PM says 1982 flaws removed 'flexibility' in Meech Lake talks," *Globe and Mail*, June 13, 1988.

13. Penny Kome, *The Taking of Twenty-Eight: Women Challenge the Constitution* (Toronto, 1983).

14. Peter H. Russell, "The Political Purposes of the Canadian Charter of Rights and Freedoms," *Canadian Bar Review*, 61 (March, 1983).

15. "[T]he Charter would become part of the Constitution immediately so far as matters within federal competence are concerned, and would become constitutionalized in respect of a province when adopted by that province. The Charter would become an *entrenched* part of the Constitution (and henceforth alterable only pursuant to a constitutional amending procedure) at such time as it is endorsed by a formal process for amendment of the Constitution." Hon. Otto E. Lang, *Constitutional Reform: Canadian Charter of Rights and Freedoms* (Ottawa, 1978), p. 4.

16. The "Highlights of the Kirby Memorandum" are reproduced in Appendix 2 of David Milne, *The New Canadian Constitution* (Toronto, 1982), pp. 219-37. The same antithesis was repeated by Trudeau in his anti-Meech Lake speeches and writings in which he summed up the constitutional struggles of the previous two decades as "much more than the struggle between two levels of government. It had been a struggle to establish the sovereignty of the people over all levels of government." Donald Johnston, ed., *With a Bang, Not a Whimper: Pierre Trudeau Speaks Out* (Toronto, 1988), p. 94.

17. Legislative Assembly of New Brunswick, Select Committee on the 1987 Constitutional Accord, *Final Report on the Constitution Amendment 1987*

(Fredericton, 1989), pp. 42, 44; Manitoba Task Force on Meech Lake, *Report on the 1987 Constitutional Accord* (Winnipeg, 1989), pp. 4, 25-27.

18. Some of the factors behind the different responses that had developed to the Charter among the Quebec Francophone majority and in Anglophone Canada by the late eighties are discussed in "The Lessons of Meech Lake," ch. 4, in Alan C. Cairns, *Charter versus Federalism* (Montreal, 1992).

19. See Sally M. Weaver, *Making Canadian Indian Policy: The Hidden Agenda 1968-1970* (Toronto, 1981), for an excellent case study.

20. Douglas Sanders, "The Renewal of Indian Special Status," in A.F. Bayefsky and M. Eberts, eds., *Equality Rights and the Canadian Charter of Rights and Freedoms* (Toronto, 1985).

21. *Re Eskimos* [1939] SCR 104.

22. These included "(a) any rights or freedoms that have been recognized by the Royal Proclamation of 7 October 1763; and (b) any rights or freedoms that may be acquired by the aboriginal peoples of Canada by way of land claims settlement."

23. The conflict between the Charter and Aboriginal values is sensitively explored in Mary Ellen Turpel, "Aboriginal Peoples and the Canadian *Charter*: Interpretive Monopolies, Cultural Differences," in Michelle Boivin *et al.*, eds., *Canadian Human Rights Yearbook* (Ottawa, 1990).

24. *The 1987 Constitutional Accord: The Report of the Special Joint Committee of the Senate and the House of Commons* (Minutes of Proceedings and Evidence, No. 17, September 9, 1987), Appendix "A"; *Report of the Special Committee to Study the Proposed Companion Resolution to the Meech Lake Accord* (the Charest Report) (Minutes of Proceedings and Evidence, No. 21, May 8-15, 1990), Appendix A.

25. *Report of the Special Committee to Study the Proposed Companion Resolution to the Meech Lake Accord*, Appendix A. As organizational names are sometimes ambiguous, another researcher might produce slightly different totals. However, the basic orders of magnitude would not change. To facilitate comparison, I have used the categories employed in the New Brunswick Select Committee *Final Report*, immediately noted below.

Similar trends emerge in the group presentations to other Meech Lake committees. For example, the New Brunswick hearings had the following breakdown, using the Select Committee's own categories: Aboriginals 3, linguistic lobbies 6, women 14, commercial 5, multicultural 3, unions 5. New Brunswick Select Committee, Final Report, Appendix F.

Applying the New Brunswick categories to the Manitoba Task Force presentations generates the following: Aboriginals 23, linguistic lobbies 3, women 28, commercial 7, multicultural 14, unions 4. Manitoba Task Force, *Report on the 1987 Constitutional Accord*, Appendix A.

The Senate heard from the following in its Committee of the Whole and special Submissions Group hearings: Aboriginals 10, linguistic lobbies 4, women 9, commercial 1, multicultural 4, unions 2. Senate of Canada, *Committee of the Whole on the Meech Lake Constitutional Accord, Third Report* (June, 1988), Appendices IV and V. The Manitoba and Senate data contain some double counting. The caveat on the precision of the data expressed at the beginning of this footnote bears repeating.

26. Robert M. Campbell, "Eleven Men and a Constitution: The Meech Lake Accord," in Robert M. Campbell and Leslie A. Pal, *The Real Worlds of Canadian Politics: Cases in Process and Policy* (Peterborough, Ont., 1989), p. 290.

## The Charlottetown Accord

1. See Philip Resnick, "Canada: Three Sociological Nations," *Canadian Forum*, October, 1992, for a brief discussion of Canada as a three-nation multinational federation. Ten academics from the University of Toronto and York University and the writer Christina McCall recently supported a three-nations view of the desired direction of constitutional change. See "Three Nations in a Delicate State," *Toronto Star*, February 4, 1992. See also "Speaking Notes by Ron George, President, NCC, to the Policy Conference on 'Identity, Rights and Values,'" February 6-9, 1992, Toronto, for advocacy of a three-nations view of Canada and for a "National Covenant" negotiated and signed by their representatives.

2. For a powerful expression of this view, see Ovide Mercredi, Assemblée nationale, *Journal des débats*, Commission parlementaire spéciale, Commission d'étude des questions afférentes à l'accession du Québec à la souveraineté, no. 27 (February 11, 1992): CEAS 826.

3. See, for example, many of the essays in Duncan Cameron and Miriam Smith, eds., *Constitutional Politics: The Canadian Forum Book on the Federal Constitutional Proposals 1991-92* (Toronto, 1992), which view Canada through a two- or three-nation lens. See also Arthur Keppel-Jones and Hugh G. Thorburn, "Why Not a Two-Nations Canada?" *Policy Options*, May, 1992, pp. 21-22. As far as Quebec/ROC constitutional aspirations are concerned, this approach frequently leads to support for asymmetrical federalism. See Duncan Cameron, "The Asymmetrical Alternative," A.W. Johnson, "A National Government in a Federal State," pp. 89-91, and Philip Resnick, "The West Wants In," pp. 198-99, all in Cameron and Smith, *Constitutional Politics*. Two- or three-nation perspectives are central themes in the post-referendum analyses of Kari Levitt, "Requiem for a Referendum," Mel Watkins, "A Flawed Process," Philip Resnick, "Beyond October 26," and Frank

Cunningham, "Democracy and Three-Nation Asymmetry," all in *Canadian Forum*, December, 1992.

4. See the report of the Constitutional Committee of the Quebec Liberal Party, *A Québec Free to Choose* (January 28, 1991) (Allaire Report), for a good example.

5. *Report of the Commission on the Political and Constitutional Future of Québec* (Québec, 1991), p. 1 (Bélanger-Campeau Report).

6. Levitt, "Requiem for a Referendum," p. 13. See also Casey Vander Ploeg, *The Referendum on the Charlottetown Accord: An Assessment* (Calgary, January, 1993), pp. 16-20.

7. Guy Laforest, "The Referendum and Its Aftermath in Quebec," *Canada Watch*, November/December, 1992, p. 57.

8. For this genre of analysis, see John McCallum, "What If the Vote Is NO?" *Network*, 2, 8 (October, 1992), pp. 7-8.

9. Resnick, "Canada: Three Sociological Nations," p. 27.

10. J.L. Granatstein and Kenneth McNaught, "Introduction," p. 12, Reg Whitaker, "With or without Quebec?" p. 18, and Tom Kent, "An Emergency Operation for the Constitution," p. 324, all in Granatstein and McNaught, eds., *"English Canada" Speaks Out* (Toronto, 1991).

11. Whitaker, "With or without Quebec?" p. 18. Tom Kent agrees with Mulroney: "No federal government elected to run the federal affairs of the country as a whole, has any right, legal or moral, to represent one part of the country in constitutional negotiations with another part . . . no entitlement to respond to Quebec on behalf of Canada outside Quebec"; Kent, "An Emergency Operation for the Constitution," p. 323.

12. Whitaker, "With or without Quebec?" p. 19.

13. Reg Whitaker, "Bearing It without a Grin," *Canadian Forum*, October, 1992, p. 29.

14. See, for example, the various essays in Granatstein and McNaught, eds., *"English Canada" Speaks Out*, especially comments by the editors, p. 12; see also the various essays in Daniel Drache and Roberto Perin, eds., *Negotiating with a Sovereign Quebec* (Toronto, 1992). The emergence of a distinct ROC or English-Canadian constitutional self-consciousness was frequently noted in the Spicer Report: *Citizens' Forum on Canada's Future: Report to the People and Government of Canada* (Ottawa, 1991).

15. Barbara Cameron, "A Constitution for English Canada," in Drache and Perin, eds., *Negotiating with a Sovereign Quebec*, pp. 230-31. Mel Watkins detects "recurring evidence over the years that English-speaking Canadians outside Quebec, their regionalism notwithstanding, think and act like a distinct people." Watkins, "A Flawed Process," p. 14.

16. For the latter, see David J. Bercuson and Barry Cooper, *Deconfederation:*

*Canada without Quebec* (Toronto, 1991), and various essays in Granatstein and McNaught, eds., *"English Canada" Speaks Out.*

17. This discussion of the Quebec components of the Charlottetown Accord is based on *Consensus Report on the Constitution, Charlottetown, August 28, 1992, Final Text,* and *Draft Legal Text, October 9, 1992.*

18. Report of the Constitutional Committee, *A Québec Free to Choose.*

19. *Reformer,* special edition, Fall, 1992.

20. Both this discussion of the Aboriginal components of the Charlottetown Accord and the discussion in the following sections are based on the *Consensus Report* and *Draft Legal Text.*

21. Radha Jhappan, "Aboriginal Self-Government," *Canadian Forum,* October, 1992, pp. 15-16.

22. Tony Hall, "Aboriginal People and the Third Option in the Referendum," October 6, 1992, mimeo, p. 1.

23. Douglas Sanders, "Lesbians and Gays and the Charlottetown Accord," October 10, 1992, mimeo, p. 8.

24. Bradford Morse, "Indigenous Peoples in Quebec and Canada," *Literary Review of Canada,* October, 1992, p. 12.

25. Ron George, "Saying NO to a Generation of Hope," *Network,* 2, 8 (October, 1992), p. 3. Elsewhere he described the Aboriginal components of the Accord as marking "an historic shift in our relationship with the government . . . the dawn of a new era. The future is ours." George, "Equity of Access for Aboriginal Peoples," in Kate Sutherland, ed., *Referendum Round-Table: Perspectives on the Charlottetown Accord,* Points of View, no. 3 (Edmonton, 1992), p. 34.

26. An undated "best efforts draft" for final review by first ministers and Aboriginal leaders described the "Métis Nation . . . as a unique nation with its own language, culture and forms of self-government." For the purposes of the Accord: (a) " 'Métis' means an Aboriginal person who self-identifies as Métis, who is distinct from Indian and Inuit and is a descendant of those Métis who received or were entitled to receive land grants and/or scrip under the provisions of the *Manitoba Act, 1870,* or the *Dominion Lands Acts,* as enacted from time to time. [And] (b) 'Métis Nation' means the community of Métis persons in subsection (a) and persons of Aboriginal descent who are accepted by that community." Métis Nation Accord, mimeo, Best Efforts Draft.

27. Jhappan, "Aboriginal Self-Government," p. 16.

28. *Native Women's Association of Canada, Gail Stacey-Moore and Sharon McIvor v. Her Majesty the Queen,* Federal Court of Appeal, August 20, 1992.

29. The Report of the Special Joint Committee of the Senate and the House of Commons, *The Process for Amending the Constitution of Canada* (Ottawa, 1991), p. 16.

30. Conference Report of Co-Chairs Joseph A. Ghiz and Mary Simon, *First Peoples and the Constitution* (Ottawa, 1992).
31. Commissioner's Report, Assembly of First Nations, *To the Source: First Nations Circle on the Constitution* (Ottawa, 1992).
32. *Report of the Royal Commission of Inquiry on Constitutional Problems* (Quebec, 1956) (Tremblay Report).
33. Mary Ellen Turpel, "Does the Road to Quebec Sovereignty Run through Aboriginal Territory?" in Drache and Perin, eds., *Negotiating with a Sovereign Quebec*, pp. 105-06.
34. Hall, "Aboriginal People and the Third Option," p. 5.
35. Hall, "The Assembly of First Nations and the Demise of the Charlottetown Accord," November 30, 1992, mimeo, p. 1.
36. *Consensus Report*, p. 22, indicated that "the issue of Aboriginal representation in the House of Commons should be pursued by Parliament, in consultation with representatives of the Aboriginal peoples of Canada, after it has received the final report of the House of Commons Committee studying the recommendations of the Royal Commission on Electoral Reform and Party Financing."
37. *Shaping Canada's Future Together: Proposals* (Ottawa, 1991), pp. 4-9.
38. Shawn Henry, *Public Opinion and the Charlottetown Accord* (Calgary, January, 1993), p. 4.
39. Jean-François Lisée, "Les dossiers secrets de Bourassa," *L'Actualité*, November 1, 1992, pp. 67-69.
40. Guy Laforest, "L'Accord d'Ottawa-Charlottetown et la réconciliation des aspirations nationales au Canada," in Claude Bariteau *et al.*, *Référendum, 26 octobre 1992: les objections de 20 spécialistes aux offres fédérales* (Montréal, 1992). In the same work, Daniel Latouche makes a similar comparison, focusing on the division of powers, in "le partage des pouvoirs: ceux des Autochtones, ceux du Québec et ceux qu'on peut-être oubliés."
41. Trudeau's views are cogently, indeed polemically, presented in his *Trudeau: "A Mess that Deserves a Big NO"* (Toronto, 1992).
42. Assistance in tracing this policy evolution is provided by Douglas Sanders, "The Renewal of Indian Special Status," in Anne F. Bayefsky and Mary Eberts, eds., *Equality Rights and the Canadian Charter of Rights and Freedoms* (Toronto, 1985); and Sally M. Weaver, "A New Paradigm in Canadian Indian Policy for the 1990s," *Canadian Ethnic Studies*, 22, 3 (1990).
43. *Transition*, 6, 1 (January, 1993), p. 10.
44. Richard Gwyn, "A Second Sovereignty," in Granatstein and McNaught, eds., *"English Canada" Speaks Out*, p. 387.
45. Douglas Sanders, "An Uncertain Path: The Aboriginal Constitutional Conferences," in Joseph M. Weiler and Robin M. Elliot, eds., *Litigating the Values*

*of a Nation: The Canadian Charter of Rights and Freedoms* (Toronto, 1986), pp. 72-73; Bryan Schwartz, *First Principles, Second Thoughts: Aboriginal Peoples, Constitutional Reform and Canadian Statecraft* (Montreal, 1986), p. 324.

46. For another example, see Ed Finn, "A Vote to Reject," *Canadian Forum*, October, 1992, p. 31.

47. Thomas J. Courchene and Lisa M. Powell, "A First Nations Province," School of Policy Studies, Queen's University, April, 1992, mimeo, p. 49.

48. "Referendum File: What Happens Next," *Maclean's*, November 2, 1992, p. 17. The question was: "Which of the following reasons for voting No comes closest to your main reason?" See also Henry, *Public Opinion and the Charlottetown Accord*, p. 4, for the far greater antipathy to the "Quebec concessions" than to the Aboriginal constitutional package. (The gap is much greater if Quebec is excluded from the comparison, but Henry does not provide this data.) Even where dislike of Aboriginal self-government was greatest (12 per cent of respondents in British Columbia and Saskatchewan), opposition to the Quebec concessions was still four times greater, at 47 per cent.

49. P.A. Monture-Okanee and M.E. Turpel, "Aboriginal Peoples and Canadian Criminal Law: Rethinking Justice," *University of British Columbia Law Review*, special edition (1992), pp. 256, 258, 264. Andrew Bear Robe concurs, asserting that Indian First Nations had no voice in the constitutional settlements of 1867 or 1982. "We have," he continued, "no sense of ownership regarding the federal and provincial laws that apply to us simply because those laws were forced upon us without our consent, consultation or input, especially the much despised federal *Indian Act*." See "Treaty Federalism," *Constitutional Forum*, 4, 1 (Fall, 1992), p. 6.

50. Bercuson and Cooper, *Deconfederation*, p. 169.

51. Tony Hall, "Aboriginal Issues and the New Political Map of Canada," pp. 136-39, and Bruce W. Hodgins, "The Northern Boundary of Quebec: The James Bay Crees as Self-Governing Canadians," both in Granatstein and McNaught, eds., *"English Canada" Speaks Out*.

52. See also Turpel, "Does the Road to Quebec Sovereignty Run through Aboriginal Territory?"; Kent McNeill, "Aboriginal Nations and Quebec's Boundaries: Canada Couldn't Give What It Didn't Have," in Drache and Perin, eds., *Negotiating with a Sovereign Quebec*. Turpel (p. 95) refers to "embittered relationships between aboriginal peoples and the [Quebec] provincial government." McNeill states: "The Québécois cannot assert a right of self-determination for themselves and at the same time deny that right to the aboriginal nations. . . . The aboriginal nations may decide to

align themselves with Canada, or go with Quebec, or set off on their own. If the country disintegrates, the choice must be up to them."

Ovide Mercredi's blunt presentation to the Quebec National Assembly committee studying sovereignty, and the hostile reactions of nationalist committee members, graphically revealed the tensions and conflicts between rival views of "Who is a people?," "Who has the right to self-determination?," and "Can a seceding Quebec depart with all its territory, taking all of its peoples with it?" See Assemblé nationale, *Journal des débats*, no. 27. Criticism of Quebec's relation to Aboriginal peoples needs to be tempered by the recognition that in many policy areas Quebec's response has been very positive and enlightened compared with that of other provinces in Canada. For a discussion, see Bradford Morse, "Indigenous Peoples in Quebec and Canada," *Literary Review of Canada*, October, 1992.

53. Roger Tassé, "Finding the Balance: Comments on the Proposals to Amend the Division of Powers," *Network Analysis*, Analysis no. 6, October, 1992, pp. 10-11. *De facto* asymmetries would, of course, emerge as different provincial governments struck different arrangements with the federal government.

54. Courchene and Powell, "A First Nations Province," pp. 3, 55. Their proposal would apply to on-reserve Indians, about 60 per cent of the status population. See also David. J. Elkins, *Where Should the Majority Rule? Reflections on Non-Territorial Provinces and Other Constitutional Proposals*, Points of View, no. 1 (Edmonton, 1992).

55. If the proposals were implemented, presumably it would mean that Aboriginal Canadians would not be considered citizens of the traditional ten provinces, but only of the new territorially fragmented Aboriginal province, and hence that they would have no vote or voice in, for example, British Columbia elections.

56. See Native Women's Association of Canada, *Native Women and the Charter: A Discussion Paper* (Ottawa, n.d.), and *Native Women and Self-Government: A Discussion Paper* (Ottawa, n.d.). The first round of public hearings of the Royal Commission on Aboriginal Peoples elicited recurrent expressions of fear that Aboriginal self-government would be an instrument for the domination of Aboriginal women by Aboriginal men and that the application of the Charter of Rights and Freedoms was an essential safeguard. See "Royal Commission on Aboriginal Peoples, Public Hearings: Overview of the First Round" (prepared by Michael Cassidy Ginger Group Consultants, October, 1992), pp. 4, 27, 36, 40-41, 46.

57. Commissioners' Report, Assembly of First Nations, *To the Source*.

58. Mary Ellen Turpel, "Aboriginal Peoples and the Canadian *Charter*: Interpretive Monopolies, Cultural Differences," *Canadian Human Rights Yearbook* (1989-90).

59. According to law professor L.E. Weinrib, basing her interpretation primarily on the strengthening of the existing section 25 Charter exemption of Aboriginal, treaty, or other rights or freedoms of the Aboriginal people from the Charter's application, its application to Aboriginal government would be minimal. She also noted that the section 33 override made available to Aboriginal governments might not be subject to the same safeguards and political costs that attend the open political process of federal and provincial legislatures, a weakness that might be especially pronounced when self-government, including Aboriginal leadership selection, followed traditional norms. See "Charlottetown Accord Constitutional Proposals: Legal Analysis of Draft Legal Text of October 12, 1992" (prepared by Professor L.E. Weinrib, Faculty of Law, University of Toronto, October 21, 1992, mimeo), pp. 23, 26-27. Weinrib argued that the overall impact of the Accord, not just its Aboriginal sections, was Charter weakening. Thirteen legal colleagues agreed with the Weinrib analysis.

    Professor Anne Bayefsky concurs with the Weinrib analysis, stating that "the insulation of aboriginal self-government from Charter rights and freedoms has been greatly expanded." Although she was referring to an earlier draft legal text, the final wording appears to confirm the validity of her statement. See Anne F. Bayefsky, "The Effect of Aboriginal Self-Government on the Rights and Freedoms of Women," *Network Analysis: Reactions; Comments on Analysis no. 4*, October, 1992, p. 2.

60. An Aboriginal third order was, of course, much more threatening to the Québécois' sense of themselves as a national people in possession of Quebec territory, and doubly so to the advocates of independence.

## Dreams versus Reality in "Our" Constitutional Future

1. Julian Beltrame, "Canada rated 'best place to live' in world," *Vancouver Sun*, May 28, 1994, based on a report from UN Development Program, using 1992 statistics.

2. Scott Feschuk, "Chrétien shuns debate on the C-word," *Globe and Mail*, May 28, 1994.

3. Richard Mackie, "Breakup talks must include all regions, experts say," *Globe and Mail*, June 7, 1994.

4. See Maurice Pinard, "The Secessionist Option and Quebec Public Opinion, 1988-1993," *Canada Opinion: A Newsletter Published by the Council for Canadian Unity*, 2, 3 (June, 1994), pp. 1-5, for a discussion of the markedly different responses of Québécois to polling questions using these terms.

5. *Ibid.*, p. 3. Similar confusion emerged in a July, 1994, *Globe and Mail*/Léger

and Léger poll. In the poll, "substantial numbers of Quebeckers say a sovereign Quebec would continue to be part of Canada, would use the Canadian
passport, would send M PS to Ottawa and even would pay taxes to Ottawa."
Richard Mackie, "50% see win as mission nod for P Q: July survey reveals
confusion in province about term 'sovereign Quebec,'" *Globe and Mail*, July
15, 1994.

6. According to B.C. Premier Mike Harcourt, "An independent Quebec may
have very different borders, a very bitter fight over the division, insurrec-
tions with natives and a mass exodus of people and capital." Cited in Kenneth Whyte, "Bouchard shouldn't mistake weariness with indifference or
resignation," *Globe and Mail*, May 7, 1994. Harcourt's hardline position is
elaborated in Miro Cernetig, "Harcourt hardens on Quebec," *Globe and
Mail*, May 17, 1994 – "if they decided to separate we wouldn't be the best of
friends; we'd be the worst of enemies.... There will be great bitterness and a
nasty split." For Premier Roy Romanow's support for Harcourt's tough position, which "tapped into the sentiment of a lot of people in Western Canada," see David Roberts, "Quebec hot topic for western premiers," *Globe and
Mail*, May 18, 1994. For more on Romanow's tough position, see David
Roberts, "Quebec separatist leaders pulling a con job, Romanow says," *Globe
and Mail*, May 19, 1994. See also Richard Mackie, "Independent Quebec
could expect hostility, Clark warns," *Globe and Mail*, October 14, 1994, for
Joe Clark's prediction of a hostile, unsympathetic reaction from Canadians
outside Quebec.

7. See, for example, Douglas M. Brown, "Quebec Independence: Examining
the Assumptions," *Canada Opinion: A Newsletter Published by the Council
for Canadian Unity*, 2, 4 (August, 1994); Desmond Morton, "Reflections on
the Breakup of Canada, Conflict, and Self-Determination," in Stanley H.
Hartt *et al.*, *Tangled Web: Legal Aspects of Deconfederation* (Toronto, 1992),
pp. 86-98; Stanley H. Hartt, "Sovereignty and the Economic Union," in
Hartt *et al.*, *Tangled Web*, p. 28. A *Globe and Mail* editorial (May 20, 1994),
"Time to be honest about Quebec," listed a battery of problems that would
follow Quebec's secession, a scenario summed up as an "ungodly mess." As
Richard Simeon correctly observes, Quebec independence would require
the R O C to rethink its *raison d'être* "under social and economic conditions
hostile to reasoned debate." *In Search of a Social Contract: Can We Make
Hard Decisions as if Democracy Matters?* (Toronto, 1994), p. 54. The possibility of cool reason prevailing in negotiations with Quebec in these circumstances would be minimal.

8. As Hartt observes, the dominance of economic self-interest in R O C bargainers "is almost the entire basis for the presumption that business flows
and special institutional arrangements, which now stimulate economic and

trading relationships between Quebec and the other provinces, would be renewed or continue undisturbed." "Sovereignty and the Economic Union," p. 8.

9. Guy Laforest, "Quebec Beyond the Federal Regime of 1867-1982: From Distinct Society to National Community," in Ronald L. Watts and Douglas M. Brown, eds., *Options for a New Canada* (Toronto, 1991), p. 103.

10. Charles Taylor, "Shared and Divergent Values," in Watts and Brown, eds., *Options for a New Canada*, p. 65.

11. "La réponse du Québec à la double crise canadienne, Discours de . . . Lucien Bouchard . . . devant les membres des Amitiés parlementaires France-Québec et France-Canada," mimeo, Paris, 18 mai 1994, p. 1.

12. Albert O. Hirschman, *Shifting Involvements: Private Interest and Public Action* (Princeton, N.J., 1982).

13. See Graham Fraser, "Quebec election lights no fire; Lack of passion seen in early Liberal, PQ campaigning," *Globe and Mail*, August 20, 1994. A few months earlier Lysiane Gagnon observed that "the sense of urgency is gone, and so is the passion" in the sovereigntist movement. "The young separatists of the seventies aren't today's sovereigntists," *Globe and Mail*, April 16, 1994. See also Anne McIlroy, "'Separation anxiety' running low among Quebecers," *Vancouver Sun*, June 3, 1994.

14. See Lucien Bouchard, "Québec-Canada at Crossing Roads," mimeo, speech before members of the Canadian Bar Association, Constitutional Law Section, Vancouver, May 2, 1994, pp. 2, 5, 6; Lucien Bouchard, "The French-Speaking Community and Québec," notes for a speech to the forty-fifth Annual General Assembly of the Association canadienne-française de l'Ontario, June 3, 1994, mimeo, p. 11; Claude Castonguay, "Un cul-de-sac politique," *Le Devoir*, 17 juillet 1994. The *Globe and Mail* responded in a bitter editorial, "The suffering of Claude Castonguay," reprinted in the same issue of *Le Devoir*. Susan Delacourt, "Liberals must address national unity," *Globe and Mail*, May 16, 1994, for Chrétien's view; Rhéal Séguin, "PQ looking toward independence talks," *Globe and Mail*, December 28, 1993, for the views of Parizeau and Claude Ryan; David Roberts, "Western premiers seek more powers," *Globe and Mail*, May 21, 1994, for Romanow's view. A *Globe and Mail* editorial, "Good Morning, Mr. Parizeau," December 14, 1993, stated that Quebecers face a "clear choice between as-is federalism and outright separation." This was repeated in another editorial, "The only choice for Quebec," *Globe and Mail*, January 14, 1994.

15. Miro Cernetig, "Harcourt hardens on Quebec," *Globe and Mail*, May 17, 1994.

16. See Rhéal Séguin, "Native self-rule talks plunged into disarray," *Globe and Mail*, May 19, 1994; David Roberts, "Manitoba Indians demand autonomy,"

and Rudy Platiel, "Chrétien disliked system that made him 'great white father'," both in *Globe and Mail*, March 11, 1994, for the federal government's non-constitutional, step-by-step pragmatic approach.

17. The thesis is argued in Stefan Dupré and Paul Weiler, "A Sense of Proportion and a Sense of Priorities: Reflections on the Report of the Task Force on Canadian Unity," *Canadian Bar Review*, LVII, 3 (September, 1979), pp. 446-71.

18. Peter H. Russell, *Constitutional Odyssey: Can Canadians be a Sovereign People?* (Toronto, 1992), pp. 74-76.

19. The summary of a 1994 poll described the rest of Canada as "adamant about not providing Quebec with any arrangements that would give Quebec powers not held by other provinces." John Laschinger, "How about setting a few stretch targets for Canada?" *Globe and Mail*, May 20, 1994. According to Kenneth McRoberts, "asymmetry is clearly beyond the pale." "New faces offer hope," *Globe and Mail*, October 4, 1993.

20. Bouchard, "La réponse du Québec à la double crise canadienne," p. 4.

21. E. Preston Manning, "Remarks on Reform Motion Affirming Commitment of Canadians to Federal Union . . . House of Commons, June 7, 1994," mimeo, p. 6.

22. Bouchard, "Québec-Canada at Crossing Roads," pp. 5-6.

23. Robert Sheppard, "Talking tough to the dream-spinners," *Globe and Mail*, May 18, 1994.

24. "Consensus Report on the Constitution, Charlottetown, August 28, 1992, Final Text," s. 41. Reproduced in Curtis Cook, ed., *Constitutional Predicament: Canada after the Referendum of 1992* (Montreal, 1994), p. 243.

25. These usages of "normal" by Parizeau and Bouchard are taken from Rhéal Séguin, "PQ won't say how it would govern after referendum loss," *Globe and Mail*, September 1, 1994; John Gray, "Rain puts damper on PQ victory parade," *Globe and Mail*, September 13, 1994; Anne McIlroy and Bertrand Marotte, "Separatists failed to capture landslide they had expected," *Vancouver Sun*, September 13, 1994.

26. Bouchard, "The French-Speaking Community and Québec," p. 13; see also Bouchard, "Québec-Canada at Crossing Roads," pp. 7-8.

27. Menno Boldt, *Surviving as Indians: The Challenge of Self-Government* (Toronto, 1993), pp. xvi, 50, 74.

28. See Richard Mackie, "Outside attacks incite separatism, Quebec observer warns," *Globe and Mail*, May 23, 1994, for the thesis of the article's headlines.

29. Cited in Scott Reid, *Canada Remapped: How the Partition of Quebec Will Reshape the Nation* (Vancouver, 1992), p. 74.

30. Lysiane Gagnon, "How the word 'nationalist' changed its meaning in the Quebec lexicon," *Globe and Mail*, April 23, 1994.

31. Philip Resnick, *Thinking English Canada* (Don Mills, Ont., 1994).

32. J.L. Granatstein and Kenneth McNaught, eds., *English Canada Speaks Out* (Toronto, 1991); David J. Bercuson and Barry Cooper, *Deconfederation: Canada without Quebec* (Toronto, 1991); David J. Bercuson, "Building the will to rebuild," *Globe and Mail*, September 13, 1994.

33. David Mitchell, independent B.C. MLA, observed prior to the Quebec provincial election that the western Canadian status as "bystanders" in processes that might break up the country strengthened the latent separatism of western Canada. Miro Cernetig and Scott Feschuk, "Western separatism reviving," *Globe and Mail*, July 29, 1994.

34. Canada, Task Force on Canadian Unity, *A Future Together*, chaired by Jean-Luc Pepin and John Robarts (Ottawa, January, 1979), pp. 113-14.

35. Reid, *Canada Remapped*, pp. 6, 69. The acceptance at the political level of Quebec's right to self-determination is documented and analysed in Daniel Turp, "Quebec's Democratic Right to Self-Determination," in Hartt *et al.*, *Tangled Web*, pp. 103-07.

36. Hartt, "Sovereignty and the Economic Union," p. 28.

37. See, for example, Edward Greenspon, "Yes not enough, Romanow asserts," *Globe and Mail*, May 27, 1994; Peter O'Neill, "Non-Quebecers must have vote on separation, Manning says," *Vancouver Sun*, May 25, 1994.

38. According to a *Globe and Mail* editorial, the Meech Lake and Charlottetown episodes have "taken constitutional reform forever out of elite hands, and thrown it into the public arena. There will never be another major change to the Constitution without a referendum." "Good morning, Mr. Parizeau," December 14, 1993. The Quebec situation is no different. "The Slovakian way – in which the separation of Slovakia from the Czech Republic was decided by leaders without a general vote – is absolutely unthinkable in Quebec." Lysiane Gagnon, "There's no way PQ could parlay separation without assent of voters," *Globe and Mail*, April 2, 1994.

39. This hardline posture was supported by 47 per cent outside of Quebec versus 44 per cent who were willing to make concessions – based on an Angus Reid poll between May 30 and June 1, 1994. Anne McIlroy, "Non-Quebec Canadians won't budge, poll suggests," *Vancouver Sun*, June 3, 1994.

40. Simeon, *In Search of a Social Contract*, pp. 24-25.

41. Miro Cernetig, "Harcourt hardens on Quebec," *Globe and Mail*, May 17, 1994.

42. For some anticipatory provincial positioning in western Canada for a future without Quebec, see Gordon Gibson, "B.C. separatism is no joke, Mr. Chrétien," *Vancouver Sun*, May 10, 1994. Premier Harcourt stated "that a Canada without Quebec would have little appeal to his province. 'I mean, a Canada dominated by Ontario? British Columbians wouldn't want that." Cernetig, "Harcourt hardens on Quebec." *Globe and Mail*, May 17, 1994. See

William Boei, "Bash the BQ, not the PQ, Alberta premier says," *Vancouver Sun*, May 25, 1994, for the post-breakup speculations of Premier Klein of Alberta.

43. "PQ loss won't end debate: Bouchard," Montreal *Gazette*, June 15, 1994.

44. Canadian Press, "52% in Quebec poll shun breakup," *Globe and Mail*, May 23, 1994.

45. Richard Mackie, "PQ likely to win majority, poll finds," *Globe and Mail*, August 13, 1994.

46. Robert Sheppard, "Accepting the notion of two Quebecs," *Globe and Mail*, September 13, 1994.

47. Richard Mackie, "Separation not simple, Quebeckers say," *Globe and Mail*, June 30, 1994.

48. Jacques Henripin, "Population Trends and Policies in Québec," in Alain G. Gagnon, ed., *Quebec: State and Society*, 2nd ed. (Scarborough, Ont., 1993), p. 312.

49. Richard Gwyn, "An east-coast view of the coming Quebec contretemps," *Vancouver Sun*, August 12, 1994.

50. Susan Delacourt, "Quebec land not inviolable, PM says," *Globe and Mail*, May 25, 1994.

51. David Roberts, "Harcourt, Romanow tone down rhetoric," *Globe and Mail*, May 20, 1994.

52. Reid, *Canada Remapped*, p. 134, notes that the population in the territory transferred in 1898 and 1912 is four-fifths French-speaking, and the traditional Cree territory now has more French Canadians than Natives.

53. *Ibid.*, ch. 7, "Quebec's Native Peoples," is a good summary of the issues involved.

54. Canadian Press, "Liberal convention delegate raises native fears of independent Quebec," *Vancouver Sun*, May 13, 1994.

55. Kalyani Vittala, "Natives uneasy over PQ prospects," *Globe and Mail*, September 9, 1994. See also Canadian Press, "Mohawks ban Quebec enumerators from reserves," *Globe and Mail*, August 10, 1994.

56. Canadian Press, "Mohawks vow to stay part of Canada," *Globe and Mail*, July 5, 1994.

57. Canadian Press, "Crees plan parallel referendum," *Globe and Mail*, August 27, 1994.

58. Southam News, "Cree warning: Quebec split could bring violence, U.S. told," *Vancouver Sun*, September 20, 1994.

59. John Gray, "Stay or go, our choice too, Crees say," *Globe and Mail*, October 15, 1994. This position is also supported by Ovide Mercredi, national chief of the Assembly of First Nations. Susan Delacourt, "Be careful, premiers advise Parizeau," *Globe and Mail*, September 14, 1994.

60. Rhéal Séguin, "Irwin reassures Quebec natives," *Globe and Mail*, May 18, 1994.

61. Alan Toulin, "Quebec 'No' for independence," *Financial Post*, June 28, 1994. See also John McGarry, "The native spanner in the separatist works," *Globe and Mail*, May 16, 1994, for support for Native peoples in Quebec by Canadians outside Quebec.

62. Turp, "Quebec's Democratic Right to Self-Determination," p. 120. Turp's views caused Bouchard to retreat from his previously unequivocal statement that Quebec's territory is sacrosanct. Geoffrey York, "Bouchard's stand on natives clashes with adviser's opinion," *Globe and Mail*, May 27, 1994. Additional legal support, from a slightly different perspective, is offered by Patrick Monahan of Osgoode Hall Law School. "International law isn't on Mr. Parizeau's side," *Globe and Mail*, May 19, 1994.

63. Reid, *Canada Remapped*, ch. 3, presents and analyses various partition proposals of the last two decades applied to Quebec. Reid's own proposals are presented in chs. 4 to 7. The historian Kenneth McNaught supports Reid's proposals in "How to avoid a bitter battle: Partition Quebec," *Globe and Mail*, June 13, 1994.

64. "Consensus Report on the Constitution," s. 60, in Cook, ed., *Constitutional Predicament*, p. 248.

65. Edward Greenspon and Martin Mittelstaedt, "Natives warn premiers about PQ," *Globe and Mail*, September 2, 1994.

66. Simeon, *In Search of a Social Contract, passim*.

67. Rhéal Séguin, "Bourassa playful to the end," *Globe and Mail*, December 17, 1993.

68. See the section, "Why English Canada Cannot Turn Its Back on Quebec's Natives," in Reid, *Canada Remapped*, pp. 125-26, for a brief discussion.

69. Teressa Nahanee, "Dancing with a Gorilla: Aboriginal Women, Justice and the Charter," in Royal Commission on Aboriginal Peoples, *Aboriginal Peoples and the Justice System: Report of the National Round Table on Aboriginal Justice Issues* (Ottawa, 1993), p. 360.

70. R. Pierre Gauvin and Diane Fournier, "Marriages of Registered Indians: Canada and Four Selected Bands, 1967 to 1990," Technical Paper 92-1, Department of Indian Affairs and Northern Development (July, 1992), p. 8.

71. Stewart Clatworthy and Anthony H. Smith, "Population Implications of the 1985 Amendments to the Indian Act: Final Report," mimeo (December, 1992), p. ii. The rate is 25 per cent for the on-reserve population and 62 per cent for off-reserve (p. ii). The authors assume that the current 34 per cent rate will increase to 44 per cent over the next four decades (p. vii).

72. *Ibid.*, ch. 5, "Inequality after C-31."

73. Colin Irwin, "Lords of the Arctic: Wards of the State: The Growing Inuit

Population, Arctic Resettlement and Their Effects on Social and Economic Change. A Report ... for the Review of Demography and Its Implications for Economic and Social Policy, Health and Welfare Canada," mimeo, 1988 [?]), pp. 41-42.

74. See National Executive Council of the Parti Québécois, *Quebec in a New World: The PQ's Plan for Sovereignty*, trans. by Robert Chodos (Toronto, 1994), for a strongly argued case for independence.

75. Irwin, "Lords of the Arctic," pp. 34, 44.

76. Edward W. Said, *Culture and Imperialism* (New York, 1993), pp. xxv, 15. Italics in original.

77. Salman Rushdie, *Imaginary Homelands: Essays and Criticism 1981-1991* (London, 1992), p. 394. Italics in original.

# Selected Publications of Alan C. Cairns since 1988

A Selected Bibliography of earlier publications is included in *Constitution, Government, and Society*.

"The Limited Constitutional Vision of Meech Lake," in Carol Rogerson and Katherine Swinton, eds., *Competing Constitutional Visions: The Meech Lake Accord* (Toronto: Carswell, 1988), 247-62.

*"Citizens (Outsiders) and Governments (Insiders) in Constitution-Making: The Case of Meech Lake," *Canadian Public Policy*, XIV Supplement (September, 1988), 121-45.

*"Ottawa, the Provinces, and Meech Lake," in Roger Gibbins, ed., *Meech Lake and Canada: Perspectives from the West* (Edmonton: Academic Publishing, 1988), 105-19.

*"Federalism and the Provinces," in H.P. Oberlander and Hilda Symonds, eds., *Meech Lake: From Centre to Periphery* (Vancouver: Centre for Human Settlements, 1988), 45-54.

*"Political Science, Ethnicity, and the Canadian Constitution," in David P. Shugarman and Reg Whitaker, eds., *Federalism and Political Community: Essays in Honour of Donald Smiley* (Peterborough, Ont.: Broadview Press, 1989), 113-40.

"The Senate – in Need of Reform?" in *The Canadian Senate: What is to be Done?* Proceedings of the National Conference on Senate Reform, May 5-6, 1988 (Edmonton: Centre for Constitutional Studies, University of Alberta, n.d.), 39-43.

*"Ritual, Taboo, and Bias in Constitutional Controversies in Canada, or Constitutional Talk Canadian Style," The Timlin Lecture, November 13, 1989, *Saskatchewan Law Review*, 54 (1990), 121-47.

"Reflections on Commission Research," in A. Paul Pross *et al.*, eds., *Commissions of Inquiry* (Toronto: Carswell, 1990), 87-108.

---

\* Reprinted in *Disruptions*.
\*\* Reprinted in this volume.

**"The Past and Future of the Canadian Administrative State," *University of Toronto Law Journal*, 40 (1990), 319-61.

**"Constitutional Minoritarianism in Canada," in Ronald Watts and Douglas Brown, eds., *Canada: The State of the Federation, 1990* (Kingston: Institute of Intergovernmental Affairs, 1990), 71-96.

*Disruptions: Constitutional Struggles, from the Charter to Meech Lake*. Toronto: McClelland & Stewart, 1991.

"Roadblocks in the Way of Constitutional Change," *Constitutional Forum*, (Winter, 1991), 54-58.

**"The Charter, Interest Groups, Executive Federalism, and Constitutional Reform," in David Smith *et al.*, eds., *After Meech Lake: Lessons for the Future* (Saskatoon: Fifth House Publishers, 1991), 13-31.

**"Constitutional Change and the Three Equalities," in Ronald Watts, ed., *Options for a New Canada* (Toronto: University of Toronto Press, 1991), 77-100.

*Charter versus Federalism: The Dilemmas of Constitutional Reform*. Montreal and Kingston: McGill-Queen's University Press, 1992.

"Who Should the Judges Be? Canadian Debates About the Composition of a Final Court of Appeal," in Harry N. Scheiber, ed., *North American and Comparative Federalism: Essays for the 1990's* (Berkeley: University of California Press, 1992), 57-88.

**"The Case for Charter-Federalism," *The Network*, (June-July, 1992), 25-29.

"Citizenship and the New Constitutional Order," *Canadian Parliamentary Review*, 15, 3 (Autumn, 1992), 2-6.

**"Reflections on the Political Purposes of the Charter: The First Decade," in G.A. Beaudoin, ed., *The Charter: Ten Years Later* (Cowansville, Quebec: Les Éditions Yvon Blais, 1992) 163-91.

"Constitutional Theory in the Post-Meech Era: Citizenship as an Emergent Constitutional Category," in Janet Ajzenstat, ed., *Canadian Constitutionalism: 1791-1991* (Ottawa: Canadian Study of Parliament Group, 1992), 30-37.

**"Barriers to Constitutional Renewal in Canada: The Role of Constitutional Culture," in *Canadian Politics: Past, Present and Future*, A Series of Lectures Given to Commemorate the Twenty-Fifth Anniversary of the Department of Politics, Brock University, 1990-91 (St. Catherines, Ont., 1992), 17-30.

**"The Fragmentation of Canadian Citizenship," in William Kaplan, ed., *Belonging: The Meaning and Future of Canadian Citizenship* (Montreal and Kingston: McGill-Queen's University Press, 1993), 181-220.

"The Charter: A Political Science Perspective," in Patrick Monahan and Marie Finkelstein, eds., *The Impact of the Charter on the Public Policy Process* (North York, Ont.: York University Centre for Public Law and Public Policy, 1993),

156-68; also published in the *Osgoode Hall Law Journal*, 30, 3 (Fall, 1992), 614-25.

"A Defense of the Citizens' Constitution Theory: A Response to Ian Brodie and Neil Nevitte," *Canadian Journal of Political Science*, XXVI, 2 (June, 1993), 261-67.

\*\*"The Charlottetown Accord: Multinational Canada vs. Federalism," in Curtis Cook, ed., *Constitutional Predicament: Canada After the Referendum of 1992* (Montreal and Kingston: McGill-Queen's University Press, 1994), 25-63.

"History, Memory and Constitutional Reform," in Jean Laponce and John Meisel, eds., *Debating the Constitution* (Ottawa: University of Ottawa Press, 1994), 19-24, plus commentaries pp. 24-25, 38-39, 60-62, 85-88.

"Conflict and Integration in Canada: The Role of the Constitution," *Zeitschrift fur Kanada-Studien/Journal for Canadian Studies* (forthcoming).

"An Election to be Remembered: Canada 1993," Conference Proceedings of the Centro de Investigaciones Sobre America del Norte (Universidad Nacional Autonoma de Mexico, forthcoming), and *Canadian Public Policy*, xx, 3 (September, 1994), 219-34.

\*\*"The Constitutional World We Have Lost," in C.E.S. Franks *et al.*, eds., *Governing in a Maturing Society: Essays in Honour of John Meisel* (Montreal and Kingston: McGill-Queen's University Press, 1995).

"Constitutional Government and the Two Faces of Ethnicity," in Karen Knop *et al.*, eds., *Rethinking Federalism: Citizens, Markets and Governments in a Changing World* (Vancouver: University of British Columbia Press, forthcoming).

"States and Nations: A Comment," in Stephen J. Randall and Roger Gibbins, eds., *Federalism and the New World Order* (Calgary: University of Calgary Press, 1994), 71-75.

# Acknowledgements

The following individuals and institutions are gratefully acknowledged for per-mission to reprint articles included in this book:

Keith Banting and University of Toronto Press for "The Embedded State: State-Society Relations in Canada," in Keith Banting, ed., *State and Society: Canada in Comparative Perspective*, Volume 31 of the Research Studies for the Royal Commission on the Economic Union and Development Prospects for Canada (Toronto, 1986);

*University of Toronto Law Journal* and Stephen Waddams, editor, for "The Past and Future of the Canadian Administrative State," *University of Toronto Law Journal*, 40/3 (1990). Reprinted by permission of University of Toronto Press Incorporated;

McGill-Queen's University Press for "The Constitutional World We Have Lost," in C. E. S. Franks *et al.*, *Canada's Century: Governance in a Maturing Society* (Montreal and Kingston, forthcoming);

Institute of Intergovernmental Affairs, Queen's University and Ronald Watts and Douglas Brown for "Constitutional Minoritarianism in Canada," in Ronald Watts and Douglas Brown, eds., *Canada: The State of the Federation, 1990* (Kingston, 1990);

Department of Politics, Brock University, and William Hull for "Barriers to Constitutional Renewal in Canada: The Role of Constitutional Culture," in *Canadian Politics: Past, Present and Future*, A Series of Lectures Given to Commemorate the Twenty-Fifth Anniversary of the Department of Politics, Brock University (St. Catharines, Ont., 1992);

McGill-Queen's University Press for "The Fragmentation of Canadian Citizenship," in William Kaplan, ed., *Belonging: The Meaning and Future of Canadian Citizenship* (Montreal and Kingston, 1993);

University of Ottawa and Don Lenihan for "The Case for Charter-Federalism," *The Network* (June-July, 1992);

Les Editions Yvon Blais Inc. for "Reflections on the Political Purposes of the Charter: The First Decade," in G. A. Beaudoin, ed., *The Charter: Ten Years Later* (Cowansville, Quebec, 1992);

Ronald Watts and University of Toronto Press for "Constitutional Change and the Three Equalities," in Ronald Watts, ed., *Options for a New Canada* (Toronto, 1991). Reprinted by permission of University of Toronto Press Incorporated;

McGraw-Hill Ryerson and Paul Fox for "Aboriginal Canadians, Citizenship, and the Constitution," in Paul Fox, ed., *Politics: Canada* (forthcoming);

David E. Smith and Fifth House Publishers for "The Charter, Interest Groups, Executive Federalism, and Constitutional Reform," in David Smith *et al.*, eds., *After Meech Lake: Lessons for the Future* (Saskatoon, 1991);

McGill-Queen's University Press for "The Charlottetown Accord: Multinational Canada vs. Federalism," in Curtis Cook, ed., *Constitutional Predicament: Canada After the Referendum of 1992* (Montreal and Kingston, 1994).

The index was prepared by Jenefer A. Curtis.

# Index

Abella, Judge Rosalie Silberman, 97

Aboriginal nationalism, 83-84, 162, 164, 166, 168, 172-73, 184, 207-08, 210, 240, 245, 283, 301-14; as challenge to ROC, 184; and Quebec nationalism, 166-68, 224; *see also* Aboriginal self-government, Constitutional future

Aboriginal peoples, 11-12, 13, 16, 18, 21, 26-27, 47-48, 57, 76-77, 93, 105-07, 109, 116, 117, 125-27, 131-32, 134-38, 140, 146, 153, 163-68, 173, 175, 187-88, 193, 196, 204-15, 223-24, 238-60, 262, 264, 274-76, 283, 292-314, 317-18, 326, 339-41, 342, 384 n41, 392 n62, 394-95 n10; and administrative state, 76-77; categories defined, 164, 179, 240; and Charlottetown Accord, 245-57, 292-96, 296-314; and the Charter, 204-15, 223, 264, 275, 310; Charter antipathy to, 205-06; separate Aboriginal charters, 207-08; stakes in Charter federalism, 187-88, 193; citizenship in, 26, 173, 188; congruity with other Charter groups, 224; constitutional identity of, 16, 125-27, 204, 317-18; in constitutional change, 105, 109, 116, 117, 124, 132, 140, 146, 153, 164, 166-68, 223, 238-60, 262, 275-76, 283, 292-301; future of, 251-60, 317;

First Nations women, 210-11; history of, 26-27; international context, 47-48, 135; opposition to Meech Lake, 272-74; representation of, 174-75, 180-81; role in territorialism, 188-91; *see also* Assembly of First Nations, Inuit, Native Council of Canada, Métis, White Paper

Aboriginal self-government, 11-12, 165, 170, 172-73, 180, 188, 191, 210, 214, 224, 240, 263-68, 302-05, 306-07, 354 n17, 381 n19, 386 n61; Penner Report, 172; separate justice systems, 180, 210, 305; third order of government, 172-73, 184, 187, 206, 239, 294, 299, 302-03, 306-07; *see also* Aboriginal nationalism, Assembly of First Nations, Métis, Nunavut

Acton, Lord, 7

Affirmative action, *see* Canadian Charter of Rights and Freedoms

Akwesasne Mohawks, 338

Alan B. Plaunt Memorial Lectures, 138

Alberta, 43, 152

Allaire Report, 167, 283, 285, 290, 292

Amending formula, 13, 16, 17, 29, 43, 109-10, 140, 145, 147-52, 155, 159, 190, 194, 216, 232, 327; and failure of

419

Meech Lake, 263-69; Fulton-
Favreau formula, 110, 147, 263, 268;
"Gang of Eight," 110, 148, 190, 194,
232; and the three equalities, 216; in
new constitutional culture, 148-52,
223; Victoria Charter, 147, 152, 220,
263; *see also* Constitutional future,
Executive federalism
"Amending the Constitution of
Canada" (1990), 150
Archilochus, 8
Ash, Timothy Garton, 137
Assembly of First Nations, 153, 166,
168, 177, 181, 191, 204, 207-10, 240,
279, 297-98, 311, 343; *To the Source,*
207-11, 298
Association of Métis and Non-Status
Indians of Saskatchewan, 126
Asymmetrical citizenship, 386 n67
Asymmetrical federalism, 146, 217,
219, 225-28, 231, 234, 235, 236;
Charter dimension and
jurisdictional dimension, 225-28;
dynamics of, 236; erosion of
"sharing," 230; lack of controlling
external models, 229; viability of,
228-31; as weak counterfoil to
Quebec nationalism, 229; *see also*
Constitutional future, Quebec

Beauvoir, Simone de, 129
Becker, Carl, 25
Bélanger-Campeau Commission, 146,
163, 167, 208, 209, 221, 226, 234, 283,
285
Bercuson, David, 306
Berger, Tom, 204, 223
Berlin, Sir Isaiah, 7-9
Berra, Yogi, 158
Bill of Rights (1960), 21, 42, 79, 82, 112,
148, 188, 189, 198, 260, 326

Bird, Richard, 66
Bish, Robert L., 168
Bismarck, 56
Black, Edwin, 11, 127
Blakeney, Allan, 74
Bliss, Michael, 185
Bloc Québécois, 316, 323-34
Boldt, Menno, 205, 206, 211-12, 256
Boli-Bennett, John, 56
Borden, Robert B., 85
Bouchard, Lucien, 316, 318-23, 335
Bourassa, Robert, 70, 147, 151, 225, 231,
250, 273-74, 286, 291, 309, 313, 316,
342, 378 n14; accommodation of in
constitutional change, 225, 231;
government of, 70, 195; and
Victoria Charter, 147
Boyle, Christine, 178, 180, 385 n56
Brady, Alexander, 108, 111
Breton, Raymond, 79
British Canadians, 111, 140, 144, 158,
372 n40
British Columbia, 60, 108
British North America Act, *see*
Constitution Act, 1867
Brown, George, 97
Bryden, Kenneth, 90
Bundesrat proposals, 43
Bureaucracy, 45, 47, 54, 57, 69, 87-88,
95, 130-31; *see also* Elites

Cameron, David, 68, 136, 176
Campbell, Robert, 277
Canada Shipping Act, 85
Canadian Charter of Rights and
Freedoms, 13, 17, 21-25, 27, 29, 32,
39-46, 50-52, 55, 70, 72-78, 79, 82,
96, 122, 124-26, 176, 196-200,
203-15, 218-19, 222-28, 270-72,
321-22; and the administrative
state, 43, 72-78, 96; affirmative

Mulroney, Brian, 150, 152, 245, 267,
    289
Multiculturalism, 26, 42, 77, 136, 176,
    203-04; *see also* Constitutional
    minoritarianism, Ethnicity,
    Minorities
Multinationalism, 280-314, 326; in
    Charlottetown Accord, 280-314;
    and Charter, 306, 310; emergence
    of, 281; the four nationalisms in,
    282; replacing two nations view,
    326
Murray, Lowell, 140, 267

National Action Committee on the
    Status of Women, 279, 304
Nationalism, *see* Aboriginal
    nationalism, Multinationalism,
    Quebec nationalism
Native Council of Canada, 165, 166,
    168, 207, 293, 380-81 n15
Native Women's Association of
    Canada, 191, 211-12, 297, 310
New Brunswick Select Committee on
    the 1987 Constitutional Accord,
    219
Newfoundland, 21, 71, 81, 111;
    government of, 81; maximizing
    community income, 92; Science
    Research Tax Credit program, 71;
    referenda in, 21
*Non-People, The*, 129
Northwest Territories, 162, 165,
    172
Nunavut, 131, 172, 210, 239, 257, 309,
    341, 384 n41

Oakeshott, Michael, 13
O'Connor, W.F., 100
O'Connor Report (1939), 99-100
Offe, Claus, 36, 65, 84, 93

Olson, Mancur, 17
Ontario Human Rights Commission,
    75
Ontario human rights legislation, 82,
    88-89
Open society, 16, 36
Owram, Douglas, 69, 71

Pal, Leslie A., 76, 85
Parizeau, Jacques, 70, 286, 316, 321,
    323
Parti Québécois, 57, 146, 152, 159, 195,
    225, 229, 265, 268, 284, 285, 286,
    287, 316-18, 320, 338
Pearson, Lester B., 43, 270
Peckford, Brian, 197
Penner Report, 172
Pepin-Robarts Task Force on
    Canadian Unity, 43, 114, 163, 230,
    285, 329
Peters, B. Guy, 33, 59
Petter, Andrew, 73
Polanyi, Karl, 56
Porter, John, 57, 58, 109
Powell, Lisa, 304
Prince Edward Island, 70, 283
Provincialism, 19, 39, 40, 43, 73, 74,
    114, 117, 161, 172, 199, 220-21, 231,
    271; challenged by three nations
    view, 161, 172; emergence of, 114;
    limited by Charter and the three
    equalities, 198-99, 231

Quebec, 17, 21, 40-43, 99, 113, 122-25,
    144-45, 148-52, 163, 167, 171, 197, 217,
    220-22, 228-29, 231-36, 284-92,
    316-39, 343-44, 389 n22;
    accommodation of, 163, 171;
    challenge to dualism, 122-25; and
    Charter, 197, 219; in constitutional
    change, 17, 99, 113, 144-45, 148-52,